STRANGE VISITORS

STRANGE VISITORS

Documents in
Indigenous–Settler Relations
in Canada from 1876

Edited by
KEITH D. SMITH

UNIVERSITY OF TORONTO PRESS

LIBRARY AND ARCHIVES CANADA CATALOGUING IN PUBLICATION

Strange visitors : documents in Indigenous–settler relations in Canada from 1876 / edited by Keith D. Smith.

Includes bibliographical references and index.

Issued in print and electronic formats.

ISBN 978-1-4426-0824-5 (bound).—ISBN 978-1-4426-0566-4 (pbk.).—ISBN 978-1-4426-0567-1 (pdf).—ISBN 978-1-4426-0568-8 (epub)

1. Native peoples—Canada—Government relations—History—Sources. 2. Native peoples—Government policy—Canada—History—Sources. 3. Native peoples—Legal status, laws, etc.—Canada—History—Sources. 4. Native peoples—Canada—History—Sources. 5. Canada—Ethnic relations—History—Sources. I. Smith, Keith D. (Keith Douglas), 1953–, editor of compilation

E92.S77 2014   323.1197'071   C2013-908649-8   C2013-908650-1

We welcome comments and suggestions regarding any aspect of our publications—please feel free to contact us at news@utphighereducation.com or visit our Internet site at www.utppublishing.com.

North America
5201 Dufferin Street
North York, Ontario, Canada, M3H 5T8

2250 Military Road
Tonawanda, New York, USA, 14150

ORDERS PHONE: 1–800–565–9523
ORDERS FAX: 1–800–221–9985
ORDERS E-MAIL: utpbooks@utpress.utoronto.ca

UK, Ireland, and continental Europe
NBN International
Estover Road, Plymouth, PL6 7PY, UK
ORDERS PHONE: 44 (0) 1752 202301
ORDERS FAX: 44 (0) 1752 202333
ORDERS E-MAIL: enquiries@nbninternational.com

Every effort has been made to contact copyright holders; in the event of an error or omission, please notify the publisher.

The University of Toronto Press acknowledges the financial support for its publishing activities of the Government of Canada through the Canada Book Fund.

Cover image: Eskimos watch landing of helicopter from C.G.S. "C.D. Howe," Eastern Arctic Patrol Vessel, at Arctic Bay (Ikpiarjuk/Tununirusiq), Nunavut, N.W.T. (July 1951). W. Doucette / National Film Board of Canada / Library and Archives Canada / PA-131766.

"Our first encounters with Europeans were friendly. We welcomed these strange visitors—visitors who never left. The Europeans also valued their encounters with us. They thought we were fair and tough entrepreneurs and—no doubt today—negotiators. In 1832 traders from the Hudson's Bay Co. found our people living, in their words, 'in two-storey wooden houses the equal of any in Europe.' For a time our people prospered, but there were dark days yet to come."

CHIEF JOSEPH GOSNELL TO THE BRITISH COLUMBIA
LEGISLATIVE ASSEMBLY, 1998 (FROM DOCUMENT 15.2)

Contents

CHAPTER 4

"FOR THE GENERAL GOOD": RESTRICTING MOVEMENT
AND CULTURAL PRACTICE

81

CHAPTER 5

"OUR OBJECT IS TO CONTINUE UNTIL THERE IS NOT A SINGLE
INDIAN IN CANADA THAT HAS NOT BEEN ABSORBED INTO
THE BODY POLITIC": ASSIMILATION AND ORGANIZED RESISTANCE

113

CHAPTER 6

"PLEASE DON'T BLAME YOURSELVES": RESIDENTIAL SCHOOLS

151

CHAPTER 7

"WE DO NOT ASK FOR SPECIAL FAVOURS FROM ANYONE":
INDIGENOUS PEOPLE AND GLOBAL CONFLICT

191

CHAPTER 8

A "COMPLETE AND FINAL SOLUTION":
PREPARING FOR THE NEW INDIAN ACT OF 1951

231

CHAPTER 9

"WE HAD NO HESITATION IN USING THE WORD 'EXPERIMENT'":
THE HIGH ARCTIC RELOCATION OF 1953

256

CHAPTER 10

"A FAULTY UNDERSTANDING OF FAIRNESS":
THE WHITE PAPER OF 1969

287

CHAPTER 15
"A UNIQUE TRUST-LIKE RELATIONSHIP": MODERN TREATY MAKING
427

Acknowledgements

✳

The completion of this project required the help of many more people than I would have ever imagined. Natalie Fingerhut of the University of Toronto Press Higher Education Division provided indispensable advice and assistance as she patiently shepherded this project from conception to publication. Others at UTP as well, Ashley Rayner, Anna Del Col, Megan Pickard, and Beate Schwirtlich, contributed in various important ways throughout the creation of this book. Karen Taylor went well beyond the strict job description of a copy editor to check factual details and offer suggestions that served to clarify many of this work's more complicated characteristics. Securing the permissions necessary for the more than 90 documents included in this collection was a journey in itself and I appreciate all of those publishers, First Nations organizations, government departments, archives, and others who were willing to have material under their control reproduced here. I especially thank William Wuttunee and Sharon McIvor who gave permission to reprint their own work and Tanya Harnett who sorted out the permission of her family necessary to allow me to include the writing of their late relative, Chief Dan Kennedy. Mary Wood, the now retired interlibrary loan librarian at Vancouver Island University (VIU), was tireless in bringing material to me from obscure locations that I would never have been able to trace on my own. I would also like to thank the anonymous reviewers at both the conceptual and final manuscript stages. I have done my best to incorporate all of your valuable suggestions in this collection. Further, I would like to thank the many friends, colleagues, students, and elders at VIU and beyond who challenge me to rethink my interpretations of the past on a daily basis. Clayton Smith helped with the early proofreading of many of the documents in this collection, but his real contribution was and is in ensuring that I not take myself too seriously. Finally, I would be remiss indeed not to acknowledge Leanne Schultz who contributed enormously to this project in numerous ways, both directly and indirectly. Any errors or omissions that remain in this publication are, of course, solely my responsibility.

Introduction

✳

Imagine that you are a young Métis student in your first university-level history course. You have listened to your grandparents and other family elders speak of your people's history for as long as you can remember, but the stories you grew up with often stood in opposition to what you read in high school and saw on TV. In particular, the version of the events often referred to as the North-West Rebellion or North-West Resistance of 1885 presented by your family has always been at odds with some of the more widely available accounts. Whereas in the latter your ancestors were often portrayed as unreasonable and hasty in their decision to take up arms against the legitimate authority of the Canadian government, your grandparents spoke of the long-standing undemocratic and unfair treatment faced by the Métis in the mid and late 1800s. By the time you reached high school, you began to wonder why it was that, by the 1880s, British Columbia had already become a province with its own democratically elected legislature based on representation by population whereas the region that became Saskatchewan and Alberta, then known as the North-West Territories, was controlled by an unelected lieutenant governor and a small, mostly appointed, council consisting solely of non-Indigenous men.[1] At family gatherings, you heard that Canada did not recognize Métis title to their farms while at the same time these lands were coming under increasing pressure from land speculators who had no intention of ever settling in the area. You listened to stories about how your ancestors were not consulted in the appointment of officials and about how health care and education for your people were well below the standard taken for granted elsewhere in Canada. All the while, First Nations people were being increasingly confined to reserves, and treaty promises, including promises of adequate food supplies, were ignored or glacially slow in being kept. You grew up understanding that both First Nations people and Métis, along with non-Indigenous settlers, had exhausted every legal method of seeking redress before violence broke out in early 1885.

In many other accounts that you read or saw, these events were portrayed as solely the machinations of Louis Riel, a single charismatic leader of questionable sanity who duped other Métis and naive First Nations people into believing they had grievances where none

---

1 It should be noted that, although British Columbia gained provincial status and an elected legislature after 1871, those defined as Indians were denied the vote in provincial elections until 1949. As in the rest of Canada, First Nations people living on reserves in BC had to wait until 1960 to vote in federal elections.

actually existed. The federal government was on the verge of settling all outstanding issues when violence erupted by peoples naturally and historically inclined to brutality and the love of plunder.

You decide to try to sort all of this out by writing your term paper in first-year post-Confederation Canadian history on these events. In the process of researching this topic you come across the 1885 *Annual Report of the Department of Indian Affairs* (DIA) on line. You see that this report includes a statement by Prime Minister John A. Macdonald (see document 3.2 in this reader) that seems in direct opposition to what your grandparents have told you and appears to confirm the popular accounts. So how do you reconcile the differences between these virtually polar opposite versions? The document was written by Canada's first prime minister, so surely it must be true? Did your grandparents misrepresent the story in order to present your ancestors in a more positive light? Did they simply misunderstand what happened or get the story muddled? You bring the problem to your professor who suggests that you evaluate Macdonald's report more critically. She asks you to consider the kinds of questions listed below and introduces you to the strategy of reading "against the grain."

You begin by reading the way you normally would in order to determine what Macdonald is trying to tell his readers. This approach is called "reading with the grain." Reading in this way, you determine that the author was primarily interested in defending his government's program. According to Macdonald, Canada had created a benevolent program in relation to First Nations, and the employees under his supervision were conscientious and sensitive to the needs of Indigenous people. The author maintains, for example, that, contrary to the stories told by the elders in your family, food had been provided in abundance. Macdonald suggests, then, that there was no reason for extra-legal activity to resolve any perceived injustices. Those involved were quite simply criminals interested only in plunder or, as Macdonald puts it, "great benefits, in the shape of rich booty";[2] they were *not* interested in securing the necessities of life or advancing Indigenous rights. Besides, he suggests, the decision to take up arms was facilitated by "[t]heir old instincts for the warpath."[3] Macdonald is careful, too, to show that the North-West Mounted Police and Indian agents were instrumental both in limiting the action and in restoring calm in its aftermath. Reading with the grain, then, provides readers with an understanding of what the author wants them to believe.

Once you have deduced the author's overt message, you switch to a more critical evaluation of the document and to reading it against the grain to uncover hidden or unintentional elements imbedded within it. You start by asking yourself who the author was. You are already aware that John A. Macdonald was a respected Conservative politician and lawyer who is routinely credited for bringing Canada together. From the document itself, you find that, in addition to being prime minister, he was also the superintendent of Indian affairs, a position that gave him direct responsibility for those in Canada defined as Indians but not for other Indigenous peoples who did not have that status, including

---

2 Dominion of Canada, Department of Indian Affairs, *Annual Report of the Department of Indian Affairs for the Year Ended 31st of December, 1885* (Ottawa: MacLean, Roger & Co., 1886), x.

3 Dominion of Canada, Department of Indian Affairs, *Annual Report, 1885*, x.

the Métis. You find yourself curious as to whether Macdonald's political orientation, his geographic location distant from Canada's North-West, and his cultural isolation from Indigenous peoples might have had some impact on his interpretation of these events. You could look more closely into Macdonald's background, but, for now, you decide to move on to considering the document's intended audience.

You see that Macdonald's report was written to the governor general, the Queen's representative in Canada. This is not a private communication though, meant for the governor general's eyes alone, but part of the annually published report of the Department of Indian Affairs. You notice on the Library and Archives Canada website, where you found this document, that in 1886 the department's annual report consisted of over 600 pages and included information presented in narrative and tabular format that touched on virtually every aspect of the administration of Indian affairs. Even without further research into Macdonald's background, his attitudes toward any group of Indigenous people, or his limited exposure to any of these populations or to Canada's North-West, you see clearly that Superintendent of Indian Affairs Macdonald had a vested interest in presenting his department's efforts in a positive light and in demonstrating that there was no reason for grievance on the part of those Indigenous people for whom he was responsible. Rather, the confrontation was "due to circumstances over which this Department had no control."[4]

You understand that in his published report, which would be read by politicians and those within settler society interested in these issues, he would be inclined to present Indians as locked in the past, impulsive, and easily led astray and so reliant on the department's benevolent guidance. That even the dedicated employees of Macdonald's department had no indication of dissatisfaction among those they were responsible for prior to their succumbing to the deceptions of the Métis is offered as evidence of their tendency to act without careful and reasoned reflection. If the author were to conclude that First Nations people were capable of making intelligent and competent independent decisions about their own future, then what would justify conferring an inferior legal status on them and maintaining an entire federal department dedicated to supervising and modifying their actions and behaviour? On the other hand, the Métis were beyond the responsibility of the DIA and so could conveniently be presented as the antagonists of the story who misled their gullible First Nations cousins.

In the next step of "reading against the grain," you think about why the document was created, which, in this case, you have already gone a long way to answering for yourself. Because the primary function of the DIA was to supervise the transition from Indigenous lifeways to the acceptance of Euro-Canadian culture, institutions, and structures, its annual reports were created to provide a portrait of the success of the DIA's efforts in that direction. They identified individuals and groups who were adhering to state policies and singled out those who were not—for further departmental intervention. It was politically important for Macdonald, and vital for the success of future departmental funding requests, to show the DIA in the best possible light. The DIA's annual reports had to illustrate progress, but they also needed to show that there was still work to be done by the department. By emphasizing the positive contributions of DIA employees and those of

---

4 Dominion of Canada, Department of Indian Affairs, *Annual Report, 1885*, ix.

the North-West Mounted Police for whom, as prime minister, Macdonald was also ultimately responsible, the author furthers these objectives. The next issues you need to consider are when and where the document was written.

Macdonald's report was published in 1886 and dated on January 1st of that year. At most, then, the document must have been written little more than six months after the events described and only a month after the execution of Riel and eight Cree men.[5] Though perhaps not written at the precise moment of the events described, the document, you can reasonably conclude, retained a considerable degree of immediacy, and the events surely remained in the public consciousness and played a role in the DIA's policy decisions. The timing of the document's creation means that Macdonald's view of the events and of their participants is relatively uncluttered by any potential re-evaluation.

You cannot be absolutely certain exactly where the document was written, but because Macdonald would not visit Western Canada for the first time until his travels there later in 1886, it could not have been written anywhere near where the events occurred. More likely, it was written in Ottawa or in Macdonald's home town of Kingston, Ontario, in either case, thousands of kilometres away from Fort Battleford or Duck Lake, Saskatchewan.

Reading this document against the grain and armed with critical evaluations of who the author was, what constituted his intended audience, the reasons for the document being created, and when and where it was written gives you considerable insight into the motivations and foundational understandings that influenced its content and tone. It is difficult for you to imagine how the cultural location of the author as an elder statesman and member of Canada's social and political elite could not have influenced how he saw the world. You notice that Macdonald clearly demonstrates a number of preconceptions. For example, he seems to see Indigenous people as inherently violent when he refers to their "old instincts for the war path."[6] But, you wonder, didn't Europeans and their descendants in North America have a past rife with violent confrontation? So what in Macdonald's view could be the salient difference?

You feel that you now have a good indication of the potential biases and preconceptions that went into the creation of this document, and, by reading against the grain, you have also considered some of what was left unsaid or possibly misrepresented or misinterpreted. But there is more that troubles you. You quickly realize that although Macdonald presents a racially informed and, in your view, not particularly satisfying explanation for First Nations involvement in the events of 1885, there is no attempt at understanding why the Métis would engage in such drastic action nor is there any indication of the many attempts made to resolve their concerns through legal means. From other research, you are aware that the Canadian government had received numerous reports from missionaries and policemen warning of widespread dissatisfaction in the North-West and advising that a solution should be found quickly, but Macdonald is silent on this as well. Further, there is no mention of the dissatisfaction of non-Indigenous settlers who were unhappy for many

---

5 The eight Cree men who were hanged in the aftermath of the resistance were Wandering Spirit, Round the Sky, Bad Arrow, Miserable Man, Iron Body, Little Bear, Crooked Leg, and Man Without Blood.

6 Dominion of Canada, Department of Indian Affairs, *Annual Report, 1885*, x.

of the same reasons as their Indigenous neighbours. Taken together, the frustration felt by these diverse groups of people appears to you to indicate problems that were much more extensive than those presented by Macdonald; it also suggests that the government was, or should have been, well aware of the potential for serious consequences. Although you might not necessarily agree with specific tactics or actions, you are beginning to understand the level of exasperation that led to armed resistance, despite Macdonald's overt message.

Original documents like this, then, need to be read with the same critical eye as books and articles written after the fact. Further, reading against the grain to uncover what is left unsaid can give a voice to people reduced to silence and highlight events that have often been ignored. It can uncover Indigenous agency and action in pursuit of an independent political destiny, economic future, and cultural survivance. This, in turn, serves to offset the notion of docile and tradition-bound Indigenous people passively awaiting their cultural superiors to set their fate.

Most often, students who are new to postsecondary academic work will already have some familiarity with what historians and others refer to as "secondary sources." These are books and articles generally written after the fact by commentators who have no first-hand experience with the events or processes they describe. Some students may also already recognize that not all secondary accounts are equal and that the author of a story in a magazine that they might find at a grocery store checkout has perhaps not had the same time or opportunity to examine a subject as deeply or as broadly as an author whose work appears in a scholarly journal. These students may understand further that, before crafting their accounts, academic authors especially have spent considerable time collecting and assessing "primary sources," the various forms of evidence that were created at the time of the matter under investigation, such as Macdonald's report discussed above.

This evidence—the government records, personal papers, church files, newspapers, statistical representations, court documents, police reports, oral testimony, poetry, novels, photographs, maps, paintings, drawings, carvings, modified landscapes, architecture, household goods, music, and a variety of other materials created during the period under investigation—makes up the building blocks or "primary sources" that historians evaluate and weave together in the process of crafting their articles and books. They recognize that as they collect more and more of these sources a clearer understanding of the situation at issue will begin to emerge. For most historians, the detective work involved in locating and assessing these primary sources is among the most enjoyable and interesting aspects of their work. It often takes time, though, for students to recognize that these primary sources do not provide neutral, unfiltered windows onto the past. Like secondary accounts, primary sources of all sorts (e.g., oral, material, textual) must be interrogated and evaluated according to certain criteria and with a sharp critical eye, a healthy degree of scepticism, and with a number of questions in mind. In the case of a textual source for example, one should ask the following:

> **Who is the author of the document?** What impact does the author's sociocultural location, political orientation, gender, age, or occupation have on what is written or how it is written? For example, when writing about an Indigenous community's economic strategies, Indian agents, who were almost exclusively White and

male, tended not to recognize, and so to understate, the economic and political contributions of Indigenous women.

Who is the intended audience or for whom was the document written? If the document is a report for an employer, the author might include different observations and structure the account differently than if he or she was describing the same events to a family member. Students might ask themselves whether they would describe their weekend's activities to their grandmothers in the same way that they would to their best friends. I would not presume to present myself as an expert on family dynamics, but I suspect that few would answer in the affirmative.

Why was the document created in the first place? Is it meant to shape someone's view of a particular issue? Is it intended to serve as a justification for some action or proposal or to protect someone's job? For example, the reports of individual employees of the Department of Indian Affairs that were published in the department's annual reports were meant, in part at least, to show the movement of First Nation communities toward lifeways deemed appropriate by the Euro-Canadian majority. Their contents, however, were highly regulated by senior departmental bureaucrats. The DIA did not want "complaints from Indians" to enter into the published public record and considered non-compliance in this regard as "insubordination."[7]

As no document is created without a purpose or without a particular agenda in mind, none can be considered absolutely neutral. Yet intent is not always easy to determine, and sometimes it is purposefully or unconsciously obscured. Researchers must be alert to possible embellishments, oversights, and misrepresentations, even if these might be unintentional. Further, though proclamations, orders, dictates, and the like, especially those of the state and its agencies, can provide conduits into official thinking, a researcher must bear in mind that demands do not necessarily ensure compliance, either from those for whom they were intended or even from those charged with enforcement in the field. Based on this type of document alone, there is no way of evaluating the extent to which official stipulations were implemented, resisted, or ignored. Most would argue, for example, that the anti-potlatch provisions of the Indian Act had a detrimental effect on First Nations communities on the West Coast, but, despite the potential risk of jail terms and the confiscation of significant spiritual objects, the practice continued in many locations even if in modified form.

When was the document written? Was it created during or immediately following the events it describes, or did a period of time pass during which the immediate reactions and impressions of the author might have shifted? Over time, outside influences or a reconsideration of what might be left behind could cause an author to alter his or her account. During one research trip, I met a man in his late

---

7 L. Vankoughnet, Deputy Superintendent of Indian Affairs, Circular, 10 April 1890, LAC, RG 10, vol. 3905, file 104,939.

70s who wrote in his daily journal unfailingly over the course of several decades. He told me he was glad that he had recently switched to a computer-based journal because now he was able to go back and "readjust" his entries when the situation became clearer to him. This gentleman might be happier with his textual legacy, but his immediate impressions are lost.

Where was the document written? Was it created at or near the location it describes or from some distant site? When evaluating a primary source, one should consider the extent to which the physical location of the writer had an impact on what that writer saw and wrote. We could ask ourselves, for example, whether a news report about an emerging situation in Nunavut written in Toronto is as compelling as one written in Iqaluit.

Researchers must also confront a variety of other thorny issues that will affect their reading of any document they discover. Was it published? If so, how was the original altered during the editorial and publishing processes? Was the document translated or ghostwritten? If so, how much of the document reflects the relative skill of the translator or the views of ghostwriter? Did the specific language of the document mean the same thing to its creators as it does to readers in the twenty-first century?

In addition to the specific explicit content they include, primary sources can also implicitly reveal much about the socio-economic, cultural, and political environments of their creators. Often, if these documents are read carefully, researchers can catch glimpses of prevailing relations of power, class structures, racial hierarchies, gender roles, and family structures among many other features of the creator's world.

Beyond all of the above, students of any history involving Indigenous people must navigate a constellation of other issues when examining primary textual sources. First, most of the written record, especially until very recently, was created by a particular segment of society: typically White men who had some degree of economic, social, and political privilege. Though they most definitely did not constitute a homogenous or monolithic body, these individuals tended to share common cultural understandings that inevitably shaped how they viewed the world and therefore what they wrote. As a result, one must be sensitive to the assumptions, misunderstandings, misinterpretations, misconstructions, errors in judgement, and simple self-interests that are intrinsic to the documents they created.

Even though there is a preponderance of White male voices in the historical record, whispers, and even the shouts, of Indigenous people can still be heard through the written documents left behind. In order to hear them, researchers in this area often use the technique introduced above. When historians read documents "with the grain," they strive to understand the material presented, and what the author is attempting to communicate about it, through the author's eyes and in the author's terms. To read against the grain, one must work counter to the author's overt message and endeavour to unmask or uncover contradictions, inconsistencies, absences, preconceptions, and biases even if these may not have been intentional on the part of the author. For example, a reference to "troublesome," "lazy," or "backward" Indigenous people might easily be read as a sign of their resistance to some offensive act, policy, or administrator. Similarly, comments about "begging" or "theft" could be read as an attempt by Indigenous people to extract a kind of rent or tribute for the use of their territories or resources. "Illegal" occupations of public land could be efforts to claim, or reclaim, sovereignty over traditional territory.

There should be little doubt that language has a unique power to convey meaning and conjure up images in the mind of the reader or listener. Along the same lines, the naming of objects, places, and people is a manifestation of the power of the person or people doing the naming. The decision of the British imperial government and later Canadian authorities to name the Indigenous people resident in what became Canada Indians and then to define, and continually refine, the attributes of who fit within that category is a demonstration of the power of Britain and Canada. More recently, the new Canadian Constitution of 1982 presents the omnibus term "aboriginal" to refer to Indians, Métis, and Inuit. "Aboriginal,"[8] then, is also a construction of the Canadian state and a manifestation of its power. The decision in this reader is to avoid that particular term in favour of what appears to me to be the more neutral word "Indigenous" when referring to First Nations people, Métis, Inuit, and non-status persons collectively, realizing, of course, that this choice too is a manifestation of power, my power as editor, and that my decision will not meet universal approval. It is also understood here that being as specific as possible and referring to specific nations or communities is always preferable and more accurate than using sweeping expressions. Pan-Indianism, or the tendency to write and think about all Indigenous people as one homogenous mass, is rife in Canadian history and is responsible for many misunderstandings and policy blunders. It would be like expecting all the peoples of Europe to have experienced a single history, to adhere to one culture, and to respond to life's challenges in the same way.

In addition to all of the specific considerations discussed above that need to be reflected upon when first encountering any primary source, students must also be aware that nothing was or can be created in a vacuum, uninfluenced by the world around it. Whether it is a government report, a piece of poetry, a diary, an oral account, a photograph, or an altered landscape, every source emerges within a particular context. It is caught within a specific web of time, place, culture, and circumstance. Not unlike the author of a document, a student or professional researcher is also subject to outside influences. Their socio-economic position, cultural background, political orientation, and a host of other factors will affect the way they read and interpret the source. It follows, then, that any secondary material that is necessarily based on an author's interpretation of the primary sources they use cannot be absolutely objective or value free.

Researchers often encounter primary sources that they find offensive. Even these documents, though, help to draw back the curtains keeping us from a fuller understanding of the past. If you were writing a history of Germany in the 1930s, you would hardly avoid consulting and perhaps quoting the writings of Adolph Hitler because you found them repulsive. Similarly, readers of this volume might find some of the works that have

---

8 The decision in this reader is to avoid that particular term in favour of what appears to me to be the more neutral word, "Indigenous," when referring to First Nations people, Métis, Inuit, and non-status persons collectively. Of course, this choice too is a manifestation of power, my power as editor, and my decision will not meet universal approval.

been included to be less than stellar examples of human compassion, understanding, and foresight. Nonetheless, the objective in including these documents here is to lay bare the missteps, poorly conceived policies, selfishness, and draconian actions along with the advances and cooperative efforts that illustrate the relationships between Indigenous peoples and settler society in Canada after 1876. The hope is that the more people in the present can engage with the actual documents created in the past, the more they will be in a position to challenge the standard narrative of Canadian history as a raceless, heroic, unilinear, and unilateral nation-building effort. Arming ourselves with an understanding of Canada's complex and multifaceted past will affect, in turn, how we see and act in the present.

Learning to read critically is a life skill—some might say even a duty—in a democratic society and certainly not one that should be limited to academic pursuits. As the tools of persuasion become more sophisticated and increasingly subtle, heightened vigilance and the development of new skills, like reading against the grain, become ever more essential so that we are able to assess and utilize effectively the masses of information that constantly swirl around us. Reducing our complacency will hopefully limit the possibility of future historians finding documents about us that they find offensive. The purpose of this volume, then, is twofold. Primarily, it is meant to encourage students to assess for themselves some of the building blocks in the relations between Indigenous peoples and Canadian society. In the process, they will perhaps challenge both their own assumptions and popular presentations of the specific events and the larger processes behind these events.

Choosing a start date for a reader like this created its own set of issues. Dates that have significance to Canada or settler society might have little relevance for Indigenous communities. Similarly, dates important to eastern Canada might be relatively unimportant to the North or the West. The start date settled on here, 1876, was chosen primarily because that year was witness to the introduction of Canada's first Indian Act. While the act had more immediate impact where there was a longer history of interaction between Europeans and Indigenous communities, it came to affect virtually every aspect of the lives of those that Canada defined as Indians. The Métis, the Inuit, and non-status Indigenous people, too, have been affected by the Indian Act of 1876, if only, in some cases, because they are not included in its provisions and so have had to struggle in different ways to assert their own distinct identities and legal rights. The relationship between Indigenous people and settler society in post–Indian Act Canada is laced with misunderstandings and contradictions that are often poorly understood or not acknowledged at all. One of the objectives of this volume is to subject some of those issues to the critical analysis of readers.

The documents in this collection were drawn from a variety of sources and include multiple themes and perspectives. Further, a variety of different kinds of primary sources have been included here, each with its own potential strengths and weaknesses. Readers of this collection will have the opportunity not only to interrogate individual letters, transcripts of oral accounts and testimony, official reports, reminiscences, legislation, poetry, photographs, and other materials provided here but also to consider the relative value of different kinds of sources to the different sorts of projects that a historian might undertake. At the same time, in addition to this volume's focus on issues that are significant in their own right, there are also a number of overarching themes represented here. For example Canada's goals of acquiring land and resources and assimilating Indigenous people run through virtually every chapter of this reader, as does Indigenous resistance in its many forms.

Each document and each chapter includes an introductory note meant to provide a little background and context. Students who would like more background information should consult the "further readings" section of each chapter and one of the several survey texts available on the history of the relationship between Indigenous peoples and Canadian society. Three of the most popular of these are J.R. Miller's *Skyscrapers Hide the Heavens: A History of Indian–White Relations in Canada*, Olive Dickason's *Canada's First Nations: A History of Founding Peoples from the Earliest Times*, and Arthur Ray's *I Have Lived Here Since the World Began*. Although each has its own interpretations and focus, the indexes and tables of contents of all can lead readers of this volume to additional contextual and related material if they wish to seek it out.

Even though an effort has been made to incorporate a diverse range of sources on a wide array of topics in this reader, I have, nonetheless, had to make difficult choices about which topics and documents to include. As a result, some readers might find that many important issues and views have been omitted. Similarly, I have made an effort to maintain the integrity of every document (including punctuation style, which varies from reading to reading), but since many of the original pieces are very long, are parts of large collections, or are drawn from transcriptions of months of testimony, some editing was necessary. Given all that has been said above, I must acknowledge that even a light editorial pen undoubtedly causes some strands of the past to be lost. Nonetheless, I hope that this collection goes some way in serving to illustrate the contours in the relationships between Indigenous peoples and the relative newcomers to their territories in the period after 1876. Hopefully, too, it will shed some light on the reasons behind the headlines of the present.

CHAPTER I

"IN A STATE OF TUTELAGE"[1]

THE INDIAN ACT OF 1876

The principles at the heart of Canada's policies related to those defined as Indians are rooted in British imperial strategies that predate the starting point of this reader. Peace, friendship, and alliance marked the earliest British imperial objectives in relation to Indigenous people, but when the need for military alliance was removed after the War of 1812, the final major conflict among European and Euro-American powers and their Indigenous allies for control of North America, policy shifted to include "civilization of the Indian" as a major component. Reserves were established as locations where First Nations people could be trained to better manage their relations with settler society. Next, by the mid-nineteenth century, this policy too was modified from being merely a training exercise to a more profound project of assimilation and indoctrination into settler culture. This shift in direction was codified in legislation passed in the United Canadas in 1857 as An Act to Encourage the Gradual Civilization of the Indian Tribes in this Province, and to Amend the Laws Respecting Indians, otherwise known as the "Gradual Civilization Act."[2] It defined who was an Indian and set out what conditions that person would have to meet to be allowed the rights and privileges granted to Euro-Canadians.

The British North America Act, Canada's constitution between 1867 and 1982, included the provision in Section 91(24) that "Indians and lands reserved for the Indians" would fall under the legislative authority of the Parliament of Canada, as opposed to that of provincial legislatures. With that authority, Canada's parliament moved first to pass An Act for the Gradual Enfranchisement of Indians in 1869 (known as the "Gradual Enfranchisement Act").[3] This act represented a further extension of the goal of assimilation. European-style

---

1 Hector-Louis Langevin in Canada, House of Commons, *Debates*, 4 April 1876, p. 1039. This quotation appears in document 1.1 below.

2 *Statutes of the Province of Canada*, 20 Vic. (1857), c. 26.

3 *Statutes of Canada*, 32–33 Vic. (1869), c. 6.

political structures would be imposed, for example, and elected leaders could be removed by Canadian authorities without the necessity of community consent.

In 1876, as Canada was moving to consolidate its authority over the Prairie West through the numbered treaties, presented in Chapter 2 of this reader, parliament passed the first Indian Act to consolidate and expand existing legislation. The Indian Act of 1876 codified prevailing Euro-Canadian attitudes concerning the superiority of European cultures and world views, the "White man's burden" of "elevating" Indigenous peoples perceived to be backward and in dire need of such assistance, the essential normality of gender relations based on patrilineal descent and male authority, and the necessity of acquiring land for an economy based primarily on agriculture. Although these paternal and racialized attitudes are evident, several of the provisions include a degree of voluntariness in a way that later legislation did not, at least until 1951.

First Nations did not sit by passively and watch these developments but rather organized to at least have input into the content of the Indian Act. The Grand General Indian Council of Ontario and Quebec, for instance, met in conference to craft proposals to amend the legislation. While this and other Indigenous groups and individuals sought a political space to guide Canada's Indian policy, Canada pursued cooperative partners who would support and legitimize its overall policy directions. Some, like the group of Haudenosaunee chiefs presented in document 1.3 refused to accept this kind of role and maintained that Canada had no right to sovereignty over them. Nonetheless, while the Indian Act of 1876 has seen many amendments and modifications since it was passed, it remains in force today and continues to have a profound impact on the lives of those it defines as Indians.

QUESTIONS FOR DISCUSSION

1. What were the federal government's objectives in the 1876 Indian Act?
2. What attitudes toward Indigenous people are reflected in these documents? What specific passages draw you to these conclusions?
3. According to the Indian Act, who is an "Indian"? How could a person cease to be an Indian?
4. How might the Haudenosaunee (Six Nations) respond to the passage of the Indian Act? Why?

DOCUMENTS

1.1   House of Commons Debates on the Proposed Indian Act, 1876

The selections below come from the debates that occurred over a number of days in Canada's House of Commons in 1876 leading up to the passage of the first Indian Act. They illustrate what was important to the parliamentarians of the day and the particular parameters within which discussion on the act was limited, irrespective of partisan differences. There were, of course, no Indian members of parliament, nor were there any women; thus, with these and other absences, the diversity of interests expressed was arguably quite limited. Nonetheless, the issues raised concerning land and the nature of consent required to surrender it, as well as those involving gender relations and the role of government in modifying Indigenous lifeways, continued to inform official discussions and Indigenous grievances for many decades to come.

Source: Canada, House of Commons, *Debates*, 2 March 1876, pp. 342–43; 21 March 1876, p. 753; 28 March 1876, p. 869; 30 March 1876, pp. 928–29; 4 April 1876, pp. 1037–39.

[2 March 1876]

THE INDIANS

Hon. Mr. [David] LAIRD introduced a Bill entituled [sic] "An Act respecting the Indians of Canada." He said: The principal object of this Bill is to consolidate the several laws relating to Indians now on the statute books of the Dominion and the old Provinces of Upper and Lower Canada. We find that there are three different statutes on the Dominion law books, as well as portions of several Acts that were in operation under the laws of Old Canada, and which are still in operation. It is advisable to have these consolidated in the interests of the Indian population throughout the Dominion, and have it applied to all the Provinces. Several amendments of various kinds are introduced. The principal amendment relates to the enfranchisement of Indians. Under the present law an Indian who becomes enfranchised only obtains a life interest in the land set apart for him, and his children have no control over it after his death. The present Act proposes that his children can control the land after his death by will from him. The operation of this it is considered will be an inducement for the Indians to ask for enfranchisement. Hitherto the inducement has been so small that very few of the Indians have asked for the privilege. This Bill proposes to go further; any Indian who is sober and industrious can go to one of the agents appointed for the purpose, to see whether he is qualified for the franchise or not; if qualified he receives a ticket for land, and after three years he is entitled to receive a patent for it which will give him absolute control of the portion allotted to him for his own use during his lifetime, and after that it will be controlled by whoever it is willed to. It is thought that this will encourage them to improve their land, and have a tendency to train them for a more civilized life. It is also intended that after they have obtained the patent for their land, if they wish to go on further and get possession of their share of the invested funds of the land, they can make application accordingly, and after three years further they will be entitled to a distribution of the funds; thus after six years of good behaviour they will receive their land and their share of the moneys in the hands of the Government, and will cease in every respect to be Indians according to the acceptation of the laws of Canada relating to Indians. We will then have nothing more to do with their affairs, except as ordinary subjects of Her Majesty.

Sir JOHN A. MACDONALD—The Bill is a very important one. It affects the interests of the Indians who are especially under the guardianship of the Crown and of Parliament. From the statement of the hon. gentleman, I have a great deal of doubt whether it would be well to give every Indian, when he becomes 21 years of age, the right of absolute disposal of his lands. I am afraid it would introduce into this country a system by which land-sharks could get hold of their estates. However, we will have a better opportunity of discussing the question on the second reading.

. . .

[21 March 1876]

THE LAWS RESPECTING INDIANS

. . .

Mr. [William] MCGREGOR thought that the Bill was a step in the right direction, as Indians should have it within their power to obtain the full privileges of the white men. The Leader of the Opposition had had the honour of attending at a banquet given to an Indian residing in the County of Peel. The latter's brother, if in the House, would hardly be supposed to be an Indian, and indeed, many hon. members would sooner be so considered than this person.

The Minister of the Interior had visited his county last year, and settled a dispute, which had long existed there between the whites and Indians, the males being allotted 100 and the females 50 acres of the land, the balance being sold. They occupied about 8,000 acres. He regretted that the term of probation was not shorter, as three-quarters of the Indians in his county might very properly be enfranchised at once.

Mr. [George] SNIDER had had a great deal to do with Indian Reserves and with Indians, who he knew were very grateful to the Minister of the Interior for the interest the hon. gentleman had taken in their welfare. He had with great pleasure shown educated Indians around the Parliament Buildings, and these he could say would do the House no discredit if they occupied seats on this floor, being more intelligent than the great majority of white men. This was a great improvement on former similar Bills, and the Indians were perfectly satisfied with its provisions. He did not think that Indians could be so easily tempted with bribes as whites; and he hoped that the Bill would be made as perfect as possible.

Mr. [Gavin] FLEMIMNG [sic] contended that the policy to be pursued with regard to the Indians, must be either one of preservation or one of absorption and amalgation [sic]. Legislation during the past twenty years had a tendency in the former direction. In 1857 he believed the first Bill having relation to the enfranchisement of Indians had been introduced by the right hon. member for Kingston, who explained that the object was to raise them to the position of white men. If it had failed this was to be ascribed to the fact that the machinery provided had not been sufficient for the purpose. Indians should be placed precisely on the same footing with whites; and they should be made more self-reliant and self-dependent. He was greatly gratified on account of the introduction of the Bill; and he would have been better pleased had it gone still further, offering them greater inducements for self-advancement.

. . .

[28 March 1876]

INDIAN LEGISLATION

Hon. Mr. [David] LAIRD moved the House in to Committee of the Whole on the Bill to amend and consolidate the laws respecting Indians.

The first and second clauses were adopted without amendment.

On clause 3,

Mr. [William] PATERSON suggested that the word "male" be struck out.

Hon. Mr. [David] LAIRD said it made no difference, because when an Indian man married a white woman she became a member of the band, but when an Indian woman married a white man, her children did not share in the lands.

Mr. [William] PATERSON doubted if it was wise to impose a penalty on an Indian woman for marrying a white man. He contended it would be a benefit to the country to encourage such intermarriages.

Hon. Mr. [David] LAIRD said there was a great deal of force in the remarks of the hon. member, and an endeavour was made in another sub-section to meet the objection. It was proposed to allow an Indian woman who married a white man to retain her annuity moneys during her life time, and if she wished to receive the capital sum, she could do so by drawing ten years' purchase of annuity money. Of course she and her husband would then cease to have any connection with the band, and their children would not be considered.

The sub-section was passed.

. . .

[30 March 1876]

THE INDIAN LAWS

. . .

Hon. Mr. [Hector-Louis] LANGEVIN, with reference to Section 26th which provides for the release or surrender of Reserves, held that the majority of the band should be required to be present when this was in consideration.

Hon. Mr. [Alexander] MACKENZIE remarked that an officer of the Government would be present on such occasions, preventing any chance of a mistake.

Hon. Mr. [David] LAIRD was of the opinion that the section gave more protection than when simply the presence of the majority of the Chiefs was required.

Hon. Mr. [Hector-Louis] LANGEVIN—At all events the majority of the band should be present.

Hon. Mr. [Alexander] MACKENZIE—It will never be done without the assistance of the majority.

Mr. [John Christian] SCHULTZ entirely agreed with this hon. friend from Charlevoix [Langevin] in this relation. It was perfectly well known that some of the recent difficulties with Indians in the States has arisn [sic] from the fact that such assent was not obtained.

Hon. Mr. [David] LAIRD—The provision confers quite sufficient protection; an officer of the Government will be in attendance, and if any serious complaint is made attention can be given to it.

Hon. Mr. [Alexander] MACKENZIE—That is substantially provided for in another part of the Bill.

Hon. Mr. [Hector-Louis] LANGEVIN—In what part?

Hon. Mr. [Alexander] MACKENZIE—In the 61st section.

Hon. Mr. [Hector-Louis] LANGEVIN—I cannot prevent the clause from passing but I say once more that the protection is not sufficient. When I was at the head of the Department, complaints were preferred against our officers. They were very jealous—and properly so—of their rights.

Hon. Mr. [Alexander] MACKENIZE [sic]—Is the hon. gentleman satisfied with a majority?

Hon. Mr. [Hector-Louis] LANGEVIN—The majority of the band should be present.

Hon. Mr. [Alexander] MACKENZIE—That is is [sic] required in the 61st Section.

The section was passed.

. . .

[4 April 1876]

THE INDIAN LAWS

[On section 86, the enfranchisement provisions of the act]

Hon. Mr. [Hector-Louis] LANGEVIN stated, that after three years of probation, if he remembered right, the Indian would obtain under this Act full title to his property; consequently he might sell it at any time, and white men purchasing might intrude on the reserves. He knew that this had been the objection to the law as it now stood and which was enacted in 1869. The consent of the band to enfranchisement would be obtained for this reason: it would introduce whites on the reserves, and bring about all the evils which followed the mingling of the two races. Great difficulty, at least, would be experienced in obtaining the assent of a band to the enfranchisement of one of their number fitted to enjoy this privilege. He was aware of the delicate nature of this question, but it nevertheless must be settled. They should have in view the gradual enfranchisement of all the Indians living amongst us. He thought that the intention of the Government was good, but he did not consider that the result would meet the views of the Minister of the Interior. He drew attention to these matters, because this clause of course contained the principle of this section of the Bill.

Hon. Mr. [David] LAIRD agreed with a great portion of the remarks of the hon [sic] member for Charlevoix; but in the first place the Government thought that it would be very undesirable to frame any scheme for enfranchisement which would not be acceptable to the Indians. If this were done regardless of the consent of the band, confusion, want of harmony, and dissatisfaction would be produced. They knew from experience, and from the deliberations of the Council held the other year at Sarnia, that the Indians generally in these Provinces, were willing to accord enfranchisement to intelligent members of these Bands. By the 88th clause of the Bill, while the enfranchisement enabled them to hold their lands in fee simple, they also had the right to sit in Council and draw their annuities; and this was precisely what the Indians desired. The hon. member remarked that white men might settle on the reserves if these provisions were enforced; but if the great privilege in question was not accorded they would run counter to the whole policy of the Government regarding the surrenders which had existed for years. It was our boast that we did not take an acre of land from the Indians without their consent; and if this privilege were denied them, they would have a right to complain. This

Act was in entire harmony with the surrender principle; and he did not think that much trouble would be met in carrying it into effect. The Six Nation Indians did not seem quite prepared for it, but when they saw other Bands accept it, they would soon follow their example. As regarded the North-West Territories, Manitoba and British Columbia, they did not expect that these provisions would be applicable to the Indians living in these regions for some years to come. This was the best they could do under the circumstances; and while they could offer counsel and advice to the Indians at all times, he thought that they should not attempt to act in any way contrary to the views of the Indians, at least as far as their rights to property were concerned. This was the policy of the Administration.

Mr. [William] PATERSON remarked that in 1857 the right hon. member for Kingston [John A. Macdonald] had introduced a Bill, in which this feature of enfranchisement was recognised. This law was amended by the hon. member for Charlevoix in 1869 [Simon-Xavier Cimon], and though the principle was recognised, the law had remained inoperative—in fact a dead letter in this respect. Only one Indian he believed had sought to obtain this privilege under it, but when he had secured it, no land was allotted to him. The Minister of the Interior dwelt upon this subject in his report in language full of eloquence and of truth, stating that he was firmly persuaded that the true interests of the aborigines and the State alike require that every effort should be made to aid the red man in lifting himself out of his condition of tutelage and dependence. It was the duty of the Government then to consider whether every aid was given the Indian seeking enfranchisement. He feared that in some of the tribes the consent of the majority of the Band required by the Acts would not be given, and thus the desire of the Indian seeking enfranchisement be denied.

He would suggest that it should be so amended that when the majority of the tribe refused to allow one of their number the right of enfranchisement, he could have the right of appeal to the General Superintendent; without such a remedy the Bill would, he feared, be defective.

Hon. Mr. [David] LAIRD said this Bill was found to meet the wishes of the Indians themselves, and consequently they expected it to be more effective than the Bill of 1857. If it was found after a year or two that the suggestion of the hon. gentlemen would be any improvement the law would be easily amended.

Mr. [Gavin] FLEMING said the Indians of the Six Nations were too shrewd and intelligent to accept of the enfranchisement offered under the Acts of 1857 and 1869. If we would enfranchise the Indians we must offer them such inducement as would make it worth their while to ask for. They should first be located on their reserves; first decide what land they should have, and let them feel that this land was theirs forever, but do not give them the power to alienate it to white men, and as soon as they knew exactly what they possessed then they would look for enfranchisement; but the most intelligent Indians were debarred from it by this clause, which would put them in a worse position than they now occupied.

Mr. [John Christian] SCHULTZ said that as the discussion on this Bill had already occupied much time, he would content himself with making some observations generally on the clauses under the heading of enfranchisement. The clauses under this head, he thought objectionable for the following reasons:—They are merely a repetition in a modified form of existing rules which have been found to be utterly inapplicable and are so complicated and cumbersome that it would be next to impossible for an Indian, however well qualified otherwise, to become enfranchised under them; and this is proven by the fact that although the law has been long in existence, no Indian, as far as he knew, has ever availed or attempted to avail himself of its provisions. Again, these clauses would make enfranchisement contingent, not only on the breaking up of the reserves into separate freehold allotments, but also on the Indians ceasing to be Indians under the meaning of the Statutes. It would therefore follow that Indians, no matter how wealthy, intelligent or well-educated, must continue to be without civil rights, unless they comply with rules which, even if they could be complied with, would have the effect of breaking up the whole system of Indian management, thus depriving the Indians of the protection they have hitherto enjoyed, and it is well known, or at least, generally supposed that these rules were adopted in the first instance, with a view to breaking up the tribal system and enabling the white man to get possession of the lands of the Indians.

Again—these causes being, as proved by practical experience of similar ones, inapplicable, will continue to be inoperative, in fact a dead letter, except in so far as that they will, as heretofore, deprive a large number of very deserving people in Ontario at least, of civil rights, and a well-to-do Indian will still have the mortification of seeing his white labourers voting at elections, while he, the son of the soil, finds himself in an inferior position, branded in fact as an outlaw, and unfit to share in the common privileges of a white man. The Act will thus have the very opposite effect to that which was no doubt intended. Instead of imbuing the Indian with a sense of self-respect, and leading them to feel that when they have advanced in civilization they are to stand on an equal footing with the white man, it will have a tendency to degrade them in their own eyes and in the estimation of those around them. The Indians are everywhere so attached to their tribal system that they will not abandon it, and some way should be found of leading them to civilization and independence without trenching on this, their most cherished institution. In Ontario the Indians have, in many cases, passed the probationary period and are in a position to exercise the franchise as judiciously as the majority of white men.

The interpretation of the word "enfranchisement," section 3, sub-section 5, does not make the matter any better, but the clause might be relieved to some extent of its objectionable features by using the words "freehold" and "freeholder" for "enfranchised" and "enfranchisement;" and it should be left entirely to the Provinces to say who shall, or who shall not vote at elections, which is the spirit at least, of the present election law.

Hon. Mr. [David] LAIRD said that the term "enfranchised" was defined in the Bill, and in view of hls [sic] hon. friend's representations he proposed introducing an amendment.

Mr. [John Christian] SCHULTZ said he was aware of it, but the definition did not relieve the objectionable features of these clauses. However, he was glad to learn that, in view of the different condition of the Indians of the North-West as compared with those of the older Provinces, the hon. Minister intended to make an amendment to the Bill and as he (Mr. Schultz) had before explained the different circumstances of the Indians of the North-West, he hoped the amendment would be of such a character as would render the Bill applicable to both.

Hon. Mr. [Hector-Louis] LANGEVIN said the Minister of Interior would agree with him it would not be wise to give the Superintendent General the power to enfranchise Indians who had been refused that privilege by the band. It would be better to fix a time—say a period of fifteen years—at the expiration of which all the members of a band should be enfranchised.

Hon. Mr. [David] LAIRD—They would not all be fit.

Hon. Mr. [Hector-Louis] LANGEVIN said there were many white men who were not fit for enfranchisement, yet they enjoyed all the rights of freemen. By being educated all the members of a band would become fit for taking their places in Society. The object of this Bill was to keep the Indians, with the exception of a few, in a state of tutelage. Looking to the future of the race, he believed the true policy should be to do away with that system, by the gradual emancipation of all the Indians who lived in villages and were settled on lands.

Hon. Mr. [David] LAIRD said that would offer no inducement to them to become fit for enfranchisement. Under this Bill they were given some aim to better themselves, and he believed that was the true policy.

Mr. [William] PATERSON said at the same time it struck a blow at the very root of the tribal relation. The very fact of an Indian seeking enfranchisement implied that he no longer wished to be recognized as an Indian.

Hon. Mr. [David] LAIRD—An Indian is not cut off from his band by enfranchisement. He belongs to the tribe as much as ever he did.

Mr. [William] PATERSON said it was impossible at the same time to preserve the tribal relations and facilitate the enfranchisement of the Indians. If the Government were prepared to take the position that the tribal relations must continue for all time to come, then it was a mistake to do any thing in the way of enfranchisement at all. It was evident the proposition of the hon. member for Charlevoix would have to be adopted ere long—a time must be fixed when all Indians living in the midst of civilized communities and refusing to move to the North West, must be enfranchised. Take the Brant reserve for instance. The Indians there are increasing rapidly, and something must be done to meet their case. They would not remove to a larger reserve, and there remained only the alternative of enfranchising the whole band at a certain time.

The clause passed.

. . .

1.2 The Indian Act of 1876

The Indian Act of 1876 consolidated and expanded legislation already passed by the parliaments of the United Kingdom and Canada. Though its main precursors were the 1857 "Gradual Civilization Act" and the 1869 "Gradual Enfranchisement Act," other pieces of legislation, too, were brought together in this single piece of legislation. Like the Debates *in the last section, the Indian Act itself demonstrates what was considered important to Canada's parliamentarians and the society they represented, though the issues presented were not necessarily those that Indigenous people believed needed attention. As mentioned in the introduction to this chapter, the 1876 act codified the prevailing Euro-Canadian view that Indigenous people would have to become more like them if they were to survive and thrive. Although the segments from the Indian Act reproduced here focus primarily on identity broadly defined, including who was an "Indian" and who was a "person," what political identity a community would be compelled to accept, and the rules regarding the land it would be allowed to retain, this legislation affected virtually every aspect of an Indian's life. The intrusive aspects of the act and its provisions that promoted assimilation were to become even more numerous and profound over time.*

Source: Canada, An Act to Amend and Consolidate the Laws Respecting Indians, *Statutes of Canada*, 39 Vic. (1876), c.18.

CHAP. 18.
An Act to amend and consolidate the laws respecting Indians.

[Assented to 12th April, 1876.]

Preamble.

WHEREAS it is expedient to amend and consolidate the laws respecting Indians: Therefore Her Majesty, by and with the advice and consent of the Senate and House of Commons of Canada, enacts as follows:—

Short title and extent of Act.

1. This Act shall be known and may be cited as "*The Indian Act*, 1876;" and shall apply to all the Provinces, and to the North West Territories, including the Territory of Keewatin.

Superintendent General.

2. The Minister of the Interior shall be Superintendent-General of Indian Affairs, and shall be governed in the supervision of the said affairs, and in the control and management of the reserves, lands, moneys and property of Indians in Canada by the provisions of this Act.

TERMS.

Meanings assigned to terms in this Act.

3. The following terms contained in this Act shall be held to have the meaning hereinafter assigned to them, unless such meaning be repugnant to the subject or inconsistent with the context:—

Band.

1. The term "band" means any tribe, band or body of Indians who own or are interested in a reserve or in Indian lands in common, of which the legal title is vested in the Crown, or who share alike in the distribution of any annuities or interest moneys for which the Government of Canada is responsible; the term "the band" means the band to which the context relates; and the term "band," when action is being taken by the band as such, means the band in council.

Irregular Band.

2. The term "irregular band" means any tribe, band or body of persons of Indian blood who own no interest in any reserve or lands of which the legal title is vested in the Crown, who possess no common fund managed by the Government of Canada, or who have not had any treaty relations with the Crown.

Indians.

3. The term "Indian" means

First. Any male person of Indian blood reputed to belong to a particular band;

Secondly. Any child of such person;

Thirdly. Any woman who is or was lawfully married to such person;

(a) Provided that any illegitimate child, unless having shared with the consent of the band in the distribution moneys of such band for a period exceeding two years, may, at any time, be excluded from the membership thereof by the band, if such proceeding be sanctioned by the Superintendent-General: *As to illegitimates.*

(b) Provided that any Indian having for five years continuously resided in a foreign country shall with the sanction of the Superintendent-General, cease to be a member thereof and shall not be permitted to become again a member thereof, or of any other band, unless the consent of the band with the approval of the Superintendent-General or his agent, be first had and obtained; but this provision shall not apply to any professional man, mechanic, missionary, teacher or interpreter, while discharging his or her duty as such: *Absentees.*

(c) Provided that any Indian woman marrying any other than an Indian or a non-treaty Indian shall cease to be an Indian in any respect within the meaning of this Act, except that she shall be entitled to share equally with the members of the band to which she formerly belonged, in the annual or semi-annual distribution of their annuities, interest moneys and rents; but this income may be commuted to her at any time at ten years' purchase with the consent of the band: *Women marrying other than an Indian.*

(d) Provided that any Indian woman marrying an Indian of any other band, or a non-treaty Indian shall cease to be a member of the band to which she formerly belonged and become a member of the band or irregular band of which her husband is a member: *Marrying non-treaty Indians.*

(e) Provided also that no half-breed in Manitoba who has shared in the distribution of half-breed lands shall be accounted an Indian; and that no half-breed head of a family (except the widow of an Indian, or a half-breed who has already been admitted into a treaty), shall, unless under very special circumstances, to be determined by the Superintendent-General or his agent, be accounted an Indian, or entitled to be admitted into any Indian treaty.   *As to half-breeds.*

4. The term "non-treaty Indian" means any person of Indian blood who is reputed to belong to an irregular band, or who follows the Indian mode of life, even though such person be only a temporary resident in Canada.   *Non-treaty Indian.*

5. The term "enfranchised Indian" means any Indian, his wife or minor unmarried child, who has received letters patent granting him in fee simple any portion of the reserve which may have been allotted to him, his wife and minor children, by the band to which he belongs, or any unmarried Indian who may have received letters patent for an allotment of the reserve.   *Enfranchised Indian.*

Reserve.	6. The term "reserve" means any tract or tracts of land set apart by treaty or otherwise for the use or benefit of or granted to a particular band of Indians, of which the legal title is in the Crown, but which is unsurrendered, and includes all the trees, wood, timber, soil, stone, minerals, metals, or other valuables thereon or therein.
Special Reserve.	7. The term "special reserve" means any tract or tracts of land and everything belonging thereto set apart for the use or benefit of any band or irregular band of Indians, the title of which is vested in a society, corporation or community legally established, and capable of suing and being sued, or in a person or persons of European descent, but which land is held in trust for, or benevolently allowed to be used by, such band or irregular band of Indians.
Indian lands.	8. The term "Indian lands" means any reserve or portion of a reserve which has been surrendered to the Crown.
Intoxicants.	9. The term "intoxicants" means and includes all spirits, strong waters, spirituous liquors, wines, or fermented or compounded liquors or intoxicating drink of any kind whatsoever, and any intoxicating liquor or fluid, as also opium and any preparation thereof, whether liquid or solid, and any other intoxicating drug or substance, and tobacco or tea mixed or compounded or impregnated with opium or with other intoxicating drugs, spirits or substances, and whether the same or any of them be liquid or solid.
Superintendent General.	10. The term "Superintendent-General" means the Superintendent-General of Indian Affairs.
Agent.	11. The term "agent" means a commissioner, superintendent, agent, or other officer acting under the instructions of the Superintendent-General.
Person.	12. The term "person" means an individual other than an Indian, unless the context clearly requires another construction.
	. . .

SURRENDERS.

Necessary conditions previous to a sale.	25. No reserve or portion of a reserve shall be sold, alienated or leased until it has been released or surrendered to the Crown for the purposes of this Act.
On what conditions release or surrender to be valid.	26. No release or surrender of a reserve, or portion of a reserve, held for the use of the Indians of any band or of any individual Indian, shall be valid or binding, except on the following conditions:—
Assent of band.	1. The release or surrender shall be assented to by a majority of the male members of the band of the full age of twenty-one years, at a meeting or council thereof summoned for that purpose according to their rules, and held in the presence of the Superintendent-General, or of an officer duly authorized to attend such council by the Governor in Council or by the Superintendent-General; Provided, that no Indian shall be entitled to vote or be present at such council, unless he habitually resides on or near and is interested in the reserve in question;
Proviso.	
Proof of assent.	2. The fact that such release or surrender has been assented to by the band at such council or meeting, shall be certified on oath before some judge of a superior, county, or district court, or stipendiary magistrate, by the Superintendent-General

or by the officer authorized by him to attend such council or meeting, and by some one of the chiefs or principal men present thereat and entitled to vote, and when so certified as aforesaid shall be submitted to the Governor in Council for acceptance or refusal;

Superintendent-General may grant license to cut trees, &c.

3. But nothing herein contained shall be construed to prevent the Superintendent-General from issuing a license to any person or Indian to cut and remove trees, wood, timber and hay, or to quarry and remove stone and gravel on and from the reserve; Provided he, or his agent acting by his instructions, first obtain the consent of the band thereto in the ordinary manner as hereinafter provided.

Proviso.

No intoxicant to be permitted at council of Indians.

27. It shall not be lawful to introduce at any council or meeting of Indians held for the purpose of discussing or of assenting to a release or surrender of a reserve or portion thereof, or of assenting to the issuing of a timber or other license, any intoxicant; and any person introducing at such meeting, and any agent or officer employed by the Superintendent-General, or by the Governor in Council, introducing, allowing or countenancing by his presence the use of such intoxicant among such Indians a week before, at, or a week after, any such council or meeting, shall forfeit two hundred dollars, recoverable by action in any of the superior courts of law, one half of which penalty shall go to the informer.

Invalid surrenders not confirmed hereby.

28. Nothing in this Act shall confirm any release or surrender which would have been invalid if this Act had not been passed; and no release or surrender of any reserve to any party other than the Crown, shall be valid.

. . .

COUNCILS AND CHIEFS

Votes at election of chiefs.

61. At the election of a chief or chiefs, or the granting of any ordinary consent required of a band of Indians under this Act, those entitled to vote at the council or meeting thereof shall be the male members of the band of the full age of twenty-one years; and the vote of a majority of such members at a council or meeting of the band summoned according to their rules, and held in the presence of the Superintendent-General, or an agent acting under his instructions, shall be sufficient to determine such election, or grant such consent;

In ordinary cases.

Provided that in the case of any band having a council of chiefs or councillors, any ordinary consent required of the band may be granted by a vote of a majority of such chiefs or councillors at a council summoned according to their rules, and held in the presence of the Superintendent-General or his agent.

Periods of election how fixed: and term of office.

62. The Governor in Council may order that the chiefs of any band of Indians shall be elected, as hereinbefore provided, at such time and place, as the Superintendent-General may direct, and they shall in such case be elected for a period of three years, unless deposed by the Governor for dishonesty, intemperance, immorality, or incompetency; and they may be in the proportion of one head chief and two second chiefs or councillors for every two hundred Indians; but any such band composed of thirty Indians may have one chief: Provided always, that all life chiefs now living shall continue as such until death or resignation, or until their removal by the Governor for dishonesty, intemperance, immorality, or incompetency.

Number of Chiefs.

Proviso: as to life chiefs.

63. The chief or chiefs of any band in council may frame, subject to confirmation by the Governor in Council, rules and regulations for the following subjects, viz.:

1. The care of the public health;
2. The observance of order and decorum at assemblies of the Indians in general council, or on other occasions;
3. The repression of intemperance and profligacy;
4. The prevention of trespass by cattle;
5. The maintenance or roads, bridges, ditches and fences;
6. The construction and repair of school houses, council houses and other Indian public buildings;
7. The establishments of pounds and the appointment of pound-keepers;
8. The locating of the land in their reserves, and the establishment of a register of such locations.

. . .

ENFRANCHISEMENT

86. Whenever any Indian man, or unmarried woman, of the full age of twenty-one years, obtains the consent of the band of which he or she is a member to become enfranchised, and whenever such Indian has been assigned by the band a suitable allotment of land for that purpose, the local agent shall report such action of the band, and the name of the applicant to the Superintendent-General; whereupon the said Superintendent-General, if satisfied that the proposed allotment of land is equitable, shall authorize some competent person to report whether the applicant is an Indian who, from the degree of civilization to which he or she has attained, and the character for integrity, morality and sobriety which he or she bears, appears to be qualified to become a proprietor of land in fee simple; and upon the favorable report of such person, the Superintendent-General may grant such Indian a location ticket as a probationary Indian, for the land allotted to him or her by the band.

(1.) Any Indian who may be admitted to the degree of Doctor of Medicine, or to any other degree by any University of Learning, or who may be admitted in any Province of the Dominion to practice law either as an Advocate or as a Barrister or Counsellor or Solicitor or Attorney or to be a Notary Public, or who may enter Holy Orders or who may be licensed by any denomination of Christians as a Minister of the Gospel, shall *ipso facto* become and be enfranchised under this Act.

87. After the expiration of three years (or such longer period as the Superintendent-General may deem necessary in the event of such Indian's conduct not being satisfactory), the Governor may, on the report of the Superintendent-General, order the issue of letters patent, granting to such Indian in fee simple the land which had, with this object in view, been allotted to him or her by location ticket.

88. Every such Indian shall, before the issue of the letters patent mentioned in the next preceding section, declare to the Superintendent-General the name and surname by which he or she wishes to be enfranchised and thereafter known, and on his or her receiving such letters patent, in such name and surname, he or she shall be held to be also enfranchised, and he or she shall thereafter be known by such name or surname, and if such Indian be a married man his wife and minor unmarried children also shall be held to be enfranchised; and from the date of such letters patent the provisions of this Act and of any Act or law making any distinction between the legal rights, privileges, disabilities and liabilities of Indians and those of Her Majesty's other subjects shall cease to apply to any Indian, or to the wife or minor unmarried children of any Indian as aforesaid, so declared to be enfranchised, who shall no longer be deemed Indians within the meaning of the laws relating to Indians, except in so far as their right to participate in the annuities and interest moneys, and rents and councils of the band of Indians to which they belonged is concerned: Provided always, that any children of a probationary Indian, who being minors and unmarried when the probationary ticket was granted to such Indian, arrive at the full age of twenty-one years before the letters patent are issued to such Indian, may, at the discretion of the Governor in Council, receive letters patent in their own names for their respective shares of the land allotted under the said ticket, at the same time that letters patent are granted to their parent: and provided, that if any Indian child having arrived at the full age of twenty-one years, during his or her parents' probationary period, be unqualified for enfranchisement, or if any child of such parent, having been a minor at the commencement of such period, be married during such period, then a quantity of land equal to the share of such child shall be deducted in such manner as may be directed by the Superintendent-General, from the allotment made to such Indian parent on receiving his probationary ticket.

Wife and minor children enfranchised. Effect of such enfranchisement.

Proviso as to children attaining majority before their father's probation expires.

Proviso as to children found unqualified, or being married.

89. If any probationary Indian should fail in qualifying to become enfranchised, or should die before the expiration of the required probation, his or her claim, or the claim of his or her heirs to the land, for which a probationary ticket was granted, or the claim of any unqualified Indian, or of any Indian who may marry during his or her parents' probationary period, to the land deducted under the operation of the next preceding section from his or her parents' probationary allotment, shall in all respects be the same as that conferred by an ordinary location ticket, as provided in the sixth, seventh, eighth and ninth sections of this Act.

Case of Indian dying before expiration of probation or failing to qualify.

90. The children of any widow who becomes either a probationary or enfranchised Indian shall be entitled to the same privileges as those of a male head of a family in like circumstances.

As to children of widows probationary or enfranchised.

91. In allotting land to probationary Indians, the quantity to be located to the head of a family shall be in proportion to the number of such family compared with the total quantity of land in the reserve, and the whole number of the band, but any band may determine what quantity shall be allotted to each member for enfranchisement purposes, provided each female of any age, and each male member under fourteen years of age receive not less than one-half the quantity allotted to each male member of fourteen years of age and over.

Rules for allotting lands to probationary Indians.

Proviso: as to power of Band in this behalf.

92. Any Indian, not a member of the band, or any non-treaty Indian, who, with the consent of the band and the approval of the Superintendent-General, has been permitted to reside upon the reserve, or obtain a location thereon, may, on being assigned a suitable allotment of land by the band for enfranchisement, become enfranchised

As to Indians not members of the Band, but permitted to reside on their reserve.

on the same terms and conditions as a member of the band; and such enfranchisement shall confer upon such Indian the same legal rights and privileges, and make such Indian subject to such disabilities and liabilities as affect Her Majesty's other subjects; but such enfranchisement shall not confer upon such Indian any right to participate in the annuities, interest moneys, rents and councils of the band.

Proviso.

Provision when Band decides that all its members may become enfranchised.

93. Whenever any band of Indians, at a council summoned for the purpose according to their rules, and held in the presence of the Superintendent-General or of any agent duly authorized by him to attend such council, decides to allow every member of the band who chooses, and who may be found qualified, to become enfranchised, and to receive his or her share of the principal moneys of the band, and sets apart for such member a suitable allotment of land for the purpose, any applicant of such band after such a decision may be dealt with as provided in the seven next preceding sections until his or her enfranchisement is attained; and whenever any member of the band, who for the three years immediately succeeding the date on which he or she

Or when Indian becomes qualified by exemplary conduct.

was granted letters patent, or for any longer period that the Superintendent-General may deem necessary, by his or her exemplary good conduct and management of property, proves that he or she is qualified to receive his or her share of such moneys, the Governor may, on the report of the Superintendent-General to that effect, order that the said Indian be paid his or her share of the capital funds at the credit of the band, or his or her share of the principal of the annuities of the band, estimated as yielding five per cent. out of such moneys as may be provided for the purpose by Parliament; and if such Indian be a married man then he shall also be paid his wife and minor unmarried children's share of such funds and other principal

If such Indian be a married man or widow.

moneys, and if such Indian be a widow, she shall also be paid her minor unmarried children's share: and the unmarried children of such married Indians, who become of age during either the probationary period of enfranchisement or for payment of such moneys, if qualified by the character for integrity, morality and sobriety which they bear, shall receive their own share of such moneys when their parents are paid, and if not so qualified, before they can become enfranchised or receive payment of such moneys they must themselves pass through the probationary periods; and all

And as to unmarried children of such enfranchised married Indians.

such Indians and their unmarried minor children who are paid their share of the principal moneys of their band as aforesaid, shall thenceforward cease in every respect to be Indians of any class within the meaning of this Act, or Indians within the meaning of any other Act or law.

Provision as to Indians in British Columbia, N.-W. Territories or Keewatin.

94. Sections eighty-six to ninety-three, both inclusive, of this Act, shall not apply to any band of Indians in the Province of British Columbia, the Province of Manitoba, the North-West Territories, or the Territory of Keewatin, save in so far as the said sections may, by proclamation of the Governor-General, be from time to time extended, as they may be, to any band of Indians in any of the said provinces or territories.

1.3 Letter from George Buck and 32 Other Six Nations Chiefs, 1876

The Haudenosaunee Confederacy, also known as the Six Nations Confederacy or the Iroquois Confederacy, has consistently maintained that it is independent of Canadian authority. The confederacy draws this position from treaties such as the covenant chain of peace and friendship and the two-row wampum, which were entered into beginning in the seventeenth century. The document included here is a letter from 1876, the same year as the first Indian Act. It was signed by 31 Haudenosaunee chiefs belonging to the Onondaga, Cayuga, and Seneca nations and also by two chiefs of their Delaware allies.

The spelling of the original is retained.

Source: Notice from Six Nations Reserve—George Buck and 32 Other Chiefs to David Laird, SGIA, 17 August 1876, Library and Archives Canada, Department of Indian Affairs, RG 10, vol. 1995, file 6897, reel C-11130.

Oshweken Council House of the Six Nation Chiefs Indians

August 17th 1876,

To the Honourable
    Mr. D. Laird
        Supt General of Indian Affairs

We the undersigned Chiefs & Members of the Six United Nation Indian Allies to the British Government residing on the Grand River, Township of Tuscarora, Onondaga and Oneida, in the counties of Brant and Haldimand Ont, To your Honourable our Brother "by the treaty of Peace" we thought it is fit and proper to bring a cirtin things under your Notice which it is a very great hindrance and grievance in our Council for we believe in this part it is your duty to take it into consideration with your government to have this great hindrance and grivance to be removed in our Council and it is this, one says we are subjects to the British Government and ought to be controled under those Laws which was past in the Dominion Parliament by your Government you personally, and the others (that is us) says we are not subjects but we are Allies to the British Government, and to your Honourable our Brother we will now inform you and your Government, personally that we will not deny to be Allies, but we will be Allies to the British Government as our forefathers were we will further inform your Honourable our Brother and to your Government that we do now seprate from them henceforth we will have nothing to do with them any more as they like to be controled under your Laws we now let them go to become as your own people, but us we will follow our Ancient Laws and Rules, and we will not depart from it.

[signed by George Buck and 32 other chiefs]

SUGGESTIONS FOR FURTHER READING

Most surveys of Canadian history, and especially those that focus on the relations between Indigenous people and settler society (such as those by Miller, Dickason, and Ray noted in the main introduction to this reader), will have at least a brief section on the Indian Act of 1876, and they will often also discuss its legislative precursors and comment on later amendments to it. For additional context related to how the official thinking and policy objectives that lay behind Canada's first Indian Act had their roots firmly located in pre-Confederation British programs and strategies, see John S. Milloy, "The Early Indian Acts: Developmental Strategy and Constitutional Change," in *Sweet Promises: A Reader on Indian-White Relations in Canada*, ed. J.R. Miller (Toronto: University of Toronto Press, 1991), 145–54. For an exploration of the objectives of policy related to First Nations people and the ways in which these were translated into legislation during the period beginning before Confederation and concluding with the withdrawal of the *Statement of the Government of Canada on Indian Policy, 1969* (known as "The White Paper"), see John Tobias, "Protection, Civilization, Assimilation: An Outline History of Canada's Indian Policy," *Western Canadian Journal of Anthropology* 6, no. 2 (1976): 13–30. For a detailed exploration of the development of policy and legislation from the pre-Confederation period through to the 1951 amendments to the Indian Act, see John Leslie and Ron Maguire, *The Historical Development of the Indian Act* (Ottawa: DIAND, 1978). For an examination of the difficulties established by the Indian Act of 1876, its precursors and later amendments, see Canada, Royal Commission on Aboriginal Peoples, "The Indian Act," *Report of the Royal Commission on Aboriginal Peoples*, vol. 1, *Looking Forward, Looking Back* (Ottawa: Indian and Northern Affairs Canada, 1996), ch. 9. This report is available on line at http://www.collectionscanada.gc.ca/webarchives/20071124124337/http://www.ainc-inac.gc.ca/ch/rcap/sg/sgm9_e.html.

CHAPTER 2

"NO MORE FIGHTING BETWEEN ANYONE"[1]

THE NUMBERED TREATIES

Indigenous nations and communities in what became Canada were making treaties with each other for millennia before the first Europeans arrived in their lands. Treaties might be made to clarify access to resources, to end or prevent conflict, to secure alliance, to facilitate trade, or for any one of the other reasons that any nation or community in Europe or elsewhere might treat with another party. Similarly, treaty making between Indigenous people and the newcomers to their territories has taken place since the earliest days of the encounter and continues through to the present. These agreements have varied in intent and content, and, though each of the parties to the treaties had their own reasons for entering into a relationship of this sort, all understood the importance of a establishing a bond that would protect their interests. A century before Canada came into being, the Crown codified its position on treaties and treaty making with the Royal Proclamation of 1763. The Royal Proclamation committed Britain and then Canada to gaining the consent of Indigenous communities before asserting control over their territories. Still, the meaning and significance of the treaties made in the past continues to be disputed by the descendants of treaty principals, by academics, and in the courts in the twenty-first century, as can be seen in later chapters of this reader.

Seven of these historic treaties were signed between 1871 and 1877 in a region that encompasses southern Canada from Lake Superior to the Rocky Mountains. Although each treaty has distinctive clauses, all of these agreements are quite similar in content overall. With this in mind, and in order to allow more depth and opportunity for analysis than might be available in a broader survey of the numbered treaties, I have included here the documents that relate to solely the last of these treaties, Treaty 7, which includes the area

---

1 Interview with Mrs. Cecile Many Guns conducted by Dila Provost and Albert Yellowhorn Sr., n.d. University of Regina, *oURspace*, http://ourspace.uregina.ca/handle/10294/586. This quotation appears in document 2.6.

that is now southern Alberta. Treaty 7 was signed in 1877 between the Crown and the Siksika (Blackfoot), Piikani (Peigan), and Kainai (Blood) nations of the Blackfoot Confederacy, as well as the Tsuu T'ina (Sarcee) and Nakoda (Stoney) First Nations.

Like all treaties, Treaty 7 must be understood in its historical context. The First Nations signatories were aware of the dwindling buffalo herds that were so important to their physical and spiritual well-being. With the declining herds and the movement of Cree and Métis hunters west, they were growing increasingly concerned about protecting their territories and resources. They were also conscious of the growing Euro-Canadian presence to the east. Ensuring their material and cultural survival, then, and, at the same time, retaining their position as independent nations were paramount considerations as they prepared for a somewhat uncertain future in a country shared with newcomers. Peace was essential, both with other Indigenous peoples and with settler society. The Canadian government wanted peace too in order to facilitate western expansion, and the Blackfoot especially were perceived to be volatile and dangerous. There was also a growing concern by 1877 that Sitting Bull and the Lakota, who had moved into the Canadian Cypress Hills after their defeat of the American Seventh Cavalry under Lieutenant Colonel George Custer, might ally with the Blackfoot. Even if it had wanted too, Canada did not have the resources to mount an American-style military campaign. Further, Canadian authorities were compelled by the Royal Proclamation of 1763 to treat with resident First Nations in order to acquire land for non-Indigenous settlement. Finally, Canada wanted to assert its sovereignty over the West and to protect this territory from American incursion. Though both the First Nations and the Canadian government wanted peace, their visions for the future, and of Indigenous participation in that future, were not necessarily in harmony.

When the treaty commissioners arrived at Blackfoot Crossing with their North-West Mounted Police escorts in red serge and hauling artillery, they were clearly prepared for a show, a theatre of sorts, meant to awe Indigenous observers. They were not as equipped, though, to offer adequate translation to the speakers of three distinct First Nations languages who were assembled for the meetings. Nor were they ready to explain the meaning of concepts that might have been obscure to Indigenous signatories or to clarify their views on the status of verbal agreements that were made at Blackfoot Crossing but would never find their way into the written treaty. All of these issues taken together, then, make it improbable that the First Nations people present, despite their experience with treaty making, fully grasped the underlying intentions of the Canadian government, even if these were fully disclosed, a notion that is suspect at best. As well, it must be remembered that Treaty 7 was "negotiated" against the visible and implied threat that force might be applied at any time.

QUESTIONS FOR DISCUSSION

1. Based on the documents presented here, what were the objectives of the First Nations signatories in concluding Treaty 7? What were the objectives of the Canadian government and its representatives?

2. What indications do we have of David Laird's views of Indigenous people? Are there any instances when he may have misinterpreted or misreported on First Nations political structures, words, actions, or desires?
3. Does it appear that the treaty was made as an equal respectful relationship?
4. What are the problems with the treaty as advanced by Constantine Scollen, Cecile Many Guns, and Annie Buffalo? Are there any others?

2.1 Area of Treaty 7 and the Traditional Territory of the Blackfoot Confederacy

Reproduced from Treaty 7 Elders and Tribal Council with Walter Hildebrandt, Dorothy First Rider, and Sarah Carter, *The True Spirit and Original Intent of Treaty 7* (Montreal: McGill-Queen's University Press, 1996), xvii, with permission from McGill-Queen's University Press.

2.2 Boundaries of the Numbered Treaties

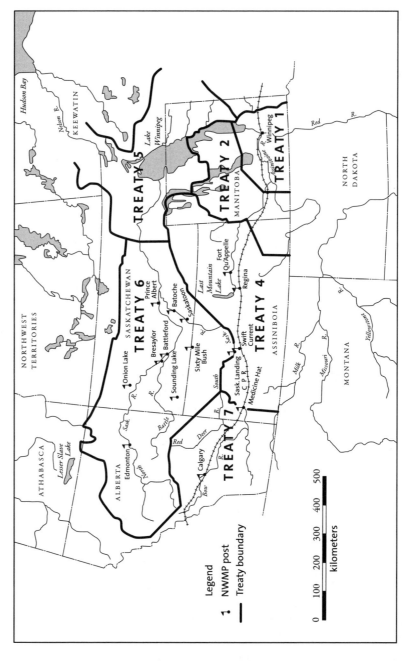

Reproduced from Treaty 7 Elders and Tribal Council with Walter Hildebrandt, Dorothy First Rider, and Sarah Carter, *The True Spirit and Original Intent of Treaty 7* (Montreal: McGill-Queen's University Press, 1996), xviii, with permission from McGill-Queen's University Press.

2.3 Treaty 7, 1877

The final textual version of Treaty 7 was presented to the First Nations a year after the negotiations took place between their leaders and Crown representatives at Blackfoot Crossing in September of 1877. Questions soon arose regarding the extent to which the text included all of the understandings that were arrived at in 1877, especially those of importance to the First Nations. There have also been questions regarding the adequacy of translation during the meetings of 1877. It is clear that the text of the treaty represents the issues of importance to the Crown and to settler society, their understandings of geography, and the kind of economic activity that Canada thought appropriate for First Nations people to pursue and was prepared to encourage. Less apparent are the provisions for the long-term cultural and material security sought by the First Nations signatories. The entire text of the treaty appears here.

Source: Copy of Treaty and Supplementary Treaty No. 7, Made 22nd Sept., and 4th Dec., 1877, between Her Majesty the Queen and the Blackfeet and Other Indian Tribes, at the Blackfoot Crossing of Bow River and Fort MacLeod, rpt. from 1877 ed. (Ottawa: Queen's Printer, 1966).

ARTICLES OF A TREATY

Made and concluded this twenty-second day of September, in the year of Our Lord, one thousand eight hundred and seventy-seven, between Her Most Gracious Majesty the Queen of Great Britain and Ireland, by Her Commissioners, the Honorable David Laird, Lieutenant-Governor and Indian Superintendent of the North-West Territories, and James Farquharson MacLeod, C.M.G., Commissioner of the North-West Mounted Police, of the one part, and the Blackfeet, Blood, Piegan, Sarcee, Stony and other Indians, inhabitants of the Territory north of the United States Boundary Line, east of the central range of the Rocky Mountains, and south and west of Treaties numbers six and four, by their Head Chiefs and Minor Chiefs or Councillors, chosen as hereinafter mentioned, of the other part.

WHEREAS the Indians inhabiting the said Territory, have, pursuant to an appointment made by the said Commissioners, been convened at a meeting at the "Blackfoot Crossing" of the Bow River, to deliberate upon certain matters of interest to Her Most Gracious Majesty, of the one part, and the said Indians, of the other;

And whereas the said Indians have been informed by Her Majesty's Commissioners that it is the desire of Her Majesty to open up for settlement and such other purposes as to Her Majesty may seem meet, a tract of country, bounded and described as hereinafter mentioned, and to obtain the consent thereto of Her Indian subjects inhabiting the said tract, and to make a Treaty, and arrange with them, so that there may be peace and good will between them and Her Majesty, and between them and Her Majesty's other subjects; and that Her Indian people may know and feel assured of what allowance they are to count upon and receive from Her Majesty's bounty and benevolence;

And whereas the Indians of the said tract, duly convened in Council, and being requested by Her Majesty's Commissioners to present their Head Chiefs and Minor Chiefs, or Councillors, who shall be authorized, on their behalf, to conduct such negotiations and sign any Treaty to be founded thereon, and to become responsible to Her Majesty for the faithful performance, by their respective Bands of such obligations as should be assumed by them, the said Blackfeet, Blood, Piegan and Sarcee Indians have therefore acknowledged for that purpose, the several Head and Minor Chiefs, and the Stony Indians, the Chiefs and Councillors who have subscribed hereto, that thereupon in open Council the said Commissioners received and acknowledged the Head and Minor Chiefs and the Chiefs and Councillors presented for the purpose aforesaid;

And whereas the said Commissioners have proceeded to negotiate a Treaty with the said Indians; and the same has been finally agreed upon and concluded as follows, that is to say: the Blackfeet, Blood, Piegan, Sarcee, Stony and other Indians inhabiting the district hereinafter more fully described and defined, do hereby cede, release, surrender, and yield up to the Government of Canada for Her Majesty the Queen and her successors for ever, all their rights, titles, and privileges whatsoever to the lands included within the following limits, that is to say:

Commencing at a point on the International Boundary due south of the western extremity of the Cypress Hills, thence west along the said boundary to the central range of the Rocky Mountains, or to the boundary of the Province of British Columbia, thence north-westerly along the said boundary to a point due west of the source of the main branch of the Red Deer River, thence south-westerly and southerly following on the boundaries of the Tracts ceded by the Treaties numbered six and four to the place of commencement;

And also all their rights, titles and privileges whatsoever, to all other lands wherever situated in the North-West Territories, or in any other portion of the Dominion of Canada:

To have and to hold the same to Her Majesty the Queen and her successors for ever:—

And Her Majesty the Queen hereby agrees with her said Indians, that they shall have right to pursue their vocations of hunting throughout the Tract surrendered as heretofore described, subject to such regulations as may, from time to time, be made by the Government of the country, acting under the authority of Her Majesty and saving and excepting such Tracts as may be required or taken up from time to time for settlement, mining, trading or other purposes by Her Government of Canada; or by any of Her Majesty's subjects duly authorized therefor by the said Government.

It is also agreed between Her Majesty and Her said Indians that Reserves shall be assigned them of sufficient area to allow one square mile for each family of five persons, or in that proportion for larger and smaller families, and that said Reserves shall be located as follows, that is to say:

First.—The reserves of the Blackfeet, Blood and Sarcee Bands of Indians, shall consist of a belt of land on the north side of the Bow and South Saskatchewan Rivers, of an average width of four miles along said rivers, down stream, commencing at a point on the Bow River twenty miles north-westerly of the Blackfoot Crossing thereof, and extending to the Red Deer River at its junction with the South Saskatchewan; also for the term of ten years, and no longer, from the date of the concluding of this Treaty, when it shall cease to be a portion of said Indian Reserves, as fully to all intents and purposes as if it had not at any time included therein, and without any compensation to individual Indians for improvements, of a similar belt of land on the south side of the Bow and

Saskatchewan Rivers of an average width of one mile along said rivers, down stream; commencing at the aforesaid point on the Bow River, and extending to a point one mile west of the coal seam on the said river, about five miles below the said Blackfoot Crossing; beginning again one mile east of the said coal seam and extending to the mouth of Maple Creek at its junction with the South Saskatchewan; and beginning again at the junction of the Bow River with the latter river, and extending on both sides of the South Saskatchewan in an average width on each side thereof of one mile, along said river against the stream, to the junction of the Little Bow River with the latter river, reserving to Her Majesty, as may now or hereafter be required by Her for the use of Her Indian and other subject, from all the reserves hereinbefore described, the right to navigate the above mentioned rivers, to land and receive fuel cargoes on the shores and banks thereof, to build bridges and establish ferries thereon, to use the fords thereof and all the trails leading thereto, and to open such other roads through the said Reserves as may appear to Her Majesty's Government of Canada, necessary for the ordinary travel of her Indian and other subjects, due compensation being paid to individual Indians for improvements, when the same may be in any manner encroached upon by such roads.

Secondly—That the Reserve of the Piegan Band of Indians shall be on the Old Man's River, near the foot of the Porcupine Hills, at a place called "Crow's Creek."

And Thirdly—The Reserve of the Stony Band of Indians shall be in the vicinity of Morleyville.

In view of the satisfaction of Her Majesty with the recent general good conduct of her said Indians, and in extinguishment of all their past claims, she hereby, through her Commissioners, agrees to make them a present payment of twelve dollars each in cash to each man, woman, and child of the families here represented.

Her Majesty also agrees that next year, and annually afterwards forever, she will cause to be paid to the said Indians, in cash, at suitable places and dates, of which the said Indians shall be duly notified, to each Chief, twenty-five dollars, each minor Chief or Councillor (not exceeding fifteen minor Chiefs to the Blackfeet and Blood Indians, and four to the Piegan and Sarcee Bands, and five Councillors to the Stony Indian Bands), fifteen dollars, and to every other Indian of whatever age, five dollars; the same, unless there be some exceptional reason, to be paid to the heads of families for those belonging thereto.

Further, Her Majesty agrees that the sum of two thousand dollars shall hereafter every year be expended in the purchase of ammunition for distribution among the said Indians; Provided that if at any future time ammunition become comparatively unnecessary for said Indians, Her Government, with the consent of said Indians, or any of the Bands thereof, may expend the proportion due to such Band otherwise for their benefit.

Further, Her Majesty agrees that each Head Chief and Minor Chief, and each Chief and Councillor duly recognized as such, shall, once in every three years, during the term of their office, receive a suitable suit of clothing, and each Head Chief and Stony Chief, in recognition of the closing of the Treaty, a suitable medal and flag, and next year, or as soon as convenient, each Head Chief, and Minor Chief, and Stony Chief shall receive a Winchester rifle.

Further, Her Majesty agrees to pay the salary of such teachers to instruct the children of said Indians as to Her Government of Canada may seem advisable, when said Indians are settled on their Reserves and shall desire teachers.

Further, Her Majesty agrees to supply each Head and Minor Chief, and each Stony Chief, for the use of their Bands, ten axes, five handsaws, five augers, one grindstone, and the necessary files and whetstones.

And further, Her Majesty agrees that the said Indians shall be supplied as soon as convenient, after any Band shall make due application therefor, with the following cattle for raising stock, that is to say: for every family of five persons, and under, two cows; for every family of more than five persons, and less than ten persons, three cows; for every family of over ten persons, four cows; and every Head and Minor Chief, and every Stony Chief, for the use of their Bands, one bull; but if any Band desire to cultivate the soil as well as raise stock, each family of such Band shall receive one cow less than the above mentioned number, and in lieu thereof, when settled on their Reserves and prepared to break up the soil, two hoes, one spade, one scythe, and two hay forks, and for every three families, one plough and one harrow, and for each Band, enough potatoes, barley, oats, and wheat (if such seeds be suited for the locality of their Reserves) to plant the land actually broken up. All the aforesaid articles to be given, once for all, for the encouragement of the practice of agriculture among the Indians.

And the undersigned Blackfeet, Blood, Piegan and Sarcee Head Chiefs and Minor Chiefs, and Stony Chiefs and Councillors on their own behalf and on behalf of all other Indians inhabiting the Tract within ceded do hereby solemnly promise and engage to strictly observe this Treaty, and also to conduct and behave themselves as good and loyal subjects of Her Majesty the Queen. They promise and engage that they will, in all respects, obey and abide by the Law, that they will maintain peace and good order between each other and between themselves and other tribes of Indians, and between themselves and others of Her Majesty's subjects, whether Indians, Half Breeds or Whites, now inhabiting, or hereafter to inhabit, any part of the said ceded tract; and that they will not molest the person or property of any inhabitant of such ceded tract, or the property of Her Majesty the Queen, or interfere with or trouble any person, passing or travelling through the said tract or any part thereof, and that they will assist the officers of Her Majesty in bringing to justice and punishment any Indian offending against the stipulations of this Treaty, or infringing the laws in force in the country so ceded.

In WITNESS WHEREOF HER MAJESTY'S said Commissioner, and the said Indian Head and Minor Chiefs, and Stony Chiefs and Councillors, have hereunto subscribed and set their hands, at the "Blackfoot Crossing" of the Bow River, the day and year herein first above written.

[The signatures of 21 Crown and North-West Mounted Police (NWMP) representatives and missionaries and the marks of 51 First Nation representatives follow.]

2.4 Report of Lieutenant Governor and Special Indian Commissioner David Laird, 1877

Prince Edward Island born David Laird served as minister of the interior from 1873 and was at the helm when his ministry created the Indian Act in 1876. That same year, he was appointed lieutenant governor of the "North-West Territories," which included present day Saskatchewan and Alberta, and he was present at the signing of Treaty 6. In 1877, he was selected as a special Indian commissioner along with Lieutenant Colonel James F. MacLeod of the North-West Mounted Police to negotiate Treaty 7 on behalf of Canada. Laird's report on the negotiations was sent to newly appointed Minister of the Interior David Mills and published in the *1877* Annual Report of the Department of the Interior. *In addition to Laird's views of the negotiations themselves and of the First Nations people present, his report includes insight into the challenges of travel in Western Canada at this point in time, the state of the buffalo herds, and resources that might be important to potential non-Indigenous settlers. His attitude on a variety of other issues is also apparent if sometimes implicit.*

Source: Canada, Department of the Interior, *Annual Report of the Department of the Interior, 1877* (Ottawa: Maclean, Roger & Co., 1878), xxxiv–xliii.

SPECIAL APPENDIX C.

GOVERNMENT HOUSE,

BATTLEFORD, NORTH-WEST TERRITORY

Sir,—I have the honour to inform you that on the 4th August I received at Swan River your telegram dated on the first of that month.

It notified me that a Commission appointing Lieutenant Colonel James F. McLeod, C.M.G., and myself, Commissioners to negotiate a treaty with the Blackfeet and other Indians of the unsurrendered parts of the North-West Territories adjoining the United boundary, had been forwarded to Fort MacLeod.

I immediately made preparations for the journey. These occupied me a week, as arrangements had to be made for the removal of furniture and other property to Battle River, where the Government House for the Territories in course of construction, would probably be ready for occupation on my return from the treaty negotiations.

On the 11th August I left Swan River for Fort McLeod, *via* Battleford, proposing to go from the latter place by Cypress Hills to my destination.

I took the Quill Lake trail and came to the telegraph line, about four miles from Big Stone Lake. Thence I followed that line until I came to the trail at the elbow of the North Saskatchewan leading to Battle River.

Where the telegraph crosses the South Saskatchewan, I found an excellent ferry scow, and a ferryman placed there by the Public Works Department. I arrived at the Ferry about noon on the 20th, and though a high wind rendered it difficult to manage the scow, the horses, with the vehicles and their contents, were safely ferried before sunset.

On the following evening I reached the Elbow, and the morning thereafter before leaving camp, Inspector Walker, of Battleford, drove up, on his way to Carlton, to arrange for the distribution of certain of the articles intended for the Indians of Treaty No. 6, which had not arrived when he paid the annuities at that post in the early part of the month. Some of the Indians had not dispersed since they received their payments, and interested parties were causing dissatisfaction among them by reporting that the provisions intended for them, while assembled to receive their annuities, having now arrived, should be distributed to them as well as the agricultural implements and other articles promised.

I advised Inspector Walker to distribute to those Indians still around Carlton, their share of the presents, and to give them a small quantity of provisions from the Government supplies, to enable them to proceed without delay to their hunting grounds.

I then continued my journey to Battleford, which I reached on Monday, the 24th at noon.

Here I was happy to meet Major Irvine, who had come straight from Fort McLeod, across the Great Plains, to conduct me on my journey, and to inform me that for satisfactory reasons adduced by "Crowfoot," the leading chief of the Blackfeet, Lieutenant Colonel McLeod, my associate Commissioner, had consented that the meeting of the Treaty should be held at the Blackfoot Crossing of the Bow River, instead of at Fort McLeod.

Major Irvine had reached Battleford only a few hours before me, and having a Blackfoot Indian as guide, I abandoned my intention of going to Fort McLeod by Cypress Hills, and resolved to take the more direct and much shorter course by which that officer came.

On Friday I had interviews with several parties on business, among whom were "Red Pheasant," the Chief of the Battle River Crees, and a portion of his Band. He desired explanations about the articles promised in the treaty of last year, and the reason they were so late in being forwarded. I explained that the unusually heavy rains in Manitoba and the eastern portion of the Territories had made the travelling so bad that the freighters had not been able to overtake the journey in the time which they expected; that the Government were very sorry at the disappointment, as it was their desire to faithfully carry out all their promises. The officers here had done their best to meet the difficulty and satisfy the Indians, though at no little expense to the country.

The Chief appeared to be quite satisfied with the explanation, and after some further conversation about the Reserve, which he desires to be located at Eagle Hills, he and his companions retired to their lodges, situated for the present close to the south side of Battle River, under the bank in front of Government House.

Inspector Walker having kindly given instructions to the non-commissioned Officer in charge of the Mounted Police, in his absence that every assistance in his power was to be afforded to me for continuing my journey, I was enabled to leave Battleford for Fort McLeod with Major Irvine, on the 25th August. Besides us two, the party consisted of four police constables, my personal servant and the guide.

For the first day we followed a trail leading southward, but afterwards our course was across the trackless plains until we approached near our destination.

On the third day out we first sighted buffalo, and every day subsequently that we travelled, except the last, we saw herds of the animals. Most of the herds, however, were small, and we remarked with regret that very few calves of this season were to be seen. We observed portions of many buffalo carcasses on our route, from not a few of which the peltries had not been removed. From this circumstance, as well as from the fact that many of the skins are made into parchments and coverings for lodges, and are used for other purposes, I concluded that export of buffalo robes from the Territories does not indicate even one half the number of those valuable animals slaughtered annually in our country.

Antelope, though not very abundant, are widely scattered over the plains. The numerous lakelets abound with water fowl. Some of the pools contain alkali, but we experienced no inconvenience on the journey from scarcity of fresh water.

The grass in many places is short and thin, but in the hollows, feed for horses is easily obtained. Altogether, though the plains are perfectly treeless, not even a shrub being visible, a journey across them in fine weather, such as we experienced, when the "buffalo chips" are sufficiently dry to make a good campfire, is not disagreeable.

On the afternoon of the 29th we reached the lowest ford of the Red Deer River, 168 miles by our course from Battleford. On the north side of the river at this ford there is quick sand. The water too, in mid-stream was deep enough to flow over the side boards of our waggons, and at one place the current was dangerously rapid. After repeated trials by some of the men on horse-back to find the best footing, we made the attempt, and the whole party got safely across by night-fall. On Saturday evening, the 1st of September, we arrived at the Blackfoot Crossing of the Bow River, 118 miles from where we forded the Red Deer River. The Bow River is a noble stream. The current is pretty rapid, but at this "ridge under the water" (which is the literal translation of the Blackfoot name for the ford) the bed of the river is pebbly and the footing consequently good. Though we found the water almost as deep as at the Red Deer River, yet under the guidance of Mr. French, a small trader who lives near the ford, we, without almost any delay, crossed bravely over and camped until Monday morning on the south bank of the river.

At this crossing, where the Indians had latterly been notified to assemble for the treaty, there is a beautiful river bottom on the south side of the river. It extended about one mile back from the river, and is some three miles in length. The river, as far as the eye can reach, is skirted close to the water by a narrow belt of cotton-wood and other trees.

When I surveyed the clear waters of the stream, the fuel and shelter which the wood afforded, the excellent herbage on hill and dale, and the Indians camped in the vicinity crossing and re-crossing the river on the "ridge" with ease and safety, I was not surprised that the Blackfeet were attached to the locality, and desired that such an important event in their history as concluding a treaty with Her Majesty's Commissioners should take place at this spot.

On Saturday evening and Sunday several of the Indians called to shake hands with me, among them was "Rainy Chief" of the North Bloods. Here also I met with Monsieur Jean L'Heureux, a French Canadian, who had spent nearly twenty years of his life among the Blackfeet. From him I obtained much valuable information respecting the numbers and wishes of the Indians, together with an elaborate list of the different Chiefs and minor Chiefs of the Blackfeet, Bloods, Piegans, and Surcees, with the principal families of their respective tribes and clannss [sic] of divisio [sic].

This list the Commissioners found very useful in enabling them to understand the relative influence of several Chiefs and the strength of their Bands.

On our journey, while within the limits of Treaty No. 6, we met scarcely any Indians, but after we crossed Red Deer River we met a few Crees and Half-breeds and several hunting parties of Blackfeet. The former generally use carts in travelling, but the Blackfeet and their associates are always on horseback.

The Crees appeared friendly, but were not so demonstrative as the Blackfeet, who always rode up at once with a smile on their countenances and shook hands with us. They knew the uniform of the Mounted Police at a distance, and at once recognized and approached them as their friends.

We resumed our journey on Monday, and arrived at Fort McLeod on the Old Man's River, on Tuesday, the 4th September. The distance between the Blackfoot Crossing of the Bow River and the Fort is about 79 miles, thus making the length of our journey from Battleford 365 miles, as measured by Major Irvine's odometer.

A few miles from Fort McLeod I was met by the Commissioners of the Mounted Police and a large party of the Force, who escorted me into the Fort, while a salute was fired by the Artillery Company from one of the hills overlooking the line of march. The men, whose horses were in excellent condition, looked exceedingly well, and the officers performed their duties in a most efficient manner.

The villagers presented me with an address of welcome, and altogether my reception at Fort McLeod was such as to satisfy the most fastidious lover of display, and more than enough to satisfy the writer.

At Fort McLeod, on my arrival, I received your despatch of first August, covering the commission relating to the treaty and a copy of the Order in Council of 12th July, in terms in which the commission was issued. Also your letter of 27th July, informing me that it had been thought desirable to place the services of the Rev. Father Lacombe at the disposal of the Commissioners while negotiating the treaty. A few days afterwards, I was sorry to learn by telegraph that the Reverend gentleman had been taken by illness on the journey and would be unable to be present at the meeting with the Indians. Here, however, I was happy to meet Rev. Father Scollen, a Roman Catholic missionary, who has laboured for some years among the Crees and Blackfeet in the western portion of the territories. He kindly furnished me such information as he possessed, and afterwards went to the treaty where his assistance was of some value, particularly in dealing with the Crees present.

While at the Fort I had interviews with several of the Blood Chiefs, who called upon me to enquire if they could not be treated with there instead of at Bow River.

I explained that hereafter the Government would endeavour to pay them their annuities at places most convenient for them, but that on the occasion of making a treaty it was desirable that the several Chiefs and their principal headmen should meet together to talk over the matter, so that all might feel that they had been consulted as to the terms of the agreement. They went away satisfied, said they would do as the great Father advised, and go to Bow River.

I cannot speak too highly of the kind manner in which the officers and men of the Mounted Police at Fort McLeod treat their Indian visitors. Though the red man is somewhat intrusive, I never heard a harsh word employed in asking him to retire. The beneficial effects of this treatment, of the exclusion of intoxicants from the country, and of impartially administering justice to whites and Indians alike, were apparent in all my interviews with the Indians.

They always spoke of the officers of the Police in the highest terms, and of the Commissioners of the Force, Lieut. Colonel McLeod especially, as their great benefactor.

The leading Chiefs of the Blackfeet and kindred tribes, declared publicly at the treaty that had it not been for the Mounted Police they would have all been dead ere this time.

Having rested a week after my tedious journey of over 700 miles, I then occupied myself for a few days in viewing the surrounding country.

In the village I found some excellent stores, supplied with almost every article of dry goods, hardware and groceries, that any inland community requires. Notably among these were the stores of J.G. Baker & Co. and Messrs. T.C. Power & Bro. There is also a good blacksmith's shop in the village, in which coal is used from the Belly River, at a place some twenty miles distant from Fort McLeod. I was told by the proprietor of the shop that the coal answers tolerably well for blacksmithing purposes, and in the Fort it is extensively used for fuel. It burns nearly as well in a stove as some varieties of Pictou coal.

The land around the Fort, and indeed for almost the whole distance between the Bow and Old Man's Rivers, is well adapted for grazing, and where cultivation has been fairly attempted this season, grain and vegetables have been a success.

In short, I have very little doubt, that this portion of the Territories, before many years will abound in herds of cattle, and be dotted with not a few comfortable homesteads.

Lieut.-Colonel McLeod having attended to forwarding the supplies to Bow River, which had been previously delivered at the Fort, left for the Blackfoot Crossing with some eighty officers and men of the Police Force, on Wednesday, the 12th September. I followed on Friday and reached Bow River on Sunday morning. The Police having arrived on Saturday, the Commissioners were fully prepared for business on Monday, the 17th, the day which I had from the first appointed for the opening of the treaty negotiations.

The Commissioners were visited by "Crowfoot," the principal Chief of the Blackfeet, shortly after their arrival. He desired to know when he and his people might meet us. We ascertained that most of the Indians on the ground were Blackfeet and Assiniboines or Stonies, from the upper part of the Bow River.

But as the 17th was the day named the Commissioners determined to adhere to the appointment, and sent a messenger early in the morning to invite the Indians camped around to meet them at the Council tent at two o'clock, p.m.

Half an hour before the time appointed a gun was fired as a signal for the Indians to assemble.

The meeting was well attended.

The Chiefs came forward first and were introduced to the Commissioners, and their followers on being invited sat up close to the tent.

I addressed them, stating that the Queen's Government had last year promised that they would this year be visited by Commissioners to invite them to make a treaty.

That months ago I had named this very day to meet them, and that in accordance with the promises made the Commissioners were now here to discuss the terms of a treaty.

Yet as we had learned that very few of the Bloods, Surcees or Piegans had arrived, we would not unduly press forward the negotiations, but wait until Wednesday to give the others time to arrive.

The Indians listened attentively to what was said, and several of the Chiefs expressed their satisfaction at not being asked to meet us on the morrow. The Commissioners then told them there were rations provided for them by the Government, and that those who were in need of provisions might apply to certain of the police officers detailed to see to their proper distribution.

The Stonies and one Blood Chief applied for flour, tea, sugar, and tobacco, but said they were not then in need of beef. "Crowfoot" and some other Chiefs under his influence, would not accept any rations until they would hear what terms the Commissioners were prepared to offer them. He appeared to be under the impression that if the Indians were fed by the bounty of the Government they would be committed to be proposals of the Commissioners, whatever might be their nature. Though I feared this refusal did not augur well for the final success of the negotiations, yet I could not help wishing that other Indians whom I have seen, had a little [of] the spirit in regard to dependence upon the Government exhibited on this occasion by the great Chief of the Blackfeet.

Among the visitors at the treaty I was pleased to meet the Rev. John McDougall, Wesleyan Missionary at Morley Villa, and son of the late lamented Rev. George McDougall, so well and favorably known in connection with Indian affairs in the North-West. Mr. McDougall was present at the first interview the Commissioners held with the Indians, and acted as interpreter for the Stonies, who do not understand the Blackfeet language. He, as well as the Rev. C. Scollen, rendered the Commissioners all the assistance in their power. Traders with large supplies of goods were arriving on the ground. They desired to erect buildings of logs to protect their property, but as some of the Indian Chiefs objected to the trees along the river being cut down for such a purpose until after the treaty, the Commissioners deemed it prudent, to prevent complications, to ask the traders to erect only temporary stanchions sufficient to support canvas coverings.

They complied with our wishes, and the Indians gave us no further trouble on the subject.

On the evening of Monday I also received a message from "Bobtail," a Cree Chief, who, with the larger portion of the Band, had come to the treaty grounds.

He represented that he had not been received into any treaty. He, however, had not attended the meeting that day, because he was uncertain whether the Commissioners would be willing to receive him along with the Blackfeet. I asked him and his Band to meet the Commissioners separate from the other Indians on the following day.

On Tuesday, at two o'clock, the Cree Chief and his Band assembled according to appointment.

The Commissioners ascertained from him that he had frequented for some time the Upper Bow River country, and might fairly be taken into the present treaty, but he expressed a wish to have his Reserve near Pigeon Lake, within the limits of Treaty No. 6, and from what we could learn of the feelings of the Blackfeet towards the Crees, we considered it advisable to keep them separate as much as possible.

We therefore informed the Chief that it would be most expedient for him to give in his adhesion to the treaty of the last year, and be paid annually, on the north of Red Deer River, with the other Cree Chiefs. He consented. We told him that we could not pay him until after the Blackfeet had been dealt with, as it might create jealousy among them, but that in the meantime his Band could receive rations.

He said it was right that he should wait until we had settled with the Blackfeet, and agreed to come and sign his adhesion to Treaty No. 6 at any time I was prepared to receive him.

During Tuesday several parties of Indians came in, but the principal Blood Chiefs had not yet arrived. According to appointment, however, the Commissioners met the Indians at two o'clock on Wednesday.

An outline was given of the terms proposed for their acceptance. We also informed them we did not expect an answer that day, but we hoped to hear from them to-morrow.

That day we again intimated to the Indians that rations would be delivered to such as applied for them.

We told them the provisions were a present, and their acceptance would not be regarded as committing the Chiefs to the terms proposed by the Commissioners.

Most of the Chiefs at once applied for flour, tea, sugar, and tobacco, and in a day or two they also asked for meat. Even Crowfoot at last thankfully accepted his share of the rations, and the beef cattle began to decrease rapidly.

On Tuesday we met the Indians at the usual hour. We further explained the terms outlined to them yesterday, dwelling especially upon the fact that by the Canadian law their Reserves could not be taken from them, occupied or sold without their consent.

They were also assured that their liberty of hunting over the open prairie would not be interfered with, so long as they did not molest settlers and others in the country.

We then invited the Chiefs to express their opinions. One of the minor Blood Chiefs made a long speech.

He told us the Mounted Police had been in the country for four years, and had been destroying a quantity of wood.

For this wood he asked that the Commissioners should make the Indians a present payment of $50 a head to each Chief, and $30 a head to all others.

He said the Blackfeet, Bloods, Surcees and Piegans were all one; but he asked that the Crees and Half-breeds should be sent back to their own country.

The Queen, he remarked, had sent the Police to protect them; they had made it safe for Indians to sleep at night, and he hoped she would not soon take these men away.

"Crowfoot" said he would not speak until to-morrow. "Old Sun," another influential Blackfoot Chief, said the same. "Eagle Tail," the head Chief of the Piegans, remarked that he had always followed the advice the officers of the Mounted Police gave him. He hoped the promise which the Commissioners made would be secured to them as long as the sun shone and water ran.

The Stony Chiefs unreservedly expressed their willingness to accept the terms offered.

Fearing that some of the Indians might regard the demands of the Blood Chief who had spoken, if not promptly refused, as agreed to, I told them he had asked too much.

He had admitted the great benefit the Police had been to the Indians, and yet he was so unreasonable as to ask that the Government should pay a large gratuity to each Indian for the little wood their benefactors had used.

On the contrary, I said if there should be any pay in the matter it ought to come from the Indians to the Queen for sending them the Police.

Hereupon "Crowfoot" and the other Chiefs laughed heartily at the Blood orator of the day.

I also said the Commissioners could not agree to exclude the Crees and Half-breeds from the Blackfoot country; that they were the Great Mother's children as much as the Blackfeet and Bloods, and she did not wish to see any of them starve.

Of course, the Crees and Half-breeds could be prosecuted for trespassing on their Reserves.

In this the Indian Act secured them.

The Local Government had passed a law to protect the buffalo.

It would have a tendency to prevent numbers from visiting their country in the close season.

But to altogether exclude any class of the Queen's subjects, as long as they obeyed the laws, from coming into any part of the country, was contrary to the freedom which she allowed her people, and the commissioners would make no promise of the kind.

On the following morning there was a rumor that the Indians in their own Councils could not agree, that a small party was opposed to making a treaty.

The opposition, however, could not have been very formidable.

The principal Chief seemed fully to understand the importance of accepting some terms.

About noon, "Crowfoot," with Mr. L'Heureux, as interpreter, came to my tent and asked for explanations on some points, which I cheerfully gave him.

During the forenoon a large party of Bloods came in, among whom was "Bad Head," an aged minor Blood Chief, of considerable influence, who attended the meeting in the afternoon.

When the Commissioners intimated that they were ready to hear what the Chiefs had to say, "Crowfoot" was the first to speak.

His remarks were few, but he expressed his gratitude for the Mounted Police being sent to them and signified his intention to accept the treaty.

The Blood Chief who made the large demands on the previous day said he would agree with the other Chiefs. "Old Sun" head Chief of the North Blackfeet, said "Crowfoot" spoke well. We are not going to disappoint the Commissioners. He was glad they were all agreed to the same terms.

They wanted cattle, guns, ammunition, tobacco, axes and money. "Bull's Head," the principal Chief of the Surcees, said we are all going to take your advice.

"Eagle Head," the Piegan head Chief, remarked, "I give you my hand." ["]We all agree to what Crowfoot says." "Rainy Chief," head of the North Bloods, said he never went against the white man's advice. Some of the minor Chiefs spoke to the same effect.

The Commissioners expressed their satisfaction at the unanimity among the Indians, and said they would prepare the treaty and bring it to-morrow for signature.

The only difficult matter then to be arranged was the Reserves. The Commissioners thought it would take unnecessary time to discuss this question in open meeting, and resolved that one of them should visit the head Chiefs at their camps and consult them separately as to the localities they might desire to select.

Lieut.-Colonel McLeod undertook this duty, while I attended to the preparation of the draft treaty.

On Saturday, 22nd September, we met the Indians to conclude the treaty.

"Mekasto" or "Red Crow," the great Chief of the South Bloods, had arrived the previous evening or morning on the ground, and being present came forward to be introduced to the Commissioners.

The assemblage of Indians was large. All the head Chiefs of the several tribes were now present, only two Blackfoot and two Blood minor Chiefs were absent.

The representation was all that could be expected.

The Commissioners had previously informed the Indians that they would accept the Chiefs whom they acknowledged, and now close in front of the tent sat those who had been presented to the Commissioners as the recognised Chiefs of the respective bands.

The conditions of the treaty having been interpreted to the Indians, some of the Blood Chiefs, who had said very little on the previous day, owing to "Red Crow's" absence, now spoke, he himself in a few kind words agreeing to accept the treaty.

"Crowfoot" then came forward and requested his name to be written on the treaty.

The Commissioners having first signed it, Mr. L'Heureux, being familiar with the Blackfoot language, attached the Chief's names to the document at their request, and witnessed to their marks.

While the signing was being proceeded with a salute was fired from the field guns in honour of the successful conclusion of the negotiations.

I may mention in this connection that on Saturday also I was waited upon by a deputation of Half-breeds, who presented me with a petition, expressing the hope that the buffalo law might not be stringently enforced during the approaching winter, and praying that they might receive some assistance to commence farming. With respect to the buffalo ordinance, I told them that the notice having been short, the law would not be very strictly enforced for the first winter, and in regard to their prayer for assistance to farm, I said I would make it known at Ottawa.

On Monday, the 24th, the Commissioners met the Indians at 10 a.m.

Some minor Chiefs who had not remained until the close of the proceedings on Saturday, signed the treaty this morning.

The Chiefs were then asked to stand up in a body, their names were read over and the Indians once more asked to say whether they were their recognized Chiefs.

"Heavy Shield," a brother of "Old Sun," at the request of the latter took the place of head Chief of his Band. It was, however, afterwards ascertained that this arrangement caused dissatisfaction, and "Old Sun" was restored to his position, and the Band adhering to his brother, was called the Middle Blackfoot Band.

After their names were called over, I gave the head Chiefs of the Blackfeet, Bloods, Piegans, and Surcees their flags and uniforms, and invested them with their medals.

While I was shaking hands with them, acknowledging their Chiefs in the name of the "Great Mother," the band played "God save the Queen."

The payments were then immediately begun by the officers of the Mounted Police, one party taking the Blackfeet, and another the Bloods, while a third was detailed to pay the Assiniboines, or Stonies, near their encampment some two miles up the river.

The Commissioners went in the afternoon with the latter party, and before the payments were commenced, presented the Chiefs with their medals, flags and uniforms.

The Stonies received us with quite a demonstration. They are a well-behaved body of Indians

The influence of the Christian missionary in their midst is apparent, polygamy being now almost wholly a thing of the past.

On Tuesday I took the adhesion of "Bobtail," the Cree Chief, and his Band, to Treaty No. 6, and they were paid out of the funds which I had brought with me from Swan River.

On the invitation of the Blackfoot, Blood, and kindred Chiefs, the Commissioners went on Wednesday to the Council tent to receive an address of thanks.

A large number of Indians were present.

Mr. L'Heureux spoke on their behalf, and expressed their gratitude to the Commissioners generally for the kind manner in which they conducted the negotiations, to me personally for having come so far to meet them, and to Lieutenant-Colonel McLeod for all that he and the Mounted Police had done for them since their arrival in the country.

To this address the Commissioners feelingly replied, and expressed their confidence that the Indians before them would not regret having agreed to the treaty.

The Cree Chief and his Band also waited upon us in the evening at my tent, and through Father Scollen, as interpreter, thanked us for the manner in which we had treated them. The presents sent for the Indians were distributed to each Band, after payment. On Wednesday also the Commissioners drove to see the coal seam about five miles east of the Blackfoot crossing.

Under the guidance of Mr. French, they found an outcrop of the seam at a coulee some three miles south of the river.

The seam there is from three to ten feet in thickness, and the coal, some of which was burned every day in the officers' mess tent at the treaty, is of a very fair quality.

About noon on Friday the payments were completed, and the Commissioners proceeded to close the accounts.

They found that the number of Indians paid, who had accepted the terms of the new Treaty, was as follows:—

Head Chiefs	10 at $25 00	$250 00
Minor Chiefs and Councillors	40 at 15 00	600 00
Men, women and children	4,342 at 12 00	52,104 00
Total	4,392	$52,954 00

The Crees who gave in their adhesion to Treaty No. 6 were only paid the gratuity, this year's annuity being still due them.

These were paid from the funds of Treaty No. 6, as follows:—

Chief	1 at $25 00	$25 00
Councillors	2 at 15 00	30 00
Men, women and children	429 at 12 00	5,148 00
Total	432	$5,203 00

The officers of the Police Force who conducted the payments, discharged this duty in a most efficient manner.

Not in regard to the payments alone were the services of the officers most valuable.

With respect to the whole arrangements, Lieut-Col. McLeod, my associate Commissioner, both in that capacity and as commander of the Police, was indefatigable in his exertions to bring the negotiations to a successful termination.

The same laudable efforts were put forth by Major Irvine and the other officers of the Force, and their kindness to me, personally, I shall never fail to remember.

The volunteer band of the Police at Fort McLeod deserve more than a passing notice, as they did much to enliven the whole proceedings.

The Commissioners at first had not a good interpreter of the Blackfoot language, but on Wednesday they secured the services of Mr. Bird, a brother of Dr. Bird, of Winnipeg.

He has been many years among the Piegans and Blackfeet, and is a very intelligent interpreter.

Mr. L'Heureux also rendered good service in this respect.

The accounts being closed and certified to by the Commissioners, I commenced my return journey on the evening of the 28th September. I came by a crossing of the Red Deer River some fifteen miles east of the Hand Hills, travelled across the prairies further west than my former route, and arrived at Battleford on the evening of Saturday of the 6th October.

I transmitted herewith the treaty as signed by the Commissioners and Chiefs, and also the adhesion of the Cree Chief to Treaty No. 6.

In conclusion, I beg to offer a few observations on the treaty, and subjects connected therewith.

1. With respect to the Reserves, the Commissioners thought it expedient to settle at once their location, subject to the approval of the Privy Council.

By this course it is hoped that a great deal of subsequent trouble in selecting reserves will be avoided.

The object of the ten years reserve on the south side of the Bow River is to keep hunters from building winter shanties on the river bottom.

This practice has a tendency to alarm the buffalo, and keep them from their feeding grounds on the lower part of the river.

After ten years it is feared the buffalo will have become nearly extinct, and that further protection will be needless.

At any rate by that time the Indians hope to have herds of domestic cattle.

The country on the upper part of the Bow River is better adapted for settlement than most of that included in the Blackfoot Reserve, consequently the Commissioners deemed it advisable to agree that a belt on the south side of the river should be exempt from general occupation for ten years, particularly as the Indians set great value on the concession.

2. The articles promised in addition to the money payments may to some appear excessive.

The Stonies are the only Indians adhering to this treaty who desired agricultural implements and seed.

The promises, therefore, respecting these things may be understood as merely applicable to that tribe.

The Blackfeet and Bloods asked for nothing of this kind; they preferred cattle, and the Commissioners being fully of opinion that such were likely to be much more serviceable to them than seed and implements, encouraged them in their request.

The number of cattle promised may appear large, but when it is considered that cows can be readily purchased at Fort McLeod for twenty or twenty-five dollars per head, and their delivery to the Indians will cost an inconsiderable sum, the total expense of supplying the articles promised to this treaty will, I am convinced, cost less than those under either Treaty No. 4 or No. 6.

3. I would urge that the officers of the Mounted Police be entrusted to make the annual payments to the Indians under this treaty.

The Chiefs themselves requested this, and I said I believed the Government would gladly consent to the arrangement.

The Indians have confidence in the Police, and it might be some time before they would acquire the same respect for strangers.

4. The organization of the Blackfoot Bands is somewhat different from that of the Saulteaux and Crees.

They have large Bands with head and minor chiefs, and as they preferred that this arrangement should remain unchanged, the Commissioners gladly acceded to their desire, as expense would be saved to the Government in clothing, were councillors and headmen not named.

The Stonies, however, asked to be allowed councillors, and their request was granted to the extent of two to each chief.

5. Copies of the treaty printed on parchment should be forwarded to Fort McLeod in good time to be delivered to each Head and Minor Chief at next year's payment of annuities.

I have the honor to be, sir,
Your obedient servant,

DAVID LAIRD,
Lieutenant-Governor, and Special Indian Commissioner.

2.5 Letter from Father Constantine Scollen, 1879

Catholic priest Constantine Scollen, with the Oblates of Mary Immaculate (OMI), was born in Ireland and arrived in the region that became Alberta in 1862 at age 22. Like David Laird, he was present at the meetings leading to Treaty 6. He also served as an interpreter at the Blackfoot Crossing discussions preceding Treaty 7. Scollen portrayed the Cree in comparatively favourable, though still ethnocentric, terms but perceived the Blackfoot as particularly dangerous and volatile. He was apparently quite interested in having First Nations settled and brought under treaty, probably for a variety of reasons including that doing so would ease his own work. With these attitudes and interests in mind, examine his handwritten letter to Major Irvine of the North-West Mounted Police, and discover what it reveals about the efforts taken by the treaty commissioners in 1877 to explain their intentions, the inadequacy of translators, the First Nations delegates' understanding of what they were agreeing to, and the non-fulfilment of even the written treaty promises.

Source: Father Constantine Scollen to Major A.G. Irvine, 13 April 1979, Library and Archives Canada, Department of Indian Affairs, RG 10, vol. 3695, file 14,942, reel C-10122.

Fort Macleod
April 13th 1879

Dear Major

Having come to Fort Macleod a week ago, and being somewhat disappointed by not finding you here in order to communicate with you verbally, I now undertake to forward you this letter containing some facts relative to the condition of the Indians, and some of my views thereon.

You are aware, Dear Major, that I have always abstained from meddling, either publicly or privately with anything pertaining to the political economy of these N.W. Territories, although others perhaps far less versed than myself in Indian affairs, have vauntingly, and very often erroneously advanced their opinions on every subject, and worked hard to have these opinions adopted; and, I am not afraid to say it, most of the time having some private end in view.

For my own part I have always confined myself to explaining to the Indian, from a Christian point of view, the relation existing between the whiteman and himself, and to giving the whiteman the information which to my mind seemed necessary for the proper government of the Indian. The former I still continue to do, it being a part of the duty attached to my position, the latter I had resolved to abandon forever, seeing with what bad grace some information I gave last fall was received by some of our head officials.

However, this extreme resolution has been changed by a circumstance. Since I came to Macleod this time, I have talked considerably with some of the officers on the Indian question; and as they think it my duty to make a statement thereof, and have pressed me strongly to do so, I now reluctantly undertake the task; and knowing, Dear Sir, that nobody has the interest of the Indians more at heart than yourself, I address this statement to you.

In speaking of Indians in this paper I refer exclusively to the Blackfeet properly so called, the Bloods, the North Piegans, and the Sarcees, all of whom comprise the great Blackfoot nation.

Now, in the van of my statements stands this all important question, which to my mind is the pivot on which all others revolve: Did these Indians, or do they now, understand the real nature of the treaty made between the Government and themselves in 1877? My answer to this question is unhesitatingly negative, and I stand prepared to substantiate this proposition.

It may be asked: If the Indians did not understand what the treaty meant, why did they sign it? Because previous to the treaty they had always been kindly dealt with by the Authorities, and did not wish to offend them: and although they had many doubts in their mind as to the meaning of the treaty, yet with this precedent before them, they hoped that it simply meant to furnish them with plenty of food and clothing, and particularly the former every time they stood in need of them; and besides this, many outside influences were brought to bear upon them; but I repeat, they were not actuated by any intuitive comprehension of what they were called upon to do.

Again: What was the cause of the Indians not understanding the treaty? The immediate cause was the absence of competent Interpreters, although they could have been procured, and I myself did recommend some long before the treaty. The remote causes were many, such as the dullness of the Indian mind &c which cannot comprehend a thing until after many repetitions. It is true, Crowfoot, who, beyond a doubt, is considered the leading Chief of the Plains, did seem to have a faint notion of the meaning of the treaty, as his last speech would go to shew. If you remember his speech ran thus: "Great Father! Take pity on me with regard to my Country; with regard to the mountains, the hills, and the valleys: with regard to the prairies the forests and the waters: with regard to all the animals that inhabit them, and do not take them from myself and my children forever!!!["]

All the other Chiefs followed Crowfoot, and the substance of their speeches was that they agreed with him in all he had said.

Then followed the signing of the treaty, and if you remember, Crowfoot would not touch the pen. This recalls to my mind a conversation between him and me last fall. After the payments, I and my companion travelled with the Blackfoot Camp until late in October.

Crowfoot one day asked me what was the meaning of making the Indians touch the pen at the treaty. I explained to him that when making a bargain, the contracting parties draw it up in writing and sign their names so as to make it binding, and as the treaty was a bargain between the Government and the Indians, and the latter could not write they were made to touch the pen which was equivalent to signing their names. "Ah! Said he, they are out there, for I did not touch it." Of course I explained to him that he had taken the money and that was enough, but I dare say after all, the old gentleman still had his own opinion.

It is now important to consider what the Indians think of the treaty, two years having already elapsed since it was first made. Being very superstitious, they often attribute to the white-man any misfortune that may befall them shortly after they have had any dealing with him; and so the death of three of their Chiefs during the first year, alarmed them considerably, and was looked upon as a very bad omen for the future. This bad omen is now being realized amongst them. Since the conclusion of the treaty the decrease of the buffalo has been more apparent than ever before, and during the winter just past, the sufferings of the Indians from hunger have been something unparalleled heretofore in this section of the country.

This of course to the Indian mind, is the terrible consequence of the treaty.

I have now been acquainted sixteen years with the Blackfeet. I have seen them in all their phases—in their days of prosperity and opulence; when their braves mustered double the number they can muster now; when they were entire masters of the immense prairies from Benton to Edmonton, and the terror of their enemies on every side, North, South, East, and West. I have seen them in those days mourn the loss of numerous relatives fallen in deadly combat against their foes. I have seen them later on, when reduced to the last stage of poverty and disorganization from the effects of intoxicating liquor, but through all these stages I have never seen them so depressed as they are now; I have never seen them before in want of food: last winter for the first time have they really suffered the pangs of hunger, and for the first time in my life have I seen a Blackfoot brave withdraw from his lodge that he might not listen to his crying children when he had not meat to give them! Such, Dear Sir, has been the state of the Blackfoot Indians last winter. They have suffered fearfully from hunger. Two poor women on Elk River, fell victims to the scourge, a thing never heard of before amongst the Blackfeet. Many sustained life by eating the flesh of poisoned wolves. Some have lived on dogs; and I have known others to live several days on nothing else but old bones which they gathered and broke up, wherewith to make a kind of soup.

This state of affairs has disheartened the Indians wonderfully. They can no longer live together in big camps under control of their Chiefs. They have been, during the Winter, and are now, scattered all over the country. They are in utter dejection, and from a state of dejection, if they continue to suffer, I have no doubt that there will be a transition to a state of desperation.

In fact hunger has driven them to commit many acts of dishonesty which they always abstained from before, around the posts. Many of those whose skeleton horses were able to plod through the deep snow hastened around the settlements in order to live. The consequence is, they have become a burden and a cause of anxiety to the Settlers. They have begged and stolen all they could, and got into the way of helping themselves to white-men's cattle. [Italicized section following was written in the margins in another hand, perhaps Irvine's, with an arrow to this point in the text. Italics added.] *The Mounted Police have done what they could to alleviate the sufferings of the Indians but* The Mounted Police were not prepared for the emergency.

White-men, farmers, are becoming disgusted. There is now at Fort Macleod, an industrious hard working man from Calgary on his way across the line. He is leaving the country because after working hard all last summer and raising a magnificent crop, he could get no market for his produce; and the Indians have been robbing him all Winter. If things continue without a change, others will do the same.

Men will begin to think of driving their Stock across the line for security, as many Indians are now thinking of crossing it in order to get something to eat from the American Agents. It is an undeniable fact that there is in the country a *money-making monopoly*; the members of the monopoly will, of course, put up with a great deal, in order to hold their grasp, but the poor hard working man, the bone and sinew of the land, will not be inclined to linger where there is no security for his property.

In my opinion, give us another Winter like the past, and we are done for. We shall either have to provide for the Indians or fight them; there is no other alternative.

The sooner they are provided for then, the better, and of course the best way to provide for them is to teach them habits of industry.

It was with a view to this that I wrote to Lieut. Gov. Laird last fall, at the request of the Blackfeet and Bloods, and asked him to grant me a breaking plow and some seed potatoes.

With this help I intended in the Spring to work with the Indians on their re-serve at the Crossing, and put in twenty five or thirty acres of potatoes. The Indians would all willingly have worked with me, and in the fall, would be able to enjoy the fruits of their own labor.

This would encourage them for next year, and others would join in with them; and so the Government would see a great good done amongst them with very little expense.

I was willing to give my time and labor to forward the work, but imagine my deep regret when I received the Governor's answer with a refusal to my request on the plea that I am not an "Indian Agent" forsooth![,] that the Indians might not wish to have me upon their reserve, and that he would require to know more about it before he could recommend the affair to the Dominion Govern-ment. Is it not strange that the Dominion Government who can endow a man with power to hang another for murder, has not endowed the Lieut. Gov. with power to grant so paltry a thing as the above, which might be the means of sav-ing a few Indians from starvation!

And then, as to my going upon the Reserve!!! The Lieut. Gov. must know that I lived amongst the Blackfeet long before there was any thought of bringing law into the country, and was kindly treated by them when it was not safe for other white-men to travel through their country. And even now they make an important distinction between those who sacrifice their lives for their benefit; and those whose principal object amongst them is lucre.

But the Piegan Indians, according to the treaty are entitled to farming imple-ments and seed, and now is the time they should be using them—yet they have received neither, nor has their reserve ever been surveyed.—Surely this is too much procrastination at a time when the Indians are in extreme want.

It will now *be another year before the* Piegans can use their farming implements; and when they do get them, suppose they will be useless flimsy plows without colters &c. Such as have been sent to the Stoney Indians, whereas they ought to be furnished some good strong breaking plows, Strong Hoes &c such as one would suppose Government paid for.

And now, Dear Major, I am done *for the present* on the Chapter of the Indian question: In the course of this letter I have stated facts and given my views with entire freedom. It is far from my intention either to flatter or offend. What I have written, I have done so with only one view, and that is to be useful to both the white-man and the Indian, and the country at large.

Knowing, Dear Major, your unswerving love of justice and order, and your in-defatigable efforts for the welfare of every grade of society in the country, I send this communication to you with the request that you make it known at Ottawa; hoping if not palatable it may at least be useful; for I can assure you I have writ-ten it with all frankness.

In the mean time I shall retain a copy myself, in readiness for publication, if circumstances should require it

With kindest regards
I remain Dear Sir
Your humble Servt.
(Sgd) Constantine Scollen

Miss. Prst O.M.I.

> Major Irvine
> Asst. Comm.
> N.W.M.P.

Forwarded for the information of the Honbl The Minister of the Interior

Fort Walsh

> 4th May 1879   (Sgd) A.G. Irvine
> Asst. Comm.

2.6 Interview with Cecile Many Guns (Grassy Water), 1973

This document is a selection from the transcript of an interview with Piikani (Peigan) elder Mrs. Cecile Many Guns (Grassy Water) conducted by Dila Provost and Albert Yellowhorn Sr. The interview took place on the Piikani reserve at Brocket, Alberta, in 1973. There are many indications here of the differences between the text of the treaty and the oral tradition of the Treaty 7 First Nations regarding what was agreed to at Blackfoot Crossing in 1877.

> *This selection of the transcript has been reproduced without alteration.*

Source: Interview with Mrs. Cecile Many Guns conducted by Dila Provost and Albert Yellowhorn Sr., n.d. University of Regina, *oURspace*, http://ourspace.uregina.ca/handle/10294/586.

Reprinted with permission from the University of Regina.

Albert: *Now, we are going to talk about the original Treaty No. 7. Now, did you get interpreters concerning the land surrenders and promises of this treaty with the Crown? What knowledge did you have about what happened? What is your understanding?*

Mrs. Many Guns: At the time of the treaty the Queen made a lot of promises. The main interpreter for the Indians was Rising Buffalo. He announced to make peace, no more fighting between anyone, everybody will be friends he said. Everybody will be in peace.

Albert: *What about the treaty promised?*

Mrs. Many Guns: As long as the sun shines and the rivers flow we will be looked after by the Queen and benefit from her bounties. This was the biggest promise. When the sun quits shining and the river quits running then the promises will cease. Also rations were to be issued and $12.00 annually. These also were to be given as long as the sun shone and the rivers flowed, but they broke the promise about the $12.00 annually. We were never told that the $12.00 would lessen (decrease) after the first year. The next year only $5.00 was issued which was a surprise to these people after the impression had been given that we would always receive $12.00. When questioned about the balance of the $7.00, the government said it was being held in trust for us to be used for our benefit in the future, such as ammunition money. They never heard that this first payment of $12.00 would be later reduced to $5.00. Only after a payment of $5.00 was issued they told us the balance would be put away for our people's use in the future. All the people living at the time of this promise wondered what happened to the money. The ammunition (for hunting) was not given to us as scheduled under the treaty. Sometimes they didn't get it all, then finally it was stopped completely.

Albert: *At the present, Treaty No. 7 claims this promise is being worked on.*

Cecile: We, the Indian people, always thought it was put away for us and that some day we would get it back.

Albert: *What about food rations?*

Cecile: At the treaty, rations were issued. The people took only the tea and sugar, coffee and other dry stuff. The rest they had no use for and left them behind. They did not like the smell of domestic meat (beef, bacon). They would rather hunt for this, as the buffalo was yet plentiful then.

Albert: *Were they any beans?*

Cecile: I don't remember.

Albert: *After the camp was broken, where did you go?*

Cecile: After the treaty we all moved South. Our leader was Sitting on the Eagle Tail Feathers. He said, "We'll go back to the Crow Lodge country, so I can be back to the Porcupine Hills, which is our home. They will always be there and my children and their children will make use of the timber there." He asked for land using three land marks to describe the country he wished, (1) Old Man's Playground, known today as Living Stone District (2) Porcupine Hills, (3) The Crow Lodge area (indications were that they did not have knowledge concerning the white man's geographical methods[)]. Jerry Potts (Bear Child) had visited (Sitting on Eagle Tail Feather's) camp earlier before he chose the area and had advised our leader to ask for the country beginning at the International line along the immediate foothills of the Rockies going north (there today oil has been discovered). Jerry Potts (Bear Child) said, "Tomorrow is the day when you have to choose land. Ask for the foothills up to the Porcupine Hills. Someday this land will be beneficial to you and your people, as hunting in this area is always plentiful." Sitting on Eagle Tail Feathers made a bad mistake and chose this area we live in today.

When the treaty was over, we scattered. We went home and the Blood Indians went back to their area. In my girlhood days I remember there was no fences. This country was wide open. I remember going with my father to visit on the Blood area. There was no fences, no houses, no white people from the Porcupine Hills, the Crow Lodge Creek to the Belly Buttes. We thought all this space was ours. My belief was that this land was our principal natural asset. Suddenly it was surveyed and fenced and it was small and we were told to stay in this corral.

After this land was fenced it turned out to be much smaller than we always thought was ours. When we visited the Bloods my father believed that all this land was ours from the Kootenay River to Waterton Lakes, the Mountain Range, to the Porcupine Hills to the present town site of Pincher Creek to the Crow Lodge area known to the Indians to expand to [the] west of Lethbridge.

Southeast of Pincher Creek was our main camping grounds. We used to cut hay there and haul water from the creek. It was during the time we used the travois. In later years this was all taken for white man's homes and the land broken. We used to tell stories about how this was once our home. All our favorite area was taken by the white people who built their settlements on it, this land they took away from us [w]as our home. We did not understand geographical ways of measuring land, they did this without explaining it to us.

When we left the reserve we had to have a paper (permit) and if we did not have it, we had to pay a fine, or go to jail if we didn't have any money.

One day a group of Blood Indians came to visit without this paper. Yellow Boy and Yellow Feather, both old men, were involved and the police came and took them from East Camp to Brocket town site late in the afternoon. They slept in a little house without blankets. The next day they were sent back home. One Indian talked to the police and told them that they had no heart and showed no mercy for locking them up just for visiting which was a very common procedure among us. This kind of treatment from the police to the Indian caused the Indians to lose faith and trust in the white man.

There were letters or notes given to the Indians by the missionaries whenever we went to town. These were to take with us to be presented to the white people in town to obtain food because we were always starving. These were known as starving people's letters. In some instances the clerk would issue these.

Albert: *Were there medical services?*

Mrs. Buffalo: There was never any real medical service. Sometimes a doctor would travel through the reserve. He never told anyone to go to the hospital. He gave castor oil to the children. The Indians called him "Castor Oil Doctor." Many times the Indian doctors saved their own people, so most of the Indians used their own doctor's methods. They crushed roots and herbs and threw them in heated rock and water and benefitted from the evaporation of the steam.

. . .

2.7 Interview with Mrs. Annie Buffalo (Sitting Up High), 1975

The document below is the transcript of an interview with another Piikani (Peigan) elder, Mrs. Annie Buffalo (Sitting Up High). The interview was conducted by Johnny Smith on March 12, 1975 and also includes Smith's grandfather, Tom Yellowhorn, along with Mrs. Buffalo's sons, Arthur Crow Shoe and Richard Crow Shoe, and Mrs. Black Plume who was visiting Mrs. Buffalo from the Kainai (Blood) reserve at the time. As with the Many Guns interview we can get a sense of the objectives sought by First Nations in the treaty negotiations and the conviction that promises made at Blackfoot Crossing were not upheld.

The entire transcript appears here without alteration.

Source: Interview with Mrs. Buffalo conducted by Johnny Smith, 12 March 1975, University of Regina, *oURspace*, http://ourspace.uregina.ca/handle/10294/504.

Reprinted with permission from the University of Regina.

Introduction: My name is John Smith. The purpose of this interview is to obtain an Indian understanding of the treaty and of the promises made to the Indians by the government representatives at the signing of the treaty. We are here today at Mrs. Buffalo's place and my grandfather Tom Yellowhorn has explained in Blackfoot to the group about the work I am doing. The people that will be taking part in this interview are Arthur Crow Shoe, Richard Crow Shoe, Mrs. Buffalo and Mrs. Black Plume (Mrs. Black Plume is from the Blood Reserve and is visiting Mrs. Buffalo[).]

John: *It is time to talk into the tape recorder. I will start off by asking your name. What is your name?*

Mrs. Buffalo: Mrs. Buffalo. My Blackfoot name is Sitting Up High.

John: *How old are you?*

Mrs. Buffalo: I am past 90 now. Yes.

Tom Yellowhorn: She is past 90 now. Yes?

Richard Crow Shoe: She's 93.

John: *Where were you born?*

Mrs. Buffalo: Here. I was born here.

John: *I will now ask everyone else their names and ages.*

Mrs. Black Plume: I am 69. I was born at the Belly Buttes.

Tom Yellowhorn: On the Blood reserve, she's a member of the Blood tribe.

John: *Arthur, how old are you?*

Arthur Crow Shoe: Fifty.

John: *Richard, how old are you?*

Richard Crow Shoe: Fifty-nine.

John: *And you were all born here?*

Interviewees: Yes. All born here (Peigan reserve).

Tom: Richard and Arthur are both children of Mrs. Buffalo.

John: *Tom will now ask you these questions I have.*

Tom: *The question is, saying those people who have left you, your old people, your fathers and grandfathers, did their lives depend a lot on the buffalo and the use of the buffalo?*

Mrs. Buffalo: The buffalo? My mother lived at the time of the buffalo and they really depended on the buffalo for their livelihood, for everything, for living and shelter and everything else like that.

Tom: *When did the buffalo disappear, before the signing of the treaty or after?*

Mrs. Buffalo: Myself, I did not know the buffalo. But the stories that I hear from my elders, they say that the buffalo disappeared shortly after the signing of the treaty. It was sometime soon after the first payment.

Tom: *The old people, did they talk about how the buffalo disappeared or why they disappeared?*

Mrs. Buffalo: The old people were saying that the white people, they took away all the buffalo. That was the reason why there were no more buffalo around here. The white people just took away all the buffalo.

Tom: *Did the disappearance of the buffalo change the Indian way of life?*

Mrs. Buffalo: Did it change their way of living?

Tom: *Yes, did it change their way of living?*

Mrs. Buffalo: When the buffalo disappeared, the white man gave us cattle to eat. They fed us cow meat instead of us eating buffalo.

Tom: *Did the signing of the treaty change the way the people were living?*

Mrs. Buffalo: The old people told me that after the signing of the treaty, that's when the Indian peoples' way of living changed. They no longer lived the way of the buffalo. It really changed their customary way of life.

Tom: *Did the people from here hear anything about the peace treaties being made across the border?*

Mrs. Buffalo: We heard that everything was stopped. There was no more fighting. Our relatives across the border and all the other tribes of Indians, they were told, "Now you are going to end all the fighting amongst yourselves. You are all going to be friends." My mother was one of the last persons to receive a medal from some officials. It was a medal with a stamp of shaking hands and a peace pipe. This meant that the Indians have agreed to stop fighting amongst themselves. There will be no more wars between the Indians.

Tom: *What did the old people think of the signing of the treaty?*

Mrs. Buffalo: Well, at first they thought it was really good. This was right at the signing of the treaty. They said that was the time when they gave us the five dollars. And the rest of the money was supposed to be put away for our use later.

Tom: *Did the Indian people think they were going to go on using the land as they had always done after the signing of the treaty?*

Mrs. Buffalo: After the signing of the treaty the leaders of each group of Indians chose the area in which they were to live thereafter. Each tribe claimed a tract of land for their own use. But as time went on these areas claimed by the different headmen was reduced by the white man's fences and surveyors. The Indians felt they could go on living the way they used to. It was not until they were put on reserves that they realized they could no longer live the way they used to. And each tribe lost a lot of land after they were put on reserves. It was Chief Sit Against the Eagle Tail who chose this area, the Old Man River, the Porcupine Hills. He thought this area he chose was going to be the land where his people lived. He was the head chief of the Peigans at that time.

Tom: *There are papers, which have recently been uncovered by the government, of treaties that have been signed. They seem to be all different. We are trying to understand these written treaties now to see if they were true. The promises that were made at the signing of the treaty, were those promises kept?*

Mrs. Buffalo: At the time of the signing of the treaty, our chief, Chief Sitting Against the Eagle Tail, was promised that his people will get five dollars—the rest of which will be put away until later need—and rations as long as the river flows. They have broken their promises. It is no longer so. They are saying that the old legislations are wiped out, that they no longer exist. New laws that have changed these promises are no longer in effect.

Tom: *Did the Indian people think that anything above the ground was of any value or anything below the ground was of any value?*

Mrs. Buffalo: The old people, they said the land held much that could be made use of. This is Indian use, not white man use. The old Indian people also found wealth of the land under the ground in the form of paint and medicine.

Tom: *Did the old people make any request as to what they wanted that was not in the treaty?*

Mrs. Buffalo: The old people say there was a lot of promises and these promises have never been kept, such as the money that was set aside for ammunition. Today we still have not seen anything of it yet.

Tom: *How was the treaty signed?*

Mrs. Buffalo: The understanding was made to Crowfoot that the people that signed treaty were to get twelve dollars. It was about the third payment when the Queen's men said, "We will give you five dollars from now on. The rest will be put away for you until you need it." They understand that they had some money coming to them. To this day, they have not received this money.

Tom: *Did the white people have everything on paper before they came to sign [the] treaty as to how we were to be governed from there on?*

Mrs. Buffalo: The Indians were not familiar with writing. That was the white man's form. The white man had been writing for a long time before we knew how to write. Whether or not everything was written down before the signing of the treaty, I do not know.

Tom: *Was there anything that the Indian people said they gave up at the signing of the treaty?*

Mrs. Buffalo: No, they didn't know that they gave up anything.

Tom: *Was there anything they asked for that was not written in the treaty?*

Mrs. Buffalo: Yes, the people at the time of the signing of the treaty did ask for a lot of things. But whether or not it was written down, I do not know.

Tom: *What did you hear about the fur trade from the elders?*

Mrs. Buffalo: All the furs gotten by the men are tanned by the women and then brought to Edmonton, Hudson Bay. They were traded for food and cloth to make clothing. There was no money given for them.

Tom: *What did you hear about the whiskey runners from the old people?*

Mrs. Buffalo: They used their furs to buy this whiskey.

Tom: *When was the smallpox epidemic?*

Mrs. Buffalo: Well, I don't know. But across the river from Fort Macleod east, the people . . . sometimes some of the tipis were empty, no one was living in them. Sometimes all the people from one tipi were wiped out by smallpox. They were struck really bad.

Tom: *Was that before the signing of the treaty?*

Mrs. Buffalo: No, it was after the signing of treaty that the smallpox epidemic struck the people.

Tom: *Do you know what it was all about when Sitting Bull was fighting with the white men in the United States?*

Mrs. Buffalo: I don't know. I never heard what the trouble started from.

Tom: *Why did the Indian people refer to land as our mother?*

Mrs. Buffalo: Yes, that's right they refer to her as our mother.

Tom: *Why did they call it our mother, the earth?*

Mrs. Buffalo: When we pray, we say, "Help us, our earth, our mother." It was part of the religion. This is where our life comes from because we walk on this land. And whenever we pray for our relatives, whenever we want to wish them well, we tell them to walk happily on this earth as long as they live. I do not know who first called the earth our mother. We always pray to our mother the earth that we may ever live good and ever travel in safety and always be happy. Everything that the Indians thought was holy came from the earth and their needs, such as tobacco and berries. It was more referred to as the earthly spirit, because whenever they offered anything in sacrifice it always went back into the earth.

Tom: *At the signing of the treaty did they know anything about buying or selling of land?*

Mrs. Buffalo: No, they did not know.

SUGGESTIONS FOR FURTHER READING

There has been much work done on treaty making in Canada and on the numbered treaties specifically, but only a few published works have been listed here. For a detailed account of Treaty 7 that explores what the treaty meant and means to the First Nations signatories, an account conveyed through the voices of elders, see Treaty 7 Elders and Tribal Council with Walter Hildebrandt, Dorothy First Rider, and Sarah Carter, *The True Spirit and Original Intent of Treaty 7* (Montreal: McGill-Queen's University Press, 1996). This book also includes the first-hand accounts of government officials involved in the making of the treaty and analyses of later secondary accounts and academic arguments related to the numbered treaties. For a sweeping historical survey of treaty making in Canada from early commercial compacts to the treaties and claims of the twenty-first century, see J.R. Miller, *Compact, Contract, Covenant: Aboriginal Treaty Making in Canada* (Toronto: University of Toronto Press, 2009). For an exploration of the motivations of Siksika and Kainai representatives at the treaty talks, see the biographies of Crowfoot and Red Crow written by Hugh Dempsey: *Crowfoot: Chief of the Blackfeet* (Edmonton: Hurtig, 1972) and *Red Crow: Warrior Chief* (Saskatoon: Western Producer Prairie Books, 1980). For an account that compares the post-treaty experience of the First Nations of Treaty 7 with those residing in the British Columbia interior, see Keith D. Smith, *Liberalism, Surveillance, and Resistance: Indigenous Communities in Western Canada, 1877–1927* (Edmonton: Athabasca University Press, 2009). For a study that explores government policy, restriction of post-treaty economic activity, and Indigenous response with a focus on the Treaty 4 area of Saskatchewan, see Sarah Carter, *Lost Harvests: Prairie Indian Reserve Farmers and Government Policy* (Montreal: McGill-Queen's University Press, 1990).

CHAPTER 3

"THEN GO, AND STRIKE FOR LIBERTY AND LIFE"[1]

THE 1885 RESISTANCE IN THE NORTH-WEST

By the spring of 1885, many in the Prairie West were markedly dissatisfied with their treatment at the hands of Canadian authorities. Euro-Canadian farmers were frustrated with their lack of representation in the formal political affairs of Canada. They were also disappointed with the sluggish pace of the land registry procedure, particularly because having a registered title was a mandatory requirement for obtaining improvement loans for their farms. Finally, they were displeased with the non-completion of the transcontinental railway through their region.

First Nations witnessed the rights and protections they had agreed to at the various treaty talks being systematically violated. Canada's policy toward them was becoming increasingly restrictive, coercive, and unresponsive to their needs and wishes. To make matters much worse, the buffalo herds that were central to their economies and cultures had disappeared. Many Indigenous people were hungry and desperate. Elders and the senior leadership of the Cree, such as Big Bear and Piapot, continued to advise restraint and diplomacy, but the more militant young men advocated direct action in the effort to press for remedial action.

In addition to the Cree and other First Nations, the Métis were also an important population in the North-West Territories. The Métis had established a number of settlements along the South Saskatchewan River and elsewhere that included all that one might expect in the way of amenities: churches, ferries, river-lot farms, sellers of goods and provisions, grist mills, fire brigades and other facilities and services.

---

1 E. Pauline Johnson, "A Cry from an Indian Wife," *The Week*, June 18, 1885, 457. This quotation appears in document 3.7 below.

As with the First Nations, the disappearance of the buffalo had a significant effect on Métis well-being and on their confidence in the future.

Land was a primary concern for the Métis, especially as large grants were provided to the Hudson's Bay Company and the Canadian Pacific Railway and as Métis communities came to be surrounded by newly arrived non-Indigenous settlers. They wanted surveys and protection for their river-lot system of land holding against Canada's square-grid practice. Most of all, they wanted title to their lands and protection from encroachment.

The Métis forwarded petitions to officials and politicians in Ottawa outlining their concerns, and these were augmented by the words of warning and advice sent by missionaries, policemen, and others. In the early summer of 1884, the Métis sent a delegation to Montana to attempt to persuade Louis Riel to return to Saskatchewan and assist them in their campaign to protect their lands.

Since leaving Canada after the resistance of 1869–70 centred at Red River in Manitoba, Riel had married and become an American citizen and schoolteacher. He had been elected three times to represent a constituency in Manitoba, but was never allowed to take his seat. He had spent two years in asylums in Quebec and wrote that he was receiving divine revelations. He came to see the Métis as a chosen people and himself as a prophet selected to renew religious faith.

Upon his return to Canada's North-West, Riel continued to advocate a diplomatic solution to Métis grievances, but government responses were either non-existent or glacially slow. Métis representations and appeals continued to go unheeded. When talk turned to the use of force in the spring of 1885, the support of non-Indigenous settlers and the Roman Catholic clergy fell away. Nonetheless, believing they had little choice, the Métis seized arms and ammunition and, on March 19, elected a provisional government as they had at Red River in 1869.

The documents in this chapter provide different perspectives on some of the events that followed. Even when one considers the few documents that appear here, it is easy to see how placing particular emphasis on one over another can drastically alter an historical account. It is understandable, then, that there is no unanimity among scholars or other observers concerning the causes of the events most often referred to as the North-West Rebellion or the Resistance of 1885—or concerning the actions or motivations of the principal actors in them. In fact, there are few events in Canadian history about which such a wide range of views have been expressed and published as these. There is little doubt, though, that the 1885 resistance was a watershed moment in Canadian history, especially for the Prairie West. Although these events are multifaceted, the documents in this chapter relate primarily to the initial confrontation at Duck Lake on March 26, 1885. Some of Canada's responses in the aftermath of the events of 1885 are presented in Chapter 4, Section A of this reader.

Certainly distinct Métis communities were established and recognized long before 1885, but issues related to Métis identity and the legal rights attached to that identity continue to be subjects of debate in the twenty-first century. See document 13.4 in Chapter 13 for a selection from *R. v. Powley*, a case heard before the Supreme Court of Canada that dealt with Métis identity and rights.

1. What are Prime Minister John A. Macdonald's explanations for the actions of the First Nations and the Métis?

2. In your view, was it unreasonable to expect the Canadian government to accept the items listed in the "Bill of Rights," as reprinted in the *Daily Mail*? If so, which items are problematic and why? If not, why do you think the Bill of Rights was not simply accepted by the government as the basis for settlement?

3. The documents created by L.N.F. Crozier and Gabriel Dumont are written in different styles and from different perspectives. Which do you find more compelling? Why?

4. Which, if any, of the punishments and rewards suggested by Hayter Reed or presented by others do you think would help ameliorate the strained relations between Canada and First Nations that, in part at least, led to the events of 1885? Why would these be helpful?

5. What reasons does Pauline Johnson give for the resistance?

6. In what ways does the position of these authors (e.g., their employment, cultural background) affect what they have to say?

DOCUMENTS

3.1 Riel's Case, 1885

This selection is from the Daily Mail *newspaper published in Toronto in April of 1885, a few weeks after the first real confrontation between the Métis and Canadian forces at Duck Lake at the end of March. It reproduces a version of the "Métis Bill of Rights," which summarizes the grievances of disaffected Métis and Euro-Canadian settlers in present-day Saskatchewan. Among other things, this document outlines where settlers broadly support Métis initiatives and where settlers and Métis differ in regard to strategy. Though a longer "Petition of Rights" penned in December of 1884 still exists and has been published, the original "Bill of Rights" would be an important one to recover. Unfortunately it appears to no longer exist.*

Source: "Riel's Case," *Daily Mail*, April 13, 1885.

Riel's Case

An Important Statement from the Rebel Leaders

Special to the *Mail*

FORT QU'APPELLE, N.W.T., April 12.—An important letter was received last night by a person here who has long had close relations with the half-breeds, from an influential person at St. Laurent, giving the rebel account of recent events. The substance of it is as follows:—

On March 6 or 7, a large meeting of half-breed delegates was held at St. Laurent. Three white delegates were present purporting to speak for the discontented white settlers of the Prince Albert district. Riel submitted the following "Revolutionary Bill of Rights," which the meeting adopted, most of the points having been discussed at many public meetings during the winter:

THE REBEL PLATFORM

(1) That the half-breeds of the North-West Territories be given grants similar to those accorded to the half-breeds of Manitoba by the Act of 1870.

(2) That patents be issued to all half-breed and white settlers who have fairly earned the right of possession on their farms.

(3) That the provinces of Alberta and Saskatchewan be forthwith organized with legislatures of their own, so that the people may be no longer subject to the despotism of Mr. Dewdney [lieutenant governor of the North-West Territories].

(4) That in these new provincial legislatures, while representation according to population shall be the supreme principle, the Metis shall have a fair and reasonable share of representation.

(5) That the offices of trust throughout these provinces be given to residents of the country, as far as practicable, and that we denounce the appointment of disreputable outsiders and repudiate their authority.

(6) That this region be administered for the benefit of the actual settler, and not for the advantage of the alien speculator.

(7) That better provision be made for the Indians, the Parliamentary grant to be increased and lands set apart as an endowment for the establishment of hospitals and schools for the use of whites, half-breeds, and Indians, at such places as the provincial legislatures may determine.

(8) That all the lawful customs and usages which obtain among the Metis be respected.

(9) That the Land Department of the Dominion Government be administered as far as practicable from Winnipeg, so that settlers may not be compelled as heretofore to go to Ottawa for the settlement of questions in dispute between them and the land commissioner.

(10) That the timber regulations be made more liberal, and that the settler be treated as having rights in this country.

THE REBEL GOVERNMENT FORMED

The writer of the letter does not pretend to give the actual language of the resolutions, but merely the substance of it. At this meeting speeches were made on behalf of the half-breeds by Riel, Maxime Lepine, and Charles Nolin; and on behalf of the white settlers by Archibald Davidson, George Fisher, and Alexander Waller (or Walter). It is determined to embody this bill of rights in a memorial and send it to the newspapers, and to leading members of Parliament, and to the Dominion authorities. Nolin and Riel then moved that, as the Government had for fifteen years neglected to settle the half-breed claims, though it had repeatedly (and more especially by providing for their adjustment in the Dominion Land Act of 1883) confessed their justice, the meeting should assume that the Government had abdicated its functions through such neglect; and should proceed to establish a Provisional Government based upon the principles involved in the bill of rights. This was agreed to, and a Government was there and then formed with Riel as President. He announced that no hostile movement would be made unless word were received from Ottawa refusing to grant the demands in the bill of rights. If, however, the Government should appoint a commission to deal with the half-breed claims and pledge itself to deal with the questions affecting white settlers, then the Provisional Government, on obtaining reasonable guarantees that this would be done, would disband. Bloodshed was to be avoided unless the provocation amounted to life or death for the revolted settlers. In the meantime, the authority of the Dominion would be repudiated, and supplies collected to provide against the emergency of war. Immediately after the meeting Alexander Fisher, Lavallée and Lepine, who had charge of supplies, began to levy on the freighters and settlers. Riel, Dumont, and others turned their attention to the Indians, with whom they had had talks during the winter; and tobacco men were sent out in all directions informing the chiefs and head men regarding what had been done.

THE DUCK LAKE FIGHT

This is how matters stood when the fight at Duck Lake occurred. The half-breeds solemnly declare that, while they had repudiated Dominion authority, they had no hand or part in provoking the collision there. They say that if they had intended to fight they would not have sent twenty men but five hundred, and would have wiped out Crozier's command altogether. Their small force was out looking for Government *caches* (hidden supplies) in order to be in a position, should the Government precipitate war by refusing to treat with the Provisional Government, to secure provisions. But, and on this point the half-breeds are most urgent and explicit, Dumont did not attempt to interfere with Crozier. On the contrary he was so careful in obeying Riel's instructions that, to avoid even the risk of a collision, he ordered his men to disperse into the bush, while he talked with Crozier. The latter, however, supposed that his force was being surrounded, and ordered his men to fire. The fight then followed. There were two hundred armed half-breeds within ear-shot of the firing, but when they arrived at the scene Crozier was in full retreat, and, still, acting according to Riel's orders, they did not attempt to go in pursuit, though they might easily have destroyed Crozier before he reached Carleton, encumbered as he was with wounded men. The half-breeds say that Captain Moore, who was wounded, will testify that Crozier lost his head, and ordered his men to fire without cause or provocation.

RIEL'S PRESENT POSITION

The news of this bloodshed reached Riel on the 27th of March, the fight having taken place at 3 p.m. on the previous day. Riel at once issued an order, of which the substance is as follows:—

The police have suffered in an attack upon the forces of the Provisional Government, having fired upon our men without provocation and even without knowing that this Government had been established. No doubt they acted under orders from Mr. Dewdney, who, to our entreaties and remonstrances so often conveyed to Ottawa by letters and by deputation since 1870, replies with a volley. It is therefore evident that war is being thrust upon us. We shall not continue hostilities, however, unless we are again attacked, until we know for certain that Mr. Dewdney has been instructed to deal with us, settlers struggling for our rights, as public enemies of Canada. In the meantime it is necessary for us to prepare to resist. We remain on the defensive, but the emissaries of the Government are evidently determined to make us the aggressors. Justice must triumph, however, and we must trust in God. For God and our rights!

The white settlers who had taken part in the preliminary movement, and who had opposed the levying for supplies, were now greatly alarmed at the news of the fight, and most of them abandoned the half-breeds, though Riel argued all through that the police were to blame, Riel then sent out other messengers, telling the Indians that Mr. Dewdney had determined to kill them as well as the half-breeds and all other persons who had complained of him and his Administration. Lepine and others renewed their efforts to secure supplies, promissory notes of the so-called Provisional Government being given to those levied upon.

. . .

3.2 Report of Superintendent of Indian Affairs John A. Macdonald, 1885

In the spring of 1885, the then 70-year-old John A. Macdonald was both prime minister of Canada and superintendent general of Indian affairs (SGIA). The fact that Macdonald was responsible both for Indian policy generally as prime minister and for implementation of that policy as SGIA would seem certainly to have affected how he presented Indigenous grievances and the events of 1885, especially since he knew his report would be published and because the Department of Indian Affairs was not responsible for the Métis. The department's annual reports were published individually and also appeared in Canada's Sessional Papers *for the following year. The reports included a massive amount of community, agency, provincial, national, and, in some cases, individual-level data in both tabular and narrative form based on the observations of departmental employees stationed across the country. This selection comes from the Department's annual report for 1885.*

Source: John A. Macdonald, Superintendent of Indian Affairs, in Canada, Department of Indian Affairs, *Annual Report*, 1885 (Ottawa: Maclean Roger and Co., 1886), ix–xiv.

REPORT

OF THE

DEPARTMENT OF INDIAN AFFAIRS

FOR THE

YEAR ENDED 31ST DECEMBER, 1885

DEPARTMENT OF INDIAN AFFAIRS,
OTTAWA, 1st January, 1886

To His Excellency the Most Honorable The Marquess of Lansdowne, Governor General of Canada, &c., &c., &c.

MAY IT PLEASE YOUR EXCELLENCY :—

I have the honor to submit for Your Excellency's information the Report of this Department for the year 1885.

The condition of Indian matters in the several Provinces of the Dominion has been generally satisfactory during the past year. And if the same cannot be said with regard to the North-West Territories as a whole, it is due to circumstances over which this Department had no control, but which were the result of specious inducements held out to the Indians of the North-West Territories by the leader of the half-breed insurgents and his lieutenants, and to which several of the Indian bands on the North Saskatchewan lent too ready an ear, which resulted in some of them forgetting the allegiance they owed their Sovereign, and becoming involved in the rebellious movement, and eventually committing crimes, for the more serious of which those whose guilt was confessed or proven suffered the extreme penalty of the law, and others convicted of having been guilty of outrages of a less criminal nature were sentenced to and are undergoing imprisonment for long or short terms, as the extent of the offences committed by them justified. That the Indians who revolted had no reason for doing so, in so far as their treatment was concerned, is sufficiently established by the concurrent testimony of all those connected with the management of the Indians in the North-West Territories, as also by the fact that they had no intention of joining in the insurrection until messages reached them from the leaders of the half-breed insurgents, assuring them that great benefits, in the shape of rich booty, would accrue to them in the event of success attending the rebels, which they were also told was a foregone conclusion. Moreover, the fact of the Indians being connected by blood relationship with the half-breeds had, of course, great influence with the former. These messages were more successful in misleading the Indians after the encounter had by the Nort-West

[sic] Mounted Police with the rebels at Duck Lake—that affair having been represented by the runners sent by the insurgents to the Indians as having been a great success for the rebels. Their old instincts for the war path were thus aroused in several of the bands, more especially in those wandering tribes not settled on reserves, such as Big Bear's following at Frog Lake, by some of whom the majority of the more revolting atrocities were perpetrated, such as the massacre at that place of two clergymen of the Roman Catholic Church, and of the Indian agent, the farming instructor, and several other white people.

The last advices received from the above officials before they were thus ruthlessly slain indicated no apprehension on their part of an Indian outbreak, but, on the contrary, that they were on the best of terms with the Indians, and that the latter were working well and were quite contented. The same good accounts were received just previous to the uprising from the other points at which the Indians were induced to act with the insurgent half-breeds. On the 17th of March Mr. Acting Indian Agent Lash wrote from Carlton: "I have the honor to state I visited Duck Lake yesterday, and remained over night in that neighborhood, and am pleased to report the Indians are all quiet, and not interfering with the half-breed movement. The latter are still a little uneasy, but I trust the precautions taken by the Police have cooled their ardor, as they are starting on freighting trips, and I am inclined to think their excitement will blow over."

As will be observed from the same officer's report, which will be found with the appendices attached to this report, on the 18th of March, only three days after the date of this letter above quoted, being apparently the next occasion of his visiting the above locality, which he did in consequence of a rumor having reached him that the half-breeds were tampering with the Indians, he "was surrounded by an armed mob of about forty half-breeds, commanded by Riel,["] who gave orders to make him and his interpreter prisoners. "This," he adds, "was done, and I remained a prisoner in the rebel camp, until released by General Middleton's column, on the 12th May." It should be here stated, that at about the same time the farming instructor at Duck Lake, and other loyal subjects, were also made prisoners, and that these men were subjected to great indignities at the hands of the rebels. During the last ten days of their captivity they were kept in a dark cellar, from which they were not allowed egress for any purpose whatever, the cellar being at the same time without any means of ventilation, except that afforded by a few chinks in the foundation.

The agent at Battleford reports that the Indians of that vicinity were better clothed last winter than usual; that there were sufficient provisions on the different reserves to last until June, and that all seemed happy and contented until the half-breed insurgents began to trouble them with messages. The purport of these false missives was, among other things, that the troops were on the way northward, and that the Indians would either be enlisted as soldiers or be massacred. The effect which attended the receipt of these messages was afterwards only too evident. The town of Battleford was sacked: the farming instructor on the Assiniboine or Stony Indian reserve at Eagle Hills, and one of the settlers of the vicinity, were murdered; the farming instructor and his family on the Cree Indian reserve, in the same locality, barely escaped with their lives, by fleeing to Swift Current, the nearest point on the Canadian Pacific Railway; and the inhabitants of the town and of the adjacant [sic] country were forced to seek refuge in the fort of the North-West Mounted Police at Battleford, which was besieged by the half-breeds and Indians for several weeks, until reinforcements came to the relief of the garrison. The Indians who revolted do not plead grievances in extenuation of their having done so. On the contrary, they express regret for the part they took, and say they were led into it by the leader of the half breed insurrection. And those of them who suffered for their crimes on the gallows publicly acknowledged that they deserved the punishment, and advised their compatriots to be warned by their fate not to follow their example.

The Department had taken especial care, inasmuch as their crops had proved a failure, to provide, in the autumn of 1884, an extra large supply of provisions for the districts in which they afterwards became disaffected, and the Indians consequently had an abundance of food. The excitement extended as far west as Edmonton, and to the Bear Hills south of that place; but with the exception of the looting of the farming instructor's house and the storehouse at Saddle Lake, and the pillaging of the Hudson Bay Company's store and the house of the Methodist missionary on Battle River, in the Bear Hills, no deeds of rapine were committed, although the Indians were greatly excited, and for some time there were grave apprehensions of an uprising; but wiser counsels prevailed with them, and the arrival of the military effectually removed the difficulties of the situation.

It is gratifying to be able to bear testimony to the loyalty, during this most trying time, of several of the most prominent chiefs, and the bands represented by them, whose reserves are situated in the districts affected by the late rebellion. I would mention especially the names of Chiefs Mis-to-was-sis and At-tak-a-koop, the most important Indian leaders of the Carlton section, and those of Chiefs John Smith, James Smith and William Twatt, leading chiefs in the vicinity of Prince Albert. Chiefs Moosomin and Thunder Child, whose reserves are situated near Battleford, also deserve mention; the latter, however, owing to his band having run short of supplies, and the impossibility of obtaining any elsewhere, had to seek the rebel's camp. All of the above chiefs and their followers removed to a distance from the scene of the trouble, as they had no sympathy with it. Chief Pecan *alias* Seenum, of Whitefish Lake, deserves special mention. He is the most influential of the chiefs of that section of country east of Victoria and west of Frog Lake, and has the most numerous band: which he managed to control, and they, led by their chief, successfully resisted an attempt made by a war party from Big Bear's band to pillage the store of the Hudson Bay Company at Whitefish Lake, one man having been killed in the encounter. Chief Blue Quill, of Egg Lake, south of Victoria, and his band, likewise remained loyal; as did also chief Muddy Bull, of Pigeon Lake, and Chief Chepoostiquahn, or Sharphead, of Peace Hills, south of Edmonton, and their followers. The other chiefs and bands of the country adjacent to Edmonton, although they were considerably excited, committed no overt acts, if we except the raiding by some of Chief Bobtail's band of the Hudson Bay Company's Store at Battle River and the residence of the missionary of the Methodist Church at Bear Hills, which matters have already been referred to; and I should state that those Indians have consented that the cost of the damage done by them shall be paid for from their annuities.

None of the Indians in the southern part of the district of Alberta took any part in the rebellion, notwithstanding that messages urging them strongly to do so were constantly being received by them. The chiefs remained true to their allegiance, and their followers obeyed them, by abstaining from any interference in the matter. Many of the young men of the Blackfeet, Bloods and Piegans were anxious to be allowed to fight on behalf of the Crown against the insurgents. The chiefs in this section of the Territories whose names deserve special mention are, Red Crow, head chief of the Bloods; Crowfoot and Old Sun, head chiefs of the Blackfeet; Eagle Tail (recently deceased), head chief of the Piegans; Jacob, Bear's Paw, and Chinniquy, head chiefs of the Stoneys or Assiniboines, of Morleyville.

In the district of Assiniboia, which, from its geographical position, wasmore [sic] readily reached from the Saskatchewan district by the emissaries of the rebels than other parts, the Indians were constantly besieged with messages from the half-breed insurrectionists, urging them in the strongest terms to revolt and assist in the movement. With the exception of about twenty or thirty, who plundered the houses and property of a few settlers, none of the Indians responded to the call; although they were naturally greatly excited by the messages received, as well as by seeing so many troops moving north; for all of them had to pass that way to the scene of the troubles, and a considerable force was also stationed in their vicinity. The rebels did not omit to inform these Indians, as they had done elsewhere, that they would be massacred by the soldiers in the event of the insurgents being defeated, whether they had fought or not. It required all the influence which the Indian agents for the locality, Col. McDonald, of Indian Head, and Mr. Lawrence Herchmer, of Birtle, and those acting under them, could bring to bear upon the Indians, to remove the false impression engendered by these messages in their minds. Those officers were indefatigable in moving about among them and quieting their fears. And I beg here to state that all the officials connected with the Indian service in the North-West Territories, Manitoba and Keewatin, from the Indian Commissioner, Assistant Indian Commissioner and Superintending Inspector at Winnipeg, downwards, deserve great commendation for the zealous efforts made by them to keep the Indians loyal, and which endeavors, I am sure, all are thankful to know were, as regards the great majority of the Indians, entirely successful. And I would also be lacking in a recognition of what is properly due to those who assisted us with their wise counsel and active sympathy in that trying time did I omit to acknowledge the eminent services rendered by several clergymen and other gentlemen, who, though not directly connected with the Indian management in the North-West, voluntarily and magnanimously lent their services; and, by their influence with the Indians, were, doubtless, largely instrumental in preserving order amongst them. In this connection I would especially mention the Rev. Father Lacombe, Principal of the St. Joseph's Industrial School at High River; the Rev. Father Scollen, of the St. Albert Mission; Mr. C. E. Denny, of Fort McLeod, and the officers of the Honorable the Hudson Bay Company generally.

Despatches expressive of their loyalty and attachment to their Sovereign, and of their disapproval of the insurrection, were received from time to time, from Indian chiefs in several parts of the North-West Territories, Manitoba and Keewatin.

It is encouraging to learn, from the report of the Indian commissioner for these portions of the Dominion, that notwithstanding the excitement incident to the rebellion, educational progress among the Indian children was not seriously retarded in the North-West Territories, as shown by seven new schools having been opened during the year, and the increase generally in the number of children attending the schools. It is much to be regretted, however, that the industrial institution established at Battleford was pillaged by the half-breeds and Indians, and the building greatly damaged. So soon as the rebellion was quelled and the troops had been withdrawn from Battleford, this institution was re-opened, the Indian children being glad to return to it. But, later, when the artillery was sent to that point, it had again to be vacated and given over to them, as no accommodation could be found elsewhere for the troops. The Department, however, succeeded in securing two vacant houses, where the children are at present lodged and taught, until more suitable arrangements can be made. The two industrial institutions at High River, in the district of Alberta, and at Qu'Appelle, in the district of Assiniboia, have continued their operations. It is proposed, provided Parliament will vote money for the purpose, to establish another institution of the same type in the vicinity of Long Lake, in the district of Assiniboia, and to select the Principal and other officers of the institution from the Presbyterian denomination.

Except on the reserves on the North Saskatchewan, a considerable quantity of land was brought under cultivation, and the Indians worked well. Especially was this the case on the reserves in the southern part of the district of Alberta, where the Indians generally remained steadily at work, as did those, also, in the western part of Manitoba, and the large majority of the Indians in the district of Assiniboia.

As elsewhere intimated, the Indians of Manitoba, and of the district of Keewatin, generally, had no sympathy with the insurgents, but denounced the rebellion in no measured terms.

. . .

3.3 Report of North-West Mounted Police Assistant Commissioner L.N.F. Crozier, 1885

Irish born Leif Newry Fitzroy Crozier (1846–1901) settled with his family in Belleville, Ontario, in the early 1860s. He served in the volunteer militia and then joined the North-West Mounted Police in time for its march west in 1874. He rose fairly quickly in the ranks of the police to the position of assistant commissioner, but his career was punctuated with actions that can only be described as injudicious at best. Crozier served at a number of posts across the western plains and was a witness to the signing of Treaty 7 at Blackfoot Crossing. This report, written by Crozier to his superior, NWMP Commissioner A.G. Irvine, was published in the force's 1885 annual report. Crozier resigned from the force a year later when he was not appointed to replace the retiring Irvine as commissioner.

Source: L.N.F. Crozier, Assistant Commissioner, N.W.M.P., in *Report of the Commissioner of the North-West Mounted Police Force, 1885* (Ottawa: MacLean, Roger & Co., 1886), 43–46.

PRINCE ALBERT, 29TH MAY, 1885.

SIR,—I am asked to make a further report as to the affair at Duck Lake on the 26th March last. In addition to what I have already said in former reports, I may further state as follows:

Between the 19th and 26th March Riel and his followers had robbed, plundered, pillaged and terrorized the settlers and country; they had sacked stores, seized and held as prisoners officers of the Government, merchants, settlers and others; they had risen in armed rebellion or insurrection, they patrolled the country with armed parties, who seized, with the muzzles of rifles at their heads, loyal subjects, or any one else they chose, declaring that they had the choice of submitting to be made prisoners or of being shot; their orders were to massacre all those who would not allow themselves to be made prisoners; they had incited the Indians to take up arms and rebel against authority, a condition of affairs which must lead to murders, massacres and the most frightful atrocities; they had cut the telegraph wires and cut down the telegraph poles, and stopped all mail and other communication and traffic; had committed highway robbery, seized and plundered freighters and freight, and had fired upon and driven into the fort I was commanding, my patrols; they had denounced and repudiated the authority of the Queen, and had plunged the country into a state of war, terror and anarchy; they had paralyzed all trade and business, and the legitimate and peaceful occupations and callings of the people.

Riel, the leader of the rebels, had sent word to me, demanding the unconditional surrender of Carlton, and on my failing to comply with his request, the alternative was to be, he said, "a war of extermination." Upon one occasion he sent word that he wished to see me, in order to negotiate. I replied that I would meet him at a certain place named, half way between Duck Lake and Carlton, and that I would go without an escort, and promised that he might have a chance of saying whatever he wished; and further, that upon that occasion I would not arrest him. I said to the messenger: "Give the man my word of honor that I will not arrest him this time." He replied that he would not meet me, but would send emissaries. I therefore, instead of going myself, sent two gentlemen to represent me. They were told, on meeting Riel's men, that they had nothing more to say than that Fort Carlton must be surrendered unconditionally. The gentlemen I sent out were Captain Moore and Captain Thomas McKay, of Prince Albert. I had told them to tell Riel's men that the gravest offences had been committed against the law, and that the leaders and instigators of the rebellion would have to be delivered up to the authorities, to be dealt with according to the law; and as to the others, I said, tell them that I think many have been led astray or forced into rebellion. I believed that they would be pardoned at any rate, that I would do all in my power to get for them an amnesty. Through these gentlemen I advised the rebels to disperse, lay down their arms and go to their homes. Upon another occasion Captain Thomas McKay, a gentleman well known to the French half-breeds, had gone to their headquarters at Batoche, and then entreated them to go to their homes, and used every conceivable argument to induce them to see how foolishly they were acting. I published also, written and printed notices in French and English, offering any and all those who had been forced into rebellion, or were held against their will, protection, on presenting themselves to the officers commanding at Carlton or Prince Albert; but all this was of no avail. Riel said, among other violent utterances, to one of the messengers I had sent out to try and induce the rebels to go to their homes: "We want blood! blood! If Carlton is not surrendered it will be a war of extermination; I must have an answer by 12 o'clock or we will attack and take the fort."

Such was the condition of affairs when, on the morning of the 26th March last, Sergeant Stewart's party was prevented from going on to Duck Lake (to get the stores which I desired to fetch from Mitchell's store) by an armed party of rebels. Their number was reported to me as being about 100. From the latest information brought in by my scouts I believed the rebel headquarters and main body of insurgents were at Batoche's, on the south side of the river, and therefore I was led to believe that the party north of Duck Lake was but a detachment from the main body engaged in a marauding expedition, and I considered that with the 100 men I had with me I would be able to overcome their resistance, if any, and get the stores in spite of them. I also took with me a 7-pr. gun in charge of Mr. Howe (who was wounded in the subsequent engagement). It was not until after the action had been in progress for some time that I discovered that the numbers of rebels opposed to me was greatly in excess of what I had been informed were within striking distance of me. I found then that I was outnumbered at every point, and in imminent danger of being surrounded. The snow was, as I have before reported, very deep and badly crusted, and my men found the greatest difficulty in moving about at all. The deep snow also badly interfered with the use of the 7-pr. gun in action. Four shots, at least, were fired from the gun—two shrapnel, one case and one common shell.

When I found that the enemy were more numerous by far than we were, that they were ambushed almost all round me, and had every advantage of ground and cover on their side, while we had every disadvantage of position to contend against, I deemed it prudent to abandon my attempt to push on to Duck Lake, and to withdraw my force from the action, which was done, as before reported, in perfect order by the men under my command. Five of my horses having been killed or disabled by gun shot wounds, I was obliged to abandon two of my sleighs and one jumper, in which there were a few rounds of ammunition for the 7-pr. gun, and which fell into the hands of the rebels. The rest of my command—horses, sleighs and all the wounded—as was reported to me, were brought safely off the field. Such of the dead as I could gather I also brought with me. Most of the killed, however, were off to the extreme right, in situations most exposed to the rebel fire from shelter, and could not have been collected without incurring the gravest risk of putting my entire command into the greatest possible jeopardy, with an absolute certainty of losing many more lives from the terrible and continuous fire from the enemy ambushed on the right. Three different times I gave the order to put the killed and wounded on the sleighs, and I held the column until it was reported to me that all were on; but even to have endeavored to get the bodies from the extreme right would have been, in the situation we were in, impossible. Besides, if I had delayed leaving the field but a few minutes my party would have met total destruction. Reference to the diagram attached will show the position of the rebel forces, the trap in which we were, and from which they intended we should never escape.[2] I contend that no man desirous of taking action necessary to the performance of his duty could have foreseen, or escaped under the circumstances, getting into the affair on the 26th March, as I did, and having got into it, our getting out was most fortunate. Had the rebel plan succeeded and a few minutes more would have made it successful—there would not have been one of us left. With our gun in their possession, and flushed with victory, and following it up, Carlton must have fallen, and if Colonel Irvine's party, then coming through a difficult country, had suffered a reverse, it would have exposed the whole of the eastern part of the territory to the rebel attack and occupation, which would have been most probable, for it must be remembered that many of the men of Prince Albert were with Colonel Irvine and myself at Carlton.

I have stated already that I was going out for provisions and ammunition, not expecting or intending to meet the rebels in full force. The force with me was ample for what I intended it. Had I delayed, I considered I would have no chance to secure what I wanted, but with prompt action I certainly expected to succeed. Therefore, I acted promptly. I thought at the time and still think that

---

2 The diagram described was not included in this report.

the securing of the provisions and ammunition at that stage of the rebellion was a matter of the very greatest importance, for though the rebels had already secured a large quantity of supplies by plunder, they must, from their numbers, and what they had given to the Indians, in endeavoring to secure and retain their allegiance, have greatly reduced their store. Again, I argued if the Indians see that a party of half-breeds can contemptuously drive back and prevent officers of the Government from doing their duty, thus defiantly seizing property with impunity, they would be able to gain the firm allegiance of the wavering Indian tribes by what is stronger to them than any argument—namely, giving them plenty to eat.

A person understanding the nature of Indians as well as you do, and the situation as it was on the 26th March last, will readily understand what a gain to us it would be, and how the prestige of the rebel half-breeds would have suffered and ours gained, among the Indians, had I succeeded in carrying out the object of my expedition, more especially after we had made an attempt and being unsuccessful in the morning; and further, you will see that had I waited for you the chance and time in which it would be possible to get the stores would have passed; therefore, a day or even a few hours was of vital importance. But withall, had I known or even suspected that the rebels were in full force, or had I expected that I should be attacked by them as I was, I certaintly [sic] would not have taken the matter in hand. With the number of available men at my disposal the risk would have been too great—even to secure the great advantage that would in all probability, have been a consequence of the securing the provisions and ammunition.

My former reports show how I met the rebels. I admit I was deceived as to their strength. When I left Carlton I considered I would probably meet, if they did not run away, not to exceed 100 of them. From the numbers I first saw in the field I was justified in thinking that there were no more than that number.

The Prince Albert volunteers lost more heavily than the police, because several of them happened to be extended on the right of our line, where they were more exposed to the fire of the enemy in ambush and in houses. When I felt the fire pouring in on us from that quarter, I said to Mr. Howe, commanding the gun Detachment: "Shell those fellows," pointing in the direction from which the fire was coming. He replied: "Our own men are extended there, and I may fire into them." I then said, pointing to the coulée opposite our left front, from whence a very heavy fire was coming on us: "Throw a shell over there," which was done. The gun did good service, and no men could have worked better than the gunners did that day, under conditions that would have tried soldiers, no matter how well disciplined. I did not know, when the line extended, that there was a house on our right, and that the enemy were ambushed about it in large numbers, so that I did not purposely expose one part of the line to fire more than another. The sleighs I threw out for no other purpose than for cover, and they were taken advantage of as such by the volunteers and police indiscriminately; and if unkind and unfeeling remarks have been made, it was not by any of those who fought so gallantly together, and received, without flinching, as hot a fire as men ever were exposed to. The strongest feeling of friendship exists between the Prince Albert volunteers and the Mounted Police, because all who were present on that day know that no man shirked from his duty, or from danger, but that each unflinchingly and bravely took his chances and did his work.

Though unsuccessful in getting possession of the stores I strove to bring in, and enforcing the rebels to withdraw, I considered that one consequence of my action was to force the rebels to give up, for the time, the attack on Fort Carlton, which they had mediated and would otherwise have made on the night of the 26th March, and prevented the bloodshed which must have occurred there, and the by no means impossible disaster to our arms, which, owing to the position of the fort, might have occurred there.

It is to be regretted that I was not made aware of the fact that the rebels were in force at Duck Lake at the time I engaged with them, but my scouts did not learn that such was the case in time to apprise me of it. The movement of the main body of the rebels to Duck Lake was sudden and unexpected, and was, so far, a surprise to me.

Before concluding this supplementary report, I may repeat that it was the rebels who attacked me and began the action. They had their dispositions most skillfully made, and nearly succeeded in cutting off my command, which they would have done but for the steady valor and good discipline of the men under me, on which I justly relied before setting out on the 26th March last.

I attach a rough sketch of the ground upon which the action at Duck Lake was fought.[3] It will give a fairly good idea of the disposition of the opposing forces on the 26th March last, and show their numbers to have been between 300 and 400 fighting men.

I have the honor to be, Sir,

Your obedient servant,
  L.N.F. CROZIER,
    Assistant Commissioner, N.W.M.P.
  Lt.-Col. IRVINE
    Commissioner, N.W.M.P., Prince Albert.

Forwarded,
  A.G. IRVINE
    Commissioner.

---

3 As above, the sketch was not included in this report.

3.4 The Account of Gabriel Dumont, 1888 (1949)

Gabriel Dumont was born in the area around Red River in 1837, and, although he never learned to read or write, he spoke six different languages. He was skilled on horseback and as a marksman and was leader of the large-scale annual Métis buffalo hunts. Dumont played only a small role in the Red River Resistance of 1869–70, but he served as a military leader during the events of 1885. The selection below comes from an article published in 1949 by George F.G. Stanley, the foremost early historian of the Canadian Prairie West. According to Stanley, this account was originally dictated by Dumont in 1888, transcribed by the recorder of Montreal (B.A.T. de Montigny), and then read back to and approved as accurate by Dumont.

The footnotes from Stanley's article, many referring to other texts and which include Stanley's voice, have been removed with the exception of those identifying persons mentioned in the text.

Source: George Stanley, "Gabriel Dumont's Account of the North West Rebellion, 1885," *Canadian Historical Review*, 30, no. 3 (Sept. 1949): 251–56.

Reproduced with the permission of the University of Toronto Press.

On March 25th, 1885, being at St. Antoine de Padoue, which is half a mile from Batoche, when the mounted police appeared on the other side of the river, I asked Riel to give me 30 men so that we could go to Duck Lake and ransack our opponents' storehouses. When I got there, Mitchell had fled.[4] I got Magnus Burnstein, his clerk, to give me the keys to his warehouse, and helped myself to the contents.

I then left with ten men to reconnoitre the road to Carlton, taking care to send scouts in advance.

After midnight, my scouts, Baptiste Ouellet and Baptiste Arcand, saw two men on horseback go by, Ross and Astley.[5] My brother Edouard, Philippe Gariépy, Baptiste Deschamps, an Indian and I pursued them. Although my men were armed, I gave orders that they were not to harm anyone who did not resist.

We caught up to them at Duck Lake, and I swooped down upon them. I took aim at them saying in Indian: "Don't try to escape, or I'll kill you". Ross said to me "I'm a surveyor". I knocked him down off his horse. Seeing his revolver, I grabbed it from him, telling him "You're no surveyor, you're a liar".

Astley escaped, and as my men wanted to kill him, I ordered them not to do anything to him. However, he fell off his horse and they seized him. We took them both disarmed to Duck Lake, and kept them prisoners. I told them that if they behaved, they would be well treated.

---

4 Hillyard Mitchel was a trader at Duck Lake.

5 Harold Ross was Deputy Sheriff at Prince Albert. John W. Astley was a civil engineer and land surveyor and a resident of Prince Albert.

We took possession of their horses.

This man Ross whom I had taken into custody in this manner was a sheriff. He must have been very frightened because, in his testimony, he said we numbered fifty when there were only 5 of us. He also claimed in the same testimony that his companion had kept him from shooting, he certainly didn't have time to do so, because I jumped on him too fast.

We were going out to stable our horses when someone shouted: "Here come the police", but it was only three scouts whom my brother Edouard, Patrice Fleury, my brother-in-law James Short, and I chased and who escaped. Patrice Fleury said he saw Mackay[6] among those scouts.

My companions had a lead over me in the chase after the fugitives, and I realized that they had fallen into an ambush of some forty mounted policemen who were taking aim at them. I galloped my charger towards my comrades shouting at them to get off their horses. I myself dismounted, because I heard a sergeant swear he was going to kill me. I immediately aimed at him yelling "It is I who will kill you". Then he emptied his rifle, putting it across his knees. I promptly pounced on him and knocked him over with the barrel of my rifle. When I lifted my gun again a shot went off by accident. Then Thomas Mackay rushed at me saying "Be careful Gabriel". I answered him, "You'd better be careful yourself, or I'll blow your brains out". And I flung myself upon him. He turned his horse which had its back feet sunk in snow, and it reared up. I gave Mackay a push in the back with my rifle. He spurred his horse and it gave a leap forward and got away. Meanwhile, Mackay kept telling me, "Watch out Gabriel" and I kept repeating too, "You'd better be careful yourself, or I'll slaughter you" and I followed him with my gun.

My brother had jumped into one of the police vehicles to capture the two men in it. But they whipped their horses and made him tumble out. The cart passed over him.

There were about twenty double-yoked sleighs, and there were two men in each. Mackay commanded the retreat. I shouted at him, "What did you come here for?" He replied that he had come to talk to us. "But don't run away like this," I answered him, "we were told that you would come with men, Where are they? You're only one blockhead".

When I saw they were going to run away, I stopped my men from running after them. They weren't numerous enough to check them, there were only three of them.

We went back to Duck Lake, and we had scarcely let our horses out to eat, when we heard someone shout again, "Here come the police". We immediately jumped on horseback, and without delay I had my men occupy a hillock which commanded the plain, and from where the enemy would have been able to level their guns on us.

We were only a few men on horseback and a few men on foot, waiting for the police who had been reinforced by eighty men commanded by Crozier, who had rejoined Mackay's forty runaways. They had a cannon with them.

I sent in pursuit of their scouts several men to whom I gave orders not to shoot, because Riel had asked us not to be the first to fire.

I gave orders to my horsemen, who numbered 25, to go down into a hollow, where we were under shelter from the cannon.

---

6 Thomas Mackay (or McKay) was of Scottish and First Nation decent and a resident of Prince Albert.

Crozier, accompanied by an English half-breed, approached one of our Indians who was unarmed and, it seems, gave him his hand. The Indian then tried to grab the gun out of the hands of the English Métis who was, I believe, John Dougall Mackay. This English Métis fired, and I think it was this rifle shot which killed my brother Isidore and made him fall from his horse, stone dead.

What makes me think that it was this shot which killed my brother is that this Métis had an interest in killing him, seeing that my brother was the only one armed.

As soon as the shot was fired, the police and the volunteers commanded by Crozier, fired a round, and the Indian who was with my brother, was killed.

All this happened without any parley taking place between the two sides.

Charles Nolin, who at first had been full of boasting, had come with us to the fight, against his will. At the first shot, he fled, taking his sister-in-law's cart, going off in the direction of Prince Albert where he gave himself up.

As soon as the shooting started, we fired as much as we could. I myself fired a dozen shots with my Winchester carbine, and I was reloading it to begin again, when the English alarmed by the number of their dead, began to withdraw. It was time they did, for their cannon which until then had kept my infantry men from descending the slope, was silenced because the gunner, in loading it, put in the shot before the powder. My infantrymen then began to surround them.

This first encounter had lasted half an hour.

In their flight they had to go through a clearing, so I lay in wait for them saying to my men, "Courage, I'm going to make the red coats jump in their carts with some rifle shots". And then I laughed, not because I took any pleasure in killing, but to give courage to my men.

Since I was eager to knock off some of the red coats, I never thought to keep under cover, and a shot came and gashed the top of my head, where a deep scar can still be seen; I fell down on the ground, and my horse, which was also wounded, went right over me as it tried to get away. We were then 60 yards from the enemy. I wanted to get up, but the blow had been so violent, I couldn't. When Joseph Delorme saw me fall again, he cried out that I was killed. I said to him, "Courage, as long as you haven't lost your head you're not dead". I told Bte Vandal to take my cartridges and my rifle which was famous and which had a range of 800 yards.

All during the battle, this Delorme was at my side fighting like a lion. But before the fight, he had said to me: "I have never been under fire, if I am afraid, don't spare me but keep me keyed up".

While we were fighting, Riel was on horseback, exposed to the gunfire, and with no weapon but the crucifix which he held in his hand.

Seeing me fall, my brother Edouard rushed forward to drag me down into the ravine, but I told him to go first to our men who seemed to be discouraged by my fall. He rallied them; they began to shout with joy and started shooting again. It was then my cousin Auguste Laframboise whom I had, only a few minutes before, been urging not to expose himself so much, fell close to my side. A bullet had struck his arm and passed through his body. I crawled and dragged myself over to him, saying to myself: "I am always going to say a little prayer for him", but wishing to make the sign of the cross with my left hand, since my right side was paralysed, I fell over on my side and, laughing I said, "Cousin, I shall have to owe it to you".

I should have liked to say for him the prayer which I made up when we had been blessed by the priest at Belton, in Montana, "Lord, strengthen my courage, my faith and my honour that I may profit all my life from the blessing I have received in the Thy holy name".

This is an invocation which I have always said after my prayers, morning and night. This blessing we had received on leaving Montana had impressed Riel so much that he often asked me if I remembered it.

When Riel saw Laframboise fall, he said to me, "Uncle, I am going to have our men on foot advance." I told him that would be like sending them into the lion's den, and that he would do better to maintain the morale of those still on the battle field.

The enemy was then beginning to retire, and my brother, who had taken command after my fall, shouted to our men to follow and destroy them. Riel then asked, in the name of God, not to kill any more, saying that there had already been too much bloodshed.

However, there was a captain whom the police called Morton,[7] a good shot, who was behind a tree and had killed two of our men; he was hit in the back while trying to get away. As he was screaming and suffering horribly, Guillaume Mackay thought he did him a service by shooting him in the head.

The retreating men left behind nine dead and one man wounded in the leg. Since this last man wanted to continue shooting, Philippe Gariépy threw himself on him, wrenched his gun and bayonet from him and tried to hit him with his weapon. One of our men restrained Gariépy, and urged him to have pity on the miserable creature who was taken to Duck Lake.

In the haste of their flight, Clarke forgot to take along his wild cat fur cap.[8]

The vanquished left behind 4 or 5 carts and 8 uninjured horses, as well as several dead ones. In their carts we found some stove tops behind which they had hidden while firing.

They did, however, remove the bodies of the dead mounted policemen, who could easily be recognized by their red uniforms, but they left on the ground the bodies of nine volunteers. I think they lost 16 men including captain Moore, who had a leg broken and amputated.

After the enemy had fled, my companions tied me on my horse, and we went to Duck Lake, where my wound, which was a deep one, was dressed. They also brought in the carts.

We lost five men in this encounter: J.-Bte Montour, Joseph Montour, Auguste Laframboise, Isidore Dumont, and an Indian Joseph Trottier (named after his godfather).

The next day, March 26, 1885, Riel assembled his forces in two ranks and said to them, "Give three cheers, Hurrah for Gabriel Dumont! thank God who gave you so valiant a leader".

---

7 Captain John Morton was a farmer from Bruce County Ontario, and a volunteer officer in the Prince Albert Volunteers.

8 Lawrence Clarke was the Chief Factor of the Hudson's Bay Company and a member of the Council of the Northwest Territories for the district of Lorne.

We spent the whole day in prayer for our dead whose bodies we laid out in a house. They were buried the next day at St. Laurent.

We had captured from the enemy 12 or 13 muskets, some ammunition, and five double waggons; but they had saved their cannon.

The day after the funeral of our friends, I told Riel that it was a shame to leave exposed to the dogs the bodies of our dead enemies who, perhaps bore no more ill will against us than we against them. I suggested that we send a prisoner to Carlton to tell the English to come and get their dead. Riel intimated that perhaps they would be afraid to come and ask for them. So I told Riel that I would send a letter with this prisoner giving my word of honour that neither Indian nor Métis would harm them while they performed this duty. On Riel's agreeing, I signed a safe conduct for whoever should come to claim the bodies.

When the man carrying my message arrived at Fort Carlton, the authorities took him prisoner as a spy, and panic took possession of the police, who abandoned the fort during the night after setting fire to it and destroying the stores. They marched out, guided by an old Canadian Métis called Flat Side of a Dog. But the French Métis in the fort tried to save the stores. As a matter of fact they succeeded in putting out the fire in the shop, but the warehouse was destroyed.

The police took refuge at Prince Albert, fifty miles from Fort Carlton. I wanted to prepare an ambush with a few of my men in a large spruce wood through which the men of the police would have to pass. We could have killed a lot of them, but Riel, who was always restraining us, formally opposed the idea.

It was only at Prince Albert, three days later, that the prisoner we had released, and whom they had taken as a spy, was able to get the refugees to understand that the letter he carried might contain a good proposal. The English Métis then demanded that it be shown to them. How surprised they were to find that it left them free to go and get their dead, and even offered them help in this task. The English Métis were especially interested in this proposition, because it was their dead who lay on the field of battle, the police having taken care to collect their own.

They therefore sent three men from Prince Albert to fetch their dead, whom we had placed in an old house, where they would be sheltered from any desecration. Several of our men helped them put the dead into wagons, and turned over their wounded man to them.

The next day or the day after, Riel made us leave Duck Lake, after setting fire to the buildings, with the exception of the mill.

We crossed the river in order to go to Batoche.

. . .

3.5 The Recommendations of Assistant Indian Commissioner Hayter Reed, 1885

Canadian-born Hayter Reed was still serving in the volunteer militia when he was called to the Manitoba bar in 1871. By the late 1870s, he was working at the Department of the Interior, and then, a year after the Department of Indian Affairs was created in 1880, Reed moved on to take up the position of Indian agent at Battleford. For the next three decades, Reed served in several capacities within the department, eventually rising to its highest civil-service position, that of deputy superintendent general in 1893. The document here was created by Reed in the wake of the events of 1885 following the instructions of his immediate superior, Indian Commissioner Edgar Dewdney. Then Assistant Commissioner Reed put into writing 15 proposals meant to provide a framework for the future administration of First Nations people.[9]

Source: Hayter Reed, "Memorandum for the Honourable the Indian Commissioner relative to the future management of Indians," 20 July 1885, Library and Archives Canada, Department of Indian Affairs, RG 10, vol. 3710, file 19550–3, reel C-10124.

Memorandum for the Honble the Indian Commissioner relative to the future management of Indians.

(1) All Indians who have not during the late troubles been disloyal or troublesome should be treated as heretofore, as they have not disturbed our treaty relations, and our treatment in the past has been productive of progress and good results.

(2) As the rebellious Indians expected to have been treated with severity as soon as overpowered, a reaction of feeling must be guarded against. They were led to believe they would be shot down & harshly treated. Though humanity of course forbids this, unless severe examples are made of the more prominent participants in the rebellion much difficulty will be met with in their future management, & future turbulence may be feared. It is therefore suggested that all leading Indian rebels whom it is found possible to convict of particular crimes, such as instigating & inciting to treason, felony, arson, larceny, murder &c, be dealt with in as severe a manner as the law will allow, & that no offences of their most prominent men be overlooked.

(3) That Half-breed offenders who it is found have been really guilty of such serious offences as the above mentioned should be punished for their crimes in order to deter them from rebellious movement in future.

(4) That the tribal system should be abolished in so far as is compatible with the treaty, i.e., in all cases in which the treaty has been broken by rebel tribes; by doing away with chiefs & councillors, depriving them of medals & other appurtenances of their offices. Our instructors & employees will not then be hampered by Indian consultations & interferences but will administer direct orders & instructions to individuals, besides, by this action & careful repression of those that become prominent among them by

---

9 There are handwritten marginal notes in the original document, which are not reprinted here. These were penned by Edgar Dewdney (ED), Indian commissioner for the North-West Territories (and Reed's immediate superior). In most of these notes, Dewdney expresses his approval of Reed's suggestions (1–4, 7, 9–13, and 15). For the rest, he agrees, but with some qualification, or says that a report will follow (#8). For #5 he states that he wants to elicit the views of the Department of Indian Affairs regarding annuities. Only for #14 does he write, "I do not think this can be done."

councilling [sic] medicine dances & so on a further obstacle will be thrown in the way of future united rebellious movements.

(5) No annuity money should be now paid any bands that rebelled, or to any individuals that left well disposed bands & joined the insurgents. As the treaty expressly stipulated for peace & good-will as well as an observance of law & order, it has been entirely abrogated by the rebellion. Besides this fact such a suggestion is made because in the past the annuity money which should have been expended wholly in necessaries has to a great extent been wasted upon articles more or less useless & in purchasing necessaries at exorbitant prices, entailing upon the Department a greater expenditure in providing articles of clothing, food & implements, not called for by the terms of the treaty, than need have been entailed if the whole of the annuity money had been well & economically applied to the purchase of such necessaries. All future grants should be regarded as concessions of favor, not of right, & the rebel Indians be made to understand that they have forfeited every claim as matter of right.

(6) Disarm all rebels, but to those rebel Indians north of the North Saskatchewan who have heretofore mainly existed by hunting, return shot guns (retaining the rifles) branding them as I.D. [Indian Department] property and keeping lists of those to whom arms are lent. Those to whom arms are thus supplied if left to their own resources—under careful supervision—would suffer great hardship & doubtlessly be benefitted by experiencing the fact that they cannot live after their old methods. They would soon incline to settlement & be less likely to again risk losing the chance of settling down.

(7) No rebel Indians should be allowed off the Reserves without a pass signed by an I.D. official. The dangers of complications with white men will thus be lessened, & by preserving a knowledge of individual movements any inclination to petty depredations may be checked, by the facility of apprehending those who commit the first of such offences.

(8) The leaders of the Teton Sioux who fought against the troops should be hanged & the rest be sent out of the country, as there are certain of the settlers who are greatly inclined to shoot them on sight, & the settlements are more in fear of such marauders as these than of anything else.

(9) Big Bears band should either be broken up & scattered among other bands or be given a Reserve adjacent to that at Onion Lake. The action in this regard could be decided better when it is known, after their surrender, the number that will have to be dealt with. If the band is kept intact & settled as suggested the Instructor stationed at Onion Lake would be sufficient for the two bands.

(10) One Arrows band should be joined with that of Beardy & Okemasis & their present Reserve surrendered & dealt with by the Department for their benefit. Chakaotapayoins band [perhaps the Chekastapaysen (Chakastaypasin) First Nation now part of the James Smith First Nation] should be broken up & their Reserve surrendered, the band being treated as suggested with One Arrows. Neither of these bands are large enough to render it desirable to maintain Instructors permanently with them & as they are constituted of bad & lazy Indians nothing can be done without constant supervision for them. The action suggested therefore would have been wise in any case, their rebellion justifies its pursuit.

(11) All Half-breeds, members of rebel bands, although not shewn to have taken any active part in the rebellion, should have their names erased from the Paysheets, & if this suggestion is not approved of, by directing that all belonging to any bands should reside on the Reserves, most of these half-breeds would desire to be released from the terms of the treaty. It is desirable however that the connection between such people & the Indians be entirely severed as it is never productive of aught but bad results.

(12) There are one or two Canadians, not possessed of Indian blood, on the Pay-sheets; these should be struck off.

(13) James Seenum's band especially should receive substantial recognition of its loyalty, & all Indians like Mistawasis and Ahtahkakoop & other bands that have held aloof from rebellion should receive some mark of the government's appreciation of their conduct. If such a mark is conferred carefully it will at once confirm them in their loyalty & assist in ensuring it in future, whilst increasing the contrast between their treatment & that of those who have acted differently, & this without leading them to believe that it is for the purchase of good behaviour, an effect to by guarded against.

(14) Agents should be particularly strict in seeing that each & every Indian now works for every pound of provisions given to them, & I would urge that so soon as possible directions be given to treat Indians that receive assistance in provisions & clothing in excess of Treaty stipulations as coming under the *Masters & Servants* Act until such time as they become self-dependent. Unwilling ones can then be made to give value for what they receive, a policy heretofore most difficult to carry out.

(15) Horses of rebel Indians should be confiscated, sold, & cattle or other necessaries be purchased with the proceeds of such sale. This action would cripple them for future rebellious movements, & they do not require ponies if made to stop on Reserves & adhere to agricultural pursuits. They would be retained on Reserves too with greater ease if the means of travelling expeditiously were taken from them. In view of the desirability of keeping the Indians from wandering where confiscation is impossible endeavors might be made to induce a voluntary exchange of ponies for cattle &c.

Hayter Reed
Ass^t Comm^r
Regina
July 20th / 85

3.6 Address Presented to Chief Crowfoot from the Council of the Corporation of the City of Ottawa, 1886

For his decision not to participate in the resistance of 1885, Siksika Chief Issapo'-mahkikaaw (Crowfoot) was praised by Prime Minister John A. Macdonald and his cabinet, by the governor general on behalf of Queen Victoria, as well as by several missionaries, members of the press, and the general settler public. To honour his allegiance to the Crown, Crowfoot was invited on a tour of Montreal and Quebec with a small group of other Blackfoot leaders. On his way home, he also visited Ottawa, where he met Macdonald and received this address from the mayor. This document demonstrates not only the appreciation for Crowfoot's allegiance to the Crown but is also fairly clear on the future that settler society envisioned for Indigenous people generally.

Source: Address Presented to Chief Crowfoot from the Council of the Corporation of the City of Ottawa, 1886, with W.M. Graham, Indian Commissioner, to Norman H.H. Lett, City Clerk, Ottawa, 14 October 1925, Glenbow Museum and Archives, William Morris Graham Papers, M8097, box 1, file 1.

Reproduced with the permission of the Glenbow Museum Archives.

ADDRESS PRESENTED TO CHIEF CROWFOOT:

GREAT CHIEF:

We, the Council of the Corporation of the City of Ottawa, on behalf of the Citizens of the Metropolis of the Dominion of Canada, hail with great pleasure your arrival amongst us. We appreciate the visit of such a powerful and distinguished Sagamore of the aboriginal tribes of the great North West.

We have witnessed with profound satisfaction your personal loyalty, and have marked the devotion of your Tribe to the person and Government of Her Most Gracious Majesty the Queen, a devotion the more worthy of admiration when it is considered that notwithstanding national ties, in the midst of strong temptation when other Chiefs and tribes forgot their allegiance, that your people proved true to the Flag of the Empire.

We welcome you heartily to the City of Ottawa, and wish you and your people peace and prosperity for many years. We trust that your sojourn in the East may prove not only interesting and gratifying to yourself and your fellow-warriors, but, also, that it may be frought [sic] with lasting lessons of wisdom and prudence to the great branch of the Indian Nations of North America over which you have ruled so long, so wisely, and so well.

Great Chief of the Redmen of the North West, your pale-faced brothers of the chief City of the Dominion where our Great Mother Victoria commanded the Council Fires of the people to be lighted, bid you welcome! We present you with the wampum belt of friendship. We offer you the pipe of peace. Our hearts are glad when we see your face, for we know that should the hatchet ever be dug up, the voice of Crowfoot will not be heard in the ranks of our enemies. We know that he will not forget the old traditions of his race; and that he will walk in the paths trodden with bravery and honour for so many moons by the Chiefs and warriors of his Tribe.

The Buffalo is no more—the Wapiti has fled to the Mountains—the Grizzly Bear, the Deer and the Antelope will soon follow them. The hand of man has slain them; the smoking monster of the fire path has frightened them from the prairie. They are gone—the Manitoo has said it, and the voice of the Great Spirit never changes. What is left? The land, the plow, the cattle, the sheep, the Reaper, and the Threshing Machine, the iron horse and the steel road, the fruits of the soil, with peace and plenty for the Redman and his White brothers. Let the Great Chief and his People till the land and live in houses warmed by the black diamonds of the Saskatchewan. Let Crowfoot cast away his blanket—and arrayed in better garb let him stand up beside his white brothers, a man—a man who has deserted the war path and taken the bread trail of prosperity and progress.

Great Chief, we have been glad to see you; we shall remember you when you are gone. We wish you a safe journey home again over the long trail to the Setting Sun. We have welcomed you as a friend of loyalty and peace. Go and tell your people that our hearts wish that never again shall the skalping [sic] knife be unsheathed nor the war-whoop heard on the boundless prairies of the Great North West. I have said.

City Clerk. Mayor of Ottawa.

3.7 The Poetic Interpretation of Pauline Johnson, 1885

Emily Pauline Johnson—also known as Tekahionwake—(1861–1913) was born on the Six Nations Reserve near Brantford, Canada West (Ontario), to an English mother and a Mohawk father. Johnson toured across Canada performing her poetry and is one of the few Canadian women ever to make her living writing and performing poetry. Though the popularity of Johnson's work suffered a decline after her death in Vancouver in 1913, it has enjoyed a resurgence in the last half-century as it came to be re-evaluated by feminist and post-colonial scholars and others. This poem portrays an Indigenous perspective on the Resistance of 1885.

Source: E. Pauline Johnson, "A Cry from an Indian Wife", *The Week,* June 18, 1885, 457.

A CRY FROM AN INDIAN WIFE

———

My Forest Brave, my Red-skin love—farewell;
We may not meet to-morrow—who can tell
What mighty ills befall our little band,
Or what you'll suffer from the white man's hand?
Here is your knife. I thought 'twas sheathed for aye.
No roaming bison calls for it to-day;
No hide of prairie cattle will it maim—
The plains are bare—it seeks a nobler game;
'Twill drink the life-blood of a soldier host.
Go—rise and strike—no matter what the cost.
Yet stay. Revolt not at the Union Jack,
Nor take revenge upon this stripling pack
Of white-faced warriors, marching west to quell
Our fallen tribe that rises to rebel.
They all are young, and beautiful, and good;
Curse to the war that spills their harmless blood.
Curse to the fate that brought them from the east
To be our chiefs—to make our nation least

That breathes the air of this vast continent.
Still, their new rule and council is well meant.
They but forget we Indians owned the land
From ocean unto ocean; that they stand
Upon a soil that centuries agone
Was our sole kingdom, and our right alone.
They never think how they would feel to-day,
If some great nation came from far away,
Wresting their country from their hapless braves,
Giving what they gave us—but wars, and graves.
Then go, and strike for liberty and life,
And bring back honour to your Indian wife.
Your wife? Ah, what of that—who cares for me?
Who pities my poor love and agony?
What white-robed priest prays for your safety here
As prayer is said for every volunteer
That swells the ranks that Canada sends out?
Who prays for vict'ry for the Indian scout?
Who prays for our poor nation lying low?
None—therefore take your tomahawk and go.
My heart may break and burn unto its core,
Yet I am strong to bid you go to war.
But stay. My heart is not the only one
That grieves the loss of husband and of son:
Think of the mothers o'er the inland seas;
Think of the pale-faced maiden on her knees;
One pleads her God to guard some sweet-faced child
That marches on toward the North-West wild.
The other prays to shield her youth from harm,
To strengthen his young, proud uplifted arm.
Ah, how her white face quivers thus to think
Your tomahawk his life's best blood will drink.
She never thinks of my wild, aching breast,
Nor dreams of your dark face and eagle crest
Endangered by a thousand rifle balls.
My heart the target, if my warrior falls.
O! coward self—I hesitate no more.
Go forth—and win the glories of the war.
O! heart o'erfraught—O! nation lying low—
God, and fair Canada have willed it so.

E. PAULINE JOHNSON.

There are few topics in Canadian history that have engendered a greater diversity of published opinion than the many aspects of the North-West Resistance of 1885. For an influential early account that presents Indigenous people as ill-equipped to adapt to changing circumstances, see George F.G. Stanley, *The Birth of Western Canada: A History of the Riel Rebellions* (London: Longmans, Green, 1936). For reminiscences of these events by the man who is probably Canada's most famous Mountie, see Samuel B. Steele, *Forty Years in Canada: Reminiscences of the Great North-West with Some Account of His Service in South Africa* (1914; repr., Toronto: McGraw-Hill Ryerson, 1972), especially pages 201–31. For an account more sympathetic to the Métis, see D.N. Sprague, *Canada and the Metis, 1869–1885* (Waterloo, ON: Wilfrid Laurier University Press, 1988). For the perspectives of a Métis author that focuses on the causes of the events of 1885, see Howard Adams, *Prison of Grass: Canada from a Native Point of View* (1975; repr., Saskatoon, SK: Fifth House Publishers, 1989), especially Chapter 8. For a study that challenges the notion that First Nations disregarded treaty promises, see Blair Stonechild and Bill Waiser, *Loyal till Death: Indians and the North-West Resistance* (Calgary: Fifth House, 1997). For a concise exploration of the events of 1885 and their aftermath, see Chapter 10 of J.R. Miller, *Skyscrapers Hide the Heavens: A History of Indian-White Relations in Canada*, 3rd ed. (Toronto: University of Toronto Press, 2000). For an examination of the published narratives of two women held in the camp of Cree leader Big Bear, see Sarah Carter's introduction to *Two Months in the Camp of Big Bear* (1885; repr., Regina: Plains Research Center, 1999) by Theresa Gowanlock and Theresa Delany. For a biography of Gabriel Dumont, see George Woodcock, *Gabriel Dumont*, ed. J.R. Miller (Peterborough, ON: Broadview Press, 2003). For an overview of the resistance from a different perspective see Bob Beal and Rod Macleod, *Prairie Fire: The 1885 North-West Rebellion* (Edmonton: Hurtig Publishers, 1984). For an account that is very sympathetic to government actions and downplays the depth and spread of grievance, see Thomas Flanagan, *Riel and the Rebellion: 1885 Reconsidered* (Saskatoon, SK: Western Producer Prairie Books, 1983). For a published version of the "Petition of Rights" mentioned in the introduction to document 3.1, as well as some related correspondence, see L.H. Thomas, "Documents of Western History: Louis Riel's Petition of Rights, 1884," *Saskatchewan History* 23, no. 1 (Winter 1970): 16–26.

CHAPTER 4

"FOR THE GENERAL GOOD"[1]

RESTRICTING MOVEMENT AND CULTURAL PRACTICE

Most Canadians take the rights to move about freely and to engage in the spirituality of their choice largely for granted. But in their continuing campaign to assimilate Indigenous people and advance the economic, political, and cultural structures of settler society in the late nineteenth and early twentieth centuries, Canadian and church authorities felt it necessary to restrict Indigenous people to their reserves whenever possible and to prohibit a range of spiritual practices that had been followed since time immemorial. Confined to reserves, individuals could be tutored in Anglo-Canadian values, institutions, structures, and beliefs. Within the boundaries of reserves, too, communities could be observed persistently, so any behaviour that was contrary to or appeared to challenge Anglo-Canadian ideals or state authority and policy could be subjected to enhanced remedial action. Although reserves offered residents a refuge from the outside world, a world where they might be discriminated against in a multitude of ways, for church and government officials these small pockets of land served as laboratories of reform. On reserves, "Indianness" could be instructed, cajoled, legislated against, or, if necessary, coerced out of the original inhabitants of Western Canada. This chapter, then, examines two strands in the web of restrictions imposed on Indigenous people.

In Canada, the free movement of Indigenous people was constrained through a variety of means that included enforcing the provisions in the Indian Act that prohibited trespass—so that visiting family, friends, and children in schools and coming together for cultural events and other gatherings could be limited—and enforcing the criminal code, the prohibitions against vagrancy, for example, so that access to urban and other centres could be prohibited. In the Prairie West, though, a more comprehensive policy, referred to as the pass system, was adopted. Under the pass system, discussed in more detail in

---

1 Hayter Reed to Edgar Dewdney, 16 August 1885, LAC, Edgar Dewdney Fonds, MG 27- IC4. This quotation appears in document 4a.2 below.

Section 4a below, any individual wishing to leave his or her reserve for any reason had first to ask permission and receive a written pass from the appropriate Indian agent, the local representative of the Department of Indian Affairs.

At the same time, Indigenous spiritual practices, which were fundamental to community identity, continuity, and well-being but were contrary to church and state objectives, were especially singled out for suppression. On Canada's West Coast the cultural complex known as the potlatch received considerable attention from both missionaries and Canadian officials and politicians. Section 4b below describes the potlatch and outlines, from various perspectives, its significance, the reasons it should be saved or eradicated, some of the effects of its being prohibited, and more recent community revitalization efforts.

The prohibition against the potlatch and the introduction of the pass system in the late nineteenth century further demonstrate the growing authority of the federal government and its Department of Indian Affairs over the lives of First Nations people. These actions also serve to further illustrate the matrix of laws, regulations, and policy meant to "elevate" Indigenous people while at the same time helping to secure the interests of non-Indigenous newcomers.

SECTION 4A: THE PASS SYSTEM

Even before 1885, correspondence between the Department of Indian Affairs (DIA) and the North-West Mounted Police (NWMP) indicates that there was a desire and willingness at all levels of the DIA, NWMP, church, and political hierarchies (and supported by Prime Minister John A. Macdonald) to restrict and monitor the movement of Indigenous people. An early concern, which subsequently became part of the discussion on passes, was related to the cross-border movement of Indigenous people and the possibility of alliance or joint action between those living in the United States and those resident in Canada. Within Canada itself, the vagrancy provisions of the Criminal Code and the restrictions against trespass in the Indian Act were used both before and after 1885 to limit access to towns and travel to neighbouring reserves. But, although there was early discussion about the advisability of a more coordinated and comprehensive approach, neither an officially approved nor a generally applied system was developed. The events of 1885, however, provided a justification to monitor movement, and a procedure was developed that required all individuals wishing to leave their reserve, for any reason, to first attain a pass from their Indian agent. Their pass listed the dates and individuals covered and the purpose of absence from the reserve. Even those who did not participate in the resistance and were considered "loyal" by Canadian officials were subjected to this policy.

The pass system did not have any legal foundation. It was never part of the Indian Act, the Criminal Code, or any other legislation. It was employed primarily in the Prairie West, with other jurisdictions continuing to rely on other methods of restricting and monitoring the movement of Indigenous people. Though the pass system was most widely implemented in the decade after 1885, there is documentary evidence of it continuing in some areas into the 1920s and, in certain situations, into the 1940s. The system's extension into the interwar period at least is supported by oral tradition as well. Further, even while the pass system was in full operation, other measures continued to be employed to restrict movement. The pass system should not, though, be confused with the permit system, within which First Nations communities had to gain governmental approval to sell any goods produced, grown, or extracted from their reserves.

This section contains a number of short documents that provide a survey of some of the justifications presented for different applications of the pass system. Readers will also be exposed to the concerns and attitudes of police officers, DIA employees, and the press related to the pass system and toward Indigenous people more generally. Of special interest is where the different writers place the emphasis for their concerns. One can also find hints in this section of Indigenous opposition and resistance, and readers might want to revisit the short comment on the pass system in the interview with Mrs. Many Guns reprinted in Chapter 2. With the exception of the first document, which provides a brief general overview of the pass system, all others appear in chronological order. While all of the writers were important players in the story of the pass system, responsibility rests with the highest levels of political and regulatory authority and ultimately with the citizens of Canada.

QUESTIONS FOR DISCUSSION

1. Was the implementation of the pass system an appropriate response to the events of 1885? Explain your answer.
2. What reasons does A.E. Forget give for restricting the visits of parents to their children attending residential schools?
3. Compare the documents written by the two members of the North-West Mounted Police, Sam Steele and Fred White. What might account for any differences?
4. According to Fred White, what are the major problems with the policy?
5. What are the various justifications for restricting movement presented in these documents?
6. What might be the effects of this policy on First Nations people?

DOCUMENTS

4a.1 Letter from Robert Sinclair to Edgar Dewdney, 1892

This handwritten letter from Acting Deputy Superintendent General of Indian Affairs Robert Sinclair to his superior, Minister of the Interior and Superintendent General of Indian Affairs Edgar Dewdney, provides a general overview of the background, functioning, and police concerns related to the pass system. As mentioned in the introduction to this section, the pass system had no legal basis, so the leadership of the North-West Mounted Police was understandably concerned that enforcement of the policy could reflect badly on the force, not to mention the worry that Indigenous resistance might cause operational difficulties for individual policemen on the ground. The references to "disloyal" and "loyal" bands indicate those who participated, or were suspected of participating, in the events of 1885 and those who did not. The document containing the suggestions of Assistant Commissioner Hayter Reed that is referred to here is included in Chapter 3 of this reader as document 3.5.

Department of Indian Affairs
Ottawa 23 June 1892

To the Hon. E. Dewdney
Supt. General of
Indian Affairs

Memorandum

With respect to the subject of the letter addressed to the Deputy Sup^t General by the Comptroller of the N. W. M. Police on the 17th instant, enclosing copy of a letter from the Commissioner of the Mounted Police respecting the escorting back of Indians who leave their Reservations without passes, a custom which has now become an almost daily occurrence, the undersigned has the honor to report that the granting of passes to Indians in the North West, permitting them, for certain ~~reasons~~ approved reasons to leave their Reservations, commenced in 1885 when the Department was advised, by letter from the then Indian Commissioner for Manitoba and the N. W. Territories, that at his request the Assistant Commissioner Mr. Hayter Reed had put into writing a number of suggestions with regard to future management of the Indians in the Territories xxxx Amongst these suggestions which were reduced to writing by the Assistant Indian Commissioner was the following marked No 7:—

"No rebel Indians should be allowed off the Reserves without a pass signed by an I.D. [Indian Department] official. The danger of complications with white men will thus be lessened and by preserving a knowledge of individual movements any inclination to petty depredations may be checked by the facility of apprehending those who commit the first of such offences."[2]

In a letter addressed to the Indian Commissioner by the Department on 28th Oct. of that year, with reference to the granting of passes, the Indian Commissioner was informed that the Sup^t General was of opinion that if the pass system could be generally introduced with safety it would be in the highest degree desirable, and that with respect to *disloyal* Bands the system should be strictly carried out as a consequence of their disloyalty, and that it should be introduced as far as practicable amongst the ~~disloyal~~ Bands, but *no punishment* could be inflicted in the case of members of such Bands for breaking bounds, and that should

---

2 Beside this quotation in the original document are comments, signed "E.D." [Edgar Dewdney]: "This should be done and insisted upon as far as practicable. It might be thought well another year to legislate in that direction."

resistance be offered on the ground of Treaty rights the obtaining of a pass before leaving the Reserve would not be insisted upon in regard to loyal Indians.

The form of pass which it was proposed to use was submitted to the Sup.^t General in May 1886 and was approved of in the following June, and a number of books of passes were accordingly prepared.

The system appears to have worked without much trouble until recently, when it appears by the letter of the 17th June instant, herein, enclosing copy of a report from the Commissioner of the N. W. M. Police, that the Commissioner had recently sent back 100 Sarcees to their Reserves, and it is pointed out that there is a possibility that the Police might at any time be liable to perform the same service with respect to the Bloods or Blackfeet leaving their Reserves in large bodies. These Sarcees undoubtedly left their Reserve without the authority of the Agent and had no passes or they would not have been turned back; but it appears to be a subject worthy of consideration whether or not, as the Comptroller of the N. W. M. Police remarks, the escorting back of large bodies of Indians who leave their Reserves without passes—a custom which has now become of almost daily occurrence—may not sooner or later lead to complications by Indians defying the Police. The Comptroller points out the hesitancy with which the Blackfeet signed the Treaty from fear that they would be compelled to stay on the Reserves, and that positive assurances were given them by the Commissioner that such would not be the case.

The undersigned begs to add that no report appears to have been received from the Indian Commissioner for Manitoba and the N. W. Territories upon this subject; and perhaps before considering it further it would be well to request him to report fully and state his views with regard to the possibility of a conflict with the Indians, which is pointed to in the letter from the Comptroller of the N. W. M. Police above referred to.

R Sinclair
    Acting Deputy Sup.^t General of Indian Affairs

P.S. An important factor in this question appears to be the opinion quoted by [NWMP] Commissioner Herchmer given by one of the Supreme Court Judges that the proceedings (it is presumed by this he means the turning back of the Indians) are illegal. . . .
RS

4a.2 Letter From Hayter Reed to Edgar Dewdney, 1885

This letter from Assistant Indian Commissioner Hayter Reed to his immediate superior, Indian Commissioner Edgar Dewdney, was written seven years before the one from Sinclair to Dewdney that appears above and only a few months after the resistance of 1885 had been subdued. It had only been a few weeks since Reed had made a series of recommendations to Dewdney that appears in this reader as document 3.5. Reed presents his views here on, among other things, the legal status of passes, the importance of manual labour, the rights of Indigenous people, and the conduct of local policemen.

Source: Hayter Reed to Edgar Dewdney, 16 August 1885, LAC, Edgar Dewdney Fonds, MG 27-IC4.

Battleford Aug 16th 1885.

Dear Mr. Dewdney,

I have just finished a tour through the Reserves in this neighborhood & find that all the Indians excepting those of Little Pine—and there are exceptions to those—are inclined to work well, and I am endeavoring to impress upon our employees that now is the time to work them into a proper groove in which they must be retained—but many circumstances tend to cripple our efforts at the start, such as shortness of cattle on some reserves and lack of implements on others. I am endeavoring at all events for this year to make Instructors discard mowers as much as possible & in no case encourage their use as the work is to be done with scythes, thus providing work where otherwise it might be lacking. One is at a great loss to know what to do for good Instructors. There are good men in the country but some do not care to trust themselves on the Reserves while in other cases the wages are not a sufficiently tempting bait—and although it would be well if we had more men among our Indians still I consider it wiser to wait and endeavor to get the class we want. As it now stands we have only one man in the Eagle Hills one for all the Battle River Indians and two on the Sas" [Saskatchewan] Reserves—this is not sufficient to handle them properly, especially when it is considered that the numbers of the bands have been materially augmented by members of other bands. I am sending Ballendine and another out with lists of the names of the Indians and finding out exactly who we have about us & where the rest are, for as it now stands we are greatly in the dark in this respect—I find that not a few of Big Bears band are anxious to go west to Buffalo Lake—no doubt with a view of joining Big Bear's eldest son whom you may remember you met in the Peace Hills last fall. I think it would be well to have the few lodges of this band now wandering in the Edmonton District sent to this, and distributed, as they will be a disturbing element where they now are. I hope you will not allow them to have any Reserve near Buffalo Lake if they still desire it as their time is now over to dictate or even have a voice in the matter. I am adopting the system of keeping the Indians on their respective Reserves & not allowing any leave them without passes. I know this is hardly supportable by any legal enactment but one must do many things which can only be supported by common sense and by what may be for the general good. I get the Police to send out daily and send any Indians without passes back to their Reserves—but unless one is at their heels Police duties here are done in a half hearted manner. Some good Officers should be here as those now in command are perfectly useless.

Fancy after my taking the trouble to hunt up Little Poplar's[3] exact whereabouts, which they had not the energy to do, and requesting a party be sent on his trail, it is found a party certainly were sent out but with only four days provisions & of course about the time it struck the trail it had to turn back owing to shortness of food.

. . .

4a.3 Letter from A.E. Forget to Blackfoot Indian Agent, 1889

This circular letter is from Assistant Indian Commissioner Amédée Emmanuel Forget to Magus Begg, the Indian agent for the Siksika (Blackfoot) at Blackfoot Crossing, where the meetings for Treaty 7 took place. It illustrates another aspect of the pass system—the restrictions imposed on parents wishing to visit their children at the residential schools. The letter also presents the department's justification for this move.

Source: A.E. Forget, Assistant Indian Commissioner, to Indian Agent at Blackfoot Crossing, 29 March 1889, Library and Archives Canada, Department of Indian Affairs, RG 10, vol.1137, reel T-1467.

© Government of Canada. Reproduced with the permission of the Minister of Public Works and Government Services Canada (2012).

OFFICE OF THE
    Indian Commissioner,
      NORTH-WEST TERRITORIES

Indian Agent
Blackfoot Crossing
Gleichen P.O.
Alta.

Regina, March 29th, 1889

Sir,

I have the honor to inform you that the visits of Indians to Industrial Schools, for the ostensible purpose of seeing their children, have grown to be so frequent that they have come to be regarded by the Department as a very serious evil, to be discouraged, because they tend to unsettle the minds of the children,

---

3 Little Poplar was among the more militant of the Cree leadership whose popularity among his own people was growing quickly. Reed accused Little Poplar of agitating for the executions of local government officials and also wrote to Prime Minister Macdonald recommending that Little Poplar be taken into custody, a suggestion that the prime minister supported. See for example John L. Tobias, "Canada's Subjugation of the Plans Cree, 1879–1885," in *Sweet Promises: A Reader on Indian-White Relations*, ed. J.R. Miller (Toronto: University of Toronto Press, 1991), 226 and Blair Stonechild and Bill Waiser, *Loyal till Death: Indians and the North-West Rebellion* (Calgary: Fifth House Publishers, 1997), 112.

confirm and foster idle and wandering habits in the parents, and cause an unjustifiable expenditure of supplies both on the reserves and at the school.

I have therefore to request that you will be good enough to allow no Indians to leave the reserves under your charge for the purpose of visiting any Industrial School without a pass, showing the time and purpose of their permitted absence, and bearing the name of each individual of the party covered by it. During the absence of such Indians their names must be removed from the ration lists of the reserve to prevent their drawing rations there as well as at the school visited, or if rations are given them for the visit, the same should be stated on the pass for the information of the Principal.

You will please keep a record, and make a monthly return of all such passes.

I have the honour to be,

Sir,

Your obedient servant,

   A. E. Forget
   Asst. Commissioner.

4a.4 Extract from NWMP Superintendent Steele's Monthly Report, June 1890

Samuel Benfield Steele (1849–1919) is perhaps Canada's most famous Mountie. He was one of the original members of the North-West Mounted Police and participated in the march west in 1874. He led the Alberta Field Force during the resistance of 1885, though he did not get the recognition for his service in the conflict that he thought he deserved. Before being posted to Fort McLeod in what became southern Alberta, Steele was stationed in British Columbia at what later became Fort Steele. During the Klondike Gold Rush, he commanded the Mounted Police in the Yukon area. At the outbreak of the South African War, Steele went on leave from the force and soon took up the position of first commander of Lord Strathcona's Horse. After that conflict was over, Steele became a divisional commander with the South African Constabulary where he was particularly conciliatory to the Afrikaner citizenry, often at the expense of the majority Black population. Steele continued his military career after he returned to Canada in 1907, and, upon the outbreak of World War I, he requested active duty. He was by then in his mid-60s and was initially rejected for command because of age. Nonetheless, he was soon promoted to the rank of major-general, and, in early 1915, he took command of the 2nd Canadian Division until it departed for France. He died in the influenza epidemic that followed the war.

Even though the First Nations resident in the Treaty 7 area of southern Alberta did not participate in the resistance of 1885, this document outlines Steele's views on their character, especially that of the Kainai (Blood), and the necessity, in his view, of restricting their movement. This extract from his monthly report is reproduced below in its entirety.

Source: "Extract from Supt. Steel's monthly report, Fort Macleod, June 1890," Library and Archives Canada, Royal Canadian Mounted Police Fonds, RG 18, series A-1, vol. 45, file 953–90.

INDIANS

The Indians this month as usual have required most careful watching, especially the Bloods, who are truculent and mischievous, and constantly giving trouble. I must give St. Sergt. Hilliard and his detachment at Stand Off great credit for the thorough way they have performed their duties, but as long as Indians are allowed to roam about the way they do at present, it is impossible to prevent their causing trouble on the ranger [sic], but even were there three times the available force of Police, it would of course, be utterly impossible to prevent occasional crimes, both from whites and Indians.

These Indians are both numerous and cunning, and watch carefully the movements of anyone whom they suspect can be in any way inimical to their love of plunder. A large number of ranches have sprung up exactly opposite the Blood Reserve, and thousands of cattle are grazing along the left bank of the Belly, and on the banks of the Kootenai River. Great temptation is thus constantly before the Indians, and it is not to be wondered at, if they occasionally take advantage of a dark night to steal across and slaughter a calf or two. It is far more wonderful that it is not more frequently indulged in, and it is to my mind a standing proof of the moral force possessed by the Police over the Indians. Not a single report has come in from the settlers complaining of want of vigilance on the part of the Police. All are perfectly satisfied. *There is however, an universal desire on the part of all the ranchers to have the Indians confined to their reserve, and prevented from roaming at will over the prairie. I think the time has come when something should be done in this matter.* They have no excuse for wandering about, there is no longer any game, and they are well fed and looked after. There is plenty of opportunity for good and industrious Indians to make large wages if there were more of them to be relied on. In the hay-field, on the round-up, and night herding, they are occasionally seen, and there is nothing to prevent their competing with white men as wage earners in a field in which they are as familiar as amongst horses and cattle. The following is an extract from a report of St. Sergt. Hilliard, dated 28th June, 1890—"I have the honour to report that a cow has been killed at Cochrane Crossing on Wednesday night last. The animal belongs to Mr. Black of Belly River. None of the meat has been taken away. The animal has been butchered and the meat put in a pile. I certainly think it has been done by an Indian. I had the meat watched, thinking someone would come after it, but so far no one has been . . . . I have been looking for a case of cattle killing for the last week, and have been very careful with my patrols, sending them out early and late".

Subjoined is a list of cases against Indians tried at this post.

4a.5 "The Mounted Police and the Sarcees," *Calgary Herald*, June 8, 1892

This brief newspaper article from Calgary gives a hint at popular opinion in settler society toward the NWMP and its activities. It is also indicative of the paper's view of local

Indigenous people, the Tsuu T'ina (Sarcee), and, by implication, of how insignificant the reporter considered the restrictions placed on their freedom of movement, a right taken for granted by other Canadians.

Source: "The Mounted Police and the Sarcees," *Calgary Herald*, June 8, 1892.

Reproduced with the permission of the *Calgary Herald*.

The Mounted Police and the Sarcees

When eight of the Mounted Police went after the Sarcee Indians who left the Reserve lately without leave, as they approached Sheep Creek, which was in high flood, they met a horse with harness on, and taking him in charge they soon discovered a buckboard stranded in the middle of the Creek with a white man and woman sitting in it! Although the water was running over the skirts of the lady's dress she laughed good naturedly at their strange dilemma. On enquiry it was found that one trace broke while crossing the Creek, and the buckboard being liable to be upset, the owner cut the other. The police, always equal to any emergency, procured ropes and hauled out the buckboard, to the great relief of the occupants, who stated that they meant to sit there until help arrived.

The Indians on being overtaken when camped at High River showed considerable length of face, and as some growled over their disappointment the sub-chief shook his head and said:—"We must go back now they have come for us." The party composed of men, women, pappooses [sic], horses, dogs, and travoys [sic], extended over a distance of about two miles, and some colts being too young to cross the Creek were lifted on to the backs of the mothers and landed safely. Altogether it was a picturesque and funny sight and these varied experiences were apparently much enjoyed by the good natured police who always treat the Indians with kindly forbearance.

4a.6 Letter from Fred White to L. Vankoughnet, 1893

This letter from Frederick White, comptroller of the NWMP, to Lawrence Vankoughnet, deputy superintendent general of the Department of Indian Affairs, gives further indication of the position that the Mounted Police felt that they were put in. Readers might want to take note of where the leadership of Canada's premier law enforcement agency chose to put the emphasis when speaking about the problems associated with the pass system.

Source: Fred White, Comptroller, NWMP to L. Vankoughnet, DSGIA, DIA, 16 June 1893, Library and Archives Canada, Department of Indian Affairs, RG 10, vol. 6817, file 487–1-2, pt. 1.

© Government of Canada. Reproduced with the permission of the Minister of Public Works and Government Services Canada (2012).

North West Mounted Police
Office of the Comptroller,

Ottawa, 16th June 1893

L. Vankoughnet, Esq.,
Deputy Supt. General of Indian Affairs,
Ottawa

Sir,

Referring to your letter of 13th inst, with enclosures from Mr. Commissioner Reed, respecting the authority of the Mounted Police to order back, or to arrest, Indians who have left their Reserves without passes.

Mr. Reed, while admitting that there is no legal authority either to prevent Indians leaving, or to compel them to return to their Reserves, considers that the Police should not stand too literally upon the extent of their powers in dealing with Indians, although the greatest discretion should be used in avoiding measures calculated to provoke a contest of authority, possibly ending in a victory for the Indians, which would make them more defiant thereafter.

He is also of opinion that the Police should avoid the possibility of actual conflict with the Indians; that should they find that their numbers are not enough to present such show of force as will overawe and prevent danger of resistance, they should govern themselves accordingly.

No one can question the importance of using, to the fullest extent, the moral effect of a display of force when dealing with Indians, but the danger which now faces us lies in the fact that many of them are aware that the Police have no legal authority to arrest or punish them for refusal to return to their Reserves, and thus we are courting the humiliation, loss of prestige, and victory for the Indians, which would result from a refusal to return to their Reserves when ordered by a body of armed men representing the executive powers of the law.

In my last communication to you on this subject, I quoted written instructions from an Indian Agent to a member of the Mounted Police to order an Indian and his family back to their Reserve, but not to make an arrest if satisfied that they were on their road back. The Indians returned to their Reserve when ordered, and the Constable very properly asked, for his future guidance, whether he would have been justified in arresting them had they refused.

The untenable position assumed by the Police when carrying out the requests of Indian Agents suggested to me the desirability of our endeavouring to frame instructions, or a form of request to be used by Agents, which would enable the Police to act with a feeling of confidence in their authority and I am still of opinion that something in the way of an order to return, with a warning of the deprivation of privileges allowed them under, or in excess of, their Treaty rights, should be adopted.

Of course this would not apply to Indians loitering in the vicinity of settlements and rendering themselves liable to punishment under the Vagrant Act.

I have the honour to be,

Sir,

Your obedient servant,

Fred White
Comptroller.

4a.7 Letter from Hayter Reed to the Deputy Superintendent General of Indian Affairs, 1893

As Indian commissioner since 1888, Hayter Reed was responsible for the oversight of the Department of Indian Affairs policy and the supervision of the department's employees in the region that became the Prairie Provinces. As assistant commissioner, he recommended the implementation of the pass system (document 3.5) and was one of the first to restrict Indigenous people to reserves irrespective of the lack of legal foundation for such a policy (document 4a.2). Given the views that led to these actions, he became frustrated over the stance taken by the North-West Mounted Police, which is evident in the following document.

Source: Hayter Reed, Indian Commissioner, to DSGIA, 14 Jun 1893, Library and Archives Canada, Department of Indian Affairs, RG 10, vol. 6817, file 487–1-2, pt. 1, reel C-8539.

© Government of Canada. Reproduced with the permission of the Minister of Public Works and Government Services Canada (2012).

OFFICE OF THE
Indian Commissioner,
MANITOBA AND THE NORTH-WEST TERRITORIES

Regina, June 14th, 1893

Sir,

I have the honor to refer to my letter to Department of even number, of 5th inst., in reply to its No. 47554 of 18th ultimo, and to inform you that the Commissioner of N. W. M. Police has informed me that under order from his Department and pending further instructions on the subject, the police will not order or take any Indians back to their Reserves, but will merely ask them to return.

I cannot refrain from an expression of extreme regret that such order should have been given. If the Police are unable to do anything more than request Indians to return, then it will be better for them to abstain from doing that, since it will only draw the Indians' notice to and emphasize the fact that they are powerless to enforce their requests.

It will however, in any case, before long become apparent to Indians that they can leave their Reserves when they like.

Prosecution under the Vagrancy Act may still serve in a measure to prevent Indians loafing about towns, with all the attendant evils of such practice, but the difficulties will certainly be aggravated and the evil much more widely spread.

Ranchers and settlers will soon be complaining, and unless a remedy be found, it is hard to see how conflict between them and the Indians can be avoided.

Among other evils sure to follow, if the Indians are to be allowed to wander about at will, are the impossibility of enforcing the Game Laws, and the increase of prairie fires.

The very root of the policy by which Indians are kept on their Reserves and taught to farm for their maintenance will receive a blow, the effects of which can not be estimated, and a retrograde step will be taken. The longer matters remain on their present footing, the greater will be the difficulty in dealing with the Indians, when the Police control may be re-asserted, as it most assuredly will have to be sooner or later.

It is, I think, to be further regretted that before such a step was taken I was not notified sufficiently far in advance to have enabled me to have endeavored to devise measures to counteract as far as possible, the consequences which must inevitably follow. Had the order been kept quiet, the Indians might have remained for some time in ignorance, but as I have already seen references to it in the public press, no expectation of withholding it from them need now be entertained.

I have the honour to be,

Sir,

Your obedient servant,

Hayter Reed

Commissioner.

4a.8 Chief Dan Kennedy, *Recollections of an Assiniboine Chief*, 1972

In this account from oral tradition, Assiniboine Chief Dan Kennedy of Carry the Kettle First Nation in Saskatchewan gives readers a brief sense of how it felt to be restricted to a reserve. He also gives us an example of how some might have been able to circumvent pass policy restrictions, and he outlines the differences between passes and permits.

Source: Dan Kennedy, *Recollections of an Assiniboine Chief*, ed. James R. Stevens (Toronto: McClelland and Stewart, 1972), 87–88.

Reproduced with the permission of Tanya Harnett for the family of Chief Kennedy.

The Warpath "Pass"

Chant of the Warrior
"Long have I wooed Dame Fortune of the warpath

Behold this day our tryst is at hand"

"Long have I wooed Dame Fortune of the warpath
Behold this day our tryst is at hand"

"Long have I wooed Dame Fortune of the warpath
Behold this day our tryst is at hand"

At the signing of Treaty No. 4 in 1874 at Fort Qu'Appelle, the Treaty Commissioners told the tribesmen that the Great White Queen across the big waters was a woman with a woman's heart and had asked all tribesmen to bury their tomahawks and live in peaceful co-existence with other tribesmen.

To forego our glorious traditions of the warpath was a bitter pill to swallow. Even though the Redcoats kept a watchful eye, the war-drums echoed across the Prairies.

It was quite obvious why the government decided to move the Assiniboines to the present site although their hunting territory was at Cypress Hills. The objective of the government was to put a distance barrier between the Assiniboines and their hereditary enemies, the Blackfoot Confederacy. This would put an end to the warpath craze and bring peace to the waring [sic] tribesmen—at least they thought so, but did not reckon with the Indians' craftiness.

In the early days of reservation life, the Indians were plagued with all kinds of restrictions, imposed on them by the guardian government. We could not sell grain, cattle, horses, wood, hay, etc., unless we got a permit from the Indian Agent. We also had to get passes from the Indian Agent to go anywhere on social visits or business trips. The Indian reserve was a veritable concentration camp.

It was in such a setting that the Indians' craftiness outwitted the Indian Agent. Our kinsmen from Fort Peck reservation in Montana arrived on our reserve, ostensibly on a social visit. When it was time for these visitors to go home, some of our young braves went and asked the Indian Agent for passes. The Indian Agent was reluctant to issue the passes, but they told him that these visitors from the Fort Peck reservation had brought urgent messages that their close relative was critically ill, and so the Indian Agent had no choice but to issue them passes—unwittingly the warpath passes.

When they arrived at their destination, they were glad to know that their kinsmen waited for them to embark on the warpath.

The chief actors in this historic drama have gone to the Happy Hunting ground to rejoin their ancestors.

SECTION 4B: RESTRICTING THE POTLATCH

The term "potlatch" does not refer to a single practice but rather to an assortment of strictly regulated ceremonies of central importance to West Coast peoples. As an integral component of the cultural, political, social, and economic structures of the Kwakwaka'wakw, Nuu-chah-nulth, Coast Salish, Haida, Tlingit, Tsimshian, Heiltsuk, and others, potlatches play an essential role in holding those societies together. They can be held to confirm leadership, alliances, and the ownership of land and resources. Names can be given or passed down, debts repaid, dishonour erased, marriages performed, births announced, or the loss of loved ones memorialized. Potlatches provide a forum for history to be transmitted and verified, and gifts are given to witnesses who are obliged to remember and confirm what they have seen, heard, and experienced. In addition to handling and healing earthly concerns, potlatches also have important spiritual components.

Many in late nineteenth- and early twentieth-century settler society supported the continuation of the ceremonies, even if representations by non-Indigenous observers were most often simplistic. Still, those who were fortunate enough to be present appreciated the experience. Others benefited from providing supplies and gifts. For most missionaries and representatives of the state, however, potlatches were absolutely inimical to their goals of assimilation and Christianization. Indian agents thought them wasteful and unsettling, while missionaries saw them simply as the manifestation of evil. Potlatches represented an opposition to the individual accumulation of goods and capital that was central to most in settler society. Even more fundamentally, they manifested a challenge to the understanding of "wealth" as solely the accumulation of material goods.

In 1884, the potlatch was banned along with the expressly spiritual dances that the legislation refers to as "tamanawas," though the move to eliminate these and other cultural practices had begun much earlier. Unlike the pass system discussed in the previous section, the ban against the potlatch was included in the Indian Act and so had the force of law. The legislative restrictions against the potlatch became ever more comprehensive over time. Though there were arrests and prosecutions in some locations, the law remained ostensibly dormant until after World War I. Even then, many communities felt they had no choice but to continue to hold potlatches, and considerable effort was expended to keep them away from the surveying eyes of missionaries and Indian agents and in making the ceremonies more portable. Finally, in 1951, the prohibition against the potlatch was simply dropped from the act. The documents in this section include a range of views on potlatches and their prohibition. The first documents are the various amendments to the Indian Act related to the potlatch; these are presented in chronological order. They are followed by a newspaper report on early Indigenous resistance to the ban and by the reminiscences of a missionary, an Indian agent, and a Kwakwaka'wakw elder.

QUESTIONS FOR DISCUSSION

1. In what specific ways did the amendments to the Indian Act become more restrictive?
2. What, according to Thomas Crosby and W.M. Halliday, are the problems associated with the potlatch?
3. What examples of Indigenous resistance can be found in W.M. Halliday's account and elsewhere in this section?
4. According to the *Victoria Daily Colonist*, how did Nisga'a representatives defend the potlatch?
5. What, according to Harry Assu, were the effects of the potlatch ban on his family and community?
6. Based on the evidence provided here, was the potlatch ban an appropriate policy measure? Why or why not?

4b.1 Legislation Restricting Indigenous Ceremonies, 1884–1933

This series of excerpts from amendments to the Indian Act illustrate the act's evolution over time from the first move to restrict Indigenous ceremonies, including the potlatch, in 1884. The amendments below also demonstrate the act's growing comprehensiveness in this area and hint at the mounting authority of the Department of Indian Affairs over the lives of those defined as Indians. There is also irony implied here. Though few in settler society thought assimilation was a bad idea, they wanted authentic Indians for their stampedes and other public entertainments. In studying the amendments below, readers should note that the numbering of sections of the Indian Act changed over time and between the issuance of the Statutes of Canada *and the* Revised Statutes of Canada. *As a result, references to the numbers of sections being altered may not line up with the numbers of the earlier amendments presented here.*

Sources: (4b.1a) *An Act further to amend "The Indian Act, 1880,"* S.C. 1884, 47 Vict., c.27, s.3; (4b.1b) *An Act further to amend the Indian Act,* S.C. 1895, 58 and 59 Vict., c.35, s.6; (4b.1c) *An Act to amend the Indian Act,* S.C. 1914, 4 & 5 Geo. V, c.35, s.8; (4b.1d) *An Act to amend the Indian Act,* S.C. 1933, 23–24 Geo V, c.42, s.10.

4b.1a Indian Act Amendment, 1884.

Celebrating or inciting to celebrate "Potlatch" or "Tamanawas" to be a misdemeanor punishable by imprisonment.

3. Every Indian or other person who engages in or assists in celebrating the Indian festival known as the "Potlatch" or in the Indian dance known as the "Tamanawas" is guilty of a misdemeanor, and shall be liable to imprisonment for a term of not more than six nor less than two months in any gaol or other place of confinement; and any Indian or other person who encourages, either directly or indirectly, an Indian or Indians to get up such a festival or dance, or to celebrate the same, or who shall assist in the celebration of the same is guilty of a like offence, and shall be liable to the same punishment.

4b.1b Indian Act Amendment, 1895.

Section 114 amended.

6. Section on hundred and fourteen of *The Indian Act* is hereby repealed and the following substituted therefor:—

Celebrating certain festivals, dances or ceremonies whereat presents are made or human or animal bodies are mutilated.

"114. Every Indian or other person who engages in, or assists in celebrating or encourages either directly or indirectly another to celebrate, any Indian festival, dance or other ceremony of which the giving away or paying or giving back of money, goods or articles of any sort forms a part, or is a feature, whether such gift of money, goods or articles takes place before, at, or after the celebration of the same, and every Indian or other person who engages or assists in any celebration or dance of which the wounding or mutilation of the dead or living body of any human being or animal forms a part or is a feature, is guilty of an indictable offence and is liable to imprisonment for a term not exceeding six months and not less than two months;

Indictable offence.

but nothing in this section shall be construed to prevent the holding of any agricultural show or exhibition or the giving of prizes for exhibits thereat." *Proviso.*

4b.1c Indian Act Amendment, 1914.

8. Section 149 of the said Act is amended by adding the following subsection thereto:— *S. 149 amended.*

"2. Any Indian in the province of Manitoba, Saskatchewan, Alberta, British Columbia, or the Territories who participates in any Indian dance outside the bounds of his own reserve, or who participates in any show, exhibition, performance, stampede or pageant in aboriginal costume without the consent of the Superintendent General of Indian Affairs or his authorized Agent, and any person who induces or employs any Indian to take part in such dance, show, exhibition, performance, stampede or pageant, or induces any Indian to leave his reserve or employs any Indian for such a purpose, whether the dance, show, exhibition, stampede or pageant had taken place or not, shall on summary conviction be liable to a penalty not exceeding twenty-five dollars, or to imprisonment for one month, or to both penalty and imprisonment." *Restriction.*
Indian dances, &c.

4b.1d Indian Act Amendment, 1933.

10. Subsection three of section one hundred and forty of the said Act is amended by striking out the words "in aboriginal costume" in the fifth line thereof. *Restrictions on Indian*
dances, etc.

4b.2 Thomas Crosby, *Among the An-Ko-me-nums*, 1907

Thomas Crosby (1840–1914) first came to British Columbia, at his own expense, in 1862 as a lay missionary for the Methodist Church. In 1863, he secured a position with Cornelius Bryant at a Methodist mission in Nanaimo. He was successful enough in his work that he was first transferred to missions in the lower mainland of British Columbia and then ordained in 1871. Crosby is perhaps best known, though, for his work with the Tsimshian near Port Simpson in northern BC, where he worked for over two decades beginning in 1874. The selection here concerns Crosby's work among the Hul'q'umi'num and Halq'eméylem speaking peoples of south central Vancouver Island and the lower Fraser Valley. Like many missionaries of the time, Crosby was forceful in his efforts to eliminate many aspects of Indigenous cultures and in his attempts to implant Euro-Christian structures and beliefs in their place.

Source: Thomas Crosby, *Among the An-Ko-me-nums or Flathead Tribes of Indians of the Pacific Coast* (Toronto: W. Briggs, 1907), 102–10.

MUSIC AND DANCING.

With most feasting is usually associated dancing and other merriment.

The readiness with which the Indians pick up our beautiful hymn tunes and learn to play our musical instruments has been remarked. Indeed, these people are naturally very musical, and in their heathen state were passionately fond of singing their own native melodies. Of songs they had a great variety: war songs, marriage songs, songs for feasts and public gatherings, mourning songs for the dead, songs when the fish came, dancing songs, canoe songs, and many others. When we asked the old dance-song maker where they got their music, he replied:

> We get it from the wind in the trees, from the waves on the sea-shore, from the rippling stream, from the mountain side, from the birds, and from the wild animals.

As for musical instruments, we are all familiar with the simple Indian drum, made by stretching a deerskin tightly over a hoop. Besides this they used as a drum a big square box, painted in different colors, with figures of birds and animals upon it.

When the drummer was at work crowds would accompany him, beating time with sticks upon boards. The sound was weird in the extreme, if heard at the dead of night, coupled with the shouts of the heathen dancers.

Besides the drums were rattles of various shapes, used by the chiefs and conjurers, and pipe whistles—indeed, whistles of many kinds, imitating birds and animals—some of which were used by the hunters in pursuit of game.

With much of their music is associated their pagan dancing. There are professional dancers among the tribes, who as a rule are identified with the clans of the medicine men. The heathen dances are very fascinating to the heathen mind, and in nothing is the "backsliding" of the Indian more noticeable than in his return to the dance.

At the dancing season certain persons become possessed, or as the An-ko-me-nums say, "the you-an, or dance spirit, is on them." They dream dreams and see visions, and move about in a hypnotic state, unable, or at least declining, to work, and roaring out at intervals a sort of mournful sobbing, "Oh-oh-oh-oh-oh." Then they go from house to house, hunting up every kind of food they can get hold of, and gorging themselves many times a day. At night these dancers, all daubed and plastered with grease and paint, would gather in the large houses, where the people were assembled, and work themselves up into a frenzy, prancing up and down and round about, performing numerous contortions. Then they would break out in song, or in monotonous recitation relate their dreams and visions and tell many weird tales. Then round and round, and up and down again, they would prance, until they dropped from sheer exhaustion, or fell, perhaps, into the fire, and another took their place. All this time the onlookers watched and listened to the chanting and the story, or screamed and pounded in frantic accompaniment to the dancing.

The heathen dance is certainly demoralizing, and, like everything of heathenism, is of the devil.

WHITE MAN'S DANCE VS. INDIAN DANCE.

Early in my stay at Nanaimo four or five of the leading chiefs came to me with the proposition that if I would allow them to go on with their potlatching and wild dancing every day in the week, they would come to church and rest on Sunday.

"No; you had better stop all your heathenism," was my answer.

Nothing daunted, they came back again later. Now they would all be good on Sabbath and stand by me if they could dance. It was not very bad, and they had to keep up a little of what their fathers told them. And if I would not speak against it or pray against it they would all be good soon and would have all their children go to school.

"No, I cannot have anything to do with the old way, the dance, the potlatch, etc., it is all bad," I said.

Then they whispered to each other, "Oh, he is like a post; you cannot move him."

To give an idea of the scenes witnessed on these dancing occasions: Old Sna-kwe-multh, a man who had been taken a slave by some northern tribe, but who had found his way home, wished to demonstrate his bravery. At a great feast he came rushing in half naked and danced before the people. As his frenzy increased he slashed at his thighs with some kind of sharp instrument, and then with both hands caught up his own blood and drank it, to prove himself a brave.

A number of white men, who had been witnesses of the shameful scene, ran out and cried, "The devil is in the man."

I denounced the custom and pleaded with them to give it up. Speaking to the Old Chief Squen-es-ton, I said, "You must stop it. It is of the devil."

"Oh," said he, "the white man's dance worse than the Indian's dance."

"How do you make that out?" I said.

"Oh, Indian man, alone, dance all round the house and sit down. And then Indian woman she dance all round and she sit down. But white man take another man's wife and hug her all round the house."

What could I say to the argument? What would you have said?

POTLATCHING.

Of the many evils of heathenism, with the exception of witchcraft, the potlatch is the worst, and one of the most difficult to root out.

At one time its demoralizing influence was so manifest that the Government passed a law prohibiting it, but this excellent law was seldom properly enforced.

"Potlatch"—the word is from the Chinook and means "to give." Literally the idea is the giving away of everything a man possesses to his friends. In return he gets nothing except a little flattery, a reputation for generosity, and poverty.

"Tlaa-nuk" is the An-ko-me-num word, and it suggests something more than "a giving," or a feast, or an entertainment, or a ceremony, for it is all of these and more. It is a system of tribal government which enforces its tyrannical rule upon all, and overrides all other laws of the nation or the individual.

Its outward manifestation of the heathen feast and dance, with the giving of gifts to all present, is bad enough, but this is as nothing to the unseen influence behind it all.

The potlatch relates to all the life of the people, such as the giving of names, the raising into social position, their marriages, deaths and burials.

A man desires, or thinks himself entitled to, some coveted position, property or distinction, and for years, perhaps, makes preparation to secure it. This can only be done by the law of "tlaa-nuk" (potlatch), and so when ready he calls together from far and near his friends and relatives, when, after much feasting and dancing and speech-making, he gets up on a high platform and proceeds to give away all that he possesses.

The ambition of an Indian to be thought greater, richer and more influential than any of his neighbors leads him not only to give away a large part of his goods—which, as a matter of fact, he expects returned with interest on some future occasion, at another such gathering—but wantonly to destroy very much in such a manner that it can never be restored. For instance, think of a man taking a fine large canoe, valued at, perhaps, one hundred and fifty dollars, and smashing it into pieces; or of another seizing a number of beautiful new guns or rifles and bending and breaking them so that they would be utterly useless; or of another setting fire to piles of food and of goods. Some few years ago, at one such gathering, the poor, foolish creatures took rolls of new bills, the product of their summer's work, and threw them into the fire.

I knew a man at Nanaimo who, together with his wives and children, worked for years saving and getting together much property; and then a great potlatch was given, and everything went, to the last stitch of clothing, and he and his family were left practically naked to face the winter, without any provisions. His children nearly starved, while he contracted a cold which led to consumption, from which he died.

Some time ago it was rumored that the law against the potlatch was to be repealed. This drew a strong protest from several quarters, among them from some of the Indians themselves.

About that time the following letter, which explains itself, appeared in the local press signed by an Indian whose identity was vouched for by a gentleman who knew him well:

Having heard that in the last session of the provincial parliament a resolution was passed asking Dominion Government to reconsider the potlatch question with a view to repealing section 114, and that there is to be an inquiry as to the evils of the potlatch, we should like to tell the public what the potlatch is.

Really and truly it is destruction to life and property, as we shall show. The first is that the women go from home to other places for immoral purposes, to get money or blankets to give away, or potlatch, as people call it. The second is that they sell their daughters to other men as soon as possible, sometimes twelve or thirteen years old, marriage they call it; the people do not care so long as they get blankets to potlatch with. And the third is that they hate each other so much because of their trying to get one above the other in rank, as it is according to how many times they potlatch that they get the rank, and keep it, too. If they could they would even poison one another. Even now they think they kill one another by witchcraft, with intent to kill, and they believe that they do kill. A man does not care for any relatives when the potlatch is in question. The potlatch is their god; they will sacrifice everything to it—life, property, relatives, children, or anything, must go for him to be a 'tyee' (chief) in the potlatch.

A man after giving a potlatch will sit down, his children, too, without knowing where he is going to get his food and clothes, as he has given away everything, and he has borrowed half of it, for which he has to pay back double.

And another thing is, when they are mad with one another they will break canoes or tear blankets or break a valuable copper, to shame their opponent. The potlatch is one fight, with quarrelling and hating one another.

And another is the desecration of the dead. The hamatsa, or medicine man, when he first comes from the woods, carries a dead body in his arms, professing to have lived on such things when in the woods, and as soon as the hamatsa comes in the house the other hamatsas all get up and go and tear the body to pieces among them like dogs; besides all this they bite the arms of one another; and the other thing is that when a man gets ill he thinks he is witchcrafted, and then his relatives will go and take the dead body that they think he is fixed with: they cut and mutilate it to undo the work that they think has been done to him. We have just heard of such a case from Kurtsis, of a woman's dead body having been taken out and cut, to undo the work that they think has been done to a certain man. All these things are pure facts, and we are prepared to prove them if need be, and could tell other evils, but we are afraid of tiring the public.

. . .

4b.3 W.M. Halliday, *Potlatch and Totem*, 1935

William May Halliday first began working with Indigenous people in 1897 when he took a job at Alert Bay, off the north-east coast of Vancouver Island, as an assistant to St. Michael's Indian Residential School principal A.W. Corker. Nine years later, Halliday was made Indian agent for the Kwakwaka'wakw people living in the DIA's Kwakewlth Agency. The agency included 90 reserves and fishing stations scattered over the northern part of Vancouver Island and the many smaller islands off its north-east coast. Halliday served as an agent stationed at Alert Bay until 1932, when he retired to Victoria. During his time as Indian agent, Halliday was one of the department's most active opponents of the potlatch. The excerpt below is a full chapter from Halliday's published recollections, primarily concerning his time at Alert Bay. Document 4b.5 later in this section presents a contrasting Kwakwaka'wakw understanding of some of the events discussed here.

Source: W.M. Halliday, "Matters Judicial," in *Potlatch and Totem and the Recollections of an Indian Agent* (London and Toronto, J.M. Dent, 1935), 188–95.

CHAPTER VII

MATTERS JUDICIAL (continued)

THE greater part of the serious offences that have occurred within the boundaries of this agency have been enumerated, but possibly the most interesting cases of offences against any statutory enactments would come under the prosecutions that arose from infringements of that portion of Indian Act that deals with the *potlatch*. The Act had been on the statute-book for many years without being enforced. It was thought that education and missionary training amongst the Indians would so open their minds to the folly of the custom that the custom itself would die a natural death without any legal proceedings having to be taken to compel it to die.

However, things gradually got worse and worse; the *potlatch* was assuming greater and greater proportions, and instructions were received from the Department of Indian Affairs to enforce the regulations and see that this custom was done away with entirely. Notice was given to all the Indians both by letter and personally, as I made it my business to call on every Indian village in the agency, and when the people were all assembled together, to tell them that the Department was being compelled to put into force the legislation against the *potlatch,* and they were warned to govern themselves by what they were being told. It was a matter that so far as the agent was concerned admitted of no argument, as instructions had come direct from headquarters. At that time the Act made it an indictable offence to engage in these ceremonies, and the first prosecutions were entered by the provincial police against two Indians living at Alert Bay, both of whom were particularly good fellows in other ways.

I committed them for trial, and they went to Vancouver and were let out on bail, pending a meeting of the assize court. When they appeared in the assize court before Mr. Justice Gregory, they pleaded 'Guilty.' I was present at the court, and Mr. Justice Gregory asked me as to the character of these two men, and I told him that they were good fellows, law-abiding in every other way. Consequently, they were given a reprimand and told to warn the other Indians, and were allowed their liberty on suspended sentence.

It seemed apparent that to operate this section of that Act properly, the Act itself should be amended, as that was the only section of the Indian Act which did not admit of some jurisdiction by the Indian agent or two justices of the peace, and accordingly the Act was amended, making it a summary conviction.

Four Indians from Kingcome Inlet were brought up for summary trial. They had been having a big feast and had broken a copper as a sort of spite against some enemy they had, and in conjunction with the breaking of the copper they were compelled by custom to give away some considerable quantity both of money and goods, which brought it under the category of an offence against Section 149 of the Indian Act, as it was at that time. Mr. E.K. De Beck of Vancouver, whose father had at one time been Indian agent of this agency, defended them, but they were convicted and sent to Okalla prison for two months. An appeal was made against my decision, but the appeal was dismissed by Chief Justice Hunter.

Several more Indians were arrested by the Royal Canadian Mounted Police, who at that time were sent here to assist in the maintenance of law and order and to carry out certain other work in connection with the government of the Dominion of Canada. Mr. Frank Lyons of Vancouver undertook their defence, and Mr. H.C. Senkler, K.C., of Vancouver was instructed by the Department to attend and prosecute. The trial lasted all day, and was adjourned until the next morning. Mr. Lyons was very desirous that his clients should not be imprisoned (the Act allows no other penalty), and after talking the matter over with the Indians themselves in court, he made the proposition that the

Indians should refrain from this custom for all time, as it never was the desire of the Department that the Indians should be punished unnecessarily, their sole aim and object being to better their conditions by having them give up the *potlatch* custom. This was assented to, and an agreement was drawn up and signed by the Indians in question, also assented to by the counsel for the Crown and the counsel for the Indians, and countersigned by the Indian agent. The Indians in this agreement not only pledged themselves to refrain from potlatching any more, but to use their influence to prevent any other Indians from holding any of these prohibited ceremonies. In order that the court should be made more impressive, both counsel wore their gowns during the proceedings, and by so doing added a certain dignity and impressiveness to the court, which afterwards bore good fruit. Suspended sentence was given to all these Indians subject to their good behaviour in the future. It was explained to them that this did not take away their right to make what efforts they could to have the law amended, but no hope was held out that they would be successful in these efforts.

For some considerable time the Indians obeyed the law, and it was thought that in a very short time they would have forgotten all about this ancient custom. Some two years later a big gathering was held at Village Island the home of the Mamilillikulla tribe, and not only was the ancient custom of the redemption carried out, whereby one man was enabled to give a very big *potlatch*, but in addition an unusually large amount of property had been collected and was given away in due and ancient form. Sergeant Angerman of the mounted police acted very promptly in the matter, and about eighty Indians were summoned to appear to answer to the charge of the violation of this section of the Indian Act.

Sergeant Angerman was an old hand at conducting prosecutions and was as efficient as the average counsel, and he had such strong evidence that he did not think it necessary for the Crown to engage a counsel to prosecute as he was quite competent to do the prosecuting himself, and an array of legal talent came to Alert Bay for the defence.

Mr. Findlay, who is now the assistant police magistrate in the city of Vancouver, a Mr. Ellis, Mr. Campbell, and one or two others, all appeared for various members of those who were charged with potlatching. The trial lasted some considerable time, and then their counsel made another proposal to the Indians to the effect that as the first agreement had only been signed by a limited number of Indians, none of whom was concerned in the present offence, an additional opportunity would be given them to escape from punishment. The conditions attached to it were that they were not only to promise that for all time they would refrain from potlatching, but that they were also to use their influence to see that nobody else took part in any of these proceedings; and in addition to this, they agreed to surrender all their *potlatch* paraphernalia, such as dancing-masks, head-dresses, coppers, and various other things, which would be sold to the various museums by the Department of Indian Affairs and the proceeds given over to the Indians. Those who had been most active in the carrying on of this *potlatch* were the most active in trying to persuade their friends to join with them in signing the agreement or in assenting to it, and thirty days was given them to collect the paraphernalia in question. At the expiration of the thirty days it was found that practically all the Indians with the exception of those at Kingcome Inlet had signed the agreement and surrendered the paraphernalia. This was all carefully tabulated and shipped to Ottawa, and, later on, cheques were received reimbursing the owners.

The sum realized the Indians considered entirely inadequate, but this is a matter on which opinions differed very much. Some of the things for which good prices were paid, the ordinary individual would not consider worth anything at all, while some of the things were more or less new and though in many instances were much better looking, they only brought fair to low prices, as to those learned in the antiquities of the Indians they had little historic value. When all had been completed, the whole of the offenders, numbering sixty-four, were collected together for sentence. Those who had refused to accept the conditions as laid down were sent to prison for two months, and the rest were given suspended sentence.

It so happened that there were two amongst the defendants to whom suspended sentence could not be given, as theirs was a second offence, but as the part taken by them had been very minor, their sentence was delayed and a recommendation sent through the Department of Indian Affairs to the Department of Justice, asking for special authority to allow suspended sentence to these two.

Later on another prosecution was entered by the mounted police against some Indians of the Nakwakto band, whose headquarters were at Blunden Harbour, and they were sent to jail for two months.

It may be noted here that these prosecutions and the sentences imposed made the Indian agent extremely unpopular amongst the Indians, and extremely unpopular with a certain number of outsiders who were not interested in the matter at all, and who, not realizing the reasons which lay behind the whole thing, were inclined to think the proceedings very arbitrary, and that the personal liberties of the Indians were being taken away from them. I received two anonymous letters, which were treated with the contempt they deserved. One of these referred to certain actions done by the Ku-Klux-Klan, and they stated that people of my type should be treated in the same manner as the Ku-Klux-Klan had done, and should either be put out of the way or tarred and feathered.

Since that time the *potlatch* has been gradually dying away, and in no instance has it been done openly. Under the statute it has to be proved that it is an Indian festival, dance, or ceremony, and also it must be proved that at this Indian festival, dance, or ceremony the giving away of money goods, or articles of any sort formed a part or was a feature. There have been a number of instances where people who felt they must give away have done it surreptitiously. They would travel in a boat to the village where they felt it was incumbent on them to give something away, and, while there, call the people individually to the boat and give them what they intended. This method, of course, freed them from any prosecution, as there was neither ceremony, dance, nor festival in connection with it; but on the other hand, there was no *éclat* attached the one who gave it, and the affair would fall very flat.

This *potlatch* custom has tended very materially to retard progress amongst the Indians. It has set up false ideas amongst them, and has been a great waste of time, a great waste of energy, and a great waste of substance. However, apparently it will take some time before the idea of the *potlatch* will be entirely eliminated, and when that is done progress will be extremely rapid, as the Indian of to-day, apart from these ideas, is inclined to be progressive.

As matters have turned out, these prosecutions came at the right moment for many of the tribes. Some of the younger men were fully conscious of the evils of the system, and wanted to break away from it. The older ones, who were wedded to the custom, were very much concerned over these young and thinking men trying to get free from their laws and regulations, and had even gone so far as to warn them that if they carried out their intention they would be obliged to sever all connection with the Indians living on the reserves. When the Act was enforced, it strengthened the hands of the young men and weakened the influence of the older ones, with the result that in those villages there has been a very rapid improvement and advancement.

4b.4 "A Plea for Potlatches," 1896

First Nations had been hosting and attending potlatches for untold centuries before Canada decided to enact legislation prohibiting them. In hindsight, it seems patently unreasonable to assume that such an important institution would be cast aside simply because a foreign entity passed laws against it from a distant location. Resistance took many forms. In some instances, potlatches were shortened in duration and made more portable so that the ceremonies could be continued surreptitiously. In other cases, such as the one presented here, in which a missionary who was also a justice of the peace exceeded even the remedial action stipulated in the Indian Act, First Nations might attempt to use Canadian law to protect themselves. On this occasion, a Victoria newspaper reported that leaders of the Nisga'a and other First Nations from the Nass River region of north coastal British Columbia had travelled from their homes to meet with legal representa-tion and then the DIA's superintendent for British Columbia, Arthur Wesley Vowell.

Source: "A Plea for Potlatches," *Victoria Daily Colonist*, February 20, 1896, 5.

Reproduced with the permission of the *Victoria Times Colonist*.

A PLEA FOR POTLACHES

———

A Delegation of Northern River Indians

Visit Victoria to Crave

Favor for the Gift-Feast.

———

If Necessary Will Fight the Legality

of Its Prohibition Through

the Courts.

———

Amos Gosnell, William Jeffrey and Billy Williams, three intelligent and representative chiefs of the Nass River Indians, reached Victoria yesterday by the arrival of the Boscowitz on business fraught with peculiar importance to not only their Important tribe but to all the native races of British Columbia. Their mission is to place before the public the Indians' side of the story so far as potlaches in particular are concerned, and—such action being necessary—to test in the highest courts of the land the constitutionality of that portion of the Dominion statute relating to Indian affairs wherein the holding of "potlaches" or "gift feasts" is declared illegal and prohited [sic] under heavy penalties. It is the intention of the delegation, who come as the accredited representatives of 153 chiefs of the northern river nations, to retain legal advice this morning and forthwith wait upon Mr. A. W. Vowell, superintendent of Indian affairs for British Columbia, with the object of presenting the following petition:

> We your humble petitioners, being a deputation from our people living on the Naas river, beg that you will take such steps as will prevent clergymen and missionaries from interfering with our people in the holding of potlaches, as Rev. J. A. McCullough [probably J. B. McCullagh], of Naas river, has, we believe, unduly interfered with us in our holding or giving of potlaches. The holding of potlaches has been a custom prevalent among our people for many generations, and a method we have of showing our good will toward one another, and we believe that it is our right just as much as it is the right of our white brethren to make presents to each other.
>
> We assure you that our potlaches are conducted in the most orderly manner, and we expect to keep and do observe the laws of our great and good mother, Queen Victoria, whom we all love. We not only feel very keenly this interference but we know that it is the opinion of many intelligent and good white men that the clergymen's meddling in our affairs is very often uncalled for, and creates a feeling against them among us which prevents the accomplishment of any amount of good that might be realized to our advantage. By answering our supplications we, as in duty bound, will ever pray.

This statement of the case was drafted as long ago as the 30th of last August, when the Northern tribes were notified of the changes in the Indian act prohibiting the potlatch. Since then, however, the authorities of the North have been energetic in the enforcement of the new law, hence the presence of Amos Jeffery and his two companions in Victoria. Matters were brought to an issue so far as the Naas men are concerned, a little more than a month ago when a potlatch was held about one mile above Rev. Mr. McCullough's place. The clergyman, who is also a justice of the peace, promptly summoned six of the tribe including Scotteen, the head chief. The latter with Stephen Light, Stephen Gransey and Nis-kit-iskh, was according to the story of Amos and the two Williams, held prisoner in a dark cabin for four days prior to any court being held, and each of the Indians summoned was then fined $70 and costs. The reverend magistrate, as they understood him, gave the option to the prisoners of paying these fines or of going to jail at Nanaimo for one year, the tribe at the same time to pay $900 for each man. It is a result of the apprehension, trial and sentence referred to, that the head men of the northern tribes gathered in council and decided to send their representatives to Victoria to invoke the aid of the law. The tribes interested have plenty of money at command, and their delegates have authority to spend liberally in order to accomplish the object of their mission.

It was in the spring of last year that the Dominion government decided that the potlach must follow its contemporaneous festival, "the tamanawas," into the list of aboriginal celebrations proscribed by Canadian law, and the agents of the Indian department lost no time in notifying their wards in British Columbia accordingly. From the first it has been questioned whether the prohibition would be or could be enforced, for the potlach has ever been the joy and delight of the Western Indian's soul, and the prospect that he would relinquish its pleasures without a struggle were not of the brightest hue. The "tamanawas" is still practiced far up North, at the heads of the rivers, in the interior mountains—anywhere remote from civilization and beyond the reach of the officers of the law. And so doubtless it will be with the potlatch—less barbarous by far.

4b.5 *Assu of Cape Mudge*, 1989

Harry Assu (1905–1999) was born at Cape Mudge on Quadra Island just off Campbell River on the east coast of Vancouver Island. He was an elected chief of the We Wai Kai Nation of the Lekwiltok or southern Kwakwaka'wakw in 1954, succeeding his father, Billy Assu. Harry Assu was a fisher and a member of the Native Brotherhood; he helped found the Nuyumbalees Society, which was partly responsible for the return of some of the goods and regalia confiscated during the potlatch ban. He was also involved in the United Church and was a Freemason and Shriner. In this excerpt from the book he wrote with Joy Inglis, Assu speaks of his own experience with the post–World War I crackdown on the potlatch and the efforts to have the material returned. The ceremonial objects that have been brought back are currently housed at the Nuyumbalees Cultural Centre on Quadra Island and at the U'mista Cultural Centre at Alert Bay. Both are run by Kwakwaka'wakw boards.

Source: Harry Assu with Joy Inglis, "Renewal of the Potlatch at Cape Mudge," in *Assu of Cape Mudge: Recollections of a Coastal Indian Chief* (Vancouver: UBC Press, 1989), 103–8.

The footnotes are reproduced here as in the original.

Many of the Kwagiulth people were arrested for taking part in a big potlatch given by Dan Cranmer on Village Island in 1921. Dan's wife Emma was from Village Island, and her family were giving away a lot of things that went into that potlatch because that's what the family is expected to do for the daughter who is married. My father and eldest brother Dan were called to go there because my father was related to Emma. I don't know if anyone else went from the villages around here.

My father and brother were arrested. Charges were laid against them under a law that had been on the books for a long time. They were told they would go to jail unless they signed a paper that said they wouldn't potlatch any more. They were told that our people would have to hand over everything they used for the potlatch, whether they were there or not. Anybody arrested who didn't give up their family's masks and other things went to jail. Twenty-two of our Kwagiulth people went to Okalla. They were prisoners from two months to six months.[1]

My father had to go to court in Alert Bay two or three times. I was only a young fellow then, and I wasn't too concerned—older men were handling it anyway; but I remember thinking, "Why would the Indian agent start all that?" I was around seventeen at the time and walked every day to Quathiaski Cove from the village and back home at night after spending all day learning to use machine tools with W. E. Anderson. He was the manager and the best mechanic we had at the cannery. I felt lucky to learn and was working hard at it. I didn't know what the government was doing to our people, taking away our culture.

The scow came around from the cannery and put in at the village to pick up the big pile of masks and headdresses and belts and coppers—everything we had for potlatching. I saw it pull out across Discovery Passage to the Campbell River side where more stuff was loaded on the *Princess Beatrice* for the trip to Alert Bay. Alert Bay was where the potlatch gear was gathered together. It came mainly from our villages around here and from Alert Bay and Village Island. It was sent to the museum in Ottawa from Alert Bay by the Indian agent. Our old people who watched the barge pull out from the shore with all their masks on it said: "There is nothing left now. We might as well go home." When we say "go home," it means to die.

When that shipment went to Ottawa they were supposed to send $1,415 to pay for all the things our Kwagiulth people had been forced to give up under threat of jail. But people are still alive who didn't get paid, and they never knew anybody who did get paid. You can't by *one* of those old pieces now for $1,415! They took away around six hundred pieces.

A collector named Heye turned up at Alert Bay, the Indian agent Halliday sold him some of our stuff before he shipped off the rest to the museum in Ottawa.[5] Even the government who were getting all the rest didn't like that! They wanted it all for themselves, I guess. Heye had his pick of all those hundreds and hundreds of pieces. One of them belonged to my father; some to my grandfather, Jim Naknakim; to my wife's uncle, John Dick; and to other Lekwiltok men in this area, as well as people from farther north at Alert Bay and Village Island. None of the pieces that went to Heye's museum in New York were ever returned, though we sent a delegation there to negotiate with them.

---

4 For the circumstances surrounding the potlatch suppression and its effects on the native people in the Kwagiulth area with evidence from native people involved in the proceedings of that time, see *Prosecution or Persecution* by Daisy (My-yah-nelth) Sewid-Smith (1979). For confiscation and return of Kwagiulth potlatch gear as part of an international trend to repatriation, see "Cultural Readjustment, a Canadian Case Study" by Stephen Inglis in *Gazette: Quarterly of the Canadian Museums Association* 12 (Summer 1979). See also, Marie Mauzé, "The Potlatch Law and the Confiscation of Ceremonial Property among the Kwakiutl," *Bulletin Amérique Indienne* (July 1983), translated by Katherine Odgers, Kwagiulth Museum, Cape Mudge.

5 George Heye, founder and collector for the Museum of the American Indian, Heye Foundation, New York.

In 1978 the National Museum in Ottawa returned the part of the collection they still held because they knew it was wrong to force us to stop our custom of potlatching and take all our goods away from us. But early on Indian Affairs had gone ahead and loaned around 135 pieces of our masks and regalia to the Royal Ontario Museum, and it took us much longer to get that museum to return what is ours. This is our family inheritance I am talking about. You don't give up on that! Finally, in 1987 the Royal Ontario Museum returned what they had taken.

Our people figured that all that potlatch gear that was taken away to museums was still theirs by rights and that they still owned it, so it would have to be given back. Those old people kept trying to have it returned to them. A lot of people worked to get it back. I know Jimmy Sewid went to Ottawa with Guy Williams in 1963, and he went into the museum for the Kwagiulth people and demanded our stuff back. He had his wife's mother with him to be sure of what was ours. He told them he was ready to buy it back for the $1,415 they claimed to have paid for it and to bring a truck around and load it in; and he told them he was ready to go to the newspapers and tell how the museum had got hold of our stuff.

Back then, they wouldn't show us the potlatch regalia or listen. Finally, in 1973 they informed our chiefs meeting in the Kwakiutl District Council that they were going to return the "Potlatch Collection." But they didn't want to give it back to the families who own it. They wanted it put in a museum. So it was voted that the museum should be built at Cape Mudge. Well, the Nimpkish band at Alert Bay wanted the museum to be built up there. So in the end two museums were built, and each museum could show what was taken away from their own area. Village Islanders had to decide where their goods would go because they didn't live on Village Island anymore.

Here at Cape Mudge we set up the Nuyumbalees Society to get a museum going and bring back the potlatch regalia. We chose the name Kwagiulth Museum because we wanted it to be for all our people not just our Lekwiltok tribe. At Cape Mudge we are located where all people can easily call in on their way down from our northern villages to the city—Victoria or Vancouver. It's a good place for getting together. Nuyumbalees means "the beginning of all legends." The legends are the history of our families. That is why the chiefs show our dances in the potlatch, so that our legends are passed on to the people.

It has all worked out pretty well. All our stuff that was brought back from Ottawa is in glass cases in the museum according to the family that owns them. That's what the masks and other things mean to us: family ownership. We are proud of that! It tells our family rights to the people. With our people you don't talk about what rights to dances you've got; you call the people and show them in the potlatch. A few families had only a few pieces of what was taken away from their family returned and put in the museum. That wasn't right, and they were really angry. That's another reason why *all* the pieces that were taken away in 1922 and are in museums in Canada and other countries have to be brought back.

On museum opening day, 29 June 1979, my son Don brought his seiner around to the beach in front of the museum. Chiefs of all our Kwagiulth villages were on board, drumming and singing. Jim Sewid was our speaker. He welcomed everybody from the beach. There were about five hundred people. He called to the chiefs of each band in our language, welcoming the people from that village.

That's when they threw "Klassila," the spirit of dancing, from the boat to the shore, where it was caught by a fellow who started up dancing. Then he threw it back up and into the museum.[6]

Everyone moved up the beach and around the ramp outside the museum doors. We didn't have a ribbon cutting. That's not our custom. We had a cedar-bark cutting. The chiefs were holding a long piece of dyed red cedar bark in a circle. I chose Colleen Dick from Cape Mudge to be our princess and stand in the middle of the ring. She is the daughter of two families with a lot of masks on display in the museum. Her father was Dick, and her mother is Assu.

All the important people pressed close in to the bark ring so that nobody saw the knife passed hand to hand. The cedar bark was slashed and there was a scream. All the chiefs got excited, and each shouted out the cries of the animals they can show in the potlatch: the Whales blew, the Bears growled, the Hamatsas cried out. It sounded like a big roar.

When the museum doors were opened, the chiefs came first, followed by the people. Everybody was given a piece of the cedar ring as they came inside, just the way it was done in the old days. Then our chiefs gathered in the open space in the middle of the museum. After fifty-seven years we had our family possessions back! A big shout went up. It was the sound of Klassila, the spirit of dancing, now back again in the house.

My boys and I put up a totem pole to my father inside the museum. Sam Henderson and his sons carved it with Assu family crests. It's big and heavy, around twenty-nine feet tall and fifteen hundred pounds. It had to be lowered in from above before the museum roof was put on. When you raise a pole you have to potlatch. I potlatched for all the tribes when they gathered here for the museum opening. Our fishermen donated the salmon we roasted over the open fires for everybody—fifteen hundred pounds.

A year later another pole was put out in the open area outside the museum and beside the entrance door. That pole was carved by Sam Henderson and his sons and has the crests of their family on it. Sam was from Blunden Harbour, but he married the oldest daughter of Johnny Quocksister of Campbell River, and they raised their family over there. When he put up that pole, there was another big celebration when the Hendersons called the people to the potlatch.

The museum has been good for the Kwagiulth people. Our people who want to learn about native customs come to the museum. When the Ainu or Hawaiians or other people come to visit, we bring them here. Many of our young people have been trained to teach school classes and the public in the museum. They are learning the Kwakwala language, and there is carving, dancing, button-blanket-making, and work with cedar bark. They learn about the potlatch and how everything was used. The elders teach it to the kids. One of the museum programs won first prize for a program in the schools.

I've been on the museum board from the start. I think that getting our potlatch goods back has done a lot to teach our youth who we really are. It will help us to hold on to our history.

. . .

---

6 The Spirit of Dancing, referred to as "Klassila," had been imprisoned in Ottawa for many years and was now being released to the Kwagiulth people. The Power of the Spirit was symbolically thrown from ship to shore, where it was "caught" and set the catcher dancing. He in turn hurled the spirit across the beach and through the museum doors. The spirit had entered the ceremonial house (museum).

Pass System

Readers of additional sources related to the pass system should keep in mind that there is some confusion in the secondary literature between the pass system, as discussed in this chapter, and the permit system, which required reserve residents to secure permission from their Indian agent before selling any goods located or produced on reserves. This problem is compounded by the use of the term "permit" in primary sources to refer to the document that allowed the holder to leave their reserve—to what is referred to here as the "pass." Some authors also refer to a "pass law" that was added as an amendment to the Indian Act, but it never was included in the act nor did it ever have any other legislative foundation. On the pass system as discussed in this chapter, see Keith Smith, "'A Splendid Spirit of Cooperation': Churches, Police Forces, and the Department of Indian Affairs," in *Interpreting Canada's Past*, ed. J.M. Bumstead, Len Kuffert, and Michel Ducharme, 4th ed. (Don Mills: Oxford University Press, 2012), 46–55. See also Sarah Carter, *Lost Harvests: Prairie Indian Reserve Farmers and Government Policy* (Montreal: McGill-Queen's University Press, 1990), especially pages 149–58. See further, Brian Hubner, "Horse Stealing and the Borderline: The NWMP and the Control of Indian Movement, 1874–1900," *Prairie Forum* 20, no. 2 (Fall 1995): 281–300 and Laurie Barron, "The Indian Pass System in the Canadian West, 1882–1935," *Prairie Forum* 13, no. 1 (Spring 1988): 27–29.

Potlatch

Like many other topics in this reader, the potlatch has had a significant amount of material written about it from different perspectives, by scholars from different disciplines and by Indigenous authors. Beyond the book by Harry Assu excerpted above, see Daisy Sewid-Smith (My-yah-nelth), *Prosecution or Persecution* (Cape Mudge, BC: Nu-Yum-Baleess Society, 1979) for more context related to the restriction of the potlatch and the impact of the confiscation of ceremonial objects from the perspective of Kwakwa-ka'wakw elders. For an exploration of the potlatch itself through the eyes of a Tseshaht (Nuu-chah-nulth) elder, artist, and storyteller, see George Clutesi, *Potlatch* (Sidney, BC: Gray's Publishing, 1969). For a more traditionally academic work that tends to downplay the significance of the ban and its effects, see Douglas Cole and Ira Chaikin, *An Iron Hand Upon the People: The Law against the Potlatch on the Northwest Coast* (Vancouver, BC: Douglas & McIntyre, 1990). For a wide-ranging exploration with a special focus on southern Vancouver Island, follow the index entries for "potlatch" in John Sutton Lutz's fully illustrated *Makúk: A New History of Aboriginal White Relations* (Vancouver, BC: UBC Press, 2008). For a cinematic presentation that explores the significance of the potlatch, the post-ban prosecutions, and late twentieth-century resurgence from a Kwakwa-ka'wakw perspective, see *Potlatch: A Strict Law Bids Us Dance* (1979; rpt., Vancouver, BC: Moving Images Distribution, 2005).

"OUR OBJECT IS TO CONTINUE UNTIL THERE IS NOT A SINGLE INDIAN IN CANADA THAT HAS NOT BEEN ABSORBED INTO THE BODY POLITIC"[1]

ASSIMILATION AND ORGANIZED RESISTANCE

It should be noted at the outset that Indigenous resistance to the appropriation of land and resources and the extension of European economic, political, cultural, and social structures and institutions began at the moment of contact and continues through to the present. Although there were important waves of activism in many spheres following World War I, most Euro-Canadians were perhaps even more convinced than previously that their economies were more efficient, their political configurations more responsive, and their cultures more advanced than those of Indigenous peoples. Within this framework of understanding, which provided little room for Indigenous needs, desires, or future ambitions, Canadian policy makers continued to assume that leaving behind Indigenous ways of life offered the best prospect for everyone's future. At the same time, the economic structures of settler society produced a voracious demand for land and resources. The solution to both of these issues was the assimilation of Indigenous people into settler society and the appropriation of their territories, which were presented as not used to their full potential. Not only would the removal of Indigenous people from their lands pave the way for Euro-Canadian development, but assimilation would abolish any existing aboriginal or treaty rights and eliminate federal responsibilities for "Indians and lands reserved for the Indians" under Section 91(24) of the British North America Act.

---

1 Evidence of D.C. Scott to the Special Committee of the House of Commons examining the Indian Act amendments of 1920, Library and Archives Canada, Department of Indian Affairs, RG 10, vol. 6810, file 470–2-3, pt.7, p. N-3, reel C-8533. This quotation appears in document 5a.3 below.

The policy of assimilation was given a patina of fairness through the strategy of enfranchisement whereby Indigenous people could, if they gave up their aboriginal and treaty rights, take on the rights and privileges of Canadians. They could, then, become full citizens but only if they gave up their identity as Indigenous people.

The federal body responsible for implementing and overseeing this policy of assimilation and land and resource acquisition, the Department of Indian Affairs (DIA), had, by the end of the nineteenth century, already developed into an extensive, hierarchical, military-like network that intervened in every aspect of the lives of those defined as Indians. Though cabinet oversight of this large cadre of employees on reserves, in field offices across the country, and at Ottawa rested in the minister of the interior, the day-to-day operations fell to his deputy superintendent general of Indian affairs (DSGIA). In addition to overseeing the implementation of policy, the DSGIA also often took the initiative to recommend strategy or policy on his own. Between 1913 and 1932, the man leading the department as DSGIA was Duncan Campbell Scott.

Scott served in a number of capacities within the department since his first appointment in 1880, and although there were other important actors in the DIA over time, there is little doubt that during the period that Scott was at the helm at least, he was the major instigator and overseer of policy related to First Nations people, and particularly the policy of assimilation. For this reason, many of Scott's writings are included in this chapter. In addition to his long career as a civil servant with the DIA, Scott was also an accomplished and respected poet, and both elements of Scott's work are represented here. Readers can determine to what extent there are similarities between Scott the poet and Scott the civil servant and can explore how one identity informs the other.

With the high level of Indigenous participation in World War I, both on the front lines and through other sacrifices, Indigenous people and their leaders hoped that the prevailing Euro-Canadian assumptions concerning their backwardness and cultural inferiority would finally be laid to rest. Some expected, for example, that Indigenous ways of life and identity would be respected and accepted. It was becoming obvious that most Indigenous people were not willingly going to give up their rights and identity as Indians in order to accept enfranchisement. This fact left federal politicians and the DIA with a problem. They wanted to enfranchise those who had the longest experience with Euro-Canadian tutelage, and those they believed to be the most "civilized" and "advanced," but many of those educated and successful by Western standards were the most resistant to enfranchisement. Further, the contradictions between being civilized enough to fight for Canada and understand its ideals and yet not being advanced enough to know what was best for them without DIA oversight had become evident to many. The only way to deny real equality, including the right to self-governance, was to continue to endorse the notions of Indigenous backwardness—to argue for their incapacity to govern themselves and their inability to understand what was in their own self-interest.

Within this milieu, the government's plan for enfranchisement was added to a multitude of other grievances as resistance became more organized and sophisticated in its understanding of Canadian institutions. Official response to the new mode of organized resistance did not take the form that one might expect of a liberal democracy. Protests were ignored, Indigenous leaders deposed, majority decisions circumvented, and legislation revamped to meet the challenges posed to the expansion of liberal Canada.

This chapter includes two sections, one focusing on assimilation and enfranchisement and the other concentrating on organized resistance. In both, documents are from the period immediately following World War I. Through the documents included in this chapter, readers will be exposed to policy, legislation, resistance, and response both in relation to enfranchisement and to Indigenous organization itself.

SECTION 5A: ASSIMILATION

The long-held view of Canadian policy makers was that Indigenous cultures were doomed to fall by the wayside, overpowered by superior Euro-Canadian ones. This notion was reflected in the first Indian Act of 1876 and is evident in the examples of Duncan Campbell Scott's poetry included here. It remained the dominant view through to the late twentieth century at least. Scott and his predecessors thought it obvious, for example, that Indigenous people, especially those they considered more advanced, educated, and intelligent, would naturally see the superiority of European-based culture and willingly give up all that made them Indigenous in order to be a part of it. Yet, in hindsight, it seems unremarkable that there was so little interest within Indigenous communities to accept either the concept of European superiority or enfranchisement, especially if the latter meant giving up their cultures and rights. Although Scott gives a slightly higher number in his testimony below, his annual report for 1920 states that only 102 people had accepted enfranchisement since Confederation in 1867.[2] As a result, and in keeping with Canada's paternalistic attitude toward Indigenous people, both the Indian Act and Indian policy became increasingly restrictive and coercive, even though these mounting compulsory elements continued to be presented as being in the best interests of Indigenous people. The 1918 version of the Indian Act simplified enfranchisement procedures, but band councils, the political unit established for First Nations people under the act, retained veto authority over an individual band member's enfranchisement. Though some band councils argued that enfranchising some community members and not others would destroy community unity and cohesiveness, Scott and the DIA felt the councils' authority on this issue was excessive and counterproductive to Canada's long-term goals. Scott's views and the resultant remedial legislation appear in the documents included in this section. There is more of a concentration on organized resistance in the following section of this chapter, but there was almost universal Indigenous opposition to the inclusion of compulsory school attendance and enfranchisement within the Indian Act. To ensure that his proposals for amending the Indian Act would get legislative approval, Scott requested letters of support from missionaries, those involved in the residential schools, and others he believed would be in agreement with the changes. Although some trade unions and others opposed the compulsory nature of the amendments, the most sustained and articulate opposition came from Indigenous organizations. The statement of one of those groups, which included the Six Nations and others, appears below as well.

---

2 D.C. Scott, DSGIA, in DIA, *Annual Report, 1920* (Ottawa: King's Printer, 1921), 13.

1. What are the differences in perspective between Pauline Johnson's poem in the previous chapter and Duncan Campbell Scott's in this one?
2. What are the similarities and differences between Scott's poetry and his presentations as a DIA employee?
3. What does "consultation" mean according to Scott's presentation to the Special Committee of the House of Commons?
4. Why was there Indigenous opposition to enfranchisement if they were to "enjoy all the legal powers, rights and privileges of His Majesty's other subjects"?
5. What concerns about the proposed amendments are expressed by the Six Nations delegation?

DOCUMENTS

5a.1 Duncan Campbell Scott, "Onondaga Madonna," 1898

As mentioned in the introduction to this chapter, Duncan Campbell Scott was both a senior official with the Department of Indian Affairs and a respected poet. This selection of Scott's poetry succinctly illustrates Scott's view of Indigenous people and his predictions for their future.

Source: Duncan Campbell Scott, "Onondaga Madonna", in *Labor and the Angel* (Boston: Copeland & Day, 1898), 15.

THE ONONDAGA MADONNA

SHE stands full-throated and with careless pose,
This woman of a weird and waning race,
The tragic savage lurking in her face,
Where all her pagan passion burns and glows;
Her blood is mingled with her ancient foes,
And thrills with war and wildness in her veins;
Her rebel lips are dabbled with the stains
Of feuds and forays and her father's woes.
And closer in the shawl about her breast,
The latest promise of her nation's doom,
Paler than she her baby clings and lies,
The primal warrior gleaming from his eyes;
He sulks, and burdened with his infant gloom,
He draws his heavy brows and will not rest.

5a.2 Duncan Campbell Scott, "The Half-Breed Girl," 1906

As in "Onondaga Madonna," in this poem, Scott once again outlines his impressions of Indigenous cultures, explores the encounter between Indigenous people and Europeans, and presents his views on the result. The existence of a kind of "blood memory" manifests itself in a form of self-hatred for the protagonist's Indigenous lifestyle. Scott's prescription for a remedy remains consistent here as well.

Source: Duncan Campbell Scott, "The Half-Breed Girl," in *Via Borealis* (Toronto: William Tyrell, 1906), 12–14.

THE HALF-BREED GIRL

SHE is free of the trap and the paddle,
The portage and the trail,
But something behind her savage life
Shines like a fragile veil.

Her dreams are undiscovered,
Shadows trouble her breast,
When the time for resting cometh
Then least is she at rest.

Oft in the morns of winter,
When she visits the rabbit snares,
An appearance floats in the crystal air
Beyond the balsam firs.

Oft in the summer mornings
When she strips the nets of fish,
The smell of the dripping net-twine
Gives to her heart a wish.

But she cannot learn the meaning
Of the shadows in her soul,
The lights that break and gather,
The clouds that part and roll,

The reek of rock-built cities,
Where her fathers dwelt of yore,
The gleam of loch and shealing,
The mist on the moor,

Frail traces of kindred kindness,
Of feud by hill and strand,
The heritage of an age-long life
In a legendary land.

She wakes in the stifling wigwam,
Where the air is heavy and wild,
She fears for something or nothing
With the heart of a frightened child.

She sees the stars turn slowly

Past the tangle of the poles,
Through the smoke of the dying embers,
Like the eyes of dead souls.
Her heart is shaken with longing
For the strange, still years,
For what she knows and knows not,
For the wells of ancient tears.
A voice calls from the rapids,
Deep, careless and free,
A voice that is larger than her life
Or than her death shall be.
She covers her face with her blanket,
Her fierce soul hates her breath,
As it cries with a sudden passion
For life or death.

5a.3 Evidence of D.C. Scott on the Indian Act Amendments of 1920

Amendments were made to the Indian Act in 1918 and 1919 to facilitate enfranchisement and to reduce community control over reserve lands. D.C. Scott, however, felt that more rigorous measures were required and was supported in this by Arthur Meighen, Canada's cabinet minister responsible for Indian Affairs. A further amendment to the Indian Act was introduced in the spring of 1920 as Bill 14. Due to the controversial nature of the bill, especially its aspects related to compulsory enfranchisement, Parliament decided to submit Bill 14 to a special committee of the House of Commons formed to consider the amendment. Excerpts from Scott's testimony before the committee appear here. Of special interest to the issues of this chapter are the discussions on the scope of Indigenous consultation and the conditions required for state compulsion. In the end, the committee recommended virtually no changes to the legislation as it was proposed.

Source: Evidence of D.C. Scott to the Special Committee of the House of Commons Examining the Indian Act Amendments of 1920, Library and Archives Canada, Department of Indian Affairs, RG 10, vol. 6810, file 470–2-3, pt.7, pp. K-4, L-1 to L-4, M-1 to M-4, N-1 to N-4, reel C-8533.

© Government of Canada. Reproduced with the permission of the Minister of Public Works and Government Services Canada (2012).

...

MR. SCOTT: It has been stated that the franchise provided for under this Bill is a compulsory franchise, and I have been asked the question whether that is so. I have been asked that question in the hope apparently that I would endeavour to conceal that fact, but it is a compulsory system, and I hope the Committee will support it. The present law as it exists has not been satisfactory, it placed it too much in the hands of the band. In the first place when an Indian wished to be enfranchised he had to undergo a probatory period which is imposed upon the Indian by the Act, and it forced them out. Under the present system he has to apply for enfranchisement, but he has to be located for a certain piece of land, then his application has to go before the band at a certain time, to see whether or not they approve of his being enfranchised. After all these preliminary steps, and after three years' probation he gets his share of the capital money of the band, and after another probationary period of three years, during which he must behave himself, he gets a patent on his land. That is to say it is six years before he can take his position as a citizen of the country. The result has been that since confederation we have only been able to enfranchise about 150 individuals, and it is a crying shame that people should not be able to be enfranchised immediately, when they desire to do so. During 1917, I recommended to the Minister that any Indians who have any land located on the reserve may apply for enfranchisement and become immediately enfranchised if they have the proper qualifications.

Since the passage of that Act, and it has been in operation less than two years, we have enfranchised nearly three hundred individuals. That shows that there is a class which that amendment certainly reaches, and that they are men who are willing and anxious to take their places as Canadian citizens. It shows that there is such a class of reserves, there is no doubt about it whatever. You have heard evidence from people who are, in all respects, thoroughly qualified to be enfranchised, no matter what their reasons are for not being enfranchised, sentimental and other reasons. You have had oral and visible evidence that there are Indians in the Country who are perfectly able to stand alone, whether they are willing or not. The Bill empowers the Superintendent to appoint an officer or person to make enquiry and report, and when that report is satisfactory, the Governor in Council may enfranchise, and from that date the Indian is a Canadian citizen; that is, he takes his place free of any disabilities of the Indian Act as a citizen after having received his equitable share of the property and funds. The clauses of the Act have been carefully thought out, and I think they would be easily operated. There is no doubt about it. We provide that the Governor in Council may make regulations for any special cases that may arise. There will be minute differences in the franchise of an individual or of a whole band. We intend to take that step. The Governor in Council shall have the power to make regulations. It is not the intention of the Department that there should be any wholesale enfranchisement. What I want is to have on the statute books a progressive franchise, so that when any Indians ask for it I will have the privilege, or the Department will have the privilege, of saying to the Indian, "Don't you think it is time you should be enfranchised"? To my mind, the word "investigation" carries with it consultation. They say that there is no measure of consultation in this Bill. There is, because you cannot investigate without consulting. You must consult the Indian. You must know all about his personal affairs, and how he is fixed before you allow him to go out.

MR. DELISLE: On that very point, it does not seem very clear that it is on your initiative that you have the power to declare that I should be enfranchised. I would be the first one to suffer.

MR. SCOTT: What do you mean by that?

MR. DELISLE: I will be the first one to be enfranchised, and from my point of view I will suffer.

MR. SCOTT: The Bill provides for investigation.

MR. DELISLE: Suppose I did not want it. I won't ask for it, but you know me, and you will say Mr. Delisle should be enfranchised because you consider him fit.

MR. SCOTT: Yes.

MR. DELISLE: That is where I consider it is not right.

MR. SCOTT: I will not say it; it is the Governor in Council.

MR. HAROLD: Our time is very limited, and I think Mr. Scott should be allowed to finish.

MR. SCOTT: That is the purpose of the Bill, and if the Committee wish to ask me any questions or to express any opinion upon the evidence, I am at their service.

MR. WILSON: We are a new country and a great many people are coming to us. After a time they become enfranchised, but we have no law compelling these people to become enfranchised, and I would like you to give us the reason why you wish to obtain the enfranchisement of the Indian by compulsion.

MR. SCOTT: I want to get rid of the Indian problem. I do not think as a matter of fact, that this country ought to continuously protect a class of people who are able to stand alone. That is my whole point. I do not want to pass into the citizens' class people who are paupers. That is not the intention of the Bill. But after one hundred years, after being in close contact with civilization it is enervating to the individual or to a band to continue in that state of tutelage, when he or they are able to take their position as British citizens or Canadian citizens, to support themselves, and stand alone. That has been the whole purpose of Indian education and advancement since the earliest times. One of the very earliest enactments was to provide for the enfranchisement of the Indian. So it is written in our law that the Indian was eventually to become enfranchised. It will be may [sic] years before this will apply to the Indians in the West, although I have a petition from the Moshelle Tribe to become enfranchised. They have a very good system by which under this Bill they will become enfranchised. While they are a race of half-breeds, it is quite possible that they will be able to stand alone, although I do not know that I am quite in favour of their enfranchisement. But they are progressive enough to ask for it.

MR. STACEY: Your interpretation of the phrase is entirely different from my experience of some thirty years of the Indian peoples' meaning. Their idea of compulsion is literal, your interpretation is not. You suggest an initiation on the part of the Department, which will result in enfranchisement as a result of conversations, consultation, agreement.

MR. SCOTT: Certainly that is my reading of the Act, and if the Act does not explain it properly, it is the Committee's privilege to suggest amendments.

MR. STACEY: From all the evidence we have heard I am satisfied that their idea is that it is absolutely compulsory.

MR. SCOTT: The compulsory power is in the Act, there is no doubt; but all the relations of the Indians are on that basis. There is very little compulsion exercised in the clauses of the Act that empower it.

THE CHAIRMAN: It would only be exercised after inquiry.

MR. SCOTT: I don't want to give up the initiation. I would like this Bill to go through, and I would like the Committee to be unanimous. It would be a tremendous help to me and a tremendous advance if it could go through as it is.

MR. LICKERS: How far does that word "investigation" mean consultation?

THE CHAIRMAN: Perhaps we could insert the word "consultation".

MR. LICKERS: If you had a band of chickens and you go to feed them, that is investigation, but it is not consultation.

MR. SCOTT: But you are not chickens.

MR. LICKERS: We are domestic animals.

MR. SCOTT: All this feeling is pure fiction. There is no such relation between the Department and the Indians as Mr. Lickers tries to make out.

MR. LICKERS: How far does the word "investigation" carry consultation.

MR. SCOTT: It carries it fully.

THE ACTING CHAIRMAN: It goes further—to make inquiry.

MR. LICKERS: So that there is no compulsion.

THE ACTING CHAIRMAN: After the inquiry the report was made, and no action is based on the report.

MR. HAROLD: Would it be well to put that word there.

THE ACTING CHAIRMAN: Yes.

MR. SCOTT: As to the way the investigation should be made, we say the Superintendent General should appoint an officer or person. I have no objection to making a change there. I do not want to set up a commission, because it costs money, and I do not want to add to the staff of the Department a person to be specially assigned to conduct these investigations. I want to make use of my experienced officers in making these investigations. The Committee might think of that.

THE ACTING CHAIRMAN: That will be a detail.

MR. STACEY: Will you tell us to what extent there have been requests similar to the one you have quoted?

MR. SCOTT: There have been quite a few of them lately, from individuals from Moravian town. Albert Tobias spoke to is [sic] about that. A large number of them wished to be enfranchised. I have not investigated, and I cannot say whether they could stand alone. We have had a petition from Walpole Island, the reserve the Rev. Mr. Brigham came from, for enfranchisement.

MR. HAROLD: A point has been brought up several times that the old method of franchisement was too hard, and that the new one is going to another extreme, and it has always appealed to me that if this were framed along lines so that the Indian had not to make the application, or take the initiative, and have it arranged so that he could automatically become a citizen, it would be better. Why do you approach it the way you do instead of the other method.

MR. SCOTT: Because if you understood the Indian mind you would know. Surely we have had enough illustrations of it here. These gentlemen are perfectly able to address the Committee—far better than I am—as far as the form goes. But these are the people who will never move.

MR. LAPOINTE: What do you say about the argument of the young gentlemen yesterday, Mr. Moses and Mr. Martin. They impressed me very much. They are in favour of the enfranchisement of the Indians but they do not want it compulsory. I think the proper way is to encourage them, because if you force them against their will, they will have a sense of wrong in their heads. The old Act requires the consent of the band. I would be opposed to that. There should not be any obstacle in the way of an Indian who wants to be enfranchised. He should be encouraged, but on the other hand if you compel him, it seems to [me] you are going to the other extreme.

MR. SCOTT: We have not gone to the other extreme.

MR. LAPOINTE: They all know that as long as you are there they will be well treated.

MR. SCOTT: That has nothing to do with it. I accept the responsibility of recommending the legislation, and for the few years that I have to remain here I will endeavour to carry it out. All the legislation is in the interest of the band. The purpose of the Act is not to rush in everywhere and enfranchise people. I do not believe it would be possible to enfranchise the Six Nations or the Caughawagas [sic].

MR. HAROLD: Or any person on those reserves.

MR. SCOTT: Take the Caughnawagas Indians—I would not want to touch the thing at all. Their land rights and villages are in such an entangled condition that whoever takes that question up in future is going to have an awful time—we attempted to survey the reserves a few years ago and spent a whole lot of the Indian money doing it, I think in an extravagant fashion, and the survey is not worth the paper it is written on.

MR. DESLISLE [DELISLE]: Why all that tangle?

MR. SCOTT: All the lots are irregular, and it is very difficult to make a survey. But take the Caughnawagas, why is it that a judge of the Quebec Superior Court should be a Caughnawagas Indian? That is one thing. Judge Delemimiere has rights on your reserve just as much as you have.

MR. DESLISLE [DELISLE]: How did he get them?

MR. SCOTT: There is no use in arguing about that. There was a time when a white man could sit down on a reserve and marry an Indian woman, or because [sic] associated with the tribe. Individual cases of that kind could be dealt with under the law.

MR. HAROLD: Your proposition is not to pass legislation now with the idea of going into the Six Nations and picking out a certain number of men and enfranchising them?

MR. SCOTT: No. One of our intelligent Indians said "Give us notice" and this is just what I am doing. I am giving them notice "Here you are to be enfranchised", and I want to make it plain that this is a thing that is coming and has got to come. It has not arrived yet for the Caughnawagas and Six Nations, but it has arrive[d] for some reserves.

THE ACTING CHAIRMAN: The objection was raised that the Six Nation Indians were not ready for the enfranchisement now, and that has been considered by the Department.

MR. SCOTT: Yes, and in reference to the provision that I spoke of, the amendment to the Act, nearly all these people who are enfranchised are members of the Six Nation Reserve. The Six Nations have got rid of that element that was living in Toronto and who would come under that amendment. Of cource [sic] they can be enfranchised under this provision as easily, but we have not gone to the furthest extreme in the matter of enfranchisement. The people who have gone the furthest are the Americans. Their new Bill of enfranchisement which has passed Congress, and which they intend to carry out, simply provides that two Commissioners shall be provided for the whole country. Those

Commissioners will have to finish their business in two years. They are empowered to make lists of the different bands in the country showing who are t[h]e Indians belonging to that band.

When these lists are made up and filed with the proper authorities in Washington, ipsofacto, all these people on these lists are enfranchised and become citizens of the United States.

MR. LAPOINTE: Are there any exceptions?

MR. SCOTT: Yes, not because they were Six Nations at all, but because their affiars [sic] are in such a complicated condition that Congress has appointed a special commisssion [sic] to go into them.

MR. LAPOINTE: It is the law of the United States to-day?

MR. SCOTT: It is the law of the United States, and the only reason why the Six Nations are exempt, not because they are Six Nation Indians, but because, I have the decision here showing that Congress has exempted them from the provisions of the Bill because their affairs, in the State of New York, are of such a complicated condition. There is no comparison between our Bill and that of Congress. Just as soon as the affairs of the Six Nations in New York have been adjusted, they will, be enfranchised because the United States are determined not to continue their Indians in a state of tutilage [sic]. We are not going as far as that, but I want to safeguard the interests of every Indian and every band in this country, and, at the same time, put on the statute books a provision that will enable us to enfranchise them so that the Indian, well knowing that we have the power to go to him and say "Do you not think it is time to be enfranchised"? will prepare himself for it.

MR. HAROLD: It is not the desire to force any one to do anything against their own interests?

MR. SCOTT: No.

THE CHAIRMAN: And it can only be done after thorough investigation by the Department and by an officer appointed for the purpose.

MR. DESLISLE [DELISLE]: On the application of the Indian?

MR. SCOTT: No. I cannot give up the initiative which must be with the Government, because we have had the other way long enough and have made no progress.

MR. HAROLD: The idea of this enfranchisement is that it gets away from the point of the Indian being the ward of the nation, because as soon as he is enfranchised then he has got to stand alone, he is no longer a ward, and the Department will have no further responsibility.

MR. SCOTT: No, he becomes thoroughly self-supporting and subject to the law of the country and it lifts him from under the shadow of the Indian Act; he exercises all his rights as a citizen. Mr. Cook mentioned the enfranchisement Bill of Wyandottes and I am glad he did so as it is an illustration of the time it takes to make a change such as proposed by this Bill. That Bill was passed 25 years ago, but we did not suceed [sic] in accomplishing it until 20 years afterwards. We were unable to distribute the funds of the band because one old woman called Laforest objected and we had to wait until she died. They were perfectly capable of looking after their own affairs and the reserve was divided amongst them. There was a great many difficulties in connection with this work and we had to get a man specially trained in order to straighten up the affairs of that band, I remember I was afraid he would die before we could get the work completed, but he didn't, and after ten years' delay we were able to get the funds distributed. The officer visited every member of the band individually and the facts in connection with it were published in the report because I wanted the public to read it. He found that at that time one member of the band was manager of a large factory in Detroit getting $6,000 a year, and at the bottom of the social scale, as you might say, was a char woman supporting herself, as hundreds of other women are supporting themselves here, and there was not one bit of hardship suffered by any member of the band. They had all been absorbed into the life of the country and had dissapeared [sic] in the mass. Our object is to continue until there is not a single Indian in Canada that has not been absorbed into the body politic. [A]nd there is no question, and no Indian Department, that is the whole object of this Bill.

MR. LAPOINTE: There was an argument made here that this Bill constituted an infringement of the rights of the Six Nations under the Treaty.

MR. SCOTT: They had no treaty. In fact I think their own people criticize that argument, there were two or three Indians who spoke here yesterday and said they were British subjects. They hold their reserve, they surrendered all their lands to the Crown except the reserve at Brantford, there are two townships there, everything else they surrendered to the Crown, because they mismanaged their lands so horribly when handling it themselves by issuing title which they had no right to. [T]hey squandered their property and in 1841 they surrendered it to the Government and asked us to administer it, which we have done as well as we could since that date, but the rights of the Six Nations are just like those of the other Indians. They are under the Indian Act, they are just as all the other Indians are in every other respect, there is no difference whatever, their rights are thoroughly safeguarded, I do not think the progressive element of [t]he reserve will object to that sentiment at all. This is what I have always told the Indians, it is exactly what I have told them for ten years, I do not know what they want. The last thing I would like to see done is the splitting up of the Six Nations. I want to see them all live in peace and contentment, I will not live long enough perhaps to see it myself, but my aim is that they shall be absorbed in the county of Brant. I know there is a reactionary element on the reserve and it will probably take 30 years to accomplish the result.

The committee adjourned.

5a.4   Memorandum of the Six Nations of Brantford and Other Haudenosaunee First Nations on the Indian Act Amendments of 1920

Contrary to the views of D.C. Scott above, but as presented in document 1.3 in Chapter 1, the Six Nations Iroquois (Haudenosaunee) had treaty relationships with the Crown long before Confederation. Although they do not rely on that relationship in this written submission to the Special Committee of the House of Commons formed to consider the proposed amendment to the Indian Act in 1920, this document illustrates their frustration with growing governmental control over their affairs and identity. The authors identify the contradictions that they see in the amendment and express a far different perception of its terms and effects than does Scott, especially on the meanings of consultation and compulsion.

Source: Memorandum of the Six Nations of Brantford, the Mohawks of Tyendinaga, the Mohawks of St. Regis, the Caughnawaga near Montreal, and the Iroquois of Oka, to the Special Committee of the House of Commons, 30 March 1920, Library and Archives Canada, Department of Indian Affairs, RG 10, vol. 6810, file 470–2-3, pt.7, reel C-8533.

<hr>

Memorandum

re Bill 14

(An Act to Amend the Indian Act)

The Six Nations of Brantford, the Mohawks of Tyendinaga, the Mohawks of St. Regis, and the Caughnawaga near Montreal, and the Iroquois of Oka, unite in respectfully representing to your Honourable Committee the following, among other objections to the said Bill.

1. Objections to Paragraph 3 or Compulsory Enfranchisement

(a) The proposed new Paragraph No. 107, of the Indian Act replaced the present voluntary right to become enfranchised by giving the Superintendent General practically compulsory power without the Indian in question being consulted.

(b) This Bill is obviously illogical, since if he is so intelligent as to be fit for enfranchisement he is sufficiently intelligent to be consulted about it.

(c) On the contrary, he is treated as a serf.

(d) Such enfranchisement involves his compulsory separation from the community of his relatives as a member of the Band or Tribe.

(e) This can be done on the simple report of an "officer or person" who may have a dislike to him.

(f) It is feared that the effect will be, that if an agent finds an intelligent Indian asserting a right the agent will be able to get rid of him by encompassing his compulsory enfranchisement.

(g) The entire arrangement as set forth in Section 107 (1) is extremely indefinite and gives no grounds for limitation or conditions under which the arbitrary power of the "officer or person" or the Superintendent General is to be exercised.

(h) Under sub-section 4, the lands and monies of a Band, Tribe or Nation can be broken into by the same arbitrary process.

(i) In the same way the land and money of the minor children may be paid to the father or even in the case of the father's death to a person arbitrarily selected and the land and money of the wife shall be paid to the husband or maybe paid to the husband.

(j) By the proposed section 109, it is evident that a compulsory enfranchisement may be made of a whole community and its lands and property can be sold to outsiders without any of the owners being in any way consulted.

(k) The Bill being based upon the obvious theory that Indians are far advanced in development, the reasonable process should be to consult them more about their own affairs, whereas the Bill adopts the backward step of abolishing consultation and replacing it by compulsion,—the principle of the whole Bill.

2. The Aforesaid Indians respectfully represent:—

(a) That the Indians of Canada are annually making considerable advancement in education, and improving their conditions and include a large proportion of individuals of equal standing in these respects to the white population.

(b) They cannot now be regarded as a kind of children.

(c) They have every right to be consulted regarding their own welfare and interests.

(d) They ask your Committee and the gentlemen of Parliament to definitely introduce this principle of granting them the right of consultation and consent in regard to their property and affairs.

(e) They particularly ask that their personal liberty to choose enfranchisement or not, be left to their own will and discretion.

(f) There is a Constitutional objection of considerable interest to the Six Nations based on the Bill being an interference with their internal affairs and which is at present the subject of a Petition to the Governor in Council.

3. In conclusion they request that the Compulsory enfranchisement clauses of Bill 14 be entirely dropped.

4. The first portion of the Bill regarding education is one on which opinion is divided and they need more time for its consideration than the present Parliamentary Session will allow and they ask that it be held over for the present.

5. They desire to add that they are all practically in favor of more and better education and all desire to support any truly progressive measures and furthermore they appreciate the fact that Bill 14 has its source in a desire on the part of the Superintendent General to advance their welfare although they feel compelled to reject the method. They also thank the members of the House of Commons who have taken a kindly interest in their affairs.

6. We would also urge upon your attention the necessity of our being allowed sufficient funds to carry on our case against the present Bill as well as the proceedings under our said Petition and other similar business to engage a proper counsel independently of the Department and to meet the outlays of our delegation.

Secretary, Six Nations
Council, and also for
The Delegation.
Ottawa, March 30, 1920.

5a.5 Amendment to the Indian Act, 1920

There was universal opposition among Indigenous leaders to the enfranchisement and other provisions of Bill 14, and their objections were articulated repeatedly in submissions to the Special Committee of the House of Commons. Nonetheless, the committee approved the bill virtually unchanged, and the following was incorporated into the

Indian Act in 1920. This amendment also continues the gendered understandings of earlier versions of the act. The portion of this legislation included here is part of a modification of Section 107 of the Indian Act.

Source: *An Act to Amend the Indian Act*, S.C. 1919–20, 10–11 Geo. V., ch. 50, s.3.

107.

. . .

(2) On the report of the Superintendent General that any Indian, male or female, over the age of twenty-one years is fit for enfranchisement, the Governor in Council may by order direct that such Indians shall be and become enfranchised at the expiration of two years from the date of such order or earlier if requested by such Indian, and from the date of such enfranchisement the provision of the *Indian Act* and of any other Act or law making any distinction between the legal rights, privileges, disabilities and liabilities of Indians and those of His Majesty's other subjects, shall cease to apply to such Indian or to his or her minor unmarried children, or, in the case of a married male Indian, to the wife of such Indian, and every such Indian and child and wife shall thereafter have, possess and enjoy all the legal powers, rights and privileges of His Majesty's other subjects, and shall no longer be deemed to be Indians within the meaning of any laws relating to Indians.

Governor in Council may enfranchise Indians, on approval of report of Superintendent.

Effect of enfranchisement.

SECTION 5B: ORGANIZED RESISTANCE

Armed with a growing understanding of Canadian laws and political structures and faced with a declining economic base, the loss of territory, the growth of Euro-Canadian settlements near Indigenous communities, and increasingly restrictive policy and legislation, First Nations people from across the country organized to protect their interests. Given the context, their actions seem inevitable. The documents in this section are from the interwar period and provide examples of their organizing efforts and Canada's responses.

The first three documents are from Ontario. Fred Loft, a Mohawk veteran of World War I wrote a circular letter in 1919 suggesting that the First Nations leaders join his fledgling League of Indians, which he hoped to develop into a national organization to protect the interests of First Nations people by legal means. Though Loft was not particularly radical, especially on the issue of assimilation, he and the league offered a challenge to the paternalistic authority and public image of the DIA. In addition to Loft's circular, this section also includes the views of an Indian agent and a response from his superior, DSGIA D.C. Scott.

On the other side of the country, when British Columbia became part of Canada in 1871, the terms of union that brought the new province into Confederation included Article 13: "[t]he charge of the Indians, and the trusteeship and management of the lands reserved for their use and benefit, shall be assumed by the Dominion Government, and a policy as liberal as that hitherto pursued by the British Columbia Government shall be continued by the Dominion Government after the Union."[3] What "liberal" meant became a bone of contention between the two governments, especially when the term related to the lands for which First Nations would be permitted to retain the use. British Columbia

---

3 "Terms of Union, 1871" in British Columbia, *Revised Statutes of British Columbia, 1979*, vol. 7 (Victoria: Queen's Printer, 1981), 85.

insisted that the clause allowed for far less reserve lands west of the Rockies than was the norm in the rest of Canada. This circumstance helps explain not only why there are so few treaties in British Columbia but also the diminutive size of reserves there.

Despite their differences, the two governments shared underlying assumptions concerning the propriety of individual land ownership, European-style agriculture, and Christian religious beliefs. The main issue, then, was to resolve differences between them over land, not necessarily to promote First Nations interests or desires. In 1912, a royal commission was established to "settle all differences between the governments of the Dominion and the Province respecting Indian lands and Indian affairs."[4] This commission, popularly known as the McKenna-McBride Commission and named for federal representative J.A.J. McKenna and BC Premier Richard McBride, travelled the province and spoke to reserve residents and settler representatives. In the end, it recommended adding more land to reserves than it proposed reducing or cutting off. The added land was, though, of far less value than that which would be cut off.

Throughout the on-reserve meetings, First Nations were continually assured that land would not be removed from reserves without their consent. After the McKenna-McBride Commission submitted its report, BC Premier John Oliver requested a response from the Allied Indian Tribes of British Columbia. The Allied Tribes, formed in 1916, included First Nations from every region in BC and represented a coalescence of previously organized regional groups. The position of the Allied Tribes on the McKenna-McBride report and on what actions would be necessary for an acceptable solution is included in their statement below.

Although the Allied Tribes did not rule out a made-in-Canada solution, it believed that the issue of Aboriginal title to land, which was never acknowledged by British Columbia, would likely need to be addressed by the Judicial Committee of the Privy Council (JCPC). The JCPC, though in Britain, was the highest court for Canada until 1949. For his part, D.C. Scott believed that any refusal to accept the recommendations of the commission by First Nations could only be the result of outside agitation, so, in 1920, the British Columbia Land Settlement Act confirmed that Indigenous consent to cut-offs of reserve land would not be necessary. In 1924, the Canadian government accepted the commission's recommendations despite the opposition of the Allied Tribes.

In the meantime, Cayuga hereditary Chief Deskaheh (Hi-wyi-iss or Levi General) travelled to London and Geneva on behalf of the Haudenosaunee (Iroquois) to seek support from Britain and the League of Nations in the struggle against Canada's attempt to eliminate the traditional governing structures on the Six Nations reserve and elsewhere and impose the political system mandated by the Indian Act. Though ultimately unsuccessful, Deskaheh's presentation to the League of Nations, *The Redman's Appeal for Justice* included below, is illustrative of the Haudenosaunee position, many items of which remain unresolved in the present.

---

4 "Memorandum of Agreement arrived at between J.A.J. McKenna, Special Commissioner appointed by the Dominion Government to investigate the condition of Indian Affairs in British Columbia and the Honourable Sir Richard McBride as Premier of the Province of British Columbia" in "Orders-in-Council and Agreement re: Powers and Functions of The Royal Commission on Indian Affairs for British Columbia," LAC, RG 10, vol. 3821, file 59,335, Part 4.

Scott and the DIA thought that the issues advanced by Indigenous organizations and activists during this period were inimical to Canada's policy objectives. Although the Allied Tribes were initially optimistic when a special joint committee of the Senate and House of Commons was appointed to inquire into their claims in 1926, their optimism soon waned. The committee accepted the DIA's interpretations regarding the wisdom of its policy initiatives and Scott's view that it had to be outside agitators who were responsible for any opposition because there was no reason for any dissatisfaction amongst reserve residents. Brief excerpts from the special committee's report and the legislation that was the result of its recommendations appear below.

Although this generation of Indigenous leaders was ultimately unsuccessful in attaining what they sought, they represented a new era in political activity that should not be underestimated. The Indigenous activism of the present is clearly not a new phenomenon, and it can be understood only in the context of the efforts and challenges of past leaders. In many ways, they served as models for present-day Indigenous activists.

QUESTIONS FOR DISCUSSION

1. In what ways is Fredrick Loft's position different from that of Deskaheh and the Six Nations Council?
2. Are what D.C. Scott identifies as contradictions in Frederick Loft's position actually contradictions? Why or why not?
3. What might be the reasons for governmental resistance to Frederick Loft's organizing efforts?
4. What are the Six Nations' grievances? What does the organization seek as remedial action?
5. Why were the Allied Tribes opposed to the McKenna-McBride agreement?
6. Why would D.C. Scott and others argue that Indigenous agitation must have originated from external sources?

5b.1 Letter from F.O. Loft to Chiefs and Brethren, 1919

Frederick Ogilvie Loft or Onondeyoh (1861–1934) was born of Mohawk parents on the Six Nations Reserve in present-day Ontario. He married a non-Indian and strove to meld his Mohawk culture with his desire to participate in Euro-Canadian society. In 1906, he applied for enfranchisement, but it was turned down by his band council. Loft underrepresented his age by over a decade to serve as a lieutenant in World War I. On his return, he was instrumental in the formation of the League of Indians. This circular letter, written to recruit membership to the league, briefly outlines some of Loft's concerns and the reasons for his attempts to organize. The local Indian agent's view of Loft and the League of Indians, and those of DSGIA D.C. Scott, can be seen in the two documents that follow this one.

Source: Chief F.O. Loft, President, League of Indians of Canada to Chief and Brethren, 14 November 1919, Library and Archives Canada, Department of Indian Affairs, RG 10, vol. 3211, file 527,787, pt.1, reel C-11340.

Chief F.O. Loft, President.
75 Madison Ave.,
Toronto.

League of Indians of Canada,

Toronto. 14th November 1919

Dear Chief and Brethern [sic]

For and in behalf of the League of Indians of Canada and its Executive, I have the honor to address you and the members of your band, to seriously urge upon the important necessity of all Indians becoming united into one great association; in this way to stabilize our interests, protect and advance them in ways that will be of national benefit.

Union is the outstanding impulse of men today, because it is the only way by which the individual and collective elements of society can wield a force and power to be heard and their demands recognized by governments. Look at the force and power of all kinds of labor organizations, because of their unions. Now we see the great development and strength of the farmers, who are uniting to uphold and advance their interests. In a recent election in Ontario, they have been able to control the Government and Legislature of Ontario. How is this? Because each and all have combined to work together for an end, to elevate their position and noble calling as producers.

In politics, in the past, they have been in the background, scarcely heard or noticed in parliaments or in nature of laws passed, but now they are getting right into the front because they have wakened up to the great duty of uniting.

We as Indians, from one end of the Dominion to the other, are sadly strangers to each other; we have not learned what it is to co-operate and work for each other as we should; the pity of it is greater because our needs, drawbacks, handicaps and troubles are all similar. It is for us to do something to get out of these sad conditions. The day is past when one band or a few bands can successfully—if at all— free themselves from the domination of officialdom and from being ever the prey and victims of unscrupulous means of depriving us of our lands and homes, and even deny us of the rights we are entitled to as free men under the British Flag.

As peaceable and law-abiding citizens in the past, and even in the late war, we have performed dutiful service to our King, Country and Empire, and we have the right to claim and demand more justice and fair play as a recompense for we, too, have fought for the sacred rights of justice, freedom and liberty so dear to mankind, no matter what their colour or creed.

The first aim of the League then is to claim and protect the rights of all Indians in Canada by legitimate and just means; second, absolute control in retaining possession or disposition of our lands; that all questions and matters relative to individual and national wellbeing of Indians shall rest with the people and their dealing with the Government shall be by and through their respective band Councils at all times to be consulted, and their wishes respected in like manner as other constituted bodies conducting public affairs.

All these matters are formulated in the constitution of the League, which was passed and adopted at the first congress of the League held at the "Soo" Ontario, September 2–4th 1919, which was attended by a large delegation from Ontario, and Manitoba was also represented.

Union then has started; it is for all who are not yet members to join with the forces to create a permanent national brotherhood with a great national policy of progress and advancement to lift ourselves up by our own efforts to better conditions, morally, socially, politically and industrially. The aim also is to demand better educational advantages for our children, also to encourage our people to be farmers, stay on the land and work it, for it is the most independent way of living. We will co-operate with the Government, but we must have its sympathy, encouragement and assistance so as to make good. To force or coerce us will do no good; justice and fair dealing is what we ask for. We are men, not imbeciles; from our view and standpoint we must be heard as a nation when we have to speak for ourselves.

I urge your band and Council's early decision to join the League, if you are really concerned in the peace and welfare of your brother Indians in Canada.

Let me hear from you as soon as possible, or when you decide to join the League, send me $5.00 registration fees. This is only a first payment. For payment of yearly dues as a member, a band pays on the basis of 5 cents per head of the population.

Money is always required to pay for paper, stamps and other expenses. A fund to be created by us will be used to pay our Children's fees in high schools. By doing this you are helping your race to get better schooling. Our success is in our own hands, so let us strive to be true to ourselves, our families, our brethern [sic] and our country. This is good citizen ship [sic].

When you write let me know how many are in your band and [the] name and post office address of [the] person I am to write to.

Tendering my kind regards to all

I remain in truth and regard your brother.
    Chief F.O. Loft,
      President

Written by pen [In spite of this note regarding the paragraph below, all the copy was typed in the document consulted for this anthology.]

Please let me know when you get this letter, so that I will know you have it. There are many bands in Kenora Agency who have joined the League. I am writing to most of [the] Chiefs of Fort Frances Agency. Talk about this matter to others up there. Get together and consider this great Indian union. I hope some of you will try and meet me in Elphinstone, Manitoba next June. I expect to go there to a great Congress of League.

5b.2 Letter from J.P. Wright to D.C. Scott, 1919

This letter from J.P. Wright, the DIA's Indian agent for the Fort Frances Agency, outlines the agent's concerns to his superior D.C. Scott about Loft's circular letter that appears as document 5b.1 above. Scott's response follows as document 5b.3.

Source: J.P. Wright, Indian Agent at Fort Frances, to Duncan C. Scott, DSGIA, 20 December 1919, Library and Archives Canada, Department of Indian Affairs, RG 10, vol. 3211, file 527,787, pt. 1, reel C-11340.

INDIAN OFFICE,
Fort Frances, Ont. 20th Dec. 1919

Duncan C. Scott, Esq.
Deputy Supt. General of Indian Affairs
Ottawa,
Ont.

Dear Mr. Scott, —

I enclose a copy of a letter received by the Chief of the Coucheching band, regarding a new League of Indians of Canada. I do not know if you are aware of this movement but I am suspicious of it, I don't like the tone of it, it looks like the I.W.W. [Industrial Workers of the World] or O.B.U. [One Big Union] or Balshevick [sic]. I have advised my Indians to have nothing to do with it, at least not until it had your sanction. I hear that nearly all the bands have received a similar letter.

Sincerely yours
Jno. P. Wright
Indian Agent.

5b.3 Letter from D.C. Scott to J.P. Wright, 1919

This letter from D.C. Scott is in response to the circular from F.O. Loft and to the correspondence from Indian Agent J.P. Wright (above). It displays Scott's commitment to his own particular views, his administrative agenda, and his perspective on how Indigenous people should respond to his department's efforts.

Source: Duncan C. Scott, DSGIA, to J.P. Wright, Indian Agent at Fort Frances, 31 December 1919, Library and Archives Canada, Department of Indian Affairs, RG 10, vol. 3211, file 527,787.

© Government of Canada. Reproduced with the permission of the Minister of Public Works and Government Services Canada (2012).

J. P. Wright, Esq.
Indian Agent,
Fort Frances, Ont.

December 31st. 1919.

My dear Wright,

I have yours of the 20th. December enclosing a circular from F.O. Loft. You are quite right in advising your Indians to have nothing to do with it. The circular is a peculiar mixture. With one side of his mouth he says he wants to be "free from the domination of officialdom and from being ever the prey and victims of unscrupulous means, etc. etc." and with the other side of his mouth he says he wants to "co-operate with the Government", and he says to "Force and co-erce" the Indians will do no good.

I took a particular interest in this fellow's daughter and we strained ourselves to give the girl advantages at Toronto University and this is the sort of thanks one gets for it.

Wishing you a very happy New Year.

Yours very truly,
    DCS [Duncan C. Scott]
    Deputy Superintendent General.

5b.4 Statement of the Allied Indian Tribes of British Columbia, 1919

The Royal Commission on Indian Affairs for the Province of British Columbia, a.k.a the McKenna-McBride Commission, tabled its report in 1916. Because BC Premier Frank Oliver, elected in 1918, understood that Indigenous consent would be required to cut off or reduce reserves as recommended by the royal commission, he asked the Allied Tribes for its opinion of the report. The Allied Tribes met in general assembly and formed a committee to draft a response to Oliver's request. The draft was approved by the Executive Committee of the Allied Tribes and presented to Premier Oliver in December of 1919.

Source: *Statement of the Allied Indian Tribes of British Columbia for the Government of British Columbia* (Vancouver: Cowan & Brookhouse, 1919) in Library and Archives Canada, Department of Indian Affairs, RG 10, vol. 3821, file 59335, part 4A, reel C-10143.

STATEMENT OF THE ALLIED INDIAN TRIBES OF

BRITISH COLUMBIA FOR THE GOVERNMENT

OF BRITISH COLUMBIA

Part I.—General Introductory Remarks

The Statement prepared by the Committee appointed by the Conference held at Vancouver in June, 1916, and sent to the Government of Canada and the Secretary of State for the Colonies, contained the following:

> The Committee concludes this statement by asserting that, while it is believed that all the Indian tribes of the Province will press on to the Judicial Committee, refusing to consider any so-called settlement made up under the McKenna Agreement, the Committee also feels certain that the tribes allied for that purpose will always be ready to consider any really equitable method of settlement out of court which might be proposed by the Government.

A resolution, passed by the Interior Tribes at a meeting at Spence's Bridge on the 6th December, 1917, contained the following:—

> We are sure that the governments and a considerable number of white men have for many years had in their minds a quite wrong idea of the claims which we make, and the settlement which we desire. We do not want anything extravagant, and we do not want anything hurtful to the real interests of the white people. We want that our actual rights be determined and recognized. We want a settlement based upon justice. We want a full opportunity of making a future for ourselves. We want all this done in such a way that in the future we shall be able to live and work with the white people as our brothers and fellow citizens.

Now we have been informed by our Special Agent that the Government of British Columbia desires to have from us a statement further explaining our mind upon the subject of settlement, and in particular stating the grounds upon which we refuse to accept as a settlement the findings of the Royal Commission on Indian Affairs for the Province of British Columbia, and what we regard as necessary conditions of equitable settlement.

In order that our mind regarding this whole subject may be understood, we desire first to make clear what is the actual present position of the Indian land controversy in this Province of British Columbia.

Throughout practically the whole of the rest of Canada, tribal ownership of lands has been fully acknowledged, and all dealings with the various tribes have been based upon the Indian title so acknowledged.

It was long ago conceded by Canada in the most authoritative way possible that the Indian tribes of British Columbia have the same title. This is proved beyond possibility of doubt by the report to the Minister of Justice, which was presented on January 19, 1875, and was approved by the Governor-General in Council on January 23, 1875. We set out the following extract from that report:

> Considering then these several features of the case, that no surrender or cession of their territorial rights, whether the same be of a legal or equitable nature, has been ever executed by the Indian Tribes of the Province—that they allege that the reservations of land made by the Government for their use have been arbitrarily so made, and are totally inadequate to their support and requirements and without their assent—that they are not averse to hostilities in order to enforce rights which it is impossible to deny them, and that the Act under consideration not only ignores those rights, but expressly prohibits the Indians from enjoying the rights of recording or pre-empting land, except by consent of the Lieutenant-Governor; the undersigned feels that he cannot do otherwise than advise that the Act in question is objectionable as tending to deal with lands which are assumed to be the absolute property of the Province, an assumption which completely ignores as applicable to the Indians of British Columbia, the honor and good faith with which the Crown has in all other cases since its sovereignty of the territories in North America dealt with their various Indian tribes.
>
> The undersigned would also refer to the British North America Act, 1867, section 109, applicable to British Columbia, which enacts in effect that all lands belonging to the Province, shall belong to the Province, "subject to any trust existing in respect thereof, and to any interest other than that of the Province in the same."
>
> That which has been ordinarily spoken of as the "Indian title" must of necessity consist of some species of interest in the lands of British Columbia.
>
> If it is conceded that that they have not a freehold in the soil, but that they have an usufruct, a right of occupation or possession of the same for their own use, then it would seem that these lands of British Columbia are subject, if not to a "trust existing in respect thereof," at least "to an interest other than that of the Province alone."

Since the year 1875, however, notwithstanding the report of the Minister of Justice then presented and approved, local governments have been unwilling to recognize the land rights which were then recognized by Canada, and the two governments that entered into the McKenna-McBride Agreement failed to recognize those land rights.

If now the two governments should be willing to accept the report and Order-in-Council of the year 1875 as deciding the land controversy, they would thereby provide what we regard as the only possible general basis of settlement other than a judgment of the Judicial Committee of His Majesty's Privy Council.

By means of the direct and independent petition of the Nishga Tribe, we now have our case before His Majesty's Privy Council. We claim that we have a right to a hearing, a right which has now been made clear beyond any possibility of doubt. Sir Wilfrid Laurier, when Prime Minister, on behalf of Canada, met the Indian Tribes of Northern British Columbia, and promised without any condition whatever that the land controversy would be brought before the Judicial Committee. Moreover, the Duke of Connaught, acting as His Majesty's representative in Canada, gave positive written assurance that if the Nishga Tribe should not be willing to agree to the findings of the Royal Commission, His Majesty's Privy Council will consider the Nishga petition. In view of Sir Wilfrid Laurier's promise, and the Duke of Connaught's assurances, both of which confirm what we regard as our clear constitutional right, we confidently expect an early hearing of our case.

Before concluding these introductory remarks, we wish to speak of one other matter which we think very important. No settlement would, we are very sure, be real and lasting unless it should be a complete settlement. The so-called settlement which the two governments that entered into the McKenna-McBride Agreement, have made up is very far indeed from being complete. The report of the Royal Commission deals only with lands to be reserved. The reversionary title claimed by the Province is not extinguished, as Special Commissioner McKenna said it would be. Foreshores have not been dealt with. No attempt is made to adjust our general rights, such as fishing rights, hunting rights and water rights. With regard to fishing rights and water rights, the Commissioners admit that they can make nothing sure. It is clear to us that all our general rights, instead of being taken from us as the McKenna-McBride Agreement attempts to do by describing the so-called settlement thereby arranged as a "final adjustment of all matters relating to Indian affairs in British Columbia" should be preserved and adjusted. Also we think that a complete settlement should deal with the restrictions imposed upon Indians by Provincial Statutes and should include a revision of the Indian Act.

Now, having as we hope made clear the position in which we stand, and from which we look at the whole subject, we proceed to comply with the desire of the Government of British Columbia.

Part II.—Report of the Royal Commission

Introductory Remarks

The general view held by us with regard to the report of the Royal Commission was correctly stated in the communication sent by the Agents of the Nishga Tribe to the Lord President of His Majesty's Privy Council on 27th May, 1918.

We now have before us the report of the Royal Commission, and are fully informed of its contents, so far as material for the purposes of this statement. The report has been carefully considered by the Allied Tribes, upon occasion of several meetings, and subsequently by the Executive Committee of the Allied Tribes.

Two general features of the report which we consider very unsatisfactory are the following:—

1. The additional lands set aside are to a large extent of inferior quality, and their total value is much smaller than that of the lands which the Commissioners recommend shall be cut off.

2. In recommending that reserves confirmed and additional lands set aside be held for the benefit of bands, the Commissioners proceeded upon a principle which we consider erroneous, as all reserved lands should be held for the benefit of the Tribes.

In addition to the grounds shown by our general introductory remarks, we mention the following as the principle [sic] grounds upon which we refuse to accept as a settlement the findings of the Royal Commission:—

1. We think it clear that fundamental matters such as tribal ownership of our territories require to be dealt with, either by concession of the governments, or by decision of the Judicial Committee, before subsidiary matters such as the findings of the Royal Commission can be equitably dealt with.

2. We are unwilling to be bound by the McKenna-McBride Agreement, under which the findings of the Royal Commission have been made.

3. The whole work of the Royal Commission has been based upon the assumption that Article 13 of the Terms of Union contains all obligations of the two governments towards the Indian Tribes of British Columbia, which assumption we cannot admit to be correct.

4. The McKenna-McBride Agreement, and the report of the Royal Commission ignore not only our land rights, but also the power conferred by Article 13 upon the Secretary of State for the Colonies.

5. The additional reserved lands recommended by the report of the Royal Commission, we consider to be utterly inadequate for meeting the present and future requirements of the Tribes.

6. The Commissioners have wholly failed to adjust the inequalities between Tribes, in respect of both area and value of reserved lands, which Special Commissioner McKenna, in his report, pointed out and which the report of the Royal Commission has proved to exist.

7. Notwithstanding the assurance contained in the report of Special Commissioner McKenna, that "such further lands as are required will be provided by the Province, in so far as Crown lands are available." The Province, by Act passed in the spring of the year 1916, took back two million acres of land, no part of which, as we understand, was set aside for the Indians by the Commissioners, whose report was soon thereafter presented to the governments.

8. The Commissioners have failed to make any adjustment of water-rights, which in the case of lands situated within the Dry Belt, is indispensable.

9. We regard as manifestly unfair and wholly unsatisfactory the provisions of the McKenna-McBride Agreement relating to the cutting-off and reduction of reserved lands, under which one-half of the proceeds of sale of any such lands would go to the Province, and the other half of such proceeds, instead of going into the hands or being held for the benefit of the Tribe, would be held by the Government of Canada for the benefit of all the Indians of British Columbia.

Part III.—Necessary Conditions of Equitable Settlement

Introductory Remarks

1. In the year 1915, the Nishga Tribe and the Interior Tribes allied with them, made proposals regarding settlement, suggesting that the matter of lands to be reserved be finally dealt with by the Secretary of State for the Colonies, and that all other matters requiring to be adjusted, including compensation for lands to be surrendered, be dealt

with by the Parliament of Canada. Those proposals the Government of Canada rejected by Order-in-Council, passed in June, 1915, mainly upon the ground that the Government was precluded by the McKenna-McBride Agreement from accepting them. For particulars we refer to "Record of Interviews," published in July, 1915, at pages 21 and 105. It will be found that to some extent these proposals are incorporated in this statement.

2. Some facts and considerations which, in considering the matter of additional lands, it is, we think, especially important to take into account, are the following:—

(1) In the three States of Washington, Idaho and Montana, all adjoining British Columbia, Indian title has been recognized, and treaties have been made with the Indian tribes of those States. Under those treaties, very large areas of land have been set aside. The total lands set aside in those three States considerably exceeds 10,000,000 acres, and the per capita area varies from about 200 acres to about 600 acres.

(2) Portions of the tribal territories of four tribes of the Interior of British Columbia extend into the States above-mentioned, and thus portions of those tribes hold lands in the Colville Reservation, situated in the State of Washington, and the Flathead Reservation, situated in the State of Montana.

(3) By treaties made with the Indian Tribes of the Provinces of Saskatchewan and Alberta, there has been set aside an average per capita area of about 180 acres.

(4) For the five Tribes of Alberta that entered into Treaty No. 7, whose tribal territories all adjoin British Columbia having now a total Indian population of about 3,500, there was set aside a total area of about 762,000 acres, giving a per capita area of 212 acres.

(5) The facts regarding the Indian Tribes inhabiting that part of Northern British Columbia lying to the East of the Rocky Mountains shown in Interim Report No. 91 of the Royal Commission at pages 126, 127 and 128 of the Report show that the Royal Commission approved and adopted as a standard for the Indians of that part of the Province occupying Provincial lands the per capita area of 160 acres of agricultural land per individual, or 640 acres per family of five, set aside under Treaty No. 8.

(6) As shown by the facts above stated, all the Tribes that are close neighbours of the British Columbia Indians on the South and East have had large areas per capita set aside for their use and benefit, and the Indians inhabiting the Northeastern portion of British Columbia have also been fairly treated in the matter of agricultural lands reserved for them. Notwithstanding that state of affairs, the areas set aside for all the other British Columbia Tribes average only thirty acres per capita, or from one-fifth to one-twentieth of the acreage of Reserves set aside for their neighbours.

(7) It may also be pointed out that at one time even this small amount of land was considered excessive for the needs of the Indian Tribes of British Columbia, as is shown by the controversy which in the year 1873 arose between the two Governments on the subject of acreage of lands to be reserved for the Indians of British Columbia. (See Report of Royal Commission at pages 16 and 17.) At that time the Dominion Government contended for a basis of 80 acres per family or 16 acres per capita, and the British Columbia Government contended for a basis of 20 acres per family or 4 acres per capita.

(8) It may further be pointed out that at that very time, while the Governments were discussing the question whether each individual Indian required 16 acres or 4 acres, the Provincial Government was allowing individual white men each to acquire by pre-emption 160 acres West of the Cascades and 320 acres East of that Range, each pre-emptor choosing his land how and where he desired.

(9) All the facts which we have above stated when taken together prove conclusively, as we think, that the per capita area of 30 acres recommended by the Royal Commission is utterly inadequate, and that a per capita area of 160 acres would be an entirely reasonable standard. That conclusion is completely confirmed by our knowledge of the actual land requirements of our Tribes.

(10) At the same time it is clear to us that, in applying that standard, the wildly differing conditions and requirements of various sections of the Province should be taken into consideration.

(11) We proceed to state what are the conditions and requirements of each of the sections to which we have referred.

(12) For that purpose we divide the Province into five sections as follows:

I. Southern Coast.
II. Northern Coast, together with the West Coast of Vancouver Island.
III. Southern Interior.
IV. Central Interior.
V. Northern Interior.

In the case of Section I all conditions are favourable for agriculture, and the Indians require much more agricultural land.

In the case of Section II the conditions are such that the country is not to any great extent agricultural. The Indians require some additional agricultural land together with timber lands.

In the case of Section III the conditions are more favourable to stock raising than to agriculture. Throughout the Dry Belt irrigation is an absolute necessity for agriculture. The Indians require large additional areas of pasture land.

In the case of Section IV there is abundance of good agricultural land but the climatic conditions are not favourable for stock raising and fruit growing. The Indians require additional areas of agricultural land.

In the case of Section V the conditions are wholly unfavourable to both agricultural and stock raising. The main requirement of the Indians is that, either by setting aside large hunting and trapping areas for their exclusive use or otherwise, hunting and trapping, the main industry upon which of necessity they rely, should be fully preserved for them.

3. It is quite clear to us that these conditions of settlement require to be considered by the Government of Canada as well as the Government of British Columbia.

Conditions Proposed as Basis of Settlement

We beg to present for consideration of the two Governments the following which we regard as necessary conditions of equitable settlement:

1. That the Proclamation issued by King George III in the year 1763 and the Report presented by the Minister of Justice in the year 1875 be accepted by the two Governments and established as the main basis of all dealings and all adjustments of Indian land rights and other rights which shall be made.

2. That it be conceded that each Tribe for whose use and benefit land is set aside (under Article 13 of the "Terms of Union") acquires thereby a full, permanent and beneficial title to the land so set aside together with all natural resources pertaining thereto; and that Section 127 of the Land Act of British Columbia be amended accordingly.

3. That all existing reserves not now as parts of the Railway Belt or otherwise held by Canada be conveyed to Canada for the use and benefit of the various Tribes.

4. That all foreshores whether tidal or inland be included in the reserves with which they are connected, so that the various Tribes shall have full permanent and beneficial title to such foreshores.

5. That adequate additional lands be set aside and that to this end a per capita standard of 160 acres of average agricultural land having in case of lands situated within the dry belt a supply of water sufficient for irrigation be established. By the word "standard" we mean not a hard and fast rule, but a general estimate to be used as a guide, and to be applied in a reasonable way to the actual requirements of each tribe.

6. That in sections of the Province in case of which the character of available land and the conditions prevailing make it impossible or undesirable to carry out fully or at all that standard the Indian Tribes concerned be compensated for such deficiency by grazing lands, by timber lands, by hunting lands or otherwise, as the particular character and conditions of each such section may require.

7. That all existing inequalities in respect of both acreage and value between lands set aside for the various Tribes be adjusted.

8. That for the purpose of enabling the two Governments to set aside adequate additional lands and adjust all inequalities there be established a system of obtaining lands including compulsory purchase, similar to that which is being carried out by the Land Settlement Board of British Columbia.

9. That if the Governments and the Allied Tribes should not be able to agree upon a standard of lands to be reserved that matter and all other matters relating to lands to be reserved which cannot be adjusted in pursuance of the preceding conditions and by conference between the two governmnts [sic] and the Allied Tribes be referred to the Secretary of State for the Colonies to be finally decided by that Minister in view of our land rights conceded by the two Governments in accordance with our first condition and in pursuance of the provisions of Article 13 of the "Terms of Union" by such method of procedure as shall be decided by the Parliament of Canada.

10. That the beneficial ownership of all reserves shall belong to the Tribe for whose use and benefit they are set aside.

11. That a system of individual title to occupation of particular parts of reserved lands be established and brought into operation and administered by each Tribe.

12. That all sales, leases and other dispositions of land or timber or other natural resources be made by the Government of Canada as trustee for the Tribe with the consent of the Tribe and that of all who may have rights of occupation affected, and that the

proceeds be disposed of in such way and used from time to time for such particular purposes as shall be agreed upon between the Government of Canada and the Tribe together with all those having rights of occupation.

13. That the fishing rights, hunting rights, and water rights of the Indian Tribes be fully adjusted. Our land rights having first been established by concession or decision we are willing that our general rights shall after full conference between the two Governments and the Tribes be adjusted by enactment of the Parliament of Canada.

14. That in connection with the adjustment of our fishing rights the matter of the international treaty recently entered into which very seriously conflicts with those rights be adjusted. We do not at present discuss the matter of fishing for commercial purposes. However, that matter may stand, we claim that we have a clear aboriginal right to take salmon for food. That right the Indian Tribes have continuously exercised from time immemorial. Long before the Dominion of Canada came into existence that right was guaranteed by Imperial enactment, the Royal Proclamation issued in the year 1763. We claim that under that Proclamation and another Imperial enactment, Section 109 of the British North America Act, the meaning and effect of which were explained by the Minister of Justice in the words set out above, all power held by the Parliament of Canada for regulating the fisheries of British Columbia is subject to our right of fishing. We therefore claim that the regulations contained in the treaty cannot be made applicable to the Indian Tribes, and that any attempt to enforce those regulations against the Indian Tribes is unlawful, being a breach of the two Imperial enactments mentioned.

15. That compensation be made in respect of the following particular matters:

(1) Inequalities of acreage or value or both that may be agreed to by any Tribe.

(2) Inferior quality of reserved lands that may be agreed to by any Tribe.

(3) Location of reserved lands other than that required agreed to by any Tribe.

(4) Damages caused to the timber or other natural resources of any reserved lands as for example by mining or smelting operations.

(5) All moneys expended by any Tribe in any way in connection with the Indian land controversy and the adjustment of all matters outstanding.

16. That general compensation for lands to be surrendered be made:

(1) By establishing and maintaining an adequate system of education, including both day schools and residential industrial schools, etc.

(2) By establishing and maintaining an adequate system of medical aid and hospitals.

17. That all compensations provided for by the two preceding paragraphs and all other compensation claimed by any Tribe so far may be found necessary be dealt with by enactment of the Parliament of Canada and be determined and administered in accordance with such enactment.

18. That all restrictions contained in the Land Act and other Statutes of the Province be removed.

19. That the Indian Act be revised and that all amendments of that Act required for carrying into full effect these conditions of settlement, dealing with the matter of citizenship, and adjusting all outstanding matters relating to the matter of citizenship,

and adjusting all outstanding matters relating to the administration of Indian affairs in British Columbia be made.

20. That all moneys already expended and to be expended by the Allied Tribes in connection with the Indian land controversy and all adjustment of all matters outstanding be provided by the Governments.

PART IV.—Concluding Remarks

In conclusion we may remark that we have been fully informed on all matters material to the preparation of this Statement, and have been advised on all matters which we considered required advice. We have conducted a full discussion of all points contained in the Statement, and have been careful to obtain the mind of all the principal Allied Tribes on all the principal points. These discussions have taken place at various large inter-tribal meetings held in different parts of the Province, together with a meeting of the Executive Committee. As result, we think we thoroughly understand the matters which have been under consideration. Having discussed all very fully, we now declare this Statement to be the well-settled mind of the Allied Tribes.

We have carefully limited our Statement of what we think should be conditions of settlement to those we think are really necessary. We are not pressing these conditions of settlement upon the Governments. If the Governments accept our basis and desire to enter into negotiations with us, we will be ready to meet them at any time. In this connection, however, we desire to make two things clear. Firstly, we are willing to accept any adjustment which may be arranged in a really equitable way, but we are not prepared to accept a settlement which will be a mere compromise. Secondly, we intend to continue pressing our case in the Privy Council until such time as we shall obtain a judgment, or until such time as the Governments shall have arrived at a basis of settlement with us.

To what we have already said we may add that we are ready at any time to give whatever additional information and explanation may be desired by the Governments for the further elucidation of all matters embraced in our Statement.

We may further add that the Allied Tribes as a whole and the Executive Committee are not professing to have the right and power to speak the complete mind of every one of the Allied Tribes on all matters, particularly those matters which specially affect them as Individual Tribes. Therefore, if the Governments should see fit to enter into negotiations with us, it might become necessary also to enter into negotiations regarding some matters with individual tribes.

We certify that the Statement above set out was adopted at a full meeting of the Executive Committee of the Allied Tribes of British Columbia held at Vancouver on the 12th day of November, 1919, and by the Sub-Committee of the Executive Committee on the 9th day of December in the same year.

PETER R. KELLY,

Chairman of Executive Committee
and member of Sub-Committee

J. A. TEIT

*Secretary of Executive Committee
and member of Sub-Committee*

5b.5 Deskaheh, *The Redman's Appeal for Justice*, 1923

Deskaheh or Hi-wyi-iss or Levi General (1873–1925), chief of the Younger Bear Clan, was born on the Six Nations Reserve on the Grand River in present-day southern Ontario to an Oneida mother and Cayuga father. Even though he received a Western education by Christian teachers in early childhood, he remained an adherent of Haudenosaunee (Iroquois) longhouse spirituality. By 1923, the Federal Government was making moves to replace traditional Haudenosaunee governing structures on the Six Nations Reserve with the elective system as prescribed by the Indian Act. On behalf of the Six Nations governing council, Deskaheh took his opposition to this and other government actions first to the British government in London and then to the League of Nations in Geneva to request their assistance. Deskaheh and the Haudenosaunee Confederacy were ultimately unsuccessful in these initiatives, and, in September of 1924, Prime Minister Mackenzie King and Governor General Byng signed an order in council replacing the traditional Haudenosaunee council. In December, acting on the order, the RCMP raided the Ohsweken Council House and the homes of wampum keepers, read the order, and confiscated documents and sacred belts.

Source: Deskaheh, *The Redman's Appeal for Justice* (London: Kealeys Limited, 1923).

THE REDMAN'S
APPEAL
FOR JUSTICE

———

The Honourable Sir James Eric Drummond, K.C.M.G., C.B., Secretary-General of the League of Nations, Geneva.

Sir,

Under the authority vested in the undersigned, the Speaker of the Council and the Sole Deputy by choice of the Council composed of forty-two chiefs, of the Six Nations of the Iroquois, being a state within the purview and meaning of Article 17 of the Covenant of the League of Nations, but not being at present a member of the League, I, the undersigned, pursuant to the said authority, do hereby bring to the notice of the League of Nations that a dispute and disturbance of peace has arisen between the State of the Six Nations of the Iroquois on the one hand and the British Empire and Canada, being Members of the League, on the other, the matters in dispute and disturbance of the peace being set out in paragraphs 10 to 17 inclusive hereof.

2. The Six Nations of the Iroquois crave therefore invitation to accept the obligations of Membership of the League for the purpose of such dispute; upon such conditions as may be prescribed.

3. The constituent members of the State of the Six Nations of the Iroquois, that is to say, the Mohawk, the Oneida, the Onondaga, the Cayuga, the Seneca and the Tuscarora, now are, and have been for many centuries, organised and self-governing peoples, respectively, within domains of their own, and united in the oldest League of Nations, the League of the Iroquois, for the maintenance of mutual peace; and that status has been recognised by Great Britain, France and the Netherlands, being European States which established colonies in North America; by the States successor to the British Colonies therein, being the United States of America, and by the Dominion of Canada, with whom the Six Nations have in turn treated, they being justly entitled to the same recognition by all other peoples.

4. Great Britain and the Six Nations of the Iroquois (hereinafter called "The Six Nations") having been in open alliance for upwards of one hundred and twenty years immediately preceding the Peace of Paris in 1783, the British Crowns in succession promised the latter to protect them against encroachments and enemies making no exception whatever, and King George the Third, falling into war with his own colonies in America, promised recompense of all losses which might be sustained by the Six Nations in consequence of their alliance in that war and they remain entitled to such protection as against the Dominion of Canada.

5. Pursuant to such alliance and to his promise of protection and recompense King George the Third, about the year 1784, acquired the territorial rights of the occupants of certain domains bordering the Grand River and Lake Erie, over which the Six Nations had exercised suzerain rights, and lying northerly of the boundary line then recently fixed between him and the United States of America, such rights of the occupants being so acquired by His Britannic Majesty to induce the Six Nations to remove to that domain as a common home-land in place of their separate ancient homes on the south of the line. Thereupon the Six Nations (excepting certain numbers of those people who elected to remain), at the invitation of the British Crown and under its express promise of protection, intended as security for their continued independence, moved across the Niagara and thereafter duly established themselves and their league in self-government upon the said Grand River lands, and they have ever since held the unceded remainder thereof as a separate and independent people, established there by sovereign right.

6. The Six Nations crave leave to refer, in support and verification of their status and position as an independent State, and of their recognition as such, to (inter alia) the following documents, facts and circumstances:—
The Treaties between the Six Nations and the Dutch.

The Treaties between the Six Nations and France.

The Treaties between the Six Nations and the British and particularly the treaty between the Mohawk and others of the Six Nations electing to become parties thereto, and the British under date of October 25th, 1784.

The Memorial of His Britannic Majesty's Government in support of the claim of the Cayuga Nation being one of the components of the Six Nations against the United States of America filed the 4th December, 1912, in the Arbitration of outstanding Pecuniary Claims between Great Britain and the United States.

In regard to the said Memorial, lastly referred to, the Six Nations desire particularly to note (inter alia) the following passage contained in the said Memorial:—"The Six Nations were recognised as independent nations and allies by the Dutch and afterwards by the English to whom the Dutch surrendered their possessions in 1664."

7. The Six Nations have at all times enjoyed recognition by the Imperial Government of Great Britain of their right to independence in home-rule, and to protection therein by the British Crown—the Six Nations on their part having faithfully discharged the obligations of their alliance on all occasions of the need of Great Britain, under the ancient covenant chain of friendship between them, including the occasion of the late World War.

8. Because of the desire of Great Britain to extend its colonial domain, and of the Six Nations to dispose of domain not deemed by them at the time as of future usefulness, the British Crown prior to 1867, the year in which the Dominion of Canada was established, obtained from the Six Nations cessions of certain parts of their Grand River domain for purpose of sale to British subjects, retaining, by consent of the Six Nations, the stipulated sale moneys for the cessions, but in express trust for the use of the Six Nations and the British Crown at the same time promised to pay to the Six Nations the interest moneys annually earned by those funds; but subsequently the Imperial Government of its sole accord handed over to the Dominion Government such funds, but for administration according to the terms of that trust and promise, and the fund is now in the actual possession of the Dominion Government, the beneficial rights remaining as before in the Six Nations.

9. The circumstances and causes leading up to the matters in dispute and the said matters in dispute are set out in the next following paragraphs.

10. The Parliament of the Dominion of Canada, in or about the year 1919, enacted a measure called an Enfranchisement Act amendatory of its Indian Act so-called, imposing or purporting to impose Dominion rule upon neighbouring Red men, and the administrative departments undertook to enforce it upon citizens of the Six Nations, and in the next year those departments undertook to apply Canadian laws for the tenure of private property to the remaining

territory of the Six Nations which had long before been sub-divided by and among the people thereof; and mortgages of proprietary title to those private parcels under those laws have recently been taken by authorised Officials of the Dominion from certain citizens of the Six Nations, tempted by loans of the public funds of Canada and, under cover of Canadian laws, but in violation of Six Nation Laws, administration over such titles and parcels has since been undertaken by various departments of the Dominion Government at the instance of the Mortgagees.

11. The Dominion Government is now engaged in enforcing upon the people of the Six Nations certain penal laws of Canada, and, under cover thereof, the Dominion Government is violating the Six Nation domain and has wrongfully seized therein many nationals of the Six Nations and cast them into Canadian prisons, where many of them are still held.

12. Large sums of the Six Nations' funds held by the Dominion Government have been misappropriated and wasted without consent of the Six Nations and misappropriation thereof is still being practised by the Dominion Government and accountings thereof, asked for by the Six Nations, have never been made.

13. All the measures aforesaid have been taken without the consent of the Six Nations, and under protest and continued protest of the duly constituted Council thereof, and with the manifest purpose on the part of the Dominion Government to destroy all de jure government of the Six Nations and of the constituent members thereof, and to fasten Canadian authority over all the Six Nations' domain, and to subjugate the Six Nation peoples, and these wrongful acts have resulted in a situation now constituting a menace to international peace.

14. The Dominion Government for the manifest purpose of depriving the Six Nations of means for self-defence, has withheld for three years last past moneys earned by the said trust funds, and is now disbursing the principal thereof, together with such earnings, for such objects as it sees fit, and has ignored the request of the Six Nations, recently made upon it, that the said funds in its hands be turned over to the Six Nations; and the Dominion Government, after firm opposition by the Six Nations to these aggressive measures, and for about two years last past, has been using these trust funds to incite rebellion within the Six Nations, to furnish occasion for setting up of a new Government for the Six Nations, tribal in form but devised by the Dominion Parliament and intended to rest upon Canadian authority under a Dominion Statute known as the "Indian Act."

15. To the manifest end of destroying the Six Nations Government, the Dominion Government did, without just or lawful cause, in or about December of the year 1922, commit an act of war upon the Six Nations by making an hostile invasion of the Six Nations domain, wherein the Dominion Government then established an armed force which it has since maintained therein, and

the presence thereof has impeded and impedes the Six Nations Council in the carrying on of the duly constituted government of the Six Nations people, and is a menace to international peace.

16. The aforesaid acts and measures of the Dominion Government are in violation of the nationality and independence of the Six Nations, and contrary to the successive treaties between the Six Nations and the British Crown, pledging the British Crown to protect the Six Nations; and especially in violation of the treaty pledge of October 25th, of the year 1784, of the same tenor, entered into between King George the Third of Great Britain and the Six Nations, hereinbefore referred to which, never having been abrogated by either party, remains in full force and effect and all of which were and are binding upon the British Crown and the British Dominion of Canada; and the said acts and measures were and are in violation as well of the recognised law of Nations, the Six Nations never having yielded their right of independence in home-rule to the Dominion of Canada, and never having released the British Crown from the obligation of its said covenants and treaties with them, but they have ever held and still hold the British Crown thereto.

17. In the month of August of the year 1921, the Six Nations made earnest application to the Imperial Government of Great Britain for the fulfilment on its part of its said promise of protection, and for its intervention thereunder to prevent the continued aggressions upon the Six Nations practised by the Dominion of Canada, but the Imperial Government refused.

18. The Six Nations have within the year last past and with the acquiescence of the Imperial Government of Great Britain, negotiated at length through its Council with the Government of the Dominion of Canada for arbitration of all the above-mentioned matters of dispute, when the Six Nations offered to join in submission of the same to impartial arbitration, and offered also to treat for establishing satisfactory relations, but those offers were not accepted.

19. The Six Nations refrained from engaging the armed Canadian troops, making the invasion aforesaid, in reliance on protection at the hands of the League of Nations under the peaceful policies of its covenant and they continue so to rely.

20. The Six Nations now invoke the action of the League of Nations to secure:—
    (1) Recognition of their independent right of home-rule.
    (2) Appropriate indemnity for the said aggressions for the benefit of their injured nationals.
    (3) A just accounting by the Imperial Government of Great Britain, and by the Dominion of Canada of the Six Nations trust funds and the interest thereon.
    (4) Adequate provisions to cover the right of recovery of the said funds and interest by the Six Nations.

(5) Freedom of transit for the Six Nations across Canadian territory to and from international waters.

(6) Protection for the Six Nations hereafter under the League of Nations, if the Imperial Government of Great Britain shall avow its unwillingness to continue to extend adequate protection or withhold guarantees of such protection.

The Six Nations invoke also the action of the League of Nations to secure interim relief as follows:—

(a) For securing from the Dominion of Canada for unrestricted use by the Six Nations, sufficient funds for the purposes of this application from the moneys of the Six Nations held in trust as aforesaid, the balance of which as admitted by the Dominion Government, approximates seven hundred thousand dollars, but which in truth largely exceeds that amount.

(b) For securing suspension of all aggressive practices by the Dominion of Canada upon the Six Nation peoples pending consideration of this application and action taken thereunder.

Done in behalf of the SIX NATIONS this Sixth day of August, in the year One Thousand nine hundred and twenty-three.

DESKAHEH,
Sole Deputy and Speaker of the Six Nations Council.

5b.6 Special Joint Committee of the Senate and House of Commons Appointed to Inquire into the Claims of the Allied Indian Tribes of British Columbia, 1926

As mentioned in the introduction to this section, a special joint committee of the Senate and House of Commons was appointed to inquire into the claims of the Allied Tribes in 1926. This short excerpt from the report of the committee is included here because it acts as a kind of bridge between the "Statement of the Allied Tribes" in 5b.4 and the Indian Act amendment of 1927 (see 5b.7). The full document includes testimony and questioning as members of the Allied Tribes reiterate and defend the position advanced in their statement, which was also reproduced in the committee's report. The special committee also heard representations from Duncan Campbell Scott and other government officials. Though brief, this excerpt is indicative of the views held by Canada and its politicians concerning the legitimacy of the claims not only of the Allied Tribes but also of the First Nations in Canada more generally. As mentioned in relation to other documents in this chapter as well, Canada and its representatives presented Indigenous grievances as originating from and advanced by external sources for nefarious purposes.

Source: Special Joint Committee of the Senate and House of Commons Appointed to Inquire into the Claims of the Allied Indian Tribes of British Columbia, as Set Forth in Their Petition Submitted to Parliament in June 1926, "Report and Evidence," *Appendix to the Journals of the Senate of Canada, 1926–27* (Ottawa: F.A. Acland, 1927), vii–viii.

... The fact was admitted that it was not until about fifteen years ago that aboriginal title was first put forward as a formal legal claim by those who ever since have made it a bone of contention and by some a source of livelihood as well.

The Committee note with regret the existence of agitation, not only in British Columbia, but with Indians in other parts of the Dominion, which agitation may be called mischievous, by which the Indians are deceived and led to expect benefits from claims more or less fictitious. Such agitation, often carried on by designing white men, is to be deplored, and should be discountenanced, as the Government of the country is at all times ready to protect the interests of the Indians and to redress real grievances where such are shown to exist.

. . .

5b.7 Amendment to the Indian Act, 1927

Following the growth of organized resistance and the parallel increase in the understanding of Canadian legal and political structures by Indigenous activists in the early part of the twentieth century, the Canadian government grew increasingly concerned that Indigenous grievances would find their way into Canadian courts and ultimately be presented to the Judicial Committee of the Privy Council. All court actions required financial support, though, and, in 1927, the Indian Act was amended to prevent the possibility of legal action.

Source: Canada, *Revised Statutes of Canada*, 1927, vol. II, ch. 98, s. 141.

141. Every person who, without the consent of the Superintendent General expressed in writing, receives, obtains, solicits or requests from any Indian any payment or contribution or promise of any payment or contribution for the purpose of raising a fund or providing money for the prosecution of any claim which the tribe or band of Indians to which such Indian belongs, or of which he is a member, has or is represented to have for the recovery of any claim or money for the benefit of the said tribe or band, shall be guilty of an offence and liable upon summary conviction for each such offence to a penalty not exceeding two hundred dollars and not less than fifty dollars or to imprisonment of any term not exceeding two months.

Receiving money for the prosecution of a claim.

SUGGESTIONS FOR FURTHER READING

For an evaluation of the work of Duncan Campbell Scott, the long-serving senior civil servant in the Department of Indian Affairs, an assessment that includes an interpretation of his views on Fred Loft and Indigenous political organization and his efforts toward assimilation, treaties, and the eradication of the potlatch, among other issues, see Brian Titley, *A Narrow Vision: Duncan Campbell Scott and the Administration of Indian Affairs in Canada* (Vancouver: UBC Press, 1986). For a brief exploration of the Six Nations response to the 1920 Indian Act amendments, the efforts of Deskaheh (Levi General) at the League of Nations, and Canada's restructuring of Haudenosaunee political organization and power, see Edward S. Rogers and Donald B. Smith, eds., *Aboriginal Ontario:*

Historical Perspectives on the First Nations (Toronto: Dundurn Press, 1994), 247–49. For an exploration of Indigenous political activism that focuses on Frederick Ogilvie Loft and the League of Indians, see Peter Kulchyski, "'A Considerable Unrest': F.O. Loft and The League of Indians," *Native Studies Review* 4, nos. 1 and 2 (1988): 95–115. For more on Loft, see Donald B. Smith, "Loft, Frederick Ogilivie," *Dictionary of Canadian Biography* XVI, 1931–1940, available at http://www.biographi.ca/en/bio.php?id_nbr=8419. For Donald Smith's entry in the *Dictionary of Canadian Biography* on Deskaheh (Levi General) see http://www.biographi.ca/en/bio/deskaheh_15E.html. For a work on Indigenous political organizing in British Columbia, see Paul Tennant, *Aboriginal Peoples and Politics: The Indian Land Question in British Columbia, 1849–1989* (Vancouver: UBC Press, 1989). Chapters 7 and 8 focus on the Royal Commission on Indian Affairs for the Province of British Columbia (the McKenna-McBride Commission), the Allied Tribes, and the 1927 amendment to the Indian Act. For a further examination of these issues, see Keith Smith, *Liberalism, Surveillance and Resistance: Indigenous Communities in Western Canada, 1877–1927* (Edmonton: University of Athabasca Press, 2009), especially pages 179–95. For background on the McKenna-McBride Commission, the impact it caused and its connection to more recent land claims activity, see the Union of BC Indian Chiefs, "Our Homes are Bleeding" Digital Collection at http://www.ubcic.bc.ca/Resources/ourhomesare/narratives/index.html. This collection also includes audio and video content featuring Indigenous activists and leaders, mostly from the 1970s, and a searchable database of transcripts of testimony presented by Indigenous people and their neighbours to the McKenna-McBride Commission between 1913 and 1916.

CHAPTER 6

"PLEASE DON'T BLAME YOURSELVES" [1]

RESIDENTIAL SCHOOLS

All of the Christian churches have now apologized for their involvement in residential schools. Prime Minister Stephen Harper, too, delivered an official apology in Parliament to residential school survivors on June 11, 2008. That same year, the Truth and Reconciliation Commission of Canada was formed with a five-year mandate to examine the documentary record and to hear testimony from those who had operated the schools as well as survivors and their families. The goal of the commission was to facilitate healing and eventually reconciliation and the inauguration of more positive relationships moving into the future. Only time will tell if the commission's efforts will be successful, but most see its work as a positive step.

Residential, industrial, or boarding schools for Indigenous children were in operation in Canada for over three centuries—from the first half of the seventeenth century until the last federally funded school, on the Gordon Reserve in the Touchwood Hills area of south central Saskatchewan, closed in 1996. The modern version of these schools came into being in the 1880s with institutions run by Anglican, Presbyterian, United, and Roman Catholic churches and funded by Canadian taxpayers. Over the course of their operation, the over 130 residential schools in Canada housed more than 150,000 children. Though pressure was always applied to parents to have them send their children to these schools, attendance became compulsory after 1920.

Residential schools were developed to further the objective of assimilation, discussed throughout this reader, by removing children from the influences of their families and working to supplant the structures, values, and beliefs of their people with Anglo-Canadian ones. Ideally, assimilated residential school graduates would then act as agents of assimilation themselves, promulgating their new-found understandings to their home

---

1 Imelda Brooks quoted in Isabelle Knockwood, *Out of the Depths*, 3rd ed. (Lockport, NS: Roseway Publishing, 2001), 157. This quotation appears in document 6.5.

communities. Because the officials of the Department of Indian Affairs and the churches feared that the influence of families and communities would reverse any steps made toward assimilation, vacations home and visits from parents were discouraged. Further, in many cases, visits in either direction were a practical impossibility for much of the late nineteenth and early twentieth century due to travel distances and restrictions on off-reserve movement, as discussed in Chapter 4. Making communication with pupils even more difficult was that church administrators often insisted that any correspondence home be written in English, which parents could rarely read.

Certainly, both parents and community leaders saw the benefit of having children educated in Euro-Canadian practices and in the functioning of their institutions. Often, though, residential schools offered substandard education and limited classroom time in favour of religious pursuits or manual labour that would help raise funds for the school. Further, as the overall goal was assimilation and not education in the sense offered to non-Indigenous students, teachers were chosen for their potential to advance this assimilative agenda, not necessarily for their professional teaching qualifications.

There were, and continue to be, complaints offered by students, family members, and others of poor food, overcrowding, and insufficient medical care. Some of these complaints are evident in the documents below. Students were taught that their cultures and lifestyles were inferior. Even worse are the reports of sexual abuse, shocking physical brutality, emotional cruelty, and many other forms of mistreatment perpetrated on children by the church officials running the schools. Removed from their families, students got no exposure to healthy family life and, all too often, passed on the trauma of the residential school experience to their own children. Thus began what is often referred to as the generational effect of the schools.

Even when graduates returned to their home communities, many found that they no longer fit in. Because their native language was forbidden at school, most could not carry on conversations with their parents or elders. Because many were emotionally unable to speak about their experiences at school, even with other survivors, they continued to suffer from isolation and its effects.

Even if one were to consider all the policies, laws, and institutions that Canadians have aimed at Indigenous people, it would be difficult to find a system that had a more dramatic effect on families and communities than the long-lived residential school system. There seems little doubt that the violent and lengthy assimilative venture undertaken by the residential, industrial, and boarding schools is one of the darkest chapters in all of Canadian history. Yet there are those, former students and commentators alike, who portray the schools in much more positive terms. They point to the acquisition of English language skills, which helped usher in a new era of Indigenous activism, and to other constructive outcomes of the schools. Undoubtedly, not all teachers and administrators were abusive, and many were involved out of the best of intentions, but, on balance, the systemic flaws in the residential school system and the reasons for its creation were overwhelmingly devastating to the students, their future families, and their communities.

The documents in this chapter cover the period from 1879 to 1920 and present a variety of perspectives on the schools. They include the reminiscences and views of two survivors from very different parts of the country. Taken together, they examine the reasons for creating the schools, some of the problems associated with their management, and several of the effects experienced by those who attended them. Readers may find it remarkable that even in this dark period, residential school students found creative ways to resist the authority of school administrators. As they did in the past, Indigenous families and communities today continue to educate their young people using the time proven methods of their communities, despite the array of forces concentrated to suppress and replace such practices.

QUESTIONS FOR DISCUSSION

1. What reasons does N.F. Davin give for the introduction of residential schools for Indigenous children? What examples do we have here of his views on Indigenous people?
2. What concerns regarding the schools are presented in the debates in the House of Commons? Explain whether or not these seem like the most important issues that could have been discussed in this forum?
3. What are P.H. Bryce's specific concerns? Do you think these concerns are legitimate, or is he just upset because he was forced to retire?
4. Isabelle Knockwood says her manuscript would be different if she had used books and archives. What would be different?
5. Who should "foot the revitalization bill" that Mary Carpenter talks about? Why?
6. What specific elements in the photographs of Thomas Moore represent his apparent assimilation?
7. In hindsight, what alternatives to residential schools could have been developed to prepare Indigenous children for a life that would include negotiating the institutions of settler society?

DOCUMENTS

6.1 N.F. Davin, Report on Industrial Schools, 1879

Nicholas Flood Davin (1840–1901) was born in Ireland but left for England in 1865. After being called to the bar and working for several years as a journalist in London, he moved to Toronto in 1872. In Canada, he continued this work but also did freelance writing and lecturing. Davin was a loyal Conservative, and, although he lost his first electoral contest for a federal seat in Ontario, he was rewarded with a patronage appointment to a one-person team to investigate industrial schools created for Indigenous children in the United States. The document below includes excerpts from Davin's confidential report to Minster of the Interior and Superintendent General of Indian Affairs John A. Macdonald. Davin's views on the character, nature, and abilities of Indigenous people come through quite clearly. Following this report, Davin moved west, became editor of the Regina Leader, *and served as a Conservative member of parliament.*

Source: N.F. Davin, "Report on Industrial Schools for Indians and Half-Breeds," 14 March 1879, Library and Archives Canada, MG 26A, Sir John A. Macdonald Papers, vol. 91, 35428, pp. 1–2 and 9–16, reel C-1518.

REPORT ON INDUSTRIAL SCHOOLS FOR
INDIANS AND HALF-BREEDS

OTTAWA, 11th March, 1879

To the Right Honourable
The Minster of the Interior.

SIR,—I have the honour to submit the following report on the working of Industrial Schools for the education of Indians and mixed-bloods in the United States, and on the advisability of establishing similar institutions in the North-West Territories of the Dominion.

In accordance with your directions of the twenty-eighth of January, I went to Washington. His Excellency Sir Edward Thornton, the Honourable Carl Schurtz, Secretary of the Interior, and the Honourable E.A. Hayt, the Commissioner of Indian Affairs, secured for me every facility for becoming acquainted with the establishment, cost and practical value of industrial schools among Indian populations of the United States.

The industrial school is the principal feature of the policy known as that of "aggressive civilization." This policy was inaugurated by President Grant in 1869. But, as will be seen, the utility of industrial schools had long ere that time been amply tested. Acting on the suggestion of the President, Congress passed a law early in 1869, providing for the appointment of the Peace Commission. This Commission recommended that the Indians should, as far as practicable, be consolidated on few reservations, and provided with "permanent individual homes"; that the tribal relation should be abolished; that lands should be allotted in severalty and not in common; that the Indian should speedily become a citizen of the United States, enjoy the protection of the law, and be made amenable thereto; that, finally, it was the duty of the Government to afford the Indians all reasonable aid in their preparation for citizenship by educating them in industry and in the arts of civilization. After eight years' experience of the partial carrying out of these recommendations, the Board pressed for a still more thorough policy; they urged, among other things, that titles to land should be inalienable from the family of the holder for at least three generations. From 1869 vigorous efforts in an educational direction were put forward. But it was found that the day-school did not work, because the influence of the wigwam was stronger than the influence of the school. Industrial Boarding Schools were therefore established, and these are now numerous and will soon be universal. The cry from the Agencies where no boarding industrial schools have been established is persistent and earnest to have the want supplied.

The experience of the United States is the same as our own as far as the adult Indian is concerned. Little can be done with him. He can be taught to do a little at farming, and at stock-raising, and to dress in a more civilized manner, but that is all. The child, again, who goes to a day school learns little, and what little he learns is soon forgotten, while his tastes are fashioned at home, and his inherited aversion to toil is in no way combated.

There are two ways of conducting the industrial schools. In the one, the Government carries on the school through the Agency; the other, by contract. A contract is made, for instance, with the Episcopal Church authorities, or the Roman Catholic Church authorities, or with the authorities of any other body of Christians, to carry on an industrial boarding school among the Indians. One hundred and twenty-five dollars a year is paid for each pupil boarder, when the attendance at the school does not exceed thirty; in larger schools, one hundred dollars; and even less when the school is of considerable size. The Honourable the Commissioner of Indian Affairs is not in favour of the contract system, because the children at schools under contract do not, as a rule, get a sufficient quantity of food. The contractor, in addition to supplying the food, prepares the clothing, the raw material of which is found by the Government. The Commissioner was emphatic in his testimony as to the happy results which had attended the industrial schools wherever established. . . .

At Winnipeg, I met most of the leading men, clerical and lay, who could speak with authority on the subject of the inquiry, and to the experience, knowledge and courtesy of Mgr. Taché, Pere Lacombe, Hon. Jas. McKay, and many others, this report is much indebted.

Among the Indians there is some discontent, but as a rule it amounts to no more than the chronic querulousness of the Indian character, and his uneasiness about food at this time of year will unfortunately leave no trace in his improvident mind when spring opens and fish are plentiful. The exceptions are furnished by one or two chiefs whose bands are starving, that is in the Indian sense of that word, without a certain prospect of food in the future. Distress will always exist among improvident people, and undoubtedly distress and misery exist in many Bands. The attitude of the chiefs referred to, and the language held by the chief on the occasion of a visit to the St. Peter's Reservation—language which showed that he was in communication with the unsettled Bands—open up, in the event of the disappearance of the buffalo (a disappearance no protective legislation can long retard), a prospect which demands the serious consideration of the Department. No race of men can be suddenly turned from one set of pursuits to another set of a wholly different nature without great attendant distress. But, suddenly, to make men long accustomed to a wild unsettled life, with its freedom from restraint, its excitement and charm, take to the colourless monotony of daily toil, the reward of which is prospective, is impossible.

The half-breeds or mixed-bloods are thoughtful, if not anxious, regarding the Government's intentions respecting them. But the problem before the Department cannot be settled by the issue of scrip. That problem can be solved only by gradually educating Indians and mixed-bloods in self-reliance and industry.

. . .

The lesson would also be taught, were that lesson necessary, that the mixed-blood or half-breed is a man of capacity, intelligence and power. But that lesson does not need to be taught in the Dominion, where we have leading barristers and competent statesmen from that interesting and useful class of our fellow-citizens. The Indian himself is a noble type of man, in a very early stage of development. His temperament is for the most part lymphatic. That temperament might or might not be modified by advance in civilization in the course of generations. This temperament, united with the nervous or nervo-sanguine temperament of Saxon or Celt, a type is produced of great staying power, often highly intellectual, vigorous, of quick perceptions and large resource.

There is now barely time to inaugurate a system of education by means of which the native populations of the North-West shall be gradually prepared to meet the necessities of the not distant future; to welcome and facilitate, it may be hoped, the settlement of the country; and to render its government easy and not expensive.

I would respectfully warn the Department against listening to alarmists who would press them to act in a manner which would develop, with tropical rapidity, in every chief, the pestilent character of the demagogue. But as far as we can judge from approximate returns, there are some twenty-eight thousand Indians in the seven territorial divisions covered by treaty. There are about twelve hundred half-breed families. Chief Beardy and Big Bear are malcontent. Beardy's Band is put down in the official returns as not more than thirty-nine. His Band is, however, many times larger than this. We have warlike and excited refugees within our territory. A large statesmanlike policy, with bearings on immediate and remote issues, cannot be entered on too earnestly or too soon.

The Indian character, about which some persons fling such a mystery, is not difficult to understand. The Indian is sometimes spoken of as a child, but he is very far from being a child. The race is in its childhood. As far as the childhood analogy is applicable, what it suggests is a policy that shall look patiently for fruit, not after five or ten years, but after a generation or two. The analogy is misleading when we come to deal with the adult, and is of course a mere truism and not a figure of speech when we take charge of the Indian in the period of infancy. There is, it is true, in the adult, the helplessness of mind of the child, as well as the practical helplessness; there is, too, the child's want of perspective; but there is little of the child's receptivity; nor is the child's tractableness always found. One of the prime conditions of childhood is absent—the abeyance of the passions. Anybody who has tried to educate grownup civilized men, with untrained minds, as are the minds of most civilized men, will understand the disturbing and dwarfing influence of the complex interests which crowd in on the adult. The Indian is a man with traditions of his own, which make civilization a puzzle of despair. He has the suspicion, distrust, fault-finding tendency, the insincerity and flattery, produced in all subject races. He is crafty, but conscious how weak his craft is when opposed to the superior cunning of the white man. Not to speak of him—even some of the half-breeds of high intelligence are incapable of embracing the idea of a nation—of a national type of man—in which it should be their ambition to be merged and lost. Yet he realises that he must disappear, and realizing this, and unable to associate himself with the larger and nobler idea, the motive power which inspired a Pontiac and a Tecumseh, is absent. The Indian's stolidity is in part assumed, in part the stupor produced by external novel and distasteful conditions, and in both respects has been manifested in white races at periods of helplessness and ignorance, of subjection to, and daily contact with, the power and superior skill and refinement of more advanced races, or even more advanced branches of the same race. We need not, therefore, recall the names of Indian heroes to make us respect the latent capacities of the red man. We have only to look to the rock whence we were hewn. The Indian, I repeat, is not a child, and he is the last person that should be dealt with in a childish way. He requires firm, bold, kindly handling and boundless patience. He exacts, and surely not unreasonably, scrupulous honesty. There ought to be a special exemplary punishment provided for those persons who, when employed by the Government to supply the Indian with stores, cheat him.

It would be travelling beyond the record to comment on our Indian policy and our treaties with the Indians, though I have formed very decided opinions respecting both. But this remark is pertinent. Guaranteeing schools as one of the considerations for surrendering the title to land, was, in my opinion, trifling with a great duty and placing the Government in no dignified attitude. It should have been assumed that the Government would attend to its proper and pressing business in this important particular. Such a guarantee, moreover, betrays a want of knowledge of the Indian character. It might easily have been realized, (it is at least unthinkable), that one of the results would be to make the Chiefs believe they had some right to a voice regarding the character and management of the schools, as well as regarding the initiatory step of their establishment. Chief Prince is giving some trouble on this head. There are cases where a denominational would be more suitable than a secular school, and *vice versa*; there are other cases where no Government school is needed, and where the true policy is to utilize the mission schools. The establishment and conduct of schools are matters which should have been left in a position to be considered apart from the disturbing, and sometimes designing predilections of a Chief; the needs and aptitudes of the settlement are alone worthy of being weighed. The moment there exists a settlement which has any permanent character, then education in some form or other should be brought within reach of the children. This is not merely a matter of policy. It is that, of course, in the highest degree. It is a sacred duty.

One ill result of promising the Indians schools, is that the Church Missionary Society is withdrawing its aid to the mission schools—a step which adds to conditions already sufficiently imperative, calling for a prudent, far-seeing and vigorous educational policy.

The first and greatest stone in the foundation of the quasi-civilization of the Indians, wherever seen, was laid by missionaries, men who had a supreme object and who did not count their lives dear unto them. Schools are scattered over the whole continent, wherever Indians exist, monuments of religious zeal and heroic self-sacrifice. These schools should be utilized as much as possible, both on grounds of efficiency and economy. The missionaries' experience is only surpassed by their patient heroism, and their testimony, like that of the school teachers, like that of the authorities at Washington is, that if anything is to be done with the Indian, we must catch him very young. The children must be kept constantly within the circle of civilized conditions. Mgr. Taché in his work, "Sketch of the North-West of America"—points out that the influence of civilized women has issued in superior characteristics in one portion of the native population. This influence in and out of the school must be constantly present in the early years. "Hitherto," says Mr. Meeker, a man who could speak with authority of a large portion of the Indians of the United States, "young men have been boarded and clothed and instructed, but in time they were off to the hunting ground. The plan now is to take young children, give them the care of a mother, and have them constantly in hand." Such care must go *pari passu* with religious training.

There are, as we have seen, some twelve hundred families of half-breeds—or mixed-bloods—in the North-West. Some of these are men of education and set-tled pursuits. But the great majority of them live under conditions which turn on the vanishing axle-tree of the buffalo's existence. It is no reproach to these men and their children to say that they will require training, whether supplied from within or without, before they can happily and effectively settle down as farmers. Archbishop Taché's sketch of the virtues and vices of the mixed bloods (*Sketch of the North-West of America*, pp. 98–110) a sketch drawn at once by a masterly and loving hand, can leave no doubt on the mind that training will be needed. Nor, as I have said, is this a reproach. The same thing has been true of men belonging to the best white races, and in modern times. The mixed-blood has already in high development many of those virtues which would make him a useful official, where activity, intelligence, horsemanship and fidelity were required. But if the mixed-blood is to hold his own in the race for existence, which will soon be exigent, in lands where, even yet, for the greater part of the year, primeval silence reigns, it is not enough that he should know all the arts of the voyageur and trader; not enough even that he should be able to do a little farming; he must be educated, and become susceptible to the bracing influences of complex wants and varied ambitions.

I should recommend, at once, an extensive application of the principle of industrial boarding schools in the North-West, were it not that the population, both Indian and half-breed, is so largely migratory that any great outlay at present would be money thrown away.

The recommendations I venture to submit are as follows:—

(1) Wherever the missionaries have schools, those schools should be utilized by the Government, if possible; that is to say, a contract should be made with the religious body controlling the school to board and educate and train industrially a certain number of pupils. This should be done without interfering with the small assistance at present given to the day mission schools.

(2) Not more than four industrial boarding schools ought to be established at first. If the Department should determine to establish more than four, the Reservation recommended by Mr. McColl, (Appendix B.) [not included] would possess many advantages. Here the population is settled and to some extent civilized. The soil is rich. The Missionary Society is withdrawing its aid from the school, which will henceforth be dependent on Government aid, and voluntary contributions. The Rev Mr. Cook assured me that here there would be no difficulty in getting a sufficient number of children from eight years old to twelve to attend the boarding industrial school.

(3) An industrial boarding school should be established somewhere in the fork of the North and South Saskatchewan, near Prince Albert, in connection with the Episcopalian Church. The land is wonderfully fertile. There are a good many Indians in the neighborhood. There are Bands of Indians near Carlton and near Dutch Lake. There is plenty of fish and timber.

(4) In no place could an industrial boarding school in connection with the Methodist body be more properly placed than near Old Bow Fort. The Blackfeet and Stoneys, wild but noble types of Indians, would thus be reached. There are numbers of good places between the Saskatchewan and the Athabasca rivers; but the needs in those quarters are not so pressing, as the Methodists and Roman Catholics have here been very successful, the boarding school principle having been tried with great success by the Roman Catholics in at least one instance. The want in the Blackfeet country is pressing. A Wesleyan mission exists to the east of Old Bow Fort. Timber and fish are at hand, and a vast tract of the finest grazing soil in the world. There ought to be no difficulty here, in a few years, in rivalling the Cheyenne and Arapho Agency with its promising herd.

(5) At Qu'Appelle it might well be thought we should find an appropriate site for an industrial boarding school to be conducted by Roman Catholics. The soil, it is true, is generally poor, but where the river narrows it leaves a good deal

of fair land. To the north is Touchwood, a trading post of the Hudson Bay Co. Around are lakes in which much fish is found, and when the buffalo is gone the Indians will flock hither to fish. A good many half-breeds are here now. It is a central point. Roads run south and west and north. The Blackfeet country, or that covered by Treaty 7, is sure to be a great grazing country in the not distant future. The advantages of the route thence to Qu'Appelle, on and alongside of the river, are unmistakeable. There is a permanent settlement. There is also a Roman Catholic mission. But there is no timber, and it is said the frosts menace the crops; but this is true of a good many other places where men, not with bad results, take the risks; and, notwithstanding these last drawbacks, I should have recommended Qu'Appelle as a site for a Roman Catholic industrial boarding school, were it not that other considerations of a weighty nature point to Buffalo Lake or some spot on the Red Deer River running by it. The advantages of Qu'Appelle should, however, be utilized in the near future, either on the contract system, or by means of a boarding school, immediately controlled by the Government, on a denominational or secular basis. On the shores of Buffalo Lake the school would have the advantage of being removed far from possible contact with whites for many years at least. Timber is sufficiently near along the river to the east and west. The land, I am assured, is good. The most pressing considerations of workableness point to those shores as the site for a Roman Catholic boarding industrial school.

(6) An industrial boarding school, in connection with the Presbyterian Church, should be established on Riding Mountain. The Presbyterans [sic] have already been very successful here. There is plenty of timber and the land is excellent. There is, it is true, no abundant supply of fish in the Little Saskatchewan. In all other respects, however, the locality is every thing that could be desired. The Indians here are represented as intelligent, and the children eager to acquire.

The importance of denominational schools at the outset for the Indians must be obvious. One of the earliest things an attempt to civilize them does, is to take away their simple Indian mythology, the central idea of which, to wit, a perfect spirit, can hardly be improved on. The Indians have their own ideas of right and wrong, of "good" Indians and "bad" Indians, and to disturb this faith, without supplying a better, would be a curious process to enlist the sanction of civilized races whose whole civilization, like all the civilizations with which we are acquainted, is based on religion. A civilized sceptic, breathing, though he does, an atmosphere charged with Christian ideas, and getting strength unconsciously therefrom, is nevertheless, unless in instances of rare intellectual vigour, apt to be a man without ethical backbone. But a savage sceptic would be open to civilizing influences and moral control only through desires, which, in the midst of enlightenment, constantly break out into the worst features of barbarism. Where, however, the poor Indian has been brought face to face with polemics and settlements are divided, or think they are divided, on metaphysical niceties, the school should be, as at the White Earth Agency, Minnesota, undenominational.

(7) Some distinction should be made between the treatment of parents who send their children regularly to the day-school, and of those who are either careless whether their children go to school or not, or who are wholly opposed to their children attending school, as some are. To the first, an additional ration of tea and sugar might be given.

(8) Where practicable, some inducement of a special nature should be held out to the child.

(9) As Bands become more amenable to the restraints of civilization[,] education should be made compulsory.

(10) The character of the teacher, morally and intellectually, is a matter of vital importance. If he is morally weak, whatever his intellectual qualifications may be, he is worse than no teacher at all. If he is poorly instructed or feeble in brain, he only enacts every day an elaborate farce. It must be obvious that to teach semi-civilized children is a more difficult task than to teach children with inherited aptitudes, whose training is, moreover, carried on at home. A teacher should have force of character, and when he presides over an industrial school should have a knowledge of farming. Such a man must be adequately paid. The advantage of calling in the aid of religion is, that there is a chance of getting an enthusiastic person, with, therefore, a motive power beyond anything pecuniary remuneration could supply. The work requires not only the energy but the patience of an enthusiast. The teacher's appointment to an industrial boarding school should be made by the Government, after consultation with the religious body immediately interested, and the whole machinery should be carefully guarded against the suspicion of having any character of religious endowment, or any likelihood of issuing therein.

(11) In order to secure that the education given would be efficient, there ought to be competent inspection. Failing this, when industrial boarding schools come to be widely established, large sums will be thrown into the sea. The education given in Indian schools is, as a rule, of a very poor sort, mechanical to the last degree.

(12) Where boys or girls, whether Indian or half-breed, show special aptitudes or exceptional general quickness, special advantages should be offered them, and they should be trained to become teachers and clerks in connection with the Department, as well as fitted to launch out on commercial and professional careers.

(13) The salary of a teacher must be such as will induce good men to offer themselves. The teacher should be paid according to his qualifications. In the future, when the manual labour boarding school is an established institution, those teachers who manage their schools in a manner tending towards self-support, should have a percentage on the reduction in the cost of management.

I have the honour to be,

Sir,

Your obedient servant,

NICHOLAS FLOOD DAVIN.

6.2 House of Commons Debates, 1920

Though there were other topics related to Indigenous people discussed in the House of Commons on June 8, 1920, this selection includes the entirety of the debate on the appropriation for "Indian Schools" held that day. This exchange is indicative of the extent to which there was debate on the appropriateness of boarding, industrial, or residential schools for Indigenous children and what shape that debate took. The discussion concludes with an exchange between two Conservatives over spending for a more advanced education for Indigenous children. The either/or attitude presented hints at the tension between class and race and how members of disadvantaged groups can be, and were, played off against one another.

Participants here are Conservative Minister of the Interior and Superintendent General of Indian Affairs Arthur Meighen, representing Portage la Prairie, Manitoba; Daniel McKenzie a Liberal representing the North Cape Breton and Victoria constituency in Nova Scotia; Jacques Bureau, a Liberal from Trois-Rivières and St. Maurice in Quebec; William F. Cockshutt, Conservative, representing Brantford, Ontario; Henri Sévérin Beland, a Liberal from Beauce, Quebec; and John Best, Conservative, representing Dufferin, Ontario.

Source: Canada. House of Commons, *Debates*, 8 June 1920, pp. 3277–80.

Indian education, $1,064,425.

MR. [DANIEL DUNCAN] MCKENZIE: In our part of the country we find that the Indian's capacity for education is rather circumscribed. The Indian child is able to read and write pretty well and has a fair knowledge of arithmetic, but the teachers tell me that beyond that, in the field of English grammar, composition, history, etc., it shows an aversion to concentrated study. I should like to know how the Indians in the West get on, and what results are obtained from their educational training.

MR. [ARTHUR] MEIGHEN: As regards the day schools in the West, I fear there has not been any great success. The chief difficulty has been to get the Indian child to attend with sufficient regularity to make progress. The boarding school is the proper system of Indian education for Western Canada. In the boarding school I have never heard of any special class of subjects in which the Indians are deficient or in which, indeed, they are not the equal of the white children, if they would attend with the same regularity and give the same attention to their studies. I have discussed the matter very frequently with teachers in those Indian schools and they speak in the highest terms of the capacity of the Indian children as a general rule. But the great trouble is that just as soon as the child gets out his tendency is to revert back to the reserve. Those of his own blood are not earning their living out in the world and he has not his own class with whom he can associate outside; consequently his tendency is to go back to the reserve, and in a short time the value of his education is largely lost. That fact also has a bearing on the question of the wisdom of encouraging and enabling the Indian to the utmost extent possible, consistent with his own fitness, to be enfranchised and be out away from the reserve fighting his way in the world like other people. Undoubtedly, the education will help the Indian children when they come out of the Indian school for they will be equipped, so far as education goes, to make a living.

MR. [JACQUES] BUREAU: A question was asked by the hon. member for Last Mountain (Mr. Johnston) as to the appropriation for a particular school, and the letter which he read showed a pitiful condition of things in that school. Now, the amount we are asked to vote is $1,064,415 for 34,000 people.

MR. [ARTHUR] MEIGHEN: Over 100,000.

MR. [JACQUES] BUREAU: The total population of Indians?

MR. [ARTHUR] MEIGHEN: Yes.

MR. [JACQUES] BUREAU: Are these schools built on the reserves? I had the impression the schools were on the reserves?

MR. [ARTHUR] MEIGHEN: Boarding schools usually are on the reserves but not always. There is an Indian boarding school at Portage la Prairie and that is not on a reserve, but they usually are on reserves.

MR. [JACQUES] BUREAU: The policy, as I understand the minister, of improving the condition of the Indian is to take him away from the habits and environment he has on the reserve would not seem to help to improve the Indian very fast, if the idea is to take him away from his environment. Suppose a white child were to go amongst Indians and to live with them. Although he is supposed to be superior to the Indians he would have a hard time of it if he were not allowed to go back among white people again. It seems hard—I will not say cruel—to take an Indian child away from his people and to mix him up with white people in one of these schools. If it is necessary, in order to improve the condition of the Indian, to take him away from his environment and to place him in one of these schools, it would be well that the schools should be outside of the reserve. But on the other hand, from a purely humanitarian point of view it would be cruel to take that child from the reserve and put him among white people without giving him a chance to go back to his people and choose the life he would like to live. Does this amount of over a million dollars that we are asked to vote include buildings, or the improvement of the schools? Or is it just for the purpose of carrying on the schools and paying the teachers and various staffs? If so it seems to be rather a large amount for the number of schools under the control of the department.

MR. [ARTHUR] MEIGHEN: It is exactly the same as last year, and certainly it is none too much; we would like to be able to afford more. There ought to be more Indian boarding schools built and we would like to build the one in Last Mountain if we could afford to undertake it with the money in hand, as well as others equally urgent.

MR. [JACQUES] BUREAU: How many are there? Take Manitoba where the population is the largest.

MR. [ARTHUR] MEIGHEN: In Manitoba there are 39 day schools and 8 boarding schools; in Quebec 28 day schools and no boarding schools. Day schools seem to be a success in Eastern Canada at all events.

MR. [HENRI SÉVÉRIN] BELAND: Is the school at Qu-Appelle a boarding school?

MR. [ARTHUR] MEIGHEN: It is an industrial school. It really is a boarding school.

MR. [HENRI SÉVÉRIN] BELAND: Is not that one of the best Indian schools you have now?

MR. [ARTHUR] MEIGHEN: It is out of the Qu'Appelle school that the File Hills colony has come. The File Hills colony is undoubtedly a phenomenal success. The number of day schools in the Dominion is 248, boarding schools 58, industrial schools 16, total 322. This is a vote for the maintenance of these schools.

MR. [JACQUES] BUREAU: It is not too much.

MR. [ARTHUR] MEIGHEN: And for the construction of such school buildings as are contemplated for next year.

MR. [JACQUES] BUREAU: And the maintenance of the old schools?

MR. [ARTHUR] MEIGHEN: The maintenance of the whole of them.

MR. [JACQUES] BUREAU: Is it not possible to comply with the request of the hon. member for Last Mountain (Mr. Johnston) under the conditions existing there? It seems a pitiful state of things if the letter contains the truth.

MR. [ARTHUR] MEIGHEN: It was not altogether right; it was not up to date in some respects.

MR. [JACQUES] BUREAU: Out of this amount will there be any money which can be used to improve the condition there?

MR. [ARTHUR] MEIGHEN: No.

MR. [JACQUES] BUREAU: Is there any other amount which will be used for that purpose.

MR. [ARTHUR] MEIGHEN: No.

MR. [WILLIAM FOSTER] COCKSHUTT: Before passing from the question of the education of the Indians, I would like to make a few remarks in regard to the Indians in the county of Brant. We have there the largest number of Indians to be found on any one reserve in Canada, or in North America—I think about 4,500. The hon. member for North Cape Breton (Mr. McKenzie) raised a question about them being circumscribed in their education. I have been in very close touch with a good many of the Indians and I think that does not apply to this tribe. The Six Nation Indians are amongst the most intelligent, if not the most intelligent, on the North American continent and they are capable of a very fine education if they have the opportunity. I know that in several instances they have taken very important positions almost immediately after they have passed out of the public schools. I heard of one last week who entered on a commercial course and, just fresh from school, received a salary of $20 per week for her services. That goes to show that if the Indian has a fair chance he is capable of very substantial advancement. I would like to know if there is any fund, or whether there can be any fund, provided for those Indian boys and girls, who wish to push on beyond the common school and take a high school course. There are some few in our city who are taking the high school course at the present time. There has been a contention between the city and the county as to who shall pay the fees of these children coming in from the Mohawk institution and from the reserve and completing their course in the high school of the city. The city keeps up the high school and it is customary to charge country pupils for the education they receive. It appears to me that if the department wishes to advance the education of Indian children there should be a fund provided that might be drawn upon in order that these boys and girls who have got as far as they can in the common school have an opportunity of prosecuting their studies farther in the high schools of Ontario particularly. I am not sure that any fund of that kind exists; I have not heard of it. But I know that recently there has been quite a sharp controversy in the county of Brant on that very point. I would like the minister to say whether or not there is an opportunity for those who wish to take the higher branches that are taught in the high schools and collegiate institutes, where the parents are not able to pay the fees, and whether the department has a fund out of which it can pay a whole or a part of the expenses of those students while they pursue the higher branches of education. I feel certain that if these facilities were extended and if such a fund were provided, a very large number of children on the Six Nations Indian Reserve would take advantage of it, and that a large number of them would take a place among the most advanced of the white population. I am sure they have the capacity to do that and we only need to look to what has been accomplished in the last generation for confirmation of my statement. One Indian at least became one of the foremost citizens of Toronto and received a salary of $12,000 a year as head of the Independent Order of Foresters.

DR. [HENRI SÉVÉRIN] BELAND: Oronhyatekha.

MR. [WILLIAM FOSTER] COCKSHUTT: He was a well known Indian, a credit to the country and to the reserve from which he came. I mention that case in order that the committee may realize that there are sons of the soil among our own original population who are capable of the highest education. I certainly think that the department, if they desire to encourage higher education, should make it easy for these scholars who wish to press on from the common schools of the reserve or the country schools which they attend, and to go to collegiate institutes and high schools and that, if necessary, a fund should be provided to help them while they are passing through. I believe in many cases you will find that no inconsiderable number of Indians have made their way in the world by reason of education they have received. I know several of them from our reserve that have gone to New York, and other great cities of [the] United States, and hold very high positions indeed at very fine remuneration. I feel confident that the Six Nations Indian is capable of higher education to a considerable extent, and if the minister would give us assurances that they would be treated a little more liberally with regard to the fees in these higher branches of education I feel confident that more of them would take advantage of it.

AN HON. MEMBER: Have they got a vote?

MR. [WILLIAM FOSTER] COCKSHUTT: Some of them have the vote. I believe that of the number that went overseas nearly four hundred had the vote, and that nearly all of them voted at the last election. That is a matter, though, that does not particularly concern myself as they belong to the North Riding of Brant. I am speaking now on behalf of the Indian, and I trust the minister will give that feature to which I have alluded his serious consideration so that those Indians who desire to pursue the higher branches of education should be induced to do so.

MR. [ARTHUR] MEIGHEN: There are quite a number of Indians, particularly of the Six Nations reserve, who do desire and do obtain a high school education. With respect to that reserve, the Indian parents for the most part, are quite capable financially of supplying their children with that education, and as to them the department has merely encouraged the attendance of those children at school by awarding scholarships to help them through. But there are others, fewer in number, who are not in the same position, and in those cases the department has always sympathetically received any application for help, and a large number of pupils are being helped by the department in the securing of a high school education at the present time. The ear of the department has been sympathetic to the ambitions of any pupils whose parents are not able to provide them with the fees and the necessary books for the purpose.

MR. [JOHN] BEST: I realize that many of these Indians are capable of a very high education, but in view of the conditions in which the finances of the country are to-day I hope the minister will not for one moment think of laying aside tens or hundreds of thousands of dollars for any such purpose. I have brought to the notice of some of the departments instances where the parents of young white men,—young men who went overseas and fought for this country—were poor and were not able to put their sons through high school; these had to do the best they could to get through. Why then should we set aside hundreds of thousands of dollars to give higher education to young Indians when our own white people cannot put themselves through? I realize that many Indians went overseas and fought for the Empire and we ought to treat them just the same as we would any other class of people, but we are not in a financial position to do what has been suggested; and to my mind no hon. member should get up here and advocate that we pay out a lot of unnecessary money for this purpose. I believe in fair play to every one in the Dominion, but I am also of the opinion that if we were to do more to assist our white people we would better serve the interests of our country. There is no doubt whatever that the sons of poor people are just as capable of learning as the sons of the rich; but in many cases they have to do without the education they need because they are not able to put themselves through. I hope the minister will not for one moment consider laying aside hundreds of thousands of dollars for any such purpose as suggested.

MR. [WILLIAM FOSTER] COCKSHUTT: Who is asking for hundreds of thousands of dollars?

MR. [JOHN] BEST: Well the hon. member advocated the expenditure of money for this purpose.

. . .

6.3 P.H. Bryce, *The Story of a National Crime*, 1920

Peter Henderson Bryce (1853–1932) worked as secretary of Ontario's Board of Health for over 20 years before being appointed as medical inspector for the Department of the Interior and the Department of Indian Affairs in 1904. In this capacity, and at the request of the deputy superintendent general of Indian affairs, Bryce carried out a thorough investigation of residential schools in the Prairie Provinces. He found that the conditions in the schools were so dangerous that they threatened health in Indigenous communities throughout the Prairie West. From Bryce's perspective, his concerns went largely unheeded and his recommendations remained unrealized. After he was forced out of his position in 1921, Bryce went public and published the document presented here. It is an important publication for what it says about the schools but also for its information about Canada's provision of health care and preventative services to Indigenous communities. It is included in its entirety here with the exception of the epilogue, which contains the reasons Bryce should not have been forced to retire.

Source: P.H. Bryce, *The Story of a National Crime: Being an Appeal for Justice to the Indians of Canada; the Wards of the Nation, Our Allies in the Revolutionary War, Our Brothers-in-Arms in the Great War* (Ottawa: James Hope & Sons, 1922), 3–14.

THE STORY OF A NATIONAL CRIME
BEING A

Record of the Health Conditions of the Indians of Canada from 1904 to 1921

–BY–
DR. P. H. BRYCE, M. A., M. D.
Chief Medical Officer of the Indian Department.

I. By Order in Council dated Jan. 22nd, 1904, the writer was appointed Medical Inspector to the Department of the Interior and of Indian Affairs, and was entrusted with the health interests of the Indians of Canada. The Order in Council recites:—

The undersigned has the honour to report that there is urgent necessity for the appointment of a medical inspector to represent the Department of the Interior and Department of Indian Affairs. The undersigned believes that the qualifications for the position above mentioned are possessed in an eminent degree by Mr. Peter Henderson Bryce, M. D., at present and for a number of years past Secretary for the Provincial Board of Health of Ontario, and who has had large experience in connection with the public health of the province.

(Signed) CLIFFORD SIFTON,
Minister of the Interior and
Superintendent General of Indian Affairs.

For the first months after the writer's appointment he was much engaged in organizing the medical inspection of immigrants at the sea ports; but he early began the systematic collection of health statistics of the several hundred Indian Bands scattered over Canada. For each year up to 1914 he wrote an annual report on the health of the

Indians, published in the Departmental report, and on instructions from the minister made in 1907 a special inspection of thirty-five Indian schools in the three prairie provinces. This report was published separately; but the recommendations contained in the report were never published and the public knows nothing of them. It contained a brief history of the origin of the Indian Schools, of the sanitary condition of the schools and statistics of the health of the pupils, during the 15 years of their existence. Regarding the health of the pupils, the report states that 24 per cent. of all the pupils which had been in the schools were known to be dead, while of one school on the File Hills reserve, which gave a complete return to date, 75 per cent. were dead at the end of the 16 years since the school opened.

Briefly the recommendation urged, (1) Greater school facilities, since only 30 per cent. of the children of school age were in attendance; (2) That boarding schools with farms attached be established near the home reserves of the pupils; (3) That the government undertake the complete maintenance and control of the schools, since it had promised by treaty to insure such; and further it was recommended that as the Indians grow in wealth and intelligence they should pay at least part of the cost from their own funds; (4) That the school studies be those of the curricula of the several Provinces in which the schools are situated, since it was assumed that as the bands would soon become enfranchised and become citizens of the Province they would enter into the common life and duties of a Canadian community; (5) That in view of the historical and sentimental relations between the Indian schools and the Christian churches the report recommended that the Department provide for the management of the schools, through a Board of Trustees, one appointed from each church and approved by the minister of the Department. Such a board would have its secretary in the Department but would hold regular meetings, establish qualifications for teachers, and oversee the appointments as well as the control of the schools; (6) That Continuation schools be arranged for on the school farms and that instruction methods similar to those on the File Hills farm colony be developed; (7) That the health interests of the pupils be guarded by a proper medical inspection and that the local physicians be encouraged through the provision at each school of fresh air methods in the care and treatment of cases of tuberculosis.

II. The annual medical reports from year to year made reference to the unsatisfactory health of the pupils, while different local medical officers urged greater action in view of the results of their experience from year to year. As the result of one such report the Minister instructed the writer in 1909 to investigate the health of the children in the schools of the Calgary district in a letter containing the following:—

> As it is necessary that these residential schools should be filled with a healthy class of pupils in order that the expenditure on Indian education may not be rendered entirely nugatory, it seems desirable that you should go over the same ground as Dr. Lafferty and check his inspection.

Recommendations based upon examination of 243 school children.

These instructions were encouraging and the writer gladly undertook the work of examining with Dr. J. D. Lafferty the 243 children of 8 schools in Alberta, with the following results:—

(a) Tuberculosis was present equally in children at every age; (b) In no instance was a child awaiting admission to school found free from tuberculosis; hence it was plain that infection was got in the home primarily; (c) The disease showed an excessive mortality in the pupils between five and ten years of age; (d) The 10,000 children of school age demanded the same attention as the thousand children coming up each year and entering the schools annually.

Recommendations, made in this report, on much the same lines as those made in the report of 1907, followed the examination of the 243 children; but owing to the active opposition of Mr. D. C. Scott, and his advice to the then Deputy Minister, no action was taken by the Department to give effect to the recommendations made. This too in spite of the opinion of Prof. George Adami, Pathologist of McGill University, in reply to a letter of the Deputy Minister asking his opinion regarding the management and conduct of the Indian schools. Prof. Adami had with the writer examined the children in one of the largest schools and was fully informed as to the actual situation. He stated that it was only after the earnest solicitation of Mr. D. C. Scott that the whole matter of Dr. Bryce's report was prevented from becoming a matter of critical discussion at the annual meeting of the National Tuberculosis Association in 1910, of which he was then president, and this was only due to Mr. Scott's distinct promise that the Department would take adequate action along the lines of the report. Prof. Adami stated in his letter to the Deputy Minister:—

> It was a revelation to me to find tuberculosis prevailing to such an extent amongst these children, and as many of them were only suffering from the early incipient form of the disease, though practically everyone was affected, when under care it may be arrested, I was greatly impressed with the responsibility of the government in dealing with these children. . . . I can assure you my only motive is a great sympathy for these children, who are the wards of the government and cannot protect themselves from the ravages of this disease.

III. In reviewing his correspondence the writer finds a personal letter, written by him to the Minister dated March 16th, 1911, following an official letter regarding the inaction of the Department with regard to the recommendations of the report. This letter refers to the most positive promises of Mr. D. C. Scott that the Department would at once take steps to put the suggestions contained in the report into effect. The letter further says:—

> It is now over 9 months since these occurrences and I have not received a single communication with reference to carrying out the suggestions of our report. Am I wrong in assuming that the vanity of Mr. D. C. Scott, growing out of his success at manipulating the mental activities of Mr. Pedley, has led him to the fatal deception of supposing that his cleverness will be equal to that of Prospero in calming any storm that may blow up from a Tuberculosis Association or any where else, since he knows that should he fail he has through memoranda on file placed the responsibility on Mr. Pedley and yourself. In this particular matter, he is counting upon the ignorance and indifference of the public to the fate of the Indians; but with the awakening of the health conscience of the

people, we are now seeing on every hand, I feel certain that serious trouble will come out of departmental inertia, and I am not personally disposed to have any blame fall upon me.

It will then be understood with what pleasure the writer hailed the appointment of Dr. W. A. Roche as Superintendent General of Indian Affairs after the year's term of the Hon. R. Rogers, whose chief activity was the investigation of the Deputy Minister, which led up to his retirement. Now at last he said, "A medical minister exists who would understand the situation as relates to the health of the Indians." So an early opportunity was taken to set forth in a memorandum to Dr. Roche, dated Dec. 9th, 1912, data and statistics relating to the several hundred scattered bands on whose health the total expenditure was but little more than $2 per capita, while the death rate in many of the bands was as high as forty per thousand. The reply acknowledging receipt of this memorandum contained the following:—

Dr. Roche is urged to act.

There is certainly something in your suggestion that should meet with every consideration, and some time when I can find an opportunity and it is convenient for you, I shall be pleased to discuss this matter with you.

As Dr. Roche became ill and was absent for some months nothing further was done; but on his return the writer in a personal interview urged that this serious medical Indian problem be taken up in earnest. It was stated that medical science now knows just what to do and what was necessary was to put our knowledge into practice. Dr. Roche stated that on his return from the West he would certainly take the matter up. Since that moment however, to the present, the matter has awaited the promised action.

The writer had done no regular inspection work since Mr. D. C. Scott was made Deputy minister in 1913, but had in each year up to 1914 prepared his medical report, printed in the annual report of the Department. About this time the following letter was received :—

P. H. Bryce, M. D.
Medical Inspector,
Immigration Branch.

Ottawa,
June 17, 1914.

Dear Sir,

In reply to your letter of the first instant, asking that the files of the Department, containing our medical officers' reports be placed at your disposal, so that you may peruse them to enable you to furnish a report for publication, I desire to point out, that by the organization of this Department, under the Civil Service Act of 1908 you were not included therein and since that time your whole salary has been a charge against the Department of the Interior. It is true that since then we have availed ourselves of your services on a few occasions; but during the past year, so far as I am aware, you have not been called upon to do any duty for the Department. I may say also that Dr. Grain of Winnipeg, has lately been appointed to oversee the Western schools and reserves and his time is fully occupied in the work. Under these circumstances, I do not think that you should be asked to furnish a report on the medical work in connection with Indians during the fiscal year. I must thank you cordially for the offer to again prepare a report for publication.

Yours sincerely,
DUNCAN C. SCOTT,
D. S. G. I. A.

Mr. Scott's malign influence.

The transparent hypocrisy contained in this remarkable communication sent, not by the Minister Dr. W. A. Roche, but by his deputy, will be seen in the fact that from 1908, five annual reports had been prepared by the writer, while the special report on the eight schools of the Calgary district with the recommendations already referred to had been made on the instructions of the Department in 1909. The other reason given, to the effect that a certain physician, since retired for good cause, quite inexperienced in dealing with Indian disease problems, had been appointed as Medical Inspector for the Western Provinces, showed how little the Minister cared for the solution of the tuberculosis problem. As a matter of fact the Order in Council appointing the writer had neither been changed nor rescinded, while the transfer to the Interior Department of the payment of the total salary was made in 1908 in order that his regular increase of pay under the new classification of the Civil Service Act of that year might be made.

Dr. Roche's culpable apathy.

IV. As the war broke out in 1914 and immigration was largely suspended, an unexpected opportunity occurred through the greater time at his disposal for the writer's special knowledge and experience to be utilized in improving the health of the Indians; but in no single instance, thereafter, were the services of the writer utilised by this medical Minister, who in 1917 was transferred to preside over the Civil Service Commission, and who must be held responsible for the neglect of what proved to be a very serious situation. In 1917, the writer prepared, at the request of the Conservation Commission, a pamphlet on "The Conservation of the Man Power of Canada," which dealt with the broad problems of health which so vitally affect the man power of a nation. The large demand for this pamphlet led to the preparation of a similar study on "The Conservation of the Man Power of the Indian Population of Canada," which had already supplied over 2000 volunteer soldiers for the Empire. For obvious reasons this memorandum was not published, but was placed in the hands of a minister of the Crown in 1918, in order that all the facts might be made known to the Government. This memorandum began by pointing out that in 1916 4,862,303 acres were included in the Indian reserves and that 73,716 acres were then under cultivation; that while the total per capita income for farm crops in that year in all Canada was $110, that from the Indian reserves was $69, while it was only $40 for Nova Scotia. It is thus obvious that from the lowest standard of wealth producers the Indian population of Canada was already a matter of much importance to the State. From the statistics given in the "Man Power" pamphlet it was made plain that instead of

Value of man power of Indians.

the normal increase in the Indian population being 1.5 per cent. per annum as given for the white population, there had been between 1904 and 1917 an actual decrease in the Indian population in the age period over twenty years of 1,639 persons whereas a normal increase would have added 20,000 population in the 13 years. The comparisons showed that the loss was almost wholly due to a high death rate since, though incomplete, the Indian birth rate was 27 per thousand or higher than the average for the whole white population.

The memorandum states, "As the Indian people are an unusually strong native race, their children at birth are large and sturdy, and under good sanitary conditions have a low mortality. Thus of the 134 children born in the File Hills Farm Colony in 17 years only 34 died, while of 15 births in 1916 only 1 died, giving the unusually low rate of 77 per thousand within the year."

As it was further desirable to obtain the latest returns of deaths by age periods and causes the writer communicated with the Secretary of the Indian Department asking for such returns. In reply he received the following letter.

Ottawa, May 7, 1918.

Dear Dr. Bryce,

I have your letter of the third instant asking for certain vital statistics. I am unable to give you the figures you ask as we are not receiving any vital statistics now, and last year we obtained only the total number of births and deaths from each Agency. These were not printed and are not therefore available for distribution. The causes of deaths have never been noted in our reports and we have no information.

Your obedient servant,
(Signed) J. D. McLean,
Asst. Deputy and Secretary.

Entire absence of causes of deaths.

Thus after more than a hundred years of an organized Department of Indian Affairs in Canada, though the writer had at once begun in 1904 on his appointment the regular collection of statistics of diseases and deaths from the several Indian bands, he was officially informed that in a Department with 287 paid medical officers, due to the direct reactionary influence of the former Accountant and present Deputy Minister no means exists, such as is looked upon as elementary in any Health Department today, by which the public or the Indians themselves can learn anything definite as to the actual vital conditions amongst these wards of the nation.

A study of the 1916–17 statistics shows that in the wage earning period of life, from 21 to 65 years, the Indians of Alberta had 161 less population, of British Columbia 901 less, of Ontario 991 less and of Nova Scotia 399 less. In order however to show how an Indian population may increase, the writer obtained from Mr. W. M. Graham, at that time Superintendent of the File Hills colony from 1901 to 1917, the complete record for this period. In all there were 53 colonists from the neighbouring Indian schools, starting with five in 1901, who had taken up homesteads in the colony. Most of them married although 15 either left or had died previous to marriage. In June 1917 there were resident 38 men, 26 women and 106 children, or 170 colonists in all. Thus we have the picture of a young Indian population of 49 males who remained in the colony, of whom 10 died of tuberculosis after an average sickness there of 2.7 years and of 29 females of whom 3 died and to whom had been born in all 134 children. In 1916 the colony had 3,991 acres under cultivation or over a hundred acres per farmer. This was one nineteenth of the total area cultivated by 105,000 persons in all the Indian bands in Canada, while 87,498 bushels of grain were grown, and 33,052 head of live stock were kept. That this variation from the normal is viewed as an anomaly may be judged from the following extract from the Deputy Minister's Annual Report for 1917; "The Indian population does not vary much from year to year." How misleading this statement is may be judged from the fact that between 1906 and 1917 in the age periods over 20 years in every Province but two the Indians had decreased in population by a total of 2,632 deaths.

The famous File Hills Farm colony.

Naturally it is asked; Why this decrease should have taken place? In 1906 the report of the Chief Medical Officer shows that statistics collected from 99 local medical officers having the care of a population of 70,000 gave a total of 3,169 cases of tuberculosis or 1 case for every seven in a total of 23,109 diseases reported, and the death rates in several large bands were 81.8, 82.6, and in a third 86.4 per thousand; while the ordinary death rate for 115,000 in the city of Hamilton was 10.6 in 1921. What these figures disclose has been made more plain year by year, namely that tuberculosis, contracted in infancy, creates diseases of the brain, joints, bones, and to a less degree of the lungs and also that if not fatal till adolescence it then usually progresses rapidly to a fatal termination in consumption of the lungs.

Extraordinary mortality from tuberculosis.

The memorandum prepared by the writer in 1918 further showed that the city of Hamilton with a population greater than the total Indian population had reduced the death rate from tuberculosis in the same period, from 1904 to 1917, by nearly 75 per cent. having in 1916 actually only 68 deaths. The memorandum further states, "If a similar method had been introduced amongst the bands on the health-giving uplands of Alberta, much might have been done to prevent such a splendid race of warriors as the Blackfeet from decreasing from 842 in 1904 to 726 in 1916, or, allowing for natural increase, an actual loss of 40 per cent. since they should have numbered at least 1,011."

The amazing reduction of tuberculosis in Hamilton.

V. Such then is the situation made known to the Hon. N. W. Rowell, who applied to the writer in 1918 to supply him with such facts and arguments as would support the Bill he proposed to introduce into Parliament for the creation of a Federal Department of Health.

It was with pleasure that the memorandum dealing with Indian health matters was given him, along with a proposed Bill for a Department of Health, which contained amongst its provisions one for including the Indian Medical Service along with the other Medical Federal services in the new Department. In the special medical committee called by Mr. Rowell to discuss the Bill, such inclusion was of course approved of and the clause appeared in the First Reading in Parliament. But something then happened: What special occult influences came into action may be imagined, when the Second Reading of the Bill took place with this clause regarding the Indian Medical Service omit-

Occult influences again rob the Indians of a chance.

ted. It has been noted that from 1913 up to the time when Dr. W. A. Roche was eliminated from the government in 1917 to make room for a more hardy and subtle representative of Unionism the activities of the Chief Medical Inspector of the Indian Department, had in practice ceased; yet now he was to see as the outcome of all this health legislation for which he had been struggling for years, the failure of one of his special health dreams, which he has hoped to see realized.

One who failed them in their agony.

If the writer had been much disturbed by the incapacity or inertia of a medical Minister in the matter of the Indian health situation, he now saw that it was hopeless to expect any improvement in it when the new Minister of Health, who had posed as the Bayard of Social Uplift, the Protagonist of Prohibition, the Champion of Oppressed Labour, the Sir Galahad of Women's rights, and the *preux Chevalier* of Canadian Nationalism, could with all the accumulated facts and statistics before him condemn to further indefinite suffering and neglect these Wards of the Canadian people, whom one Government after another had made treaties with and whom deputies and officials had sworn to assist and protect.

A side light however, may serve to illumine the beclouded situation. With the formation of the Unionist Government the usual shuffle of portfolios was made and the then dominating Solicitor General, grown callous and hardened over a franchise Bill, which disfranchised many thousands of his fellow native-born citizens, had now become Minister of the Interior. That the desire for power and for the control appointments should override any higher consideration such as saving the lives of the Indians must be inferred from the following statement of the Hon. A[.] Meighen, Minister of the Interior and now Prime Minister. On June 8th, 1920, the estimates of the Indian Department were under consideration in Parliament. Page 3275 of Hansard has the following:—

> Mr. D. D. McKenzie, "I understand that frightful ravages are being made amongst them (Indians) by tuberculosis and the conditions of life are certainly not such as to preserve them from the ravages of that dread disease. I should be pleased to know at the earliest possible moment if that branch of the Department was going to be transferred to the Department of Health."
>
> Mr. Meighen, "The Health Department has no power to take over the matter of the health of the Indians. That is not included in the Act establishing the department. It was purposely left out of the Act. I did not then think and do not think yet that it would be practicable for the Health Department to do that work, because they would require to duplicate the organization away in the remote regions, where Indian reserves are, and there would be established a sort of divided control and authority over the Indians."
>
> Mr. Beland, "Is tuberculosis increasing or decreasing amongst the Indians?"
>
> Mr. Meighen, "I am afraid I cannot give a very encouraging answer to the question. We are not convinced that it is increasing, but it is not decreasing.["]

In this reply of the Minister we see fully illustrated the dominating influence, stimulated by the reactionary Deputy Minister, which prevents even the simplest effective efforts to deal with the health problem of the Indians along modern scientific lines. To say that confusion would arise is the equivalent of saying that co-operation between persons

Red tape condemns the Indians because of pitiable inertia.

toward a desired social end is impracticable; whereas co-operation between Provincial and Federal Health Departments is the basis upon which real progress is being made, while further a world peace is being made possible in a league of once discordant nations. The Premier has frankly said he can give no encouraging answer to Dr. Beland's question, while at the same moment he condemns the Indians to their fate by a pitiable confession of utter official helplessness and lack of initiative, based upon a cynical *"non possumus."*

Thus we find a sum of only $10[,]ooo has been annually placed in the estimates to control tuberculosis amongst 105,000 Indians scattered over Canada in over 300 bands, while the City of Ottawa, with about the same population and having three general hospitals spent thereon $342,860.54 in 1919 of which $33,364.70 is devoted to tuberculous patients alone. The many difficulties of our problem amongst the Indians have been frequently pointed out, but the means to cope with these have also been made plain. It can only be said that any cruder or weaker arguments by a Prime Minister holding the position of responsibility to these treaty wards of Canada could hardly be conceived, and such recall the satirical jibe of Voltaire, regarding the Treaty of Shack[a]maxon between Wm. Penn and the Indians, which he describes as "the only known treaty between savages and Christians that was never sworn to and never broken."

The degree and extent of this criminal disregard for the treaty pledges to guard the welfare of the Indian wards of the nation may be guaged [sic] from the facts once more brought out at the meeting of the National Tuberculosis Association at its annual meeting held in Ottawa on March 17th, 1922. The superintendent of the Qu'Appelle Sanatorium, Sask., gave there the results of a special study of 1575 children of school age in which advantage was taken of the most modern scientific methods. Of these 175 were Indian children, and it is very remarkable that the fact given that some 93 per cent. of these showed evidence of tuberculous infection coincides completely with the work done by Dr. Lafferty and the writer in the Alberta Indian schools in 1909.

It is indeed pitiable that during the thirteen years since then this trail of disease and death has gone on almost unchecked by any serious efforts on the part of the Department of Indian Affairs, placed by the B. N. A. Act especially in charge of our Indian population, and that a Provincial Tuberculosis Commission now considers it to be its duty to publish the facts regarding these children living within its own Province.

. . .

6.4 Mary Carpenter, "No More Denials Please," 1991

Mary Carpenter is an Inuvialuit Inuit woman who was born in the western Arctic and attended the Catholic-run Immaculate Conception Residential School in Aklavik, which is also referred to as the Aklavik Immaculate Conception Boarding School (AICBS). The school, located on the west side of the Mackenzie River Delta, was opened in 1925. The opening of AICBS was followed by the launch of the Anglican All Saints Residential School in 1936. Both schools were funded by Canadian taxpayers. In 1959, AICBS was closed in favour of a new school, the Inuvik Federal School. Two residences were built in Inuvik for the children who attended this school: Grollier Hall, which was operated by the Catholic Missionary Oblates of Mary Immaculate, and Stringer

Hall, its Anglican counterpart, run by the Missionary Society of the Church of England in Canada. Carpenter is no friend of the residential schools but extends the blame for the attendance of Inuit children in the schools beyond the churches and the Canadian state. She also hints at the relative absence of attention paid to Inuit and, by extension, to Métis children in discussions and publications related to this issue. The piece below contains the entire English text of Carpenter's article published in Inuktitut *magazine.*

Source: Mary Carpenter, "Recollections and Comments: No More Denials Please," *Inuktitut* 74 (1991): 56–61.

Reprinted with the permission of *Inuktitut* magazine.

Recollections and Comments: No More Denials Please

by Mary Carpenter

I am 48 years old and I am still crawling out from a very private nightmare. I was six years old when my parents enrolled me in the Aklavik Immaculate Conception Boarding School and Hospital, operated by the Oblates of Mary Immaculate (OMI). My mother had tuberculosis. She never left this infirmary except to transfer to the All Saints Anglican Hospital across town. My mother died when I was twelve years old. I was never to know the warmth and security of family life.

It still hurts me today that men like my late father, Fred Carpenter, reconciled himself to a government and to a religious institution that was stealing his children.

I firmly disagree with some modern Inuit political leaders who say that the generation of my parents never had a choice. The buck can no longer be passed to the white people. My father was reputed to be an excellent hunter. Did he not learn that the mother polar bear was most vicious when she had young? A mother bear fights to the death for her cubs. In my little heart I wished that my father had battled for me. My lifelong torment from this parental abandonment is that I have never felt secure in love.

It is time for my people, the Inuit, to take part of the blame for what happened to my generation of children in those wretched residential schools. It is time for Inuit to accept their fair share for the breakup of our family unit, the loss of Inuit values, spouse and child neglect, and alcohol induced indifference.

In July, the Rev. Doug Crosby OMI apologized to 10,000 Indians at a religious pilgrimage at Lac Ste-Anne, Alberta. This Oblate priest and the Vatican need to apologize to the Inuit of Canada also. We attended those cultural-extermination institutions too!

The primary objective of these residential schools, staffed by Roman Catholic and Anglican church missionaries, was to sever the primal bonds between grandparents, parents, and children, and imprint another. These missionaries were as capable and able as the Nazi machine.

Though the missionaries had discovered a healthy Eskimo culture with its own laws and language, they recast the tundra in their own image. They baptized the Inuit and renamed en masse, creating an instant nation of names reflecting Old and New Testaments, and the British Crown. The disc numbers and the English names were a mere convenience for the conquerors' English and French tongues, and not a sign of equality with our fellow Canadians.

I entered the missionary schools fluent in Inuvialuktun and I did not know any other language. When I transferred from Immaculate Conception School to the All Saints Anglican Mission School across town, it was not Inuvialuktun that I learned. The English language of the Anglican mission was as opaque and unfamiliar to me as the French spoken by the Grey Nuns.

After a lifetime of beatings, going hungry, standing in a corridor on one leg, and walking in the snow with no shoes for speaking Inuvialuktun, and having a heavy, stinging paste rubbed on my face, which they did to stop us from expressing our Eskimo custom of raising our eyebrows for "yes" and wrinkling our noses for "no", I soon lost the ability to speak my mother tongue. When a language dies, the world it was generated from is broken down too.

My Inuit world is now broken and self-destructing very fast. We have been uprooted from our families and our security as a race is shattered. The big troubles are wide use of drugs and alcohol, babies making babies, violence, and suicide. Many of our Inuvialuit youth feel the walls are closing in on them. Somehow we must convince them that life is worthwhile. We must teach them to turn to each other and not on each other.

My Inuvialuit culture did not know about religions. Nature was our religion. I do not believe in any of the organized religions of today. I think the crosses are on the wrong buildings. I think Jesus is in the Alcoholics Anonymous meetings and in some of the more enlightened welfare offices across the nation. I know many people who feel empowered after their sessions with A.A. I feel that it is best to have an individual spiritual guide.

The impact of boarding schools and other outside pressures has been devastating to the Inuvialuit. In an informal survey that was done in the six Inuvialuit communities of Inuvik, Aklavik, Tuktoyaktuk, Paulatuk, Sachs Harbour, and Holman, it was estimated that out of a population of 2,500 Inuvialuit, about 500 were fluent in the three dialects of Siglitun, Uummarmiutun, and Kangiryuarmiut.

The language can be revitalized but the political will of the Inuvialuit leaders toward this project must be one of commitment to its growth. I personally feel that the Vatican and the Anglican Church of England should fully finance the revitalization of Inuvialuktun, since they were the primary instruments of cultural genocide. If the religious bureaucrats say that they were only following orders from the Federal Government, then there needs to be serious discussion of who foots the revitalization bill. It will be costly.

6.5 Isabelle Knockwood, *Out of the Depths,* 2001

Isabelle Knockwood, a respected Mi'kmaq elder by the time she wrote the book excerpted below, was born in Wolfville, Nova Scotia, and attended the Shubenacadie Indian Residential School from age four in 1936 until she was a teenager in 1947. The only residential school in Atlantic Canada, the school at Shubenacadie was operated by the Roman Catholic Church and funded by Canada from its inception in 1930 until it was closed in the late 1960s. After leaving the school, Knockwood raised six children and later in her life, beginning at age 58, attended St. Mary's University in Halifax. She graduated with a degree in anthropology and a minor in English in 1992, the same year as the first edition of her book, from which the excerpts below are drawn, was published. Knock-wood's account is situated about as far away in Canada as is geographically possible from Mary Carpenter's. Still, though Knockwood's book-length narrative is far more detailed than Carpenter's, there are some striking parallels.

Source: Isabelle Knockwood, *Out of the Depths*, 3rd ed. (Lockport, NS: Roseway Publishing, 2001), 32–34, 88–89, 99–100, 124–26, 143, and 157–61.

Reprinted with the permission of Fernwood Publishing.

The square brackets in this excerpt are duplicated from the original.

. . .

Everyday Life at the School

. . .

The dormitories were kept spotless, with polished hardwood floors which were always cold. I was never warm at school. There were never enough blankets. Sometimes at night I would get up and put on my stockings. Sometimes I kept my stockings on when I went to bed. I missed my nice warm bed at home. Rosie and I had always slept together. It was always warm in our house. The fire was always going and at night I'd wake up and hear the tea kettle simmering. I missed that sound at night and I missed the sound of the clock. Sometimes I crawled into my sister's bed, knowing full well that if I was caught we both would be strapped. Later, when I told Mom about the cold sheets, she explained that was the reason why so many children were bed-wetters—they had a cold in their kidneys.

Bed-wetting was common and punishable by humiliation and horrible beatings. I wet my bed once because I found the floor too cold to walk on and tried to hold my bladder in till morning. Poor Rosie was so scared when she found it, she tried to cover it up and save me from a beating. But the nun noticed and told Susie, my charge, to change my sheets. After that, Susie used to get me up after study hour to go to the bathroom.

One night, on my way to the bathroom, I bumped into a girl carrying a pan of boiling water for the Sister's hot water bottle, The water spilled all over my face, neck and chest. Someone ripped off my nightdress and carried me to the bathroom and splashed cold water on me. I must have fainted because the next thing I remember is being rubbed down with a yellow salve. Blisters were already forming all over. During the night, I started to cry and Rosie heard me.

"Isabelle, what's wrong?"

"My face hurts."

She jumped out of bed and led me by the hand to the windows. There was no snow on the window sill but she held her hands on the marble to cool them and told me to do the same. Then we placed our hands on my face and neck until I stopped crying and then went to bed. In the morning, Rosie had to go to Mass but I got to sleep in. She never complained about losing her sleep to look after me. She was seven and I was five.

Sometimes the little girls would get thirsty during the night and go to the bathroom for a drink of water. If they were caught, they were dragged out of the room by the hair or ear and sent back to bed, so we figured out how to get a drink without turning the light on. The water taps had been turned off, so we drank out of the toilet tanks and sometimes out of the toilet bowl. Later as we grew older, we learned how to turn the taps back on and go to the bathroom in groups of three or four, then turn the taps back off after everyone had a drink.

It didn't take long to figure out the daily routine. It was so dominated by praying at every stage that one student now jokes that his knees hurt every time he thinks of his schooldays. Betsey Paul remembers:

> First thing in the morning, we were awakened by the nun's clapping. Then we'd hit the cold floor and say our morning prayers. Then we'd get ready for Mass which lasted for an hour. This was 365 days a year with no let-up.
>
> All we did was pray. We prayed so much. Prayers were going out to everybody—this bishop, that priest, this nun, that nun's father, even the Pope, and our boys overseas because the war broke out in 1939 and that's all we did— no play hardly. Before bedtime, we had to kneel on the cold floor with every window open and we just had nightgowns on.

Attendance at Mass seemed to be an obsession, and even seriously ill children were required to go. I remember boys and girls fainting during Mass, being picked off the floor, placed on the benches, revived and then made to go to communion just barely walking and pale as ghosts. Sometimes they would collapse in the pews onto the floor, hitting their faces and heads on the kneelers and prayer book holders on the way down. If a child felt faint and sat down during Mass one of the nuns would open all the windows regardless of the weather until the child woke up and the rest of us had to attend Mass shivering from the cold. We were not permitted to leave or to close the windows.

Though I adapted to having to spend so much time on my knees, the reason for doing so remained obscure. It took me a long while before I could grasp the idea of sin. I began to question whether I wanted to go to Heaven if my parents were not going to be there, as well as all the Indians who were never baptized. I worried about them, but the Sister told me not to worry because God would excuse them because they didn't know. Excuses were made for everyone except me it seemed and my parents who had conceived me in sin and who would not go to Heaven if they missed Mass on Sunday. My parents missed a lot of Masses on Sundays because we lived down the meadow, which was two miles through the woods, and sometimes the meadow flooded over. I began to wonder how the priests and nuns were conceived and the Pope and all the white people. It remained a puzzle for me all through my childhood.

I felt betrayed when I was older and began to understand English and discovered that the people whom I feared the most in the whole world as a child were being called "father" and "sister" and even, "mother superior"—the very words used for those dearest to me. I was sickened by the thought that I had been calling the nun, Wikew, "Sister." We found a text in the Bible that said, "Call no man Father." But when we asked the nuns if that didn't prohibit calling the school's principal "Father" Mackey, she answered, "This is different." Even at the time I was not impressed with this reasoning.

. . .

. . .

Throughout both Father Mackey's and Father Collins' regimes the biggest crime was running away. Runaways were brought back in a cop car by the RCMP. Their heads were shaved and they were kept in the dark broom and soap closet, sometimes for several days and nights. They were strapped and fed only dry bread and water. In one case, the boys were tied to a chair and left there for two days. Matthew Thomas and his wife Katie Copage were both students in 1934 when Bruce Labrador and Joe Toney ran away and were brought back. They told me that the two boys had their heads shaved and their hands tied behind their backs. They were strapped to a chair with Bibles on their laps which they were supposed to read. They had to sit in the broom closet all day and all night and all the next day without permission to go to the bathroom. These were Father Mackey's orders. Then they ran away again and were brought back and the same thing happened.

Peter Julian recalls the treatment given to runaways:

When I first landed there, I think it was the first time that I ever seen my brother Joe and I heard that he ran away. He was picked up by the RCMP and brought back. Sister Paul of the Cross stripped him down to the waist and shaved off all his hair. Bald! I was just a young boy and I pitied my brother but I didn't dare cry. They had a closet which they called the dark hole that had no windows and it was located just underneath the steps where they locked runaways and bad kids and the only time they saw any light was when their meals of dry bread and water were served them. They were taken from there and up to Mackey and given the same type of beating I got. I don't know how long they were put on this bread and water, sometimes maybe a week and very light food after. There were quite a few boys who ran away and every one of them got the same treatment when they returned.

The Sister had the same kind of strap as Father Mackey's. I remember Peter Michael Stevens was acting the fool one evening in the dormitory and when he was told to keep quiet he kept it up so he was told to pull his pants and underwear down and lay across his bed. Sister Paul of the Cross put a strapping across his bum and after the first blow he rolled right over on his back with his front showing. But Sister didn't stop at that. She laced it right across his privates and the poor boy let out a scream that could be heard all over the dormitory and Sister hollered, "The longer you lay that way, the longer I'm going to keep whacking." So he rolled back again. She was a sadist.

. . .

One day during my first year, I came into the recreation hall to find Wikew slapping a little girl and yelling at her. The nun had the little girl backed up against the presses, which were shelves where we kept shoes, mitts, and our precious junk boxes. The little girl was looking in her junk box when the nun came up from behind her and swung her around and began beating her up. From where I was standing by the toilet door,

I could see the nun's back. Her arms were swinging. At first, the nun's size obstructed my view but it also blocked the girl's escape, When Wikew hit with her right hand, her black veil swung left and when she slapped with the right, the veil went in the opposite direction. I could see the girl's feet. At first, she was standing with both feet on the floor. Then the Sister pinched her cheeks, and her lips were drawn taut across her teeth and her eyes were wide with terror. I stood hypnotized with fear. I had never been so scared in my whole life before and I almost voided a puddle right there on the spot. Then the nun picked the little girl clean off the floor by the ears or hair and the girl stood on her tiptoes with her feet dangling in the air so that one of her shoes fell off. The nun was yelling, "You bad, bad girl." Then she let go with one hand and continued slapping her in the mouth until her nose bled. The little girl was still holding her junk box, while tears and drops of blood were falling in it. Wikew hit the box, and the girl's precious posses-sions went flying in every direction onto the floor. Suddenly Wikew turned around and screeched at us, who were standing paralyzed with fear. "Get out, you little savages, and don't let me hear anyone else talking that mumbo-jumbo again." We all went scrambling up the cement steps that led into the yard. Out of nowhere came Susie. She pushed me gently and firmly out the door. I couldn't even imagine what the little girl had done. When we got out of hearing from everyone else, she told me, "Don't talk Mi'kmaw, Aniap has spies." The next day, I saw the little girl. She had bruises on both cheeks and her throat where Wikew had pinched her and her lips were swollen with a cut on the upper one. When one of her little friends tried to comfort her, Wikew called out, "Get away from her, she's a bad girl and if I see you near her again, I'll give you the same thing." When little children first arrived at the school we would see bruises on their throats and cheeks that told us they had been caught speaking Mi'kmaw. Once we saw the bruises begin to fade, we knew they'd stopped talking.

Although many of those who so relentlessly punished the children entrusted to them are now dead, the effect of their savage punishments has outlived them. Not only were little children brutally punished for speaking their mother tongue, reducing them to years of speechlessness, but the Mi'kmaw language was constantly referred to as "mumbo-jumbo" as if it were some form of gibberish. The ruthless banning of Mi'kmaw in the school drove a wedge between family members. Freda Simon, for example, re-members that when she arrived at the school two years after her older sister, they were completely unable to communicate with each other since Freda spoke only Mi'kmaw and her sister spoke only English. The punishment for speaking Mi'kmaw began on our first day at school, but the punishment has continued all our lives as we try to piece together who we are and what the world means to us with a language many of us have had to re-learn as adults.

. . .

Resistance

. . .

I admired the girls who had the courage to fight back. Some of them tried to give me some tips on how it was done. My friend Leona told me once, "Isabelle, if you ever get a beating, grab the strap." She demonstrated this one day in Skite'kmuj's class by grabbing the strap. You should have seen the look of surprise on Sister's face! You should have seen the look of admiration and surprise on my own face! I was sitting at my desk just shivering with fear. They stood in front of the room, each pulling on the strap, until finally Skite'kmuj went to get Sister Superior who came walking in quietly and said, "Leona, give me the strap," and Leona gave it to her. When Superior left, Leona looked at me and grinned. That's how it's done.

But me—I used to start shivering and biting my nails at the first sign of the strap. I was only a scared little girl—not brave at all, but just waiting for the day when I would get big and could confront Wikew. That day came when I was twelve.

I remember Wikew was going to shave my sister's hair. Rosie was standing in front of her with her head down and Wikew had her left hand on her shoulder and her right hand was holding the electric razor. We were standing in three lines of twos, waiting to go to Sunday school.

Suddenly, Wikew flipped the razor on and started to cut Rosie's hair. When I saw the hair falling on her shoulders I realized she was serious. Mostly to get her attention, I yelled "Leave her alone, you big fat pig." And it worked. She stopped, but by this time, she had shaved a strip of about one inch wide and one inch from Rosie's neck up into her hair.

"Who said that?"

"Isabelle Knockwood."

"Who? What did you say? Get over here or you'll get the same." I walked across the room, but my knees were not shaking for once. Try it, you big fat pig. As I got closer—Boy, she's tall. How am I going to get that razor away from her? Her pets will overpower me so I better act fast. My mind was working fast because I knew that she had the power to do whatever she wanted. By the time I reached her, she had turned off the razor and was holding it over her head and that's when I saw my chance to hit her in the chest. It felt like a pillow. She pushed Rosie away by the shoulder and Rosie took a step backward. Rosie stood nearby with her head bowed down. "Got to bed, you dirty girl." I found out later, she was having her period and didn't know what was happening to her. There were two of us, looking at each other. Her blue eyes were just dilating as if she could see through me. She preached bout hitting a nun and scolded me, but I kept my eye and my mind on that electric razor. I thought I was next. Try it, pig, I was thinking: I'm telling Mom when she comes this afternoon. I didn't move. I noticed every move in the room—all the girls were watching—not saying a word. Wikew told one of them to sweep up the hair. She was sweeping really close to my feet but I wouldn't move—I couldn't. I was sent to Sister Superior, who seemed as if she might be on my side. She sent for Rosie and appeared shocked when she saw her head, but all she kept saying to Wikew was, "Well now, Sister, I'll talk to you later."

When Mom came to visit, Wikew walked in while Rosie's head was on Mamma's lap and Mom was rocking her in the rocking chair. The rest of us were watching them silently, feeling the pain and trying to understand what was going on. Wikew said in a sweet voice, with her gold teeth showing. "Mrs. Knockwood, I had to cut your daughter's hair because she did something bad." But what she did bad was never explained.

Mom just looked at her in disgust and wouldn't respond. Mom knew she was lying and refused to talk to her after that.

Despite the fact that speaking Mi'kmaw was so absolutely forbidden, children would use their knowledge of the language to undermine the nuns' authority. Clara Julian could reduce us all to helpless laughter in church when she would take a line from one of the Latin hymns for Benediction, "*Resurrecsit sicut dixit*" [He said he would rise again]. But Clara would sing at the top of her voice, "*Resurrecsit kisiku piktit,*" which in Mi'kmaw means, "When the old man got up, he farted." The whole choir would start laughing and poor Sister Eleanor Marie thought we were laughing at Cara for mispronouncing Latin and she'd stop and patiently teach Clara the proper pronunciation. Clara would just stand there and grin. Even the holy ones had to laugh.

. . .

The Official Story

If I had never attended the Indian Residential School and had based this book on material in libraries and archives, rather than on the students' own experiences, I would have told a quite different story. The photographs accompanying newspaper accounts of the school show rows of smiling neatly-dressed children. The newspaper stories refer to "this fine institution" run according to "humanitarian and democratic principles." I remember how we used to have to change our prison-style, broad-striped blouses for dresses on the day of the photograph. Then we lined up in rows according to height with Wikew yelling, "Smile, smile," as the photographer snapped the picture.

As students we all knew that a special show was put on whenever the school came into contact with the outside world. The monthly letters home were written in class, and anyone who wrote anything critical about the school was punished and made to rewrite the letter, leaving out their complaints. Imelda Brooks remembers that, although she had no warm outdoor clothes at school, she was dressed in a new snow suit and boots to go to medical appointments in Halifax:

> I had doctor appointments in Halifax for my polio. Sister Gilberta would take me there. I told her I was going to tell the doctor how we were treated. All through the examination, she dug her nails into my shoulder and said I would get the strap. I was scared so I never said anything. Of course, when we got back, I got the strap . . . The only time I had a nice warm new snowsuit and boots was when I had doctor appointments.

. . .

Out of the Depths

Please don't blame yourselves for what happened at the Indian Residential Schools, for the Great Spirit's sake, we were only children.

Scared and frightened children who were taken hundreds of miles away from home. We were beaten to learn and live a different life and culture, children who were forced to speak English and Latin instead of Micmac.

It's time to be heard by the people of Canada. Only the ones who went to the Indian Schools know what went on because we lived it. We've lived it every day of our lives.

—*Imelda Brooks, Big Cove, N.B.*
Micmac-Maliseet News, May 1991.

How can you forget your past? It's a part of your thoughts every day. This is our history and now we're talking about it.

—*Rita Howe*

Every one of the students who attended the Indian Residential School in Shubenacadie during the nearly forty years it was open has their own story to tell. Some say, "Thank God for the Residential School" and that they learned valuable skills such as how to speak English, how to keep themselves and their homes clean, and how to sew and cook, and especially how to pray. Some of these people deny there were any beatings, while others say that the beatings were deserved and justified. Among this group were children who were "good" themselves or else had bigger sisters and brothers to look after them. Others were priests' and nuns' pets and favourites who were used as spies. Some looked on the school as a refuge from homes where they were abused, frequently by parents who had themselves attended the school and learned physical punishment as a method of child-rearing.

On the other hand many former students say that the Residential School was a terrible childhood experience and tell shocking stories of what happened to them there. Yet they all seem to make an effort to understand what motivated the priests and nuns who ran the school. "I've tried to understand why the priests and nuns acted the way they did toward us and I can't justify any of the beatings no matter how much I try," a former student, who is now a grandmother, told me.

Nearly everyone had many difficulties when they left the school finding an identity and a place in the world. Some went home to the reserves after being discharged from the school only to find out that they didn't fit in, and when they tried to point out the social ills at home were told, "You don't belong here. Go back to where you came from." Even those of us who had parents who welcomed us home were suspended in limbo because we could no longer speak Mi'kmaw.

Despite school years where religion was practised as brutal compulsion, some former students still persist in endless churchgoing and expect God to come and solve everything. Others have become addicted to gambling in the false hope of becoming rich. Many others are staying home, collecting welfare instead of earning wages, because there are no jobs on the Reserves. We have too many who are living in perpetual bliss under the influence of drugs and alcohol, thus becoming numb to the real problems and their practical solutions. However, others have claimed as adults the education they were denied as children. One person who has started on this path told me her reason for this: "The same treatment I suffered at the Resi will never again be inflicted on Native people."

These people include counsellors like Nora Bernard, who have examined their lives and traced patterns which developed in childhood. Nora realized that her alcoholism began with drinking altar wine while she was a teenager at the school, serving as an altar girl. She is now a counsellor for the Native Alcohol and Drug Addiction Center. She says, "I had to experience all this in order to do the work that I have chosen."

Several former students have told me that one of the school's most devastating effects on their lives is that it instilled a fear of touching or of being physically close to other people. When Georgina Denny went to live at Eskasoni after spending her entire childhood at the school, she says that she was "fascinated" by the way people would show physical affection, "Everybody else seemed like they were so loving—holding and touching—I couldn't even have anyone sit next to me close." Another woman I talked to traced back her fear of touching to an incident at the school and the lessons instilled there:

> When I crawled in my sister's bed during a thunderstorm to keep warm, the Sister came along checking the beds and found me and my sister. I was cuddled up next to my sister and she said that we weren't allowed to sleep together because it's not clean to sleep with someone. They taught us to stay away and not be touching. It's a natural thing to touch someone you love, be it your sister, brother, mother, father. It was pure innocence, real love. And they pushed that away from us and told us that it was dirty . . . Today I have a hard time. I don't want anybody to touch me unless I'm really close to them. I even have a hard time shaking hands. I want to be close to my family, but they're like me, afraid to hug me. The closest thing they ever tell me is, "See you tomorrow."

Her mother had also been a student at the school, and she has no recollection of ever being hugged as a child. She speculates that her mother's refusal to touch her children was taught at the school, but she herself has deliberately changed the way she treats her own child. "I broke that cycle of not touching. I hug my daughter and tell her all the time that I love her."

Those who ran the school tried to rob us of our collective identity by punishing us for speaking our language, calling us "savages" and "heathens." They also tried to take away our individual identities. Often the nuns would arbitrarily change a child's name. Margaret Knockwood remembers, "Sister wrote 'Marjorie' on the board and told me, 'Your name is not Margaret. It's Marjorie.' So I was known as Marjorie at the school." Another girl named Margaret was also renamed by the nuns. We had all been forced to call Margaret Julian "Peggy O'Neill." She had been so constantly punished at school that I somehow assumed that she must have died. But thirty years later I met her. "Oh Peggy, I thought they had killed you." She replied, "No, almost. But I'm Margaret Julian remember? It's Johnson now." She had taken back her real name and identity and built another life on it as a married woman.

Strangely enough, some of the students who were most seriously abused have been able to transform their lives and bring themselves "out of the depths." Wallis LeBillois ran away in 1939 and was hounded down by a police dog. He grew up to become a political activist, spending some of his time helping the National Indian Brotherhood, now the Assembly of First Nations (AFN), develop its policy on Native education and eventually become Elder-in-Residence for the AFN.

Others have claimed their own identity and the meaning of their lives through the rediscovery of Native spiritual traditions. Despite the efforts of those who ran the school to instill hatred and contempt for Native traditions and culture, many of us have returned to a traditional path as the source of our strength. One man I interviewed joked that he now describes himself as "a born-again savage." Some of us have come to realize that we were abused not only physically but spiritually. For us, the Native Way with its Sacred Circle and respect for all living things is a means of healing that abuse.

The Talking Stick has come full circle. When Sister Mary Leonard told us that the Catholic Church believed in the saying, "Give me a child before the age of seven, and I will show you the adult," she was speaking a larger truth than she knew. Many years will have to pass before the damage inflicted by the Residential School can be healed. I am still dealing with the mentally, emotionally and spiritually damaged child of five. It makes me angry that the people who almost destroyed me got away with it because they grew old and died before I could confront them. My anger led to frustration because there is nothing I could do to even things up. I cannot confront those who lied to me about myself and about my people and withheld knowledge from me which could have allowed me to live up to my fullest potential. It made no real difference that government officials and some representatives of the Catholic Church apologized to Native people for the schools. Those individuals who directly caused our suffering never admitted their wrongdoing and were never called to account for their actions.

My path has taken many twists and turns which eventually led to the writing of this book. Long before I began writing it, Sulian Herney, my mentor at Mi'kmaw Lodge, had counselled me by saying, "Isabelle the adult has to go back into that school and find Isabelle the child, and take her by the hand and get her out of there." I have done that, and I find myself in a safer place where people are willing to listen, which is the first step of the healing process.

There is one story which I have not fully told till now. Two days before the derelict school burned down, when I went there with my daughter and granddaughter, they went ahead of me up the steps and stopped suddenly. They had heard a voice from behind the half-open door whisper, "Come in, you're welcome." My mother, Deodis, had always talked out loud to ghosts or spirits when she felt their presence. "Who's there?" I called out. "Is that you, Father Mackey? Is that you, Sister Superior? Show yourself." There was no answer, but I shouted back, "You got me when I was a child. But I'm here now and you can't have my children and my grandchildren."

I pass the Talking Stick to you.

6.6 Thomas Moore, Before and After Photographs, 1896

These two photographs were originally published in the Department of Indian Affairs annual report for 1896. Thomas Moore, the principal subject of the photos, was a student at the Regina Industrial School and is shown here "before and after tuition" at the school. Both the clothing worn by the young Mr. Moore and the other detail and props included in these photos are symbolic of Canada's goals in relation to Indigenous peoples.

Source: Saskatchewan Archives Board, R-A 8223(1) and R-A 8223(2). Originally published in Canada, Department of Indian Affairs, *Annual Report of the Department of Indian Affairs for the Year Ended 30th June 1896* (Ottawa: S.E. Dawson, 1897), iv.

Thomas Moore at admission to Regina Industrial School. Saskatchewan Archives Board, R-A 8223(1).

Thomas Moore after attending Regina Industrial School. Saskatchewan Archives Board, R-A 8223(2).

SUGGESTIONS FOR FURTHER READING

Residential schools and the residential school experience have been the subjects of numerous published histories and fictional accounts. The two most comprehensive surveys are J.R. Miller, *Shingwauk's Vision: A History of Native Residential Schools* (Toronto: University of Toronto Press, 1996) and John S. Milloy, *A National Crime: The Canadian Government and the Residential School System, 1979 to 1986* (Winnipeg: University of Manitoba Press, 1999). For accounts built around Indigenous testimony in addition to that of Mary Carpenter and Isabelle Knockwood included above as documents 6.4 and 6.5, see, for example, Agnes Grant, *Finding My Talk: How Fourteen Canadian Native Women Reclaimed Their Lives after Residential School* (Calgary: Fifth House, 2004); Agnes Jack, *Behind Closed Doors: Stories from the Kamloops Indian Residential School* (Penticton, BC: Theytus Books, 2006); and Theodore Fontaine, *Broken Circle: The Dark Legacy of Indian Residential Schools, a Memoir* (Victoria: Heritage House, 2010). For an account of the Métis experience in the schools, which is given scant attention in many other histories, see

Larry N. Chartrand, Tricia E. Logan, and Judy D. Daniels, *Métis History and Experience and Residential Schools in Canada* (Ottawa: Aboriginal Healing Foundation, 2006). For a theoretically informed treatment of a single residential school principal that has much broader implications, see Sharon Wall, "'To Train a Wild Bird': E.F. Wilson, Hegemony and Native Industrial Education at the Shingwauk and Wawanosh Residential Schools, 1873–1893," *Left History* 9, no. 1 (Fall/Winter 2003): 7–42. For a study of the work of Peter Bryce, see Megan Sproule-Jones, "Crusading for the Forgotten: Dr. Peter Bryce, Public Health, and Prairie Native Residential Schools," *Canadian Bulletin of Medical History* 13, no. 2 (1996): 199–224. For a publication that includes personal reflections on the Truth and Reconciliation Commission, see Greg Younging, Jonathan Dewar, and Mike DeGagné, eds., *Response, Responsibility, and Renewal: Canada's Truth and Reconciliation Journey* (Ottawa: Aboriginal Healing Foundation, 2009). For fictionalized studies of the residential school and post-residential experience by Indigenous authors, see Robert Arthur Alexie, *Porcupines and China Dolls* (Penticton, BC: Theytus Books, 2009) and Tomson Highway, *Kiss of the Fur Queen* (Toronto: Doubleday Canada, 1998). For a film that presents the reminiscences and post-school experiences and challenges of survivors of the Kuper Island Indian Residential School, see Peter Campbell and Christine Welsh, *Kuper Island: Return to the Healing Circle* (Victoria, BC: Gumboot Productions, 1997).

CHAPTER 7

"WE DO NOT ASK FOR SPECIAL FAVOURS FROM ANYONE"[1]

INDIGENOUS PEOPLE AND GLOBAL CONFLICT

As mentioned briefly in Chapter 2, Indigenous peoples had been making treaties and forming alliances among themselves for a very long time before the first Europeans arrived in their territories. When the newcomers appeared, they too were brought into this pre-existing web of alliances for reasons of trade, peace, or military support. During the seventeenth and eighteenth centuries, European and Indigenous peoples fought alongside one another in what became Eastern and Central Canada, as settlers strove for supremacy and the First Nations fought for security. Following the War of 1812, the final conflict between Europeans and Euro-Americans for political and territorial control in North America, the relationship changed considerably. Europeans and their descendants in Canada no longer had any need of military or trade alliances with Indigenous nations or communities, so their focus shifted to the acquisition of Indigenous lands.

At the turn of the twentieth century, Indigenous people once again acted in support of Britain as it moved to secure control over southern Africa and the route to its imperial possessions in south Asia. Less than two decades later, Indigenous soldiers again took up arms alongside other residents of Canada to assist Britain, this time in the theatres of World War I. During World War II, the second global conflict of the twentieth century, Indigenous people could again be found on the front lines and in a myriad of supportive capacities. Later still in the Korean conflict and even later as part of Western forays into the Middle East, Indigenous people participated broadly in Canada's military efforts.

---

1 Gordon Ahenekew, Transcripts of the Hearings of the Royal Commission on Aboriginal Peoples, vol. 50, Saskatoon Indian and Metis Friendship Centre, Saskatoon, Saskatchewan, Tuesday, October 27, 1992, vol. 1, p. 104. This quotation appears in document 7b.1.

The two sections of this chapter explore Indigenous participation in the two world wars of the twentieth century. In both of these conflicts, Indigenous lands, resources, and bodies were brought into the service of the war effort. Although Canada came into its own as result of its accomplishments and sacrifices in these two wars, Indigenous people were not accorded a parallel growth of respect. Their wartime contributions were acknowledged, but legislation and policy continued to assert their inferior status in Canada. The documents below allow readers to delve into Canada's policies and actions related to Indigenous people during these challenging times and also to consider Indigenous responses to those policies and actions.

SECTION 7A: WORLD WAR I

During World War I, Indigenous people made sacrifices in various ways in aid of imperial Britain and its former Canadian colony. Despite the fact that they were officially excluded from the Military Service Act, which compelled enlistment, Indigenous people volunteered in such large numbers that their participation exceeded the national average. First Nations, Métis, and Inuit alike served overseas and were regularly found in the heat of battle. Many were cited for bravery, and many more were wounded or killed in action. Document 7a.4 below, written by Duncan Campbell Scott, the senior civil servant at the Department of Indian Affairs, outlines some of the accomplishments of Indigenous soldiers. Scott's own views on the value of military service to Indigenous soldiers and their communities are also evident.

Back home in Canada, Indigenous individuals and communities participated in the war effort through various means. For example, they contributed to patriotic funds and Red Cross drives even while their lands were being increasingly removed from their control. Before the war had even begun, reserve land across the country was expropriated for rifle ranges, training camps, and other direct military purposes, a trend that continued after 1914. The Indian Act was amended in 1906 to allow the expenditure of band funds, with community consent, for on-reserve improvements, but, in 1918, a further amendment withdrew the necessity of community approval before its funds were used by the DIA for any reason deemed "reasonable and proper." At the same time, the 1918 amendment permitted the seizure of both reserve land that was not being actively cultivated and community funds to bring the land under agricultural production. The relevant sections of both the 1906 and 1918 amendments appear below.

The 1918 amendments to the Indian Act paved the way for the introduction of an initiative known as the "Greater Production" scheme developed especially for the Prairie West. On the advice of a DIA commissioner appointed for the purpose, and on approval of the minster of the interior, reserve land could be leased to non-Indigenous farmers or put under DIA supervised cultivation with the aid of community funds, again without the requirement of first gaining community consent. Interestingly, tracts of land held for speculation by corporations such as the Hudson Bay Company and the Canadian Pacific Railway suffered no such threat of appropriation.

The commissioner responsible for Greater Production, William Morris Graham, and his superiors in Ottawa provided glowing reports on the success of the program to the House of Commons and elsewhere. At the same time, though, there were regular rebuttals and complaints from reserve residents and their supporters concerning the expropriations and the operation of the Greater Production program. The letter from Kainai Chief Shot-on-Both-Sides, reproduced here as document 7a.3, provides an example of Indigenous concerns. It was not that Indigenous people were unpatriotic, as evidenced by their participation in other areas of the war effort, but they did resent the usurpation of their land and resources without consultation. For his part, Commissioner Graham dismissed most of the allegations against Greater Production and blamed the others on the incompetence of local agents.

Although Graham and his boss, Minister of the Interior Arthur Meighen, continued to support the scheme even after the war, in the end, the Greater Production farms did not live up to expectations. By 1921, they had cost much more to set up and operate than they had returned, so the scheme was abandoned, though the leasing of reserve land continued across the country.

By all accounts, Indigenous soldiers were well treated by their comrades in arms. They served bravely and were subjected to the same risks and the same horrors as were their non-Indigenous fellows. They would seem to have every reason to expect that the equality of treatment they received in the service would be retained following the war. Yet, on their return, they found that little had changed. Though it has been said that Canada advanced from colony to nation as a result of its efforts and sacrifices during World War I, Indigenous people remained in a state of tutelage and continued to be subject to discriminatory treatment. Other returned soldiers were offered lands and finances under the Soldier Settlement Act, but Indigenous veterans remained under the administration of the Department of Indian Affairs and were only offered lands on reserves that they already had an interest in. Unlike non-Indigenous veterans, even to take up this land, they had to prove to department officials that they were "advanced" enough to make a living from farming. Even benefits owing to the families of those killed in action were withheld unless the department was convinced that the money would be spent in an approved manner. Canadian authorities clearly believed they had operated appropriately during and after World War I because the experiences of Indigenous veterans after World War II were not unlike those identified by the veterans of the earlier war (compare Sections A and B of this chapter).

QUESTIONS FOR DISCUSSION

1. What were the reasons put forward for developing the Greater Production idea on reserve lands?
2. Why do you suppose the underused land held by other interests (for example, the HBC or the CPR) was not similarly appropriated?
3. Why might Indigenous people have been dissatisfied with the Greater Production scheme?
4. What are the specific concerns raised by the Kainai?
5. Given D.C. Scott's glowing report on Indigenous soldiers, why might the department have insisted that they be treated differently than other veterans upon their return to Canada?
6. Why do you think Indigenous people decided to participate in the war effort to the extent that they did?

7a.1 Report of the Privy Council 393, 1918

This document informs Superintendent General of Indian Affairs Arthur Meighen, who is also the minister of the interior in Prime Minister Robert Borden's cabinet, that his recommendations concerning reportedly unused reserve lands have been agreed to by the monarchy's consultants in Canada, the Privy Council. The recommendations originate from ideas presented by W.M. Graham, a Department of Indian Affairs inspector for southern Saskatchewan who was related to Meighen by marriage. This scheme, which came to be known as "Greater Production," has serious implications for reserve communities. In addition, Graham is placed in a position where he reports directly to Meighen, thus bypassing Meighen's deputy, Duncan Campbell Scott.

Source: Canada, Privy Council of Canada, P.C. 393, 16 February 1918, Glenbow Museum and Archives, William Morris Graham Papers, M8097, box 1, file 1.

The Honourable
The Superintendent General of Indian Affairs

P. C. 393

*PRIVY COUNCIL
CANADA.*

Certified copy of a Report of the Committee of the Privy Council, approved by His Excellency the Governor General on the 16th February 1918.

The Committee of the Privy Council have had before them a report, dated 12th February, 1918, from the Superintendent General of Indian Affairs, representing that he has considered the possibility of utilizing the vacant Indian lands in the Provinces of Manitoba, Saskatchewan and Alberta, and also the officers and employees of the Department of Indian Affairs in these provinces with a view to increasing the production of grain and live-stock.

The Minister states that pursuant to the provisions of the several treaties with the Indians, large reserves were set aside out of the public domain, and in order to render the Indians self-sustaining, agents and farmers were appointed to instruct them in agriculture and stock-raising; a system of education in which agriculture formed a chief subject was also established for the youth of the tribes. A considerable degree of success has attended these efforts; rations are no longer issued to able-bodied Indians and they show increasing ability to provide their own maintenance. Last season they harvested 654,644 bushels of grain, their live-stock amounts to 22,362 head.

The Minister further states, however, that only a small portion of the land on Indian reserves is under cultivation and that these reserves are for the most part situated in the productive area of the three Provinces and are finely adapted for agriculture and stock-raising.

The Minister has also considered how these idle lands might be brought under cultivation and how the present officers and employees of the Department of Indian Affairs and the Indians themselves might be organized in a scheme to produce supplies of food now so greatly needed. The conclusion has been reached that the appointment of a qualified Commissioner, charged with the responsibility of developing such a scheme and carrying it out and clothed with the requisite authority to conduct its activities, would be the first essential to success.

The Minister, therefore, recommends that Mr. W.M. Graham, Inspector of Indian Agencies, South Saskatchewan Inspectorate, be appointed a Commissioner for the Department of Indian Affairs in Manitoba, Saskatchewan and Alberta, with the following duties and powers;

> To make proper arrangements with the Indians for the leasing of reserve lands, which may be needed for grazing, for cultivation or for other purposes, and for the compensation to be paid therefor;
>
> To formulate a policy for each reserve;
>
> To issue directions and instructions to all Inspectors, Agents and employees in furtherance of that policy;
>
> To make purchases and engage or dismiss any extra or temporary employees, and market the yield of grain and live-stock, and in effect to have the sole management of this work subject to the approval of the Superintendent General of Indian Affairs to whom he shall report fully at close and regular intervals,
>
> The Minister further recommends that the said Commissioner be authorized also to make recommendations to the Superintendent General of Indian Affairs, looking to the greater efficiency of such of the Indian service in the said Provinces as is not related to the said special work.

The Minister believes that in this way it will be possible to bring larger areas under cultivation and produce grain and meat supplies of great value.

The Minister recommends further that, pursuant to the provisions of the War Measures Act, 1914, and of all other authority in that behalf, the sum of $300,000.00 be advanced from the War Appropriation to the Department of Indian Affairs for the purchase of agricultural machinery and implements, seed and live-stock, fence wire and other supplies, and for rentals, salaries, and expenses necessary for the undertaking, the said amount to be refunded to the War Appropriation from revenues arising from sales as they accrue; all expenditure and revenue to be treated in the usual way and all accounts to be audited by the Department of Indian Affairs and by the Auditor General.

The Committee concur in the foregoing recommendations and submit the same for approval.

(Sgd) Rodolphe Bourdeau
Clerk of the Privy Council

7a.2 Amendments to the Indian Act, 1906 and 1918

Below are two further amendments to the Indian Act. The first, included in 1906, authorized the governor in council, which in practical terms meant the Department of Indian Affairs, to spend band funds with the approval of the community involved. The second amendment, passed 12 years later, removed the necessity of acquiring community

consent. Further, this second amendment allowed the department to lease out any re-
serve land it believed was not being used appropriately. Again, community consent was
not required either for the lease itself or for its terms. Similarly, the 1918 amendment
allowed the department to use band funds in any way it felt necessary to increase the
agricultural productivity of reserve land.

Sources: *An Act Respecting Indians*, R.S.C. 1906, ch. 81, s.90 and *An Act to Amend the Indian Act*, S.C. 1918, 8–9 Geo. V., ch.26, s.4.

7a.2a Indian Act Amendment, 1906

Power of Governor in Council as to direction of expenditure of capital of band.

90. The Governor in Council may, with the consent of a band, authorize and direct the expenditure of any capital moneys standing at the credit of such band, in the purchase of land as a reserve for the band or as an addition to its reserve, or in the purchase of cattle for the band, or in the construction of permanent improvements upon the reserve of the band, or such works thereon or in connection therewith as, in his opinion, will be of permanent value to the band, or will, when completed, properly represent capital. 57–58 V., c. 32, s. 11.

7a.2b Indian Act Amendment, 1918

4. Section ninety of the said Act is amended by adding thereto the following subsections:—

Direction of expenditure of capital of band without consent.

"(2) In the event of a band refusing to consent to the expenditure of such capital moneys as the Superintendent General may consider advisable for any of the purposes mentioned in subsection one of this section, and it appearing to the Superintendent General that such refusal is detrimental to the progress or welfare of the band, the Governor in Council may, without the consent of the band, authorize and direct the expenditure of such capital for such of the said purposes as may be considered reasonable and proper.["]

Lease of lands in a reserve if band or individual neglects cultivation.

"(3) Whenever any land in a reserve whether held in common or by an individual Indian is uncultivated and the band or individual is unable or neglects to cultivate the same, the Superintendent General, notwithstanding anything in this Act to the contrary, may, without a surrender, grant a lease of such lands for agricultural or grazing purposes for the benefit of the band or individual, or may employ such persons as may be considered necessary to improve or cultivate such lands during the pleasure of the Superintendent General, and may authorize and direct the expenditure of so much of the capital funds of the band as may be considered necessary for the improvements of such land, or for the purchase of such stock, machinery, material or labour as may be considered necessary for the cultivation or grazing of the same, and in such case all the proceeds derived from such lands, except a reasonable rent to be paid for any individual holding, shall be placed to the credit of the band: Provided that in the event of improvements being made on the lands of an individual the Superintendent General may deduct the value of such improvements from the rental payable for such lands."

7a.3 Letter from Kainai Chief Shot-on-Both-Sides and Others, 1922

Chief Shot-on-Both-Sides came from a family of powerful leaders and astute defenders of Kainai (Blood) rights. He was the son of Crop-Eared Wolf and the grandson of Red Crow, one of the signatories to Treaty 7. This letter from Shot-on-Both-Sides and other Kainai chiefs to Charles Stewart, superintendent general of Indian affairs and minister of the interior, follows an earlier memorial prepared for the Kainai by former mounted policeman and Indian agent R.N. Wilson titled Our Betrayed Wards: A Story of Chicanery, Infidelity and the Prostitution of Trust. *The document below is a response to Commissioner W.M. Graham's rebuttal of the memorial prepared by Wilson. It not only outlines, in the eyes of the Kainai, some of the problems caused by the Greater Production scheme and its administration by Graham but also hints at the tight control the DIA kept on information that it gathered.*

Source: Shot-on-Both-Sides et al. to Charles Stewart, SGIA, 20 December 1922, Library and Archives Canada, Department of Indian Affairs, RG 10, vol. 7102, file 773/3–1-1–1, pt. 2, reel C-9679.

Blood Reserve, Alberta,
December 20th, 1922.

Hon. Charles Stewart,
Superintendent General of Indian Affairs,
Ottawa, Ontario.

Dear Sir,

We have the honor to acknowledge the receipt of your letter of August 21st and enclosures, delivered to us on 4th of October with the injunction that we should not permit any outsider to see them, which was in our opinion an indirect way of telling us to drop the matter, because if we could not show the papers to an outsider we could never get a reply written to the many false statements in the Commissioner's [W.M. Graham's] report, it being of course well known that we Indians unaided are not capable of drafting an adequate rejoinder to a document of that sort.

We declined to accept the papers under any pledge of secrecy and informed the Department's representative that as the matter was one of tribal and public business we would deal with it as we saw fit. After discussing the various points amongst ourselves, while most of us were very busy finishing our haying, harvesting, threshing and gain hauling work, we have requested Mr R.N. Wilson, who so kindly prepared and presented for us the Memorial of 1920, to again assist us by putting in shape for your perusal our current views on the complaints dealt with therein and in the document which you have forwarded to us. Said views are here respectfully submitted.

At the outset, we beg to convey our sincere thanks to you for the good will towards the Blood Indians which you have expressed and for the interest in our affairs which you have shown by your visit to us and in your letter.

We regret, however, that we must tell you that the Blood Indians are profoundly disappointed to find that you should consider that our very serious charges of maladministration can be disposed of by merely forwarding to us the bald denials and evasions of the Commissioner. As one of our elder chiefs expresses it, "We were hopeful of tangible results from the long expected visit of Mr Stewart but all he has done for us is to send us a big bundle of the Commissioner's lies." Our experience is like that of a person who asked for bread and was given a stone.

After making due allowance for the probability that our meeting with you on our own Reserve was to a large extent neutralized by the pre-arranged presence of influential white beneficiaries of the maladministration complained of, accompanied by their political connections, we still hoped that the very least that you would do for us would be to grant us the investigation petitioned for in the concluding paragraph of the Memorial and thus give us a chance to prove our charges in the usual way.

That petition for an investigation we here beg to repeat and trust that upon re-consideration you will decide that we are entitled to it.

In order to facilitate the work of the enquiry and materially reduce the time and money expended upon it we request that prior to the holding of the investigation, (say 60 days in advance) we be permitted to begin an independent checking or external audit of the Indian accounts of the Blood Agency beginning at some date on the books to be fixed by ourselves and auditing all Indian personal accounts, vouchers and connecting accounts up to the present time. This auditing we request leave to have done by one or more chartered accountants selected and instructed by us and paid from any available tribal funds standing to our credit at Ottawa.

As so many irregularities involving large sums of our personal funds are well known to have occurred in recent years at the Blood Agency and as there is reasonable ground to suspect the occurrence of others, we consider it important that all such matters should be made clear in the manner suggested and we think that the Department would be well advised did it go further and allow us in future the privilege of a similar audit annually.

You will observe that the granting of this request will be in line with the policy already announced by you of giving us full information about our affairs.

The principal work of the proposed enquiry will presumably be in connection with our charge that the Government committed a breach of solemn treaty in the issuing of the 38 "Graham" grazing leases in 1918, and that the Blood Indians sustained heavy live stock losses and other damages in consequence of that act of infidelity.

As the Treaty itself is so free of ambiguity on the point we expect that an affirmative reply to the first question will be conceded almost without argument, but that a large amount of evidence, direct and technical, will have to be taken in order to establish beyond question the direct connection between our live stock losses and the 38 leases. As the investigation will thus assume the character of an important law suit we will need the services of a first class lawyer whose selection and engagement by the Indians, together with the matter of costs, will be details to be taken up with you when you have ordered the investigation, as we trust you ultimately will.

Though the Blood Indians are of the opinion that little is to be gained by swapping contradictions with the Indian Commissioner concerning provable facts and are anxious to get these claims into court without further controversy, there are certain features of the Commissioner's report and statements in it which we think should be brought to your notice while you are considering the matter.

Concerning our cattle losses, we claimed in 1920 and do yet that the "Graham" leases cost us by starvation about 1500 head out of a total of 3600.

The Commissioner informed the public press in May 1920 that those cattle losses were approximately 5%.

Dr Molloy M.P. was told in the House of Commons April 27th 1921 that said loss was 18%, the information apparently coming from the Commissioner.

In his report now before us the Commissioner states on Page 9 that these losses were "not more than from 25 to 30 per cent", and

On Page 8 he states by implication that said losses were more than 40 per cent, that they exceeded the losses in the bunch that was sent to the Stoney Reserve whence 251 were returned out of 419, a shortage of 168 head or 40%.

Of the four official figures above quoted three must be wrong, thus justifying the refusal of the Blood Indians to believe anything they are told from Regina.

To show that the officials opposed to us will stop at nothing in their efforts to defeat us we would point out that to another question of Dr Molloy M.P., same date as above, the "House" was told that 786 of our cattle were butchered for beef within a certain period of 12 months, while the slaughter house returns show that only a few over 200 head were butchered, so that some person occupying an official position falsified the figures to the extent of over 550 head in order to keep the facts of our case from Parliament, the object of this particular falsehood being to otherwise account for cattle that had died of starvation.

With the object of bringing out facts that would show the House of Commons that our complaints were worthy of the investigation refused by Mr Meighen, numerous questions were asked by Dr Molloy M.P. and W.H. White M.P. in the spring of 1921.

We charge that in a large number of cases material replies to those questions were utterly false and known to be false by officials of the Department. We consider this a very serious matter and now ask that this charge also be placed within the scope of the proposed investigation.

In his report and elsewhere, the Commissioner repeatedly argues that as we lost no greater percentage of live stock than some white ranchers, we should not complain.

Our reply is that there is no parallel between such cases and ours. Those white ranchers lost their stock because owing to the drought sufficient feed did not grow upon their single section, half section, or other small holdings of land, to support their animals. They had no grass or hay in reserve.

We Blood Indians, on the contrary, had ample grass on our reserve, the exclusive use of which was guaranteed to us by treaty, but it was forcibly taken from us and given to white men whose animals were thereby saved while ours starved to death.

In order to bring a white ranchers case into fair comparison with ours, you will have to find a case where the white man had an abundance of feed for his 6,000 head of stock but who had it wrongfully taken from him and leased to parties with more "pull" than himself, with the result that his stock starved to death in thousands, though the culprits expended in belated purchase of baled hay etc all of the lease money and much of the victims other earnings as well.

Such a case would be similar enough to ours for fair comparison, with the important difference that the other victim being a white man would have promptly secured his redress in the Law Courts, whose doors, in such cases as this, are closed against Indians, and when we memorialize the only source of justice provided for us by law, the Superintendent General, one incumbent refuses us to shield a relative, his successor does likewise rather than offend the first one and the third incumbent (your Honorable self) hesitates, why, we cannot understand.

. . .

Moreover, if we are given access to the Blood Agency files at Ottawa, we will show that the above is but one of the many spiteful distortions of our affairs sent from Regina to the Head Office in harmony with a malicious policy of belittling every worthy accomplishment that existed on our reserve before 1918.

"Waste and destruction" there has been and plenty of it, but it was in connection with the Greater Production fiasco, managed in detail from Regina.

When our system of farming, which the Commissioner criticises, "was introduced" we broke up sod for about $1.85 per acre, turned it over to our then quite inexperienced young Indians who themselves fenced, prepared and seeded the land, harvested, threshed, hauled to the railway and loaded by hand into twenty freight cars a crop which averaged over 38 bushels of No. I wheat from the whole acreage seeded. And this Commissioner now describes that work as "waste and destruction."

Though every operation after breaking the sod was performed by the Indians, excepting only the duties of steam engineer and separator man on the threshing outfit purchased by us with our own savings, the Commissioner falsely says that it "could not properly be called Indian farming at all."

Compared to our work above we see that when the Commissioner's Greater Production scheme "was introduced" the farming work though many more times more costly than ours, was so badly managed that only 6 bushels of wheat per acre were threshed from the limited acreage that was fit to cut at all.

We have discussed above the insane neglect to fence the G.P. crop, but that was not the only reason for its failure. During the years following our first crop in 1908 we became familiar with steam plow breaking of such quality that crops of 40 and 50 bushels on sod were common, and it remained for this Commissioner to show us the other extreme, to teach us how badly such work could really be done, which illustrations were furnished us in 1918 on the Greater Production farm where we saw a huge acreage of sod on our reserve so badly broken that when the Commissioner's fields were finished his men had to go into them and burn large patches of standing grass so as to make the Greater Production fields look like plowed land from a distance.

When these unplowed areas, extending sometimes half the length of the huge field, were being seeded with the $2.00 wheat, the Indian teamsters on the drills would look back and see the expensive seed lying upon the surface of the ground and wonder at the "waste and destruction" of the white man. And the Commissioner in his reports to the Government blames the dry weather for the fact that land so farmed (?) yielded no harvest. Some of these statements of ours may seem incredible but we are prepared to prove them.

The Greater Production slogan was "Acreage, acreage," irrespective of whether anything could be grown upon it. We are told that upon the Blackfoot reserve when the tractor plows stopped for the season owing to the land having become so dry that the plows could not be kept in it, they were upon orders from Regina sent back to scratch over the allotted acreage, which agrees with what we saw here. The main object seemingly was to enable Mr Meighen to boast in Parliament that with 20,000 acres under cultivation he was the "largest farmer in Canada," Hansard 4814, July 5th, 1919.

When we introduced the system of farming which we are here defending from the Commissioner's criticism, we established a Sinking Fund by taxing our farmers 5% on grain sales for the purpose of renewing our farming machinery as it became worn out. Under the Commissioner's administration they collect from us an exorbitant 10% for that fund and expend it upon automobiles for the agency staff and their families. And then we see in the A. G. reports, which you kindly sent us, that our Trust Funds were further mulcted for "automobile repairs and supplies, $523.00" in a single year.

The plea of economy forbade relief to our Indian children crying for food but there was plenty of money for joy riding gasoline.

We consider those automobile charges, which in two years involved the purchase of three cars and hundreds of dollars of their running expenses besides the $500.00 item just quoted, to be an outrage and we respectfully request you to restore the Sinking Fund tax to the former 5% and we ask you to make a ruling that if the Department desires its employees to use automobiles the expense thereof must be entirely provided by parliamentary grant (as the horse transportation was) and not taken as at present from Indian trust monies. If this suggestion is opposed we can furnish you with details in support of it.

We could give many more comparisons, creditable to ourselves, between our farming methods and those of the Commissioner. For instance, we financed our farming enterprise from our own resources, with a revolving fund drawn from our modest income at that time, $5,000 per annum, paying for all machinery and implements, including two steam plows and threshing outfits, and meeting expenses of every kind without calling upon the Government for assistance; whereas the Commissioner expended upon the farcical Greater Production scheme the colossal sum of half a million dollars of public money.

Taking again our crop of 1908 which introduced our system, described by the Commissioner as "demoralizing", each of the 15 farmers who participated in that initial effort paid back to the Trust Fund from his first crop all advances that had been made to him, including cost of breaking land, fence wire, seed and granaries.

Not only that but almost every individual had a clear cash balance of from $1,000.00 to $1,300.00, the crops being with one exception 40 acres and the wheat, if we remember rightly, being sold for 80¢ per bushel. This compares favorably with the Commissioner's administration, where, after three years operation with wheat selling at double the above price, the much advertised "Greater Production" farm was still indebted to the Government for the greater part of the borrowed half million dollars. There was too much "waste and destruction".

In his 4. C. the Commissioner advances the argument that the fall wheat of the lessees accounted for the fact that they raised 25 bushels to the acre while the G.P. farm right alongside of them, and plowed at the same time, raised but 6 bushels.

In reply we say that the lessees in selecting fall wheat for their first crop were utilizing the experience of the Blood Indians who had found out ten years before that fall wheat on new breaking is practically a sure crop on our reserve, which information was as much at the disposal of the Commissioner as the lessees. But the lessees plowed their land properly and fenced it, which two details neglected, as they were by the Commissioner, would have ruined his G.P. crop even had it been fall wheat.

Re Paragraph 24 of the Memorial, the Commissioner in his Sec 4. A. says that the 41,000 acres at the south western end:—

> was seldom if ever, used for winter grazing, but was grazed largely by the cattle of white settlers for years without any payment being made to the Indians.

In reply, we are prepared to prove that it was the winter range of thousands of cattle belonging to ourselves and to our pre-1918 lessee, who maintained a winter camp there since 1914 and who was paying us $10,000 per annum for the privilege of grazing cattle there and elsewhere on our reserve until forced off in 1919 by the 38 Graham leases.

Referring to the 52,000 acres at the north east end of the reserve the Commissioner says "This land was a public grazing ground from which the Indians received little or no benefit."

In reply we say that it was the grazing ground of the cattle and horses belonging to the Indians who lived at that end of the reserve and also the principal summer range of our aforesaid lessee from whom we were receiving $10,000 a year and a valuable hay contract which practically doubled the rental.

We earnestly request you to cancel all present leases on our reserve and restore to us the old leasing system under which a single large company were given grazing privileges over all unfenced portions of the reserve without interfering in any way with any Indians. That system was producing for us a revenue exceeding $20,000, between rentals and hay contracts, when it was without our consent extinguished by the disastrous "Graham" leases.

Re Paragraph 25 of the Memorial the Commissioner in 4.B. says "No persons were allowed to make use of the unleased portions of the reserve as grazing ground for sheep."

We are prepared to prove that no less than five flocks were seen doing so in one week, grazing in different directions, without being interfered with by the Government officials.

Under the circumstances which called forth this report from Regina, the plain untruths in it, which number a full score, cannot, by the most charitable construction, be classified as casual inaccuracies. After considering this mendacious document, which we take to be a fair sample of the official communications passing from Regina to Ottawa, we are convinced that the maintenance by the Government of a veritable fiction factory at Regina, furnishing the Departmental files at Ottawa with a constant supply of misinformation concerning our affairs, constitutes a real danger to all Indians within its jurisdiction, and if granted the comprehensive investigation we have asked for we will undertake to prove that these lines contain no unfair reference to the situation.

In our Memorial of 1920 we asked to be disconnected from the Regina office and to have our agency administered as formerly direct from Ottawa, and we made a similar request when we had the pleasure of meeting you here in August, which we beg to here renew.

Our people thoroughly distrust the Commissioner and want to have nothing to do with him.

The Blood Indians hope that we may have the pleasure next year of again greeting you personally on our reserve and we trust that meanwhile you will grant us the external audit and order a full and complete investigation of our affairs from 1917 to the present, by an Alberta judge sitting with court powers, under the Inquiries Act, Chapter 104, of the revised statutes of Canada, 1906.

> On behalf of the Blood Indians
> Shot-on-Both-Sides, Head Chief, His X mark.
> Many White Horses, Minor Chief, His X mark.
> Running Antelope, Minor Chief, His X mark.
> Left Hand, Minor Chief, His X mark.
> Witness
> Aloysius Crop Eared Wolf [signed]   Interpreter.

7a.4 D.C. Scott, "The Canadian Indians in the Great War," 1919

The excerpts below, written by long-serving Department of Indian Affairs Deputy Superintendent General Duncan Campbell Scott and published soon after the war, illustrate the author's views on the effects of military service on Indigenous soldiers and on their home communities. While the selections here include only Scott's coverage of soldiers from New Brunswick and British Columbia, the non-excerpted portions of the original chapter contain a similar treatment of other regions of the country and also present coverage of the war effort on the home front.

Source: D.C. Scott, "The Canadian Indians and the Great World War" in *Guarding the Channel Ports*, vol. 3 of *Canada in the Great War: An Authentic Account of the Military History of Canada from the Earliest Days to the Close of the War of the Nations* (Toronto: United Publishers of Canada, 1919), 285–86, 288–90, 305–6, 310–13, and 327–28.

THE CANADIAN INDIANS AND THE GREAT WORLD WAR

NOTHING in the war has more genuine interest than the action of the Canadian Indians in energetically espousing the cause of Great Britain and her Allies and spontaneously enlisting in the Expeditionary Force. The proportion of Indians in the force was small, but the power of their example was strong, and, as individual Canadians, they did not weaken the strength of our offensive, and even added something to the daring and efficiency of our troops. If to be singled out by the foe for particular mention as a component part of their enemies worthy of special opprobrium is any distinction, it may be claimed for the Indians, who were depicted by the Germans in war-paint and with feathers, with scalping knives and tomahawk complete, ready to carry out upon the childlike soldiers of the Fatherland their treacherous and cruel practices. No doubt, ere long, the Germans had a wholesome fear of the Canadian methods of fighting, of the efficiency of our sharp-shooters, and the sudden, desperate nature of our trench raids. It is not too much to claim that the alertness of our troops, their ability to make use of natural advantages, and their daring and unrivalled resource in the type of warfare that developed, had a remote Indian origin, and as for the Indian himself, there is no doubt that he excelled in the kind of offensive that had been practiced by his ancestors and was native to him.

As the original fighter of this continent, the Indian invented and perfected a system of tactics that finally gave the more powerful tribes complete ascendancy over weaker Indians, and that was often used with terrible success against the peaceful white settlements, and even against regular armies. It was not until the white man adopted Indian methods of ambuscade and foray and developed a fighter as cunning and resourceful as the Indian that he could meet his aboriginal foe on equal terms.

. . .

From the very outset of the Great War the Indians throughout the Dominion displayed a keen interest in the progress of the struggle and demonstrated their loyalty in the most convincing manner both by voluntary enlistment in the overseas forces, generous contributions to the patriotic and other war funds and energetic participation in war work of various kinds at home.

During the war more than 3,500 Indians enlisted for active service with the Canadian Expeditionary Force, according to the records of the Department of Indian Affairs. This number represents approximately thirty-five per cent. of the Indian male population of military age resident in the nine provinces of the Dominion. It has, moreover, been pointed out that there have undoubtedly been a number of Indian enlistments of which the department has been unable to secure any record.

The percentage of enlistments among the Indians appears in a remarkably favourable light when it is remembered that recruiting among them was greatly hampered by many serious difficulties of a highly obstructive nature. Although in the more settled parts of the country the special educational advantages that are provided by the Canadian Government for the Indians enable them to take an intelligent interest in current events, there are still many, residing in remote and inaccessible localities, who are unacquainted with the English language or conditions of life in civilized communities and who by their life, location, and training were not in a position to understand the character of the war, its cause or effect. Notwithstanding these circumstances the percentage of Indian enlistments was fully equal to that among the white communities and in a number of particular instances it was far higher than the average.

The Indian soldiers were not formed into an individual fighting force, but were scattered throughout the many battalions of the Canadian divisions. The story of the part played by them at the front is, therefore, of necessity a series of disconnected incidents rather than a continuous narrative. It may be mentioned that the authorities had for some time under serious consideration the question of raising one or more Indian battalions, but after some discussion it was finally deemed inexpedient to proceed with the project, a decision that was viewed with regret by many who believed that such a corps would have been a valuable asset to the Canadian Expeditionary Force, a credit to the Indian race, and a highly interesting addition to the history of Canada's share in the war.

When the Military Service Act was put into force in 1917, it was decided to exclude the Indians from its operation, and an Order-in-Council to that effect was passed on January 17th, 1918. This action was taken in view of the fact that the Indians, although natural-born British subjects, were wards of the Government, and, as such, minors in the eyes of the law, and that, as they had not the right to exercise the franchise or other privileges of citizenship, they should not be expected to assume responsibilities equal to those of enfranchised persons. It was also taken into consideration that certain old treaties between the Indians and the Crown stipulated that they should not be called upon for military service. It may, therefore, be emphasized that Indian participation in the war was wholly voluntary and not in any degree whatsoever subject to the influence of compulsory measures.

As an inevitable sequel to the large enlistment, the casualties among the Indians were heavy, and many a wooden cross marks the red man's share in the common sacrifice of the civilized world. A number of Indians, too, who survived the shells and bullets of the enemy, upon their return to Canada succumbed to tuberculosis, as a result of the hardships and exposures which they had undergone at the front. The Indian is even more susceptible than his white neighbour to the deadly menace of this disease.

. . .

The great majority of the Indians of the Maritime Provinces belong to the Micmac tribe, which, like the Ojibwa, is a subdivision of the Algonquian linguistic stock. The most notable record of enlistments among these Indians is that of the Micmacs of Prince Edward Island, who sent thirty from a total adult male population of sixty-four, or practically every eligible man. These Prince Edward Island Indians earned the highest praises from their officers for their gallantry in action; and they especially covered themselves with glory at the decisive Battle of Amiens. One of their number, Private James Francis, was recommended for the Military Medal for his performance at this engagement.

The reserves in Nova Scotia are very sparsely populated, and consequently the actual number of recruits secured upon them was small. In several cases, however, the record of enlistment was very high in proportion to the population. Every eligible man among the Micmacs of Sydney went to the front. Among others especially worthy of note there may be mentioned the Micmacs of Colchester county, who sent nine men to the front from a total adult male population of twenty-five; the Micmacs of Hants county, who sent six from a total adult male population of sixteen, one of whom, Joseph William Morris, was wounded three times, and was awarded the Distinguished Conduct Medal and also the Military Medal for conspicuous gallantry in action; the Micmacs of Lunenburg county, who sent eleven from a total adult male population of nineteen; the Micmacs of Pictou county, who sent ten from a total male population of forty; the Micmacs of Shelburne county, who sent three from a total adult male population of eight; the Micmacs of Yarmouth county, who sent three from a total adult male population of twelve; and the Micmacs of Digby county, who sent six from a total male population of twenty-four.

The Micmacs and Malecites of New Brunswick sent sixty-two men to the front from a total adult male population of three hundred and sixteen.

A strange occurrence is related of two Micmac boys named Cope from King's county, Nova Scotia. They were both very young when they enlisted; and as they were in different battalions they did not see each other again until they met by chance in the thick of the fighting at Vimy Ridge. They were then seventeen and nineteen years of age, and were so covered with grime and gore at the time that they at first failed to recognize each other. The elder of these boys was subsequently killed at Passchendaele, but the younger continued in the fight till the end of the war and accompanied the Canadian forces into Germany.

. . .

The Indians of British Columbia are not of so war-like a disposition as those of the central and eastern parts of the Dominion; and they are of a conservative type of character that renders them averse to leaving their homes upon any venture of an unfamiliar nature. Nevertheless they have contributed several hundred good soldiers to the Expeditionary Force, and some of them have records of notable distinction.

When the exemption tribunal, under the Military Service Act, for the Okanagan district in British Columbia, began its work, it was found that every Indian of the Head of the Lake band who came within the first class called, that is to say, unmarried men between the ages of twenty-one and thirty-five, had already enlisted.

One of the Okanagan Indians, Private George McLean, was awarded the Distinguished Conduct Medal, in recognition of an extraordinary feat of valour performed by him at the Battle of Vimy Ridge. Private McLean, single-handed and armed with a dozen bombs, destroyed no less than nineteen of the enemy and captured fourteen before being severely wounded himself.

A number of Indian recruits from British Columbia found their way into Mesopotamian service. One of these Indians, David Bernardan, a member of the Oweekayno band, located in the vicinity of Bella Coola, on the north coast of the province, was placed in command of a motor transport vessel on the Euphrates river.

An Indian from Alert Bay, Edwin Victor Cook, was awarded the Distinguished Conduct Medal. He was twice wounded, and finally killed in the latter months of the war. Like a number of other Indian soldiers, he was married in England.

Dan Pearson, a member of the Metlakatla band, which is located near Prince Rupert, was awarded the Military Medal for gallantry in action. He subsequently died of pneumonia.

At the front the Indian soldiers gave an excellent account of themselves, and their officers were most enthusiastic in praise of their qualities of courage, discipline, and intelligence. Many interesting letters written from the front by Indian soldiers have been preserved. Their diction is quaint but graphic, and is permeated throughout with a distinctive racial flavour that is unmistakable; the native Indian rhetoric and prodigality of language is noticeably in contrast to the terse and matter of a fact style that usually characterizes the letter of a modern soldier.

Many of the Indian recruits had spent a great part of their life in hunting, and they were naturally expert marksmen. In consequence of this experience they were able to do excellent work as snipers, and some of them have remarkable records in that branch of the service. The Indian sharp-shooter will sit by the hour, still as bronze statue, watching from a vantage-point for his prey. He has a picturesque method of recording the results of his unerring aim,—for each enemy whom he despatches he cuts a notch on the stock of his rifle.

We have already made references to Philip McDonald, an Iroquois Indian of St. Regis, Quebec, and his record as a sniper with the 8th Battalion. Two other Indian snipers of the same unit also won distinction. One of them, named Riel, was a grandson of the famous rebel, Louis Riel. The name of the other, a Western Indian, was Ballendine. When Riel was killed, thirty-eight notches were counted on his gun; and when McDonald in turn was killed, it was found that he had recorded forty successful hits in the same manner. Ballendine, the third and only surviving member of the trio, and who has returned home to his wife and family, has fifty notches on his gun.

Their method of attack did much towards demoralizing the entire German system of sniping. They were given a free hand and they originated a very effective mode of discomfiting the enemy snipers. By using sand-bags the Indians would construct a position for concealment behind which they would remain for hours at a time, awaiting the appearance of the enemy at his sniping post; and even when he would appear the Indian would not shoot too soon, but would prefer to wait the time when the German would from over-confidence show a little more of his body, and thereby add another notch to the stock of the Indian's gun.

But the greatest sniper among the Canadian Indians, and for that matter in the entire British Army, was Lance-Corporal Norwest, a full-blooded Indian who came from the vicinity of Edmonton and who enlisted with the 50th Battalion at Calgary. He was officially credited with one hundred and fifteen observed hits, which is the highest sharp-shooting record in the annals of the British Army. He is described as a rather short and powerfully built man, with a very pleasant face and a clear and remarkably steady eye, and a calmness of manner which never left him for a moment, either in a dangerous emergency or in conversation with officers of the highest rank. He carried a special rifle fitted with a telescopic sight that was the admiration and envy of all his fellow snipers. He died, shot through the head by a German sniper, on August 18th, 1918, while endeavouring with two companions to locate a nest of enemy snipers that had been causing a considerable amount of trouble to the advance posts of the Canadian front-line companies. Although his record stands as one hundred and fifteen, it has been pointed out that this by no means represents the number of casualties that must have been caused by him among the enemy, as he did not claim any hit unless his observer was present and confirmed it. Norwest would wait for days for a man and would never fire unless his position was absolutely secure from enemy observation. His patience and perseverance are said to have appeared to be almost superhuman. He spent much of his time in No Man's Land, and upon frequent occasions in the dark hours of the night he actually penetrated the enemy lines, where he would wait and watch, finally bag his quarry, with the sureness of the true Indian huntsman, at early dawn, and then return safely to his own lines. Just prior to the last drive that preceded the signing of the Armistice he was detailed to remain in the transport lines, as he had been almost constantly in action during his entire two years in France; but as a result of his persistent pleading, he was allowed to go forward with the attack, in which he rendered invaluable service by destroying enemy snipers and putting machine-gun posts out of action. He won the Military Medal and Bar. He is buried a Warvillers, a small hamlet, in the capture of which he had played a conspicuous part. Upon his grave his sorrowing comrades wrote in a spirit of profound admiration and respect, "It must have been a damned good sniper that got Norwest."

. . .

The return of the Indian soldiers from the front will doubtless bring about great changes on the reserves. These men who have been broadened by contact with the outside world and its affairs, who have mingled with the men of other races, and who have witnessed the many wonders and advantages of civilization, will not be content to return to their old Indian mode of life. Each one of them will be a missionary of the spirit of progress, and their people cannot long fail to respond to their vigorous influence. Thus the war will have hastened that day, the millennium of those engaged in Indian work, when all the quaint old customs, the weird and picturesque ceremonies, the sun dance and the potlatch and even the musical and poetic native languages shall be obsolete as the buffalo and the tomahawk, and the last tepee of the Northern wilds give place to a model farmhouse. In other words, the Indian shall become one with his neighbour in his speech, life and habits, thus conforming to that world-wide tendency towards universal standardization which would appear to be the essential underlying purport of all modern social evolution.

The unselfish loyalty, gallantry, intelligence, resourcefulness, and efficiency displayed by Indians from all the nine provinces of Canada should throw a new light upon the sterling qualities of a race whose virtues are perhaps not sufficiently known or appreciated.

The Indians themselves, moreover, cannot but feel an increased and renewed pride of race and self-respect that should ensure the recovery of that ancient dignity and independence of spirit that were unfortunately lost to them in some measure through the depletion of the game supply, their natural source of livelihood, and the ravages of vices that had no place in their life before the advent of the white man.

The Indians deserve well of Canada, and the end of the war should mark the beginning of a new era for them wherein they shall play an increasingly honourable and useful part in the history of a country that was once the free and open hunting-ground of their forefathers.

7a.5 *Annual Report of the Department of Indian Affairs, 1919*

Because of their level of service and sacrifice in World War I, which the previous document confirmed, Indigenous veterans should have had every reason to expect more generous and egalitarian treatment than they had previously been afforded. Unfortunately, many discovered this not to be the case. While reserve acreages were expropriated so that land grants could be offered to non-Indigenous veterans through the Soldier Settlement

*Board, those defined as Indians had to appeal through the DIA bureaucracy. Even then,
the latter were almost always offered land on the reserve that they already had a stake
in. In the following annotated excerpt from the 1919 annual report of the Department of
Indian Affairs, the deputy superintendent general presents the Indian Act amendment
that set this process in motion.*

Source: Canada, Department of Indian Affairs, *Annual Report of the Department of Indian
Affairs for the Year Ended March 31, 1919* (Ottawa: J. De Labroquerie Taché, 1920), 28–29.

AMMENDMENTS TO THE INDIAN ACT.

A number of amendments have been made to the Indian Act during the past year. The
most important of which is that providing for the administration of the Soldier Settlement Act by the Department of Indian Affairs in so far as returned Indian soldiers are
concerned.

SOLDIER SETTLEMENT.

The new provisions with regard to this mater are as follows:—

196. (1) *The Soldier Settlement Act, 1919* (excepting sections, three, four, eight, nine,
ten, eleven, fourteen, twenty-nine, subsection two of fifty-one, and sixty thereof,
and excepting the whole of Part Three thereof), with such amendments as may
from time to time be made to said Act shall, with respect to any "settler" as defined by said Act who is an "Indian" as defined by this Act, be administered by
the Superintendent General of Indian Affairs.

(2) For purpose of such administration, the Deputy Superintendent General of
Indian Affairs shall have the same powers as the Soldier Settlement Board has
under *The Soldier Settlement Act, 1919*, the words "Deputy Superintendent General of Indian Affairs" being, for such purpose, read in the said Act as substituted
for the words "The Soldier Settlement Board" and for the words "The Board."

(3) Said Act, with such exceptions as aforesaid, shall for such purpose, be read
as one with this Part of this Act.

197. (1) The Deputy Superintendent General may acquire for a settler who is an
Indian, land as well without as within an Indian reserve, and shall have authority to grant to such settler a location ticket for common lands of the band
without the consent of the council of the band, and, in the event of land being
acquired or provided for such settler in an Indian reserve, the Deputy Superintendent General shall have power to take security as provided by *The Soldier
Settlement Act, 1919*, and to exercise all otherwise lawful rights and powers
with respect to such lands, notwithstanding any provisions of the *Indian Act*
to the contrary.

(2) Every such grant shall be in accordance with the provisions of said *Soldier
Settlement Act, 1919*, and of this Part.

198. The Soldier Settlement Board and its officers and employees shall, upon request of the Deputy Superintendent General of Indian Affairs, aid and assist

him, to the extent requested, in the execution of the purposes of this Act, and the said Board may sell, convey and transfer to the said Deputy, for the execution of any such purposes, at such prices as may be agreed, any property held for disposition by such Board.

199. (1) In the event of any doubt or difficulty arising with respect to the administration by the Superintendent General of Indian Affairs of the provisions of *The Soldier Settlement Act, 1919,* or as to the powers of the Deputy Superintendent General of Indian Affairs, as by this Act authorized or granted, the Governor in Council may, by order, resolve such doubt or difficulty and may define powers and procedure.

(2) Such order shall not extend the powers which are by *The Soldier Settlement Act, 1919,* provided. 9–10 Geo. V. c.56, s. 4.

It is proposed to settle Indian soldiers as far as possible on reserves belonging to the bands of which they are members, with a view to relieving the claims for land on behalf of returned soldiers to that extent. When these returned Indian soldiers are thus settled on the reserve, the administration of their affairs is, under the legislation above quoted, left entirely in the hands of the Department of Indian Affairs, thus avoiding the confusion which would inevitably arise if their affairs were administered partly by the Department of Indian Affairs and partly by the Soldier Settlement Board. The Indian agents throughout the Dominion have a personal knowledge of the capabilities and needs of Indian returned soldiers belonging to their respective agencies, and are, therefore, able to supply the information and assistance required in the same manner as the qualification committee, field agents, inspectors, etc., under the Soldier Settlement Act, thus reducing the cost of the work to a minimum. This arrangement, moreover, is considered more satisfactory by the Indians themselves, who prefer to have all matters which relate to them personally in any way dealt with by their own department.

Section 21 of the Indian Act provides that:—

No Indian shall be deemed to be lawfully in possession of any land in a reserve, unless he has been or is located for the same by the band, or council of the band, with the approval of the Superintendent General.

and section 102 provides that:—

"No person shall take any security or otherwise obtain any lien or charge, whether by mortgage, judgment or otherwise, upon real or personal property of any Indian or non-treaty Indian" with respect to property in a reserve.

Subsection 1 of section 197 of the amendment above quoted provides for the taking of the common lands of the band, if any be available, for an Indian soldier without reference to the Indian council of the band, and for the taking of proper security for advances to Indian returned soldiers.

These amendments give the department practically all the powers of the Soldier Settlement except those of expropriation. A large number of returned Indian soldiers have been glad to take advantage of the provisions of the Soldier Settlement Act. On the Six Nations reserve thirty-five loans have been granted, and altogether seventy-five have been dealt with in Ontario, Quebec, and Prince Edward Island. No return has been received from the western provinces as yet. Altogether the expenditure has been more than $100,000, and it is expected that next spring a large number of applications for loans will come in. The department has endeavoured to keep the loans as low as possible in order not to burden the settler with too large a repayment; but in all cases he has been given sufficient to secure everything which he needs. Proper security and mortgages are secured in each case, and it is confidently expected that there will be very few settlers who will not be in a position to repay the amounts advanced them. The work of the settlers had been an excellent incentive to other members of the band, and the progress which they are making is very satisfactory.

SECTION 7B: WORLD WAR II

As they had in World War I, Indigenous men and women and their communities made substantial contributions during World War II. They provided resources, contributed to patriotic funds, and served with distinction in Canada's military. Even though, for the most part, those defined as Indians were denied entry into Canada's navy and air force, many in the army gave their lives and many more were wounded in combat. The much decorated Sergeant Tommy Prince of the Brokenhead Ojibway Nation in Manitoba, mentioned in two of the documents below, provides an example of the skill and bravery of Indigenous soldiers. Many Indigenous veterans speak positively of the treatment they received while in the service and of the comradeship they shared with soldiers of other cultural backgrounds in their confrontation of a common enemy.

On their return home, though, as after World War I, many found that the relatively egalitarian treatment they experienced among comrades in arms had evaporated. They found, for example, that in order to access veterans allowances they had to navigate additional layers of bureaucracy in the Department of Indian Affairs that other returned soldiers did not. There were complaints about both the difficulty of securing benefits and the outright unavailability of services provided to other veterans through the Soldier Settlement Board. Some veterans claimed that they were enfranchised and lost their status as Indians without their consent. In time, Indigenous veterans' organizations were formed to press for better treatment.

In 1991, the Royal Commission on Aboriginal Peoples (RCAP) was established with a broad mandate to explore the historical relationship between Indigenous peoples and Canada and to propose solutions to ongoing problems that were the result of aspects of that relationship. The commission was led by Georges Erasmus, former national chief of the Assembly of First Nations, and Rene Dussault, justice of the Quebec Court of Appeal. For four years the commissioners read stacks of submissions, heard from hundreds of witnesses, and held dozens of hearings across the country. In the end, the commissioners produced a five-volume, 4,000-page report making over 400 recommendations that called for extensive changes to the relationship between Indigenous people and Canadian governments. Four of the five documents below come from the testimony provided to this royal commission by representatives of Indigenous veterans' organizations. The fifth document comes from a report of the Standing Senate Committee on Aboriginal Peoples, which was published the same year that the RCAP report was released.

QUESTIONS FOR DISCUSSION

1. What grievances are raised in the testimony of Indigenous veterans reproduced here?
2. Are there any strategies that could have been employed after the war that would have alleviated some of these problems before they arose?
3. What, in your view, accounts for the fate of veterans such as Tommy Prince?
4. Why is there an apparent contradiction between legislation related to Indigenous veterans and the experience of those veterans?
5. The Senate report states that "The central question is whether the legislation covering veterans was unfair." Should the relative fairness of legislation be the central question of concern? Why or why not?
6. What problems does the Senate report identify?

DOCUMENTS

7b.1 Testimony of Gordon Ahenakew, Saskatchewan Indian Veterans Association, 1992

Gordon Ahenakew of the Ahtahkakoop Cree Nation was born in 1925 about 70 km north-west of Prince Albert, Saskatchewan, on the Sandy Lake Reserve. He attended the day school in his home community, and, when not quite 18 years of age, he volunteered for active service in the Canadian military during World War II. He was sent overseas and, near the end of the war, was injured in Germany. Though Ahenakew and other Indigenous veterans from Saskatchewan were active in promoting their rights in face of the discriminatory treatment they received after their return to Canada, broader organization around these issues did not begin until 1982, when the Federation of Saskatchewan Indian Nations formed the Saskatchewan Indian Veterans Association (SIVA), which is now the Saskatchewan First Nations Veterans' Association (SFNVA). Below is a transcript of Ahenekew's comments, on behalf of the SIVA, to the Royal Commission on Aboriginal Peoples in 1992.

Source: Transcripts of the Hearings of the Royal Commission on Aboriginal Peoples, vol. 50, Saskatoon Indian and Metis Friendship Centre, Saskatoon, Saskatchewan, Tuesday, October 27, 1992, vol. 1, pp. 101–7. Privy Council Office, 1992.

Reproduced with the permission of the Minister of Public Works and Government Services Canada, 2013.

GORDON AHENAKEW, SASKATCHEWAN INDIAN VETERANS ASSOCIATON: Hello, peoples. I work for the treaty Indian veterans. As you know, we have claimed that we were not treated justly by the Indian Affairs.

Incidentally, I prayed this morning. I lit my sweet grass and I prayed that the Creator would put something in my mind and in my lips, at least one thing that I would try and tell you.

I was in the war. I was hurt in the war in Germany just after we crossed into Germany. The thing is quite a lot of times I think at this time of the year on the 5th of May a young fellow was shot in the neck by a big gun and it almost took his head off. That was about two or three days before the end of the war. He just about made it. And as far as I know—my grandfather told me this—that in their society the brave, the hunter, the warrior, got the highest place in that society.

I have been chief of the Indian veterans and we have been largely ignored by our reservations. At one time when we first came back we were heroes. Of course, I suppose the young people hardly know that, and the other thing is that it is so long ago. You can't blame the government for a lot of times forgetting the treaties when it is 125 years old. My grandfather said that whichever way you treat people, that is how you are going to be treated.

I am not going to comment. I believe Axworthy did quite a reasonable job in that. And I don't like to talk about the referendum.

I fought in the war and I suffered, and there are not very many of us left now; very few, not 40 in Saskatchewan. That is treaty Indian veterans. Not many of them are left. And yet I am fighting for them 50 years after the fact, that the veterans did not get their treatment as their fellow veterans that were not on the reservation, including the Métis. I was in the war with one Métis. I knew him before. I think I met him just outside of Vander Zalm's town. They were just coming back. He had a machine gun on his shoulder and I had a machine gun, but we were going in from where they left off. Upon that guy coming back I think some of you will know, Victor. I think you knew that, Mr. Blakeney. You know that guy lived all his life in [a] mud shack. These are the things that I would like to tell. I doubt if you can do anything about it, but I will have to work on that. That one veteran in the 42—he joined up in Battleford. He had two kids and a wife. He joined up and he took his marriage certificate to Regina to join up and the colonel wouldn't buy that. It was signed by a Canon Matheson of Little Pine. He was stationed in Little Pine at the time. And you know, his kids and his wife never got anything while he was serving in the war. I have documented proof of that.

The other one is from Red Pheasant. They were both from Red Pheasant. That was a widow. Her husband was killed or lost in the Far East and she did not get anything until I fought for her. This is 48 years ago, after the fact. This is how they were treated. When Indians went on leave they were docked pay. I have proof of that. The legion has it.

The other thing is when we came back we got $2,300 each supposedly. But we didn't get that. The guy I was talking about that lived in a mud shack never got anything. Finally he came to McDowell. He came there and cut posts and rails and ties, and he was a sick man. He died in Saskatoon of cancer. He was sick for a long time.

What burns me up is that we do not ask for special favours from anyone. We just want our rights. You see, we were supposed to get—when you went into farming—and that's all you could do is go into farming, because even if you were a qualified truck driver that you learned overseas and in Canada, whatever that is, you were not allowed to go into the trucking business in Canada in Saskatchewan. I cannot speak about Manitoba or Alberta. These are the wrongs.

When you go into farming, they are supposed to give you—they call it a waiting return to us, but they only gave it to us in July and August while the other—I know my buddies that are outside in town there now, living in town, that they got that. But because of the Indian agent at the time—it was called Indian Department—they had the right to decide whatever I suppose in their sense may be good for the Indian, and they gave about five of that $2,300 grant to the veterans at that time. The rest we were short-changed. What happened to the money? I know the Department of Mines and Resources got that money. What about that?

The claims that I am making, the Indian Affairs Minister wrote back to the former Chief that we were treated equally, no different from any veteran. I presume he means the outside veterans. That's what that letter says. So there would be no cause—but I have accused them of short-changing us. In all departments you got money while incapacitated. But we didn't. Waiting returns. And some of the money that—while you are in the Army in Canada you get $7.50 a month put away for you. When you go overseas it is $15 a month. And one Indian woman—I know her name—when she came back she applied for the $2,300 and it was approved by the Veterans Land administration people and the War Allowance Board and the Indian Department at the time. She had a shack. But her gratuities was $700, the money that was put away for her. And the Indian agent told her that the $2,300 was paid to buy shingles, flooring, windows, doors, and all that $2,300 had been used in that house. And they bought two horses as well. Later they found that gratuity money was used. The $2,300 was never touched. As a result, that Indian agent was fired from his job. But where is the $2,300?

These are the claims that I am making.

Of course maybe in the Indian Department's wisdom and fairness—they gave us land. I had 30 acres my dad had given me. I had 30 acres so naturally I didn't want to move into a bush. So I took my own land. They gave me 160 acres more or less, I think it says. I guess Indian Affairs is pretty generous, aren't they, to give me my own land. Somehow, I don't want land outside the reservation because look at what I have to go through. A least I know what the TLE [Treaty Land Entitlement], the land entitlement, I know what they have had to go through. I know how much they are going to have to pay the municipalities to get that land and yet at the same time as I understand it, this was our land. Why should we buy it back? Why should we negotiate? Why should we go to the table where I don't know how much money is spent on those meetings to get where they are, and they haven't got there yet. Those things burn as [sic] up.

As far as the pension is concerned, I am getting some now. But these people were short-changed. They were never given anything. If you are a war veteran, you get war veteran's allowance when you are 60 years of age automatically, if you are a qualifying veteran. If you are sick or there is something wrong with you, you can get it at 55, the same with women. But they never informed them. We weren't in existence. They weren't informed. Naturally they knew that they had to apply for old age, and GIS, and whatever. They got that at 65. So now they remember that they had war veteran's allowance coming or disability pension coming. But it is too late because they go by ceiling. If you get $882 a month, you don't get anything else, unless it is CPP or superannuation.

. . . .

7b.2 Testimony of Norman Quinney, Indian Veterans Association, 1992

This short transcription from Royal Commission on Aboriginal Peoples' hearings includes the comments of Norman Quinney whose Indian Veterans Association was forced to close due to lack of funding. In addition to presenting some of the inequities faced by Indigenous veterans, Quinney is especially interested in the recognition of those veterans. To this end, he briefly mentions the fate of Tommy Prince, one of the most decorated Indigenous soldiers in Canada.

Source: Transcripts of the Hearings of the Royal Commission on Aboriginal Peoples, vol. 36, Edmonton Inn, Edmonton, Alberta, Thursday, June 11, 1992, vol. 1B, pp. 301–4. Privy Council Office, 1992.

Reproduced with the permission of the Minister of Public Works and Government Services Canada, 2013.

NORMAN QUINNEY, INDIAN VETERANS ASSOCIATION: At this time I would like to thank Brenda Blyan for having me on the list. Also, I would like to thank the honourable Commissioners, Commissioners Chartrand, Blakeney and Shirt.

My name is Norman Quinney and on my left is Joe Houle, a 1939 war veteran, wounded in Italy and I am a 1951 Korean War veteran, 2nd Battalion PPCLI and my partner here was with the Edmonton Royal Regiment.

The issues that confront native veterans have never been brought out properly. They haven't been administered. I think one example is that with the DVA over the Veterans Land Act. The white counterparts got better treatment after they got out of the war than the Indian veterans. The Indian veterans could not obtain any land holdings and also they weren't qualified to that $6,000 that was available to better their lives after they came back from the war.

Some of the veterans that have passed on, I think one of the issues I am working on or the objectives is the headstones. There are no headstones for the veterans who have passed on. There is no recognition given to these veterans. Also, some of the monies that was allotted after they came out of the services was $2,220. There are 1,330 veterans on the list that have received this amount of money, but there were more veterans that have been left out.

I also find out by asking questions that these 1939 war veterans that didn't go overseas weren't entitled to any benefits that the people who went overseas [got]. They didn't have the same benefits. Now that I find out that there is a legislative thing that is brought out in Ottawa, that if you were in the services from 1939 to 1946 for 365 days you qualify. You qualify for the gratuities that are allotted to other veterans.

The owners of awards are not distributed properly to people who should be receiving it. Also, I would like to bring to your attention at this time that one of the most decorated native soldiers in the Canadian army, Sgt. Prince, who was my Sergeant too, died in a police cell in Winnipeg. There is no recognition about him, no honours about him. The most decorated soldier in the Canadian army.

Also, some of these veterans, it was brought to my attention that when they receive the old age pension their army pension is cut down. The question I ask you is why? These are the issues that I would like to bring forward.

. . .

7b.3 Testimony of Ray Prince, Northern Region of National Aboriginal Veterans Association, BC Chapter, 1992

Ray Prince, from the Fort St. James area of northern British Columbia, served in Europe for over five years during World War II. In this exchange with former Assembly of First Nations National Chief Georges Erasmus during the RCAP hearings, Prince outlines some of the issues that Indigenous veterans faced, including the effect of forced enfranchisement and loss of Indian status. This testimony also speaks of the postwar life of Tommy Prince, the decorated First Nations veteran of World War II and Korea.

Source: Transcripts of the Hearings of the Royal Commission on Aboriginal Peoples, vol. 141, Prince George, British Columbia, Monday, May 31, 1993, vol. 1, pp. 58–63 and 66–70. Privy Council Office 1993.

Reproduced with the permission of the Minister of Public Works and Government Services Canada, 2013.

CO-CHAIR GEORGES ERASMUS: Okay. Could we call the meeting back to order, please, or the proceedings.

We have had a small change in our agenda, for those of you who have one. We have been asked by a respected Elder of this territory who is a representative of the National Indian Veterans Association, an Elder from the Fort St. James area, Mr. Ray Prince—-

Ray, would you like to come up and say a few words for us, please?

MR. RAY PRINCE: Mussi cho (Native language).

I would like to introduce myself. I am originally from Fort St. James and president of the Linguistic Committee. I am a Christian, also a General Director for Northern Region of National Aboriginal Veterans' Association, B.C. Chapter.

I am going to speak on behalf of the Aboriginal veterans of Canada, particularly in this northern region. We are just under way with our visiting of our Native war veterans in isolated areas. Some places we have to walk in six (6) miles with no roads and all these places like Lorapost . . . and Kitselas . . . we are going to visit and all these are where the veterans are. There aren't many of [them] left now, as you know.

The people I serve—myself, I served overseas for five and a half years. I served two (2) years in Italy, fighting, and when I give you indication that when I first—when I celebrated my twentieth birthday in Nice, France and already I served two (2) years in Italy. I served also Continental Europe and was under General George S. Patton, Third Army. But mainly about our Native veterans, Mr. Chairman, I would like to tell you about how war veterans of the Korean War, the First and Second World War and their spouses who are not really right up to standard compared with our non-Native war veterans.

I know for two (2) of the veterans right now—one is wounded pretty bad, the other one he had a pretty bad wound in Sicily in Italy—and they both haven't got no—what do you call—wheelchair. They request it but I don't know why they cannot get it. But we will give you a further report on that in the future.

But after the war—again, I will use myself as—-

I was kicked out of the reserve right after the war, in 1946, when I came back from overseas because I was away from the reserve for seven (7) years, they told me, at that time. That was in 1946. And then in 1987 one of the MP's from this area asked me if I wanted to get back on the reserve. I said "I'll get back if I wanted to." So he asked me if I wanted to get back. "Yes," I said, "okay."

So they put me back on the reserve in 1987. All these years when I came back from overseas after the war I did not receive my full soldier's settlement which the other people got. My cheque from the Department of Veterans Affairs from Ottawa come through the Indian Department in Vanderhoof, from there he made another cheque to me. And about a few months later they said I had no more money from my war gratuity money, also they call it war veteran's allowance or soldier's settlement.

And a lot of us are like that because of in between there is the Indian Department and us and the Department of Veteran Affairs. I know a lot of these people that fought in the war, First and Second World War, also in Korean War and the Pacific with some of them across the border. They went across the border, they joined United States Marine Corp. We have evidence here, now here and there, and if people want to ask us that, they are welcome to do that. We have people that are suffering right now because they are not getting proper treatment and their level of income is very minimum, of $18,000.00 I think.

The biggest complaint is that one time in—I guess you remember, all of you—as you will remember in Ottawa in 1991 I was there that time and we were not allowed to march with other veterans of Canada in Ottawa to the Cenotaph. I was there and the little hole they tell us to lay a wreath there for our war dead; we did that. And after I came back it was really a sad time for me because I figured I was a Canadian and I earned it and I know myself we did very well in Italy. I got honourable discharge in 1946.

And when I came back here right after the war I still had my uniform on. I was on leave when I came back from overseas. I came down here in Prince George in a little place they call Canada Hotel to have a beer, me and my white buddy. They let my buddy go in and have a beer but they wouldn't let me have a beer you know and they said I was not allowed in there. That's the way things were after the war for us.

It was really difficult. They told us to have a Veteran's Land Act and they didn't do a very good job on us either. Because they took some bushy land, not even cleared, and the people try to—they want them to settle there for veterans. There was no machinery whatsoever. It didn't work out too well.

And in these federal laws what they impose on us all the time, it was not really what you would call justice. A lot of things what they imposed on us years ago—today we cannot go ahead and do what we like in trap lines, and even in the trap lines they want to change that. It's not Native people that made them laws; it was the federal government made them laws and the provincial government. Now they are stepping in there. They said we are not supposed to do these things nowadays and all that you know.

However, myself I got a big trap line, my son has here, hereditary trap line from up in the Nation Lake areas. Ever since I was a little guy I roamed that country and I know that country like a book. I do not need a map. It's a large country and I always go back there. After the war I did go back there. And that's my land. My culture is there. My culture is my land.

. . .

I remember a few years ago when Brian Mulroney government got into office they said that they were going to do something about the veterans of Canada. Well, my brother is a veteran of Canada and he got wounded pretty bad. He got 49 cents rent since that time. I just thought I'd let you know these things you know. It's not just a laughing matter I think when they do/say things like this.

That's all I have to say and I thank you very much for listening.

If there are any questions I will answer that question.

CO-CHAIR GEORGES ERASMUS: Thank you. Thank you for your presentation.

MR. RAY PRINCE: You are very welcome.

CO-CHAIR GEORGES ERASMUS: When you came back from the war you say that they threw you off the reserve. What do you mean? Did they take you off the treaty list? Is that what you are talking about? Indian Affairs removed your name from the band list or what?

MR. RAY PRINCE: Yes. After the war you know I was sitting in the house. Somebody knocked at the door, so I opened the door. Here was an Indian agent with some documents. And he told me that "Raymond, we are going to take you off the reserve because you have been away seven (7) years." And I said "I've been away five and a half years overseas." Well, he says, "That's too bad but that's our law," he said, "We have to take you off the reserve." So he gave me a little blue card they call enfranchisement; that's what he gave me. He said "You can drink beer now and do like I do and whatever." I said "I been drinking beer all the time anyways," I told him.

So this is what—so, anyways, what they were doing to me at that time I felt in myself that "Well, they give me this little card, I can get off the reserve any time I want and go to work anywhere." So I went and worked all around; Queen Charlotte Islands, Vancouver Island. I'm a logger. I went fishing. I am a good trapper. I come back winter time.

First time I visited Prince George was 1932 and I landed down here on Cutting Wood Island. At that time we brought a lot of moose meat down and my father they were having court. This German guy shot another German guy that time. And there was no road up north, no road down east, a little caribou highway down to Vancouver, hardly any road to Vanderhoof.

And the backbone of the people were the Native people at that time. My dad had two (2) teams of horses, a couple of cows. We shared with non-Natives; they didn't have anything. In Fort St. James it was just industry; there was nothing. They was nothing, nothing. The trappers were the backbone and that's how this country came to be.

But when I joined the army everything was new to me: big ships on the coast. I didn't know the water, the tide. I didn't know nothing about it. I see lots of planes and towards the end of the war I have seen 3,000 bombers in the air, which was I never—I don't think I'll ever see it again.

But to tell you the truth—to tell you the truth that the Native war veterans they never will take a back seat to anybody because they done very well in these war theatres. And to mention a few like Dick Patrick and some of the boys that we lost quite a few men in this area. I know there was like Tony [Tommy] Prince from Winnipeg: most decorated soldier in the Allied army, in the Allied Forces—not just Canadians—in Allied armies, most decorated soldier. And yet, when he died, he was living in a four (4) by eight (8) room and he was sweeping the floor in the factory building for $3.00 an hour.

But myself I bulled my way. I work. I belonged to Operator Engineers for 31 years. I just retired five (5) years ago and I do all these work. And I work hard for our people. What I am doing for our veterans right now is that I am doing it on a voluntary basis. We are not getting any money for it. But every time we are trying to do something I know we get in the papers and they said that "Oh, the Native people are getting everything hand out."

. . . .

7b.4 Testimony of Harry Lavallee, National Aboriginal Veterans Association, 1993

Similar to the previous speakers in this section, Métis veteran Harry Lavallee served overseas during World War II. Lavallee outlines some of his experiences as a soldier and then speaks briefly about a return visit to Europe that a group of veterans made in 1989.

Source: Transcripts of the Hearings of the Royal Commission on Aboriginal Peoples, vol. 150, Vancouver, British Columbia, Wednesday, June 2, 1993, vol. 1, pp. 208–12 and 213–16. Privy Council Office 1993.

Reproduced with the permission of the Minister of Public Works and Government Services Canada, 2013.

MR. HARRY LAVALLEE: Good day, ladies and gentlemen, Royal Commission.

On February 12th, 1923 I was born to Metis parents who were Cree, So:to and French. We lived in Stonewall, Manitoba and we managed to survive the 1930's Depression even though we were a large family.

We moved to Winnipeg later and I attended school, grade 9 at Hugh John Macdonald.

After a stint with the reserve army, Winnipeg Light Infantry, I joined the Royal Winnipeg Rifles at Fort Ossen . . . Barracks on April the 22nd, 1941.

My basic training was at Portage la Prairie, Manitoba. All the men wore the same type of uniforms and I presented myself as a good soldier, considering my Metis background. But I was five foot eleven and a half in height and weighed only 133 pounds and felt somewhat ashamed that I was skinny.

I was happy with the discipline/training. I respect authority and the fellowship in the army. As a result, I was immediately chosen for a non-commissioned officer. I returned to Fort Ossen . . . Barracks to begin classes but unfortunately I got in the wrong company. I see the colonel to resign because I wanted to go overseas instead of stuck training all the recruits. Consequently, I transferred to the first regiment that was going overseas which was the Royal Canadian Ordinance Corps.

In October we left Halifax on the Ile de France ship and landed in Liverpool in November 1941. The trip had taken 11 days and nights of dangerous waters, enemy submarines, and we couldn't take any shortcuts.

On board we were fed mutton: mutton for breakfast, mutton for lunch and supper, and a great surprise! Mutton every day.

I will never order the pork chops again.

I was fortunate or naïve enough not to be seasick, but others in the company were not so lucky.

I have many stories about that trip overseas. I spent three years in England mainly at Camp Borden. There was ample opportunity to upgrade my education and skills in driving, in Canex, you name it. I could have done it, but me and my friends weren't interested; mainly because I didn't know or understand my situation. There was no counselling at that time to help me see the advantages of gaining more education skills.

In December '44 I applied for the Royal Winnipeg Rifles and by January 1945 I landed in Ghent, Belgium where I was put with the Queen's Own Cameron Highlanders. I was only in Ghent one month to prepare for the departure to the front lines by truck and arrived late at night. With artillery shells and bullets all around, laying there in the trenches with shrapnel hitting the dirt beside me, I was scared. "Scared" will have to encompass all the emotions I felt in the trenches. We lost a sergeant that first pitch black night of front line duty. The next day we were trapped too close to the enemy for 48 hours until our dive bombers wiped out the Germans.

The third division fought off the Germans and engineers put up the bailey bridges and we carried over the Rhine River, the other side being German territory.

We threw a hand grenade in the window of a house and captured 88 Huns. We went along until we got to Gronningen, Holland where the Germans convenient left all the bridges up, so we had to bring them all down.

We lost our lieutenant over the last bridge by a sniper and we also lost a major earlier.

The Germans surrendered on May 8th and 9th, 1945 when we were in Uldenburg, Germany.

I was in Winnipeg, Manitoba in July, 1945 because I had to volunteer—I had volunteered for the Japan War. But while we were training and about to leave for Texas, they surrendered.

With the assistance of the United Native Nations (UNN) and Ron George, they formed in 1989 the Native Veterans Association which was changed to National Aboriginal Veterans Association (B.C. Chapter) (NAVA).

After many meetings and a campaign to raise funds with the assistance of many people who gathered some Second World War veterans, we proceeded on a pilgrimage to Europe on June the 2nd, 1989. The veterans, some wives, Ron George and myself wanted to visit the graves of our brothers and sisters in France, Belgium and Holland, because many of our people were there and had given the supreme sacrifice for our people in Canada.

. . .

While we were visiting in 1989 we formed a sacred circle every morning for our comrades. We prayed, sang and played the drum. We held a marching ceremony in every cemetery for our comrades, some of us shedding a tear; some of us praying for our relatives; some of us alone feeling the pain of our people back home.

We arrived at Normandy Beaches with the bus. The driver accidently parked there because he lost his way. We got off and headed for the beaches. We stopped and said we have to have a sacred circle here. So we performed prayers, drummed and sang, some in our own language.

One of our brothers, Al Thomas, from Chase, B.C., couldn't stand it and left the circle. We went and got him and he said "My buddy died on my lap over here," and he was crying.

When we finally got him back to the sacred circle we began to hug while we were circling traditionally, and we all started to bawl like babies. Or rather, like men and women who seen so much pain and were releasing some of that not forgotten pain of remembered brothers and sisters.

It was mentioned later, some of us heard the moaning of the wounded, the actual shells, machine guns and dive bombers. Most of us also received some healing and were able to open and break our silence. Bless you, comrades, who gave your lives; bless you, veterans, of the First and Second World Wars who have fought to be recognized; who have been instrumental in organizing our people in the courts, in prison, in schools, on the streets, fighting for our rights, while our heroes have died in the wars—in the streets, hospitals and prisons.

Thank you [for] fighting for our rights in this country, for land, for jobs and for education, yet our veterans are not recognized as First Nations people as owners of this land.

There is no justice for us. Other people's laws like the Indian Act represent discrimination of the worst kind.

Some of us were given a number; some of us are called status, non-status, Metis, half-breed, urban Indians, savages. Some of us are called mice, bad, dirty, don't-know-nothing Indians. Some of us are given land on reserves. Native housing in cities are like reserves and we have to beg to receive adequate funding because of arbitrary funding cuts.

Some of us pay taxes; some do not. After all these years some of us are being recognized but that is all. What about all the benefits the veterans earned by defending this land? What about our rights in this day and age? What about the devil's Indian Act?

Thank you.

7b.5 *The Aboriginal Soldier after the Wars, 1995*

The Standing Senate Committee on Aboriginal People was established in 1994 with a mandate to study the treatment of the Indigenous veterans of World War I, World War II, and the war in Korea. The committee included Senator Len Marchand of the Okanagan Nation and the first status Indian elected to Canada's parliament, as deputy chairman. The committee heard from Indigenous veterans and representatives of their organizations as well as from Canadian government officials including those from the Department of Indian Affairs. The committee published its report in March of 1995. The selections below formed a part of that report.

Source: Canada, Senate, The Standing Senate Committee on Aboriginal Peoples, "Assessment," in *The Aboriginal Soldier after the Wars: Report of the Standing Senate Committee on Aboriginal Peoples* (Ottawa: The Senate of Canada, 1995), 25–34.

Reproduced with the permission of the Senate of Canada, 2013.

The footnotes appear as in the original document.

CHAPTER FOUR

ASSESSMENT

As the review of grievances heard by the Committee demonstrates, it is the opinion of many Aboriginal veterans that they were treated unfairly by veterans' legislation and its administration, by procedures that promoted enfranchisement, and in their overall recognition and treatment after the wars.

Veterans who appeared before or wrote to the Committee were genuine in their convictions and deep feelings of injustice. The Committee takes their grievances very seriously. Indeed, it was the gravity of their concerns that prompted our study in the first place.

This chapter provides the Committee's appraisal of the issues. In it, our intent is to clarify, to the extent possible, the record, and to give the Committee's conclusions based on the hearings and the documentary evidence placed before it.

. . .

VETERANS' LEGISLATION AND BENEFITS

A. The Equity of Veterans' Legislation

The central question is whether the legislation covering veterans was unfair. Much of this legislation is accessible for study and analysis. In itself, the legislation does not appear to be discriminatory. Most provisions applied to all veterans, not making any distinctions between those who were Aboriginal and non-Aboriginal. The extent to which a veteran was entitled to apply for benefits varied from act to act, depending upon other benefits received and whether or not the veteran met the necessary qualifications. Yet it is clear that all veterans, whether Aboriginal or non-Aboriginal, were eligible for them. All veterans were entitled to receive a War Service Gratuity, based on the time spent in the armed forces. All were also eligible for a re-establishment credit, which could be used for several purposes. In lieu of a re-establishment credit, veterans could opt for a grant or loan under the VLA, or training or educational benefits under the *War Rehabilitation Act*. It was an either/or situation, and all veterans could choose only one of these options.

Veterans Affairs officials emphasized in their testimony that legislation did not distinguish between veterans. The only separate reference to Aboriginal veterans was contained in the *Veterans' Land Act*. We will consider the VLA more closely, since it did contain provisions specific to status Indians, and provided the focus for most of the criticism.

1. Veterans' Land Act

Several grievances were expressed in the hearings: 1) that Indian veterans could not settle off reserve under the VLA; 2) that they were forced to settle on reserve, were deprived of access to VLA loans, and were not granted equal VLA benefits on reserve; and 3) that the type of land ownership on reserve was not equivalent to that available off-reserve.

A review of documentation shows that, to all appearances, Indian veterans who qualified for the VLA were free to settle on land outside an Indian reserve and receive all the benefits outlined in the legislation. The Chief Executive Assistant to the Minister of Indian Affairs stated in 1943 that "any Indian returned soldiers who may desire to go into farming off the Reserve will be permitted to do so if they are able to qualify in the same manner as other returned soldiers have to qualify."[2] Their cases were to be handled in the same fashion as those of other veterans. It has been suggested, however, that if an Indian veteran settled off reserve to claim VLA benefits, he would lose his status. This is not stipulated in any of the legislation, but it was a concern held by some veterans. The VLA would seem to be an improvement over the *Soldier Settlement Acts of 1917 and 1919* that provided veterans with quarter sections (160 acres) of land. This legislation seemed to contradict an amendment to the *Indian Act* of 1906 which prevented any Indian, veteran or otherwise, from acquiring homesteads off reserve in western Canada.

While many Indians wanted to return to their homes and communities on reserve, others felt that they were forced to settle on reserve land. Although veterans with land on reserve were eligible for VLA benefits, in particular the $2,320 grant, they did not have access to the $6,000 low cost loan available to qualified veterans off reserve. This was the source of significant feelings of grievance.

According to DVA officials the benefits available to qualified Indian veterans residing on reserve land were the same as those available to other qualified veterans who chose to settle on provincial or Dominion Crown land. David Nicholson of Veterans Affairs told the Committee:

> The Aboriginal veterans associations have often complained that 'Indian veterans got only $2,320 while other veterans got $6,000.' That complaint appears to arise from a misunderstanding of the act. The amount of financial assistance in the form of loans and grants provided to Aboriginal and non-Aboriginal veterans alike was dependent on the type of establishment chosen by each individual and was in no way related to whether the veteran had Indian status or was of Aboriginal origin . . . In addition to the rights enjoyed by all veterans, Aboriginal and non-Aboriginal alike, Indian veterans had the special privilege of obtaining VLA assistance to establish themselves on reserve land . . . The same amount was available as a grant to any qualified veteran, Indian or non-Indian who settled on Crown land.[3]

Testimony of our Aboriginal witnesses indicates that although the appearance is one of equality, several factors come into play that may have given rise to inequities. First of all, it is not clear whether there were significant numbers of non-Aboriginal veterans settling on Crown Land, or if these rules primarily affected status Indians settling on reserve and other Aboriginal people, often Metis, settling on "Crown Land" (such "Crown Land" in many cases being the historical area inhabited by the Aboriginal people

---

2 Quoted in A. Sweeney, *Government Policy and Saskatchewan Indian Veterans*, November 1979, p. 53.

3 *Proceedings*, 26 April 1994, p. 5:8–9, Mr. David Nicholson, DVA.

concerned). In addition, the benefits were the same, but the administration was not. In each case, the veterans did not necessarily receive an outright grant and did not receive the entire amount. They had to justify each purchase. As we heard in the case of non-Indians, or Aboriginal peoples off-reserve, the grant was administered by district offices of the VLA. In the case of Indians on reserve, the VLA rules applied, but the Indian Agent was also involved in the grant process.

Concerns were also raised about the use of the grant. In its report to the Royal Commission on Aboriginal Peoples, the National Aboriginal Veterans Association reviewed the VLA policy and regulations. It found that Article 39, paragraph 4 of the VLA regulations did state that Indian veterans' grants for household equipment could not exceed $250, and trapping or fur farming could not exceed $850. There was no stipulation of either maximum or minimum amounts for non-Aboriginal veterans in the regulations. However, NAVA concluded that:

> The review of VAC and Indian Affairs legislation indicates that, with the exception of Article 39, para. 4 of the VLA regulations, there is no evidence of any legislative attempt to discriminate against Aboriginal veterans or to in any way treat them as less important than non-Aboriginal veterans . . . In fact, sec. 35 of the VLA could be seen to indicate a desire on the part of the government to "level the playing field" when it came to the benefits available to Aboriginal veterans.[4]

The third grievance relates to the nature of individual land possession on reserves. Individual possession of land on a reserve is a unique form of land tenure. Land is held collectively for the band, and the general rule is that an individual Indian cannot possess reserve land without an allotment by the band. A certificate of possession, evidence of the right to possession of reserve land, is issued by the Minister after an allotment has been made by the band council. Rights of possession under earlier Indian Acts were referred to as "location title" and individuals held location tickets to the land. The allotment of reserve land provides a right that is similar to fee simple ownership in many respects. Land can be passed on to heirs, sold or transferred during the lifetime of the owner.[5] However, legal title to the land remains with the Crown. "The *Indian Act* does not make clear the character of a right that attaches to a Certificate of Possession, and in particular, whether it may be revoked at will by the band council or Minister."[6] Some bands, particularly on the prairies, have historically been reluctant to use Certificates of Possession or other *Indian Act* provisions for individual land holdings on reserves. They followed traditional land allotment patterns, allotting land at the discretion of the band council and avoiding Ministerial validation of the allotment. This resulted in questionable security of land tenure of the individual.

In order to be eligible for a VLA grant of $2,320, Indian veterans had to have some land; an area large enough for full time farming, or a minimum of 3 acres (a small holding) for part time farming. The three-acre requirement did not apply to commercial fishermen.

---

4 National Aboriginal Veterans Association, *Aboriginal Veterans: Service and Alliance Re-Examined*, p. 13.

5 Jack Woodward, *Native Law*, Toronto, Carswell, 1989. Note, however, that who may inherit the land or acquire a right to possession is limited by the *Indian Act*.

6 B. Morse, *Aboriginal Peoples and the Law*, Ottawa, Carleton University Press, 1985, p. 518.

To demonstrate land possession, VLA applications required: 1) where title was being acquired from another Indian, clear evidence of title by the owner; 2) where land was being allotted by the band, an application for a location ticket or a resolution of the band or council allotting the land to the Indian veteran; 3) where the Indian was already occupying the land, a resolution of the band or council confirming that the Indian veteran was the recognized owner. Some of the problems described in the hearings are likely a result of not obtaining valid Certificates of Possession, or of having rights to the land revoked.

For Indians on reserve, veterans policies operated within the constraints imposed by the *Indian Act*. Meshing the VLA requirements with the legal requirements regarding land holding under the Indian Act, as applied on any particular reserve, or as varied by traditional practices of the community, undoubtedly led to some of the problems described in our hearings. The VLA provisions appear to represent a genuine attempt to make benefits available to veterans who wanted to settle on reserves, within the laws, policies and practices of the day. They did not, however, take into account the particular needs of living situations of veterans returning to Aboriginal communities.

B. The Administration of Veterans' Benefits

While a careful study of veterans' legislation does not appear to indicate any deliberate attempt on the part of the government to discriminate against Aboriginal veterans, this is not to suggest that the grievances are simply a red herring. They are not. The legislation may not have demonstrated a maliciousness of intent, but when combined with the prejudices of the day and the strictures imposed by the *Indian Act*, the door was open for "malfeasance, misinformation and the undercutting of a relationship of trust and respect."[7]

Veterans were not automatically entitled to receive benefits by the mere fact of their participation in the war. They had first to apply for them and also to receive a recommendation from the appropriate authorities. After that, it was up to the government to deliver these benefits in an efficient and non-discriminatory manner. It is therefore in the area of administration, especially at the local level, that problems have arisen. For instance, while Indian Affairs did inform its Indian Agents in March 1945 that Indian veterans could settle off reserve, it noted, "the average Indian veteran may be confronted with a practical difficulty in seeking qualification papers from the responsible committees set up for the purpose, who may be expected to feel some diffidence about qualifying an Indian for establishment on the land on a debt basis. In other words, it is feared that few Indians could qualify under the conditions set by the Act."[8] The expectation of "diffidence about qualifying an Indian" underscores the fact that, although they had been equal on the battlefield, Indians encountered paternalism and prejudice at home.

1. The Administration of Benefits on Reserve

In addition to complying with the requirements of the DVA bureaucracy, Indian veterans who returned to reserves were confronted with the powers of the Indian Agent.

---

7 National Aboriginal Veterans Association, *Aboriginal Veterans: Service and Alliance Re-Examined*, p. 22.

8 See Davidson, *We Shall Remember: Canadian Indians and World War II*, Reprinted in appendix. [Appendix not included in original.]

Whether they received their benefits depended very much on how the Indian Agent on a particular reserve exercised his considerable discretionary powers. There is evidence to suggest that this was the weak link in the delivery of benefits to Indian veterans on reserves.

. . .

Non-Indian veterans had no such middlemen to deal with. If they wanted benefits, they had to cope with the DVA themselves, but, on the other hand, they were free to deal with the DVA bureaucracy themselves, and make their own decisions.

A significant example of the differences in administration of benefits arises in relation to obtaining goods and services from the $2,320 grant which land-holding veterans on reserve or other Crown Land received instead of the $6,000 loan available to veterans who owned other land. Both Indians and others residing on Crown Land (who also might be Metis or otherwise of Aboriginal origin) had to follow rigid procedures in order to receive goods or services. In the case of veterans settling on non-reserve Crown land, the grant was administered by district officers of the VLA. In the case of status Indian veterans settling on reserve, VLA procedures had to be complied with, but the Indian Agent played a major role.

The administration in the case of a status Indian was as follows. Indian Agents did not receive money. Once a purchase was considered to be justified within the terms of the VLA, the Indian Agent made the purchase on behalf of the veteran. For each purchase, the Agent filled out a form indicating the amount spent. Both the person selling the item and the Indian veteran receiving the goods had to sign this form, and both signatures had to be witnessed. Invoices and vouchers were then forwarded to the Indian Affairs Branch, who sent payment directly to the person or business who had sold the goods.

When the grant was to be used for hiring local people, for example, to clear land or do construction, a cheque was issued for the Agency Office Trust Fund, and the Indian Agent paid the workers directly. The Indian Affairs Branch was to report to the Director, VLA, the total amount of grants disbursed in a fiscal year, and refund to the VLA any undisbursed balance on the grants. Undisbursed balances required in the new fiscal year could be made available by application to the Director, VLA. These purchasing procedures, the signing and witnessing of forms, and how they were applied in individual cases, gave rise to many of the grievances we heard.

2. Communication about Benefits

On paper at least, all veterans should have been thoroughly briefed by demobilization officers immediately upon their return to Canada. Certain demobilization officers may have failed in this capacity, but it would be nearly impossible to determine whether only Aboriginal veterans were victims.

Certainly the means by which DVA chose to publicize and distribute updated information concerning entitlements—whether through notices to those who were already collecting some form of benefit, announcements in newspapers or posted notices in servicemen's clubs like the Royal Canadian Legion—is open to question. The department did not always take into account that many Aboriginal veterans may not have been receiving benefits early on, that they had the lowest literacy rates in the country, that they were not likely to buy a paper and were generally not members of Legions in that era and that often, especially in the case of the Metis, they lived in remote regions of the country.

3. Current Benefits

Many veterans, Aboriginal and non-Aboriginal, have tragic stories to relate about long and bitter struggles with the Department of Veterans Affairs. Many veterans complained to the Committee about the paternalistic and cumbersome nature of some programs. In the case of disability pensions in particular, the process remains problematic, and just recently the Senate Subcommittee on Veterans Affairs tabled a report recommending ways in which it could be improved for all veterans.[9]

ENFRANCHISEMENT

According to officials of the Department of Indian Affairs who testified, enfranchisement was not a condition for enlistment of Indians in the armed forces. That is, there was not an explicit policy or legal requirement for status Indians who enlisted or served to enfranchise. In its report, NAVA also concluded that there is no legislation, nor any documents in the Service Files they examined that would indicate that forced enfranchisement was an approved or even a common situation

While there was not an overall policy or legal requirement for status Indian soldiers to enfranchise, we were told of cases in which local Indian Agents or officers pressured Indians to enfranchise. In the testimony of individuals, and in the documents reviewed, there are numerous cases of veterans who felt they had been enfranchised as a result of their military service. Departmental officials acknowledged these cases, commenting that while enfranchisement was not a condition for enlistment or overseas service:

> *The record shows that it did happen. Presenters have recalled in their own experiences that there was a degree of encouragement about that.*[10]

The Department also noted that records show that there were significantly more enfranchisements around the period of World War I and World War II, but did not speculate about reasons for the increased number.[11] The Committee was unable to determine the total number of enfranchisements that resulted from direct or indirect encouragement relating to the war effort.

Enfranchisement was certainly an important part of the overall thrust of policy toward Indians at that time.

. . .

9 Subcommittee on Veterans Affairs of the Standing Senate Committee on Social Affairs, Science and Technology, *Keeping Faith: Into the Future*, October 1994.

10 *Proceedings*, 26 April 1994, p. 5:13, Rem Westland, Acting Assistant Deputy Minister, Claims and Indian Government.

11 *Proceedings*, 26 April 1994, p. 5:14, Rem Westland, Acting Assistant Deputy Minister, Claims and Indian Government.

One of the best places to start for further background material on many of the topics presented in this reader is Canada, Royal Commission on Aboriginal Peoples, *Report of the Royal Commission on Aboriginal Peoples* (Ottawa: Indian and Northern Affairs Canada, 1996). It is available in hard copy and on line. For a discussion of Indigenous military service, postwar experience, and related policy, see Chapter 12 "Veterans" or follow the links from http://www.collectionscanada.gc.ca/webarchives/20071124130133/http://www.ainc-inac.gc.ca/ch/rcap/sg/sgm12_e.html. Veterans Affairs Canada has produced a survey of Indigenous contributions during both World War I and World War II in Janice Summerby, *Native Soldiers, Foreign Battlefields* (Ottawa: Veterans Affairs Canada, 2005). This report, too, is available on line at http://www.veterans.gc.ca/eng/remembrance/history/other/native. Fred Gaffen's *Forgotten Soldiers: An Illustrated History of Canada's Native People in Both World Wars* (Penticton, BC: Theytus Books, 1985) was one of the first to consider the subject of Indigenous veterans and is still worth consulting, even if there are some shortcomings and omissions.

For an exploration of the reasons First Nations people from the prairies enlisted for service in World War I and of both their roles as soldiers and the efforts of those who remained in Canada, see L. James Dempsey, *Warriors of the King: Prairie Indians in World War I* (Regina: Canadian Plains Research Center, 1999). In "'An Infamous Proposal': Prairie Indian Reserve Land and Soldier Settlement after World War I," *Manitoba History* 37 (Spring/Summer 1999): 9–21, Sarah Carter examines Canada's acquisition of significant quantities of reserve land to make available to non-Indigenous veterans. For a study of the returned soldiers and their experience with the soldier settlement program with a focus on Ontario, see Robin Brownlee, "Work Hard and Be Grateful: Native Soldier Settlers in Ontario after the First World War," in *On the Case: Explorations in Social History*, ed. Franca Iacovetta and Wendy Mitchinson (Toronto: University of Toronto Press, 1998). For relatively brief treatments of Indigenous efforts during World War I as part of larger studies, see Sarah Carter, *Lost Harvests: Prairie Indian Reserve Farmers and Government Policy* (Montreal: McGill-Queen's University Press, 1990), 249; Brian Titley, *A Narrow Vision: Duncan Campbell Scott and the Administration of Indian Affairs in Canada* (Vancouver: UBC Press, 1986), 39–47; and Keith D. Smith, *Liberalism, Surveillance and Resistance: Indigenous Communities in Western Canada, 1877–1927* (Edmonton: University of Athabasca Press, 2009), 223–31.

Military historian Whitney P. Lackenbauer has written several pieces related to Indigenous people and their territories during the World War II period and beyond. See, for example, *Battlegrounds: The Canadian Military and Aboriginal Lands* (Vancouver: UBC Press, 2007). Fellow military historian R. Scott Sheffield writes about the images of Indigenous people presented to the Canadian public during World War II in *The Red Man's on the Warpath: The Image of the "Indian" and the Second World War* (Vancouver: UBC Press, 2004). For an exploration of the connections between the experiences of Indigenous veterans and post–World War II political activity, see Robert A. Innes, "The Socio-Political Influence of the Second World War Saskatchewan Aboriginal Veterans, 1945–1960," MA Thesis, Department of Native Studies, University of Saskatchewan, 2000. This thesis is available on line at http://ecommons.usask.ca/bitstream/handle/10388/etd-06292007-113525/Innes_robert_2000.pdf. Indigenous veterans' associations have also produced material related to wartime service and postwar treatment. For Saskatchewan, for example, see *The Saskatchewan First Nations Veterans Association Issues Paper* available at http://www.fsin.com/fsindownloads/sfnva/issues_paper_trpf.pdf. Readers may also wish to consult the film *Forgotten Warriors* by Loretta Todd (Montreal: National Film Board of Canada, 1996). This film explores Canada's policies and the experience of soldiers through the voices of Indigenous veterans.

CHAPTER 8

A "COMPLETE AND FINAL SOLUTION"[1]

PREPARING FOR THE NEW INDIAN ACT OF 1951

The interwar period in Canada was witness to even greater pressure applied to Indigenous people to assimilate into Euro-Canadian society than had been exerted earlier (see the previous chapters of this reader for evidence of earlier assimilative initiatives). Yet, like their predecessors, the strategies of assimilation through enfranchisement and other methods were much less successful than their promoters hoped. Contrary to earlier predictions, First Nations communities were growing in size rather than vanishing into the mists of time. Collective identity and connection to cultural practices remained strong despite the array of policy and legislation put in place to bring both to an end. After World War II, because of robust Indigenous participation in the war effort and increased attention to human rights globally, there was a growing interest in Indigenous affairs in Canada.

Many individuals and organizations called for the establishment of a royal commission to reconsider the Indian Act, to look into the administration of Indians, and to investigate the socio-economic conditions that prevailed in First Nations communities. Clearly, public awareness was increasing across the country concerning the discriminatory treatment faced by those defined as Indians, and the fact that they were not citizens with the ability to affect Canada's laws and political structures was beginning to be seen as unfair. In the end, Prime Minister William Lyon Mackenzie King's government did not establish a royal commission; instead, a joint committee of the Senate and House of Commons was appointed in 1946 to propose changes to both the Indian Act and the administration of Indians. Its rather unwieldy name was the Special Joint Committee of the

---

1 Evidence of Diamond Jenness, Special Joint Committee of the Senate and the House of Commons Appointed to Examine and Consider the Indian Act, *Minutes of Proceedings and Evidence*, No. 7, 25 March 1947 (Ottawa: Edmond Cloutier, 1947), 310. This quotation appears in document 8.1.

Senate and the House of Commons Appointed to Examine and Consider the Indian Act (abbreviated to SJC in this chapter). The SJC had a mandate to consider everything from treaty rights to residential and day schools and from enfranchisement to community social issues. Glaringly absent, though, was a primary concern of Indigenous people themselves: self-government and the limited control communities had in their own affairs.

The first four of the five selections in this chapter consist of evidence and submissions to the SJC during its two years of operation. The fifth document is from a summary of a meeting between 19 First Nations representatives from across Canada and the minister responsible for Indian affairs. This five-day meeting was meant to consider proposed amendments to the Indian Act. Although all of the documents in this chapter offer suggestions and recommendations for the future, they also illustrate the political and philosophical divides that existed between Indigenous peoples and Canadian politicians and civil servants. The submissions and testimony presented by Indigenous activists express a variety of perspectives and both generalizable concerns and those specific to particular communities and nations. Some call for increased Indigenous control within the system created by Canada's Indian Act while others challenge the very legitimacy of that regime.

The new Indian Act of 1951 did drop some of the more draconian provisions of earlier legislation, which, in many ways, is the most generous aspect of the new act. For example, the ban against the potlatch was no longer incorporated in the Indian Act nor was the 1927 provision that made the raising of funds to pursue land claims illegal. Gender discrimination, though, remained and will be discussed in Chapter 11. Further, the assimilative thrust of earlier acts remained intact, even if in a form more reminiscent, in some cases at least, of the voluntary expressions of the 1876 version than in its more recent incarnations, which included increasingly compulsory enfranchisement provisions. The patriarchal foundations, then, remained unshaken after 1951 as did the long-term objectives, even if the means to accomplish those objectives were altered. As the SJC recommended, assimilation remained the central goal of the Indian Act and of policy, but this absorption into Euro-Canadian society would be encouraged rather than forced on those the state defined as Indians.

QUESTIONS FOR DISCUSSION

1. What aspects of Diamond Jenness's plan might First Nations activists have had concerns about?
2. What problems with the new Indian Act do the First Nations representatives identify?
3. Outline the differences in the submissions that the various First Nations' representatives made to the SJC.
4. Which of these submissions seems to have been most favourably received by the commissioners? Which was greeted least favourably? What accounts for these differences in reception?
5. Was the form and extent of consultation offered in the conference of 1951 sufficient in your view? Why or why not?

8.1 Evidence of Diamond Jenness, 1947

This selection includes the comments of Diamond Jenness, chief of the Inter-Services Topographical Section, Department of National Defence. Jenness, originally from New Zealand, trained as an anthropologist at Oxford University before coming to Canada to begin his study of the Indigenous peoples of Canada's Arctic region in the 1910s and 1920s. For more than two decades after 1926, he served as the chief of anthropology at the National Museum of Canada and is among Canada's best-known anthropologists. Like many in the federal government, and even in academia, Jenness was of the opinion that Indigenous peoples belonged to vanishing races whose best hope for the future was to assimilate into mainstream Canadian society. His testimony at the SJC in 1947 outlines his proposals for a "final and definite" solution to the "Indian Problem."

Source: Evidence of Diamond Jenness, Special Joint Committee of the Senate and the House of Commons Appointed to Examine and Consider the Indian Act, *Minutes of Proceedings and Evidence*, No. 7, 25 March 1947 (Ottawa: Edmond Cloutier, 1947), 309–11.

The footnote included below appears in the original.

. . .

I should like to tell you off the record about a little incident.

Canada's intentions towards her Indians were good. She was quite sincere when she established the reserve system to train them for citizenship. But how long is that training to last? Some of our eastern reserves were established 150 years ago. Does it take 150 years to convert an Indian into a useful citizen, but a Maori only one generation?

I am strongly of the opinion, therefore, that Canada should cease to shut her eyes to her Indian problem and should take her obligations seriously. How can our representatives abroad continue to champion the rights of small nations or of subject peoples when here at home we continue to keep our Indians, generation after generation, in what have become, whether we like to call them so or not, confinement camps?

Last night I happened to be reading this little brochure[2] brought out this year by the Canadian Institute of International Affairs and I came across this passage which I should like to read to you:—

> Canadians are generally unaware also that some residents of the nation are "non-self-governing" and that the condition of the Eskimos and Indians may properly be considered a subject for report to the trusteeship council of the united nations. Senator Wishart Robertson speaking before the united nations on November 14, 1946, said:—

---

2 "Frontier of Destiny—The Canadian Arctic," by Trevor Lloyd, published by Canadian Association for Adult Education and the Canadian Institute of International Affairs. Vol. VI, No. 7, at page 7.

We have all pledged ourselves to accept as a sacred trust the well-being of the inhabitants of all non-self-governing territories, no matter what form of administration they enjoy. It is our solemn responsibility to contribute as best we can to the attainment of these high objectives no matter in what capacity we may serve.

That includes the Indians of Canada.

It has often been objected that the greatest opposition to abandoning the present reserve system will come from the Indians themselves. That is quite true, for by this time they have developed the warped mentality of a segregated or outcast people. For precisely the same reason many displaced persons in the central European camps bitterly protest being forced away from the shelter of those camps.

A striking example of this "reserve" or outcast mentality, as I might call it, comes from the United States. After Pearl Harbor the United States government evacuated many thousand Japanese from California and confined them in a large camp in the middle west. When all danger had passed it decided to close this camp, and to let the Japanese re-establish themselves wherever they wished. A notice was therefore posted that the camp would be closed at the end of nine months, and a number of officials were appointed to help the occupants find new homes. The Japanese violently protested this new "eviction", as they termed it; the government, they said, had forcibly confined them to this camp in violation of their rights as citizens, and now it was morally obligated to maintain them there at the public expense unless it was prepared to restore all the land and other possessions in California that they had vacated. They held one protest meeting after another; but the government stood firm. Then, one by one and family by family, some of the Japanese began to trickle away and establish new homes in different places. As the weeks went by the trickle became a stream, until, when the camp was finally closed at the end of the nine months, only a very small percentage remained to be evacuated.

Some four years ago I drew up a condensed plan for liquidating our whole Indian reserve system within a definite time limit, which I fixed, somewhat arbitrarily, at twenty-five years. The precise number of years, however, is relatively unimportant; what is important is that the time limit should be definite and not too remote.

There are undoubtedly many weaknesses in my plan which will be evident to abler and more experienced administrators. Nevertheless, as I wrote to the Hon. Mr. Claxton when I submitted it to him last year (he was at that time Minister of National Health and Welfare), it does have one real merit. Instead of proposing merely temporary or palliative measures, it attacks the Indian problem right at its roots and sets a definite term for its complete and final solution.

Have I your permission to read this plan? It is very short.

PLAN FOR LIQUIDATING CANADA'S INDIAN PROBLEM
WITHIN 25 YEARS

Objective.

To abolish, gradually but rapidly the separate political and social status of the Indians (and Eskimos): to enfranchise them and merge them into the rest of the population on an equal footing. The realization of this plan should:

A. Improve the Indians' social and economic position, now so depressed as to create "leprous" spots in many parts of the country;

B. Abolish the permanent drain on the federal treasury of the millions of dollars yearly now spent on Indian administration.

C. Fulfil the almost forgotten pledge of the government when it adopted the system of confining the Indians to special reserves.

Outline of Plan.

1. Change the present Indian educational system by abolishing separate Indian schools and placing Indian children in the regular provincial schools, subject to all provincial school regulations.

For a period of 10 or more years this may require:—

(*a*) Per capita subsidies from the federal government in lieu of school taxes levied on Indian families:

In British Columbia, may I remark, you could see in the same little district Japanese children going to the schools with white children and half a mile away Indian children going to segregate schools—not half as good.

(*b*) Morale promotion among the Indians (e.g. clothing grants, home inspection, etc.) and an educational campaign among white school communities, to mitigate any prejudice.

(*c*) Special facilities (scholarships, etc.) for Indian children to attend technical schools and colleges remote from their homes.

2. Include the Indians (and Eskimos) in all "Reconstruction" measures, e.g. those dealing with unemployment, public health, health insurance, and other phases of social security.

3. Appoint immediately a commission of 3 (the chairman to be a judge, and one member an agriculturalist) to study the various Indian reservations throughout the Dominion and to advise on the best means of abolishing them, of enfranchising the inhabitants, and giving them an economic status comparable with that of their white neighbours. The commission should be given a broad mandate so that it may adjudicate in each case the relative merits and demerits of individual versus co-operative ownership of reserve lands, the proper disposition of trust funds, timber and mining rights, and other complicated problems. It should present its report within two years of its appointment, and legislation implementing its recommendations should follow with as little delay as possible.

4. Increase the educational facilities of the migratory northern Indians (whose territory is not suited for either farming or ranching) in order to qualify them for such new types of employment as: aeroplane mechanics, mineral prospecting, wireless operation, game and forest protection, fur farming, etc. These educational facilities might include:

All of these pursuits, even that of aeroplane pilots, were carried out by the Eskimos in Greenland and even by the Eskimos in Siberia. Before the war three Siberian Eskimos who live just across the strait from Alaska were civilian aeroplane pilots, but I doubt if we have a single Eskimo who could read the instructions on the dial of an aeroplane or even the barometer or the thermometer. In Greenland they are doing that all the time, and they are doing that even in Siberia.

(*a*) Intensive classes for children in ordinary school subjects, and special courses for adults in mineral prospecting, motor mechanics, etc., during the summer months when the Indians tend to congregate:

This plan was made out before there was an investigation into Indian education by Dr. Moore.

(*b*) Free technical training for selected boys and girls at suitable centres, e.g., Le Pas, Churchill, etc.

D. JENNESS.

April/1943.

That was my plan. As I say, it was drawn up four years ago by myself. It could be best understood by an experienced administrator like Mr. Hoey who is very much more experienced than I am; but its main merit is this: it does attack the Indian problem at its root; it sets a definite term for its solution and for a solution that will be final and definite. I thank you.

THE CHAIRMAN: Thank you Dr. Jenness.

MR. [THOMAS] REID: Mr. Chairman, I think I voice the views of all the committee when I say that this is one of the finest talks we have heard, and at the same time we have had presented to this committee a real plan, and with most of what has been said by Dr. Jenness I am personally in entire accord. We might as well make the statement boldly that we have failed in our policy in this regard for the past fifty years. I think the sooner the people of this country admit their mistakes the better, in view of facts that have come before this committee. We now have a real plan with most of which I am in complete agreement.

. . .

8.2 Testimony of Andrew Paull, President of the North American Indian Brotherhood, 1946

This testimony before the SJC features Andy Paull, President of the North American Indian Brotherhood. Paull was a Skwx̱wú7mesh (Squamish) activist and community organizer. He attended St Paul's Residential School as a child and later received a traditional education from the elders and leaders of his community. When still a teenager, Paull worked for four years at a Vancouver law firm, but he decided not to follow a career in law, a decision likely influenced by fear that he would be forced to give up his status as an Indian and become enfranchised. Paull later served on the executive committee of the Allied Tribes of British Columbia, and he appeared before a joint committee of the Senate and House of Commons appointed to inquire into their claims; both are discussed in Chapter 5b. After the 1927 ban on raising funds to pursue land claims and the collapse of the Allied Tribes, Paull moved to promote Indigenous concerns in more localized ways. In 1942, he re-entered the political arena and joined the Native Brotherhood of British Columbia (NBBC). The NBBC was never as successful as the Allied Tribes in gaining support beyond coastal BC, and Paull moved on to lead the North American Indian Brotherhood (NAIB). In the document presented here, he is speaking for the NAIB. As always, enfranchisement is a primary concern for Paull.

Source: Evidence of Andy Paull, North American Indian Brotherhood, Special Joint Committee of the Senate and the House of Commons Appointed to Examine and Consider the Indian Act, *Minutes of Proceedings and Evidence*, No. 9, 27 June 1946 (Ottawa: Edmond Cloutier, 1946), 426–29.

. . .

THE WITNESS [CHIEF ANDREW PAULL]: . . . Now I will come perhaps to the matter of Indian administration; that is part of your reference, is it not?

THE CHAIRMAN: That is right.

THE WITNESS: We condemn as a piece of useless legislation whatever you white people call it, that department of your government which is called Department of Indian Affairs. And now, I commend most highly what Mr. Hoey has done, and what Mr. Quinn has done; but when you go out into the field and you have a white man that is called an agent—now, there are some Indian agents who are very good, but it is the opinion of the Indians of Canada that some of your Indian agents have no soul that they can curse. They have not even got a body that they can catch. That is the kind of man you have got out there trying to administer your wishes.

Now, I was supposed to speak in generalities. The parliament of Canada voted large sums of money for Indians. It starts out like a nice beautiful river; at its mouth it is a great big river, but by the time you follow this money upstream, the money which you gentlemen vote for the Indian, by the time you travel up the river to the agency, to the headwaters so to speak, you can't even get your feet on a piece of wet sand because of your system of political preferment.

Now, excuse me for saying that, but you are here because of political preferment; but in duty to my people I must say that. You understand that, Mr. Chairman?

THE CHAIRMAN: Quite.

ONE HON. MEMBER: Do you include Mr. MacNicol in that?

THE WITNESS: No, Chief (Mr. MacNicol) you are not in the government so you have nothing to say. You are lucky.

Now, friends—I think the highest compliment I can offer to members of the committee is to call them friends—we would like to change this kind of legislation; and I am here to say to you that the only way you can change it and put it in a good way is to let Indians administer Indians.

And now, permit me to give you an illustration. When the white people were in terror on the Pacific coast, when they were afraid that the Japs were going to invade British Columbia, they had every scow, every skiff, every boat ready to take the white people off from Vancouver Island; and they had every road mined in case the Japs invaded Vancouver Island. Now, the white people were afraid, they were in absolute terror. There was a great big military camp at Nanaimo. Those soldiers were the soldiers who were going to defend that country, the western gateway to Canada. Now, who did they have as supreme commander of the soldiers over there when the white man was afraid of his life; who did they have ready to protect those lives? They had Brigadier Martin, an Indian. And when in a time of crisis and peril like that you can trust your life to an Indian, I submit that you can trust an Indian to be an agent, a superintendent or something like that.

I say to you, honourable Mr. Chairman, that we have Indians qualified to do some of the government work that you men are doing, and we present that case as an illustration, that when your life is in peril you rely on an Indian. And now, in the United States, every boy is told that he can become president of the United States the minute he goes to school. In Canada to-day there is no Indian who can become an agent or anything like that. And now, in this war and in the last war we had many Indians who took a very prominent part. They marched shoulder to shoulder with your men. We have Indians throughout Canada who have a greater degree of learning than the illiterate Indian agent who supervises and administers your laws over those Indians. That thing must be stopped. We can quote you cases, and we can mention personalities, but we are not going to disturb the mentality of this committee with that. I am going to speak to Mr. Hoey the head man of the Indian Department.

We want you to lift up the morale of the Indians in Canada. That is your first duty. There is no use in passing legislation about this or that if you do not lift up the morale of the people. The only way you can lift up the morale of any people is to let their members look after themselves and look after their people. Do you understand what I mean, Mr. Chairman?

THE CHAIRMAN: Yes, quite clearly.

THE WITNESS: I mean by that, you should put into the Civil Service Indians that are qualified to look after Indians, and you should fire some of those rotten Indian agents you have got now. If you accept my recommendations, there will be no more white Indian agents in Canada.

While I am on that subject, I would say to you, gentlemen, that we have considered this matter of administration, and that we are of the opinion that the Indians should be given self-government; by that we mean self-government under you; we do not mean a rebellion; do you understand me clearly on that? We mean that there should be an Indian council which would meet, and there would be no Indian agent there when the Indian council meets, and we believe there should be a provincial council, and that the provincial council should be responsible to a central board of governors in Ottawa who are not responsible to the government in power, but who are responsible to the parliament of Canada. In that way, it is our well considered opinion, you would eradicate a lot of the things that are going on now in the administration of Indian affairs. We say there ought to be a board in control of each conference, and that there should be Indians on that board in each province. The council in each tribe could make their representations to that board and that board could send their recommendations to the federal board in Ottawa, and there would be Indians on that board too. I am not looking for any of these jobs myself because I won't be here when you get these things through. I may be up enjoying my heavenly privileges.

THE CHAIRMAN: Would you like to call it one o'clock now, Mr. Paull?

THE WITNESS: I should like to take a rest although we still have 15 minutes to go; perhaps you are tired of listening to me?

THE CHAIRMAN: Not at all.

THE WITNESS: For the next 15 Minutes I would like to ask your counsel and liaison officer to read this paper, then we will speak about it this afternoon.

THE CHAIRMAN: Very well, is that agreed?

MR. [WILFRID] GARIEPY: We have read the paper.

MR. [JOHN HORNE] BLACKMORE: I suggest we allow Mr. Paull to have his way.

THE CHAIRMAN: It is wholly within the province of this committee, whether you allow Mr. Lickers to read this paper and put it on the record.

MR. [JOHN RITCHIE] MACNICHOL: It would take only five minutes to do so.

THE CHAIRMAN: Very well. All those in favour? Contrary? Mr. Lickers, would you please read the statement.

MR. [SAM] LICKERS: This is a written recommendation in general terms: It reads as follows:

The Secretary having read to the meeting the telegram from the clerk to the joint committee of the Senate and House of Commons on the Indian Act addressed to Mr. Paull inviting him to give evidence before the committee on the 27th of June, the meeting resolved:

That Mr. Paull attend on behalf of the North American Indian Brotherhood, and make a statement on their behalf upon their position under, and attitude towards the present Act, and its administration, dealing with the following subjects under the reference to the joint committee, and expressing the views of this meeting as contained in the following several paragraphs viz:—

(1) That the joint committee enquire into the Treaty Rights and the encroachments upon the right as and privileges of the several bands hereunder;

(2) That the powers of the Department of Indian Affairs in respect of the admission and expulsion be abolished, and that the right of membership both as to admission and expulsion be placed under the jurisdiction of the band and council, and the Indian Act be revised accordingly and any right to appeal from the council's decision be referred to a board on which the Indians shall have representation;

(3) That by virtue of their treaty rights, Indians are not liable for payment of taxes either to the dominion or to the provincial governments;

(4) That by virtue of their treaty rights, Indians are not liable to any provincial laws within their territories respecting fishing, hunting and trapping, and, therefore, are not liable to take out licences from the provincial governments to fish, hunt and trap within their territories or within any lands covered by their treaties;

(5) That the policy of enfranchisement of Indians involving loss of treaty rights be abolished;

(6) That all denominational schools within reservations be abolished and the education of Indians be committed to regional boards upon which Indians in the regional districts shall be represented by Indians;

(7) That Indians are not now prepared to discuss the question of the right to vote at Dominion elections, but that the question of the right of Indians to elect their own member to the House of Commons should be studied;

(8) That the interests of the Indians demand that the administration of Indian affairs be decentralized and administered by provincial regional boards under a federal department or board responsible to parliament;

(9) That the administration of Indian affairs should be such that qualified Indians should be employed in all departments in the administration of Indian affairs;

(10) That local Indian councils be given full authority in the management of their local affairs;

(11) That in view of some tribes having the privilege of travelling on all railroads at half fare, that the Railway Act be amended to give that privilege to all Canadian Indians;

(12) That the band or tribe be given full authority to policing their own reserves;

(13) That no centralization scheme of any bands or tribes be carried out with the consent of the majority of the bands involved.

. . .

8.3 Submission of the Union of Saskatchewan Indians, 1947

The Union of Saskatchewan Indians (USI) was formed in 1946 by a merger of three pre-existing provincially based organizations. Its primary goals were to protect treaty rights and foster the improvement in economic, educational, and social conditions for Saskatchewan First Nations. The USI later became the Federation of Saskatchewan Indians and then, in the early 1980s, the Federation of Saskatchewan Indian Nations. In this excerpt from its submission to the SJC, the Union of Saskatchewan Indians offers a critique of the proposed amendments to the Indian Act.

Source: "Submission of the Union of Saskatchewan Indians," 8 May 1947, appendix ES of Special Joint Committee of the Senate and the House of Commons Appointed to Examine and Consider the Indian Act, *Minutes of Proceedings and Evidence*, No. 19, 8 May 1947 (Ottawa: Edmond Cloutier, 1947), 988–90, 992–94, and 999–1002.

. . .

PART II

Rocommendations [sic] respecting the Indian Act, R.S.C. 1827 [1927]

Chapter 98, as amended.

41. *Wide powers of Governor-in-Council and Superintendent-General*

The first and most obvious criticism of the Indian Act derives from the extremely wide powers which are thereby invested in the Governor-General in Council, and more particularly in the Superintendent-General. Although Part I of the Indian Act purports to be of wide and general application, section 3 endows the Governor-in-Council with power to:—

Exempt from the operations of this Part . . . Indians or non-treaty Indians, or any of them, or any band or irregular band of them, or the reserves or special reserves, or Indian lands or any portion of them . . .

Thus, upon mere proclamation, the efficacy of Part I of the Act may be abrogated, and the statutory legislative intent set at naught.

It is submitted that since this clause leaves the way clear for arbitrary judgments by the Governor-in-Council, it should be repealed. The matter of exempting Indians from the rights provided by the Act should, in line with democratic procedure, be a matter not for any one man to decide but one on which only the Courts should rule.

Qualified legal counsel to act in the behalf of the Indians should be provided by the Crown in such matters and a thorough and fair hearing should be extended to them.

Section 18 of the Indian Act provides that "the Superintendent General (Minister) may, from time to time, upon the report of an officer or other persons specifically appointed by him to make an inquiry, determine who is or who is not a member of any band of Indians entitled to share in the property and annuities of the band.["]

Sub-section 2 provides that the decision of the Superintendent General (Minister) in any such matter shall be final and conclusive, subject to an appeal to the Governor-in-Council.

Under this section, the Superintendent and the Governor-in-Council are given sole jurisdiction to determine who is and who is not an Indian and who may or who may not benefit from the treaties and other rights enjoyed by Indians. The Indians of this Organization object to this method of determining who may come under the Treaties. Because of the fact that when the Treaties were signed, the white man was content to leave it entirely to the discretion of the Indian Chiefs and their Councillors to determine who were to enjoy the Treaty rights, they feel that this section cannot be construed as anything but an abrogation of certain Treaty rights. It is necessary that these maters should be determined by the Indians themselves according to the customs and traditions of Indian bands. It is therefore, submitted that section 18 of the Indian Act should be repealed and there should be substituted therefor, a provision whereby the determination of the Indian band as to the membership of any person in such band who is entitled to share in the property and annuities of the band should be within the sole jurisdiction of the Indian band itself to determine according to democratic principles. In this regard, reference should particularly be made to Order in Council Nos. 1172 and 1182 and also the case of *Regina v Howson*, 1 Territory Law Reports 492, and also to the report of a recent inquiry of The Honourable Mr. Justice W. A. MacDonald in the Lesser Slave Lake area.

Furthermore, this Organization submits that there should be immediately undertaken an investigation of all persons and their families expelled from Treaty rights under Section 18, with the object of restoring them to Band Rolls and complete treaty privileges if the Indian Band so deems it proper and just.

42. *The position of Superintendent–General is especially anomalous*

The position of Superintendent-General is an especially anomalous one, in that the Act purports to require him to act as agent for the Crown, and also as representative of the

Indians. It is true that theoretically, Indians are wards of the Crown, and as such, enjoy the benefits and advantages which the Crown may afford and extend to them through its agents. To this extent, the Superintendent General, as agent of the Crown, may be deemed to be in a position in which he is able to extend such benefits. But there are cases in which a *cestui que trust*, i.e., the person to benefit from the existence of the trust (in the position of which the Indians may be deemed to be) are entitled to advice and services apart altogether from those extended to it by a trustee (in this case, the Crown). One of the principal difficulties appears to have arisen in Indian Affairs because the same person has sought to act and represent the interests of both the Crown and the Indians (the trustee and the *cestui que trust*). The result has been that the Superintendent-General, who has been placed in this inconsistent position, has found it impossible to advance the interests of both parties at the same time. He has, therefore, leaned heavily in favour of the Crown, it being the stronger, more vocal and the more affluent to the two parties.

43. *Indians should exercise their vote freely in matters of Indian concern*

The precedent of permitting Indians to exercise their vote freely and universally, in determining the question of release or surrender of a reservation is established by Section 51 of the Indian Act. This is a precedent which, it is submitted, should be extended to include many other fields of endeavor and matters of Indian concern, and should replace the arbitrary methods of determining questions by the Superintendent without recourse to further appeal. Under Section 32 and also under Section 52 of the Indian Act, the Exchequer Court of Canada is given the right to order the recovery of lands, and also to determine finally those facts relating to the removal of Indians from a reserve. There appears no reason why provisions of this nature ought not to replace legislation endowing the Superintendent-General or the local agent with wide and unrestrained powers.

44. *Chiefs and Councillors should be chosen in any way the Indians see fit*

Although at the time of the treaties, the Crown regarded the Indian Chiefs and Councillors, elected according to customary Indian practices, as having complete power and jurisdiction over Indian Affairs for all purposes for which the Crown had to deal with Indians, the Indian Act has changed their status or has at least purported to do so. At the time that the Indian Treaties were signed, the representatives of the Crown met the Chief and Councillors selected by the Indians according to their own method of choice, and according to their own customs and tradition. Furthermore, in negotiating the treaties with the Indians of the Plains, Lieutenant Governor Morris expressly promised that Indians would have the right to determine their own way of life without compulsion from without. The Indians today feel that they should still be able to choose their Chiefs and Councillors in any way that they see fit, by election for a term of years or otherwise, as they may desire. Therefore, they object to provisions in the Indian Act which stipulate a method whereby Chiefs are to be elected, and also which provide by section 96, that the Governor in Council has power to determine when it is advisable for the government of a band, to introduce the elective system of Chiefs and Councillors or head men. These are matters which should be left to the discretion and determination of a majority of the band and dealt with according to the customs of the band. Such representatives, whether Chiefs or Councillors, as the band may determine, should have the power to deal with the affairs of the band, and should not be required, for the purpose of altering or changing the system of choice, to obtain the permission of the Governor in Council or Indian agents. The Indians of this Organization are of opinion that one of the principal reasons for the failure of Indians to govern themselves successfully has been the interference which has consistently been present, by Indian Agents and other representatives of the Department of Indian Affairs. Only by permitting Indians the opportunity of directing their own affairs according to their best judgment and according to the custom of the band, can they develop those systems of free and democratic local government which are so desirable throughout this country. This may involve a measure of trial and error, but this is inevitable under any system of free government.

. . .

51. *Expenditures of trust funds without consent*

Section 93 of the Indian Act relates to the expenditure of moneys held in trust by the Crown for Indian bands; and subsection (1) thereof, provides that the Government in Canada may, with the consent of the band, authorize or direct certain expenditures. Subsection (2) of this section provides, however, that expenditures of such money may be made by the Superintendent General even in cases in which a band refuses to consent to such expenditure, provided the Superintendent is of opinion that it is in the interest and welfare of the band so to do. The effect of these two sections is that, even in cases in which the band requests that an expenditure be made, the Superintendent is free to ignore the request, and refuse to make the expenditure in question. On the other hand, however, even if the band definitely refuses to consent to an expenditure, the Superintendent is free to ignore the band's desires, and may proceed to spend the money in question. A most unjust situation therefore, results from the application of the terms of this section, and this Organization strongly recommends the repeal thereof, and the enactment of provisions to the effect that the desires of a band, expressed upon a free vote in favour thereof by a majority of the members of the band, shall be carried out by the Superintendent. Without such provision, Indians must remain the servile instruments of a bureaucracy which is required to take no cognizance whatsoever of the wishes, the hopes, the desires or the demands of the group of persons whose funds and very lives it controls, with responsibility to no one.

52. *Band should be empowered to recommend expenditures out of Indian Trust Funds*

The Association recommends that recognized bands be endowed with power to recommend expenditures out of Indian funds held by the Government of Canada in trust, and that all such recommendations be regarded as the unequivocal and conclusive wish of the Indians concerned, and be acted upon by the Department of Indian Affairs accordingly, in order that responsibility may be placed upon Chiefs and headsman, and with responsibility may come greater stability and confidence in the relationship between Indians and the Government.

53. *Accounting of all returns on capital investment should be rendered to Band*

Periodic statements of the condition of trust funds should be made to the chief of each recognized band, in order that the Indians thereof may become conversant with the state of their finances, and may take such action as may seem just and reasonable in view thereof. In addition, any member of the Board so requesting must be furnished with a statement. Furthermore, all returns on capital investments should be paid annually to the Indians and their children, and an accounting rendered at the time of such payment. Failure to do so breeds suspicion and distrust, with the result that it is generally believed to-day that, in many cases, the proper payment on capital investments is not, and has not been paid to the members of bands to whom such moneys are owing.

54. *Lands rightfully theirs have been expropriated*

Under the treaties, Indians are entitled to the lands designated as reserves and pre-emptions for all time in consideration of the great concessions granted by the Indians to the white man.

These rights have not always been respected since under the power of the Indian Act, Indians have been removed from their reserves and their lands have been expropriated and occupied.

Under the Indian Act as it stands and is administered to-day, wide powers are granted to the Superintendent of Indian Affairs to remove Indians from their reserves, to expropriate and occupy reserves under a variety of circumstances contrary to the provisions of the treaties and contrary to the express wishes of the Indians concerned. This Organization affirms the inviolable rights of Indians to their lands and recommends that henceforth the safekeeping of these lands must be regarded by the Government of Canada as a sacred trust, the duties of which cannot be detracted from by statute or by practice, and that the rights attaching thereto, demand complete and absolute fulfilment.

The Indians of Western Canada regard the practice whereby the Department of Indian Affairs directs building and uses land belonging to the Indians on the reserve for the purpose of administering Indian Affairs, as a further encroachment by the white man upon the reserves. While the Indians recognized the necessity of an Indian Agent being upon the reserve, any use which he or other agents or servants of the Crown may make of Indian lands should be duly paid for by the Department of Indian Affairs. Otherwise, such use can be regarded as nothing but an encroachment upon the rights of Indians to the exclusive use and enjoyment of their lands on their reserves. Therefore, it is recommended that compensation be paid to Indian bands for use by the Department of Indian Affairs of such lands.

Section 34 of the Indian Act provides that no person or Indian other than an Indian of the band shall without the authority of the Superintendent General, reside or hunt, occupy or use any land or marsh, or reside upon or occupy any road, or allowance for roads, running through any reserve belonging to or occupied by such band. The inviolability of Indian lands is recognized by this section, but the Superintendent is given the power to exempt persons from its operation. The Indians can regard this as nothing but a violation of their right to the sole use and enjoyment of Indian lands. The Superintendent-General therefore, should not be given the power to permit persons to use Indian lands or hunt upon them or otherwise encroach upon them. It is necessary that if any one come upon those lands, such person should first be approved by the band and not by the Superintendent who simply acts as servant for the bands for purposes of using such lands.

Subsection 2 of section 34 provides that all deeds, leases, contracts, agreements or instruments made or entered into by any Indian purporting to permit persons other than Indians of the band to reside or hunt upon such reserve or to occupy or use such land shall be void. This Organization agrees that no individual should be permitted to alienate Indian lands. But, if the band council at its duly authorized meetings permits such person or enters into such agreements, those agreements should be valid ones and should not be regarded as void.

55. *No leases without consent*

Subsection (3) of Section 93 empowers the Superintendent General to lease any part of reserve lands, if he is of opinion that the individual Indian require[d] to cultivate it, neglects to do so. The question of an Indian's neglect is one resolved entirely by the Indian Agent or the Superintendent, and there is no right to impeach that decision. Upon reaching such decision, the lands alleged to be uncultivated may be leased without the consent of any of the persons concerned, including the band occupying the particular reserve. The Organization strongly disapproves this method of dealing with portions of reserve land, and recommends that henceforth that no leases whatsoever of reserve land shall be entered into without the consent of the band itself, and thereafter, only according to the terms agreed to by the band.

. . .

70. *Liability to taxation*

Although the Indians of Canada have no desire to avoid their responsibility as citizens, it is the opinion of this Organization that until equality of economic opportunity and of status is achieved, and becomes a reality, the Indian population should be subject to no form of taxation whatsoever, either direct or indirect. The difficulties inherent in granting exemption from indirect taxation to Indians are appreciated, but it is recommended that all reasonable efforts be made by the Government of Canada, to relieve Indians of the liability for payment of takes [sic] of any nature whatsoever.

71. *Liability to military service*

Treaties numbered 3, 6 and 8 specifically exempt Indians from conscription for military service. In virtue of the signing of the Indian treaties, the Indians were regarded as a nation and as one with whom the British Crown entered into diplomatic relations. Because of these treaties the Indians therefore have never been regarded as British subjects nor can they ever be regarded as Canadian citizens under existing legislation. Thus, it follows that regulations pertaining to conscription for military service should not be applied to Indians.

It should be pointed out that the loyalty of the Indian people cannot be questioned. More than 2,500 young men and women from the reserves have served with efficiency and distinction in the war just completed. Most of these served voluntarily and the

Indians do not object to this since it is in accordance with their age-old traditions which have always stood for the freedom of the individual and of the group.

The Indians do object to conscription. They believe that once they laid down their arms in peace with the British Crown and signed treaties with the Crown, they should never again be asked to take up arms in behalf of the Crown. Preferential treatment has been afforded to Mennonites, Hutterites, Doukhobors, and other groups of immigrants from Central and Eastern Europe; there exists no reasons why the same exemption from military service should not be accorded by law to the Indians. Furthermore, it is submitted that the case of the Indians is a far stronger one than that of any other group, and that it deserves immediate consideration.

It should also be noted that in 1917, under the Act applicable during World War I, Indians were specifically exempted from compulsory military service. This practice should be continued and the principle reinstated in appropriate legislation for the Indians of to-day.

72. Franchise is meaningless without educational and economic liberty

This Organization does not favour the enfranchisement of Indians in Canada, but does recognize the necessity of eventually assuming the responsibilities and duties of citizenship, as well as the rights thereof, but the franchise itself is a thing which the Organization cannot approve as such. It is regarded, not as a desirable end in itself, but rather as only one of the indicia of full-fledged citizenship. The franchise, without the education and knowledge necessary to exercise it intelligently, and in the interest of the country, is an asset neither to the Indians who possess it nor to the nation of which such element is a part. Similarly, the franchise, without equality of economic opportunity simply disguises a system which perpetuates classes of freemen and bondsmen, and does not pretend to attack the inherent evils of such an order.

It is the opinion of this Organization that the rights granted to Indians by their Treaties with the Crown are adequate to raise the standards of Indian life, provided that the Treaties are sympathetically interpreted and administered by men of good will, with cognizance of Indian problems, and the *bona fides* to assist in solving them. When that has been done and the matter of citizenship placed in its proper perspective as a choice to be made *individually* by every Indian for himself, the franchise will become meaningful to Canada's oldest people—and her newest citizens. The franchise, therefore, is regarded by this Organization as the final affirmation of racial, religious, educational and economic liberty and equality, and it is only upon this basis that the franchise is desired. At present, it is not desired, in future, it may be regarded as valuable.

73. Enfranchisement must be on a voluntary and individual basis

Therefore, this Organization does not favour an indiscriminate or general enfranchisement of Indians, either in bands, or in other groups. It is of the opinion that since the rights and responsibilities of citizenship are primarily individual in nature, so enfranchisement must be upon an individual and specific basis. Laws which enfranchise an entire band upon the vote of a majority thereof, violate the treaty rights of all Indians who are members of the minority group, and who have voted against enfranchisement. More important even, they violate every principle of the Common Law and of International Law, which determine the nature of a man's citizenship, apart from the question of birth, according to individual action, individual consent and individual conduct.

74. *Enfranchisement must be confined to individuals upon application*

The Organization approves of the provisions of Section 110 of the Indian Act which relates to the enfranchisement of individual Indians, upon application by them, and upon approval of their fitness for enfranchisement, by examination. However, it strongly condemns the provisions contained in subsection (14) of this section, which empower a Board of Inquiry to determine the fitness of the Indians of any band who have not made application for enfranchisement, the report thereof to have the same force and effect, and to be dealt with in the same manner as if an application had been made for enfranchisement under that section. . . .

. . .

76. *Conclusion: Voice of Indians should be heard*

The Indians of this Organization submit that nothing should be done by the Department of Indian Affairs Branch or by the Government of Canada which at any time will serve to sever the close relationship which has existed from the commencement of the Treaties between His Majesty and the Indian Nations who have concluded treaties with the Crown.

Furthermore, all changes in the Indian Act and regulations pertaining to it should be made only after consultation with the authorized representatives of the Indian Nations of Canada in order that they may have a voice in stating such changes as they may think necessary or desirable.

Lastly, it is recommended that in the staff of the Department of Indian Affairs there should be placed progressively more and more Indians who themselves will have a real knowledge of Indian affairs and who will be able to administer their Indian affairs in a sympathetic and understanding manner. This is of utmost importance to the Indians of Canada in order that they may participate themselves in formulating the policies which govern them.

A long range policy is needed with the over-all aim of the total emancipation of the Indian, at his own pace and as he wishes. Fundamental to this, are the establishment of democratic practices, provision for opportunity to make a living, full health care and a proper educational program.

The first thought for the future should be co-operation: co-operation among Indian bands and the Indians themselves; co-operation between Indians and their white neighbours; co-operation between Indians and the Government of Canada. Not in hand shaking alone—as in the conclusion of the treaties in the 1880's—but in hands working together for the creation of a greater Canada and a happier Canadian people, can the hopes and aspirations which are mutually ours, be realized.

All of which is respectfully submitted.

8.4 Presentation of Mathew Lazare for the Mohawk of Caughnawaga, 1947

In this selection of testimony before the SJC, Mathew Lazare presents a brief on behalf of the Mohawk of Kahnawá:ke (Caughnawaga). This statement is perhaps even more forceful than the submissions of other organizations and was met with significant hostility from committee members who referred to the brief as an "ultimatum" and challenged the authority of Lazare and other delegates to represent their community. It seems that the ideas expressed in the submission were not only contrary to the views of the committee but also challenged Canada's perception of itself as a benevolent protector of Indigenous peoples' interests.

Source: Presentation of Mathew Lazare, Special Joint Committee of the Senate and the House of Commons Appointed to Examine and Consider the Indian Act, *Minutes of Proceedings and Evidence*, No. 33, 12 June 1947 (Ottawa: Edmond Cloutier, 1947), 1706–11.

Mathew Lazare, spokesman for Caughnawaga, called:

THE WITNESS: First I would like to say we have omitted the name of one of our delegates. He is Frank Small Fence, an interpreter for the band.

THE CHAIRMAN: Thank you Mr. Lazare.

Now then, gentlemen, we want you to feel as free and easy as you can feel under the circumstances. If it is more comfortable for you to stand up and speak, please do so, otherwise you may remain seated. If there is anything that you would like to draw our attention to please do not hesitate. If there are any suggestions you would like to make just make the suggestions and we will try to follow them. I am trying to say to you that you are among friends and we want you to feel as free and easy as you can.

Now would you like to go ahead with your brief, Mr. Lazare?

THE WITNESS: Mr. Chairman, ladies and gentlemen. First I would like to thank you on behalf of the council and the hereditary chiefs for the warm welcome you have extended. It is with great honour we stand here before you to discuss our many grievances. I am only authorized at the present moment to discuss what is in this brief, so I will go ahead and read the brief.

THE CHAIRMAN: I might draw to your attention Mr. Lazare that after you have read your brief there will be a period of questioning. The members of the committee may have questions in their minds which they would like to put to you as a witness when you have finished reading the brief. There will be no interruption until you have finished. If the reading becomes tiresome you can ask me and I will read a little bit. We want you to feel free to proceed without interruptions and then afterwards we will question you.

CAUGHNAWAGA, Prov. Que.,

May 10th, 1947.

THE WITNESS: Honourable members of the joint committee, we, the councillors and life chiefs, of Caughnawaga, the only authorized body to transact the affairs of this Caughnawaga, Mohawk Band of Indians.

The councillors and life chiefs duly assembled on this 10th day of May, in the year of our Lord 1947, at a grand council to discuss and consider the merits of the "Indian Act", and the (8) Eight Points Questionnaire as requested:

We have therefore unanimously approved the following:

We have duly and faithfully discussed and considered the Eight Points Questionnaire and we have come to the following conclusions:

1. We demand the restoration of our primordial rights, the respection and fulfilment of treaty obligations, the recognition as a sovereign nation.

We have no desire to be governed in the future by the "Indian Act", or any other form of government. The "Indian Act", as it stands to-day is a detriment to the progress of our people. All the power is vested in the superintendent general of Indian Affairs and the Indian agent, which leave our councillors and chiefs no power to control our own affairs and problems on our reserves, all they can do is offer suggestions in the form of resolutions which often go unanswered. For an example out of 485 resolutions passed the Department of Indian Affairs answered about 40, many unfavourably. The Indian Act is the most bureaucratic and dictatorial system ever imposed on mankind.

You have violated our treaties by making compulsory laws for us Indians, and the surrender of the dominion government of the natural resources to the provinces, because through it, you the dominion government transferred the rights of the Indian to live. You have taken the food out of the mouths of Indians and put it into the mouths of those who are going to vote for you. By the "Indian Act", Indians are subject to rulings of the Department of Indian Affairs presided over by the honourable Minister of Mines and Resources, and from his decision there is no appeal. The department acts on all matters on the report of the Indian agent under Section 99A. The agent is appointed by the Indian Affairs and he presides over all the meetings of the Indian council and controls all proceedings. He has sovereign power to govern as he sees fit.

The Indians to-day are a subject race, held down by the very Act which is supposed to help and protect them. Indians cannot discuss their own problems, they are tied down to a helpless condition and cannot move or do anything until the Indian agent so directs; Indians cannot go direct to the department for redress of any grievances, as all communications must be through the Indian agent, who in many cases is the direct cause of the grievances. The agent has the power to veto any resolution of Indian council, and any effort on their part to go over his head will be totally ignored by the Department of Indian Affairs. In truth, nothing can be accomplished unless recommended by the Indian agent. In fact his duties are becoming more and more like a dictator.

The "Indian Act" tends to divide then destroy the red man. The elected council came into being by fraud and treachery. On one of our reserves the elected council came into being by sheer force of arms and threat of violence which disbanded our government, but in the minds and understanding of our people, there can be only one government for us, "The Six Nations Government".

Therefore, we charge you, the Canadian government, aided by the Royal Canadian Mounted Police, of invading our domains and forcing foreign laws on our people by force of arms.

Gentlemen! Is this not what we fought for in this last war? The protection of the principles of freedom, to stop the brutal aggressor? Then why should you let some small nations be subjected to dictatorship right here at home?

Gentlemen! The Indian was once the ruler of this vast and rich country, now to-day he has a two-by-four reservation left and still your government is not contented until it takes all. Gentlemen! Is it too much to assume that you do not want us or a foreign government to make laws for you? Then, how can you expect us to accept or like the laws you impose on us?

The officials of the Indian department have overruled regulations in the "Indian Act" to suit their purposes. They also, especially the Indian agent, make all arrangements and agreements for companies and provincial governments to make roads, bridges, towers for electricity, etc., without the consent of the band, who are owners of the reserves.

The burning down of our town hall is a complete responsibility of an official of the Indian department, as it was in his use at the time; and had his office in it, and he was heating it by oil stove, which was the cause of the fire. Therefore we claim from the government of Canada the sum of $10,000 for damages caused by its official. By virtue of our treaty rights we demand the abolition of the "Indian Act," the exemption of all Indians from compulsory taxation and compulsory military service.

By virtue of our treaties we demand the removal of all whites from our reserve, including the officials of the Department of Indian Affairs and the Royal Canadian Mounted Police, as they afford no protection for our people. We want it known that the lands on our reserves is the sole property of the Indians, not the provincial nor dominion.

Therefore unless you advise your people especially the motorist using the many roads through our reserve, that we will tolerate no longer the wanton destruction of our animals, the killing and endangering the lives of our people, we will be forced to set up blockades on all roads and restrict the use of same thereafter.

Therefore we the councillors and chiefs unanimously resolve not to make any suggestions to the revision of the Indian Act, where our people are concerned by virtue of our ancient treaties, but demand the abolition of the Indian Act on behalf of the Six Nations confederacy. We therefore ask you, the federal government, to abandon the proposed Indian Act. You cannot hope to have us believe that the new Indian Act will be to our advantage and advancement, when we have been so often deceived in the past. The Act retards the progress of our nation, and as it stands today can be criticized from the beginning to the end, every section of the Act. It is too dictatorial and the powers vested in the Indian agent and superintendent general are too arbitrary and autocratic, and binds our people on a double chain of pauperism and mental servitude.

We therefore insist that treaties, as made by our great forefathers were in the form of agreements between two equal sovereign nations, but that you the whites took the attitude that we, the Indians, were not your equal, when you abrogated treaty clauses which guaranteed to the Indians of the Six Nations rights of self government as an independent nation.

That by virtue of our treaty rights Indians of the Six Nations are not liable to any federal or provincial laws within their territories.

That by virtue of our treaty rights, Indians of the Six Nations are not liable for payment of taxes to either the federal or provincial governments.

That by virtue of our treaties, we demand the government of Canada the proper adjustment of treaty obligations to meet our demands, the recognition and respection of our privileges and rights as a sovereign nation, who are able to govern and make laws for ourselves.

In dealing with those treaties, between Great Britain and the United States, wherein the independence of the Indians of the Six Nations, both Great Britain and the United States have confessed that the Six Nations were an independent people. The supreme courts of both countries furthermore recognized those treaties as inviolable.

. . .

We expected you to safeguard our interest, not give it away as you have done in the past.

2. The right to decide as to who or whom belongs to this band or other band of Six Nations lies within the jurisdiction of the local chief and councillors. It does not lie within provincial nor dominion government jurisdiction.

You would not want us to decide for you as to who or whom is citizen of Canada. It is only just that only the Indian can justly decide for himself, as every one knows one another in our reserves, as to who or whom is a member of this band or bands of Six Nations Indians of Canada. The Indian Act and your government has done enough, so much in fact that it has made white people members of this band.

3. As long as an Indian is domiciled on a reserve and he seeks employment in a city or town or any part of the country away from home or his reservation, it does not change his Indian status, and you, the government, cannot take his money legally. What he earns is his own personal property and that cannot be taxed.

Certain reservations are subject to provincial taxation on electrical services, and stores sales tax; the provincial government has no jurisdiction to legislate on Indian territory and cannot impose taxation within a reserve limits.

The income tax cannot be imposed on Indians domiciled on the reserve, because wherever he may be off or on the reserve he is still an Indian and the compulsory taxation on Indians is a violation of British justice—no representation, no taxation and against the proclamation of King George III and an infringement of Indian treaty rights. Therefore we demand a refund of all moneys collected from Indians on income and electric tax, etc. And another form of compulsory collection of moneys has been enforced on reservations in the form of unemployment insurance.

We base our arguments on the merits of our aboriginal heritage as we never imparted nor ceded any of our rights to any government or nation.

Our future, the future of your country and my country, will be exactly what we together make it. The preservation of the principles of the Four Freedoms, and the United Nations Charter.

4. We do not approve and will never submit to the government's demand of enfranchisement for the Indians of the Six Nations both voluntary or involuntary. We do not want enfranchisement of any form whatsoever. Voluntary enfranchisement should not be fostered or encouraged by the government and involuntary enfranchisement must be abolished for ever for all Indians.

5. We, the Six Nations Indians, by our International Treaty are allies of His Majesty's government, therefore we are also allies of Canada and the commonwealth. Therefore, we do not desire to be governed, or to be considered eligible to vote for any dominion or provincial elections. Therefore we have no interest and never will be interested in a vote for any other form of government, except our own Six Nations government.

6. The encroachment of white persons on our Indian reserves is made possible through the Indian Act. The officials of the department through powers of the Indian Act have decided that it is to the advantage of the Indians to rent houses to whites, by elevating their living conditions, this is and has been done regardless of protests and feeling of our people. The only elevating form the renting of houses has been done for our people, by burning and destruction and damaging the houses. Now gentlemen is that making our people richer or poorer? Therefore we demand the removal of all whites from our reserves, nuns, priests and government officials included.

7. The operation of Indian day or residential schools is not approved by this band, if it will be operated by any religious denomination. We do not approve the Nuns or Sisters of St. Anne's to teach our children as they do not teach our children enough, the only thing they learn is praying and singing and marching to church during school hours, also they get holidays for a priest's birthday, etc. We do not approve the rebuilding of our burnt school unless it becomes a public school which takes children of all religion and teaches them. Same as the protestant school system of Montreal, which is one of the highest form[s] of education in Canada. We demand qualified teachers with degrees for teaching, to teach our children. The creating of vocational section and also the creation of a technical branch.

We demand these things because our children deserve the best form of education this country can give, to be prepared to meet and conquer the industrial and professional world of to-morrow. We also complain and object to the behaviour and activities of the Jesuit Society, who are in control of our church. They are meddling in the affairs of this band when all they have a right to do is be spiritual advisers. We are capable of handling our affairs without interference from outsiders. They have set themselves up in business in a big way. They operate bingo and euchre games of chance, these games are in the category of gambling. This teaches our children to take chances, thereby become gamblers. They also operate a movie house, dance hall and pool room. They no longer preach in our native tongue, but insist in preaching in French and English only. This Act threatens the extinction of our beloved language, which the people will not tolerate for long.

The control of band funds by the Indian department is a gross injustice, because the owners of these funds are starving with the very little they get for relief.

Therefore we the Indians of the Six Nations cannot rest as long as the common laws overrule the laws of principality.

. . .

8.5 House of Commons, "A Summary of the Proceedings of a Conference with Representative Indians," 1951

In June of 1950, Louis St. Laurent's Liberal government introduced proposed changes to the Indian Act as Bill 267. The bill included some of the final recommendations of the

SJC and reflected the assimilative agenda of the current and preceding federal govern-
ments and administrators. Copies of the bill were sent to Department of Indian Affairs'
officials and to First Nations. Recipients were instructed to provide their comments be-
fore the end of the month, when the bill was meant to be passed by Parliament. To many
representatives of First Nations, as well as to opposition politicians and news writers, the
short time frame would not provide adequate opportunity for a meaningful consider-
ation of the bill or for the preparation of recommendations to amend it. Debate over the
content of the bill continued in the House of Commons until it was finally withdrawn.
A revised bill, Bill 79, was introduced in the fall of 1950, and only 19 representatives from
First Nations were selected to be invited to meet with the minister and deputy minister
for a five-day discussion of the revised bill. An excerpt from a summary of that meeting
appears here. As always, one of the main concerns expressed was related to non-voluntary
enfranchisement and loss of status.

Source: Canada, House of Commons, "A Summary of the Proceedings of a Conference with
Representative Indians Held in Ottawa, February 28–March 3, 1951" in *Debates*, 1951, vol. 2
(16 March 1951), 1364.

A SUMMARY OF THE PROCEEDINGS OF A
CONFERENCE WITH REPRESENTATIVE INDIANS HELD
IN OTTAWA, FEBRUARY 28–MARCH 3, 1951

1. On February 28, March 1, 2 and 3 of this year, a conference was held with representative Indians and officers of Indian associations from all of those regions of
   Canada where there is an Indian population, except the Northwest Territories.
   The minister attended all of the meetings in the capacity of chairman. The deputy minister and officials of the Indian affairs branch of the department were
   also present.
2. The main purpose of this historic conference was to discuss the provisions of
   Bill 79 to revise the Indian Act and to give the representatives an opportunity to
   present their opinions. Every section of the bill was read in the conference and
   was explained. Opinions were expressed and recorded, and if, after discussion,
   suggestions for changes were made, these were noted.
3. Upon conclusion of this phase of the work of the conference there was a general
   discussion about all matters of Indian affairs and administration of the Indian
   Act which proved most useful and, where appropriate, will be used as a guide for
   future action by the department.
4. It was evident from the discussion that the problem of Indian affairs varied
   greatly from reserve to reserve. It was recognized that the Indians of the several
   provinces appeared to have differing rights and experiences, and that these differences accounted for the variety of viewpoints expressed towards particular sections of the bill. Nevertheless, the opinions of all present were stated not only for
   the purpose of presenting the local viewpoint, but also in an effort to find a common, advantageous ground so as to advance the welfare of the Indian people.

5. One of the representatives stated that as far as he and his people were concerned, they did not wish to have any changes made to the present Indian Act since they found it to be satisfactory for their purposes.

6. Subject to this statement, the conference noted that there was unanimous support for 103 sections of the bill. Opinion varied with respect to the remaining sections as will be explained in more detail later. However, the results of the discussions by those representatives favoring new legislation may be summarized as follows: of the 124 sections, 103 were unanimously supported; 118 sections were supported by the majority of those present; only 6 sections were opposed by a majority of the representatives and of these, 2 were unanimously opposed.

7. All of the representatives present at the conference agreed that the Government of Canada should continue to extend self government to the Indian band councils consistent with their demonstrated ability to exercise increasing responsibility.

8. The representatives at this conference were assured that all of their representations had been noted and would be drawn to the attention of the government and parliament during the later stages of the Indian bill. It was also indicated that full consideration would be given to the suggestions made for alterations to those sections of the bill which did not meet with the general approval of the representatives. To this end, the representations which were made at the conference will now be outlined to the house.

9. The first sections to be dealt with will be those which were opposed by all of the representatives present.

10. With respect to section 86, all of the representatives were of the opinion that this section did not go far enough in providing tax exemption for Indians, and that they were opposed to sub-section 2 because it relates to a waiver of exemption under the Dominion Elections Act. They recommended that voting privileges should not be conditional upon signing a waiver. It was also asserted that under Article 13 of the Terms of Union between Canada and the province of British Columbia the Indians of British Columbia were not liable to be so taxed. It was suggested that some consideration should be given to amending the Dominion Elections Act in order to do away with the waiver.

11. All of the representatives were opposed to section 112 which is the section dealing with enfranchisement after enquiry and it was drawn to the attention of the conference that the opposition to this section had been recorded in a number of briefs submitted to the minister.

12. Of these six sections opposed by a majority, four (93–96) dealt with the sale to Indians, and possession by them, of intoxicants.

13. Regarding these sections, there were three views expressed,—(1) that the provisions dealing with intoxicants contained in the present act be continued; that is, complete prohibition; (2) that provincial liquor laws be made applicable to Indians; (3) a compromise measure, such as is contemplated by section 95, which would allow the Indians to consume intoxicants in public places in accordance

with the laws of the provinces, but which would not permit them to be in possession of package goods nor to take liquor on a reserve.

14. There was a wide range of opinion with respect to these sections. Many of the representatives favored provincial liquor laws, while others were strongly opposed to any change in the act. It was said that the present liquor provisions could not and should not be changed with respect to those Indians under Treaty 6 in Alberta and in other parts of the province not covered by this treaty. Some of the representatives stated that if the provincial laws could not be made applicable to the Indians, they would be prepared to accept the provisions made in Bill 79. It is apparent, therefore, that with so many different views expressed, the conference did not reach any general agreement on this subject.

. . .

SUGGESTIONS FOR FURTHER READING

As is often the case, it would be worthwhile to consult the Royal Commission on Aboriginal Peoples (RCAP) for further context. For this chapter see, "The Indian Act," in *Report of the Royal Commission on Aboriginal Peoples* (Ottawa: Indian and Northern Affairs Canada, 1996), vol. 1, chap. 9. Of particular interest are Section 10 "Post-War Indian Policy Reform: Everything Old Is New Again" and Section 11 "The 1951 *Indian Act* Revision." The RCAP report is available on line at http://www.collectionscanada.gc.ca/webarchives/20071124124337/http://www.ainc-inac.gc.ca/ch/rcap/sg/sgm9_e.html. For an examination of some of the testimony presented by First Nations organizations to the postwar Special Joint Committee of the Senate and the House of Commons Appointed to Examine and Consider the Indian Act, see John Leslie and Ron Maguire, "The Indian Act of 1951," in *The Historical Development of the Indian Act* (Ottawa: DIAND, 1978), 132–52. This chapter (9) also explains the 1951 amendments to the act. For a discussion of Diamond Jenness that presents his work and his testimony at the SJC hearings as evidence of his complicity with Canadian government policies toward Indigenous peoples, see Peter Kulchyski, "Anthropology in the Service of the State: Diamond Jenness and Canadian Indian Policy," *Journal of Canadian Studies* 28, no. 2 (1993): 21–50. For an examination of the Indian Association of Alberta's presentation to the SJC, see Laurie Meijer Drees, "Citizenship and Treaty Rights: The Indian Association of Alberta and the Canadian Indian Act, 1946–1948," *Great Plains Quarterly* 20, no. 1 (Spring 2000): 141–58. For a brief exploration of the conclusions of the SJC and the content and intent of the 1951 Indian Act amendments placed within the context of earlier policy, see John L. Tobias, "Protection, Civilization, Assimilation: An Outline History of Canada's Indian Policy," *Western Canadian Journal of Anthropology* 6, no. 2 (1976): 39–53.

CHAPTER 9

"WE HAD NO HESITATION IN USING THE WORD 'EXPERIMENT'"[1]

THE HIGH ARCTIC RELOCATION OF 1953

Almost since the time of their first encounters with Europeans, Indigenous people were, for reasons that varied over time and across geography, regularly displaced from at least parts of their traditional territories. They may have been exiled as the result of their involvement in European conflicts, forced to leave as settlers moved into their lands, or restricted from traditional territory as the result of treaties, land purchases, or the establishment of reserves. By the twentieth century, relocations became purposeful policy initiatives conducted by the federal government and presented as in the best interest of all of those involved.

As can be seen from previous chapters, Canadian politicians and administrators tended to see Indigenous peoples as problems that needed to be fixed. Further, because Indigenous people were perceived as incapable of making the necessary adaptations on their own that would allow them to take their place in liberal capitalist Canada, initiatives thought to further assimilation were often undertaken by the state with little or no meaningful consultation with those affected. Along with restricting movement, banning cultural activities, and limiting available economic strategies, relocation was one of the tools used in Canada's effort to make Indigenous people "useful" citizens and simultaneously advance what was portrayed as the national interest.

Relocation can also be seen within the broader context of dispossession and dislocation and the removal of Indigenous people from the lands and resources of their ancestors. Individuals and communities were relocated in the twentieth century when administrators believed food was no longer available; when there appeared to be too great a distance between the community and the infrastructure of settler society; when Indigenous people

1 Bent G. Sivertz, Transcripts of the Hearings of the Royal Commission on Aboriginal Peoples, vol. 173, Citadel Inn Ottawa, 29 June 1993, vol. 2, p. 411. This quotation appears in document 9.3.

were considered in the way of expanding agricultural development or urban centres; when they resided on lands wanted for mining, forestry, or other economic exploitation; or when moving them would facilitate their administration by Canadian authorities.

This chapter concerns a specific relocation, the High Arctic relocation of Inuit families in the 1950s. Given the above, it is evident that this relocation of almost 100 Inuit from Inukjuak in northern Quebec over 1,200 kilometres north to Grise Fiord and Craig Harbour on Ellesmere Island and to Resolute Bay on Cornwallis Island, only slightly less than the distance between Ottawa and Atlanta, Georgia, or Vancouver and San Francisco, California, is not unique but rather part of Canada's ongoing paternalistic effort to solve the problem of Indians, Inuit, and Métis. If other aspects of what was presented as the national interest could be advanced at the same time by the presence of Indigenous people, all the better. The story of the High Arctic relocation is a powerful one, though, and is starkly illustrative of the effects of Canada's attitudes, policies, and actions, both during and after the relocations themselves.

The reasons for the High Arctic relocations of 1953 have been hotly debated, as can be seen from the documents provided in this chapter. Government officials and those members of the RCMP involved in the relocation or in policing relocated communities have tended to present the moves as in the best interests of the Inuit and as being, all things considered, successful. Many of those relocated and their families have challenged that view and suggested that the government had other motivations. They argued further that they were not properly informed about the circumstances or conditions of the relocation. As is illustrated in their testimony below, the relocatees could hardly have imagined the difference in conditions between their traditional homes and those they moved to in the High Arctic.

The divide between these two positions continued to grow through the latter twentieth century. In 1990, the House of Commons Standing Committee on Aboriginal Affairs found that the relocated Inuit had been subjected to a significant injustice and requested that Canada apologize for its actions. Instead, Canada hired a consulting firm to present an alternative perspective. The resultant Hickling Report, excerpted below, was greeted with widespread condemnation from relocated Inuit, Indigenous organizations, and academics alike. Finally, in August of 2010, the minister responsible for the Department of Indian Affairs and Northern Development issued an apology to the relocated families and other Inuit on behalf of the government and all Canadians for the hardships caused by the relocations.

QUESTIONS FOR DISCUSSION

1. Based on the evidence you have here, do you think a concern for sovereignty played a role in the High Arctic relocations?
2. Were the incidents described in the memorandum from the Privy Council Office actual challenges to Canada's sovereignty in your view? Why or why not?
3. What differences do Markoosie Patsauq and Ben Sivertz provide on the use of the dump?
4. What do you think accounts for the very different interpretations of the relocation experience presented here?

5. Based on the Hickling Report and other documents presented here, was an apology necessary? Why or why not?
6. What does the Royal Commission on Aboriginal Peoples identify as the most important problems associated with the relocations? Other than the relocations themselves, what was the primary cause of these problems, in your view?

DOCUMENTS

9.1 The High Arctic Relocation, 1953

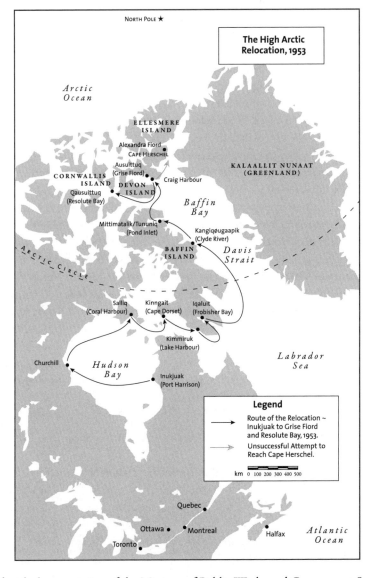

Reproduced with the permission of the Minister of Public Works and Government Services Canada, 2013.

9.2 Testimony of Markoosie Patsauq and Samwillie Elijassialuk, 1992

This selection is a transcript of testimony provided to the Royal Commission on Aboriginal Peoples at a public hearing in the community of Inukjuak, Quebec, in 1992. The two witnesses represented here, Markoosie Patsauq and Samwillie Elijassialuk, were among those Inuit taken to Resolute Bay and Grise Fiord respectively in 1953. They briefly present their experiences with the relocation experiment and its after-effects and provide their views on government motivations and conclusions.

Source: Testimony of Markoosie Patsauq and Samwillie Elijassialuk, Transcripts of the Hearings of the Royal Commission on Aboriginal Peoples, vol. 27, Inukjuak, Quebec, 8 June 1992, vol. 1, pp. 53–63.

Reproduced with the permission of the Minister of Public Works and Government Services Canada, 2013.

MARKOOSIE PATSAUQ (SPEAKING THROUGH A TRANSLATOR) I will first introduce the speakers here. On my left, is Anna Nungak who was taken to Grise Fjord in 1953. My name is Markoosie Patsauq and I was taken to Resolute in 1953. On my right is Samwillie Elijassialuk, who was taken to Grise Fjord in 1953 and on my far right Mary who was taken to Resolute in 1955. We are very happy to have a chance to address this long-standing problem we have been having for over ten years and has been very unsuccessful with the federal government up to today.

In my opening remarks I would like to have Samwillie be the first person to speak on our behalf.

SAMWILLIE ELIJASSIALUK (SPEAKING THROUGH A TRANSLATOR) Thank you. Now I am given the chance, I will try to be brief about the fact that we have gone through a hardship in the past and the fact that they told us a big lie, when the government told us the reason for sending us to the high Arctic was they said there was a lot of animals we could live off. They told us there was a lot of caribou and a lot of other animals but when we arrived there, there was hardly any caribou and they told us, we were told that we are allowed to kill one caribou in a year and they told us if we killed a muskox we would be taken unless we paid $500. They told us that they would bring us back to our communities after two years, but when we told them we wanted to go back home, the police told us it is not possible any more. The transportation is not possible. They told us that the land we were moving to is going to be plentiful and that we would come back home in the future, but once we were in the high Arctic they didn't want to move us back home.

We have experienced and seen other Inuit who have insisted on going back home, but the government representatives kept telling us that we can't go home now and they are going to build a school there for us, for our children and that is what the government was telling us. We were told there was caribou and muskox. One of us was hoping that he was going back home again, but when he learned he was not going home, he was highly touched. Often I think back and wonder if they did not send us to the high Arctic in the first place so we would have a good—maintain a good relation with our relatives.

The whole reason behind this was to maintain sovereignty in the high Arctic and they had to find people that would stay up there and not be able to go back home. They used to try to bring Inuit from the NWT to the high Arctic, but they knew how to return home and they couldn't maintain them there, so they had to find a group of people that didn't know the road back home and that would stay up there. That is the result of the relocation of the Inuit from Inukjuak to the high Arctic. Up to date it has had a really negative impact on our lives up to date.

We know that it was an experiment. It is not human to do an experiment on human beings. Thank you.

MARKOOSIE PATSAUQ (SPEAKING THROUGH A TRANSLATOR) As I was saying, me and my family were victims of the experiment for relocation in 1953. I would like to concentrate on the papers I have prepared and I would like to read it for clarity, because as I understand it we have a limited amount of time to make our presentation, unfortunately.

I would like to start with just a few words concerning the documents that we have been able to learn from over the years. This experiment in relocation was presented by the Canadian government along with the RCMP to improve Inuit standards of living, but the Inuit economic situation was not the only reason. The motives behind this decision were moral conviction in Canadian sovereignty. These are the wrongs, that we had been arguing over the years. Also the federal government was saying the area was a completely devoid way of life and I would like to make it clear this is how I saw it.

That the Nunavik area could no longer support its population was false. At this stage in the 1950s this area was a major nesting area for many of varieties of marine birds which hundreds of islands along the coast are homes to, many wildlife and fishes of every type are available from the sea and from the lakes that cover the entire area. Things like Canada geese go to that homeland each year. There are fifty or more varieties of animals which we depend on for food. To us who call this area our home, this land, this is the land of plenty and to tear us away from our roots was uncalled for. The suffering we have been forced to take over the years are unacceptable. To use us as experimental objects is illegal.

The fact is that in the 1950s the Inuit economic situation was no worse than in the 1930s or the 1940s. In fact our economic situation at that time had never been better and the government decision to provide family allowance in the 1940s greatly improved our economic conditions. The introduction of soap stone carvings meant for the aged, sick, crippled and widows, quickly improved our economic situation. These welcome reliefs were to disappear from our lives by the time we arrived on the high Arctic Islands and in the first week of September, 1953 the family arrived in Resolute Bay, which was to be our home, not for two years, as originally informed by the government, but for the next thirty years. On our arrival at the new home, we were shocked at the bareness of the land and the coldness of the air and the presence of icebergs and as far as we could see there was nothing but gravel, ice and snow. At this time of year in our original home of Inukjuak it would still be summer and we would be catching thousands of fishes with our nets for our food during the winter.

Most of the animals that we were used to back in Inukjuak were not to exist in the high Arctic, and although we were not aware of it at the time, we have since learned that [the] commanding officer of the Royal Canadian Air Force in Resolute Bay strongly objected to this experiment, since no adequate planning had been carried out. There had been no concern on the government's part that there would be no housing, no medical facilities or schools. The commanding officer also said that he was afraid there was not enough animals to support new arrivals, but still thought the government had reason to believe there was plenty of animals and besides they would make sure that the Air Force would not be inconvenienced and that Inuit families which was to arrive shortly would not become a liability to the Air Force.

The first year in our new home in Resolute was the hardest for us, mostly because we did not know the land. We did not know where to hunt and the fact was there was no daylight from November to February. We survived mostly on the garbage of the white man. If the dump had not provided us with these edible garbages, we would have had faced serious hunger or maybe even starvation and since we were not allowed to have any contact with the white people, my father and the rest of the men had to go to the dump. In the dark season which was preventing us from hunting it allowed us to sneak into the dump without being discovered by the RCMP.

When daylight returned to the land in February, we no longer sneaked into the dump as we were so desperate for food that the dump was providing for our dogs and not for ourselves. Travelling to the dump for a bit of bread became our daily labour. A certain government official who played an important part in this experiment of relocation had a dream that one day the Inuit would once again become self-reliant instead of counting on handouts from the government. With this dream the government went out to prove the Inuit were the people who could survive without any assistance from the government, and certain government officials feel that Inuit has lost a certain amount of interest in hunting and fishing for a living. The government also felt it was paying too much money, too much welfare for the Inuit in the north. A certain government official felt that a way of dealing with the Inuit problem had to be found. At the same time they were very concerned about the Inuit hunting and living freely in Canada's north and since American people were outnumbering Canadians, they were concerned that Canada's sovereignty question might be challenged. In this situation the Canadian government felt it would lead Canadian people to occupy the Islands. At this stage in time Inuit people were the only people who could survive in the harsh land without assistance from the government. Unlike white people who had to be directly paid for their services, this was an extensive venture. The simplest solution to the problem would be to use the Inuit people as the guardian of Canada's interests.

When the government personnel came once again to our home in the fall of 1954 one year after the relocation, my father, along with the rest of the men, made a request that they be returned home, having spent one year in the high Arctic and having learned about the land and its abysmal conditions, they were convinced that they were not better off in the new land and no news from the families, they knew this land had a lot less to offer. Their request was turned down and instead the government said they would bring their families, bring the rest of our families up north next ship time, which would be 1955. So the second relocation took place in 1955. My father's brother, along with his brother-in-law and three more families arrived, and this did not consist of all the family that my father had. He was fated never to see the rest of the family still living in Inukjuak.

I would like to talk about a few things that we have discussed with the federal government. At the famous relocation in 1953, I was also suffering badly from tuberculosis.

I was not sent south for treatment, but instead went along with my family to the high Arctic. The treatment subsequent was to have a very negative impact on the people who went up to Resolute in 1953. In a few years, all of us were suffering from TB. The TB I had started a chain reaction which was to affect every one of those who were relocated in '53. I would also like to say a few words about the sickness. There was my grandmother who was 73 years old at the time of relocation. She was healthy when we left here. She was strong and she was a very active worker on daily labours. She died within two years after we were relocated to the high Arctic. We know she died because of lack of different varieties of food and also because of violent change in the environment greatly contributed to her death. Also among the group we had two polio victims, my mother was one and my mother died in March of this year and Anna Mungak to my left is one of the people who are polio victims. Mother also had a heart condition, although we did not know it at the time, nobody knew that she had a heart condition. She died within eight months after we arrived in the high Arctic. It is also known she lost the will to live after finding out the government had no intention to bring us back to our home. She died a broken woman.

Lastly, right up to the present time, the government and the RCMP insisted that this experiment was successful. They are partly right, because the experiment proved that people could survive without government handouts, without aid from the government and it proved people could survive off the land in the harsh environment and continue to occupy the land despite the hardships, but the people who were used as an object had to pay a heavy price which continues to this day. Many graves of our relatives are grim proof of the suffering we had to endure and the separation of the families continues to this day. Thank you.

9.3 Examination of Bent Sivertz, 1993

Like the previous document, this one includes evidence presented to the Royal Commission on Aboriginal Peoples. Bent Sivertz had a decades-long career in the Canadian Navy and as a merchant seaman before taking up employment as a foreign service officer in the Ministry of External Affairs. By the late 1940s, he was working as an executive assistant to the deputy minister of the Department of Mines and Resources, later renamed the Department of Northern Affairs and National Resources. Sivertz refers to himself as "the person who carried out the plan from justification of the idea . . . to arranging space on the ship for the Inuit who decided to go."[2] His responses to questions from the commissioners give considerable insight into governmental interpretations of the relocation experiment.

Source: Examination of Bent Sivertz, Transcripts of the Hearings of the Royal Commission on Aboriginal Peoples, vol. 173, Citadel Inn Ottawa, 29 June 1993, vol. 2, pp. 409–17, 423–29, 438–40, and 457–60.

Reproduced with the permission of the Minister of Public Works and Government Services Canada, 2013.

. . .

---

2 Examination of Bent Sivertz, Transcripts of the Hearings of the Royal Commission on Aboriginal Peoples, vol. 173, Citadel Inn Ottawa, 29 June 1993, vol. 2, p. 389.

CO-CHAIR GEORGES ERASMUS: . . . Perhaps we could ask you a few questions now, if you would answer some.

The first question is: Could you tell us, Mr. Sivertz, what kind of planning went into the preparation of selecting the sites?

MR. BENT G. SIVERTZ: That was of a necessity. It was impossible to think of transporting a group of people to an area already occupied—and almost all accessible areas were already occupied by hunting Eskimo groups.

This area on Ellesmere Island and Cornwallis Island was empty of resident Eskimos. We were able, therefore, to propose to move these relocated people to these almost only accessible areas. There were lots more among the many islands of Canada's northland, but not accessible to the annual Eastern Arctic Patrol, not accessible to aircraft. This was a made-to-order place.

CO-CHAIR GEORGES ERASMUS: Did you have any studies done on the wildlife in the area, or were there studies done by other people that you used to figure out how many animals there would be in this area?

MR. BENT SIVERTZ: No. The Canadian Wildlife Service had almost no data. We were relying on anecdotal reports of various people. We knew a good many people who had travelled through the area, and we consulted them as to the abundance of game.

We kept the group small, because we did not want to over-tax the game resources of the immediate vicinity of the translocated people.

CO-CHAIR GEORGES ERASMUS: What were you using, then, as information that there was game there?

MR. BENT G. SIVERTZ: I just told you: anecdotal reports of Arctic hands of all kinds.

CO-CHAIR GEORGES ERASMUS: What were they telling you?

MR. BENT G. SIVERTZ: They were telling us that there was a good deal of game up there, that there was a big population of polar bears, a big population of seals and in fact, they thought, a good population of wildlife capable of supporting a moderate group of relocated people.

CO-CHAIR GEORGES ERASMUS: Were the specific sites very important or could they have been anywhere in that particular area, anywhere in the islands in that area? Was there any specific reason why these sites were chosen?

MR. BENT G. SIVERTZ: They were accessible to the Eastern Arctic Patrol, an important link to southern Canada supplies.

CO-CHAIR GEORGES ERASMUS: The term "experiment" is used in looking at the old documents. What was meant, in your understanding, when this term was being used?

MR. BENT G. SIVERTZ: Exactly what it says. It was an experiment. We used that term a great deal. We had been using it before we were talking about this subject, and we continued to use it. We had no hesitation in using the word "experiment" for the next many years of my service on this sort of work.

Each time we engaged a person to serve the department in the Arctic, we would explain to him and his family that this was an experiment. "You might not be able to work and live in this very different environment from that which you have known. After a year in the North, you and your wife may come and tell us, 'This is not for us. We have found that we do not wish to carry on with this life.' "

We used the word "experiment" in this sense quite often.

CO-CHAIR GEORGES ERASMUS: This was the Inuit that you are talking about, that this was explained to?

MR. BENT G. SIVERTZ: No. I just said: When we were engaging a person to work in the Arctic who had come from southern Canada—

CO-CHAIR GEORGES ERASMUS: These were staff people one way or another.

MR. BENT G. SIVERTZ: Yes.

CO-CHAIR GEORGES ERASMUS: Was the same kind of explanation provided to the Inuit when they were being asked to volunteer?

When the Inuit were first approached in northern Quebec in the Port Harrison area, were they provided with this same kind of explanation?

MR. BENT G. SIVERTZ: No, because they were not from a different world. They were from the north, and they were presumably going to continue with a northern life.

What you are driving at, I take it, is: Did we say to them that this could end in some kind of disappointment to them, which they would wish to withdraw from? We certainly did explain that to them. We said, "You may not like it up there. If you don't like it for any reason at all, we will return you to northern Quebec."

CO-CHAIR GEORGES ERASMUS: On that particular promise, what kind of preparation did the department take in relation to possibly bringing people back if they were un-happy? What kinds of plan were in place?

MR. BENT G. SIVERTZ: Simple. The Eastern Arctic Patrol carried them north and the Eastern Arctic Patrol would carry them south if they decided that was what they wanted done.

CO-CHAIR GEORGES ERASMUS: How did you get your information to the Inuit that they could return if they wanted to, when you were first contacting them?

MR. BENT G. SIVERTZ: By words.

CO-CHAIR GEORGES ERASMUS: Through what messengers? Through what people were you providing this information?

MR. BENT G. SIVERTZ: Everybody that we talked to.

CO-CHAIR GEORGES ERASMUS: Who were your agents who were providing the infor-mation to them? What individuals? Where you using RCMP or were you using your own officials? Who were your [sic] using?

MR. BENT G. SIVERTZ: We were using resident RCMP members and we were using special envoys from Ottawa who went north—social workers and northern hands. We had three of them who spoke Inuktitut, and we used them to go on special trips to north-ern Quebec to explain about the High Arctic and its characteristics.

We explained to them that we thought the game resources were going to be satisfac-tory. We explained to them that the characteristic of the High Arctic was different from here, that there was not very much in the matter of temperature. The temperature was somewhat lower, we thought, and I don't think we had very specific data on that, and it did not seem to be important in the minds of the Inuit people anyway.

We did explain to them that there was a difference that seemed to be important to human beings, and that is the long period when there was no sun each winter. We ex-plained to them that in the months of December and January one did not see the sun at all and that this is capable of being depressing to human beings. "You might find it so; you might find that you do not wish to live in a land where you will not see the sun for two months in the winter."

Our officers explained this to them, and it was not misunderstood. You should remember that these people of northern Quebec had long periods of approaching that, when the sun set early afternoon and rose late morning—not totally dark, but darkness.

Miss Hinds, the teacher there, entered into this. She had experience in remote places in other parts of the world. She was enthusiastic about taking some of the population of northern Quebec away for a better livelihood. She entered into the explanations to the people. She did not speak Inuktitut well. She did speak it, and she tried her best, but a woman of her age doesn't find it easy to acquire a totally new language like that and be really fluent in it, as were our other Arctic hands who had come into the north as young men and became thoroughly fluent.

She did, however, explain to them what the winter darkness was like, because she had spent some time up there as a welfare teacher.

I don't think there was any chance that she was misunderstood because she was well aware of the fact that it is not just depressing to people to have no sunlight for two months of the year, but it is a difficult matter for women who have sewing as a very important work. It is very difficult to sew in the dark. Men who are working at the dog harness or repairing weapons don't find it easy in darkness.

We said we would do our best and they would do their best with equipment that was better than old times—good coal oil burning lamps; electric-powered flashlights—that would enable people to go and get about tasks.

Margery Hinds did her best to explain this to all of the people she knew. As I said, the police officers there did the same, and our special envoys who went up, I believe, three times—that is my recollection.

. . .

CO-CHAIR GEORGES ERASMUS: In relation to the dump at the Resolute Base, what were your views on the Inuit having access to this particular dump?

MR. BENT G. SIVERTZ: I am not strongly opposed to the idea except in terminology for the name. Garbage dumps are repositories for useful articles in certain circumstances. In connection with dumps used by military establishments, this is especially the case.

The military discard equipment, materials, that you and I or a householder would usually not discard, that can be reused. My own inclination is to reuse it if it can be reused. I have, myself, in building a house [in] British Columbia gone to the local small garbage dump in the country and found a lot of useful materials, and I have personally used them.

We heard foodstuffs were sometimes thrown out on the dump and that the Inuit would retrieve these foodstuffs. This is not an easy thing to bring regulations on. This waste foodstuff from the kitchens of the military camp is actually valuable for some purposes. The ordinary purpose of pig-feeding, and that kind of thing, which is carried out with waste food in this part of the world, is not possible to arrange for in permitting or forbidding access to a garbage dump in Resolute Bay or Grise Fiord.

Therefore, as I have been reading the comments that you people have made and others here about the restrictions applied to the garbage dump in Resolute Bay and Grise Fiord, I think Constables Gibson and Fryer handled this very gently and effectively. They put up an argument that you should not be taking stuff out of the garbage dump to eat, but they certainly wanted them to take out wood, lumber, that was capable of being reused. They helped them do it.

I think they had exceptions in their minds. I recall hearing about aircraft coming north with a large number of men on board, sometimes bound for a different place, maybe Alert. This aircraft, leaving from a base in southern Canada, would have lunches for all the men on board. With changes in their plan in the aircraft flights, they would find that these lunches were not going to be required because the men would be taken off for a dinner or a breakfast or something at the camp en route. Maybe they had encountered weather that made it impossible to pass a certain place, and they had had to spend the night there. They had 45 box lunches on board and, when they got to some place, they would throw them all into the garbage dump.

I recall this sort of thing being distributed to nearby Inuit—first-class food available for their coming to get it. This happened every now and again when you were transporting service men in remote parts of the country.

The Mounted Police Officers, who were representing us and you and all the people of Canada, had to use their best judgment and their kindliness in guiding the people whom they were helping.

CO-CHAIR GEORGES ERASMUS: Thank you for that. Was there any consideration given to the fact that the foodstuffs at the Resolute dump might be used for the Inuit dogs?

MR. BENT G. SIVERTZ: Of course, yes.

CO-CHAIR GEORGES ERASMUS: There has been a lot of opinions on this. If you wouldn't mind giving an answer, I will ask you, for the record, whether or not these relocations had anything to do with Canadian sovereignty at all.

MR. BENT G. SIVERTZ: They did not.

CO-CHAIR GEORGES ERASMUS: It wasn't a secondary issue; it was not considered at all.

MR. BENT G. SIVERTZ: Not at all. I point out to you that I am in possession of a copy of a Privy Council document on sovereignty, and I have seen it in other people's hands. It is marked "Top Secret."

We never saw things marked "Top Secret." This has been declassified since that time. Certainly, documents marked "Top Secret" were not sent around to departments indiscriminately.

The one that I speak of, which I have a copy of, did mention sovereignty, but we were not instructed to take any care in that matter. We did, of our own accord, think of Canadianizing the north because we were full of thoughts of the Oblates and Mary Immaculate operating all over the north as missionaries for the Roman Catholic Church and the fact that the headquarters of the Oblates in Fedalachuk . . . and all of the men that I met in the Canadian north were from some place or other in Europe. None of them ever lived in a Canadian city. They were missionaries in the north, and they went back to

Europe for their studies and their holidays, and they went there to retire—unCanadian, incapable of describing anything of Canada to the people where they delivered service.

The Anglican Church was almost the same. They recruited nine-tenths of their missionaries from Britain, Scotland and Ireland, and they recruited replacements. The Hudson's Bay Company recruited most of its servants in Scotland. They went there for holidays and they went there to retire. They were unCanadian.

Canada had the services of wonderful people from Europe doing scientific work of all kinds in the north. Canada had benefited greatly from geographers, anthropologists, surveyors, oceanographers, glaciologists, making studies in the Canadian north and leaving their findings in our libraries—wonderful.

But we thought, as our minds turned around to these things, it would be nice if we could have these activities done by Canadian universities, by sending young Canadians out there. So we did have the idea of Canadianizing the north, and this often sort of got tangled in people's minds with sovereignty.

Actually, we didn't think there was any danger of international difficulty over ownership of the land of the Queen Elizabeth Islands. I wrote an article on the subject myself—and this is an entirely different subject—long after my retirement just a few years ago, pointing out that the danger of Canada's losing any of these lands is zero.

CO-CHAIR GEORGES ERASMUS: Did your thoughts of Canadianizing the Canadian Arctic include the relocation of Inuit? Did you see this as one of the side benefits of moving the Inuit to a better hunting place, that they would also be in the Canadian High Arctic?

MR. BENT G. SIVERTZ: Yes, we thought that here was empty land, not occupied by other Inuit hunters. This was something that we liked to see.

One of the papers that alleges that I had attributed something to sovereignty was exactly that.

CO-CHAIR GEORGES ERASMUS: When they thought the quote was sovereignty, it was really Canadianizing the north. That is really what you would have been meaning.

MR. BENT G. SIVERTZ: That's all I ever had in mind.

. . .

COMMISSIONER MARY SILLETT: When Mr. Kenney was giving your presentation, one of the things that struck me was the memory of my own childhood. I grew up in Hopedale, Labrador. There was a Canadian base there, as well, and there were rules of separation. Clearly, the local people were under instruction never to go to the base, and the base was under the same kind of instruction.

But there were times, for example, when the base people would come down and they would usually visit our family because my grandfather was a Chief Elder in my community. They would come down, and often there would be photographs taken. I still have some of those photographs, and if you look at all of us, we were happy, we were smiling, and I am sure that, if anyone had written a book, they would give a very positive impression.

I guess what I am trying to say is that sometimes there is a different side of the story to be told by people who actually live in those circumstances. I heard what you said, but I wonder if the people who gave those stories just saw or did they live there? In April we heard stories about people who had been relocated; we heard many stories about the early years of relocation, the kinds of hardship they endured.

Did you not know about those? Did you not hear those stories before? Did you ever hear that the Inuit relocatees might be unhappy?

MR. BENT G. SIVERTZ: The first time I heard any story of unhappiness concerning the relocatees that we are talking about from northern Quebec to the High Arctic was about 1975–76. I didn't hear it at the time but, looking back at it now, we heard nothing in the way of criticism until the 1970s.

. . .

A thing that was said, I think—and I don't hear very well—is that there was hardship. There was no hardship, madam. There was no hardship in 1953, 1954, 1955, 1956, 1957, 1958. There was only very great satisfaction expressed by all the Inuit people of Resolute Bay and Grise Fiord, expressed to my officers on their annual patrol, expressed to other people of the highest level of integrity—and I have given five of them as examples.

If the things that you are saying are true, then you must be implying that these five persons who appear in my letter to Madam Justice Wilson are lying. This has to be said, if you are staying with your story.

COMMISSIONER MARY SILLETT: You said earlier that the Inuit leaders at the camp were told very clearly that, if they were dissatisfied they would be able to return.

Yesterday, when we had a telephone meeting with Ross Gibson, we asked him that question, and he said that he didn't know about any promise of the Inuit being able to return if they were not satisfied.

Could you explain to me why the difference.

MR. BENT G. SIVERTZ: He had nothing to do with it. He was an agent helping with the operation of the communities. He had nothing to do with the promise or its execution, carrying it out.

Had people said to us that they wished to return to Inukjuak, what ought I to do? Had a person come to my officers and said, "I want to go back to Inukjuak," we would have said to him, "You came here as a member of a group, of a family-connected group. I am not going to respond to a request from you to be sent back all by yourself. You came to the decision to come up here as part of a group." If that group spokesman comes to me and says, "My group wants to go back," then we would send the group back.

This is the way decisions were made by the Inuit in those days. Obviously they are not being made by the Inuit nowadays.

COMMISSIONER MARY SILLETT: Could you just tell me, then, who knew about this promise.

MR. BENT G. SIVERTZ: Everybody did. It was talked about right, left and centre throughout the High Arctic and throughout northern Quebec at the time. Everybody knew that they could go back if they didn't want to stay.

But I would not deal with individuals any more than I dealt with individuals to go north. I dealt with a spokesman for the Inuit. This is the way all arrangements were made between government representatives and the Inuit people of Canada at that time. As I just said to you, obviously it is very different today.

CO-CHAIR GEORGES ERASMUS: Are there any other questions?

It has been a long morning for you. I would like to thank you for being very patient and answering these questions. I realize that at times it was emotional for you. Thank you for doing this, even though this morning you didn't feel as well as you could have.

Thank you very much for coming forward.

9.4 Memorandum from the Privy Council Office, 1952

In the early 1950s, Canada's sovereignty in the Arctic was directly challenged a number of times by actions taken by the United States. This document, written by R. A. J. Philips of the Privy Council Office, outlines some of the incidents and expresses a few of the author's concerns. Though it does not refer directly to any High Arctic relocation of Inuit, it does provide some context. Whether or not the incidents described below influenced Canada's decision to move Inuit families north is contested, as can be seen from other documents in this chapter.

Source: External Affairs and International Trade Canada, *Documents on Canadian External Relations*, vol. 18, 1952, Document 744, pp. 1195–99.

Memorandum from Privy Council Office to Clerk of Privy Council

SECRET

Ottawa, December 29, 1952

DEVELOPMENTS IN THE ARCTIC

There follows a list of possible developments in the Arctic for the coming year, mainly as a result of U.S. requests. . . .

(1) *Project Lincoln*

In 1953, the United States will wish to establish three or four experimental early warning radar stations, probably on the extreme northwest of the Canadian mainland. According to plans favoured by many U.S. officials, this will be the beginning of a chain of about 40 radar stations to be established at tremendous cost across the Canadian Arctic. The stations would probably be manned by the United States. Although Canadian defence scientists have some differing views on the value of such stations, if the United States decides to go forward with this scheme we may anticipate heavy pressure, both official and public, since the installations would be designed for the protection of North American cities.

(2) *Development of airfields at Alert and Eureka*

The U.S.A.F. wishes to develop extensively the airstrips at the two northernmost joint Arctic weather stations, on Ellesmere Island. Although the U.S. Northeast Air Command has described their requirement as "emergency landing facilities", they wish to have runways suitable for the heaviest freighters and for jet aircraft. I understand that they are considering blacktop.

At these two joint Arctic weather stations there is now a total of seven Canadians. If the airfields were developed, the installations would probably assume the character of small U.S. bases, and Canadian control might well be lost.

(3) *Loran station on Baffin Island*

The United States wishes to establish a Loran station on the east coast of Baffin Island to assist ships and aircraft en route to Thule and other Arctic destinations.

It was only in 1952 that the government decided to take over the last three Loran stations under U.S. control on the Atlantic coast, and the transfer is to take place in 1953. If the Baffin Island station is opened and operated by the United States, the pattern of Canadian control over all Loran stations in Canada will again be broken.

(4) *Radar stations in the Northeastern Arctic*

Over a year ago, the United States asked to make surveys as a preliminary to the establishment of radar stations on Ellesmere and Coburg Islands for the protection of Thule. During the spring airlift in 1952, the U.S.A.F. investigated the possibility of putting these radar stations in the vicinity of the Joint Arctic Weather Stations at Alert, Eureka and/or Resolute. Resolute, with about 35 Canadians, has the largest Canadian community in the Arctic Archipelago. Alert and Eureka have seven Canadians between them. Each U.S. radar station would probably have about 200 U.S. servicemen.

(5) *Communications facilities*

The U.S.A.F. is concerned about the inadequacy of communications links for transmission of Arctic weather information and about the inadequacy of radio aids to navigation in the North.

Some of the needed improvements which may be suggested will probably be in southern regions where they are for the support of Arctic operations. Since this is a technical matter on which I am not well briefed, I can add no further details, but I expect that the improvements will be costly and will probably have to be provided, if they are provided at all, by the Department of Transport.

It is government policy to attach importance to the maintenance of Canadian sovereignty in the Arctic. Until now the main activity in that area has been the weather station programme. We have maintained our tenuous position by providing half the staff, but in the entire Archipelago we have less than 50 men. This figure is now matched by the United States. Any new U.S. activity is bound to change the delicate balance of manpower in the northern Arctic. This in itself, of course, is not necessarily serious, but I think that our experiences since 1943 have indicated the extreme care which we must exercise to preserve Canadian sovereignty in remote areas where Canadians are outnumbered and outranked.

About a year ago Mr. Pearson remarked in private that he wondered how good our claim was to some areas of the Arctic. If it must rest on discovery and continuous occupation, it may well be in the future that our claim to some relatively unexplored areas will be shaky indeed. I am not now worried by formal claims, since the U.S. Administration has been eminently reasonable during the past six years that we have been working together in the Arctic. Probably of much greater concern is the sort of *de facto* U.S. sovereignty which caused so much trouble in the last war and which might be exercised again. There have already been incidents which, if they had reached the public ear, might have embarrassed the government. Attached to this memorandum is a list of incidents and some extracts from military reports, all of which bear on the question of sovereignty. Needless to say this list is not exhaustive, and contains references only to matters which have come to my attention in the past year or two. Most of the incidents are petty in themselves, but they indicate an atmosphere which is not ideal. And, of course, these incidents have occurred when Canada was more or less matching U.S. manpower in the Canadian Arctic, a situation which may not long continue.

In the entire Canadian Arctic Archipelago, there are only four places where there are exclusively Canadian installations. (The R.C.M.P. is, however, planning to establish a post at Cape Herschel on Ellesmere Island.) There are small weather stations at Arctic Bay and at Pond Inlet. At Resolute Bay, where there is a Joint Arctic Weather Station, there is also an R.C.A.F. station, which is manned entirely by the R.C.A.F. About two years ago, the U.S.A.F. suggested putting new radio equipment with U.S. operators there but the proposal was resisted. At Resolute, there is also a Canadian ionospheric station (6 men, 1 hut). There is at least a possibility that the United States will ask to put in a U.S.-manned radar station with between 100 and 200 men at Resolute. The other Canadian installation is the Arctic survival school open in the winter months at Cambridge Bay in the Southern Archipelago. There are three or four Canadians at each of the Joint Arctic Weather Stations (Resolute-6). The United States still mans the weather stations at Padloping Island. Although Cabinet directed that Canada should take it over by 1950, the Department of Transport has been unable to find the manpower to do so. In addition, of course, the United States also has an installation on an ice island known as T3 which, I am told, has now drifted well into the Canadian sector. Alert and Eureka have been used as staging points for supply, but I gather that the U.S.A.F. plans to use Thule as a base rather than Eielson in Alaska as hitherto. The U.S.A.F., and the U.S.N., are actively interested in finding and possibly manning other ice islands near the Pole. I understand that Canada makes no territorial claim to ice islands within the Canadian sector, and hence our main interest in these stations is in their support which may involve flights to and/over Canadian territory.

There is not a single agreement covering the presence of any Americans in the Arctic Archipelago. The Joint Arctic Weather Station Programme was established in 1947 under terms approved by Cabinet, but we never finished drafting an agreement with the Americans covering the conditions of their presence. At the present time, for instance, Canada has no clear right to increase its staff at any of the weather stations in Canada beyond 50% of the total staff. In view of the close relationships with the Americans, this is probably not a serious matter, except that it might be embarrassing if anyone asked under what terms they were operating in the Arctic. The lack of agreement may also tend to encourage the impression often held, it seems, by U.S. officers, that the Archipelago is a no-man's land. There was a general understanding that the weather station programme would last for five years but so far there has been placed before Cabinet no serious re-examination of the basis of the weather stations following that five-year period which expired almost a year ago.

. . .

Extract from Attachment to Memorandum

SECRET

INCIDENTS

1. On 5 March 1952 an RCAF Lancaster aircraft carrying out photography of the coast of Baffin Island was in touch with Thule air base. When the nature of the mission was mentioned as a photography exercise, Thule Operations inquired on whose authority the flight was being carried out. They were advised that it was on the authority of the Canadian Government. Thule then passed instructions from base operations that photography was to cease immediately and the aircraft was to proceed and land at Thule and remain there until authority to proceed was granted. The instructions were not carried out.

2. In the spring of 1952 the USAF approached Canada through service channels for permission to use Alert for the support of a party to be landed on one of the ice islands. The USAF was informed that the request would have to go through State Department/External Affairs channels. A message was received by Tac Air Group from Alaska Air Command that the operation would nevertheless proceed. The USAF party was established on the ice island, Alert being used for refuelling on the return journey. This all took place before the official U.S. request had reached the Canadian Government.

3. In giving permission for the use of Alert in the spring of 1950 to support the station on the ice island T3, the Canadian Government explicitly stated that it would expect to be informed, prior to the event, if landings were to be made on any other ice island. In fact landings were made, not only on the ice island itself, but also on Ellesmere Island and on the Ellesmere shelf ice. No request for permission for these landings was sent to Canada.

4. Permission was given in 1952 for the establishment of a temporary shore station on Banks Island by the USN icebreaker *Burton Island*. The station was established. Unfortunately the personnel at the station largely destroyed an Eskimo archaeological site by digging for curios. The site was close to a native camp where the regulations protecting such sites were known and have been respected for many years.

5. During the time that Frobisher was still operated by the USAF, immediately prior to the RCAF taking over its operation in 1950, at least one RCAF aircraft was refused permission to land as it was a USAF base.

6. At Padloping in 1951 the USAF weather station was reluctant to let the *C.D. Howe* anchor, intimating that it was a U.S. base.

7. In 1950, while the establishment at Thule was beginning, a beacon was established by the USAF at Clyde Inlet. So far as can be determined this was done without reference in any way to any Canadian authority, and it was a complete surprise when the beacon was found to be operating.

8. Scandinavian Airlines has carried out its pioneer flights on the polar route from Edmonton to Thule to Copenhagen. The major part of this route lies over north Canada. It is understood that Scandinavian Airlines were taking USAF personnel on these flights to advise on facilities and navigation. Certainly USAF charts were being used for areas where superior Canadian aeronautical charts exist. It should be noted that in much of this area Canada is responsible for search and rescue.

9. Many of the meteorological summaries on the joint weather stations are published by the U.S. Weather Bureau. It seems unfortunate that the publication of such data as the meteorological conditions at Eureka Sound is not done by Canada.

10. Although air traffic control in northeast Canada is officially an RCAF responsibility, it has become the practice at Goose Bay for Northeast Air Command, USAF, to request flights north from Goose to be cleared through Northeast Air Command Operations. Under present conditions it can only be a matter of time before this practice is extended to Frobisher and in fact for the whole Northeastern Arctic.

. . .

9.5 The Hickling Report, 1990

In 1990, the House of Commons Standing Committee on Aboriginal Affairs tabled a report concluding that significant wrong had been perpetrated on the Inuit relocated in 1953. The committee requested that Canada apologize to the relocatees, compensate them for the hardships that they had experienced, and formally recognize their contributions to Canadian sovereignty in the North. The Canadian government's response was to hire the Hickling Corporation, a consulting firm based in Ottawa, to investigate the allegations of the committee and report back to Minister of Indian Affairs and Northern Development Tom Siddon. Selections from the report, created in large part by former Department of Indian Affairs employee Bud Neville, appear below.

Source: *Assessment of the Factual Basis of Certain Allegations Made before the Standing Committee on Aboriginal Affairs Concerning the Relocation of Inukjuak Inuit Families in the 1950s: Report*, submitted to the Department of Indian Affairs and Northern Development (Ottawa: Hickling Corporation, 1990), 3–6.

Reproduced with the permission of the Minister of Public Works and Government Services Canada, 2013.

. . . Our assessment of the factual basis of the allegations included in our study is based on an extensive survey of official government files, documents, published and unpublished reports, and learned papers in the possession of the National Archives of Canada, the Department of Indian Affairs and Northern Development, various libraries in other Government departments, public libraries and sources within Makivik Corporation. We also interviewed a number of key informants, including some members of the Inuit groups that were involved in the relocations that are the subject of our study.

We found that the decision by the Government to actively encourage the relocation of Inuit families to the High Arctic in 1953, and in the two or three years subsequent to that, was not motivated by a concern to strengthen Canadian sovereignty over the Arctic Islands at that time. Canada felt secure in her claim of ownership of the Islands at that time, as a result of an exchange of Notes between Canada and Norway in 1930, and because the Canadian Government had consistently displayed in sovereignty in that area for so long and in so many ways as to firmly establish its title to all of the Arctic Islands in a manner consistent with International Law.

The R.C.M.P. participated in the exercise of Canadian sovereignty in the North by their very presence in those areas and in the various roles they were called upon to carry out on their own, and on behalf of other federal departments. They were required from time to time to deal with the illegal hunting of polar bear and muskoxen by Greenlanders, which was prohibited under the NWT Game Ordinance. In carrying our [sic] this function, they did indeed assist in asserting Canadian sovereignty.

The Inuit families in question were not relocated to the High Arctic to assist the RCMP in the administration of the NWT Game Ordinance, although, in fact, they did so on occasion. They also asserted Canadian Arctic sovereignty by the very fact of living there but that was not the purpose of their relocation.

Our study reveals that the main reason of the decision by the Government to encourage some Inuit families to relocate to the High Arctic at that time was a concern to improve the living conditions of the Inuit, particularly in the Hudson Bay region. Relocation from those depressed areas was seen, by both Government officials and the Inuit themselves, as a way of breaking out of a growing pattern of welfare dependency, and as a means of providing the Inuit with new and better economic opportunities through improved hunting, trapping and wage employment.

Reasonable steps were taken by the Government officials to establish and apply suitable criteria for the selection of families, so as to ensure the success of the project and the security of the participants. These criteria were developed over a period of several years, with input from a number of sources. Those who were transported to the new location by the "C.D. Howe" were x-rayed before their departure and appear to have been found to be free of serious infectious diseases. Some of the participants who were included were quite aged and at least one was physically disabled, but their participation in the relocation project was not out of line with Inuit cultural values nor with the realities of life in the Arctic in those years. The difficulties of life in the High Arctic were recognized and explored beforehand by the officials and a reasonable plan was articulated to ensure that those who were relocated were well supported by experienced R.C.M.P. officers who knew the families personally and who were knowledgeable of Inuit ways and language. Experienced Inuit families from the most northern settlements at the time were approached to assist with the project. They agreed to do so and to transfer their hunting and trapping skills to the Inuit participants from Arctic Quebec. The first group of Inuit relocated were not as well equipped as they might have been, but apparently this was dealt with after their arrival.

Reasonable efforts seem to have been made to explain the project to both of the Inuit groups involved before their departure, and to communicate the fact that participation in it was voluntary. It is more than likely that some of the Inuit could not completely envisage what conditions in the High Arctic would be like because these things were outside the range of personal experience at the time. While this is truly regrettable, it should not imply a deliberate attempt by the Government officials to deceive or mislead the Inuit participants.

A number of the Inuit families in the project stated in letters written to the Department in the period 1956 to 1963 that game and fur were plentiful in the vicinity of both Resolute Bay and Grise Fiord, and that hunger was not a problem. The frequency of letter-writing from Inuit at Resolute Bay dropped off considerably after 1963 and nearly completely, after 1966, with the transfer of responsibility for most aspect of Inuit affairs to the Government of the NWT. It is not possible, therefore, to say whether game and fur continued to be plentiful after the letters stopped coming but on the other hand, there is no reason to believe otherwise.

We believe that the Department gave the Inuit an understanding that they would be returned to their original communities after one, two, or three years, if this was requested. There is no evidence to suggest that the Department intended this undertaking to remain in force indefinitely.

The files show that some of the Inuit families living in Resolute Bay wrote to Ottawa, asking to return to Port Harrison for a visit. The earliest example of such a request, that we could find, occurred around 1960. The determination of the length of the proposed visits quite often required several exchanges of letters. On one known occasion, in 1961, Ottawa responded to such proposals by seeming to suggest that those wishing to visit Port Harrison should collaborate in chartering an aircraft for this purpose, at their own expense. The files would indicate that one group did this in 1962, but no further details are provided. It is uncertain if there was an official policy on the matter at that time. Our speculation is that the Department took this position because it considered the individuals involved to be economically self-sufficient. This was the practice followed with respect to Fort Chimo Inuit working at Churchill and wishing to visit their home community.

Early in the 1970s, however, the Government of the Northwest Territories arranged and paid for the transportation of several groups of Inuit, from both Grise Fiord and Resolute Bay, to Port Harrison, to visit relatives and to assess whether they wished to be returned to that community on a permanent basis. Several families subsequently requested relocation and this was done. The Department of Indian Affairs and Northern Development reimbursed the Territorial Government for the costs of both the visits and relocation.

On one occasion, the R.C.M.P. used their own aircraft to permit several families living at Grise Fiord to visit relatives in Port Harrison and subsequently relocated them. The R.C.M.P. apparently absorbed these costs.

An additional number of Inuit families living at Resolute Bay were relocated to Port Harrison in 1988, initially at their own expense or with assistance from the Makivik Corporation of Quebec. The Department agreed to re-imburse the transportation costs for those families who had already moved back to Inukjuak. This offer was subsequently extended to include the costs of transporting a number of other families who had not yet moved but who had indicated that they intended to do so. These re-imbursements, totalling approximately $250,000.00, were paid out of the Department's 1988–89 appropriations. In 1988, the Department also undertook to provide the Government of Quebec with funds, amounting to approximately $700,000, to permit Quebec to add ten houses to the pool of housing identified for Port Harrison, in recognition of the impact that this inflow of people would have on the 1989 housing plans for that community.

The evidence that we examined does not support the allegation that the Government committed wrongdoing in the planning and conduct of this project. The material we examined leads us to a different conclusion, namely that the project was conscientiously planned, was carried out in a reasonably effective manner and that the Inuit participated in it voluntarily, in their own search for a better life, and benefited from the experience.

We do not see the grounds for an apology by the Government for the manner in which the relocation project was conceived, planned and carried out. In our view, to apologize for a wrongdoing it did not commit would constitute deception on the part of the Government. It would also imply that the project had not been reasonably successful whereas this is not the case.

In our opinion, the delay in settling the matter of the return of the remaining original families still at Resolute Bay and Grise Fiord is the only real basis for criticism of the Department, as far as this project is concerned. The circumstances that caused this delay, however, have already been explained by several Deputy Ministers and Ministers since the claim was first formally raised with the Department in 1982. At this point, therefore, a concrete and definitive statement on what action the Department now intends to take on this matter would be most meaningful.

We would suggest that the Department consider extending for a further one or so years the offer previously made to the Inuit families who have already returned to Inukjuak and Pond Inlet from Resolute Bay and Grise Fiord. This would permit any of the remaining families at Resolute and Grise Fiord to undertake an exploratory visit to their original communities and to relocate on a permanent basis if they so choose.

Also, we suggest that the Department agree to support any proposal to note the contribution which Inuit throughout the Arctic have made over the years to the social, political and economic development of the High Arctic.

9.6 Report of the Royal Commission on Aboriginal Peoples, 1994

The final document in this chapter includes selections from the report prepared by the Royal Commission on Aboriginal Peoples (RCAP) on the High Arctic relocation. The commissioners travelled widely and heard from dozens of Inuit relocatees, former members of the RCMP, and other officials involved in the relocation, as well as from a number of academics and others who had studied the relocation and related issues. This selection includes a summary of the RCAP's conclusions.

Source: Royal Commission on Aboriginal Peoples, *The High Arctic Relocation: A Report on the 1953–55 Relocation* (Ottawa: Supply and Services, 1994), 134–46.

Footnotes as in original.

Chapter 9

Shedding New Light on the Relocation: Summary of the Commission's Conclusions

. . .

Over time the divergence between the position of the relocatees and that of the government has become wider. The government has also backtracked from previously stated positions. Whereas it once stated that it had no knowledge of any promise to return, the government has now acknowledged that such a promise was made and that the promise was not honoured. During the 1980s the government made various statements about the role of the relocation in maintaining Canadian sovereignty that appeared to support the relocatees' contention that sovereignty was a motivating factor. The position of the government now is that sovereignty was not a consideration. Had the government promptly acknowledged the failure to honour the promise to return and then acted to redress the wrong, the complaints might well have been resolved quickly. The reversal of the position on sovereignty only added fuel to the fire, and the government's refusal to adopt the unanimous recommendations of the Standing Committee on Aboriginal Affairs was incomprehensible to the relocatees.

Each study or report that has been critical of the government has been met with a more extensive study commissioned by the government. The government has subjected each element of the complaints, piece by piece, to extensive analysis. The apparent focus of government action has been to defend itself against these complaints and to put the government's actions in the best possible light. In adopting this approach, the government has been seen as an adversary that would argue a point so long as any evidence could be found to support it and would concede a point only in the face of overwhelming evidence. The government did not step back and begin with a reassessment of the social, political and cultural context in which the relocation took place and then consider the complaint broadly in that context. Had a different approach been adopted, the government might have been led to a new awareness that would have permitted it to see the validity in the relocatees' complaints and to move toward resolving them in a more positive way.

In short, the government's handling of the complaints has served to increase mistrust and deepen the sense of grievance.

The Commission's hearings and analysis have shed new light on the High Arctic relocation. Reconciliation of the evidence concerning the relocation provides a basis for reassessing the government's responsibilities concerning the relocation and is a first step in a more fundamental reconciliation between the relocatees and the government.

The Commission's conclusions, based on the preceding evidence and analysis, are, in summary, as follows:

Inuit Dependence and Vulnerability

1. The High Arctic relocation took place in a cultural context where Inuit typically felt dependent upon non-Inuit and powerless in their dealings with them. The power that non-Inuit held over Inuit was well understood by non-Inuit, and even the wishes of well-intentioned non-Inuit could be taken as orders by Inuit. The government was present in the Arctic in the form of the RCMP, who were held in particular awe by the Inuit.

2. Not all Inuit were equally dependent or vulnerable in their relations with non-Inuit. There are indications that the dependence and vulnerability of the northern Quebec Inuit tended to be much greater than that of the people of northern Baffin Island.

Inuit Relationship to Homeland and Kin

3. The Inuit have a particular attachment to homeland and kin. This attachment was known by non-Inuit at the time of the relocation.

4. The Inukjuak area has been inhabited by large numbers of Inuit for centuries and is a traditional hunting and fishing area.

Paternalistic Government Decision Making

5. Government decision making concerning the Inuit into the early 1950s typically did not take into account the wishes and aspirations of the Inuit. Instead, government decisions reflected a paternalistic view of what would be good for the Inuit and tended to minimize or disregard Inuit needs and desires.

Sovereignty as a Factor in the Relocation

6. The relocation took place at a time when the government was concerned about *de facto* sovereignty arising from the presence of the United States in the Arctic. The concern about the *de facto* sovereignty involved a concern that Canada would not be seen to be controlling activities in the North so that, over time, Canada's *de jure* sovereignty could be questioned. The weight of the evidence points to sovereignty as a material consideration in the relocation decision, although the primary concerns were social and economic.

Population Growth or Game Decline Not Factors in the Relocation

7. The information available to the government in the early 1950s does not indicate that the Inukjuak area was experiencing population growth. Rather, high mortality rates tended to result in a stable population. Nor were there indications of a serious decline in food game resources. In fact, the situation had not changed in 30 to 40 years.

The Preoccupation with "Handouts"

8. There was a concern in the Department about the long-term instability of the fur trade and the capacity of the fur trade to sustain the income levels to which Inukjuak Inuit had become accustomed. The government saw little prospect for

increased earned income in the Inukjuak area, with the result that periodic reliance on relief would become a permanent feature of life and that other "handouts", such as family allowance and old age pensions, would become a more significant part of Inuit income. The need for relief arose periodically as a result of the cyclical nature of the fur trade, with poor years following good years over a four-year cycle. It was considered that the Inukjuak Inuit were becoming dependent on "handouts", with a consequent loss of self-reliance and moral decline.

The Objective of Increased Reliance on Hunting

9. Officials considered that greater reliance on hunting and less reliance on the trade store would restore Inuit self-reliance and arrest the perceived moral decline. At the same time, this would resolve the perceived long-term economic concern regarding the instability of the fur trade, since a return to greater reliance on hunting would substitute for the income that fur trading would, in the long term, be unable to provide. This objective was never communicated to the Inuit.

"Overpopulations in Relation to Available Resources"

10. It was perceived that decreased reliance on the trade store through increased reliance on hunting would not be possible in the Inukjuak area unless Inuit were relocated to other parts of the Quebec coast, to the islands of Hudson Bay off the Quebec coast, or to other parts of the Arctic. In this sense, and in this sense only, the Inukjuak area was considered to be "over-populated in relation to available resources". This phrase is unfortunately ambiguous and was thought by some to refer [to] a hunting population outstripping available game food resources. In fact, it characterizes an economic concern of the government related to a desire to require Inuit to hunt more and rely less on earned income.

The Goal of "Rehabilitation"

11. The goal of restoring Inuit self-reliance and independence through greater reliance on hunting involved restoring the Inuit to what was perceived by non-Inuit to be their proper state. The goal was "rehabilitation", and the High Arctic relocation would be understood at the time—though not by the Inuit—as a rehabilitation project.

Failure to Disclose the Rehabilitation Goal to the Inuit

12. The Inukjuak Inuit were not told that the government considered them to be in need of rehabilitation and that the goal of the relocation would be rehabilitation.

Relocation Would Not Relieve the Cycles in Hunting and Trapping

13. At the time of the 1953 relocation, the fur cycle was reaching its peak, and no able-bodied Inuit were on relief at Inukjuak. Hunting was good and conditions were much improved over those of 1949–50, when the fur economy collapsed and a hard winter made hunting difficult. Such cycles occurred everywhere in the Arctic where Inuit lived by hunting and trapping. White fox trapping everywhere followed a four-year cycle.[3] Hunting, even in areas of relative abundance, could be affected by adverse weather or ice conditions or variations in migratory patterns. Relocating Inuit to other places would not relieve such variability in the conditions of life.

---

3 Cycles would not necessarily coincide in the same years in different parts of the Arctic; however, the typical cycle was of four years' duration.

The Institutional Consensus Supporting Relocations

14. There was consensus among all those with an interest in Arctic affairs, including the various government departments concerned, the RCMP, the Anglican and Roman Catholic churches and the Hudson's Bay Company, that relocations would solve perceived economic and social problems. There were, however, differences of opinion about how relocations should be undertaken, with some, such as Superintendent Larson of the RCMP, advocating the creation of small communities with wooden houses and schools, so that the adult Inuit could maintain a hunting and trapping lifestyle while children received the education that would be essential for the future.

The Relocation Plan

15. The High Arctic relocation was conceived by the Department as a way to place Inuit in areas believed to have adequate game resources and to require them to live largely by hunting, with some opportunity to trap. A small trade store would be established but would carry a limited and basic stock. The RCMP would be responsible for administering the store and, with the limited and basic stock, would be required to ration items from the store to ensure equitable distribution. It would be the role of the RCMP to "encourage" the Inuit to hunt.

The Coercive Aspect of the Plan

16. The relocation plan was inherently coercive. It was a plan designed to take people who were accustomed to an income economy, with the goods that income could purchase, and place them in a situation where they would be made to rely more heavily on game food, with all the hardship such a life naturally involved. The government did not need to use overt force. The imperative of survival achieved the desired objective.

The Coercive Aspects of Life in the Communities

17. Day-to-day life in the new communities would also have coercive elements. The RCMP were directed by the Department not to give credit to trappers, even though giving credit, or grubstaking, was the common practice of trading companies. The RCMP were also directed to exercise a firm hand in the giving of relief. Insufficient supplies in the trade stores established in the new communities would mean that the benefit of old age pensions and family allowance often would not reach the intended beneficiaries through goods issued from the store. Instead, these amounts would be recorded as a book entry in the form of forced savings. RCMP "encouragement" of the Inuit in furtherance of the project's objectives would result in the police telling the Inuit what to do and scolding them when they did not do what the police wanted. The Inuit camps were established at a distance from non-Inuit facilities to restrict contact between Inuit and non-Inuit and to prevent the Inuit from becoming a burden on the non-Inuit post or base. All these small elements of coercion became additionally coercive when carried out by a police force.

Misplaced Notions of Success

18. The overt signs of success of such a project, namely, self-reliance, would be similar regardless of the state of mind of any of the relocatees. Whether or not the

people were unhappy or had a desire to return home, they would still have to hunt. Reports by officials stating consistently that the relocatees were doing well reflect the overt state of affairs but do not address the unhappiness that many relocatees experienced and their desire to return home.

"Rehabilitation" versus Opportunities for Independent Hunters

19. Not all Inuit relied on income from trapping to the same extent. The relocation scheme might have been entirely satisfactory for people who lived largely from hunting, with income from trapping providing only a supplement, and who did not look to government support in poor fur years. There were Inuit who went to Resolute Bay from Pond Inlet who did find the relocation satisfactory. However, these Pond Inlet Inuit were not typical of all relocatees, and the relocation scheme, by its own terms, sought to relocate people who depended more heavily on an income economy, with government support as the safety net in poor years. Even the Pond Inlet Inuit at Grise Fiord, who were used to the support of a store, found conditions too hard. The recruitment of Inuit for the project was not, therefore, limited to those who had continued to live relatively distant from trading posts, with income from trading providing only a supplement to what was obtained from hunting.

Relocation [a] Regressive Step

20. At the time of the relocation, Inukjuak was a substantial settlement with a Hudson's Bay Company post, a police post, church missions, a school, a nursing station, a Department of Transport weather station and radio facility, and a port facility. The school and nursing station had been established relatively recently as part of a government program to remedy past decades of neglect. The relocation created new communities that would have no schools, no nursing stations and no missions. In this respect, the decision would turn the clock back to the era of neglect when there were no such facilities.

Further Consequences of the Rehabilitation Objectives

21. The highly generalized concern of administrators about Inuit relying too much on government "handouts" was felt by the relocatees in various ways. The concern applied both to government support programs, such as family allowance and old age security, which were available to Canadians on a universal basis, and to relief, which was available only in cases of hardship. Thus, the relocation scheme was aimed not only at changing expectations about relief, but also at discouraging reliance on the universal programs. This would involve using administrative powers to restrict or withhold the actual benefit of payments universally available to Canadians. As a result, some relocatees found that the benefit of their family allowance and old age security payments stopped after they left Inukjuak. The generalized concern about reliance on "handouts" was also applied to all Inuit. Yet, not all Inuit, even in the Quebec part of the Arctic, were equally reliant on the combination of earned and unearned income. The relocatees were not all alike. Moreover, by 1953, conditions had improved considerably since the collapse of fur prices in 1949–50, and no able-bodied Inukjuak Inuit were receiving relief. The government's generalized preoccupation abut Inuit reliance on "handouts" and the understanding of local officials that this was a "rehabilitation" project served only to reinforce stereotypical

attitudes that would adversely complicate relation between the relocatees and the local officials responsible for their well-being.

The Deputy Minister Approved Little More [T]han a Concept

22. The government plan included no indication of representations or promises that were to be made to the Inuit. The plan, as approved by the Deputy Minister, was very general in its description of what was to be done and for what purpose. The detail would be worked out as the plan was implemented. This meant that a large amount of discretion was left to those implementing the decision. The Deputy Minister approved little more than a concept.

The Promise to Return

23. The decision to extend a promise to return was made initially by Henry Larsen of the RCMP. It appears that the Department accepted this decision and, in fact, a departmental representative, Alex Stevenson, also extended a promise to return in his discussions with some Inukjuak Inuit. These promises were recorded in official memoranda and reports at the time. These documents are still in existence. No plan was developed by the Department to give effect to the promise, and the means to return were not made available to the Inuit. The content of the promise to return was never clearly defined, for example, whether it covered individuals or only an entire group, and whether it covered visits back and forth. If the promise was meant to apply only to the whole group, this was not conveyed to the Inuit.

No Special Instructions about Obtaining the Consent of the Inuit

24. The RCMP detachments in northern Quebec and Pond Inlet were responsible for recruiting Inuit for the relocation. The relocatees were to be volunteers, but the Department gave the RCMP no special instructions about how to approach the Inuit or how to secure their consent, notwithstanding the well-known difficulty of obtaining genuine consent from Inuit. The RCMP member at Inukjuak responsible for carrying out these instructions understood that it was his responsibility to sell the Inuit on a project that was for their benefit, and that is what he did.

The Absence of Free and Informed Consent

25. It cannot be said that the Inukjuak Inuit gave free and informed consent to the relocation. The Inukjuak Inuit understood that they were going to a better place where there was an abundance of large land mammals, that they would be looked after, and that they would have the support of the Canadian government. Apart, in some cases, from an understanding that there would be a dark period, the Inukjuak relocatees had no understanding of the disadvantages or risks of the project and did not believe that the relocation could change their lives fundamentally and adversely. Nor did they understand the rehabilitative character of the plan. What the Inukjuak Inuit were offered was less than what they had, in the sense that there would be less government income support available in the High Arctic and greater reliance on hunting. As a result, the relocatees, in addition to the many hardships suffered, experienced a sense of abandonment by the government and suffered considerable distress when their expectations of a significantly better life in the High Arctic were not met.

The Inukjuak Inuit Were Not Told of the Involvement of the Pond Inlet Inuit, and the Two Groups Did Not Get Along Well

26. The Inukjuak Inuit were not told that they would be joined by Pond Inlet Inuit. There are significant differences between the Inukjuak and Pond Inlet dialects, as well as differences in the two peoples' way of living. The Inukjuak and Pond Inlet groups did not get along well in the new communities. The government's desire was to have Pond Inlet Inuit involved in the relocation to help the Inukjuak Inuit adjust to High Arctic conditions. This idea failed, however, to take into account the disruptive effects of putting the different groups together in an isolated community.

Failure to Compensate Pond Inlet Inuit

27. The Pond Inlet Inuit found themselves providing a service to the government, giving guidance to the Inukjuak Inuit; they expected to be paid for this service but were not. The government failed to ensure that the conditions under which the Pond Inlet Inuit were participating were made clear to them. The government should accept responsibility for this misunderstanding.

The Last-Minute Decision to Send Inukjuak Families to Resolute Bay

28. The original plan called for Inuit from Fort Chimo to go to Resolute Bay where they could find full- or part-time employment. This aspect of the plan fell apart because the government never had any intention of providing housing for the Inuit at Resolute Bay, and the Fort Chimo Inuit were used to living in houses. The initial planning by the Department failed to accommodate the characteristics of the people. As a result, the employment aspect of the relocation to Resolute Bay was downplayed, and it was decided that Inuit from Inukjuak would go to Resolute Bay instead to make their living by hunting and trapping.

Forced Separation of the Inukjuak Inuit

29. The Inukjuak Inuit understood that they would all be going to the same place; they had been told they were going to Ellesmere Island. The Inukjuak Inuit would not learn that they were to be separated until they were already in the High Arctic, when they were separated and sent to different locations. This was painful and distressing for them and, in the circumstances, was clearly a forced separation.

Inadequate Regard for the Needs of the Relocatees

30. The government proceeded with determination to implement the plan once it had been set in motion, without regard to matters that should have been incorporated in the planning process. The relocatees would need caribou skins for bedding and clothing, which are vital for people living on the land. When the required skins were not available, the Department nevertheless proceeded with the relocation, and the relocatees went north with 60 instead of the 600 skins needed for clothing and bedding for the coming year. In addition, the relocatees arrived in the High Arctic without all the equipment they would need for life there.

The Spread of Tuberculosis to Resolute Bay

31. The Inuit community at Resolute Bay became infected with tuberculosis, which may have been carried from Inukjuak, resulting in additional hardship to the community as many members were transported south to hospital for extended periods.

The Eskimo Loan Fund was Used Improperly for Departmental Purposes

32. The trade stores in the new communities were funded through the Eskimo Loan Fund. There is no evidence that the arrangements for the loan were discussed with the relocatees before departure. The signature of one of the Inuit as the borrower would be obtained by the police after the relocatees arrived in the High Arctic. The loan arrangement lacked substance. The reality was that the Loan Fund was being used for departmental purposes, with an Inuk signing a loan agreement as a formality. The work of running the trade store was handled by the police. An Inuk signature on the loan agreement was a formality, not in the sense of being good legal form, but in the sense of something perfunctory and lacking in substance. In these circumstances, an Inuk's signature on loan documents does not imply consent to the loan.

Isolation in the High Arctic

33. The environment in the new High Arctic communities was, in addition to the dark period, considerably different from Inukjuak. Climactic conditions are more severe, and varieties of game are significantly more limited. The move to the High Arctic thus involved significant changes for the Inukjuak relocatees. The Inukjuak Inuit also suffered isolation from home and the larger community at Inukjuak as a result of separation from immediate family, extended family, and friends who remained at Inukjuak. There was also isolation from those non-Inuit facilities that did exist in the new communities as a result of the separation of the new Inuit settlements from non-Inuit facilities. Finally, isolation was created by the differences between the Inukjuak and Pond Inlet groups in very small communities consisting of only a few families.

The Hardship Adjusting to the New Land

34. The Inukjuak Inuit were placed in a situation where to survive they had to adapt to an area that was significantly different from the Inukjuak area in terms of climate, terrain and hunting conditions. There were also significant differences in the types and variety of game and fish available; this meant that the Inukjuak relocatees had to adapt their hunting techniques to the new conditions, to learn where and when various types of game could be obtained most readily, and to adjust their equipment to the different terrain, particularly in the Grise Fiord area. Changes in diet were also required. At Grise Fiord, the Inukjuak Inuit would have to learn to obtain water from grounded icebergs. The Inukjuak Inuit were also used to burning wood, and although wood could be found in the base dump at Resolute Bay, at Grise Fiord, seal oil lamps were the only means of cooking and providing heat. The more severe weather and the periods of darkness made it more difficult to carry out daily tasks and required psychological adjustment. The Inukjuak Inuit found the adjustment difficult—and certainly much harder than they expected.

Risks to Inuit Health and Life in an Experimental Project and the Inadequacy of Measures to Prevent Hardship

35. The relocation was an experiment to see whether the Inuit could adjust to life in the High Arctic. There was real risk attached to the project if it turned out that the land could not support the Inuit or if the Inuit had severe difficulty learning how

to exploit the resources of the new land. This risk would have become a reality at the Cape Herschel site if that aspect of the relocation had gone ahead. Game failed to materialize in the Cape Herschel area in the winter of 1953–54, and the land would not have been able to support the relocatees.

The supplies sent in for the trade stores at Resolute and Craig Harbour were not sufficient to support the people should they be unable to take sufficient game for food but were intended only to supplement what they could obtain from hunting. There is no evidence that the Department developed a contingency plan to take account of the possibility that game might not be sufficient to meet the communities' food needs. The inherent riskiness of the project was not discussed with the Inuit. They were simply assured that there was abundant game in the High Arctic and that they would have a better life.

Some of the supplies intended for Resolute Bay did not arrive; eventually the missing supplies were flown in by the RCAF sometime after January 1954, more than five months after they should have arrived. At both Craig Harbour/ Grise Fiord and Resolute Bay, skins for clothing and bedding arrived late in the winter, in the early months of 1954. By contrast, if a Canadian government post had been established in the High Arctic and government personnel were missing essential items such as Arctic clothing and bedding, the government certainly would have arranged for these essential supplies to be sent immediately. The fact that the Department had arranged the relocation using the device of a loan limited the Department's financial ability to respond to contingencies that developed in what was in substance a government-initiated relocation. The project was insufficiently funded, and as contingencies developed over the years, as when supplies failed to arrive, cost considerations would outweigh considerations of Inuit welfare. Contingencies were absorbed in the form of increased hardship for the relocatees.

Inadequate Provisions for Necessary Boats

36. Large boats formed an important part of life in Inukjuak and were an important aspect of status in the community. These boats had been left behind in Inukjuak. The relocatees believed that there would be boats available for them in the new land. No arrangements had been made to provide the Inuit relocatees with boats.

Hardship and Suffering the Result of an Inherently Unsound Plan

37. The relocation was not a case of an appropriate plan running into difficulty because of failures in carrying it out. The plan was inherently unsound, and the means necessary to carry it out were equally unsound. The failures in execution served only to aggravate the hardship and suffering inherent in the plan from the outset.

Inadequate Supplies for the Trade Stores

38. The small trade stores were chronically understocked and, particularly at Grise Fiord, people suffered hardship year after year through the 1950s.

Difficulty in Finding Spouses

39. The small size of the communities made it difficult for young people to find spouses.

Restrictions on Movement

40. Grise Fiord lacked the employment opportunities of Resolute Bay, yet people were effectively prevented from moving from Grise Fiord to Resolute Bay to join relatives or to pursue other opportunities.

The Failure to Honour the Promise to Return

41. The government failed to honour the promise to return, and the resulting hardship is not fully redressed by an offer to pay for a return many years after the return should have been provided. The lost years must be taken into account.

The Relocatees' Experiences were Predictable

42. The experiences of the relocatees were the predictable result of a scheme that was inherently coercive in its objective and coercive in the means chosen to achieve that objective. The other failings in planning and implementation, as well as the failure to honour the promise to return, compounded the hardship suffered by the relocatees.

SUGGESTIONS FOR FURTHER READING

The most thorough account of the High Arctic relocations discussed in this chapter, as well as of other relocations in the same general time frame, is Frank J. Tester and Peter K. Kulchyski, *Tammarniit (Mistakes): Inuit Relocation in the Eastern Arctic, 1939–1963* (Vancouver: UBC Press, 1994). For an evaluation of government policy and the motivations that led to the relocation, as well as for material on the operation of the relocation experiment itself and the later decision not to apologize for the treatment experienced by the relocatees, see Shelagh Grant, "A Case of Compound Error: The Inuit Resettlement Project, 1953, and the Government Response," *Northern Perspectives* 19, no 1 (Spring 1991), available on line at http://www.carc.org/pubs/v19no1/2.htm. For further context, see also Grant's *Sovereignty or Security? Government Policy in the Canadian North, 1936–1950* (Vancouver: UBC Press, 1988). For a study focused on the 1953–55 relocations and an assessment of the Hickling Report's findings, see Alan Marcus, "Out in the Cold: Canada's Experimental Inuit Relocation to Grise Fiord and Resolute Bay," *Polar Record* 27, 163 (1991): 285–96. Again, the Royal Commission on Aboriginal Peoples should be helpful to readers. In addition to RCAP's individual report on this topic, cited above, see "Relocation of Aboriginal Communities," in *Report of the Royal Commission on Aboriginal Peoples* (Ottawa: Indian and Northern Affairs Canada, 1996), chap. 11. This is available on line at http://www.collectionscanada.gc.ca/webarchives/20071124125856/http://www.ainc-inac.gc.ca/ch/rcap/sg/sgm11_e.html. For a report commissioned by the Department of Indian Affairs and Northern Development Canada that is quite sympathetic to government actions and motives, see Magnus Gunther, *The 1953 Relocations of the Inukjuak Inuit to the High Arctic: A Documentary Analysis and Evaluation* (Ottawa: Department of Indian Affairs and Northern Development, 1992).

CHAPTER 10

"A FAULTY UNDERSTANDING OF FAIRNESS"[1]

THE WHITE PAPER OF 1969

The first Trudeau government was elected in 1968 into a world that was rife with public displays of support for the rights of minorities and less privileged groups and against actions perceived to be imperialist in nature. In Canada, Pierre Elliott Trudeau rode to victory on the global wave of human rights consciousness by promising to create a more "just society," one that would allow for a fairer treatment of groups that had been marginalized in various ways. The 1968 election was followed only two years later by the release of the well-known Hawthorn Report, which brought together over 40 academics to conduct a federally funded survey of the living conditions of status Indians from all parts of Canada. The survey took three years to complete, and the two-volume final report made over 150 recommendations. The philosophy that framed the report was summed up by the notion that Indians should be considered as "citizens plus" due to un-extinguished rights and title to land, promises made in treaties, and their position as the original occupiers of the territories that became Canada. The Hawthorn Report made it clear that the 1951 Indian Act amendments, like previous policy and legislative initiatives, had not been effective in ameliorating the dismal socio-economic conditions that existed in many Indigenous communities.

Trudeau's liberalism, though, was based on the notion of individual not collective or community rights, so his government rejected the Hawthorn Report and especially the notion that those Canada defined as Indians should be considered in any way as "citizens plus" entitled to special rights or consideration. Historical injustice was not relevant, according to Trudeau, in his effort to be "just in our time." Instead, after hosting meetings

---

1 Indian Chiefs of Alberta, *Citizens Plus* [Red Paper] (Edmonton: Indian Association of Alberta, 1970), 4. This quotation appears in document 10.2.

with First Nations leaders, but apparently not particularly receptive to what was being said, Minister of Indian Affairs Jean Chrétien tabled a policy document titled *Statement of the Government of Canada on Indian Policy* in 1969. In Canada, a document of this sort that is approved by cabinet and made publically available is called a "white paper," an unfortunate moniker in this context. The 1969 White Paper, selections of which appear as document 10.1 below, outlined the Trudeau government's views on rights historically held by First Nations people and its plans for future policy directions.

The 1969 White Paper was met with immediate and widespread opposition from First Nations organizations. Many of the specific points of opposition appear here in documents 10.2 and 10.4 prepared by the Indian Association of Alberta and the National Indian Brotherhood, respectively. In its effort to promote its perspective and policy choices and to counter some of the opposition presented by First Nations organizations, Trudeau's government hired William I.C. Wuttunee, a Cree lawyer from Calgary. Unfortunately for the government, and especially for Wuttunee, the appointment had the tendency to inflame the situation even further. Wuttunee found himself personally ostracized in some communities and soon resigned. He presented his own perspectives in his 1971 book *Ruffled Feathers: Indians in Canadian Society*. A selection of this book, too, appears below, as document 10.3.

Finally, in the face of continuing and deepening opposition, the White Paper was withdrawn by Trudeau's government in March of 1971. The White Paper could, though, be said to represent a watershed moment, one indicative of a substantial growth in Indigenous political organizing and claims activity in Canada. It also illustrated, in the views of many First Nations leaders and activists, that the state's long-standing policy of assimilation was alive and well. Similarly, the consultation process, which was shown to be little more than posturing, illustrated that, despite the egalitarian messages presented by Trudeau's Liberals, First Nations people should still not expect meaningful involvement in the making of decisions that directly affected their lives and the future of their communities. This disjunction of message and action, in turn, led to deep-seated suspicion of all policy initiatives presented by Canada and even more acrimonious relations between Canada and First Nations for the next decade or more. Trudeau's words, from a 1969 speech promoting the new policy discussed here, were used by the Union of BC Indian Chiefs in their submission to the Russell Tribunal on the Rights of the Indians of the Americas in November 1980 as part of their opposition to the patriation of the constitution. This document is included in Chapter 12 as document 12.1.

QUESTIONS FOR DISCUSSION

1. What specific concerns did the First Nations activists whose views are presented here have with the White Paper?
2. Why would First Nations leaders want to continue the Indian Act?
3. In what ways could Canada be said to be abrogating or downloading its responsibilities for Indians under Section 91 (24) of the BNA Act, which states that "Indians and lands reserved for the Indians" are a federal responsibility?
4. What specific elements of William Wuttunee's views were in opposition to those of the other Indigenous activists represented here?

5. What parts of the White Paper and William Wuttunee's writings indicate a privileging of individual over collective rights? Identify what, in your view, are the strengths and weaknesses associated with each form of right.

6. What did consultation consist of in this case? What, in your view, should be the meaning and extent of consultation?

DOCUMENTS

10.1 *Statement of the Government of Canada on Indian Policy* (White Paper), 1969

This document includes selections from the Statement of the Government of Canada on Indian Policy, *otherwise known as the White Paper, presented by Minister of Indian Affairs and Northern Development Jean Chrétien in 1969. From the perspective of the government, this initiative would put those with Indian status on an equal footing with all Canadians. This policy would mean, over time, the abrogation of treaties, status, and any existing Aboriginal rights; the abandonment of the Indian Act; and the termination of the Department of Indian Affairs. Special services and service providers would be curtailed, and reserves would be eliminated. The document clearly outlines the Trudeau government's philosophy of rights as accruing to the individual rather than to communities, nations, or other collectivities, a notion that many see in the 1982 Charter of Rights as well.*

Source: Canada, Government of Canada, *Statement of the Government of Canada on Indian Policy, 1969* (Ottawa: Indian Affairs, 1969), 5–8, 11–15, and 18–22.

Reproduced with the permission of the Minister of Public Works and Government Services Canada, 2013.

. . .

Summary

1 Background

The Government has reviewed its programs for Indians and has considered the effects of them on the present situation of the Indian people. The review has drawn on extensive consultations with the Indian people, and on the knowledge and experience of many people both in and out of government.

This review was a response to things said by the Indian people at the consultation meetings which began a year ago and culminated in a meeting in Ottawa in April.

This review has shown that this is the right time to change long-standing policies. The Indian people have shown their determination that present conditions shall not persist.

Opportunities are present today in Canadian society and new directions are open. The Government believes that Indian people must not be shut out of Canadian life and must share equally in these opportunities.

The Government could press on with the policy of fostering further education; could go ahead with physical improvement programs now operating in reserve communities; could press forward in the directions of recent years, and eventually many of the problems would be solved. But progress would be too slow. The change in Canadian society in recent years has been too great and continues too rapidly for this to be the answer. Something more is needed. We can no longer perpetuate the separation of Canadians. Now is the time to change.

This Government believes in equality. It believes that all men and women have equal rights. It is determined that all shall be treated fairly and that no one shall be shut out of Canadian life, and especially that no one shall be shut out because of his race.

This belief is the basis for the Government's determination to open the doors of opportunity to all Canadians, to remove the barriers which impede the development of people, of regions and of the country.

Only a policy based on this belief can enable the Indian people to realize their needs and aspirations.

The Indian people are entitled to such a policy. They are entitled to an equality which preserves and enriches Indian identity and distinction; an equality which stresses Indian participation in its creation and which manifests itself in all aspects of Indian life.

The goals of the Indian people cannot be set by others; they must spring from the Indian community itself—but government can create a framework within which all persons and groups can seek their own goals.

2 The New Policy

True equality presupposes that the Indian people have the right to full and equal participation in the cultural, social, economic and political life of Canada.

The government believes that the framework within which individual Indians and bands could achieve full participation requires:

1. that the legislative and constitutional bases of discrimination be removed;
2. that there be positive recognition by everyone of the unique contribution of Indian culture to Canadian life;
3. that services come through the same channels and from the same government agencies for all Canadians;
4. that those who are furthest behind be helped most;
5. that lawful obligations be recognized;
6. that control of Indian lands be transferred to the Indian people.

The Government would be prepared to take the following steps to create this framework:

1. Propose to Parliament that the Indian Act be repealed and take such legislative steps as may be necessary to enable Indians to control Indian lands and to acquire title to them.
2. Propose to the governments of the provinces that they take over the same responsibility for Indians that they have for other citizens in their provinces. The take-over would be accompanied by the transfer to the provinces of federal funds normally provided for Indian programs, augmented as may be necessary.
3. Make substantial funds available for Indian economic development as an interim measure.

4. Wind up that part of the Department of Indian Affairs and Northern Development which deals with Indian Affairs. The residual responsibilities of the Federal Government for programs in the field of Indian affairs would be transferred to other appropriate federal departments.

In addition, the Government will appoint a Commissioner to consult with the Indians and to study and recommend acceptable procedures for the adjudication of claims.

The new policy looks to a better future for all Indian people wherever they may be. The measures for implementation are straightforward. They require discussion, consultation and negotiation with the Indian people—individuals, bands and associations—and with provincial governments.

Success will depend upon the co-operation and assistance of the Indians and the provinces. The Government seeks this cooperation and will respond when it is offered.

3 The Immediate Steps

Some changes could take place quickly. Others would take longer. It is expected that within five years the Department of Indian Affairs and Northern Development would cease to operate in the field of Indian Affairs; the new laws would be in effect and existing programs would have been devolved. The Indian lands would require special attention for some time. The process of transferring control to the Indian people would be under continuous review.

The Government believes this is a policy which is just and necessary. It can only be successful if it has the support of the Indian people, the provinces, and all Canadians.

The policy promises all Indian people a new opportunity to expand and develop their identity within the framework of a Canadian society which offers them the rewards and responsibilities of participation, the benefits of involvement and the pride of belonging.

. . .

The Case for the New Policy

In the past ten years or so, there have been important improvements in education, health, housing, welfare and community development. Developments in leadership among the Indian communities have become increasingly evident. Indian people have begun to forge a new unity. The Government believes progress can come from these developments but only if they are met by new responses. The proposed policy is a new response.

The policy rests upon the fundamental right of Indian people to full and equal participation in the cultural, social, economic and political life of Canada.

To argue against this right is to argue for discrimination, isolation and separation.

No Canadian should be excluded from participation in community life, and none should expect to withdraw and still enjoy the benefits that flow to those who participate.

1 The Legal Structure

Legislative and constitutional bases of discrimination must be removed.

Canada cannot seek the just society and keep discriminatory legislation on its statute books. The Government believes this to be self-evident. The ultimate aim of removing the specific references to Indians from the constitution may take some time, but it is a goal to be kept constantly in view. In the meantime, barriers created by special legislation can generally be struck down.

Under the authority of Head 24, Section 91 of the British North America Act, the Parliament of Canada has enacted the Indian Act. Various federal-provincial agreements and some other statutes also affect Indian policies.

In the long term, removal of the reference in the constitution would be necessary to end the legal distinction between Indians and other Canadians. In the short term, repeal of the Indian Act and enactment of transitional legislation to ensure the orderly management of Indian land would do much to mitigate the problem.

The ultimate goal could not be achieved quickly, for it requires a change in the economic circumstances of the Indian people and much preliminary adjustment with provincial authorities. Until the Indian people are satisfied that their land holdings are solely within their control, there may have to be some special legislation for Indian lands.

2 The Indian Cultural Heritage

There must be positive recognition by everyone of the unique contribution
of Indian culture to Canadian society.

It is important that Canadians recognize and give credit to the Indian contribution. It manifests itself in many ways; yet it goes largely unrecognized and unacknowledged. Without recognition by others it is not easy to be proud.

All of us seek a basis for pride in our own lives, in those of our families and of our ancestors. Man needs such pride to sustain him in the inevitable hour of discouragement, in the moment when he faces obstacles, whenever life seems turned against him. Everyone has such moments. We manifest our pride in many ways, but always it supports and sustains us. The legitimate pride of the Indian people has been crushed too many times by too many of their fellow Canadians.

The principle of equality and all that goes with it demands that all of us recognize each other's cultural heritage as a source of personal strength.

Canada has changed greatly since the first Indian Act was passed. Today it is made up of many people with many cultures. Each has its own manner of relating to the other; each makes its own adjustments to the larger society.

Successful adjustment requires that the larger groups accept every group with its distinctive traits without prejudice, and that all groups share equitably in the material and non-material wealth of the country.

For many years Canadians believed the Indian people had but two choices: they could live in a reserve community, or they could be assimilated and lose their Indian identity. Today Canada has more to offer. There is a third choice—a full role in Canadian society and in the economy while retaining, strengthening and developing an Indian identity which preserves the good things of the past and helps Indian people to prosper and thrive.

This choice offers great hope for the Indian people. It offers great opportunity for Canadians to demonstrate that in our open society there is room for the development of people who preserve their different cultures and take pride in their diversity.

This new opportunity to enrich Canadian life is central to the Government's new policy. If the policy is to be successful, the Indian people must be in a position to play a full role in Canada's diversified society, a role which stresses the value of their experience and the possibilities of the future.

. . .

3 Programs and Services

Services must . . . come through the same channels
and from the same government agencies for all Canadians.

This is an undeniable part of equality. It has been shown many times that separation of people follows from separate services. There can be no argument about the principle of common services. It is right.

It cannot be accepted now that Indians should be constitutionally excluded from the right to be treated within their province as full and equal citizens, with all the responsibilities and all the privileges that this might entail. It is in the provincial sphere where social remedies are structured and applied, and the Indian people, by and large, have been non-participating members of provincial society.

Canadians receive a wide range of services through provincial and local governments, but the Indian people and their communities are mostly outside that framework. It is no longer acceptable that the Indian people should be outside and apart. The Government believes that services should be available on an equitable basis, except for temporary differentiation based on need. Services ought not to flow from separate agencies established to serve particular groups, especially not to groups that are identified ethnically.

Separate but equal services do not provide truly equal treatment. Treatment has not been equal in the case of Indians and their communities. Many services require a wide range of facilities which cannot be duplicated by separate agencies. Others must be integral to the complex systems of community and regional life and cannot be matched on a small scale.

The Government is therefore convinced that the traditional method of providing separate services to Indians must be ended. All Indians should have access to all programs and services of all levels of government equally with other Canadians.

. . .

5 Claims and Treaties

Lawful obligations must be recognized

Many of the Indian people feel that successive governments have not dealt with them as fairly as they should. They believe that lands have been taken from them in an improper manner, or without adequate compensation, that their funds have been improperly administered, that their treaty rights have been breached. Their sense of grievance influences their relations with governments and the community and limits their participation in Canadian life.

Many Indians look upon their treaties as the source of their rights to land, to hunting and fishing privileges, and to other benefits. Some believe the treaties should be interpreted to encompass wider services and privileges, and many believe the treaties have not been honoured. Whether or not this is correct in some or many cases, the fact is the treaties affect only half the Indians of Canada. Most of the Indians of Quebec, British Columbia, and the Yukon are not parties to a treaty.

The terms and effects of the treaties between the Indian people and the Government are widely misunderstood. A plain reading of the words used in the treaties reveals the limited and minimal promises which were included in them. As a result of the treaties, some Indians were given an initial cash payment and were promised land reserved for their exclusive use, annuities, protection of hunting, fishing and trapping privileges subject (in most cases) to regulation, a school or teachers in most instances and, in one treaty only, a medicine chest.

There were some other minor considerations, such as the annual provision of twine and ammunition.

The annuities have been paid regularly. The basic promise to set aside reserve land has been kept except in respect of the Indians of the Northwest Territories and a few bands in the northern parts of the Prairie Provinces. These Indians did not choose land when treaties were signed. The government wishes to see these obligations dealt with as soon as possible.

The right to hunt and fish for food is extended unevenly across the country and not always in relation to need. Although game and fish will become less and less important for survival as the pattern of Indian life continues to change, there are those who, at this time, still live in the traditional manner that their forefathers lived in when they entered into treaty with the government. The Government is prepared to allow such persons transitional freer hunting of migratory birds under the Migratory Birds Convention Act and Regulations.

The significance of the treaties in meeting the economic, educational, health and welfare needs of the Indian people has always been limited and will continue to decline. The services that have been provided go far beyond what could have been foreseen by those who signed the treaties.

The Government and the Indian people must reach a common understanding of the future role of the treaties. Some provisions will be found to have been discharged; others will have continuing importance. Many of the provisions and practices of another century may be considered irrelevant [in] the light of a rapidly changing society and still others may be ended by mutual agreement. Finally, once Indian lands are securely within Indian control, the anomaly of treaties between groups within society and the government of that society will require that these treaties be reviewed to—how they can be equitably ended.

. . .

6 Indian Lands

Control of Indian lands should be transferred to the Indian people.

Frustration is as great a handicap as a sense of grievance. True cooperation and participation can come only when the Indian people are controlling the land which makes up the reserves.

The reserve system has provided the Indian people with lands that generally have been protected against alienation without their consent. Widely scattered across Canada, the reserves total nearly 6,000,000 acres and are divided into about 2,200 parcels of varying sizes. Under the existing system, title to reserve lands is held either by the Crown in right of Canada or the Crown in right of one of the provinces. Administrative control and legislative authority are, however, vested exclusively in the Government and the Parliament of Canada. It is a trust. As long as this trust exists, the Government, as a trustee, must supervise the business connected with the land.

The result of Crown ownership and the Indian Act has been to tie the Indian people to a land system that lacks flexibility and inhibits development. If an Indian band wishes to gain income by leasing its land, it has to do so through a cumbersome system involving the Government as trustee. It cannot mortgage reserve land to finance development on its own initiative. Indian people do not have control of their lands except as the Government allows and this is no longer acceptable to them. The Indians have made this clear at the consultation meetings. They now want real control, and this Government believes that they should have it. The Government recognizes that full and true equality calls for Indian control and ownership of reserve land.

Between the present system and the full holding of title in fee simple lie a number of intermediate states. The first step is to change the system under which ministerial decision is required for all that is done with Indian land. This is where the delays, the frustrations and the obstructions lie. The Indians must control their land.

This can be done in many ways. The Government believes that each band must make its own decision as to the way it wants to take control of its land and the manner in which it intends to manage it. It will take some years to complete the process of devolution.

The Government believes that full ownership implies many things. It carries with it the free choice of use, of retention or of disposition. In our society it also carries with it an obligation to pay for certain services. The Government recognizes that it may not be acceptable to put all lands into the provincial systems immediately and make them subject to taxes. When the Indian people see that the only way they can own and fully control land is to accept taxation the way other Canadians do, they will make that decision.

. . .

10.2 Indian Association of Alberta, *Citizens Plus* (Red Paper), 1970

The Indian Association of Alberta (IAA) was formed in 1939 to represent the interests of treaty First Nations peoples in Alberta. The IAA worked to protect treaty rights, to improve the quality of education and health services, and to publicize the conditions faced by First Nations communities. From the perspective of the IAA, there was no reason to expect that the treaties should not last forever unless both parties agreed to alterations in the relationship. When this perspective was threatened by Trudeau's vision and the introduction of the White Paper, the IAA was in the forefront of those organizations that submitted written objections. The IAA's 100-page response, known as the Red Paper, begins by outlining the organization's analysis of the process leading to the White Paper and then goes on to critique many of its most significant elements. Not included in the selection here is a detailed set of proposals, including almost 40 pages on education. The Red Paper was followed by a book written by the IAA's Cree president, Harold Cardinal, titled The Unjust Society.

Source: Indian Chiefs of Alberta, *Citizens Plus* (Edmonton: Indian Association of Alberta, 1970), 1–10.

Reproduced with the permission of the Indian Association of Alberta.
Footnote style is as in original.

A. THE PREAMBLE

To us who are Treaty Indians there is nothing more important than our Treaties, our lands and the well being of our future generation. We have studied carefully the contents of the Government White Paper on Indians and we have concluded that it offers despair instead of hope. Under the guise of land ownership, the government has devised a scheme whereby within a generation or shortly after the proposed Indian Lands Act expires our people would be left with no land and consequently the future generation would be condemned to the despair and ugly spectre of urban poverty in ghettos.

In Alberta, we have told the Federal Minister of Indian Affairs that we do not wish to discuss his White Paper with him until we reach a position where we can bring forth viable alternatives because we know that his paper is wrong and that it will harm our people. We refused to meet him on his White Paper because we have been stung and hurt by his concept of consultation.

In his White Paper, the Minister said, "This review was a response to things said by Indian people at the consultation meetings which began a year ago and culminated in a meeting in Ottawa in April." Yet, what Indians asked for land ownership that would result in Provincial taxation of our reserves? What Indians asked that the Canadian Constitution be changed to remove any reference to Indians or Indian lands? What Indians asked that Treaties be brought to an end? What group of Indians asked that aboriginal rights not be recognized? What group of Indians asked for a Commissioner whose purview would exclude half of the Indian population in Canada? The awnser [sic] is no Treaty Indians asked for any of these things and yet through his concept of "consultation," the Minister said that his White Paper was in response to things said by Indians.

We felt that with this concept of consultation held by the Minister and his department, that if we met with them to discuss the contents of his White Paper without being fully prepared, that even if we just talked about the weather, he would turn around and tell Parliament and the Canadian public that we accepted his White Paper.

We asked for time to prepare a counter proposal. We have received assurances that the implementation process would not take place. However, the Federal rhetoric has not been substantiated by action. In fact, there is every indication that the implementation process is being carried as fast and as fully as possible. For example, the Departmental officials have prepared their budgets so as to make implementation possible. They rationalize this action by saying that if the White Paper on Indians is implemented their programs must be set whereby they can achieve the implementation within five years or if it does not come about that they can have better programs. Where is the moratorium that we have asked for on activities on the implement on the White Paper?

The Minister of Indian Affairs has stated publically that he is not attempting to throw the Indians over to the provinces in spite of what is contained in writing in his White Paper. Yet, while maintaining this contradictory position he writes a letter to the Premier of Alberta dated February 20, 1970 stating that the Federal Government would transfer funds to the Province for the extension of provincial services to reserves; but these funds would be gradually phased out with the assumption that at this point the Provincial Government would bear full financial responsibility for the provision of these services.

Where is the consistency of the Minister's position when he tells Indians verbally that their reserves will not come under the Provincial tax system but his White Paper and his letter of [sic] the Premier say otherwise.

The Indian Chiefs of Alberta meeting in Calgary addressed a letter to the Honorable Pierre E. Trudeau dated January 22, 1970. That letter said:

> This assembly of all the Indian Chiefs of Alberta is deeply concerned with the action taken by the Minister of Indian Affairs and Northern Development, the Honorable Jean Chretien, regarding the implementation of the Indian policy.
>
> Time and time again, on the one hand, the Minister has declared publically to the Canadian people that the Indian Policy contained proposals to be discussed with the Indian people. On the other hand, Indian Affairs officials have been recruited for implementation teams to go ahead with the implementation of the policy paper.
>
> We find this double-headed approach contradictory. A glaring example is the appointment of the Claims Commissioner.
>
> Another example is the concentrated public relations program being conducted to impose the White Paper on the Canadian public. We find this incompatible with the Just Society. Discussions between the Federal department of Indian Affairs and provincial governments have also been initiated.
>
> This assembly of all the Indian Chiefs of Alberta reaffirms its position of unity and recognizes the Indian Association of Alberta as the voice of all the Treaty Indian people of this province. As representatives of our people we are pledge to continue our earnest efforts to preserve the hereditary and legal privileges of our people.
>
> At this meeting of Alberta Indian Chiefs, we have reviewed the first draft of our Counter Policy to the Chretien paper. We plan to complete our final draft in the near future, for presentation to the Federal Government.
>
> We request that no further process of implementation takes place and that action already taken be reviewed to minimize suspicions and to make possible a positive and constructive dialogue between your government and our people.

In his reply, dated February 19, 1970, to telegrams sent by the Chiefs' Conference of January 22nd, the Minister states that "the policy proposals, which were put forward in quite general terms will require modification and refinement before they can be put into effect." In a preceding sentence attempting to explain his Consultation and Negotiation Group which we know as the implementation team, he says "I believe that the policy that has been proposed is a correct one. I expect that my Consultation and Negotiations officers will also try to persuade the Indian people, and Canadians generally, that the direction of the policy proposals is indeed in the best interest of all concerned."

If this is his belief, where is his so called flexibility, especially when Indian people disagree with his mythical concepts of him leading the Indians to the promised land?

B. THE COUNTER POLICY

B.1. INDIAN STATUS

The White Paper Policy said "that the legislative and constitutional bases of discrimination should be removed."

We reject this policy. We say that the recognition of Indian status is essential for justice.

Retaining the legal status of Indians is necessary if Indians are to be treated justly. Justice requires that the special history, rights and circumstances of Indian People be recognized. The Chretien Policy says, "Canada cannot seek the just society and keep discriminatory legislation on its statute books". That statement covers a faulty understanding of fairness. Professor L.C. Green found that in other countries minorities were given special status. Professor Green has concluded:

> The 1969 Statement of the Government of Canada on Indian Policy is based on the assumption that any legislation which sets a particular segment of the populatiion [sic] apart from the main stream of the citizenry is ipso facto conducive to a denial of equality and therefore discriminatory and to be deplored. **Such an attitude indicates a complete lack of understanding of the significance of the concept of equality**, particularly in so far as the law concerning the protection of minorities is concerned.
>
> . . . It is perhaps not easy to define the distinction between the notions of equality in fact and equality in law; nevertheless, it may be said that the former notion excludes the idea of a merely formal equality . . .
>
> Equality in law precludes discrimination of any kind; **whereas equality in fact may involve the necessity of different treatment** in order to obtain a result which established an equilibrium between different situations . . .
>
> To attempt to maintain that the rights of the Indians result in discrimination against them or are evidence of a denial of their equality in the sense that their status is reduced thereby, is to indulge in an excessively **narrow view of the meaning of words, of the purpose of equality and of the nature of discrimination.**[2]

The legal definition of registered Indians must remain. If one of our registered brothers chooses, he may renounce his Indian status, become "enfranchised", receive his share of the funds of the tribe, and seek admission to ordinary Canadian society. But

---

2 L.C. Green, *Canada's Indians—Federal Policy* (1969) Government of Alberta.

most Indians prefer to remain Indians. We believe that to be a good useful Canadian we must first be a good, happy and productive Indian.

B.2. THE UNIQUE INDIAN CULTURE AND CONTRIBUTION

The White Paper Policy said "that there should be positive recognition by everyone of the unique contribution of Indian culture to Canadian life.["]

We say that these are nice sounding words which are intended to mislead everybody. The only way to maintain our culture is for us to remain as Indians. To preserve our culture it is necessary to preserve our status, rights, lands and traditions. Our treaties are the bases of our rights.

There is room in Canada for diversity. Our leaders say that Canada should preserve her "pluralism", and encourage the culture of all her peoples. The culture of the Indian peoples are old and colorful strands in that Canadian fabric of diversity. We want our children to learn our ways, our history, our customs, and our traditions.

Everyone should recognize that Indians have contributed much to the Canadian community. When we signed the treaties we promised to be good and loyal subjects of the Queen. The record is clear—we kept our promises. We were assured we would not be required to serve in foreign wars; nevertheless many Indians volunteered in greater proportion than non-Indian Canadians for service in two world wars. We live and are agreeable to live within the framework of Canadian civil and criminal law. We pay the same indirect and sales taxes that other Canadians pay. Our treaty rights cost Canada very little in relation to the Gross National Product or to the value of the lands ceded, but they are essential to us.

B.3. CHANNELS FOR SERVICES

The White Paper Policy says "that services should come through the same channels and from the same government agencies for all Canadians".

We say that the Federal Government is bound by the British North America Act, Section 9k [91], Head 24, to accept legislative responsibility for "Indians and Indian lands". Moreover in exchange for the lands which the Indian people surrendered to the Crown the treaties ensure the following benefits:

(a) To have and to hold certain lands called "reserves" for the sole use and benefit of the Indian people forever and assistance in the social economic and cultural development of the reserves.

(b) The provision of health services to the Indian people on the reserve or off the reserve at the expense of the Federal government anywhere in Canada.

(c) The provision of education of all types and levels to all Indian people at the expense of the Federal government.

(d) The right of the Indian people to hunt, trap and fish for their livelihood free of governmental interference and regulation and subject only to the proviso that the exercise of this right must not interfere with the use and enjoyment of private property.

These benefits are not "handouts" because the Indian people paid for them by surrendering their lands. The Federal Government is bound to provide the actual services relating to education, welfare, health and economic development.

B.4. ENRICHED SERVICES

The White Paper policy says "that those who are furthest behind should be helped most". The policy also promises "enriched services".

We do not want different treatment for different tribes. These promises of enriched services are bribes to get us to accept the rest of the Policy. The Federal Government is trying to divide us Indian people so it can conquer us by saying that poorer reserves will be helped most.

All reserves and tribes need help in the economic, social, recreational and cultural development.

B.5. LAWFUL OBLIGATIONS

The White Paper Policy says "that lawful obligations should be recognized". If the Government meant what it said we would be happy. But it is obvious that the Government has never bothered to learn what the treaties are and has a distorted picture of them.

The Government shows that it is willfully ignorant of the bargains that were made between the Indians and the Queen's commissioners.

The Government must admit its mistakes and recognize that the treaties are historic, moral and legal obligations. The redmen signed them in good faith, and lived up to the treaties. The treaties were solemn agreements. Indian lands were exchanged for the promises of the Indian Commissioners who represented the Queen. Many missionaries of many faiths brought the authority and prestige of whiteman's religion in encouraging Indians to sign.

In our treaties of 1876, 1877, 1899 certain promises were made to our people; some of these are contained in the text of the treaties, some in the negotiations, and some in the memories of our people. Our basic view is that all these promises are part of the treaties and must be honored.

Modernize the Treaties

The intent and spirit of the treaties must be our guide, not the precise letter of a foreign language. Treaties that run forever must have room for the changes in the conditions of life. The undertaking of the Government to provide teachers was a commitment to provide Indian children the educational opportunity equal to their white neighbors. The machinery and livestok [sic] symbolized economic development.

The White Paper Policy says "a plain reading of the words used in the treaties reveals the limited and minimal promises which were included in them. . . . and in one treaty only a medicine chest". But we know from the Commissioners' Reports that they told the Indians that medicine chests were included in all three.

Indians have the right to receive, without payment, all healthcare services without exception and paid by the Government of Canada.

The medicine chests that we know were mentioned in the negotiations for Treaties Six, Seven and Eight mean that Indians should now receive free medical, hospital and dental care—the same high quality services available to other Canadians.

We agree with the judgement of Policha, J. in Regina vs. Walter Johnston:

Referring to the 'Medicine chest' clause of Treaty Number Six, it is common knowledge that the provision for caring for the sick and injured in the areas inhabited by the Indians in 1876 were somewhat primitive compared to present day standards. It can be safely assumed that the Indians had limited knowledge of what provisions were available and it is obvious that they were concerned that their people be adequately cared for. With that in view and possibly carrying the opinion of Angers, J. a step further, I can only conclude that the 'medicine chest' clause and the 'pestilence' clause in Treaty No. 6 should be properly interpreted to mean that the Indians are entitled to receive all medical services, including medicines, drugs, medical supplies and hospital care free of charge. Lacking proper statutory provisions to the contrary, this entitlement would embrace all Indians within the meaning of the Indian Act, without exception.[3]

The principle thus laid down by Policha, J. is that all the provisions of the treaties are to be interpreted in favour of the Indians with full regard given to changing social and economic conditions.

The Indian people see the treaties as the basis of all their rights and status. If the Government expects the co-operation of Indians in any new policy, it must accept the Indian viewpoint on treaties. This would require the Government to start all over on its new policy.

B.6. INDIAN CONTROL OF INDIAN LANDS

The White Paper Policy says "that control of Indian lands should be transferred to Indian people".

We agree with this intent but we find that the Government is ignorant of two basic points. The Government wrongly thinks that Indian Reserve lands are owned by the Crown. The Government is, of course, in error. These lands are held in trust by the Crown but they are Indian lands.

The Indians are the beneficial (actual) owners of the lands. The legal title has been held for us by the Crown to prevent the sale or breaking up of our land. We are opposed to any system of allotment that would give individuals ownership with rights to sell.

According to the Indian Act R.S.C. 1952 the land is safe and secure held in trust for the common use and benefit of the tribe. The land must never be sold, mortgaged or taxed.

The second error the Government commits is making the assumption that Indians can have control of the land only if they take ownership in the way that ordinary property is owned. The Government should either get some legal advice or get some brighter legal advisers. The advice we have received is that the Indian Act could be changed to give Indians control of lands without changing the fact that the title is now held in trust.

---

3 Judgement dated July 12, 1965, North Battleford in District Court of Saskatchewan. The defendant Johnston was living off the reserve. It is very significant that the learned Judge examined supplemental sources and did not restrict his attention to the formal written treaty.

Indian lands must continue to be regarded in a different manner than other lands in Canada. It must be held forever in trust of the Crown because, as we say, "The true owners of the land are not yet born".

. . .

10.3 William Wuttunee, *Ruffled Feathers*, 1971

William Wuttunee was born in 1928 into the Red Pheasant First Nation, a Cree community near North Battleford, Saskatchewan. He graduated from the law school at the University of Saskatchewan and practiced law in Alberta and the Northwest Territories. Later, he became chief of the National Indian Council of Canada and began calling for more active First Nation participation in settler society. Wuttunee was hired by the federal government to promote the White Paper among First Nations people after its introduction. Rather than quelling opposition to the proposed legislation, Wuttunee was ostracized by some and barred from over a dozen First Nation communities. Though he soon distanced himself from the White Paper, Wuttunee continued actively to promote a fuller integration of Indigenous people into Canadian society. The selection below comes from Wuttunee's 1971 publication, Ruffled Feathers. *Among other issues, this work outlines the author's views on integration, First Nations organizations, the White Paper, and treaties.*

Source: William I.C. Wuttunee, *Ruffled Feathers: Indians in Canadian Society* (Calgary: Bell Books, 1971), 10–13, 23–25, 106–09, and 138–41.

Reproduced with the permission of William I.C. Wuttunee.
Footnotes as in original.

. . .

If Indians are going to see a different form of development which is more conducive to their welfare and general well-being, then they must form counter organizations which will promote integration of the Indian into the white man's society. There are many Indians who wish to integrate and who wish to have the opportunity of making a decent living side by side with the white man. There are many who are not perpetual alcoholics and who are prepared to become taxpayers. The establishment of Indian organizations opposed to Red Power—thereby forming a two-party system among the Indian people—would then enable Indians to use the democratic process within their own ranks. They would be able to stand up to people like Harold Cardinal, and obtain their own form of participation in Canadian society. They would be able to state freely that they are not reactionaries forever tied to the history of the 1800's and the treaties of that era.

This mulcting of the white man and the white man's government is an extremely negative policy. Current Indian leaders are not prepared to do their share; they are not prepared to tell the Indian people to get an education and to pull their share of the load in Canada.

Where is the dignity of the Indian people that they were once so proud of? Have they completely lost it? Or is there still some vestige of pride left in them? If so, they should immediately get rid of every dictator in their ranks; they should dispose of every racist and make sure they muzzle them adequately so that bitterness and hatred will not be further spread. Too often Indians spend their time criticizing and blaming the white man for their problems. Is it not possible that they are themselves responsible for creation and perpetuation of these problems? Is it not possible that they, too, can do something about them?

If we are to solve this dilemma there has to be a complete overhaul of the system of grants by government to Indian organizations. There has to be a toughening up of government attitude towards autocratic Indian associations. Indian people must stand up to the Red Power advocates and develop a new approach to the situation. There must be a sense of adulthood by the non-Indian people who are administering programs relating to Indians. Weak 'love' or pity for Indian people is not going to improve their lot. There must be hard-headed programs designed to increase the participation of Indians in a non-Indian society. Sociologists and anthropologists can't spend their time in apologizing for Indian people, thereby encouraging an ethnic division which will perpetuate the problem for several more generations. Their studies must be done from a positive point of view, rather than by re-affirming a separation of the two races. There is certainly something good to be said about the value of people living together peacefully, mutually, for the benefit of one another. It is time to blast the arguments against integration and to speak in favour of it.

Integration doesn't have to mean forced integration, rather it can be a gradual process which will develop Indian men and women into independent, contributing members of Canadian society. It doesn't mean the wholesale displacement of Indian people, but individual attention to individual Indians and their problems. It means giving assistance to those Indians who are now helping themselves, rather than only helping the rebellious few.

When we have re-examined our approach with a sincere desire to assist and to develop, it is possible that 'the Indian situation' can be solved within the next generation. Let the next century be one of development and self-fulfillment for Indian people. Let us establish a society within which an Indian and a white man can look each other in the eye, with mutual trust. Red Power advocates must re-channel their energy and efforts, not away from the white man, but, rather, toward helping all the poor of our land. They can join forces with the poor people of Canada, now numbering approximately 5 million, and thus form an invincible army of 'people power' against neglect, oppression and despair. In so doing, Indian leaders must not fall victim to the traditional traps of self-interest and personal aggrandisement. They must watch out for silvertongued capitalists who would take money from them, the money intended for Indian people. Their concern must always be for those people and for their right to choose freely for themselves.

. . .

On June 25, 1969 the Honourable Jean Chretien, Minister of Indian Affairs and Northern Development, announced to the House of Commons a statement of the government of Canada on Indian Policy.[4] The forward of the new policy states, in part, "The

---

4 Statement of the Government of Canada on Indian Policy, Presented by the Minister of Indian Affairs & Northern Development, 1969, Queen's Printer, Cat. No. R32–2469.

Government believes that its policies must lead to the full, free, and non-discriminatory participation of the Indian people in Canadian society. Such a goal requires a break with the past. It requires that the Indian people's role of dependence be replaced by a role of equal status, opportunity and responsibility, a role they can share with all other Canadians." The terms of the White Paper were a dramatic breakthrough for the Indian people.

The Indian Act

The government proposed that the legislative and constitutional bases of discrimination be removed, and to accomplish this it proposed to repeal the Indian Act and urged that specific references to Indians be removed from the Constitution. The Paper stated, "In the long term, removal of the reference in the Constitution would be necessary to end the legal distinction between Indians and other Canadians. In the short term, repeal of the Indian Act and enactment of transitional legislation to ensure the orderly management of Indian land would do much to mitigate the problem."

The White Paper further stated that they (the Indians) had been almost exclusively the concern of one agency of the federal government for nearly a century. Everyone left the responsibility for the development of Indians to the federal government, and provincial and municipal agencies did not participate. "The legal and administrative discrimination in the treatment of Indian people has not given them an equal chance of success. It has exposed them to discrimination in the broadest and worst sense of the term—a discrimination that has profoundly affected their confidence that success can be theirs. Discrimination breeds discrimination by example, and the separateness of Indian people has affected the attitudes of the Canadians towards them . . . The system of separate legislation and administration has also separated people of Indian ancestry into three groups—registered Indians, who are further divided into those who are under treaty and those who are not; enfranchised Indians who lost, or voluntarily relinquished, their legal status as Indians; and the Metis, who are of Indian ancestry but never had the status of registered Indians."

The proposal to repeal the Indian Act was a great step forward. For many years both Indians and non-Indians had criticized the Indian Act as being discriminatory. In fact, the Indian Act is one of the most discriminatory pieces of legislation which exists in either the provincial or federal Statutes. Parliament has exclusive jurisdiction over Indians and lands reserved for Indians by reason of The British North America Act. The Act applies only to Indians who are registered under the Act.

The provisions of the Indian Act do not give native people equality. They are saddled with disadvantages which hound them continually in their daily lives. It cannot be said that an Indian has equality before the law if he cannot enjoy his property and if he has to depend on a Minister in Ottawa to exercise and make decisions on his behalf. There is every reason to believe that the Honourable Mr. Chretien does not wish to exercise the powers which are reserved to him by the Act and that he wants to give to the Indian people the right to make decisions on their own. He states that they are now grown up and they should act like it.

The Indian Act promotes a spirit of inferiority and dependence and, coupled with the treaty mentality, is one of the main reasons for the current difficult situation. Canada will continue to have this problem unless definite steps are taken to change the provisions of the Indian Act or to repeal the Act completely.

. . .

A great injustice to Indian people is being done if we tell them that the white man did not keep his promises under the treaties. As stated in the study Indians and the Law, "This study, and others, indicates that the abrogation of treaties and laws by the non-Indian majority encourages the questioning in Indian eyes, of much of the white man's law . . . in specific terms, what the Indian people regard as the failure of successive governments to live up to the terms and the spirit of the original Treaties is, in the eyes of most Indian people interviewed, a stumbling block to their acceptance of the white man's law in the widest terms."

. . .

The treaty mentality of dependence is being prolonged by some Indian leaders today who are encouraging it among their people. It is unlikely that the government is going to renegotiate these treaties or to read more into them than was actually provided for. It is time that the Indian leaders recognized this principle. Nothing has been taken away from the Indian that was rightfully his, even though it is hard to acknowledge that the Indian at the time of the negotiation of the treaties was not in a stronger bargaining position to maintain his national independence.

The Indians have built up the treaties to such an extent that nearly everything in their lives hinges upon them. They have developed a mentality which, like the treaties, is dependent. The treaties were negotiated at a time when the Indians were no longer strong and powerful; they were peaceful and wanted good relations with the white man. They wanted the assistance which the white man was prepared to give to them and which they eventually received. It is this continuing form of dependence which the Indians cannot overcome. The Queen Victoria Treaty Protective Association was formed to put emphasis on the treaties. This organization eventually lost most of its adherents and there was some indication that this form of mentality was dying out. However, it has been regenerated with the new thrust that Harold Cardinal has put into the Indian Association of Alberta, and its emphasis on the treaties.

. . .

One cannot overstress the significance of ending these treaties and of ending the treaty mentality which has spread throughout the country. It has embedded itself so firmly in the Indian mind that it clouds all his thinking and he cannot seem to see his way clearly, for his feelings work more strongly than his mind on this subject. The Indian people cannot keep living in the past. They can never rewrite what actually transpired at the signing of the treaties because the cold facts of history have indelibly written themselves in the hearts and minds of the people. We cannot reinterpret them; we cannot give more significance to either the one side or the other; we cannot improve the bargaining position of either side, and neither can we take away. We can realistically look at the past, the present and the future, and learn from the hard lessons of history those truths which will assist us in facing the problems of the day.

. . .

The day will come when Indians will not be concerned with struggling for their basic civil rights only, but for the basic rights of all individuals. Indians who have been working with Indian people and who have gained experience in fighting for civil rights are now working with poor white people and trying to get better conditions for them as well. When the conditions for all poor people have been improved, the change will naturally also benefit Indian people.

The new breed of native cannot look at the past as a form of defeat, but only as a necessary period of transition. These people must look at today's events and the past from a viewpoint which will keep them going ever-forward into the mainstream of society. Indians had great leaders in the past, and there is no reason why they cannot continue to have great leaders in the future. If they continue only to cry about broken promises and broken treaties, they can never attain much for their people.

Merely because some Indians have chosen to leave their reserves and their people does not mean that they have no use for the Indian culture or for their language or for their families. They become tired of the poverty in which they have to live, and tired of the administration of the Indian Affairs Branch over their daily lives. They want freedom, a chance to live like an ordinary person, to grow old in peace and die without shackles.

The desire for an improvement in the standard of living must carry with it the equal desire to make a contribution to society by way of taxation. Indians cannot expect to participate in the dominant society without the resulting obligations of hard work and taxation. Indians can no longer blame the white man for their own failures. At one time they had valid arguments against Canadians for having left them to rot on the reserves, but those times have disappeared.

Old attitudes toward Indian people have to be changed. Some of these attitudes and statements which have caused a great deal of damage are statements like "The Indian is the only true Canadian." This implies that the Indian is a better type of Canadian than newly-arrived immigrants, and this is not true. The further ideas that "Indians were the first owners of this country," and "the land was taken from them" are again misconceptions. At the time of the arrival of the white man, the Indian did not occupy all of the country; therefore it cannot be said that the land was taken away from him. Those areas which were unoccupied were never taken away from anyone. Indians never owned Canada; they do not own it now, and they never will. Once this concept is clearly understood, there will be less torment in the hearts of Indians in assessing their relationship with the dominant society.

The Indian people will never regain this country from the white man. They can, however, effectively participate with the white man in its full development. Indians can work with the white men in partnership to develop a country which will provide for each of our children a legacy of great value. It is not necessary to separate from the white man, either physically or spiritually. The long period of separation of the two races has now ended.

Let us then unite in sprit, so that each of us can look forward to a peaceful old age in which we can see our children effectively participating in the creation of a new society. Many Indians have already taken the road ahead, to live in the land of the white man. They have paved the way for their brothers and sisters, on which they must learn to walk without fear.

The hard knocks of history are pushing the Indian into a new way of life, and he must learn to accept this new challenge with faith and with hope. History has taught a hard lesson, but history will vindicate itself one day when the Indian finally finds his place in Canadian society.

10.4 National Indian Brotherhood, "Statement, on the Proposed New 'Indian Policy,'" 1969

The National Indian Brotherhood (NIB) was formed in 1967 as an alliance of existing provincial and territorial organizations. In the beginning, the organization was run with the personal funds of its founding members and began to lobby various levels of government to make policy changes that would benefit status Indians. The introduction of the White Paper gave the organization a rallying point and resulted in its first major campaign. The document below includes the entire text of the NIB's 1969 statement on the White Paper with the exception of the ten signatures of representatives, and their affiliations, from across the country. The NIB remained active until it morphed into the Assembly of First Nations in 1982 to take on another national issue, the patriation of the Constitution.

Source: National Indian Brotherhood, "Statement on the Proposed New 'Indian Policy,'" 26 June 1969.

Reproduced with the permission of the Assembly of First Nations.

NATIONAL INDIAN BROTHEROOD,

230 Gloucester Street,

OTTAWA, Phone 237-7510

STATEMENT ON THE PROPOSED NEW "INDIAN POLICY"

June 26, 1969.

FOR IMMEDIATE RELEASE:

We are here before you saddled with a heavy responsibility—but it is a responsibility that all Canadians share with us. One hundred years from now our grand-children will reap the consequences of the actions we take in these next few days—just as we are the inheritors of a legacy brought about by the actions of our forefathers. Our forefathers acted in good faith, believing that the people they dealt with were of similar mind. We too have acted in good faith with your elected and appointed representatives, believing that they too were dealing in good faith.

When two partners deal in such a manner, it is presupposed that the two parties are on a somewhat equal basis—free to make their own decisions; free to make their own mistakes. In these past dealings we do not feel we took part in any decision making process and that the Minister has made a mistake.

We appreciate the Minister's concern, and do not question his good will. We agree with many of the arguments he has advanced for change in Indian policy. Indeed, we realize that some changes are inevitable no matter how we may feel about them. But in their present form, the policy proposals put forward by the Minister of Indian Affairs are not acceptable to the Indian people of Canada.

The Minister and his Department have spent months preparing this new policy and setting forth their arguments. We have had less than 24 hours to examine this policy, but feel we must issue a strong statement now lest the Canadian public believe the Indian question is solved to the mutual satisfaction of all concerned. We know it was not the intent of the new policy but we fear the end result of the proposal will be the destruction of a Nation of People by legislation and cultural genocide.

We had believed in the sincerity of the Government[']s requests for meaningful consultation to arrive at a new and just policy for Indian people. Throughout the period of consultation referred to by the Minister in his policy paper, the Indian leaders were confident they had abundantly made clear to the Minister, and through him the Government, that an essential first step in developing a new approach to the so-called Indian problem would be to honour the existing obligations; the outstanding promises and commitments made to the Indian people.

Instead of this approach, the Minister proposes to solve the problem by evading the responsibility of the Federal Government under the British North America Act.

We agree with the Minister when he says the conditions that exist today among our people must change. We must have control of our lands; our funds, and all other responsibilities. We do not impugn the Minster's motives, but we cannot accept the means proposed.

Let us consider the results of the highly-publicized consultations: At no time did the Indian people advocate the provinces take over the legal responsibilities of the Federal Government.

These contracted agreements with the Indian people are spelled out in the B.N.A. Act, yet the policy statement shows the Minister intends to abrogate Federal responsibility and turn it over to the provinces who are not bound by any means to honour these agreements.

At all times the Indian people have insisted that the areas referred to as "reserves" are in fact Indian lands, and as such cannot be taxed by any other authority. Yet the policy statement now suggests Indian lands will be taxed by authorities which have no legal claim on these lands.

At all consultations across Canada the Indian people expressed concern over the abrogation of their Treaty rights by the Migratory Birds Convention Act and Regulations. Yet in the policy statement this overriding concern receives only passing mention where the Government is prepared to "allow—transitional freer hunting" for some people, but ignores the principle involved. And the Indian people are once again asked to accept a Government proposal in good faith.

At all consultation meetings the Indian people expressed a desire to take on greater responsibility in running their own affairs. Yet the new policy will have the affairs of Indian people run by still another bureaucratic structure. At no time during the consultations did the Minister indicate to us that we would be thrown into the laps of the provinces, some of which have already established their chapters of a Department of Indian Affairs.

It is apparent to us that while there was a show of consultation, neither the Minister nor his Department really heard and understood the Indian people.

Or having heard and understood, they chose to follow the well beaten trail of the past decades and ignore our views. The Hawthorn-Tremblay Report, which was commissioned by the Department of Indian Affairs, stated that the position of the Indian people was unique in the Canadian society; that by aboriginal, residual and statutory rights we were more than just citizens of Canada—this too the Department chooses to ignore.

The policy statement was prepared unilaterally. There was no negotiation with Indian people, nor was any part of the policy discussed with Indian people while the Minister's office was preparing it.

The policy talks of "enriched programs". After all these years what new and "enriched" programs can they come up with? How does the addition of "enriched programs" aid in phasing out the Department of Indian Affairs?

The policy mentions a Claims Commission and a Commissioner to be named soon. Will we be consulted as to the make-up of this commission or will there be a unilateral appointment by government?

The question of Indian lands are of prime importance to the Indian people. As the policy reads it is apparent that the British Columbia lands question will now have to be negotiated with the provincial administration which is the beneficiary of the fact that these lands have been sequested [sic] without due process and without compensation. Land in the Maritimes, the Yukon, and the Northwest Territories have been similarly appropriated.

In Quebec, despite the fact that a constitutional amendment provided for purchase of Indian lands, there has been no compliance with this amendment, nor is there any indication that any is seriously contemplated.

History has shown us that the Indian people usually pay the highest cost when expansion and progress encroach on Indian lands. It gives us pause in considering the implications of the new policy on Indian lands when the proposed development of the Mid-Canada Corridor runs through the heart of what are presently Indian lands.

Throughout the consultation period we re-iterated that the Government must afford constitutional recognition of existing Treaties and obligations at which time the Indian people would meet in good faith with the government to clarify the meaning and intent of existing agreements. This would create a mutual sense of trust and respect so long missing in Indian-Government relations, and would enable us to proceed with the evolution of a new policy.

The Minister's policy statement appears to be a departure from the year's consultations. We view this as a policy designed to divest us of our aboriginal, residual and statutory rights. If we accept this policy, and in the process lose our rights and our lands, we become willing partners in cultural genocide. This we cannot do.

We realize all to [sic] well, perhaps better than you that the winds of change are blowing, and that we too must change to keep pace with the times. But a policy must be devised that will enable us to keep pace with you as a people. A people with not only a past but a future. A future as Indian people and as Canadians.

As we have said, we shoulder a heavy responsibility but it is a responsibly that all of you share with us. Whatever is done for or done to our Indian people will be done in your name by your Government.

. . .

SUGGESTIONS FOR FURTHER READING

For an extended response to the 1969 White Paper from the Indian Association of Alberta's president at the time, see Harold Cardinal, *The Unjust Society* (Vancouver: Douglas & McIntyre, 1999). For the perspectives of George Manuel who led the National Indian Brotherhood (the precursor to the Assembly of First Nations) from 1970 to 1976 and, at different times, headed the North American Indian Brotherhood, the Union of BC Indian Chiefs, and the World Council of Indigenous Peoples, see George Manuel and Michael Posluns, *The Fourth World: An Indian Reality* (New York: The Free Press, 1974). For a biography of Manuel that also discusses the White Paper and related issues, see Peter McFarlane, *Brotherhood to Nationhood: George Manuel and the Making of the Modern Indian Movement* (Toronto: Between the Lines, 1993). For the Hawthorn Report, mentioned several times above, see H.B. Hawthorn, ed., *A Survey of the Contemporary Indians of Canada: A Report on Economic, Political, Educational Needs and Policies in Two Volumes* (Ottawa: Indian Affairs Branch, 1966). The first part of the report focuses primarily on economic, political, and administrative issues while the second part is concerned primarily with issues of education and the internal organization of reserve communities. Both volumes are available on line from the Aboriginal Affairs and Northern Development website. Follow the links from http://www.aadnc-aandc.gc.ca/eng/1100100010186/1100 100010187. For an analysis of the Hawthorn Report, see Sally Weaver, "The Hawthorn Report: Its Use in the Making of Canadian Indian Policy," in *Anthropology, Public Policy and Native Peoples in Canada*, ed. Noel Dyck and James B. Waldram (Montreal and Kingston: McGill-Queen's University Press, 1993), 75–97. For a broader and more detailed analysis, see Weaver's *Making Canadian Indian Policy: The Hidden Agenda, 1968–1970* (Toronto: University of Toronto Press, 1981).

CHAPTER II

"AN EPIC STRUGGLE WHICH HAS LEFT ITS MARK"[1]

STRIVING FOR GENDER EQUALITY IN THE INDIAN ACT

Section 3 of the 1876 Indian Act, included in Chapter 1 of this reader, suggests that the fledgling Canadian state envisioned a future in which those it defined as Indians would adhere to a set of gender relations that reflected those permeating Euro-Canadian society. In Canada, women were the virtual property of their husbands with relatively few legal rights and restricted access to public life. It was not until 1929, for example, when Henrietta Muir Edwards, Nellie McClung, Louise McKinney, Emily Murphy and Irene Parlby pressed the issue, that the Privy Council overruled the Supreme Court of Canada and determined that women were indeed "persons" under the British North America Act, Canada's constitution at the time. From other documents included in earlier chapters, readers might have caught glimpses of the culturally based understandings regarding appropriate gender roles that were held by settler society and that its political leaders and bureaucrats strove to instil in Indigenous families and communities. Though women in many if not most Indigenous societies traditionally held powerful political roles, they were denied the right to vote by the Canadian state and so were stripped of any involvement in the formal political process, either at the community level or within the larger Canadian polity. Patrilineal descent, too, was imposed by both policy and legislation. As a result, whether or not a girl or woman was identified as an Indian was

---

1 Philo Desterres, Quebec Native Women's Association, quoted in Canada, Royal Commission on Aboriginal Peoples, *Report of the Royal Commission on Aboriginal Peoples*, chapter 2, "Women's Perspectives" in vol. 4 *Perspectives and Realities* (Ottawa: Communications Group, 1996), 38. This quotation appears in document 11.4.

determined solely by her father's and then her husband's status. If either had Indian status, she did too, even if she had no connection to any Indigenous culture and had no Indigenous ancestors. If her father or, if married, her husband did not have status, then neither did she, even if all of her ancestors were registered Indians and she had lived her entire life in a First Nations community.

The first document in this chapter is a section from the 1951 Indian Act. It was crafted at a time immediately following the revelations of the horrific human rights abuses that occurred in Europe before and during World War II. Readers will have the opportunity to determine the extent to which this section shows advancement in the area of gender equality and human rights. Certainly the rules created to determine Indian status became much more detailed, as did those spelling out who was not entitled to be registered as an Indian.

Through the next three decades, women such as Mary Two-Axe Earley, Jeannette Corbiere Lavell, Yvonne Bédard, Sandra Lovelace, Shirley Bear, and many others pressed for equal treatment through Canadian courts and at the United Nations. Because of their organizing efforts and cultural initiatives, activists were instrumental in eventually causing Canada to reformulate its policy in regard to Indigenous women. They also challenged those male leaders within their own communities who had come to see patriarchy as a traditional cultural attribute.

Following the patriation of the Constitution of Canada in 1982, which included the Charter of Rights and Freedoms, and in the wake of considerable political activity on the part of Indigenous women across the country, Canada's parliament passed Bill C-31 in 1985 and again amended the Indian Act. A selection from that amendment appears below as document 11.2. Considerable controversy continued, however, concerning what critics argued was persistent gender discrimination in the act. According to these critics, C-31 provisions were not only unnecessarily complicated but also created two levels of status in Section 6.1 and 6.2 of the amendment. In the capacity to confer status, C-31 rules continued to favour male Indians who married non-Indians and their descendants over female Indians who married non-Indians and their descendants. Other problems arose concerning women who had children outside of a marriage sanctioned by the state or who had Indigenous ancestors whose existence was not recorded. Further, the registration process itself proved to be much slower and the documentation required more onerous than many had hoped.

In 2007, after almost two decades of trying to ensure that her grandchildren could be registered as Indians, Sharon McIvor, a Nlaka'pamux woman from the Lower Nicola First Nation, pursued her case to the Supreme Court of British Columbia. Cited as *McIvor v. The Registrar, Indian and Northern Affairs Canada*, the case is excerpted and forms document 11.5 of this chapter. Following an unsuccessful appeal to the British Columbia Court of Appeal and an initial indication that it would take the case to the Supreme Court of Canada, the Conservative federal government decided on a legislative remedy as directed by the appellate court. That legislative remedy became Bill C-3, the Gender Equity in Indian Registration Act, introduced in March of 2010, but the controversy remained. In the sixth and final document included in this chapter, Sharon McIvor explains to members of parliament some of her concerns regarding Bill C-3. Despite these and other concerns, the Bill was passed by parliament on 15 December 2010 and came into force on 31 January 2011.

Though this chapter focuses on women and the Indian Act, it should be recognized that the inferior status conferred on Indian women by the Canadian state was mirrored by the discrimination they have suffered, and continue to experience, in other aspects of their lives. Systemic discrimination, in turn, continues to have serious consequences that are manifested in a myriad of ways. From the shocking socio-economic conditions in which many women and their children find themselves to the hundreds of murdered and missing Indigenous women in Canada and to their over-representation in all aspects of the criminal justice system, Indigenous women can trace their situation to the prevalent understanding in Canada that women, and especially Indigenous women, are of less value than their male counterparts. That Indigenous women continue to struggle against discrimination in all of its expressions is a testimony to their strength and resilience.

QUESTIONS FOR DISCUSSION

1. How does the 1951 amendment to the Indian Act continue to discriminate by gender?
2. According to the 1985 amendment, what would cause the children of a brother and sister who both had status before they married non-Indians in 1984 to have different kinds of status after 1985? Reading document 11.4 will also help with this question.
3. Why would the predominately male elected leadership of Indigenous organizations be less responsive to women's concerns than women activists might have hoped?
4. Outline the effects of Bill C-31 presented in the report of the Royal Commission on Aboriginal Peoples.
5. What was the decision of the BC Supreme Court in the McIvor case?
6. Why might Canada seem to be reluctant to amend the Indian Act to ensure equality?

DOCUMENTS

11.1 Amendment to the Indian Act, 1951

The 1951 amendment to the Indian Act is seen by some as a major new development and by others as simply a reversion to the somewhat less compulsory nature of the first act of 1876. Nonetheless, there were significant improvements over the 1951 Indian Act's immediate predecessors. The sections banning the potlatch and making it illegal to raise funds to pursue land claims were simply dropped in the 1951 rendition, for example. However, as can be seen in the selections below, differential treatment based on gender continued. In addition, Section 12 (a) iv introduced what came to be known as the "double mother rule" whereby a person whose mother and paternal grandmother became Indians only when they married Indian men was denied status.

Source: Canada. "An Act Respecting Indians," *Statutes of Canada*, 15 Geo. VI (1951) Ch. 29.

1951   **The Indian Act**

Chapter 29

. . .

Persons entitled to be registered.

11. Subject to section twelve, a person is entitled to be registered if that person

(a) on the twenty-sixth day of May, eighteen hundred and seventy-four, was, for the purposes of *An Act providing for the organization of the Department of the Secretary of State of Canada, and for the management of Indian and Ordnance Lands*, chapter forty-two of the statutes of 1868, as amended by section six of chapter six of the statutes of 1869, and section eight of chapter twenty-one of the statutes of 1874, considered to be entitled to hold, use or enjoy the lands and other immovable property belonging to or appropriated to the use of the various tribes, bands or bodies of Indians in Canada,

(b) is a member of a band

(i) for whose use and benefit, in common, lands have been set apart or since the twenty-sixth day of May, eighteen hundred and seventy-four have been agreed by treaty to be set apart, or

(ii) that has been declared by the Governor in Council to be a band for the purposes of this Act,

(c) is a male person who is a direct descendant in the male line of a male person described in paragraph *(a)* or *(b)*,

(d) is the legitimate child of

(i) a male person described in paragraph *(a)* or *(b)*, or

(ii) a person described in paragraph *(c)*,

(e) is the illegitimate child of a female person described in paragraph *(a)*, *(b)*, or *(d)*, unless the Registrar is satisfied that the father of the child was not an Indian and the Registrar has declared that the child is not entitled to be registered, or

(f) is the wife or widow of a person who is entitled to be registered by virtue of paragraph *(a)*, *(b)*, *(c)*, *(d)*, or *(e)*.

Persons not entitled to be registered.

12. (1) The following persons are not entitled to be registered, namely,

(a) a person who

(i) has received or has been allotted half-breed lands or money scrip,

(ii) is a descendant of a person described in sub paragraph (i),

(iii) is enfranchised, or

(iv) is a person born of a marriage entered into after the coming into force of this Act and has attained the age of twenty-one years, whose mother and whose father's mother are not persons described in paragraph *(a)*, *(b)*, *(d)*, or entitled to be registered by virtue of paragraph *(e)* of section eleven, unless being a woman, that person is the wife or widow of a person described in section eleven, and

(b) a woman who is married to a person who is not an Indian.

(2) the Minister may issue to any Indian to whom this Act ceases to apply, a certifi- *Certificate.*
cate to that effect.

. . .

14. A woman who is a member of a band ceases to be a member of that band if she *Woman marrying*
marries a person who is not a member of that band, but if she marries a member of *outside band ceases to be*
another band, she thereupon becomes a member of the band of which her husband is *a member.*
a member.

11.2 Amendment to the Indian Act, 1985

*As mentioned in the introduction to this chapter, after considerable agitation and court
challenges by Indigenous women, Canada moved to pass Bill C-31 and amended the Indian Act in 1985 to bring it in line with the Canadian Charter of Rights and Freedoms.
This amendment, though, has been criticized for, among other things, being unnecessarily complicated and creating two classes of status, as can be seen in Section 6.1 and 6.2.
Those with 6.1 status, which included non-Indian women who married Indian men but
not Indian women who married non-Indian men, had greater ability to confer status on
their children and grandchildren than their 6.2 peers.*

Source: Canada. "An Act to amend the Indian Act," *Statutes of Canada*, 33–34 Elizabeth II
(1985) Ch. 27.

Indian Register

5. (1) There shall be maintained in the Department an Indian Register in which *Indian Register*
shall be recorded the name of every person who is entitled to be registered as an Indian
under this Act.

(2) The names in the Indian Register immediately prior to April 17, 1985 shall con- *Existing Indian Register*
stitute the Indian Register on April 17, 1985.

(3) The Registrar may at any time add to or delete from the Indian Register the name
of any person who, in accordance with this Act, is entitled or not entitled, as the case may *Deletions and additions*
be, to have his name included in the Indian Register.

(4) The Indian Register shall indicate the date on which each name was added *Date of change*
thereto or deleted therefrom.

(5) The name of a person who is entitled to be registered is not required to be *Application for*
recorded in the Indian Register unless an application for registration is made to the *registration*
Registrar.

(6) (1) Subject to section 7, a person is entitled to be registered if *Persons entitled to be*
(*a*) that person was registered or entitled to be registered immediately prior to *registered*
April 17, 1985;

(*b*) that person is a member of a body of persons that has been declared by the
Governor in Council on or after April 17, 1985 to be a band for the purposes of this
Act;

(*c*) the name of that person was omitted or deleted from the Indian Register,
or from a band list prior to September 4, 1951, under subparagraph 12(1)(*a*)(iv),

paragraph 12(1)(*b*) or subsection 12(2) or under subparagraph 12(1)(*a*)(iii) pursuant to an order made under subsection 109(2), as each provision read immediately prior to April 17, 1985, or under any former provision of this Act relating to the same subject-matter as any of those provisions;

(*d*) the name of that person was omitted or deleted from the Indian Register, or from a band list prior to September 4, 1951, under subparagraph 12(1)(*a*)(iii) pursuant to an order made under subsection 109(1), as each provision read immediately prior to April 17, 1985, or under any former provision of this Act relating to the same subject-matter as any of those provisions;

(*e*) the name of that person was omitted or deleted from the Indian Register, or from a band list prior to September 4, 1951,

(i) under section 13, as it read immediately prior to September 4, 1951, or under any former provision of this Act relating to the same subject-matter as that section, or

(ii) under section 111, as it read immediately prior July 1, 1920, or under any former provision of this Act relating to the same subject-matter as that section; or

(*f*) that person is a person both of whose parents are or, if no longer living, were at the time of death entitled to be registered under this section.

Idem

(2) Subject to section 7, a person is entitled to be registered if that person is a person one of whose parents is or, if no longer living, was at the time of death subtitled to be registered under subsection (1).

Deeming provision

(3) For the purposes of paragraph (1)(*f*) and subsection (2),

(*a*) a person who was no longer living immediately prior to April 17, 1985 but who was at the time of death entitled to be registered shall be deemed to be entitled to be registered under paragraph (1)(*a*); and

(*b*) a person described in paragraph (1)(*c*), (*d*) or (*e*) who was no longer living on April 17, 1985 shall be deemed to be entitled to be registered under that paragraph.

Persons not entitled to be registered

(7) (1) The following persons are not entitled to be registered:

(*a*) a person who was registered under paragraph 11(1)(*f*), as it read immediately prior to April 17, 1985, or under any former provision of this Act relating to the same subject-matter as that paragraph, and whose name was subsequently omitted or deleted from the Indian Register under this Act; or

(*b*) a person is the child of a person who was registered or entitled to be registered under paragraph 11(1)(*f*), as it read immediately prior to April 17, 1985, or under any former provision of this Act relating to the same subject-matter as that paragraph, and is also the child of a person who is not entitled to be registered.

Exception

(2) Paragraph (1)(*a*) does not apply in respect of a female person who was, at any time prior to being registered under paragraph 11(1)(*f*), entitled to be registered under any other provision of this Act.

Idem

(3) Paragraph (1)(*b*) does not apply in respect of the child of a female person who was, at any time prior to being registered under paragraph 11(1)(*f*), entitled to be registered under any other provision of this Act.

11.3 Cathy Bailey, "Indian Women Struggle for Rights," *Poundmaker*, 1974

Poundmaker *newspaper was originally a publication created by students at the University of Alberta before cutting its ties to the U of A and becoming an alternative weekly in Edmonton. This article appeared more than a decade before Bill C-31 and outlines a few of the problems associated with the Indian Act from the standpoint of First Nations women seeking equal treatment under the law and the tensions that existed in Indigenous communities as a result of gender discrimination. The article also presents some of the actions taken by women in their simultaneous struggles for equality and to retain their status as Indians. Finally, the article mentions the Canadian Bill of Rights, passed by Parliament in 1960. The Bill of Rights seems to have been well-intentioned, but, unlike the 1982 Charter of Rights, it was never part of the Constitution, and its effectiveness proved to be limited.*

Source: Cathy Bailey, "Indian Women Struggle for Rights," *Poundmaker*, 25 February 1974.

Indian women struggle for rights

Jeannette Lavell opened a huge can of worms amongst native people when she appealed to the Supreme Court to regain the Indian status she lost when she married a non-Indian.

She lost the case because of Section 12(1)(b) of the Indian Act which states "The following persons are not entitled to be registered (as status Indians), namely . . . a woman who married a person who is not an Indian . . ."

The fact that the Canadian Bill of Rights demands equality of treatment under the law regardless of sex was overshadowed by that very clearly discriminatory clause in the Indian Act.

At present, under the Act, an Indian man may marry a white woman and maintain full treaty rights. An Indian woman upon marrying a non-Indian loses all her treaty rights and becomes a non-status Indian. This means that under the law she is really not an Indian at all in spite of her parentage, culture and upbringing.

Similarly her children have no treaty rights whatsoever.

A woman who loses her rights by marrying a non-Indian remains excluded from registration as a treaty Indian even if she loses her husband by being separated, divorced or widowed.

Ironically, a white woman who marries an Indian becomes a status Indian—she may not contain a drop of Indian blood, yet she is legally an Indian. The children resulting from the marriage are also 'legal' Indians.

Alberta non-status Indian women take exception to their unequal treatment under the Indian Act. Under the leadership of Jenny Margettes, a non-status Indian married to a white man, they have formed the association called Indian Rights for Indian Women.

The aim of the group is to see that the offending section 12(1)(b) is removed from the Indian Act.

The Lavell case has caused much dissention among native people, and was the impetus for the creation of Indian Rights for Indian Women.

Mrs. Margettes said, in an interview, that status Indian people "got pretty uptight" over the Lavell case. They feared that if Jeannette Lavell won her case it would set a threatening precedent for treaty Indians.

"They were afraid white men (husbands of Indian women) would infringe on their treaty rights or encroach on their reserve lands," she said.

BASELESS FEARS

Mrs. Margettes said there is no basis to their fears. On the contrary, Indian Rights for Indian Women does not want non-Indian husbands of Indian women to gain treaty status.

She believes that no white person should have treaty rights. "White women should never have gained Indian rights 'through marriage to an Indian'", she said.

Jenny Margettes has contempt for those who would deny Indian women their rights because to their fear of racial disintegration of Indian peoples through marriage to non-Indians. "Some Indian people are a bunch of racists—many Indians are the worst racist people in the world", she claimed.

At the time the Lavell case came up, Jenny Margettes was active in various Indian women's groups, working with treaty women at the reserve level. The treaty women refused to recognize that Jeanette Lavell, and non-status Indian women in general, had a legitimate complaint against the Indian Act.

The non-status women were told by treaty women that "if they went along with Jeanette Lavell, their relationship would be finished." It was this refusal of treaty women to support the cause of Indian women affected by the discriminatory Section 12(1)(b) of the Indian Act that led to the establishment of Indian Rights for Indian Women three years ago.

Indian Rights for Indian Women now has about 300 supporters, mostly in Alberta. Although they work mostly at the provincial and local level, they are now attempting to set up a national task force to study the situation of Indian women in all of Canada.

When asked whether her organization was attempting to deal with other Indian associations as part of its program, Mrs. Margettes replied that they have tried "for years" to reach some sort of consensus with other Indian groups, such as Harold Cardinal's Indian Association of Alberta, and the National Indian Brotherhood.

In dealing with these other Indian groups, Indian Rights for Indian Women has continually met opposition. Mrs. Margettes said:

> There is no use talking to Harold Cardinal or the National Indian Brotherhood
> any more. They only want to reserve all the rights for themselves as treaty Indi-
> ans. They are not interested in extending rights to other people who should have
> Indian rights . . . Why should we waste our energies trying to search different av-
> enues to reach a consensus amongst Indians . . . We have to deal directly with the
> parliamentarians—the people who can make the necessary legislative changes.

Indian Rights for Indian Women is directing its energies into research at the present. They have been invited to present a brief to the Standing Committee on Indian Affairs. Research papers are now being prepared on the subject of the enfranchizement [sic] of Indian women, with the aid of the University of Alberta Legal Services.

Although no specific date has been set, research papers are expected to be complete "sometime in the spring", at which time application will be made to appear before the Standing Committee.

In addition to the political stumbling blocks between non-treaty and treaty Indians there is a cultural stumbling block between Indian men and women.

Mrs. Margettes said, "Culturally we are supposed to be standing behind our men and walking a few paces behind them. . . . As far as I'm concerned if I'm going to walk a few paces behind an Indian man, I'd have to have an awful lot of respect for him and I haven't come across any Indian man that merits that kind of respect from me".

When asked whether she thought most Indian women shared her sentiments she said many Indian women no longer believe they should be subservient to men, and that formerly women played their subservient role "for political reasons".

This cultural aspect of the problem adversely affects the support Indian women give to Indian Rights for Indian Women. Jenny Margettes said while some Indian women give a great deal of support to the organization, many are apathetic. Many women have been "scared off" by criticism and social pressure from Indian women who believe in the traditional cultural system in which men play the dominant role and women are considered secondary.

For this reason much of the research outlines the evidence that women did in fact historically play more than a subservient role. During their research they have discovered that in tribal societies there was a very major role played by women. For example, the Mohawk society at Caughnawaga near Montreal had a matriarchal system called the "clan mother" system.

Through workshops and conferences, they are collecting more evidence that Indian women are not historically secondary in importance to men.

MAY WORKSHOP

A large workshop will be held in May, about 60 miles outside of Edmonton near Hobbema. It will be a "camp-out" workshop. The resource people for the "cultural awakening" have not yet been determined, but a possible speaker is Rose Auger of Faust.

Jenny Margettes was recently in Ottawa and spoke to the Indian Affairs Department. They said that changes to the Indian Act would not be considered unless all sectors of Indian society affected by the Act were consulted.

The issue of consultation came up at a conference held by Indian Rights for Indian Women in Vancouver in December. The conference, subsidized by the Secretary of State, was attended by both treaty and non-treaty women as well as some Indian chiefs.

The conference wholeheartedly rejected proposals for changes to Section 12(1)(b) drafted by the Indian Association on the grounds that not all people affected by the Act had been consulted.

She said treaty Indians constitute only about one third of Indians in Canada and that the other two thirds, non-treaty Indians, should be consulted as well.

Mrs. Margettes said that from her talks with native people in Ottawa recently, the question of "who is an Indian" is far more important in the minds of Indian peoples than even the land claims issues which are coming more and more to the forefront. She said the question of who is an Indian ought to be settled first.

Although Jenny Margettes does not believe Indian women will gain their rights in the near future, she is optimistic that in time the offending Section 12(1)(b) will be changed. She is resigned to a long slow journey towards equal treatment for Indian women.

11.4 Report of the Royal Commission on Aboriginal Peoples, 1985

In 1991, the Royal Commission on Aboriginal Peoples (RCAP) was established with a broad mandate to explore the historical relationship between Indigenous peoples and Canada and to propose remedial action, as mentioned in the introduction to Section B of Chapter 7. The selection below from the RCAP report outlines the commissioners' findings and concerns in regard to Bill C-31. This document also includes parts of the testimony of some of those who made presentations to the commission.

Source: Canada, Royal Commission on Aboriginal Peoples, *Report of the Royal Commission on Aboriginal Peoples*, chapter 2, "Women's Perspectives" in vol. 4 *Perspectives and Realities* (Ottawa: Communications Group, 1996), 33–43 and 96.

Reproduced with the permission of the Minister of Public Works and Government Services Canada, 2013.

Footnotes, square brackets, and in-paragraph ellipses as in original.

. . .

3.2 BILL C-31

The 1982 amendment of the constitution, incorporating the *Canadian Charter of Rights and Freedoms*, included the provision, in section 15, that "every individual is equal before and under the law and has the right to the equal protection and benefit of the law without discrimination based on race, national or ethnic origin, colour, religion, sex, age, or mental or physical disability". Section 15 of the Charter came into effect on 17 April 1985. The Charter accomplished overnight what the *Canadian Bill of Rights* and the *Canadian Human Rights Act*[2] had been unable to do—motivating the government to eliminate provisions of the *Indian Act* that had been criticized for discriminating against Indian women. Some influence was also exerted by the case of *Lovelace v. Canada*, in which

---

2 *Canadian Human Rights Act*, R.S.C. 1985, c. H-6. Section 67 of the act reads as follows:
> Nothing in this Act affects any provision of the *Indian Act* or any provision made under or pursuant to that *Act*.

Canada's treatment of Indian women under the *Indian Act* was strongly criticized by the United Nations Human Rights Committee.[3]

. . .

The impact of Bill C-31

The impact of Bill C-31 was enormous and profound. In 1989, the Department of Indian Affairs and Northern Development began a study to determine its effects. The study was developed and conducted in consultation with three national Aboriginal organizations— the Assembly of First Nations, through its chiefs committee on citizenship, the Native Women's Association of Canada and the Native Council of Canada (now the Congress of Aboriginal Peoples).[4]

The department of Indian affairs had seriously underestimated the number of persons likely to seek reinstatement. More than 21,000 applications, representing 38,000 individuals, were received in the first six months after enactment. A backlog of applications took five years to clear. By June 1990, 75,761 applications had been made, representing 133,134 persons. The status Indian population grew by 19 per cent in five years because of Bill C-31 alone and, when natural growth was included, by a total of 33 per cent.[5]

The report summarizing the results of the study describes the registration process, noting that responsibility for determining whether an individual is eligible for registration as a status Indian rests with the registrar, who applies the criteria outlined in section 6 of the Indian Act. The process includes searches of departmental records on the individual and/or the individual's family. If the required information cannot be located in the register, a more detailed and time-consuming search of pre-1951 records is undertaken.[6]

The documentation required to prove eligibility for Indian status and the slow pace of approval were criticized. In some instances, the existence of people had not been recorded on paper, and it became necessary to seek sworn affidavits as evidence of family relationships and declarations from elders as verification of past band affiliation. In addition, the process was particularly difficult for individuals raised by adoptive parents. Adoptees of Indian descent experienced problems because of the confidentiality of provincial adoption records. Problems also arose for status Indian women with children

---

3 [1981] 2 *Human Rights Law Journal* 158; 68 I.L.R. 17, Canada was criticized by the Human Rights Committee established pursuant to the *International Covenant on Civil and Political Rights* to which Canada is a signatory. The Covenant is one of the documents that influenced the development of the Charter and it contains many human rights provisions similar to Charter protections. The Human Rights Committee took aim at section 12(1)(b) and found that it unjustifiably denied Sandra Lovelace, who had lost Indian status and band membership upon marrying out, her rights under section 27 of the Covenant as a member of an ethnic minority to enjoy her culture and language in community with other members of her band. The Committee did not find the loss of status attendant upon her marrying out to be reasonable or necessary to preserve the identity of the Tobique Band of which she had been a member. The case is discussed in Anne F. Bayefsky, "The Human Rights Committee and the Case of Sandra Lovelace" (1982) 20 Can. Y.B. Int'l L. 244.

4 DIAND, *Impacts of the 1985 Amendments to the Indian Act (Bill C-31): Summary Report* (Ottawa: Supply and Services, 1990) (hereafter *Bill C-31 Summary Report*).

5 *Bill C-31 Summary Report*, p. ii.

6 *Bill C-31 Summary Report*, p. 5.

born out of wedlock, who had to prove that the father was a status Indian before the children could be registered.[7]

> Our children, if they are born outside the framework of a union recognized by the [*Indian Act*], are also victims of discrimination. When their father is Aboriginal, he must sign a declaration or, under [Bill] C-31, our child will be considered to have been born of a non-Indian father. [translation]

Philo Desterres
Quebec Native Women's Association
Montreal, Quebec, 27 May 1993

> They developed . . . such complex systems for re-registration. There are some things the average Canadian citizen cannot understand and doesn't have to confront, which are still aberrations, which are disguised in the way people are re-registered or even how the status is to be transmitted from one person to another, except it is necessary to understand the situation of the women who fought for it. It was that or nothing. [translation]

Michèle Rouleau
Quebec Native Women's Association
Montreal, Quebec, 27 May 1993

Of the applications received by mid-1990, 55 per cent (73,554) of all individuals seeking registration had been approved, 16 per cent (21,397) were disallowed, 8 per cent were active files, 9 per cent were inactive files, and 12 per cent were classified as "other completions". Of the 8 per cent classified as active, the majority were those requiring additional information from the applicant. Of the 16 per cent disallowed, three-quarters were denied registration under sub-section 6(2), which provides that individuals seeking registration must establish that one parent is entitled to registration under subsection 6(1).[8]

As of 30 June 1995, Bill C-31 had added 95,429 persons to the status Indian population in Canada, more than half of them (57.2 per cent, 54,589) female.[9] The enormous increase in the status Indian population did not result in an equal increase in the population of reserve communities. This is largely because most persons restored to Indian status or with first-time status under Bill C-31 still live off-reserve.[10] Through its survey of 2,000 registrants, the study found that 32 per cent of those individuals currently living off-reserve would like to live on a reserve. To a second survey question asking registrants living off-reserve if they might return to a reserve or Crown land at

---

7 *Bill C-31 Summary Report*, p. 6.
8 *Bill C-31 Summary Report*, pp. 9 and 12.
9 Figures supplied by DIAND liaison office; 5 July 1995.
10 According to *Bill C-31 Summary Report*, p. iii, 90 per cent of Bill C-31 registrants still live off-reserve.

some time in the future, 52 per cent replied in the affirmative and another 15 per cent were uncertain.[11]

Although most Bill C-31 registrants continue to live off-reserve, it is not always by choice, since it has been difficult for some of them to get reserve residency rights even when they are band members (an issue discussed later in the chapter). Some bands experienced significant population increases from Bill C-31 registrants while others had none. The average band increased in size by 19 per cent, although 80 per cent of the bands had fewer than 15 Bill C-31 registrants living on-reserve. (It is estimated that 4,600 of the Bill C-31 registrants lived on reserve in 1984 and that 2,700 more had moved to a reserve between 1985 and 1990.[12])

Clearly the full impact of Bill C-31 on reserve communities has yet to be felt. Some band leaders and community members are concerned about the possibility of crowding and disruption and have been resistant to inclusion of new band members in their communities. Services that could be affected by a population increase include housing, health and post-secondary education.

Indian women have their own concerns about Bill C-31. Women make up the majority of people reinstated under the bill, and fully three-quarters of those whose Indian status was restored—as opposed to those who gained status for the first time—are women.[13] Despite its avowed intent of bringing about sexual equality in the status and membership provisions of the *Indian Act*, Bill C-31 is nonetheless seen by many Aboriginal women as a continuation of the sexist policies of the past.

3.3 THE *INDIAN ACT* AND BILL C-31: AREAS OF *CONCERN TO FIRST NATIONS WOMEN*

There are strong concerns among Aboriginal people that, in eliminating the major forms of discrimination in the original *Indian Act,* new ones have been created. For example, as noted in the Bill C-31 study summary report, "bands that control their own membership under the Act may now restrict eligibility for some of the rights and benefits that used to be automatic with status".[14] Moreover, sex discrimination, supposedly wiped out by the 1985 amendments, remains. Thus, for example, in some families Indian women who lost status through marrying out before 1985 can pass Indian status on to their children but not to their children's children. However, their brothers, who may also have married out before 1985, can pass on status to their children for at least one more generation, even though the children of the sister and the brother all have one status Indian parent and one non-Indian parent. Such anomalies result from the fact that the Bill C-31 amendments build on past status and membership policies and provisions. They are, in this respect, somewhat reminiscent of the 1951 revisions in which the notion of 'entitlement to registration as an Indian' replace that of 'Indian blood', but without breaking with past practices.

---

11 *Bill C-31 Summary Report*, p. 17.
12 *Bill C-31 Summary Report*, p. iii.
13 *Bill C-31 Summary Report*, p. ii. The precise figure is 77 per cent.
14 *Bill C-31 Summary Report*, p. iv.

These past practices favour descent through the male line, as imposed during the Victorian era. Although Canada no longer subscribes to these values, the legacy of discrimination continues to be felt by First Nations communities:

> I married a non-Aboriginal person and was discriminated against. . . . In 1985 the act was amended and so I regained my status, along with a number of other women. And yet the discrimination continued. This is an act which has lasted 125 years, and it is difficult to change something that old because it becomes part of people's lives. It became a habit, a tradition for our Aboriginal people to discriminate against these women. Today we are still suffering this discrimination even though the law has been amended. We speak of discrimination because I returned to my community. . . . When the time came to apply for housing for the reinstated women, they were always told there was no land. Many excuses were given: "we have no money", "the band councils have no money". . . . In my community I had to fight for six years in order to meet with the chiefs. . . . There are people who cannot return to their communities for the reasons I have given you because the bands do not accept them. . . . [translation]

> *Mèrilda St. Onge*
> *Women of the Montagnais Nation*
> *Sept-Îsles, Quebec, 19 November 1992*

> What the Aboriginal leaders are unfortunately applying today, I am not saying all leaders, is the policy of exclusion. In the first years of implementation of Bill C-31, from 1985 to 1987, the approach of some band councils was simply to try to make some rules that would not accept the re-registered women. . . . I think this was extremely regrettable and the government bears a large part of the guilt . . . it is obvious that there was very strong opposition to the return of people to the communities because the people have no more houses, the people have no more room. . . . There is a terrible lack of space so the issue of re-registration is strongly linked to the issue of land. [translation]

> *Michèle Rouleau*
> *Quebec Native Women's Association*
> *Montreal, Quebec, 27 May 1993*

The testimony of many First Nations women before the Commission points to their determination to fight against discrimination and policies of exclusion:

> In short, an epic struggle which has left its mark has contributed to our understanding of the obstacles, in particular the strength of the prejudices and ravages caused by the *Indian Act*, but which has above all helped to strengthen the determination of the Aboriginal women to fight discrimination wherever it

is found, beginning with the discrimination that operates at the grassroots in the communities. [translation]

Philo Desterres
Quebec Native Women's Association
Montreal, Quebec, 27 May 1993

In the next few pages we examine the major areas that concern Indian women in the current version of the *Indian Act*. In some cases, women are not the only ones affected. However, because the majority of people restored to Indian status under the 1985 amendments were women, they feel the impact more profoundly and encounter these obstacles more often than do Aboriginal men.

Indian status under section 6

Though I regained my status under Bill C-31, my children were denied status. The children of my male cousin, who traces his descent from our common grandmother through the male line, have full status. I am challenging this inequality in another court case, pending in British Columbia.[15]

Sharon McIvor
Native Women's Association of Canada
Toronto, Ontario, 26 June 1992

First Nations women told the Commission that Bill C-31 has created a situation where, over time, their descendants may be stripped of their Indian status and rights in some circumstances in which Indian men and their descendants would be unaffected. The discrepancy arises out of the categories used to designate Indian status under Bill C-31.

The bill created two main categories of status Indians. Under subsection 6(1), legal status is assigned to all those who had status before 17 April 1985, all persons who are members of any new bands created since 17 April 1985 (none have been created), and all individuals who lost status through the discriminatory sections of the *Indian Act*. More specifically, these classes of persons are as follows:

- section 6(1)(a): this is a grandfather clause granting Indian status to persons entitled to it under the pre-1985 version of the *Indian Act*;
- section 6(1)(b): persons entitled to status as a member of a band declared by the governor in council to exist after Bill C-31 came into force (there are none: the class is therefore empty[16]);

---

15 *McIvor v. Registrar DIAND,* BCSC no. CC5/89. According to information received from the federal department of justice as of October 1995, this case is continuing.

16 Bands created since 1985 have not been declared bands in the sense in which the term is used in the *Indian Act*. Rather, they are said to result from the minister's power under section 17 to "amalgamate" or to "constitute" new bands from existing bands. According to information received from the DIAND registrar, the last band created by declaration of the governor in council was the Conne River band of Newfoundland in 1984.

- section 6(1)(c): persons regaining status under Bill C-31 who lost or were denied status because of
  - the double mother rule (former section 12(1)(a)(iv));
  - marriage out (that is, to a non-Indian) (former section 12(1)(b));
  - illegitimate children of an Indian mother and non-Indian father (former section 12(2));
  - involuntary enfranchisement upon marriage to a non-Indian, including any children involuntarily enfranchised because of the involuntary enfranchisement of the mother (former subsection 12(1)(a)(iii) and 109(2));
- section 6(1)(d): persons 'voluntarily' enfranchised upon application by the Indian man, including the Indian wife and children enfranchised along with him (former subsection 12(1)(l)(iii) and 109(1));
- section 6(1)(e): persons enfranchised because of other enfranchisement provisions, that is, residency outside Canada for more than five years (former section 13 between 1927 and 1951) and upon obtaining higher education or professional standing (former section 111 between 1867 and 1920); and
- section 6(1)(f): children whose parents are both entitled to be registered under any of the preceding subsections of section 6.

Subsection 6(2) covers people with only one parent who is or was a status Indian under any part of section 6(1). It must be stressed that the one-parent rule in subsection 6(2) applies only if that parent is entitled to status under subsection 6(1). Thus, if an individual has one parent covered by subsection 6(2) and one who is non-Indian, the individual is not entitled to status. The children or other descendants of Indian women who lost status under the discriminatory provisions described earlier will generally gain status under subsection 6(2), not subsection 6(1), since the reason their mothers lost status in the first place was that their fathers did not have Indian status when their parents were married.

As discussed earlier, the rules are complex and difficult to apply, particularly in cases where applicants may not have the required documentary proof of their ancestry. This can be a problem in some areas where written records are lacking and where oral traditions are still strong. It is also a problem where Indian children were adopted by non-Indian parents and the records are covered by the *Privacy Act* or withheld because of the confidentiality of provincial adoption records.[17]

Moreover, and more alarmingly for future generations of First Nations people, the consequences of falling within subsection 6(1) or subsection 6(2) are felt by the woman's children and grandchildren. For these descendants, the way their parents and grandparents acquired status will be important determinants of whether they will have Indian status and, if they do, whether and to what extent they will be able to pass it on to their children. The effects of the 6(1) and 6(2) designation are felt most acutely in the third generation. . . .

. . . [I]t is clear in the situation of marriage to a non-Indian that the children of a 6(1) parent and a 6(2) parent have different rights under the amended *Indian Act*. . . . When one recalls that the children of women who lost status under the discriminatory provi-

---

17 *Privacy Act*, R.S.C. 1985, c.P-21; *Bill C-31 Summary Report* (cited in note 46), p. 6.

sions of the earlier versions of the Indian Act will have gained their own status through subsection 6(2), it is clear that they will be at a relative disadvantage.

A woman who gained status under subsection 6(2) will see the impact immediately if she marries out: her children will not have Indian status. All other factors being equal, this rule creates a situation in which the descendants of a woman who married out before 1985 will have fewer Indian rights than those of her brother who married out at the same time, despite the fact that their degree of Indian ancestry is the same.

An example helps illustrate the inequality that results from these rules. The following is taken from the *Report of the Aboriginal Justice Inquiry of Manitoba* (which recommended that this form of discrimination cease):

> John and Joan, a brother and sister, were both registered Indians. Joan married a Métis man before 1985 so she lost her Indian status under section 12(1)(b) of the former Act. John married a white woman before 1985 and she automatically became a status Indian. Both John and Joan have had children over the years. Joan now is eligible to regain her status under section 6(1)(c) and her children will qualify under section 6(2). They are treated as having only one eligible parent, their mother, although both parents are Aboriginal. John's children gained status at birth as both parents were Indians legally, even though only one was an Aboriginal person.
>
> Joan's children can pass on status to their offspring only if they also marry registered Indians. If they marry unregistered Aboriginal people or non-Aboriginal people, then no status will pass to their children. All John's grandchildren will be status Indians, regardless of who his children marry. Thus entitlement to registration for the second generation has nothing to do with racial or cultural characteristics. The Act has eliminated the discrimination faced by those who lost status, but has passed it on to the next generation.[18]

The establishment of categories for Indian status was a concoction of the federal government, and instead of devising a bill that would truly repair the situation, it created a 'paper blood system' that denied thousands of individuals the opportunity to claim or reclaim their heritage. The national Aboriginal organizations had certainly not suggested such a system, nor did they consent to it. Their position was that as many individuals as possible should be registered covering at least three generations. In fact, the Assembly of First Nations and the Native Women's Association of Canada issued a joint news release on 22 June 1984 reaffirming their position: "The federal government must remedy the injustice created to people of Indian ancestry by repealing sections of the *Indian Act* that deny Indian status to Indians and reinstate all generations who lost status as a result of discriminatory laws enacted by the Parliament of Canada."[19]

---

18 Manitoba, Public Inquiry into the Administration of Justice and Aboriginal People. *Report of the Aboriginal Justice Inquiry of Manitoba*, Volume 1: *The Justice System and Aboriginal People* (Winnipeg: Queen's Printer, 1991), p. 204.

19 Assembly of First Nations/Native Women's Association, "Joint Statement on Bill C-47," 22 June 1984. Bill C-47 was the precursor to Bill C-31. The joint statement lists eight specific points relating to the right of First Nations to define their own citizenship.

In 1985, the Assembly of First Nations made a presentation to the House of Commons standing committee on Indian affairs stating that "there must be full reinstatement of all our citizens who have lost status or whose status has never been recognized. . . . [W]e cannot accept new provisions which will discriminate among different generations of our citizens, procedurally or otherwise, who have been affected by the discriminatory provisions".[20] Despite these concerns, the amendments requested by the Native Women's Association of Canada and the Assembly of First Nations were not included to Bill C-31.

The categorization of Indian status under Bill C-31 has implications for the entire Aboriginal population in coming generations. At present rates of marriage outside the 6(1) and 6(2) categories, status Indians will begin to disappear from the Indian register if the rules are not changed (see Volume 1, Chapter 2). One report on the problem supports this conclusion in the strongest of terms, noting that Bill C-31 "is the gateway to a world in which some Indians are more equal than others" because 6(1)/6(2) distinction creates "two classes of Indians: *full* Indians. . . . and *half* Indians". Moreover, the report concludes, "In the long run these rules will lead to the extinction of First Nations".[21]

> My mother married a non-Native person, and before Bill C-31 she lost her birthright, her inherent right, and her nationality right as a Native person. She, like many women who lost their status for one reason or another, regained her status through Bill C-31. This bill also allowed her children to be recognized as status, but this is where it ends. . . . As it stands now, I am a status person under section 6(2) of Bill C-31. My two girls are not Native through the government's eyes. They have one-quarter Native blood. Do I tell my daughters that they are not Native because their governments say it's so? No. And I don't think so, and neither should the government.
>
> *Corrine Chappell*
> *Charlottetown, Prince Edward Island*
> *5 May 1992*

> It was very confusing. I don't want my children to be confused as to who they are. I married a man [who regained status under] Bill C-31. And, first of all, I told my children they were Métis and all of a sudden they can be Treaty. And I decided to leave that up to them, what they want to do. It was very confusing and. . . . I want them to know who they are.
>
> *Pat Harper*
> *Metis Women of Manitoba*
> *Winnipeg, Manitoba, 22 April 1992*

---

20 Minutes of Proceedings and Evidence of the Standing Committee on Indian Affairs and Northern Development Respecting: Bill C-31, An Act to amend the *Indian Act* (Ottawa, 14 March 1985), Issue No. 16, pp. 7–8.

21 Stewart Clatworthy and Anthony H. Smith, "Population Implications of the 1985 Amendments to the Indian Act," research study prepared for the Assembly of First Nations (Ottawa: 1992) pp. vii–viii [emphasis in original].

The Commission believes that the solution to this problem lies in the process of nation building. . . .

As Aboriginal peoples develop and implement self-government, the perspectives of Aboriginal women must guide them. We offer encouragement to the Aboriginal women who came forward to speak to us, and particularly to those who could not. We acknowledge the contributions of Aboriginal women across the country; they have a critical role in providing leadership at the community and nation level. Aboriginal women are the guardians of the values, cultures and traditions of their peoples. They have a vital role in facilitating healing in families and communities. They are anxious to share their wisdom, kindness, honesty and strength with Aboriginal men so that together they can regain the self-confidence and self-esteem needed to rebuild nations governed by wise leaders dedicated to the welfare of their people and the cultural, spiritual and economic viability of their communities.

11.5 *McIvor v. The Registrar, Indian and Northern Affairs Canada,* 2007

In 1989, Sharon McIvor of the Lower Nicola First Nation in British Columbia launched a challenge under the 1982 Charter of Rights and Freedoms arguing that the Indian Act as amended by Bill C-31 still discriminated on the basis of gender. Her grandchildren, the sons of her son Jacob Grismer, were not entitled to be registered under the new rules even though their cousins, who had status Indian grandfathers but otherwise identical First Nations ancestry, were. The federal government appears not to have been interested in bringing the case to trial quickly, and, as a result of the delays it initiated, the trial did not begin at the British Columbia Supreme Court until 2006, 17 years later. Below are excerpts from the court's 2007 "Reasons for Judgment" document in the case.

In-text ellipses as in original.

___

IN THE SUPREME COURT OF BRITISH COLUMBIA

Citation: *McIvor v. The Registrar, Indian and Northern Affairs Canada,* 2007 BCSC 827
Date: 20070608
Docket: A941142
Registry: Vancouver
Between:

Sharon Donna McIvor, Charles Jacob Grismer

Plaintiffs

And

The Registrar, Indian and Northern Affairs Canada,
The Attorney General of Canada

Defendants

Before: The Honourable Madam Justice Ross

Reasons for Judgment

Counsel for the Plaintiffs	Robert W. Grant
	Gwen Brodsky
Counsel for the Defendants	Sarah P. Pike
	Glynis Hart
	Brett C. Marleau
Date and Place of Trial:	October 16 to November 10, 2006
	Vancouver, B.C.

INTRODUCTION

[1] In this action the plaintiffs, Sharon Donna McIvor ("Sharon McIvor"), and her son, Charles Jacob Grismer ("Jacob Grismer"), challenge the constitutional validity of ss. 6(1) and 6(2) of the *Indian Act*, R.S.C. 1985, c. I-5 (the "*1985 Act*"). These provisions deal with entitlement to registration as an Indian, or status as it is frequently termed. The plaintiffs do not challenge any other provisions of the *1985 Act*, and in particular, do not challenge the provisions relating to entitlement to membership in a band.

[2] Under previous versions of the *Indian Act*, the concept of status was linked to band membership and the entitlement to live on reserves. In addition, under previous versions of the *Indian Act*, when an Indian woman married a non-Indian man, she lost her status as an Indian and her children were not entitled to be registered as Indians. By contrast, when an Indian man married a non-Indian woman, both his wife and his children were entitled to registration and all that registration entailed.

[3] For years there were calls for an end to this discrimination. Eventually in 1985, the government introduced and parliament subsequently passed Bill C-31, *An Act to Amend the Indian Act*, S.C. 1985, c. 27 ("*Bill C-31*"). Part of the purpose of the legislation was to eliminate what was acknowledged to be discrimination on the basis of sex from the criteria for registration. Another significant aspect of the amendments introduced as part of *Bill C-31* was that for the first time the issue of eligibility for registration or status was separated from the issue of membership in a band.

[4] The plaintiffs submit that this remedial effort was incomplete and that the registration provisions introduced in *Bill C-31* that form the basis for registration in the *1985 Act* continue to discriminate contrary to ss. 15 and 28 of the *Canadian Charter of Rights and Freedoms* (the "*Charter*"). The plaintiffs submit that the registration provisions continue to prefer descendents who trace their Indian ancestry along the paternal line over those who trace their Indian ancestry along the maternal line.[22] The plaintiffs submit further that the provisions continue to prefer male Indians who married non-Indians and their descendents, over female Indians who married non-Indians and their descendents.

[5] In this action the plaintiffs seek the following relief:

---

22 While "descendants" is the correct spelling, both "descendents" and "descendants" are used in this document.

1. A declaration that section 6 of the *1985 Act* violates section 15(1) of the **Charter** insofar as it discriminates between matrilineal descendants and patrilineal descendants born prior to April 17, 1985, in the conferring of Indian status.

2. A declaration that section 6 of the *1985 Act* violates section 15(1) of the **Charter** insofar as it discriminates between descendants born prior to April 17, 1985, of Indian women who had married non-Indian men, and descendants of Indian men who married non-Indian women.

3. A declaration that section 6 of the *1985 Act* violates section 15(1) of the **Charter** insofar as it discriminates between descendants born prior to April 17, 1985, because they or their ancestors were born out of wedlock.

4. An order that the following words be read in to section 6(1)(a) of the *1985 Act*: "or was born prior to April 17, 1985, and was a direct descendant of such a person".

5. In the alternative:

An order that for the purposes of section 6(1)(a) of the *1985 Act*, section 11(1)(c) and (d) of the **Indian Act**, S.C. 1951, c. 29, as amended (the *"1951 Act"*), in force immediately prior to April 17, 1985 shall be read as though the words "male" and "legitimate" were omitted.

And a further order that for the purposes of section 6(1)(a) of the *1985 Act*, s. 12(1)(b) of the *1951 Act* in force immediately prior to April 17, 1985, shall be read as though it had no force and effect.

6. A declaration that the plaintiffs are entitled to register under s. 6(1)(a) of the *1985 Act*.

7. . . . .

8. An order that the relief granted in this proceeding applies exclusively to registration under section 6 of the *1985 Act* and does not alter sections 11 and 12 of the *1985 Act* or any other provision defining entitlement to Band membership.

. . .

[6] The defendants' response to the plaintiffs' claims can be organized around three principal themes:

(a) granting the relief sought by the plaintiffs would constitute an impermissible retroactive or retrospective application of the **Charter** in that it would require the court to apply the **Charter** to pre-1985 legislation and to amend repealed provisions of prior versions of the **Indian Act**;

(b) the plaintiffs suffered no injury. The only difference between the plaintiffs and Indians entitled to registration pursuant to s. 6(1)(a) of the *1985 Act* is in relation to the status of their children. There is no right to transmit Indian status, which is purely a matter of statute. Accordingly, there has been no denial of the plaintiffs' rights; and

(c) any infringement of the plaintiffs' rights is justified in light of the broad objectives of the 1985 amendments to the **Indian Act** which was a policy decision, made after extensive consultation, balancing the interests of all affected and which is entitled to deference.

[7] For the reasons that follow, I have concluded that the registration provisions contained in s. 6 of the *1985 Act* discriminate on the basis of sex and marital status contrary

to ss. 15 and 28 of the *Charter* and that such discrimination has not been justified by the government. The following conclusions form the crux of my decision:

(a) The plaintiffs' claim, properly understood, requires neither a retroactive nor a retrospective application of the *Charter*. It is rather an application of the *Charter* to the present registration provisions of the *Indian Act*.

(b) Although the concept "Indian" is a creation of government, it has developed into a powerful source of cultural identity for the individual and the Aboriginal community. Like citizenship, both parents and children have an interest in this intangible aspect of Indian status. In particular, parents have an interest in the transmission of this cultural identity to their children.

(c) The registration provisions of the *1985 Act* did not eliminate discrimination. The registration provisions contained in s. 6 continue to prefer descendents who trace their Indian ancestry along the paternal line over those who trace their Indian ancestry along the maternal line and continue to prefer male Indians who married non-Indians and their descendents, over female Indians who married non-Indians and their descendents. This preference constitutes discrimination on the basis of sex and marital status contrary to ss. 15 and 28 of the *Charter*.

(d) This discrimination has not been justified by the government pursuant to s. 1 of the *Charter*. In that regard, as part of the 1985 amendments, the government elected to sever the relationship between status and band membership. Status is now purely a matter between the individual and the state. There are no competing interests. No pressing and substantial objective has been identified with respect to the discriminatory provisions in the registration scheme.

. . .

Conclusion Regarding Discrimination

[288] I have concluded that the registration provisions embodied in s. 6 of the *1985 Act* continue the very discrimination that the amendments were intended to eliminate. The registration provisions of the *1985 Act* continue to prefer descendents who trace their Indian ancestry along the paternal line over those who trace their ancestry through the maternal line. The provisions prefer male Indians and their descendants to female Indians and their descendants. These provisions constitute discrimination, contrary to ss. 15 and 28 of the *Charter* based on the grounds of sex and marital status.

. . .

VIII. *REMEDY*

[343] I have concluded that s. 6 of the *1985 Act* violates s. 15(1) of the *Charter* in that it discriminates between matrilineal and patrilineal descendants born prior to April 17, 1985, in the conferring of Indian status, and discriminates between descendants born prior to April 17, 1985, of Indian women who married non-Indian men, and the descendants of Indian men who married non-Indian women. I have concluded that these provisions are not saved by s. 1.

[344] The final issue is that of remedy.

[345] The defendants seek a suspension of any relief for a period of 24 months. Such a suspension would, in their submission, serve two purposes. First, an immediate declaration of invalidity would "deprive deserving persons of benefits without providing them to the applicant": see *Schacter v. Canada*, [1992] 2 S.C.R. 679 at 715–716. A suspension would enable the registration process to continue and afford Parliament time to seek input from Aboriginal groups in its development and implementation of a scheme consistent with the courts ruling. In this regard, I agree with the defendants' submission with respect to the concern over judicial scrutiny of legislation as expressed in *Hunter v. Southam Inc.*, [1984] 2 S.C.R. 145 at 169 as follows:

> While the courts are guardians of the Constitution and of individuals' rights under it, it is the legislature's responsibility to enact legislation that embodies appropriate safeguards to comply with the Constitution's requirements. It should not fall to the courts to fill in the details that will render legislative lacunae constitutional.

[346] However, further delay for these plaintiffs must be measured against the backdrop of the delays that they have already experienced. The record discloses that from the late 1970's forward, successive governments recognized that the registration provisions discriminated on the basis of sex. It was not until 1985 that legislation was passed to remedy this discrimination, legislation that I have found continued to perpetuate the problem.

[347] Ms. McIvor applied for registration pursuant to the *1985 Act* on September 23, 1985. The Registrar responded some sixteen months later by letter dated February 12, 1987, granting her registration under s. 6(2) and denying registration to Jacob. Ms. McIvor protested the decision by letter dated May 29, 1987. The Registrar confirmed his decision some twenty-one months later by letter dated February 28, 1989. These proceedings were then initiated.

[348] At the time these proceeds came under case management in April 2005, the defendant's position was, and continued to be, that a substantial adjournment was required to afford the Crown sufficient time to prepare. This position was maintained notwithstanding the fact that the statutory appeal had been commenced in 1989 and the claim under the *Charter* in 1994. The defendants also asserted at that time that up to six months would be required for the trial of this action.

[349] The defendant's concession with respect to the plaintiffs' registration status, was made shortly before trial. It was based on an interpretation of the legislation and in my view could have been advanced at any time following the 1989 Decision of the Registrar. Having made the concession, the defendants immediately applied to strike the plaintiffs' claim.

[350] Against this backdrop, I conclude that the plaintiffs should not be told to wait two more years for their remedy.

[351] Plaintiff's counsel submitted that the course adopted in *Benner* should be followed, and that is the approach that I have decided to adopt. It is the intention of these reasons to declare that s. 6 of the *1985 Act* is of no force and effect insofar, and only insofar, as it authorizes the differential treatment of Indian men and Indian women born prior to April 17, 1985, and matrilineal and patrilineal descendants born prior to April 17, 1985, in the conferring of Indian status. The court remains seized of the case in order

to give the parties the opportunity to draft appropriate relief in light of these reasons. Should the parties fail to reach agreement, I will hear further submissions on the issue of remedy.

"Ross J."

11.6 Letter from Sharon McIvor to Members of Parliament, 2010

Following the conclusion of the McIvor case at the BC Supreme Court in 2007, Canada appealed the decision to the BC Court of Appeal. The court of appeal agreed with the BC Supreme Court and gave Canada until 2010 to make further amendments to the Indian Act to bring it in line with the Charter of Rights and Freedoms. Although Canada initially considered appealing this decision as well, it decided instead on a further amendment to the act. The result was Bill C-3. Even though Bill C-3 represented a further improvement, many argued that it still did not fully rectify sex-based inequality in the legislation. In this open letter to Members of Parliament, Sharon McIvor challenges the Conservative government's claims in relation to the bill and outlines some of the amendment's continued discriminatory features. Nonetheless, Bill C-3 came into effect in January 2011.

Reproduced with the permission of Sharon McIvor.

Sharon McIvor to Members of Parliament, 18 May 2010

May 18, 2010

Members of Parliament
House of Commons
Ottawa, Ontario
K1A 0A6

Dear Members of Parliament,

My name is Sharon McIvor. I am a Thompson Indian and a member of the Lower Nicola Band. I am the plaintiff in *McIvor v. Canada*, the section 15 constitutional challenge to the status registration provisions of the *Indian Act*. I am writing today to ask you to vote against Bill C-3, *Gender Equity in Indian Registration Act*.

According to the Honourable Chuck Strahl, Minister of Indian Affairs and Northern Development, Bill C-3 will make about 45,000 people newly eligible for registration as Indians. But Bill C-3 will not end the sex discrimination in the status registration provisions of the *Indian Act*.

In 1989, I decided to challenge the sex discrimination in the registration provisions because, as a woman, I was not treated equally as a transmitter of status, and, as a result, my own children and grandchildren were ineligible for registered status. I also decided to challenge the sex discrimination because I was not unique. Many thousands of other Aboriginal women and their descendants are denied Indian status because of sex discrimination.

Since I began my constitutional challenge, the support has been overwhelming. It has come from every corner: from individual Aboriginal women and their children and grandchildren who have personally thanked me for fighting for them, from national and local Aboriginal organizations, from Bands, from many women's organizations, from unions, and from church groups. Organizations and individuals have raised money to help me, held events to educate themselves and others about the continuing discrimination, and passed resolutions in their organizations to support me.

Now women from Wendake, Quebec are on a 500 kilometer march to support the complete removal of sex discrimination from the registration provisions of the *Indian Act*. So far, they have the support of the Native Women's Association of Canada, the Assembly of First Nations, the Fédération des Femmes du Québec, and Amnesty International (section canadienne-francophone). By the time they reach Ottawa, they are likely to have gathered more support.

Many people in Canada, Aboriginal and non-Aboriginal, know that this is a struggle for justice and that the discrimination against Aboriginal women and their descendants should end.

But Bill C-3 does not end it. Like the 1985 legislation—Bill C-31, Bill C-3 will provide a remedy for some Aboriginal women and their descendants, but continue the discrimination against many more. Bill C-3 will still exclude: 1) grandchildren born prior to September 4, 1951 who are descendants of a status woman who married out; 2) descendants of Indian women who co-parented in common law unions with non-status men; and 3) the illegitimate female children of male Indians. These Aboriginal women and their descendants are only ineligible for registration as Indians because of the entrenched discrimination in the *Indian Act*, which has been fiercely held onto by Canada, despite years of protest and repeated, damning criticisms by United Nations treaty bodies.

Bill C-3 will not even confer equal registration status on those who will be newly eligible. The grandchildren of Indian women who married out will only receive section 6(2) status, and never section 6(1) status. So even those who will be newly entitled to status under Bill C-3 will be treated in a discriminatory way because their Aboriginal ancestor was a woman, not a man. The "second generation cut-off" will apply to the female line descendants a generation earlier than it does to their male line counterparts.

Bill C-3 would benefit my own son and grandchildren. Nonetheless, I ask you to defeat Bill C-3 if it comes to a vote in the House of Commons. It is time for Canada to stop discriminating against Aboriginal women as transmitters of status. The Prime Minister, Stephen Harper, and the Minister of Indian Affairs and Northern Development, Chuck Strahl, should replace Bill C-3 with legislation that will do this, finally and completely.

My own struggle has taken twenty years. Before me, Mary Two-Axe Early, Jeanette Corbière Lavell, Yvonne Bedard, and Sandra Lovelace all fought to end sex discrimination against Aboriginal women in the status registration provisions in the *Indian Act*. It has been about fifty years now. Surely this is long enough.

Please stand for justice and equality for Aboriginal women and their descendants.

Sincerely,
Sharon McIvor

SUGGESTIONS FOR FURTHER READING

For more on the overview and the findings of the 1991 Royal Commission on Aboriginal Peoples, see Canada, Royal Commission on Aboriginal Peoples, *Report of the Royal Commission on Aboriginal Peoples*, chap. 2, "Women's Perspectives" in vol. 4 *Perspectives and Realities* (Ottawa: Communications Group, 1996). This chapter is available on line at http://www.collectionscanada.gc.ca/webarchives/20071124130410/http://www.ainc-inac.gc.ca/ch/rcap/sg/sjm2_e.html. For an overview of Bill C-31 written shortly after its passage, see Native Women's Association of Canada (NWAC), *Guide to Bill C-31: Explanation of the 1985 Amendments to the Indian Act* (Ottawa: NWAC, 1986). This guide is available on line from http://www.nwac.ca/research/nwac-reports. Also available at this link is *Bill C-31 Amendment: An NWAC Literature Review* (Ottawa: NWAC, 2000), NWAC's review of then existing literature and cases heard before Canadian courts related to gender discrimination in the Indian Act. (Expand the link "The Indian Act, Bill C-31" when you get to the NWAC website to access both documents.) For a review of legal challenges related to Indigenous women's rights brought forward under the 1960 Canadian Bill of Rights, the 1982 Canadian Charter of Rights and Freedoms, as well as human rights mechanisms on the international stage, see Sharon McIvor, "Aboriginal Women Unmasked: Using Equality Litigation to Advance Women's Rights," *Canadian Journal of Women & the Law* 16, no. 1 (2004): 106–36. For a video featuring Sharon McIvor speaking about her court case and the issues surrounding it, see The Institute for Feminist Legal Studies at Osgoode, "Watch Sharon McIvor talk about the case that bears her name" at http://ifls.osgoode.yorku.ca/2013/04/watch-sharon-mcivor-talk-about-the-case-that-bears-her-name/. For a discussion of the role of the Indian Act in shaping Indigenous identity and an overview of legislated discrimination by gender and some of the steps taken to resist these constructions, see Bonita Lawrence, *Real Indians and Others: Mixed-Blood Urban Native Peoples and Indigenous Nationhood* (Vancouver: UBC Press, 2004). See especially chapters 1 through 4. For a still important earlier account of the background of some of the issues presented in this chapter, see Kathleen Jamieson, *Indian Women and the Law in Canada: Citizens Minus* (Ottawa: Advisory Council on the Status of Women, 1978).

CHAPTER 12

"ITS INTENTIONS REMAIN HOSTILE"[1]

THE 1982 CONSTITUTION AND CHARTER OF RIGHTS

Following the success of their campaign to cause Pierre Trudeau's government to withdraw its White Paper of 1969, Indigenous organizations sought a more meaningful role in the delivery of services to their communities and continued working to reassert political control and self-governance. At the same time, through the 1970s, Trudeau and his government continued to press for constitutional reform and particularly for a formula that would remove the necessity of gaining the approval of Britain for any constitutional amendment. Because the existing constitution, the British North America Act, was a British statute, it could only be amended by the British Parliament.

Indigenous leaders recognized that any revision of the Constitution had the potential to alter their relationship with Canada and might have an impact on Aboriginal and treaty rights, among other things. As a result, they insisted that they be part of first minister's meetings on constitutional reform and patriation of the Constitution. After their experience with the White Paper, Indigenous representatives were justifiably concerned that Canada would use constitutional reform and patriation as a means to entrench its age-old policy of assimilation. That concern proved well-founded when Indigenous groups were, despite earlier promises, not invited to participate in talks on constitutional change in 1980 and 1981. Instead, the federal government's strategy was to present a plan in which formal consultation with Indigenous organizations would take place only after patriation, when Canada and the provinces had already achieved, between themselves, sole authority to govern Canada. As Indigenous leaders recognized clearly, enshrining rights after patriation would be extremely difficult, as the provinces would have to agree to any amendments that would benefit Indigenous people but might be at the expense of provincial authority.

---

1 Petition by the Indian People of Canada to Her Majesty Queen Elizabeth II, Ottawa, November, 1980. This quotation appears in document 12.2.

The refusal to allow Indigenous people meaningful input prior to reforming and patriating the Constitution was met with resistance and action on both legal and political fronts. For example, legal actions were begun seeking a declaration that the Constitution could not be patriated without Indigenous consent. Petitions were sent to the federal government, to the United Nations, and, as presented in document 12.2 below, to the British monarchy. The "Constitutional Express," was organized to delay patriation and allow time for the consideration of Canada's proposals, to enable Indigenous people to form a coordinated response, and to keep attention on the issues throughout. A sizable delegation boarded trains in Vancouver in November of 1980 and headed for Ottawa. Along the route, additional passengers joined in, and presentations were made in Indigenous communities across the country and to the media. By the time the Constitutional Express arrived in Ottawa to lobby government and to continue to publicize Indigenous concerns, their numbers had grown to several hundred. Some of those involved in the initiative continued on to the United Nations in New York and to Europe, where they visited the Netherlands, Germany, France, Belgium, and England. Indigenous representatives met with political leaders and media personnel to publicize and explain their opposition to patriation and to secure the alliance of similarly minded anti-colonial individuals and groups.

Indigenous representatives also made a submission to the fourth Russell Tribunal, in November of 1980, a selection of which appears below as document 12.1. The Russell Tribunal was an international body originally organized by British philosopher Bertrand Russell in the mid-1960s to investigate war crimes. The 1980 tribunal was held in Rotterdam to investigate the rights of, and aggression against, Indigenous people of the Americas.

All of this had an effect. Document 12.3 below, from the debates of the House of Commons in the United Kingdom in 1982, is indicative of the impact made by Indigenous representatives in Europe. When the Canada Act was proclaimed in April of 1982, it included some recognition of Aboriginal and treaty rights in Section 35 and in Section 15 and 25 of the Charter of Rights and Freedoms, reproduced here in document 12.4. Post-patriation constitutional conferences were also required by Section 37 of the new Constitution, and these were held, but Indigenous organizations were not included as equal participants in a tripartite forum. Rather, they were invited as guests to a conference between provincial premiers and the Government of Canada. In the end, the conferences went nowhere, so reference to the courts continues to be necessary in the attempt to define the specific rights guaranteed by Section 35.

QUESTIONS FOR DISCUSSION

1. What were the specific reasons for the concerns of the Union of British Columbia Indian Chiefs regarding patriation? Were these concerns valid in your view? Why or why not?
2. What reasons were put forward to suggest that the Queen of England should assist Indigenous people in protecting their rights in a new Canadian Constitution?
3. What, according to UK Member of Parliament Bernard Braine, are the reasons for the lack of confidence that Indigenous people had in the Government of Canada?

4. What benefits do Indigenous people gain in the 1982 Constitution? What problems might they encounter?

5. Are there any strategies, either on the part of Canada or of Indigenous people, that you think might have been more effective than the one's indicated here? If so, why do you think that these were not pursued?

12.1 Union of BC Indian Chiefs at the Russell Tribunal, 1980

The Union of BC Indian Chiefs (UBCIC) was formed in November of 1969 when representatives of 144 communities from across British Columbia met at the former Kamloops Indian Residential School. The primary purpose of the gathering was to form a coordinated response to the Trudeau government's White Paper (see Chapter 10). In the end, the White Paper was withdrawn but the UBCIC remained active in its efforts to protect Indigenous families, communities, and cultures through lobbying, awareness raising, information sharing, and capacity building. When the Trudeau Government made known its intention to patriate the Constitution, the UBCIC was one of those organizations that played an important role in attempting to ensure that Indigenous interests would be protected. The 1980 Russell Tribunal on the Rights of the Indians of the Americas provided the UBCIC an international stage upon which to present its concerns.

Source: Union of British Columbia Indian Chiefs, Submission to the Russell Tribunal on the Rights of the Indians of the Americas, November 1980, pp. 45–46, 55–57, 59–60, and 66–70.

Reproduced with the permission of the Union of the British Columbia Indian Chiefs.

Footnotes as in original.

SUBMISSIONS TO THE RUSSELL TRIBUNAL

. . .

Within the context of the Constitution of Canada, Great Britain holds the final legislative power which protects the Indian interests. The protection at present is delicately balanced between federal and provincial jurisdictions through the scheme of the B. N. A. Act and the operation of Section 91 (24) and Section 109. The only method by which the Indian interest might be abolished under the British North America Act would be through an act of the Parliament of Great Britain, patriating the British North America Act to the Dominion of Canada.

From that point onwards it would be solely within the authority of the Governments of Canada to obliterate the jurisdiction. The resolutions proposed by the Parliament of Canada to patriate the Constitution provide no assurance whatsoever that obligations presently owed to the Indian Nations will be respected.

Two centuries ago, Great Britain enabled her colony to be established in Canada by entering into political and legal obligation with the Indian Nations. Now she is being asked to confer final self-government on her former colony. The government of this former colony has never entered into or assumed such obligations with the Indian Nations. It is not conceivable that any sense of justice would allow a former colony to develop to full self-government leaving the original inhabitants severed from their long-standing protector and leaving the federal government with full power to further expropriate Indian land and culture.

Great Britain has legal obligations both to protect the self-determination of our Indian Nations as well as to facilitate the self-determination of Canada. If Great Britain chooses to deny the existence of the Indian Nations to further the self-determination of Canada, they must do so with the consequence of facing the full sanctions of international law.

. . .

C. Federal Government Policy Towards Indians

On a visit to British Columbia in 1876 the Earl of Dufferin, Governor General of Canada, summarized the position of the Crown with respect to the Indian people as follows:

> . . . no government, whether provincial or central, has failed to acknowledge that the original title to the land existed in the Indian tribes and communities [that] have hunted or wandered over them . . . and before we touch an acre we make a treaty with the Chiefs representing the Bands we are dealing with, having agreed upon and paid the stipulated price . . . we enter into possession.

What contrast between these words and those of the present Prime Minister of Canada. In a speech given on August 8, 1969 in Vancouver, British Columbia he said:

> While one of the things the Indian Bands often refer to are there [sic] aboriginal rights and in our policy, the way we propose it, we say we won't recognize aboriginal rights. We will recognize treaty rights. We will recognize forms of contract which have been made with the Indian people by the crown and we will try to bring justice in that area and this will mean that perhaps the treaties shouldn't go on forever. It's inconceivable, I think, that [in] any given society one section of the society have a treaty with the other section of the society. We must be all equal under the laws and we must not sign treaties amongst ourselves and many of these treaties, indeed, would have less and less significance in the future anyhow that things in the past were covered by the treaties like things like so much twine or so much gunpowder and which haven't been paid this must be paid. But I don't think that we should encourage the Indians to feel that their treaties should last forever within Canada so that they will be able to receive their twine or their gunpowder. They should become Canadians as all other Canadians.

With respect to the stated Indian request for a preservation of Aboriginal Rights he commented:

> And our answer—it may not be the right one and it may not be the one which is accepted but it would be up to all of you people to make your minds up and to choose for or against it and to discuss with the Indians—our answer is 'no'.

These words were said on the unveiling of the Federal Government's "New" policy with respect to Indian people. This came to be called the White Paper. It was proposed that the Indian Act be repealed, and that the Provinces take over the "same responsibility for Indians that they have for other citizens in their Provinces".

From the Federal Government's perspective the establishment of a reserve system in Canada had always been viewed as a transitional measure, to be terminated at some time in favour of individual Indian ownership of the land under a Canadian land tenure system. Indeed under the original Indian Act of 1876 it was the governments [sic] intention to survey reserves into individual lots, have Band Councils assign these lots to band members. The Band member could receive a location ticket if he could prove he was "civilized". During a three year probationary period if the Indian could demonstrate he would use the land as a Euro-Canadian might, then he was fully qualified for membership in Canadian society. He would become "enfranchised" and given title to his land. This meant that his special status as an Indian was eradicated, and he could own the land as a white person would, completely contrary to the traditional communal use of the land which had been part of the Indian land tenure system for thousands of years.[2]

As discussed above, this was clearly not the basis upon which the Royal Proclamation was enacted, nor the treaties negotiated pursuant thereto.

While this particular plan for reserves has not been implemented we submit there is abundant evidence that the federal government is ready to end this "transitional" phase and terminate the present reserve system.

As has been stated elsewhere:

> The elimination of reserve lands is termination of status and rights for Indian people. The easiest way to destroy Indian people and their culture is to eliminate the land base. The forced change of status of Indian Governments to that of municipal governments and the change of reserve land status from federal crown land to provincial crown land is a very sure means of termination of Indian rights and status and elimination of a land base.[3]

The only reason that the "White Paper" provisions were not implemente [sic] was that Indian Nations were able to unite solidly across Canada in effect of opposition.

The policy of assimilation has prevailed in Federal thinking for many years. . . .

This policy of assimilating Indian people and expropriating their land and their resources continues to be implemented by the Federal Government to date. In a policy Document #408–79, dated July 20, 1979, entitled "*Native Claims Policy—Comprehensive Claims*", the Government speaks frankly concerning the policy of native claims in Canada. In discussing the number of factors affecting the claims process which have been

---

2 Tobias, John L. "Protection, Civilization, Assimilation: An Outline History of Canada's Indian Policy" the *Western Canadian Journal of Anthropology*, Vol. VI, No. 2, 1976 at page 18.

3 "The Canadian Governments Termination Policy," Marie Smallface Marule, a paper prepared for "One Century Later," the 9th Annual Western Canadian Studies Conference, February 18–19, 1977, at page 12.

identified and which should be considered in dealing with future policy directions, the document states details:

> There has also been a spreading attitude among the native leadership that Indian title, rather than being extinguished, should be confirmed, which has been diametrically opposed to historical federal policy.

In fact, the Indian Nations of today have had the frustrating task of attempting to negotiate outstanding comprehensive claims in a climate where the federal negotiators tell our Indian leaders that Indians have no legal claim to the land, but rather only a moral or political claim.

When the Federal Government decided to support the Alcan Pipeline, the question arose as to interference with the development by Indians asserting their claim to the land. The Government's internal policy document of November 30, 1977 reveals that Indian title will not stand in the way of development:

> A few things are clear. *The Government of Canada is prepared to extinguish native land claims if necessary by legislation to support its international work and commitment but it will only do so in a way which represents the fairest possible settlement to those involved.*

The Government of Canada, in complicity with the provinces, has clearly abused the legislative reign which Great Britain conferred upon it to administer Great Britain's obligations for Indians and lands reserved for Indians. Perhaps the difficulty arises from the fact that Great Britain, having simultaneously conferred measures of self-government on Canada, ceased to monitor Canada's administration. Or perhaps Canada and the provinces, acting in a clear conflict of interest, acted in a high-handed and illegal fashion to strengthen the interest of the Canadian Confederation at the expense of our Indian Nations.

. . .

The Federal Government and Patriation

We all know deeply that the Federal Government policy to terminate Indian status, and reserve land would be fully realized through the patriation of the Canadian constitution. This is not only reasonable in terms of the past conduct of the Federal Government and particularly of the Trudeau Government, but in terms of the proposed Charter of Rights itself.

The only mention of Indian rights is Section 24 of the Charter which states:

> The guarantee in this Charter of certain rights and freedoms shall not be construed as denying the existence of any other right or freedoms that exist in Canada, including and [sic] rights and freedoms that pertain to the native peoples of Canada.

The Charter does not entrench any of the obligations to our Indian Nations. The only direction given is that the Charter shall not be construed as denying the Indian rights and freedoms that exist in Canada.

For over a hundred years now, the Federal and Provincial Governments have refused to recognize that we are the original peoples of this land and have right to the lands and resources and to our Indian Governments. They have minimized wherever possible those legal obligations owed to us and when they have been able to get away with expropriating our lands and resources, they have done so. At the 12th Annual General Assembly of the Union of British Columbia Indian Chiefs held in Vancouver on October 17th., 1980 the present Minister of Indian Affairs was asked specifically if the Federal Government recognized aboriginal rights and if those rights were incorporated in the Charter. The Minister refused to answer this question. Where then, are the protections for the obligations owed to us?

Under the guise of non-discrimination, Section 15 of the Charter states that there shall be equality without regards to race. What will that section do to our Indian people? We fought for over two years to stop the pipeline through northeastern British Columbia because of the damage which the development would do to our people. We were unsuccessful in our fight. We fought hard then to attempt to minimize the impact of the pipeline by working closely with the Northern Pipeline Agency to secure preferential hiring programs for the Indian people in the area. Those programs were scheduled to begin after the date of the proposed patriation. We recently learned that the preferential hiring program[s] are now in danger because of the Federal Government interpretation that such programs would be contrary to the Charter of Rights.

As Sam Michel, one of the elders from the Fountain Band, said earlier in this paper:

> We were the richest people in the world . . . We didn't have a penny in our pocket, but we were the richest people in the world. We had everything: we had game, we had fish, we had everything . . .

Today we are the poorest peoples in Canada suffering more than our share of social breakdown. In a recent report prepared by the Indian and Northern Affairs Canada documenting [the] "Indian Condition" (1980) the following conclusions were made:

(a) The levels of Indian juveniles considered delinquent is almost three times the national rate and is consistent with the high proportion of Indian children in care and the increasing proportion of Indian children living off reserves out of their home communities.

(b) About nine percent of the prison population is Indian compared to three percent share of the national population.

(c) The overall rate of violent deaths for Indians is more than three times the national average.

(d) The life expectancy is lower for Indians.

(e) The labour force statistics reveal massive umeployment [sic] and poverty.

We have had real difficulties trying to survive without adequate control over our lives, our governments, our resources. Matters have been made worse because the governments who do assume control in those areas continue to implement the policy of expropriation and assimilation.

As we see it, non-discrimination is another way for the Government to say to us, assimilation.

Future amendments to the constitution could be done by the Federal Government in conjunction with eight provinces with eighty percent of the population. Unless our national position is protected, there will be a tyranny by the majority over the minority rights of Indian people. We lose the supervisory protection of Her Majesty's Parliament in Britain. We will lose the protections which the Indian Nations derive from our special status and unique position within the Canadian constitution. What we really stand to lose and why we are fighting the patriation with all of our power, is our right as original peoples to continue to live on our land and carry to our future generations the culture and life which our ancestors carried to us.

Our Indian leaders attempted to be included in the constitutional discussions which took place between the Federal Government and the Provincial Governments during the Fall of 1980. Despite repeated requests, and some promises, the participation was effectively denied. The Federal Government has indicated that Indian people will be consulted *after* the patriation. Such consultation is after the fact. The purpose of patriating the constitution has been revealed in the constitutional talks. At the present time, the Provincial and Federal Government are attempting to re-order their relationships to each other and to the resources of the land to create a more workable confederation. Over forty percent of the land in Canada is presently unceded. It is our land and our resources which the Governments are currently dividing among themselves. The Federal Government carries the trust responsibility over Indians and lands reserved for Indians. Yet the Minister of Indian Affairs was not present at any of the constitutional talks as our representative. Nor were our Indian leaders permitted to represent our interests.

In the province of British Columbia, a Master Tuition Agreement exists by which the Federal Government pays to the Provincial Government a sum of money each year to educate our Indian children. For many years Indian people have attempted to change that agreement, and divert our education money to create an education system of our choice for our Indian people. We exerted considerable pressure upon the Federal Government to participate in making changes. We had been repeatedly told that Indian people may participate after the financial arrangement between the Federal and Provincial Government had been concluded. Our leaders refused to participate in discussions on that basis because the essential item of finances would have already been concluded. The decision to allow Indian participation in constitutional talks after patriation parallels the politics experienced in our fight for control of our education. Essentially the Canadian Government has blocked our effective participation.

We seek justice of Great Britain, to honour the Royal Majesty's obligations to us. We feel that patriation should be refused until the position of our Indian Nations within Canada has been resolved to everyone[']s satisfaction.

On Wednesday, November 12th, 1980 Mr. Freeland, legal counsel for the Parliamentary Standing Committee, advising [the] Parliament of Great Britain on the question of the constitution, advised the Committee that Britain did not owe any outstanding obligations to the Indians of Canada. Therefore, his opinion was that no presentation by the Indians should be heard. The Committee proceeded to deliberate as to whether or not the patriation of the constitution could take place without the agreement by the provinces.

The consultation with the provinces assumes that provincial authorities represent in some substantial way the interests of the people within the provincial boundary. However, Indian interests have never been represented by the provinces. Nor for that matter, have our interests ever been adequately represented by the Federal Government.

We have also sought a legal opinion from Professor Ian Brownlie, QC, DCL, FDA, concerning the viability of taking an action through the courts of Britain involving the rights of our Indian people. The opinion concluded that we do not have recourse through the courts of Great Britain.

We are asking this Tribunal to understand the position which we find ourselves in the world today and to lend the weight of your authority to our plea for justice.

12.2 Petition by the Indian People of Canada to Queen Elizabeth II, 1980

Frustrated by the lack of consultation on proposed constitutional changes that would permanently affect their communities and their relationship with Canada, Indigenous activists formed the Constitutional Express, as mentioned in the introduction to this chapter. The petition below was presented by its members to Governor General Edward Schreyer, the British monarchy's representative in Canada. It was one of three similar petitions sent as well to the Canadian government and to the United Nations. In preparing these petitions, Indigenous leaders hoped to apply pressure on Canada to allow Indigenous representation in a broad constitutional review process before patriation. All three of the petitions outline the issues that should form the basis of discussions on constitutional change. The entire text of the petition to Queen Elizabeth II is provided here.

Source: Petition by the Indian People of Canada to Her Majesty Queen Elizabeth II, Ottawa, November 1980.

Reproduced with the permission of the Center for World Indigenous Studies.

PETITION BY THE

INDIAN PEOPLE OF CANADA

TO HER MAJESTY QUEEN ELIZABETH II

DATED at the city of Ottawa,

November 1980.

The Indian Nations of Canada submit this petition to Her Majesty, asking that Her Majesty may graciously bring to the attention of the Parliament of the United Kingdom our most serious objections to the proposals of the Government of Canada to amend the Constitution without due regard having been given to our rightful place in the Canadian Confederation.

We urge Her Majesty to refuse the patriation of the Canadian constitution until agreement is reached between Canada, the United Kingdom and the Indian Nations which will embody in the Constitution those essential obligations, undertakings, and agreements which the British Crown solemnly caused to be made with the Indian Nations of

Canada and those conditions necessary to enable the Indian Nations to achieve self-determination within the Canadian Federation.

The petition of the Indigenous peoples of Canada, shows that:

1. We are the original Nations of Canada. Our ancestors lived in harmony with this land before the arrival of European settlers. We have been given this sacred birthright by the Creator to live in harmony with the Creator on this land through all our generations.

2. When the early settlers arrived in our Indian territory we welcomed those who respected our Sovereignty and treated them with peace and friendship. Those who disrespected our Sovereignty and our territorial boundaries were at war with us.

3. Who were these settlers? We learned that they came under the authority of the Royal Majesty in the United Kingdom and wanted to live in our land and benefit from its riches. Who was the Royal Majesty? We learned that she was the head of a large and powerful family representing a Nation, just as our leaders represented our Indian Nations. Our leaders wanted to make sure that our sovereign nations were dealing with the representatives of another sovereign nation. They asked:

> Is it true you are bringing the Queen's kindness? Is it true you are bringing the Queen's messengers' kindness? Is it true you are going to give my child what he may use? Is it true you are going to give the different Bands the Queen's kindness? Is it true you bring the Queen's hand? Is it true you are bringing the Queen's power?

> *(Qu'Appelle Treaty, 1874)*

And the leaders were told:

> What we have heard yesterday, and you represented yourself, you said the Queen sent you here, the way we understood you as a representative of the Queen. We have understood you yesterday that Her Majesty has given you the same power and authority as she has, to act in this business . . .

> *(Treaty 3, 1873)*

4. We were told that the Royal Majesty had power to protect us and would hold to her promises, we met with her representatives and agreed how our separate Nations would live together. We allowed the Royal Majesty to establish her government and her people in our land on the following terms:

a) Our Sovereignty would always be respected by the Royal Majesty and her subjects.

b) Her Royal Majesty would protect our Indian Nations against harm from other European Nations.

c) Our Indian territories would be protected against settlement by the Royal Majesty's subjects unless we consented to their occupation of our land through Treaty.

d) The Royal Majesty agreed to keep her promise which would bind her government and our Indian Nations forever.

5. Listen now to the promises made by the Royal Majesty's representatives to our Indian Nations:

No government whether provincial or central, has failed to acknowledge that the original title to the land existed in the Indian tribes . . . Before we touch an acre we make a treaty with the Chiefs representing the Bands we are dealing with, having agreed upon and paid the stipulated price . . . we enter into possession.

(Earl of Dufferin, Governor General of Canada, 1876)

The Kings rights with respect to your territory were against the Nations of Europe; . . . But the King never had any rights against you but to such parts of the Country as had been fairly ceded by yourselves with your own free consent by Public convention and sale. How then can it be said that he gave away your lands? So careful was the King of your interests, so fully sensible of your rights, that we would not suffer even his own people to buy your lands, without being sure of your free consent and of ample justice being done you . . . You desire the Kings protection, you desire his power and influence may be exerted to procure you peace and secure your rights.

(Montreal, March 10, 1771 His Excellency Lord Dorchester)

And the King[']s representatives reported to him:

I remark in the first place that the provisions of these treaties must be carried out with the utmost good faith and the nicest exactness. The Indians of Canada have . . . an abiding confidence in the government of the Queen, or the Great Mother, as they style her. This must not, at all hazards, be shaken.

(Lieutenant Governor Morris & Right Honourable Lord of Dufferin, 1880)

6. The promises and obligations of the Royal Majesty were set out in the Royal Proclamation of 1763, and in the treaties negotiated by the Royal Majesties and the Indian Nations. The Royal Proclamation says:

And whereas it is just and reasonable, and essential to Our Interest and the Security of our Colonies, that the several Nations or Tribes of Indians with whom we are connected, and who live under Our Protection should not be molested or disturbed in the Possession of such Parts of Our Dominions and Territories as, not having been ceded to, or purchases by Us, are reserved to them, or any of them as their hunting grounds.

7. The Royal Majesty and the Indian Nations have never consented to change this agreement as set out in the Royal law and treaties. For some of our Indian Nations who made Treaties with the Royal Majesty, as these Treaties continue to bind the Indian Nations, so they continue to bind the Royal Majesty and her government. However, many

of our Indian Nations did not enter into Treaties. Over 40% of the land in Canada is unceded Indian Territory, some of which is being illegally occupied by Her Majesty's subjects.

8. Our confidence has been shaken. We must talk now about the government of Canada. The government of Canada has been entrusted with the administration of Her Majesty's promises to the Indian Nations. Where did Canada get this authority? The jurisdiction to fulfill the obligation to us rests with the United Kingdom. It is through an act of Her Majesty's Parliament in Great Britain that Canada has been delegated to administer the Royal obligation. What has the government of Canada done with this trust? For years the government of Canada has been expropriating our land and re- sources, illegally settling our land and systematically trying to assimilate our people un- dermining the authority of our Indian governments.

We have protested persistently against these expropriations. For example when the Nishga Tribes asserted that their land in British Columbia was illegally claimed by the province Sir James Lougheed, leader of the government in the Senate on June 2, 1920 said:

> If Indians have claims anterior to Confederation or anterior to the creation of
> the two Crown colonies in the province of B.C. they could be adjusted or settled
> by the Imperial authorities. If its claim be a valid one . . . as to the Indian tribes
> of B.C. being entitled to the whole of the lands in British Columbia this govern-
> ment cannot disturb that claim. That claim can still be asserted in the future.

Rather than assisting Indian Nations and realizing their claim the government has passed legislation to assimilate us. In the early 1920s legislation was passed outlawing our spiritual practices. Another law passed in the same period made it illegal to form an association to press land claims. Legislation continues to exist which expropriates our hunting and fishing rights. Even by 1948 in British Columbia and in Canada we couldn't vote in provincial or federal elections if we lived on reserves.

9. In 1969 the Prime Minster of this country said:

> While one of the things the Indian Bands often refer to are their aboriginal
> rights and in our policy the way we propose it, we say we don't recognize ab-
> original rights . . . It's inconceivable I think that in any given society one section
> of the society have a treaty with the other section of the society . . . But I don't
> think that we should encourage the Indians to feel that their treaties should last
> forever within Canada . . .

He said, with respect to the stated Indian request for a preservation of aboriginal rights:

> And our answer—it may not be the right one and it may not be the one which
> is accepted . . . our answer is no.

10. In a submission to the federal Cabinet on Native Claims Policy: Comprehensive Claims dated July 29, 1979, said:

> a) Indian title is to be extinguished for money and certain concessions many of
> which would be of a temporary nature.

b) Any confirmation of Indian title is explicitly rejected as a basis for agreements.

c) Any powers or authority transferred to Indians are to be consistent with non-Indian political institutions, i.e. municipal-type administrations which can be tied later into provincial laws and institutions.

d) The concept of Indian Government, as a way of confirming Indian special status, is explicitly rejected.

e) Provincial participation in negotiating claims settlements is regarded as essential (aside from any legal requirements for this) because one important aim is to shift jurisdiction over Indians to the provinces.

This strategy was basically accepted by the government and is their policy today.

At the 11th Annual General Assembly of the Union of B.C. Indian Chiefs in October, 1979, the Indian Nations Aboriginal Rights Position Paper was accepted, and presented to the federal government. The federal government has chosen not to respond to it in any real manner.

11. The Indian Nations oppose patriation. We know that the federal government's policy to terminate Indian status and reserve land would be fully achieved through patriation. There is no mention of the obligations owed to us in the proposed resolution. We are only mentioned in Section 24 of the Charter which says that the Charter cannot be used to deny our existing rights and freedoms; but the government tells us they do not accept that we have aboriginal rights. Is it that position which is not denied? Our rights are not entrenched in the proposed patriation. After patriation the federal and provincial governments would have the full authority to eliminate the very obligations owed to us and which made Canada possible. Section 15 of the Charter adds to the problem of saying that there shall be equality without regard to race. What will happen to our Indian people? Will our reserves be ended because Indians will be seen to have a preferred position because of race?

12. The government of Canada has refused to listen to what the Indian Nations say about patriation. We have asked to be involved in the constitutional discussions between the federal and provincial governments, and we have been refused. We traveled across this country to appear in front of the Joint Parliamentary Committee on the Constitution to be told that we won't be listened to. Prime Minister Trudeau has deliberately prevented our voice from being heard . . .

It is not possible for the government of Canada to suppress our Indian Nations by refusing to listen to us. Is it possible to think that we will not exist because a government refuses to recognize us? Our Indian Nations existed long before the government of Canada did, and we have survived despite the actual neglect by this government for our physical needs and their efforts to assimilate us.

13. If her Majesty the Queen and her government in Great Britain patriate the Canadian Constitution under the terms proposed by the Federal Government of Canada, Her Majesty the Queen and her government in Great Britain will be participating in breaches of treaty, international law and breaches of international covenants of which both Canada and Great Britain are signatories.

An opportunity exists to elevate the constitutional amendment to an exercise in statesmanship and nation building.

14. This is a course which we would welcome because it offers the possibility of creating a place for us in Canada's federal system consistent with our rights as Indian Nations. We have given long and serious consideration in many assemblies of our people to the ways in which our special status can be integrated into Canada's federal system. We are convinced that this aim can be accomplished without destroying our nationhood or terminating our historical and legal rights. This process, however must take place before the Constitution is amended.

15. We propose that representative of the Indian Nations, Great Britain and Canada enter into internationally supervised discussions outside or [inside] Canada to:

1. Review and define the present roles and responsibilities of all parties involved in the existing "tri-lateral" relationship, including the Indian Nations, the Canadian Government and the British Government.

2. Define in detail the full meaning and extent of the political association between Britain and the Indian Nations in Canada.

3. Define and agree in detail on the full area and boundaries of territories occupied and/or owned by the Indian Nations of Canada.

4. Define in detail the means by which existing and future conflicts may be resolved between an Independent Canada and the Indian Nations.

5. Define and determine the extent and amount of payments owed Indian Nations of Canada by the Canadian Government for lands and natural resources already confiscated or expropriated by the Canadian Government and/or its agents; and agree to the method and terms for payment.

6. Define the terms for political existence between the Indian Nations of Canada and the Canadian Government.

7. Define the equalization payment plan between the Canadian Government and the Indian Nations.

8. Define the alternatives for individual Indian citizenship in addition to their own natural citizenship.

9. Define and agree to the necessary measures to ensure that each Indian Nation can exercise the full measure of self-government, within the Canadian confederation.

10. Define the roles and authorities of the various parties in matters related to fishing, wildlife, religious lands protection, water resource management, and control, use and development of minerals, petroleum resources, timber and other natural resources.

11. Define the terms of a Treaty which will codify the agreements above, as well as define the measures necessary to settle the unresolved lands and other territorial claims.

12. Agree upon the formation of an International Indigenous Trust Council within the United Nations to oversee future relations between indigenous peoples and countries with which they are associated.

16. As the last recourse, we propose to take whatever other measures are necessary to separate Indian Nations permanently from the jurisdiction and control of the Government of Canada, if its intentions remain hostile to our peoples, while insisting upon the fulfillment of the obligations owed to us by Her Majesty the Queen.

We humbly pray that Her Majesty gives serious consideration to this petition which is being submitted on behalf of the Indian Nations, we respect—fully request that our grievances be given an immediate remedy, and in view of the deadlines which the Government of Canada has established, that a response be provided by December 3, 1980.

12.3 United Kingdom House of Commons Debates, 1982

As suggested in the introduction to this chapter, this document from the debates of the House of Commons of the United Kingdom indicates the impact of the efforts of the Constitutional Express in Europe. In 1982, Bernard Braine, the speaker whose words are transcribed here, had been a Conservative Member of Parliament for over three decades and would continue until 1992. In this presentation, Braine explores some of the conditions that led Indigenous people to mistrust Canada's intentions in proposing patriation of the Constitution.

Source: Bernard Braine in United Kingdom, House of Commons, *Debates*, 3 March 1982, vol. 19, col. 313–19.

. . .

SIR BERNARD BRAINE:

So it is that we find a situation where, without the slightest doubt, native treaty and aboriginal rights have been extinguished by the Canadian Parliament. We find a situation in which the Canadian courts have, time after time, been rendered powerless to protect native rights. We find a situation where distinguished Canadian judges have acknowledged the solemn nature of the Crown pledges, the grave and solemn proceedings which have been pursued by the Crown, ever since the issue of the royal proclamation of King George III, when entering into treaties with the Indians for the cession or purchase of their lands. We find a situation in which those judges have been forced to acknowledge also that the Canadian Parliament, by its enactments, has caused the obligations of the Crown towards the native peoples of Canada to be regarded as a "delusive mockery", a "breach of faith", and "deceitful in the highest degree".

So much for past compliance with the Crown's promises to the native peoples which, the Committee will remember, our own distinguished Master of the Rolls has said must never be broken. Alas, once the Bill has left us, there is no way in which we, all honourable men, can say those promises will never be broken. What of the future once the Bill has left us? What will native rights amount to when, at some time in the 1990s, section 49 of schedule B to the Bill has been implemented?

Grave doubts have already been expressed in Committee as to the adequacy of the affirmation of native rights in section 35, of existing native rights—of native rights which may just have survived by the time the Bill comes into force. Perhaps some hon. Members feel that, whatever the errors in the past, the future may be counted upon to bring about something better. Perhaps cases of extinguishment of aboriginal land might simply have been unfortunate errors because the Canadian Parliament did not "expressly direct its attention to the extinguishment of aboriginal titles"; in other words, it was not in its view a matter of much moment. Perhaps in future, to repeat the hope expressed by Mr. Justice Cartwright, the treaties and the royal proclamation will be construed in Canada in such a manner that the honour of the Sovereign will be upheld and the Canadian Parliament will not be made subject to the reproach of having taken away, by unilateral action and without consideration, the rights solemnly given to Indians and their posterity by treaty.

What indications have been given by the Canadian Government of their future intentions towards native rights? Do we have anything tangible to bolster the confidence expressed by the hon. Member for Inverness or to remove the fears so genuinely expressed by the Indians who sought his help? There is considerable information available to guide the Committee in its deliberations on the need for the amendment that I have proposed.

We are fortunate to have on record many statements of policy by the present Prime Minister of Canada. Some of these pronouncements do not restrict themselves to statements of policy. They are frank and reasoned expositions of his political philosophy. On 8 August 1969 Mr. Trudeau spoke in Vancouver on aboriginal and treaty rights. He acknowledged that Canadians had no great cause to be proud of the way in which they had treated the Indian population in the past. What he considered was wrong was that Indians had been set apart as a race. They were not citizens of their provinces as the rest of Canadians were, he said. They got their services from the federal Government rather than from the provincial Governments. They had been set apart in law, and they have been set apart socially too.

The Canadian Prime Minister took the view that Indians were at the crossroads. They could continue having a special status. Other Canadians could go on adding bricks of discrimination around the ghetto in which Indians lived, helping them preserve certain cultural traits and ancestral rights. On the other hand, Indians could become Canadians of full status.

It is of very great importance that I should not misrepresent or exaggerate what the Canadian Prime Minister said on that occasion. He was speaking with the utmost frankness, and we must heed what he said. It is important that the Committee should hear his actual words, if only because this statement of policy, and all the indications of the Canadian Government's native policy which have followed since, have made the blood of Indians and Inuit run cold with apprehension.

Mr. Trudeau, referring to the crossroads that the Indians had reached, said: This is a difficult choice. It must be a very agonising choice to the Indian peoples because, on the one hand, they realise that if they come into the society as total citizens they will be equal under the law but they risk losing certain of their traditions, certain aspects of a culture and perhaps even certain of their basic rights, and this is a very difficult choice for them to make, and I don't think we want to try to force the pace on them any more than we can force it on the rest of Canadians; but here again here is a choice which is in our minds, whether Canadians as a whole want to continue treating the Indian population as something outside, a group of Canadians with which we have treaties, a group of Canadians who have as Indians, many of them claim, aboriginal rights, or whether we will say, well, forget the past and begin today; and this is a tremendously difficult choice, because, if— well one of the things the Indian bands often refer to are their aboriginal rights, and in our policy, the way we propose it, we say we won't recognise aboriginal rights.

I pause there because this was a policy statement, an expression of intent by the man who is likely to be identifying and defining those rights under section 37(2) within 12 months from now. It is a statement, therefore, of the most profound importance to the Committee in considering the need for amendments to section 49.

Mr. Trudeau said: In our policy, the way we propose it, we say we won't recognize aboriginal rights. But then he continued: We will recognise treaty rights. We will recognise forms of contract which have been made with the Indian people by the Crown, and we will try to bring justice in that area and this will mean that perhaps the treaties shouldn't go on for ever.

The Committee should recall Lord Denning's considered view: No Parliament should do anything to lessen the worth of these guarantees. They should be honoured by the Crown in respect of Canada 'so long as the sun rises and the river flows'. That promise must never be broken.

Never be broken? The view of the Prime Minister of Canada is that perhaps the treaties shouldn't go on for ever. Mr. Trudeau amplified this proposition that the treaties should be terminated. He said: It's inconceivable, I think, that in a given society one section of the society have a treaty with the other section of the society. We must all be equal under the laws and we must not sign treaties amongst ourselves and many of these treaties, indeed, would have less and less significance in the future anyhow, but things that in the past were covered by the treaties like things like so much twine or so much gun powder and which haven't been paid, this must be paid. But I don't think that we should encourage the Indians to feel that their treaties should last forever within Canada so that they be able to receive their twine or their gun powder. They should become Canadians as all other Canadians and if they are prosperous and wealthy they will be treated like the prosperous and wealthy and they will be paying taxes for the other Canadians who are not so prosperous and not so wealthy whether they be Indians or English Canadians or French or Maritimers and this is the only basis on which I see our society can develop as equals. But aboriginal rights, this really means saying, 'We were here before you. You came and you took the land from us and perhaps you cheated us by giving us some worthless things in return for vast expanses of land and we want to reopen this question. We want you to preserve our aboriginal rights and to restore them to us'. And our answer—it may not be the right one and may not be one which is accepted but it will be up to all of you people to make your minds up and to choose for or against it and to discuss with the Indians—our answer is 'No'.

I submit that we could not have had the intentions of Mr. Trudeau towards the native peoples of Canada laid barer than that. He is the Prime Minister of Canada; he is the architect and prime mover of the Bill before the Committee today. He looks to a future when the Indian, Metis and Inuit peoples of Canada are Canadians just like all other Canadians—white Canadians, like himself. He has preached with some eloquence a sermon of assimilation.

It will not escape the Committee that Mr. Trudeau was powerless in 1969—indeed, that he has remained powerless to this day—to put into legislative effect the policy of assimilation which he so frankly expounded. It would require changes in the Canadian constitution to bring the policy to fruition. To make the native peoples citizens of the provinces in which they live, to sever the special connections between them and the Canadian Government, acting for the Crown, would have required an amendment to the British North America Act. It would have required the transfer of subsection 24 of section 91 to section 92.

Mr. Trudeau has not been able to do that until now. He will be able to do it, with the support of seven out of 10 provinces, if the Bill goes on our Statute Book unamended.

In the same year, 1969, as Prime Minister Trudeau made the policy speech from which I have quoted, an official statement of the Government of Canada on Indian policy was presented to the Canadian Parliament by the Hon. Jean Chrétien, the Minister of Indian [A]ffairs and Northern Development. It was a more circumspect statement than the Prime Minister's. He paid tribute to the contribution of Indian culture and ancestry both to Canada as a whole and to the Indian peoples themselves, but he also pointed to the crossroads that the native peoples had reached. It was his recommendatiion [sic] that the Indian peoples should leave the road that had existed since confederation and before, the road of different status, a road which, he argued, had led to a blind alley of deprivation and frustration. He pointed to another road for Indians, a road that would lead gradually away from different status to full social, economic and political participation in Canadian life.

Mr. Chrétien argued that the policy of treating Indian people as a race apart should be ended. He said: ["]The tradition of federal responsibility for Indian matters inhibited the development of a proper relationship between the Provinces and the Indian peoples as citizens". He also said: ["]The ultimate aim of removing the specific references to Indians from the Constitution may take some time, but it is a goal to be kept constantly in view["].

Referring to section 91(24) of the British North America Act, which allocated to the federal Government exclusive responsibility for Indians and land reserved for Indians, Mr. Chrétien said—and I ask the Committee to ponder these words: ["]In the long term, removal of the reference in the Constitution would be necessary to end the legal distinction between Indians and other Canadians["].

The native peoples of Canada were far from reassured by that official representation of Prime Minister Trudeau's political philosophy. All that they could rely on was the knowledge that there could be no amendment to section 91(24) without the concurrence of the British Parliament.

Furthermore, there were in Mr. Chrétien's policy statement clear indications that if changes were to be made in Indian status they would be made with Indian consent. But we are considering a Bill here which, drafted and passed by resolution of the Canadian Parliament, does not have the consent of the native peoples of Canada. That is the point. They have not been consulted on matters vital to their continued existence. For that reason above all the Committee must consider the amendments, which would ensure full consultation with native interests and ensure that consent was obtained to any changes in the constitution of Canada which affect the Indians, the Metis and the Inuits.

There is further evidence of this urgent need and this is the last opportunity I shall have to give it to the Committee. Further public references to Indian policy were made after 1969, particularly in 1973 and last November, when the present Minister of Indian Affairs and Northern Development issued a document entitled "In all Fairness—a Native Claims Policy—Comprehensive Claims". These later pronouncements add nothing of significance which can be said to throw any further light on the Canadian Government's intentions towards the native peoples. They do not add to, or subtract from, the approach illustrated by Mr. Trudeau's 1969 speech and Mr. Chrétien's statement.

It has been represented to many of us by Indian representatives that any remaining confidence that their peoples had in the good faith of the Canadian Government was finally and inexorably destroyed when a confidential discussion paper was leaked to Indian interests last year. The paper, sponsored by the Hon. John Munro, Minister for Indian

Affairs and Northern Development, was entitled "Native Claims Policy—Comprehensive Claims". It was dated 5 November 1980, and thus followed upon the decision of Prime Minister Trudeau to proceed unilaterally with the patriation of the Canadian constitution.

As the paper's title suggests, detailed questions of unsettled claims based upon aboriginal rights were discussed. I shall not dwell in any great detail on what this most revealing document contains since many hon. Members who have followed this question in detail have copies in their possession. I shall come rapidly to the central policy decision which this paper recommends and which is vital to our debate on the amendments.

The paper confirmed that it was the policy of the Canadian Government to negotiate the settlement of native land claims "where the Government is satisfied that a lawful obligation exists" [o]r "where native rights based on traditional use and occupancy of the land had not been extinguished by treaty or superseded by law". But Mr. Munro's paper went on to make plain that "the policy did not mean government recognition that Natives owned the land or recognition of native title in legal terms; it was made clear that settlement would only take place in return for whatever interest they might have in the land. In adopting this position the government insisted on a clear and unequivocal legislative extinguishment of all traditional native rights, title and interests, whatever they might be, so that the claim in question could never be raised again, and to remove any possible cloud on the Crown's title that might inhibit the exercise of that title".

It is important at this point to reflect upon the fundamental importance of land rights and land title to the native peoples of Canada. Without a land base of their own, how are these people to benefit from the right to self-determination, the right by virtue of which, in the words of the international civil and political rights covenant, to which both Britain and Canada subscribe, "they freely determine their political status and freely pursue their economic, social and cultural development"?

The answer is given with stark clarity on page 5 of Mr. Munro's confidential discussion paper: the native people's claim to self-determination is to be staunchly resisted. As paragraph 14 states: "one of the most difficult issues encountered in the negotiations has proven to be native demands for future political and administrative structures which would permit varying degrees of 'self-determination' or 'autonomy'. There is also a strong belief among the native leadership that Indian title, rather than being extinguished, should be continued, which is diametrically opposed to existing federal policy".

I emphasise that statement. Is it any wonder these native people are not consulted? Is it any wonder that there are no safeguards for them in the constitution that we are being asked to enact?

Mr. Munro adds, in this revealing paper, that that belief, "together with inflated expectations of what can be obtained through a settlement in monetary compensation, land, and control over resources—as well as political autonomy—has further inhibited progress in reaching agreements". How unsatisfactory that people should trust to the solemn promises and obligations that were entered into in treaties with the Crown! How inconvenient! Let them be brushed aside.

The question that the Committee must consider is this: how is the right of the native peoples of Canada to secure their future as distinct communities within Canada to be protected, when the policy of the federal Canadian Government—to which we are fortunate enough to be privy—seeks to deny them autonomy and the ownership of land?

If we are to comply with our clear duty, we in this Parliament must propose amendments to the legislation for which we, and we alone, are responsible, so as to ensure that we do nothing, in Lord Denning's words, to lessen the worth of the guarantees which the native peoples of Canada have been given by the Crown.

Our amendments to section 49 of schedule B propose, first, that native interests be directly consulted by the Prime Minister of Canada in the course of the constitutional conference which is proposed; and, secondly, that a proper and adequate formula be devised for future amendments to the constitution affecting the native peoples of Canada, a formula that requires their consent.

Our amendment No. 40 proposes that a constitutional conference composed of the Prime Minister of Canada and the duly authorised representatives of the aboriginal peoples of Canada should take place within 15 years after part V comes into force, in order to renew its provisions in its application to the aboriginal peoples. The amendment goes on to define who the duly authorised representatives of those people should be.

I shall not detain the Committee any longer on this amendment and will advance important new arguments later, when I hope to speak on my amendment No. 41. If I have spoken at some length it is because these matters were never properly discussed in Canada, which, in itself, is justification for my comments. It is a sad commentary on the way this Bill has been rushed before us that the issues of native rights have to be discussed here, where we have no power to implement any decisions, and not in the Ottawa Parliament, where the real responsibility lies. By the time we have finished debating the matter here, the message may have reached the Canadian people. I profoundly hope so.

. . .

12.4 The Canada Act, 1982

The Canada Act became Canada's constitution in 1982, replacing the British North America Act of 1867. Included in the act and forming its first part is the Charter of Rights and Freedoms. Because the Charter is part of the Constitution, it applies to provincial and federal laws alike and has a greater scope than the 1960 Bill of Rights. Further, Section 25 of the Charter, although not conferring any new rights for Indigenous peoples, acts as a kind of shield to protect other parts of the Charter from interfering with Indigenous treaty, or other, rights. For example, equality provisions of the Charter cannot be invoked to reduce or annul special rights granted to Indigenous people by treaties or land claims. Section 35 is the only section of the Constitution itself that deals directly with Indigenous peoples. It is important to note that the shields provided by both Section 25 of the Charter and Section 35 of the Constitution are not static but are forward looking and include rights that may be acquired in the future.

Source: The Canada Act, 1982.

PART I

CANADIAN CHARTER OF RIGHTS AND FREEDOMS

Whereas Canada is founded upon principles that recognize the supremacy of God and the rule of law:

. . .

Equality before and under law and equal protection and benefit of law

15. (1) Every individual is equal before and under the law and has the right to the equal protection and equal benefit of the law without discrimination and, in particular, without discrimination based on race, national or ethnic origin, colour, religion, sex, age or mental or physical disability.

Affirmative action programs

(2) Subsection (1) does not preclude any law, program or activity that has as its object the amelioration of conditions of disadvantaged individuals or groups including those that are disadvantaged because of race, national or ethnic origin, colour, religion, sex, age or mental or physical disability.

. . .

General

Aboriginal rights and freedoms not affected by Charter

25. The guarantee in this Charter of certain rights and freedoms shall not be construed so as to abrogate or derogate from any aboriginal, treaty or other rights or freedoms that pertain to the aboriginal peoples of Canada including

(a) any rights or freedoms that have been recognized by the Royal Proclamation of October 7, 1763; and

(b) any rights or freedoms that now exist by way of land claims agreements or may be so acquired.[4]

. . .

PART II

RIGHTS OF THE ABORIGINAL PEOPLES OF CANADA

Recognition of existing aboriginal and treaty rights

35. (1) The existing aboriginal and treaty rights of the aboriginal peoples of Canada are hereby recognized and affirmed.

Definition of "aboriginal peoples of Canada"

(2) In this Act, "aboriginal peoples of Canada" includes the Indian, Inuit and Métis peoples of Canada.

Land claims agreements (3) For greater certainty, in subsection (1) "treaty rights" includes rights that now exist by way of land claims agreements or may be so acquired.

---

4 Paragraph 25(*b*) was repealed and re-enacted by the *Constitution Amendment Proclamation, 1983* (see SI/84–102).

Paragraph 25(*b*) as originally enacted read as follows:

"(b) any rights or freedoms that may be acquired by the aboriginal peoples of Canada by way of land claims settlement."

Aboriginal and treaty rights are guaranteed equally to both sexes

(4) Notwithstanding any other provision of this Act, the aboriginal and treaty rights referred to in subsection (1) are guaranteed equally to male and female persons.[5]

Commitment to participation in constitutional conference

35.1 The government of Canada and the provincial governments are committed to the principle that, before any amendment is made to Class 24 of section 91 of the "*Constitution Act, 1867*", to section 25 of this Act or to this Part,

(*a*) a constitutional conference that includes in its agenda an item relating to the proposed amendment, composed of the Prime Minister of Canada and the first ministers of the provinces, will be convened by the Prime Minister of Canada; and

(*b*) the Prime Minister of Canada will invite representatives of the aboriginal peoples of Canada to participate in the discussions on that item.[6]

. . .

SUGGESTIONS FOR FURTHER READING

For a collection of articles, written from a variety of perspectives, that focus on different aspects of the effects of Section 35 of the 1982 Constitution, see Ardith Walkem and Halie Bruce eds., *Box of Treasures or Empty Box?: Twenty Years of Section 35* (Penticton, BC: Theytus Books, 2003). For an analysis of the Constitutional Express strategy written by Louise Mandell, an attorney directly involved in the events and who represented Indigenous clients in a number of high-profile court cases both before and after 1982, see Louise Mandell, "The Union of British Columbia Indian Chiefs Fights Patriation," *Socialist Studies: A Canadian Annual* 2 (1984): 173–80. For a biography of Chief George Manuel, UBCIC president during the time of the Constitutional Express, see Peter McFarlane, *Brotherhood to Nationhood: George Manuel and the Making of the Modern Indian Movement* (Toronto: Between the Lines, 1993); especially relevant is Chapter 18. The website of the Union of British Columbia Indian Chiefs includes a section on the Constitutional Express, which provides a number of original documents, videos, sound recordings, and material that appeared in Indigenous publications related to the 1982 patriation of the Constitution. Follow the links at http://constitution.ubcic.bc.ca/node/13. For a study of the involvement of the Inuit in constitutional reform, see Simon McInnes, "The Inuit and the Constitutional Process: 1978–1981" in *As Long as the Sun Shines and the Water Flows: A Reader in Canadian Native Studies*, ed. Ian A.L. Getty and Antoine S. Lussier (Vancouver: UBC Press, 1983), 315–39. For a revealing documentary presentation of the constitutional conferences that were mandated by the 1982 Constitution, see Maurice Bulbulian, *Dancing Around the Table* (1987). Both parts of this film are available on line from the National Film Board's website. Part one is at https://www.nfb.ca/film/dancing_around_the_table_1/ and part two is available at https://www.nfb.ca/film/dancing_around_the_table_part_two/.

---

5 Subsections 35(3) and (4) were added by the *Constitution Amendment Proclamation, 1983* (see SI/84–102).
6 Section 35.1 was added by the *Constitution Amendment Proclamation, 1983* (see SI/84–102).

CHAPTER 13

"SECURING 'NECESSARIES'"[1]

THE CONSTITUTION AND THE COURTS

Following the withdrawal of the White Paper in 1971, the federal government began to take land claims more seriously than it had previously. In commenting on the 1973 Calder case concerning Nisga'a title to their ancestral land, in which six of seven Supreme Court of Canada justices ruled that Aboriginal title existed in Canadian law, Prime Minister Pierre Trudeau apparently remarked to a group of Indigenous representatives: "Perhaps you had more legal rights than we thought you did when we did the white paper."[2] By the time of Trudeau's remarks, a number of Indigenous communities had, for example, challenged Canada's somewhat narrow interpretation of treaty provisions and already had Aboriginal rights of various sorts confirmed by the courts.

Canada's new Constitution of 1982 included Section 35, presented in document 12.4 of Chapter 12, which enshrined both existing Aboriginal and treaty rights and those that might be acquired through land claims agreements or future treaties. Many Indigenous activists and their supporters believed that a new era had begun. The Constitution, though, did not define precisely what Aboriginal rights were or what specific treaty provisions meant in a contemporary context. In order to define those rights in local contexts, dozens of cases have been heard at the Supreme Court of Canada and many more at lower courts across the country since 1982.

---

1 *R. v. Marshall*, [1999] 3 S.C.R. 456. The quotation appears in document 13.3.

2 Flora MacDonald quoting P. E. Trudeau cited in J. R. Miller "Great White Father Knows Best" *Native Studies Review* 7, 1, 1991: 38. MacDonald was speaking in the House of Commons. Canada, House of Commons, *Debates*, 11 April 1973 (Ottawa: Queen's Printer, 1973), 3207. In the Nisga'a decision, 6 of 7 Supreme Court justices ruled that Nisga'a had held title to their lands even if three of those argued that their title had been extinguished by Canada's actions during the settlement period.

Presented chronologically below are four high-profile cases that were heard before the Supreme Court of Canada between 1984 and 2003. In the first, *Guerin v. The Queen* from 1984, some substance is given to the rather skeletal provisions of Section 35. The second, *R. v. Sparrow* from 1990, concerns non-treaty Aboriginal rights to a fishery. At issue in the third, the 1991 case *R. v. Marshall*, is the extent and meaning of eighteenth-century treaty provisions. Finally, *R. v. Powley*, heard in 2003, deals with Métis resource rights. In each case, rights were confirmed, but they were also limited.

The courts have tended to define rights somewhat specifically and narrowly so that each individual community has had to defend its right to access each of its resources on an individual basis. For example, if the court recognizes a community's right to harvest salmon, that does not mean that it is then legally permitted to fish for crab. In addition, Indigenous understandings and assessments of the nature of constitutionally protected rights have tended not to be given due consideration by the courts.

Even now, more than three decades after the formal protection of Aboriginal and treaty rights in the Constitution, it is still unclear to what extent the entrenchment of those rights has been a benefit to Indigenous people. Whether inclusion in the Constitution is the best way to protect rights or even whether rights-based arguments and the courts provide the best strategy to employ in the effort to ensure a secure future for Indigenous communities remains a contentious issue. Some point to victories in courts as proof of positive change in Canadian society and in Canada's relations with Indigenous people. Others, though, see the courts as part of a colonial edifice that is not equipped to offer a meaningful transformation of the lives of Indigenous people or of their relations with settler society. Aspects of this debate are occurring at the community and national level and seem unlikely to be resolved in the near future.

QUESTIONS FOR DISCUSSION

1. Why would Canada's Department of Indian Affairs not want to be absolutely transparent in its arrangement of the Musqueam lease?
2. Is it reasonable that Indigenous fisheries should be given priority over others? Why or why not?
3. The authors of a 2003 publication posed a question in the title of their book: *Box of Treasures or Empty Box?*[3] Which of these two do you think is a better metaphor? Why?
4. Should an agreement arranged in the 1760s between First Nations people and representatives of the British Crown continue to be relevant in the twenty-first century? Why or why not?
5. What limitations does the Supreme Court place on Aboriginal and treaty rights in these cases?
6. What constitutes a rights-bearing community?

---

3 Ardith Walkem and Halie Bruce, eds., *Box of Treasures or Empty Box? Twenty Years of Section 35* (Penticton, BC: Theytus Books, 2003).

7. Are the courts the best method to ensure a secure future for Indigenous communities or would some other method be more effective in your view? What other strategies in addition to or instead of reference to the courts might be employed?

DOCUMENTS

13.1 *Guerin v. The Queen*, 1984

This case involved Canada's fiduciary duty, or the trust-like responsibility, that flows from its historic relationship with Indigenous people. In 1957, representatives of the Shaughnessy Golf and Country Club, located in the prestigious Southlands area of Vancouver, wrote to the local Department of Indian Affairs office proposing to lease 162 acres of the 400-acre Musqueam reserve. The department subsequently obtained Musqueam consent for the lease by assuring community members that they would benefit financially from the arrangement. When Musqueam Chief Delbert Guerin was finally given access to the final terms of the agreement in 1970, he found that they were much less favourable than the community had been led to believe and that the lease was arranged at a fraction of market value. The case was originally filed in 1975 and, after winding its way through lower courts and an appeal by Canada, it ended up at the Supreme Court of Canada in 1984. The Supreme Court's discussion of the principle of "fiduciary duty" here became central to later interpretations of Section 35 of the Constitution.

Source: *Guerin v. The Queen*, [1984] 2 S.C.R. 335, pp. 364–71, 375–76, and 388–91.

. . .

DICKSON J.—The question is whether the appellants, the Chief and Councillors of the Musqueam Indian Band, suing on their own behalf and on behalf of all other members of the Band, are entitled to recover damages from the federal Crown in respect of the leasing to a golf club of land on the Musqueam Indian Reserve. Collier J., of the Trial Division of the Federal Court, declared that the Crown was in breach of trust. He assessed damages at $10,000,000. The Federal Court of Appeal allowed a Crown appeal, set aside the judgment of the Trial Division and dismissed the action.

I. *General*

Before adverting to the facts, reference should be made to several of the relevant sections of the *Indian Act*, R.S.C. 1952, c. 149, as amended. Section 18(1) provides in part that reserves shall be held by Her Majesty for the use of the respective Indian Bands for which they were set apart. Generally, lands in a reserve shall not be sold, alienated, leased or otherwise disposed of until they have been surrendered to Her Majesty by the Band for whose use and benefit in common the reserve was set apart (s. 37). A surrender may be absolute or qualified, conditional or unconditional (s. 38(2)). To be valid, a surrender must be made to Her Majesty, assented to by a majority of the electors of the Band, and accepted by the Governor in Council (s. 39(1)).

The gist of the present action is a claim that the federal Crown was in breach of its trust obligations in respect of the leasing of approximately 162 acres of reserve land to the Shaughnessy Heights Golf Club of Vancouver. The Band alleged that a number of the terms and conditions of the lease were different from those disclosed to them before the surrender vote and that some of the lease terms were not disclosed to them at all. The Band also claimed failure on the part of the federal Crown to exercise the requisite degree of care and management as a trustee.

II. The Facts

The Crown does not attack the findings of fact made by the trial judge. The Crown simply says that on those facts no cause of action has been made out. The following summary of the facts derives directly from the judgment at trial. Musqueam Indian Reserve (No. 2) in 1955 contained 416.53 acres, situated within the charter area of the City of Vancouver. The Indian Affairs Branch recognized that the reserve was a valuable one, "the most potentially valuable 400 acres in metropolitan Vancouver today". In 1956 the Shaughnessy Heights Golf Club was interested in obtaining land on the Musqueam Reserve. There were others interested in developing the land, although the Band was never told of the proposals for development.

On April 4, 1957, the President of the golf club wrote to Mr. Anfield, District Superintendent of the Indian Affairs Branch, setting forth a proposal for the lease of 160 acres of the Indian Reserve, the relevant terms of which were as follows:

1. The club was to have the right to construct on the leased area a golf course and country club and such other buildings and facilities as it considered appropriate for its membership.
2. The initial term of the lease was to be for fifteen years commencing May 1, 1957, with the club to have options to extend the term for four successive periods of fifteen years each, giving a maximum term of seventy-five years.
3. The rental for the first fifteen year term was to be $25,000 per annum.
4. The rental for each successive fifteen year period was to be determined by mutual agreement between the Department and the club and failing agreement, by arbitration, but the rental for any of the fifteen year renewal periods was in no event to be increased or decreased by over that payable for the preceding fifteen year period by more than 15% of the initial rent.
5. At any time during the term of the lease, and for a period of up to six months after termination, the club was to have the right to remove any buildings and other structures it had constructed or placed upon the leased area, and any course improvements and facilities.

On April 7, 1957 a Band Council meeting was held. Mr. Anfield presided. The trial judge accepted evidence on behalf of the plaintiffs that not all of the terms of the Shaughnessy proposal were put before the Band Council at the meeting. William Guerin, a Councillor, said copies of the proposal were not given to them; he did not recall any mention of $25,000 per year for rental; he described it as a vague general presentation with reference to fifteen-year periods. Chief Edward Sparrow said he did not recall the golf club proposal being read out in full. At the meeting the Band Council passed a resolution which the trial judge presumed to have been drawn up by Mr. Anfield. The relevant part of the resolution reads:

> That we do approve the leasing of unrequired lands on our Musqueam I.R. 2 and that in connection with the application of the Shaughnessy Golf Club, we do approve the submission to our Musqueam Band of surrender documents for leasing 160 acres approximately as generally outlined on the McGuigan survey in red pencil.

These events followed the Band Council meeting:

(a) Mr. Bethune, Superintendent of Reserves and Trusts of the Indian Affairs Branch, in Ottawa, questioned the adequacy of the $25,000 annual rental for the first fifteen years. At an investment return of 5 to 6 per cent, the annual rental value would be between $40,000 and $48,000 per year for the first fifteen years. The golf club proposal meant an investment return of approximately 3 per cent. Mr. Bethune suggested that the opinion of Mr. Alfred Howell be obtained. Mr. Howell, with the *Veterans Land Act* administration, had earlier made an appraisal of the reserve lands at the request of the Indian Affairs Branch.

(b) On May 16, 1957 Mr. Anfield wrote Mr. Howell asking for the latter's opinion as to whether the $25,000 per year rental for the first fifteen years was "just and equitable". Mr. Howell was not given all the details of the Shaughnessy proposal. He was not told that rent increases would be limited to 15 per cent. Nor was he made aware that the golf club proposed to have the right to remove any buildings or improvements.

(c) In this reply to Mr. Anfield, Mr. Howell expressed the view that a seventy-five-year lease, adjustable over fifteen years and made with a financially sound tenant, eliminated any risk factor. On that basis he felt the then government bond rate of 3.75 per cent was the most that could be expected.

At trial Mr. Howell said that if he had known the improvements would not revert to the Band, he would have recommended a rate of return of 4 to 6 per cent. He expressed shock at the 15 per cent clause. He had assumed that at the end of the initial term the rental could be renegotiated on the basis of "highest and best use" without any limitation on rental increase.

(d) On September 27, 1957 a Band Council meeting was held at the reserve, attended by members of the Band Council, Mr. Anfield, two other officials of the Department of Indian Affairs and representatives of the golf club. Chief Sparrow stipulated for 5 per cent income on the value of 162 acres, amounting to $44,000 per annum. The golf club people balked. They were asked to step outside while the Band Council and the Indian Affairs personnel had a private discussion. Mr. Anfield said the demand of $44,000 was unreasonable. Eventually, the Band Council reluctantly agreed to a figure of $29,000. William Guerin testified the Councillors agreed to $29,000 because they understood the first lease period was to be ten years; subsequent rental negotiations would be every five years; and the Band Council felt it could negotiate for S [sic] per cent of the subsequent values.

Mr. Grant, officer in charge of the Vancouver agency of the Department of Indian Affairs, testified that there was "absolutely no question that the vote was for a specific lease to a specific tenant on specific terms" and that the Band did not give Mr. Anfield "authority to change things around".

(e) On October 6, 1957, a meeting of members of the Band was held at the reserve, the so-called "surrender meeting". The trial judge made these findings: (i) those present assumed or understood the golf club lease would be, aside from the first term, for ten-year periods, not fifteen years; (ii) those present assumed or understood there would be no 15 per cent limitation on rental increases; (iii) the meeting was not told that the golf club had proposed that it should have the right to remove any buildings, structures, course improvements and facilities.

The trial judge found further that two matters which subsequently found their way into the lease were not even put before the surrender meeting. They were not in the original golf club proposal. They first appeared in draft leases, after the meeting. The first of these terms was the method of determining future rents; failing mutual agreement, the matter was to be submitted to arbitration; the new rent would be the fair rent as if the land were still in an uncleared and unimproved condition and used as a golf club. The second term gave the golf club, but not the Crown, the right at the end of each fifteen-year period to terminate the lease on six month's prior notice. These two terms were not subsequently brought before the Band Council or the Band for comment or approval.

The surrender, which was approved by a vote of forty-one to two, gave the land in question to Her Majesty the Queen on the following terms:

> TO HAVE AND TO HOLD the same unto Her said Majesty the Queen, her Heirs and Successors forever in trust to lease the same to such person or persons, and upon such terms as the Government of Canada may deem most conducive to our Welfare and that of our people.
>
> AND upon the further condition that all moneys received from the leasing thereof, shall be credited to our revenue trust account at Ottawa.
>
> AND WE, the said Chief and Councillors of the said Musqueam Band of Indians do on behalf of our people and for ourselves, hereby ratify and confirm, and promise to ratify and confirm, whatever the said Government may do, or cause to be lawfully done, in connection with the leasing thereof.

(f) On December 6, 1957 the surrender of the lands was accepted by the federal Crown by Order-in-Council P.C. 1957–1606, "in order that the lands covered thereby may be leased".

(g) On January 9, 1958, a Band Council meeting was held. A letter was read regarding the proposed golf club lease. The letter indicated the renewal periods were to be fifteen years instead of ten years. Chief Sparrow pointed out that the Band had demanded ten-year periods. William Guerin said the council members were "flabbergasted" to learn about the fifteen-year terms. Guerin testified the Band was told it was "stuck" with the fifteen-year terms. The Band Council then passed a resolution agreeing the first term should be fifteen years, but insisting the renewal periods be ten-year terms.

(h) The lease was signed January 22, 1958. It provided, *inter alia*:

1. The term is for 75 years, unless sooner terminated.

2. The rent for the first 15 years is $29,000 per annum.

3. For the 4 succeeding 15-year periods, annual rent is to be determined by mutual agreement, or failing such agreement, by arbitration

. . . such rent to be equal to the fair rent for the demised premises as if the same were still in an uncleared and unimproved condition [and used as a golf course.]

4. The maximum increase in rent for the second 15-year period (January 1, *1973* to January 1, 1988) is limited to 15% of $29,000, that is $4,350 per annum.

5. The golf club can terminate the lease at the end of any 15-year period by giving 6 months' prior notice.

6. The golf club can at any time during the lease and up to 6 months after termination, remove any buildings or other structures, and any course improvements and facilities.

The Band was not given a copy of the lease, and did not receive one until twelve years later, in March 1970.

(i) Mr. Grant testified that the terms of the lease ultimately entered into bore little resemblance to what was discussed at the surrender meeting. The judge agreed. He found that the majority of those who voted on October 6, 1957 would not have assented to a surrender of the 162 acres if they had known all the terms of the lease of January 22, 1958.

. . .

IV. Fiduciary Relationship

The issue of the Crown's liability was dealt with in the courts below on the basis of the existence or non-existence of a trust. In dealing with the different consequences of a "true" trust, as opposed to a "political" trust, Le Dain J. noted that the Crown could be liable only if it were subject to an "equitable obligation enforceable in a court of law". I have some doubt as to the cogency of the terminology of "higher" and "lower" trusts, but I do agree that the existence of an equitable obligation is the *sine qua non* for liability. Such an obligation is not, however, limited to relationships which can be strictly defined as "trusts". As will presently appear, it is my view that the Crown's obligations *vis-à-vis* the Indians cannot be defined as a trust. That does not, however, mean that the Crown owes no enforceable duty to the Indians in the way in which it deals with Indian land.

In my view, the nature of Indian title and the framework of the statutory scheme established for disposing of Indian land places upon the Crown an equitable obligation, enforceable by the courts, to deal with the land for the benefit of the Indians. This obligation does not amount to a trust in the private law sense. It is rather a fiduciary duty. If, however, the Crown breaches this fiduciary duty it will be liable to the Indians in the same way and to the same extent as if such a trust were in effect.

The fiduciary relationship between the Crown and the Indians has its roots in the concept of aboriginal, native or Indian title. The fact that Indian Bands have a certain interest in lands does not, however, in itself give rise to a fiduciary relationship between the Indians and the Crown. The conclusion that the Crown is a fiduciary depends upon the further proposition that the Indian interest in the land is inalienable except upon surrender to the Crown.

An Indian Band is prohibited from directly transferring its interest to a third party. Any sale or lease of land can only be carried out after a surrender has taken place, with the Crown then acting on the Band's behalf. The Crown first took this responsibility upon itself in the Royal Proclamation of 1763. It is still recognized in the surrender provisions of the *Indian Act*. The surrender requirement, and the responsibility it entails, are the source of a distinct fiduciary obligation owed by the Crown to the Indians. In order to explore the character of this obligation, however, it is first necessary to consider the basis of aboriginal title and the nature of the interest in land which it represents.

. . .

(d) Breach of the Fiduciary Obligation

The trial judge found that the Crown's agents promised the Band to lease the land in question on certain specified terms and then, after surrender, obtained a lease on different terms. The lease obtained was much less valuable. As already mentioned, the surrender document did not make reference to the "oral" terms. I would not wish to say that those terms had nonetheless somehow been incorporated as conditions into the surrender. They were not formally assented to by a majority of the electors of the Band, nor were they accepted by the Governor in Council, as required by subss. 39(1)(b) and (c). I agree with Le Dain J. that there is no merit in the appellants' submission that for purposes of s. 39 a surrender can be considered independently of its terms. This makes no more sense than would a claim that a contract can have an existence which in no way depends on the terms and conditions that comprise it.

Nonetheless, the Crown, in my view, was not empowered by the surrender document to ignore the oral terms which the Band understood would be embodied in the lease. The oral representations form the backdrop against which the Crown's conduct in discharging its fiduciary obligation must be measured. They inform and confine the field of discretion within which the Crown was free to act. After the Crown's agents had induced the Band to surrender its land on the understanding that the land would be leased on certain terms, it would be unconscionable to permit the Crown simply to ignore those terms. When the promised lease proved impossible to obtain, the Crown, instead of proceeding to lease the land on different, unfavourable terms, should have returned to the Band to explain what had occurred and seek the Band's counsel on how to proceed. The existence of such unconscionability is the key to a conclusion that the Crown breached its fiduciary duty. Equity will not countenance unconscionable behaviour in a fiduciary, whose duty is that of utmost loyalty to his principal.

While the existence of the fiduciary obligation which the Crown owes to the Indians is dependent on the nature of the surrender process, the standard of conduct which the obligation imports is both more general and more exacting than the terms of any particular surrender. In the present case the relevant aspect of the required standard of conduct is defined by a principle analogous to that which underlies the doctrine of promissory or equitable estoppel. The Crown cannot promise the Band that it will obtain a lease of the latter's land on certain stated terms, thereby inducing the Band to alter its legal position by surrendering the land, and then simply ignore that promise to the Bands detriment. See. *e.g. Central London Property Trust Ltd. v. High Trees House Ltd.*, [1947] K.B. 130; *Robertson v. Minister of Pensions*, [1949] 1 K.B. 227 (C.A.).

In obtaining without consultation a much less valuable lease than that promised, the Crown breached the fiduciary obligation it owed the Band. It must make good the loss suffered in consequence.

. . .

VII. Measure of Damages

. . .

Reviewing the record it seems apparent that the judge at trial considered all the relevant evidence. His judgment, as I read it, discloses no error in principle. I am content to adopt the *quantum of* damages awarded by the judge, rejecting, as he did, any claim for exemplary or punitive damages.

I would therefore allow the appeal, set aside the judgment in the Federal Court of Appeal and reinstate without variation the trial judge's award, with costs to the present appellants in all courts.

. . .

13.2 *R. v. Sparrow,* 1990

Prior to 1982, Canadian courts ruled that federal legislation could override the fish harvesting rights of Aboriginal peoples. Even after 1982 and Section 35(1), which stated that "The existing Aboriginal and treaty rights of the Aboriginal peoples of Canada are hereby recognized and affirmed," courts of appeal continued to hold that Section 35 rights could still be superseded by federal enactment. This interpretation was possible because the word "existing" was taken to mean that only those rights not previously extinguished by regulation were covered by constitutional protection. In R. v. Sparrow, *the British Columbia Court of Appeal and then the Supreme Court of Canada rejected that view. The Sparrow case was initiated when, in 1984, Ronald Sparrow of the Musqueam in British Columbia was caught fishing on the lower Fraser River using a drift net that violated federal fisheries regulations. This selection comes from the SCC's reasons for judgment in this case. In addition to ruling on the specifics, the court set out what became known as the "Sparrow Test," which sets the standard for identifying the conditions under which non-treaty Aboriginal rights can be infringed upon.*

Source: *R. v. Sparrow,* [1990] 1 S.C.R. 1075.

. . .

The context of this appeal is the alleged violation of the terms of the Musqueam food fishing licence which are dictated by the *Fisheries Act,* R.S.C. 1970, c. F-14, and the regulations under that Act. The issue is whether Parliament's power to regulate fishing is now limited by s. 35(1) of the *Constitution Act, 1982,* and, more specifically, whether the net length restriction in the licence is inconsistent with that provision.

Facts

The appellant, a member of the Musqueam Indian Band, was charged under s. 61(1) of the *Fisheries Act* of the offence of fishing with a drift net longer than that permitted by the terms of the Band's Indian food fishing licence. The fishing which gave rise to the charge took place on May 25, 1984 in Canoe Passage which is part of the area subject to the Band's licence. The licence, which had been issued for a one-year period beginning March 31, 1984, set out a number of restrictions including one that drift nets were to be limited to 25 fathoms in length. The appellant was caught with a net which was 45 fathoms in length. He has throughout admitted the facts alleged to constitute the offence, but has defended the charge on the basis that he was exercising an existing aboriginal right to fish and that the net length restriction contained in the Band's licence is inconsistent with s. 35(1) of the *Constitution Act, 1982* and therefore invalid.

. . .

Analysis

We will address first the meaning of "existing" aboriginal rights and the content and scope of the Musqueam right to fish. We will then turn to the meaning of "recognized and affirmed", and the impact of s. 35(1) on the regulatory power of Parliament.

"Existing"

The word "existing" makes it clear that the rights to which s. 35(1) applies are those that were in existence when the *Constitution Act, 1982* came into effect. This means that extinguished rights are not revived by the *Constitution Act, 1982*.

. . .

Further, an existing aboriginal right cannot be read so as to incorporate the specific manner in which it was regulated before 1982. The notion of freezing existing rights would incorporate into the Constitution a crazy patchwork of regulations. Blair J.A. in *Agawa, supra*, had this to say about the matter, at p. 214:

> Some academic commentators have raised a further problem which cannot be ignored. The **Ontario Fishery Regulations** contained detailed rules which vary for different regions in the province. Among other things, the **Regulations** specify seasons and methods of fishing, species of fish which can be caught and catch limits. Similar detailed provisions apply under the comparable fisheries **Regulations** in force in other provinces. These detailed provisions might be constitutionalized if it were decided that the existing treaty rights referred to in s. 35(1) were those remaining after regulation at the time of the proclamation of the **Constitution Act, 1982**.

As noted by Blair J.A., academic commentary lends support to the conclusion that "existing" means "unextinguished" rather than exercisable at a certain time in history. Professor Slattery, "Understanding Aboriginal Rights" (1987), 66 *Can. Bar Rev.* 727, at pp. 781–82, has observed the following about reading regulations into the rights:

> This approach reads into the Constitution the myriad of regulations affecting the exercise of aboriginal rights, regulations that differed considerably from place to place across the country. It does not permit differentiation between regulations of long-term significance and those enacted to deal with temporary conditions, or between reasonable and unreasonable restrictions. Moreover, it might require that a constitutional amendment be enacted to implement regulations more stringent than those in existence on 17 April 1982. This solution seems unsatisfactory.

. . .

The unsuitability of the approach can also be seen from another perspective. Ninety-one other tribes of Indians, comprising over 20,000 people (compared with 540 Musqueam on the reserve and 100 others off the reserve) obtain their food fish from the Fraser River. Some or all of these bands may have an aboriginal right to fish there. A constitutional patchwork quilt would be created if the constitutional right of these bands were to be determined by the specific regime available to each of those bands in 1982.

Far from being defined according to the regulatory scheme in place in 1982, the phrase "existing aboriginal rights" must be interpreted flexibly so as to permit their evolution over time. To use Professor Slattery's expression, in "Understanding Aboriginal Rights," *supra*, at p. 782, the word "existing" suggests that those rights are "affirmed in a contemporary form rather than in their primeval simplicity and vigour". Clearly, then, an approach to the constitutional guarantee embodied in s. 35(1) which would incorporate "frozen rights" must be rejected.

The Aboriginal Right

We turn now to the aboriginal right at stake in this appeal. The Musqueam Indian Reserve is located on the north shore of the Fraser River close to the mouth of that river and within the limits of the City of Vancouver. There has been a Musqueam village there for hundreds of years. This appeal does not directly concern the reserve or the adjacent waters, but arises out of the Band's right to fish in another area of the Fraser River estuary known as Canoe Passage in the South Arm of the river, some 16 kilometres (about 10 miles) from the reserve. The reserve and those waters are separated by the Vancouver International Airport and the Municipality of Richmond.

The evidence reveals that the Musqueam have lived in the area as an organized society long before the coming of European settlers, and that the taking of salmon was an integral part of their lives and remains so to this day.

. . .

While the trial for a violation of a penal prohibition may not be the most appropriate setting in which to determine the existence of an aboriginal right, and the evidence was not extensive, the correctness of the finding of fact of the trial judge "that Mr. Sparrow was fishing in ancient tribal territory where his ancestors had fished from time immemorial in that part of the mouth of the Fraser River for salmon" is supported by the evidence and was not contested. The existence of the right, the Court of Appeal tells us, was "not the subject of serious dispute". It is not surprising, then, that, taken with other circumstances, that court should find, at p. 320, that "the judgment appealed from was wrong in . . . failing to hold that Sparrow at the relevant time was exercising an existing aboriginal right".

. . .

At bottom, the respondent's argument confuses regulation with extinguishment. That the right is controlled in great detail by the regulations does not mean that the right is thereby extinguished.

. . .

The test of extinguishment to be adopted, in our opinion, is that the Sovereign's intention must be clear and plain if it is to extinguish an aboriginal right.

There is nothing in the *Fisheries Act* or its detailed regulations that demonstrates a clear and plain intention to extinguish the Indian aboriginal right to fish. The fact that express provision permitting the Indians to fish for food may have applied to all Indians and that for an extended period permits were discretionary and issued on an individual rather than a communal basis in no way shows a clear intention to extinguish. These permits were simply a manner of controlling the fisheries, not defining underlying rights.

We would conclude then that the Crown has failed to discharge its burden of proving extinguishment. In our opinion, the Court of Appeal made no mistake in holding that the Indians have an existing aboriginal right to fish in the area where Mr. Sparrow was fishing at the time of the charge. This approach is consistent with ensuring that an aboriginal right should not be defined by incorporating the ways in which it has been regulated in the past.

. . .

"Recognized and Affirmed"

We now turn to the impact of s. 35(1) of the *Constitution Act, 1982* on the regulatory power of Parliament and on the outcome of this appeal specifically.

. . .

For many years, the rights of the Indians to their aboriginal lands—certainly as *legal* rights—were virtually ignored. The leading cases defining Indian rights in the early part of the century were directed at claims supported by the Royal Proclamation or other legal instruments, and even these cases were essentially concerned with settling legislative jurisdiction or the rights of commercial enterprises. For fifty years after the publication of Clement's *The Law of the Canadian Constitution* (3rd ed. 1916), there was a virtual absence of discussion of any kind of Indian rights to land even in academic literature. By the late 1960s, aboriginal claims were not even recognized by the federal government as having any legal status. Thus the *Statement of the Government of Canada on Indian Policy* (1969), although well meaning, contained the assertion (at p. 11) that "aboriginal claims to land . . . are so general and undefined that it is not realistic to think of them as specific claims capable of remedy except through a policy and program that will end injustice to the Indians as members of the Canadian community". In the same general period, the James Bay development by Quebec Hydro was originally initiated without regard to the rights of the Indians who lived there, even though these were expressly protected by a constitutional instrument; see *The Quebec Boundaries Extension Act, 1912*, S.C. 1912, c. 45. It took a number of judicial decisions and notably the *Calder* case in this Court (1973) to prompt a reassessment of the position being taken by government.

. . .

It is clear, then, that s. 35(1) of the *Constitution Act, 1982*, represents the culmination of a long and difficult struggle in both the political forum and the courts for the constitutional recognition of aboriginal rights. The strong representations of native associations and other groups concerned with the welfare of Canada's aboriginal peoples made the adoption of s. 35(1) possible and it is important to note that the provision applies to the Indians, the Inuit and the Métis. Section 35(1), at the least, provides a solid constitutional base upon which subsequent negotiations can take place. It also affords aboriginal peoples constitutional protection against provincial legislative power. We are, of course, aware that this would, in any event, flow from the *Guerin* case, *supra*, but for a proper understanding of the situation, it is essential to remember that the *Guerin* case was decided after the commencement of the *Constitution Act, 1982*. In addition to its effect on aboriginal rights, s. 35(1) clarified other issues regarding the enforcement of treaty rights (see Sanders, "Pre-existing Rights: The Aboriginal Peoples of Canada," in Beaudoin and Ratushny, eds., *The Canadian Charter of Rights and Freedoms*, 2nd ed., especially at p. 730).

In our opinion, the significance of s. 35(1) extends beyond these fundamental effects. Professor Lyon in "An Essay on Constitutional Interpretation" (1988), 26 *Osgoode Hall L.J.* 95, says the following about s. 35(1), at p. 100:

> ... the context of 1982 is surely enough to tell us that this is not just a codification of the case law on aboriginal rights that had accumulated by 1982. Section 35 calls for a just settlement for aboriginal peoples. It renounces the old rules of the game under which the Crown established courts of law and denied those courts the authority to question sovereign claims made by the Crown.

The approach to be taken with respect to interpreting the meaning of s. 35(1) is derived from general principles of constitutional interpretation, principles relating to aboriginal rights, and the purposes behind the constitutional provision itself. Here, we will sketch the framework for an interpretation of "recognized and affirmed" that, in our opinion, gives appropriate weight to the constitutional nature of these words.

. . .

The nature of s. 35(1) itself suggests that it be construed in a purposive way. When the purposes of the affirmation of aboriginal rights are considered, it is clear that a generous, liberal interpretation of the words in the constitutional provision is demanded. When the Court of Appeal below was confronted with the submission that s. 35 has no effect on aboriginal or treaty rights and that it is merely a preamble to the parts of the *Constitution Act, 1982*, which deal with aboriginal rights, it said the following, at p. 322:

> This submission gives no meaning to s. 35. If accepted, it would result in denying its clear statement that existing rights are hereby recognized and affirmed, and would turn that into a mere promise to recognize and affirm those rights sometime in the future. . . . To so construe s. 35(1) would be to ignore its language and the principle that the Constitution should be interpreted in a liberal and remedial way. We cannot accept that that principle applies less strongly to aboriginal rights than to the rights guaranteed by the Charter, particularly having regard to the history and to the approach to interpreting treaties and statutes relating to Indians required by such cases as *Nowegijick v. R.*, [1983] 1 S.C.R. 29. . . .

. . .

In *Guerin*, *supra*, the Musqueam Band surrendered reserve lands to the Crown for lease to a golf club. The terms obtained by the Crown were much less favourable than those approved by the Band at the surrender meeting. This Court found that the Crown owed a fiduciary obligation to the Indians with respect to the lands. The *sui generis* nature of Indian title, and the historic powers and responsibility assumed by the Crown constituted the source of such a fiduciary obligation. In our opinion, *Guerin*, together with *R. v. Taylor and Williams* (1981), 34 O.R. (2d) 360, ground a general guiding principle for s. 35(1). That is, the Government has the responsibility to act in a fiduciary capacity with respect to aboriginal peoples. The relationship between the Government and aboriginals is trust-like, rather than adversarial, and contemporary recognition and affirmation of aboriginal rights must be defined in light of this historic relationship.

We agree with both the British Columbia Court of Appeal below and the Ontario Court of Appeal that the principles outlined above, derived from *Nowegijick*, *Taylor and Williams* and *Guerin*, should guide the interpretation of s. 35(1). As commentators have noted, s. 35(1) is a solemn commitment that must be given meaningful content.

. . .

Section 35(1) and the Regulation of the Fisheries

. . .

To determine whether the fishing rights have been interfered with such as to constitute a *prima facie* infringement of s. 35(1), certain questions must be asked. First, is the limitation unreasonable? Second, does the regulation impose undue hardship? Third, does the regulation deny to the holders of the right their preferred means of exercising that right? The onus of proving a *prima facie* infringement lies on the individual or group challenging the legislation. In relation to the facts of this appeal, the regulation would be found to be a *prima facie* interference if it were found to be an adverse restriction on the Musqueam exercise of their right to fish for food. We wish to note here that the issue does not merely require looking at whether the fish catch has been reduced below that needed for the reasonable food and ceremonial needs of the Musqueam Indians. Rather the test involves asking whether either the purpose or the effect of the restriction on net length unnecessarily infringes the interests protected by the fishing right. If, for example, the Musqueam were forced to spend undue time and money per fish caught or if the net length reduction resulted in a hardship to the Musqueam in catching fish, then the first branch of the s. 35(1) analysis would be met.

If a *prima facie* interference is found, the analysis moves to the issue of justification. This is the test that addresses the question of what constitutes legitimate regulation of a constitutional aboriginal right. The justification analysis would proceed as follows. First, is there a valid legislative objective? Here the court would inquire into whether the objective of Parliament in authorizing the department to enact regulations regarding fisheries is valid. The objective of the department in setting out the particular regulations would also be scrutinized. An objective aimed at preserving s. 35(1) rights by conserving and managing a natural resource, for example, would be valid. Also valid would be objectives purporting to prevent the exercise of s. 35(1) rights that would cause harm to the general populace or to aboriginal peoples themselves, or other objectives found to be compelling and substantial.

The Court of Appeal below held, at p. 331, that regulations could be valid if reasonably justified as "necessary for the proper management and conservation of the resource *or in the public interest"*. (Emphasis added.) We find the "public interest" justification to be so vague as to provide no meaningful guidance and so broad as to be unworkable as a test for the justification of a limitation on constitutional rights.

The justification of conservation and resource management, on the other hand, is surely uncontroversial.

. . .

. . . [I]t is clear that the value of conservation purposes for government legislation and action has long been recognized. Further, the conservation and management of our resources is consistent with aboriginal beliefs and practices, and, indeed, with the enhancement of aboriginal rights.

If a valid legislative objective is found, the analysis proceeds to the second part of the justification issue. Here, we refer back to the guiding interpretive principle derived from *Taylor and Williams* and *Guerin, supra*. That is, the honour of the Crown is at stake in dealings with aboriginal peoples. The special trust relationship and the responsibility of the government vis-à-vis aboriginals must be the first consideration in determining whether the legislation or action in question can be justified.

The problem that arises in assessing the legislation in light of its objective and the responsibility of the Crown is that the pursuit of conservation in a heavily used modern fishery inevitably blurs with the efficient allocation and management of this scarce and valued resource. The nature of the constitutional protection afforded by s. 35(1) in this context demands that there be a link between the question of justification and the allocation of priorities in the fishery. The constitutional recognition and affirmation of aboriginal rights may give rise to conflict with the interests of others given the limited nature of the resource. There is a clear need for guidelines that will resolve the allocational problems that arise regarding the fisheries. We refer to the reasons of Dickson J., as he then was, in *Jack v. The Queen, supra*, for such guidelines.

In *Jack*, the appellants' defence to a charge of fishing for salmon in certain rivers during a prohibited period was based on the alleged constitutional incapacity of Parliament to legislate such as to deny the Indians their right to fish for food. They argued that art. 13 of the *British Columbia Terms of Union* imposed a constitutional limitation on the federal power to regulate. While we recognize that the finding that such a limitation had been imposed was not adopted by the majority of this Court, we point out that this case concerns a different constitutional promise that asks this Court to give a meaningful interpretation to recognition and affirmation. That task requires equally meaningful guidelines responsive to the constitutional priority accorded aboriginal rights. We therefore repeat the following passage from *Jack*, at p. 313:

> Conservation is a valid legislative concern. The appellants concede as much.
> Their concern is in the allocation of the resource after reasonable and necessary
> conservation measures have been recognized and given effect to. They do not
> claim the right to pursue the last living salmon until it is caught. Their position, as I understand it, is one which would give effect to an order of priorities
> of this nature: (i) conservation; (ii) Indian fishing; (iii) non-Indian commercial
> fishing; or (iv) non-Indian sports fishing; the burden of conservation measures
> should not fall primarily upon the Indian fishery.

I agree with the general tenor of this argument. . . . With respect to whatever salmon are to be caught, then priority ought to be given to the Indian fishermen, subject to the practical difficulties occasioned by international waters and the movement of the fish themselves. But any limitation upon Indian fishing that is established for a valid conservation purpose overrides the protection afforded the Indian fishery by art. 13, just as such conservation measures override other taking of fish.

The constitutional nature of the Musqueam food fishing rights means that any allocation of priorities after valid conservation measures have been implemented must give top priority to Indian food fishing. If the objective pertained to conservation, the conservation plan would be scrutinized to assess priorities. While the detailed allocation of maritime resources is a task that must be left to those having expertise in the area, the Indians' food requirements must be met first when that allocation is established. The significance of giving the aboriginal right to fish for food top priority can be described as follows. If, in a given year, conservation needs required a reduction in the number of fish to be caught such that the number equalled the number required for food by the Indians, then all the fish available after conservation would go to the Indians according to the constitutional nature of their fishing right. If, more realistically, there were still fish after the Indian food requirements were met, then the brunt of conservation measures would be borne by the practices of sport fishing and commercial fishing.

. . .

We acknowledge the fact that the justificatory standard to be met may place a heavy burden on the Crown. However, government policy with respect to the British Columbia fishery, regardless of s. 35(1), already dictates that, in allocating the right to take fish, Indian food fishing is to be given priority over the interests of other user groups. The constitutional entitlement embodied in s. 35(1) requires the Crown to ensure that its regulations are in keeping with that allocation of priority. The objective of this requirement is not to undermine Parliament's ability and responsibility with respect to creating and administering overall conservation and management plans regarding the salmon fishery. The objective is rather to guarantee that those plans treat aboriginal peoples in a way ensuring that their rights are taken seriously.

. . .

Application to this Case—Is the Net Length Restriction Valid?

The Court of Appeal below found that there was not sufficient evidence in this case to proceed with an analysis of s. 35(1) with respect to the right to fish for food. In reviewing the competing expert evidence, and recognizing that fish stock management is an uncertain science, it decided that the issues at stake in this appeal were not well adapted to being resolved at the appellate court level.

. . .

According to the Court of Appeal, the findings of fact were insufficient to lead to an acquittal. There was no more evidence before this Court. We also would order a re-trial which would allow findings of fact according to the tests set out in these reasons.

The appellant would bear the burden of showing that the net length restriction constituted a *prima facie* infringement of the collective aboriginal right to fish for food. If an infringement were found, the onus would shift to the Crown which would have to demonstrate that the regulation is justifiable. To that end, the Crown would have to show that there is no underlying unconstitutional objective such as shifting more of the resource to a user group that ranks below the Musqueam. Further, it would have to show that the regulation sought to be imposed is required to accomplish the needed limitation. In trying to show that the restriction is necessary in the circumstances of the Fraser River fishery, the Crown could use facts pertaining to fishing by other Fraser River Indians.

In conclusion, we would dismiss the appeal and the cross-appeal and affirm the Court of Appeal's setting aside of the conviction. We would accordingly affirm the order for a new trial on the questions of infringement and whether any infringement is nonetheless consistent with s. 35(1), in accordance with the interpretation set out here.

For the reasons given above, the constitutional question must be answered as follows:

Question Is the net length restriction contained in the Musqueam Indian Band Indian Food Fishing Licence dated March 30, 1984, issued pursuant to the *British Columbia Fishery (General) Regulations* and the *Fisheries Act*, R.S.C. 1970, c. F-14, inconsistent with s. 35(1) of the *Constitution Act, 1982*?

Answer This question will have to be sent back to trial to be answered according to the analysis set out in these reasons.

13.3 *R. v. Marshall*, 1999

In 1971, Donald Marshall, a 17-year-old Mi'kmaq youth from the Membertou First Nation of Cape Breton Island and son of a long-serving Mi'kmaq grand chief, was arrested and convicted of the murder of another 17-year-old young man in Sydney, Nova Scotia. After serving 11 years in prison, Marshall was finally exonerated. The subsequent royal commission set up to investigate the wrongful conviction found a justice system littered with racially based discrimination against both Indigenous people and Blacks. As Marshall struggled to put his life back together, his experience became an analogy for the systemic racism embedded in Canada's legal system.

In 1996, Marshall once again found himself in the spotlight when he was charged with selling 210 kilograms of eels without a licence and contrary to federal fishing regulations. Marshall argued that his right to fish was guaranteed by mid-eighteenth-century treaties between the Mi'kmaq and the British Crown. The lower courts ruled that there was no such right to trade embodied in the treaties, so Marshall appealed to the Supreme Court of Canada. The Supreme Court's findings are excerpted here.

There was considerable opposition to the decision by some groups of non-Indigenous fishers and those opposed to the acknowledgement of Indigenous peoples' special rights more generally. Two months after its initial decision, the Court decided to take the very unusual step of issuing what it called a "clarification" of its original decision. The clarification confirmed that the Crown retained the right to regulate the fishery, provided its limitation of "the exercise of a treaty right can be justified on conservation or other grounds." [4] *It also noted that its decision was much narrower than some believed and that it was specific to this resource, eels, only. Other resources and other communities would have to await future court challenges.*

Source: *R. v. Marshall*, [1999] 3 S.C.R. 456.

Analysis

(5) The starting point for the analysis of the alleged treaty right must be an examination of the specific words used in any written memorandum of its terms. In this case, the task is complicated by the fact the British signed a series of agreements with individual Mi'kmaq communities in 1760 and 1761 intending to have them consolidated into a comprehensive Mi'kmaq treaty that was never in fact brought into existence. The trial judge, Embree Prov. Ct. J., found that by the end of 1761 all of the Mi'kmaq villages in Nova Scotia had entered into separate but similar treaties. Some of these documents are missing. Despite some variations among some of the documents, Embree Prov. Ct. J. was satisfied that the written terms applicable to this dispute were contained in a Treaty of Peace and Friendship entered into by Governor Charles Lawrence on March 10, 1760, which . . . [in part] provides as follows:

> Treaty of Peace and Friendship concluded by [His Excellency Charles Lawrence] Esq. Govr and Comr. in Chief in and over his Majesty's Province of Nova Scotia or Accadia with Paul Laurent chief of the LaHave tribe of Indians at Halifax in the Province of N.S. or Acadia.
>
> . . .
>
> And I do further promise for myself and my tribe that we will not either directly nor indirectly assist any of the enemies of His most sacred Majesty King George the Second, his heirs or Successors, nor hold any manner of Commerce traffick nor intercourse with them, but on the contrary will as much as may be in our power discover and make known to His Majesty's Governor, any ill designs which may be formed or contrived against His Majesty's subjects. And I do further engage that we will not traffick, barter or Exchange any Commodities in any manner but with such persons or the managers of such Truck houses as shall be appointed or *Established by His Majesty's Governor at Lunenbourg or Elsewhere in Nova Scotia or Accadia.*
>
> . . .

---

4 *R. v. Marshall* [1999] 3 S.C.R. 533.

(6) The underlined portion of the document, the so-called "trade clause", is framed in negative terms as a restraint on the ability of the Mi'kmaq to trade with non-government individuals. A "truckhouse" was a type of trading post. The evidence showed that the promised government truckhouses disappeared from Nova Scotia within a few years and by 1780 a replacement regime of government licensed traders had also fallen into disuse while the British Crown was attending to the American Revolution. The trial judge, Embree Prov. Ct. J., rejected the Crown's argument that the trade clause amounted to nothing more than a negative covenant. He found, at para. 116, that it reflected a grant to the Mi'kmaq of the positive right to "bring the products of their hunting, fishing and gathering to a truckhouse to trade". The Court of Appeal ((1997), 159 N.S.R. (2d) 186) found that the trial judge misspoke when he used the word "right". It held that the trade clause does not grant the Mi'kmaq any rights. Instead, the trade clause represented a "mechanism imposed upon them to help ensure that the peace was a lasting one, by obviating their need to trade with enemies of the British" (p. 208). When the truckhouses disappeared, said the court, so did any vestiges of the restriction or entitlement, and that was the end of it.

(7) The appellant's position is that the truckhouse provision not only incorporated the alleged right to trade, but also the right to pursue traditional hunting, fishing and gathering activities in support of that trade. It seems clear that the words of the March 10, 1760 document, standing in isolation, do not support the appellant's argument. The question is whether the underlying negotiations produced a broader agreement between the British and the Mi'kmaq, memorialized only in part by the Treaty of Peace and Friendship, that would protect the appellant's activities that are the subject of the prosecution. I should say at the outset that the appellant overstates his case. In my view, the treaty rights are limited to securing "necessaries" (which I construe in the modern context, as equivalent to a moderate livelihood), and do not extend to the open-ended accumulation of wealth. The rights thus construed, however, are, in my opinion, treaty rights within the meaning of s. 35 of the *Constitution Act, 1982*, and are subject to regulations that can be justified under the *Badger* test (*R. v. Badger*, [1996] 1 S.C.R 771).

. . .

Evidentiary Sources

(9) The Court of Appeal took a strict approach to the use of extrinsic evidence when interpreting the Treaties of 1760–61. Roscoe and Bateman JJ.A. stated at p. 194: "While treaties must be interpreted in their historical context, extrinsic evidence cannot be used as an aid to interpretation, in the absence of ambiguity". I think this approach should be rejected for at least three reasons.

(10) Firstly, even in a modern commercial context, extrinsic evidence is available to show that a written document does not include all of the terms of an agreement. Rules of interpretation in contract law are in general more strict than those applicable to treaties, yet Professor Waddams states in *The Law of Contracts* (3rd ed. 1993), at para. 316:

> The parol evidence rule does not purport to exclude evidence designed to show whether or not the agreement has been "reduced to writing", or whether it was, or was not, the intention of the parties that it should be the exclusive record of

their agreement. Proof of this question is a pre-condition to the operation of the rule, and all relevant evidence is admissible on it. This is the view taken by Corbin and other writers, and followed in the Second Restatement.

. . .

(11) Secondly, even in the context of a treaty document that purports to contain all of the terms, this Court has made clear in recent cases that extrinsic evidence of the historical and cultural context of a treaty may be received even absent any ambiguity on the face of the treaty. MacKinnon A.C.J.O. laid down the principle in *Taylor and Williams, supra*, at p. 236:

> . . . if there is evidence by conduct or otherwise as to how the parties understood the terms of the treaty, then such understanding and practice is of assistance in giving content to the term or terms.

The proposition is cited with approval in *Delgamuukw v. British Columbia*, [1997] 3 S.C.R. 1010, at para. 87, and *R. v. Sioui*, [1990] 1 S.C.R. 1025, at p. 1045.

(12) Thirdly, where a treaty was concluded verbally and afterwards written up by representatives of the Crown, it would be unconscionable for the Crown to ignore the oral terms while relying on the written terms, *per* Dickson J. (as he then was) in *Guerin v. The Queen*, [1984] 2 S.C.R. 335. Dickson J. stated for the majority, at p. 388:

> Nonetheless, the Crown, in my view, was not empowered by the surrender document to ignore the oral terms which the Band understood would be embodied in the lease. The oral representations form the backdrop against which the Crown's conduct in discharging its fiduciary obligation must be measured. They inform and confine the field of discretion within which the Crown was free to act. After the Crown's agents had induced the Band to surrender its land on the understanding that the land would be leased on certain terms, it would be unconscionable to permit the Crown simply to ignore those terms.

The *Guerin* case is a strong authority in this respect because the surrender there could only be accepted by the Governor in Council, who was not made aware of any oral terms. The surrender could *not* have been accepted by the departmental officials who were present when the Musqueam made known their conditions. Nevertheless, the Governor in Council was held bound by the oral terms which "the Band understood would be embodied in the lease" (p. 388). In this case, unlike *Guerin*, the Governor did have authority to bind the Crown and was present when the aboriginal leaders made known their terms.

. . .

(14) . . . as more recently discussed by Cory J., in *Badger, supra*, at para. 52:

> . . . when considering a treaty, a court must take into account the context in which the treaties were negotiated, concluded and committed to writing. The treaties, as written documents, recorded an agreement that had already been reached orally and they did not always record the full extent of the oral agreement. . . . As a result, it is well settled that the words in the treaty must not

be interpreted *in their strict technical sense nor subjected to rigid modern rules of construction.* [Emphasis added.]

"Generous" rules of interpretation should not be confused with a vague sense of after-the-fact largesse. The special rules are dictated by the special difficulties of ascertaining what in fact was agreed to. The Indian parties did not, for all practical purposes, have the opportunity to create their own written record of the negotiations. Certain assumptions are therefore made about the Crown's approach to treaty making (honourable) which the Court acts upon in its approach to treaty interpretation (flexible) as to the existence of a treaty (*Sioui, supra,* at p. 1049), the completeness of any written record (the use, e.g., of context and implied terms to make honourable sense of the treaty arrangement: *Simon v. The Queen,* [1985] 2 S.C.R. 387, and *R. v. Sundown,* [1999] 1 S.C.R. 393), and the interpretation of treaty terms once found to exist (*Badger*). The bottom line is the Court's obligation . . . to "choose from among the various possible interpretations of the *common* intention [at the time the treaty was made] the one which best reconciles" the Mi'kmaq interests and those of the British Crown (*Sioui, per* Lamer J., at p. 1069 (emphasis added)).

. . .

The 1760 Negotiations

(22) I propose to review briefly the documentary record to emphasize and amplify certain aspects of the trial judge's findings. . . .

(i) The Documentary Record

(23) I take the following points from the matters particularly emphasized by the trial judge at para. 90 following his thorough review of the historical background:

1. The 1760–61 treaties were the culmination of more than a decade of intermittent hostilities between the British and the Mi'kmaq. Hostilities with the French were also prevalent in Nova Scotia throughout the 1750's, and the Mi'kmaq were constantly allied with the French against the British.

2. The use of firearms for hunting had an important impact on Mi'kmaq society. The Mi'kmaq remained dependant on others for gun powder and the primary sources of that were the French, Acadians and the British.

3. The French frequently supplied the Mi'kmaq with food and European trade goods. By the mid-18th century, the Mi'kmaq were accustomed to, and in some cases relied on, receiving various European trade goods [including shot, gun powder, metal tools, clothing cloth, blankets and many other things].

   . . .

6. The British wanted peace and a safe environment for their current and future settlers. Despite their recent victories, they did not feel completely secure in Nova Scotia.

. . .

(25) . . . It is apparent that the British saw the Mi'kmaq trade issue in terms of peace, as the Crown expert Dr. Stephen Patterson testified, "people who trade together do not

fight, that was the theory". Peace was bound up with the ability of the Mi'kmaq people to sustain themselves economically. Starvation breeds discontent. The British certainly did not want the Mi'kmaq to become an unnecessary drain on the public purse of the colony of Nova Scotia or of the Imperial purse in London, as the trial judge found. To avoid such a result, it became necessary to protect the traditional Mi'kmaq economy, including hunting, gathering and fishing. A comparable policy was pursued at a later date on the west coast where, as Dickson J. commented in *Jack v. The Queen*, [1980] 1 S.C.R. 294, at p. 311:

> What is plain from the pre-Confederation period is that the Indian fishermen were encouraged to engage in their occupation and to do so for both food and barter purposes.

The same strategy of economic aboriginal self-sufficiency was pursued across the prairies in terms of hunting: see *R. v. Horseman*, [1990] 1 S.C.R. 901, *per* Wilson J., at p. 919, and Cory J., at p. 928.

. . .

(30) It is true, as my colleague points out at para. 97, that the British made it clear from the outset that the Mi'kmaq were not to have any commerce with "any of His Majesty's Enemies". A Treaty of Peace and Friendship could not be otherwise. The subject of trading with the British government as distinguished from British settlers, however, did not arise until after the Indians had first requested truckhouses. The limitation to government trade came as a response to the request for truckhouses, not the other way around.

(31) At a meeting of the Governor's Council on February 16, 1760 (less than a week later), the Council and the representatives of the Indians proceeded to settle the prices of various articles of merchandise including beaver, marten, otter, mink, fox, moose, deer, ermine and bird feathers, etc. Prices of "necessaries" for purchase at the truckhouse were also agreed, e.g., one pound of spring beaver could purchase 30 pounds of flour or 14 pounds of pork. The British took a liberal view of "necessaries". Two gallons of rum cost one pound of spring beaver pelts. The oral agreement on a price list was reflected in an Order in Council dated February 23, 1760, which provided "[t]hat the Prizes of all other kinds of Merchandize not mention'd herein be Regulated according to the Rates of the Foregoing articles". At trial the Crown expert and the defence experts agreed that fish could be among the items that the Mi'kmaq would trade.

(32) In furtherance of this trade arrangement, the British established six truckhouses following the signing of the treaties in 1760 and 1761, including Chignecto, Lunenburg, St. John, Windsor, Annapolis and "the Eastern Battery" along the coast from Halifax. The existence of advantageous terms at the truckhouses was part of an imperial peace strategy. As Governor Lawrence wrote to the Board of Trade on May 11, 1760, "the greatest advantage from this [trade] Article . . . is the friendship of these Indians". The British were concerned that matters might again become "troublesome" if the Mi'kmaq were subjected to the "pernicious practices" of "unscrupulous traders". The cost to the public purse of Nova Scotia of supporting Mi'kmaq trade was an investment in peace and the promotion of ongoing colonial settlement. The strategy would be effective only

if the Mi'kmaq had access *both* to trade *and* to the fish and wildlife resources necessary to provide them with something to trade.

. . .

(35) In my view, all of this evidence, reflected in the trial judgment, demonstrates the inadequacy and incompleteness of the written memorial of the treaty terms by selectively isolating the restrictive trade covenant. Indeed, the truckhouse system offered such advantageous terms that it hardly seems likely that Mi'kmaq traders had to be compelled to buy at lower prices and sell at higher prices. At a later date, they objected when truckhouses were abandoned. The trade clause would not have advanced British objectives (peaceful relations with a self-sufficient Mi'kmaq people) or Mi'kmaq objectives (access to the European "necessaries" on which they had come to rely) unless the Mi'kmaq were assured at the same time of continuing access, implicitly or explicitly, to wildlife to trade. This was confirmed by the expert historian called by the Crown, as set out below.

. . .

(40) In my view, the Nova Scotia judgments erred in concluding that the only enforceable treaty obligations were those set out in the written document of March 10, 1760, whether construed flexibly (as did the trial judge) or narrowly (as did the Nova Scotia Court of Appeal). The findings of fact made by the trial judge taken as a whole demonstrate that the concept of a disappearing treaty right does justice neither to the honour of the Crown nor to the reasonable expectations of the Mi'kmaq people. It is their common intention in 1760—not just the terms of the March 10, 1760 document—to which effect must be given.

Ascertaining the Terms of the Treaty

(41) Having concluded that the written text is incomplete, it is necessary to ascertain the treaty terms not only by reference to the fragmentary historical record, as interpreted by the expert historians, but also in light of the stated objectives of the British and Mi'kmaq in 1760 and the political and economic context in which those objectives were reconciled.

(42) I mentioned earlier that the Nova Scotia Court of Appeal has held on several occasions that the "peace and friendship" treaties with the Mi'kmaq did not extinguish aboriginal hunting and fishing rights in Nova Scotia. . . . We are not here concerned with the exercise of such a right. The appellant asserts the right of Mi'kmaq people to catch fish and wildlife in support of trade as an *alternative* or supplementary method of obtaining necessaries. The right to fish is not mentioned in the March 10, 1760 document, nor is it expressly noted elsewhere in the records of the negotiation put in evidence. This is not surprising. As Dickson J. mentioned with reference to the west coast in *Jack, supra,* at p. 311, in colonial times the perception of the fishery resource was one of "limitless proportions".

(43) The law has long recognized that parties make assumptions when they enter into agreements about certain things that give their arrangements efficacy. Courts will imply a contractual term on the basis of presumed intentions of the parties where it is necessary to assure the efficacy of the contract, e.g., where it meets the "officious

bystander test".... Here, if the ubiquitous officious bystander had said, "This talk about truckhouses is all very well, but if the Mi'kmaq are to make these promises, will they have the right to hunt and fish to catch something to trade at the truckhouses?", the answer would have to be, having regard to the honour of the Crown, "of course". If the law is prepared to supply the deficiencies of written contracts prepared by sophisticated parties and their legal advisors in order to produce a sensible result that accords with the intent of both parties, though unexpressed, the law cannot ask less of the honour and dignity of the Crown in its dealings with First Nations....

. . .

(48) Until enactment of the *Constitution Act, 1982*, the treaty rights of aboriginal peoples could be overridden by competent legislation as easily as could the rights and liberties of other inhabitants. The hedge offered no special protection, as the aboriginal people learned in earlier hunting cases such as *Sikyea v. The Queen*, [1964] S.C.R. 642, and *R. v. George*, [1966] S.C.R. 267. On April 17, 1982, however, this particular type of "hedge" was converted by s. 35(1) into sterner stuff that could only be broken down when justified according to the test laid down in *R. v. Sparrow*, [1990] 1 S.C.R. 1075, at pp. 1112 *et seq.*, as adapted to apply to treaties in *Badger, supra, per* Cory J., at paras. 75 *et seq.* See also *R. v. Bombay*, [1993] 1 C.N.L.R. 92 (Ont. C.A.).

. . .

The Honour of the Crown

(49) This appeal puts to the test the principle, emphasized by this Court on several occasions, that the honour of the Crown is always at stake in its dealings with aboriginal people. This is one of the principles of interpretation set forth in *Badger, supra*, by Cory J., at para. 41:

> . . . the honour of the Crown is always at stake in its dealings with Indian peo-ple. Interpretations of treaties and statutory provisions which have an impact upon treaty or aboriginal rights must be approached in a manner which main-tains the integrity of the Crown. It is always assumed that the Crown intends to fulfil its promises. No appearance of "sharp dealing" will be sanctioned.

. . .

(52) I do not think an interpretation of events that turns a positive Mi'kmaq trade demand into a negative Mi'kmaq covenant is consistent with the honour and integrity of the Crown. Nor is it consistent to conclude that the Lieutenant Governor, seeking in good faith to address the trade demands of the Mi'kmaq, accepted the Mi'kmaq sugges-tion of a trading facility while denying any treaty protection to Mi'kmaq access to the things that were to be traded, even though these things were identified and priced in the treaty negotiations. This was not a commercial contract. The trade arrangement must be interpreted in a manner which gives meaning and substance to the promises made by the Crown. In my view, with respect, the interpretation adopted by the courts below left the Mi'kmaq with an empty shell of a treaty promise.

. . .

(57) The Crown expresses the concern that recognition of the existence of a constitutionally entrenched right with, as here, a trading aspect, would open the floodgates to uncontrollable and excessive exploitation of the natural resources. Whereas hunting and fishing for food naturally restricts quantities to the needs and appetites of those entitled to share in the harvest, it is argued that there is no comparable, built-in restriction associated with a trading right, short of the paramount need to conserve the resource. . . . The ultimate fear is that the appellant, who in this case fished for eels from a small boat using a fyke net, could lever the treaty right into a factory trawler in Pomquet Harbour gathering the available harvest in preference to all non-aboriginal commercial or recreational fishermen. (This is indeed the position advanced by the intervener the Union of New Brunswick Indians.) This fear (or hope) is based on a misunderstanding of the narrow ambit and extent of the treaty right.

(58) The recorded note of February 11, 1760 was that "there might be a Truckhouse established, for the furnishing them with *necessaries*" (emphasis added). What is contemplated therefore is not a right to trade generally for economic gain, but rather a right to trade for necessaries. The treaty right is a regulated right and can be contained by regulation within its proper limits.

(59) The concept of "necessaries" is today equivalent to the concept of what Lambert J.A., in *R. v. Van der Peet* (1993), 80 B.C.L.R. (2d) 75, at p. 126, described as a "moderate livelihood". Bare subsistence has thankfully receded over the last couple of centuries as an appropriate standard of life for aboriginals and non-aboriginals alike. A moderate livelihood includes such basics as "food, clothing and housing, supplemented by a few amenities", but not the accumulation of wealth (*Gladstone, supra,* at para. 165). It addresses day-to-day needs. This was the common intention in 1760. It is fair that it be given this interpretation today.

. . .

(61) Catch limits that could reasonably be expected to produce a moderate livelihood for individual Mi'kmaq families at present-day standards can be established by regulation and enforced without violating the treaty right. In that case, the regulations would accommodate the treaty right. Such regulations would *not* constitute an infringement that would have to be justified under the *Badger* standard.

Application to the Facts of this Case

(62) The appellant is charged with three offences: the selling of eels without a licence, fishing without a licence and fishing during the close season with illegal nets. These acts took place at Pomquet Harbour, Antigonish County. For Marshall to have satisfied the regulations, he was required to secure a licence under either the *Fishery (General) Regulations*, SOR/93–53, the *Maritime Provinces Fishery Regulations*, SOR/93–55, or the *Aboriginal Communal Fishing Licences Regulations*, SOR/93–332.

(63) All of these regulations place the issuance of licences within the absolute discretion of the Minister. . . .

. . .

(64) Furthermore, there is nothing in these regulations which gives direction to the Minister to explain how she or he should exercise this discretionary authority in a manner which would respect the appellant's treaty rights. . . . The test for infringement under s. 35(1) of the *Constitution Act, 1982* was set out in *Sparrow, supra*, at p. 1112:

> To determine whether the fishing rights have been interfered with such as to constitute a *prima facie* infringement of s. 35(1), certain questions must be asked. First, is the limitation unreasonable? Second, does the regulation impose undue hardship? Third, does the regulation deny to the holders of the right their preferred means of exercising that right? The onus of proving a *prima facie* infringement lies on the individual or group challenging the legislation.

Lamer C.J. in *Adams, supra*, applied this test to licensing schemes and stated as follows at para. 54:

> In light of the Crown's unique fiduciary obligations towards aboriginal peoples, Parliament may not simply adopt an unstructured discretionary administrative regime which risks infringing aboriginal rights in a substantial number of applications in the absence of some explicit guidance. If a statute confers an administrative discretion which may carry significant consequences for the exercise of an aboriginal right, the statute or its delegate regulations must outline specific criteria for the granting or refusal of that discretion which seek to accommodate the existence of aboriginal rights. In the absence of such specific guidance, the statute will fail to provide representatives of the Crown with sufficient directives to fulfil their fiduciary duties, and the statute will be found to represent an infringement of aboriginal rights under the *Sparrow* test. [Emphasis added.]

Cory J. in *Badger, supra*, at para. 79, found that the test for infringement under s. 35(1) of the *Constitution Act, 1982* was the same for both aboriginal and treaty rights, and thus the words of Lamer C.J. in *Adams*, although in relation to the infringement of aboriginal rights, are equally applicable here. There was nothing at that time which provided the Crown officials with the "sufficient directives" necessary to ensure that the appellant's treaty rights would be respected. To paraphrase *Adams*, at para. 51, under the applicable regulatory regime, the appellant's exercise of his treaty right to fish and trade for sustenance was exercisable only at the absolute discretion of the Minister. Mi'kmaq treaty rights were not accommodated in the Regulations because, presumably, the Crown's position was, and continues to be, that no such treaty rights existed. In the circumstances, the purported regulatory prohibitions against fishing without a licence (*Maritime Provinces Fishery Regulations*, s. 4(1)(*a*)) and of selling eels without a licence (*Fishery (General) Regulations*, s. 35(2)) do *prima facie* infringe the appellant's treaty rights under the Treaties of 1760–61 and are inoperative against the appellant unless justified under the *Badger* test.

(65) Further, the appellant was charged with fishing during the close season with improper nets, contrary to s. 20 of the *Maritime Provinces Fishery Regulations*. Such a

regulation is also a *prima facie* infringement, as noted by Cory J. in *Badger, supra*, at para. 90: "This Court has held on numerous occasions that there can be no limitation on the method, timing and extent of Indian hunting under a Treaty", apart, I would add, from a treaty limitation to that effect.

(66) The appellant caught and sold the eels to support himself and his wife. Accordingly, the close season and the imposition of a discretionary licensing system would, if enforced, interfere with the appellant's treaty right to fish for trading purposes, and the ban on sales would, if enforced, infringe his right to trade for sustenance. In the absence of any justification of the regulatory prohibitions, the appellant is entitled to an acquittal.

. . .

13.4 *R. v. Powley*, 2003

The Métis were never subject to Canada's unilateral allocation of identity that was experienced by those whom federal authorities declared to be Indians. Like the Inuit and those defined as Indians, though, the Métis were classified as Aboriginal people in Section 35 of Canada's Constitution of 1982. Though Métis identity itself has been the subject of longstanding debate, Métis communities are the products of histories and cultures that are distinct from those of other peoples included in the Constitution's definition of Aboriginal. Whatever Aboriginal rights they might possess are distinct as well, although also protected by Section 35. Only recently has the issue of Métis resource rights been given anything close to the kind of attention paid to the rights of other Aboriginal groups. The following case involves a Métis father and son, Steve and Roddy Powley, from near Sault Ste. Marie, Ontario, who were charged with hunting a moose out of season and without licences. The court more broadly considered what constitutes a Métis community that can hold constitutionally protected rights and which individuals should be included as members of that community.

Source: *R. v. Powley*, [2003] 2 S.C.R. 207, 2003 SCC 43.

I. *Introduction*

(1) This case raises the issue of whether members of the Métis community in and around Sault Ste. Marie enjoy a constitutionally protected right to hunt for food under s. 35 of the *Constitution Act, 1982*. We conclude that they do.

(2) On the morning of October 22, 1993, Steve **Powley** and his son, Roddy, set out hunting. They headed north from their residence in Sault Ste. Marie, and at about 9 a.m., they shot and killed a bull moose near Old Goulais Bay Road.

(3) Moose hunting in Ontario is subject to strict regulation. The Ministry of Natural Resources ("MNR") issues Outdoor Cards and validation stickers authorizing the bearer to harvest calf moose during open season. . . . The validation tag requirement and seasonal restrictions are not enforced against Status Indians, and the MNR does not record Status Indians' annual harvest. . . .

(4) After shooting the bull moose near Old Goulais Bay Road, Steve and Roddy **Powley** transported it to their residence in Sault Ste. Marie. Neither of them had a valid

Outdoor Card, a valid hunting licence to hunt moose, or a validation tag issued by the MNR. In lieu of these documents, Steve **Powley** affixed a handwritten tag to the ear of the moose. The tag indicated the date, time, and location of the kill, as required by the hunting regulations. It stated that the animal was to provide meat for the winter. Steve **Powley** signed the tag, and wrote his Ontario Métis and Aboriginal Association membership number on it.

(5) Later that day, two conservation officers arrived at the Powleys' residence. The Powleys told the officers they had shot the moose. One week later, the Powleys were charged with unlawfully hunting moose and knowingly possessing game hunted in contravention of the *Game and Fish Act*, R.S.O. 1990, c. G-1. They both entered pleas of not guilty.

. . .

(8) The question before us is whether ss. 46 and 47(1) of the *Game and Fish Act*, which prohibit hunting moose without a licence, unconstitutionally infringe the respondents' aboriginal right to hunt for food, as recognized in s. 35(1) of the *Constitution Act, 1982.*

II. Analysis

(9) Section 35 of the *Constitution Act, 1982* provides:

35. (1) The existing aboriginal and treaty rights of the aboriginal peoples of Canada are hereby recognized and affirmed.

(2) In this Act, "aboriginal peoples of Canada" includes the Indian, Inuit and Métis peoples of Canada.

(10) The term "Métis" in s. 35 does not encompass all individuals with mixed Indian and European heritage; rather, it refers to distinctive peoples who, in addition to their mixed ancestry, developed their own customs, way of life, and recognizable group identity separate from their Indian or Inuit and European forebears. Métis communities evolved and flourished prior to the entrenchment of European control, when the influence of European settlers and political institutions became pre-eminent.

. . .

The Métis developed separate and distinct identities, not reducible to the mere fact of their mixed ancestry: "What distinguishes Métis people from everyone else is that they associate themselves with a culture that is distinctly Métis" (*RCAP Report*, vol. 4, at p. 202).

(11) The Métis of Canada share the common experience of having forged a new culture and a distinctive group identity from their Indian or Inuit and European roots. This enables us to speak in general terms of "the Métis". However, particularly given the vast territory of what is now Canada, we should not be surprised to find that different groups of Métis exhibit their own distinctive traits and traditions. This diversity among groups of Métis may enable us to speak of Métis "peoples", a possibility left open by the language of s. 35(2), which speaks of the "Indian, Inuit and Métis peoples of Canada".

(12) We would not purport to enumerate the various Métis peoples that may exist. Because the Métis are explicitly included in s. 35, it is only necessary for our purposes to verify that the claimants belong to an identifiable Métis community with a sufficient

degree of continuity and stability to support a site-specific aboriginal right. A Métis community can be defined as a group of Métis with a distinctive collective identity, living together in the same geographic area and sharing a common way of life. The respondents here claim membership in the Métis community centred in and around Sault Ste. Marie. It is not necessary for us to decide, and we did not receive submissions on, whether this community is also a Métis "people", or whether it forms part of a larger Métis people that extends over a wider area such as the Upper Great Lakes.

(13) Our evaluation of the respondents' claim takes place against this historical and cultural backdrop. The overarching interpretive principle for our legal analysis is a purposive reading of s. 35. The inclusion of the Métis in s. 35 is based on a commitment to recognizing the Métis and enhancing their survival as distinctive communities. The purpose and the promise of s. 35 is to protect practices that were historically important features of these distinctive communities and that persist in the present day as integral elements of their Métis culture.

. . .

(16) The emphasis on prior occupation as the primary justification for the special protection accorded aboriginal rights led the majority in *Van der Peet* to endorse a pre-contact test for identifying which customs, practices or traditions were integral to a particular aboriginal culture, and therefore entitled to constitutional protection. However, the majority recognized that the pre-contact test might prove inadequate to capture the range of Métis customs, practices or traditions that are entitled to protection, since Métis cultures by definition post-date European contact. . . .

. . .

(17) . . . [T]he inclusion of the Métis in s. 35 is not traceable to their pre-contact occupation of Canadian territory. The purpose of s. 35 as it relates to the Métis is therefore different from that which relates to the Indians or the Inuit. The constitutionally significant feature of the Métis is their special status as peoples that emerged between first contact and the effective imposition of European control. The inclusion of the Métis in s. 35 represents Canada's commitment to recognize and value the distinctive Métis cultures, which grew up in areas not yet open to colonization, and which the framers of the *Constitution Act, 1982* recognized can only survive if the Métis are protected along with other aboriginal communities.

(18) With this in mind, we proceed to the issue of the correct test to determine the entitlements of the Métis under s. 35 of the *Constitution Act, 1982*. . . . Section 35 requires that we recognize and protect those customs and traditions that were historically important features of Métis communities prior to the time of effective European control, and that persist in the present day. This modification is required to account for the unique post-contact emergence of Métis communities, and the post-contact foundation of their aboriginal rights.

(1) Characterization of the Right

(19) The first step is to characterize the right being claimed: *Van der Peet, supra*, at para. 76. Aboriginal hunting rights, including Métis rights, are contextual and site-specific. The respondents shot a bull moose near Old Goulais Bay Road, in the environs of Sault

Ste. Marie, within the traditional hunting grounds of that Métis community. They made a point of documenting that the moose was intended to provide meat for the winter. The trial judge determined that they were hunting for food, and there is no reason to overturn this finding. The right being claimed can therefore be characterized as the right to hunt for food in the environs of Sault Ste. Marie.

(20) We agree with the trial judge that the periodic scarcity of moose does not in itself undermine the respondents' claim. The relevant right is not to hunt *moose* but to hunt for *food* in the designated territory.

(2) Identification of the Historic Rights-Bearing Community

(21) The trial judge found that a distinctive Métis community emerged in the Upper Great Lakes region in the mid-17th century, and peaked around 1850. We find no reviewable error in the trial judge's findings on this matter, which were confirmed by the Court of Appeal. The record indicates the following: In the mid-17th century, the Jesuits established a mission at Sainte-Marie-du-Sault, in an area characterized by heavy competition among fur traders. In 1750, the French established a fixed trading post on the south bank of the Saint Mary's River. The Sault Ste. Marie post attracted settlement by Métis—the children of unions between European traders and Indian women, and their descendants (A. J. Ray, "An Economic History of the Robinson Treaties Area Before 1860" (1998) ("Ray Report"), at p. 17). According to Dr. Ray, by the early 19th century, "[t]he settlement at Sault Ste. Marie was one of the oldest and most important [Métis settlements] in the upper lakes area" (Ray Report, at p. 47).

. . .

(22) Dr. Ray's report indicates that the individuals named in the post journals "were overwhelmingly Métis", and that Vidal's report "provide[s] a crude indication of the rate of growth of the community and highlights the continuing dominance of Métis in it" (Ray Report, at p. 53). Dr. Victor P. Lytwyn characterized the Vidal report and accompanying map as "clear evidence of a distinct and cohesive Métis community at Sault Ste. Marie" (V. P. Lytwyn, "Historical Report on the Métis Community at Sault Ste. Marie" (1998) ("Lytwyn Report"), at p. 2) . . .

(23) In addition to demographic evidence, proof of shared customs, traditions, and a collective identity is required to demonstrate the existence of a Métis community that can support a claim to site-specific aboriginal rights. We recognize that different groups of Métis have often lacked political structures and have experienced shifts in their members' self-identification. However, the existence of an identifiable Métis community must be demonstrated with some degree of continuity and stability in order to support a site-specific aboriginal rights claim. Here, we find no basis for overturning the trial judge's finding of a historic Métis community at Sault Ste. Marie. This finding is supported by the record and must be upheld.

(3) Identification of the Contemporary Rights-Bearing Community

(24) Aboriginal rights are communal rights: They must be grounded in the existence of a historic and present community, and they may only be exercised by virtue of an individual's ancestrally based membership in the present community. The trial judge

found that a Métis community has persisted in and around Sault Ste. Marie despite its decrease in visibility after the signing of the Robinson-Huron Treaty in 1850. . . .

. . .

(26) The advent of European control over this area thus interfered with, but did not eliminate, the Sault Ste. Marie Métis community and its traditional practices, as evidenced by census data from the 1860s through the 1890s. Dr. Lytwyn concluded from this census data that "[a]lthough the Métis lost much of their traditional land base at Sault Ste. Marie, they continued to live in the region and gain their livelihood from the resources of the land and waters" (Lytwyn Report, at p. 32). He also noted a tendency for underreporting and lack of information about the Métis during this period because of their "removal to the peripheries of the town", and "their own disinclination to be identified as Métis" in the wake of the Riel rebellions and the turning of Ontario public opinion against Métis rights through government actions and the media (Lytwyn Report, at p. 33).

(27) We conclude that the evidence supports the trial judge's finding that the community's lack of visibility was explained and does not negate the existence of the contemporary community. There was never a lapse; the Métis community went underground, so to speak, but it continued. Moreover, as indicated below, the "continuity" requirement puts the focus on the continuing practices of members of the community, rather than more generally on the community itself, as indicated below.

(28) The trial judge's finding of a contemporary Métis community in and around Sault Ste. Marie is supported by the evidence and must be upheld.

(4) Verification of the Claimant's Membership in the Relevant Contemporary Community

(29) While determining membership in the Métis community might not be as simple as verifying membership in, for example, an Indian band, this does not detract from the status of Métis people as full-fledged rights-bearers. As Métis communities continue to organize themselves more formally and to assert their constitutional rights, it is imperative that membership requirements become more standardized so that legitimate rights-holders can be identified. In the meantime, courts faced with Métis claims will have to ascertain Métis identity on a case-by-case basis. The inquiry must take into account both the value of community self-definition, and the need for the process of identification to be objectively verifiable. In addition, the criteria for Métis identity under s. 35 must reflect the purpose of this constitutional guarantee: to recognize and affirm the rights of the Métis held by virtue of their direct relationship to this country's original inhabitants and by virtue of the continuity between their customs and traditions and those of their Métis predecessors. This is not an insurmountable task.

(30) We emphasize that we have not been asked, and we do not purport, to set down a comprehensive definition of who is Métis for the purpose of asserting a claim under s. 35. . . . In particular, we would look to three broad factors as indicia of Métis identity for the purpose of claiming Métis rights under s. 35: self-identification, ancestral connection, and community acceptance.

(31) First, the claimant must *self-identify* as a member of a Métis community. This self-identification should not be of recent vintage: While an individual's self-identification

need not be static or monolithic, claims that are made belatedly in order to benefit from a s. 35 right will not satisfy the self-identification requirement.

(32) Second, the claimant must present evidence of an *ancestral connection* to a historic Métis community. This objective requirement ensures that beneficiaries of s. 35 rights have a real link to the historic community whose practices ground the right being claimed. We would not require a minimum "blood quantum", but we would require some proof that the claimant's ancestors belonged to the historic Métis community by birth, adoption, or other means. Like the trial judge, we would abstain from further defining this requirement in the absence of more extensive argument by the parties in a case where this issue is determinative. In this case, the Powleys' Métis ancestry is not disputed.

(33) Third, the claimant must demonstrate that he or she is *accepted by the modern community* whose continuity with the historic community provides the legal foundation for the right being claimed. Membership in a Métis political organization may be relevant to the question of community acceptance, but it is not sufficient in the absence of a contextual understanding of the membership requirements of the organization and its role in the Métis community. The core of community acceptance is past and ongoing participation in a shared culture, in the customs and traditions that constitute a Métis community's identity and distinguish it from other groups. This is what the community membership criterion is all about. Other indicia of community acceptance might include evidence of participation in community activities and testimony from other members about the claimant's connection to the community and its culture. The range of acceptable forms of evidence does not attenuate the need for an objective demonstration of a solid bond of past and present mutual identification and recognition of common belonging between the claimant and other members of the rights-bearing community.

(34) It is important to remember that, no matter how a contemporary community defines membership, only those members with a demonstrable ancestral connection to the historic community can claim a s. 35 right. Verifying membership is crucial, since individuals are only entitled to exercise Métis aboriginal rights by virtue of their ancestral connection to and current membership in a Métis community.

(35) In this case, there is no reason to overturn the trial judge's finding that the Powleys are members of the Métis community that arose and still exists in and around Sault Ste. Marie. . . .

(5) Identification of the Relevant Time Frame

(36) As indicated above, the pre-contact aspect of the *Van der Peet* test requires adjustment in order to take account of the post-contact ethnogenesis of the Métis and the purpose of s. 35 in protecting the historically important customs and traditions of these distinctive peoples. While the fact of prior occupation grounds aboriginal rights claims for the Inuit and the Indians, the recognition of Métis rights in s. 35 is not reducible to the Métis' Indian ancestry. The unique status of the Métis as an Aboriginal people with post-contact origins requires an adaptation of the pre-contact approach to meet the distinctive historical circumstances surrounding the evolution of Métis communities.

(37) The pre-contact test in *Van der Peet* is based on the constitutional affirmation that aboriginal communities are entitled to continue those practices, customs and

traditions that are integral to their distinctive existence or relationship to the land. By analogy, the test for Métis practices should focus on identifying those practices, customs and traditions that are integral to the Métis community's distinctive existence and relationship to the land. This unique history can most appropriately be accommodated by a post contact but pre-control test that identifies the time when Europeans effectively established political and legal control in a particular area. The focus should be on the period after a particular Métis community arose and before it came under the effective control of European laws and customs. This pre-control test enables us to identify those practices, customs and traditions that predate the imposition of European laws and customs on the Métis.

(38) We reject the appellant's argument that Métis rights must find their origin in the pre-contact practices of the Métis' aboriginal ancestors. This theory in effect would deny to Métis their full status as distinctive rights-bearing peoples whose own integral practices are entitled to constitutional protection under s. 35(1). . . .

. . .

(40) The historical record indicates that the Sault Ste. Marie Métis community thrived largely unaffected by European laws and customs until colonial policy shifted from one of discouraging settlement to one of negotiating treaties and encouraging settlement in the mid-19th century. The trial judge found, and the parties agreed in their pleadings before the lower courts, that "effective control [of the Upper Great Lakes area] passed from the Aboriginal peoples of the area (Ojibway and Metis) to European control" in the period between 1815 and 1850 (para. 90). The record fully supports the finding that the period just prior to 1850 is the appropriate date for finding effective control in this geographic area, which the Crown agreed was the critical date in its pleadings below.

(6) Determination of Whether the Practice is Integral to the Claimants' Distinctive Culture

(41) The practice of subsistence hunting and fishing was a constant in the Métis community, even though the availability of particular species might have waxed and waned. The evidence indicates that subsistence hunting was an important aspect of Métis life and a defining feature of their special relationship to the land (Peterson, *supra*, at p. 41; Lytwyn Report, *supra*, at p. 6). A major part of subsistence was the practice at issue here, hunting for food.

. . .

(43) Dr. Ray emphasized in his report that a key feature of Métis communities was that "their members earned a substantial part of their livelihood off of the land" (Ray Report, *supra*, at p. 56 (emphasis deleted). Dr. Lytwyn concurred: "The Métis of Sault Ste. Marie lived off the resources of the land. They obtained their livelihood from hunting, fishing, gathering and cultivating" (Lytwyn Report, at p. 2). He reported that "[w]hile Métis fishing was prominent in the written accounts, hunting was also an important part of their livelihood", and that "[a] traditional winter hunting area for the Sault Métis was the Goulais Bay area" (Lytwyn Report, at pp. 4–5). . . .

. . .

(44) This evidence supports the trial judge's finding that hunting for food was integral to the Métis way of life at Sault Ste. Marie in the period just prior to 1850.

(45) Although s. 35 protects "existing" rights, it is more than a mere codification of the common law. Section 35 reflects a new promise: a constitutional commitment to protecting practices that were historically important features of particular aboriginal communities. A certain margin of flexibility might be required to ensure that aboriginal practices can evolve and develop over time, but it is not necessary to define or to rely on that margin in this case. Hunting for food was an important feature of the Sault Ste. Marie Métis community, and the practice has been continuous to the present. Steve and Roddy Powley claim a Métis aboriginal right to hunt for food. The right claimed by the Powleys falls squarely within the bounds of the historical practice grounding the right.

(8) Determination of Whether or Not the Right Was Extinguished

(46) The doctrine of extinguishment applies equally to Métis and to First Nations claims. There is no evidence of extinguishment here, as determined by the trial judge. The Crown's argument for extinguishment is based largely on the Robinson-Huron Treaty of 1850, from which the Métis as a group were explicitly excluded.

(9) If There Is a Right, Determination of Whether There Is an Infringement

(47) Ontario currently does not recognize any Métis right to hunt for food, or any "special access rights to natural resources" for the Métis whatsoever (appellant's record, at p. 1029). This lack of recognition, and the consequent application of the challenged provisions to the Powleys, infringe their aboriginal right to hunt for food as a continuation of the protected historical practices of the Sault Ste. Marie Métis community.

. . .

III. *Conclusion*

(53) Members of the Métis community in and around Sault Ste. Marie have an aboriginal right to hunt for food under s. 35(1).

. . .

SUGGESTIONS FOR FURTHER READING

The full text of the Supreme Court decisions for each of the cases presented in this chapter are available on line by entering the appropriate search terms at http://scc-csc.lexum.com/decisia-scc-csc/scc-csc/scc-csc/en/nav_date.do. For a study that weaves together Anishinaabe and Canadian legal traditions and understandings by a leading Indigenous legal scholar, see John Borrows, "Frozen Rights in Canada: Constitutional Interpretation and the Trickster," in *Recovering Canada: The Resurgence of Indigenous Law* (Toronto: University of Toronto Press, 2002), 56–76. Readers will probably find other chapters in this book useful as well. For a detailed examination of the Guerin case and its effects, written by one of the lawyers involved in the case, see James I. Reynolds, *A Breach of Duty: Fiduciary Obligations and Aboriginal Peoples* (Saskatoon, SK: Purich Publishing, 2005). For an overview of the Sparrow decision, see Thomas Isaac, "Balancing Rights: The Supreme Court of Canada, *R. v. Sparrow*, and the Future of Aboriginal Rights," *Canadian Journal of Native Studies* 13, no. 2 (1993): 199–219. For the Marshall case, see Kenneth S. Coates, *The Marshall Decision and Native Rights* (Montreal and Kingston: McGill-Queen's University Press, 2000). For an examination of some of the impacts of the Powley decision on Métis identity and community, see Chris Anderson, "Settling for Community?: Juridical Visions of Historical Metis Collectivity in and after *R. v. Powley*" in *Contours of a People: Metis Family, Mobility, and History*, ed. Nicole St-Onge, Carolyn Podruchny, and Brenda Macdougall (Norman: University of Oklahoma Press, 2012), 392–421. For the experiences of a historian acting as an expert witness in Indigenous rights cases and an analysis of the use of history and historical evidence in such cases, see Arthur J. Ray, *Telling It to the Judge: Taking Native History to Court* (Montreal: McGill-Queen's University Press, 2011). For the work of a historian called as an expert witness in the Marshall case, see William Wicken, *Mi'kmaq Treaties on Trial: History, Land, and Donald Marshall Junior* (Toronto: University of Toronto Press, 2002). For an exploration of the use of oral narratives in the courts, see Bruce Granville Miller, *Oral History on Trial: Recognizing Aboriginal Narratives in the Courts* (Vancouver: UBC Press, 2011). For a film that explores the post Marshall experience of the Mi'kmaq community at Esgenoôpetitj (Burnt Church), New Brunswick, see Alanis Obomsawin, *Is the Crown at War With Us?* (Montreal: National Film Board of Canada, 2002).

CHAPTER 14

"IT WAS TIME TO PROTECT OUR LANDS"[1]

CONFLICT AT IPPERWASH

The late 1980s were witness to the several failed constitutional conferences that were required under Canada's new Constitution of 1982, mixed results in the settlement of land claims, and austerity measures and regulatory constraints adopted by the Mulroney government. In 1990, the Meech Lake Accord was defeated, in part, because of the opposition of Elijah Harper. Harper was an NDP member of Parliament from the Red Sucker Lake First Nation, an Oji-Cree community in northern Manitoba. These events served simultaneously to embolden and frustrate Indigenous activists. In this context, more militant action was almost certain.

Indigenous dissatisfaction was manifested in different ways across the country during the first half of the 1990s. Occupations and blockades became more common, and these actions were met with growing force by the state. Probably the best known of these incidents is the "Oka crisis" that occurred in Quebec in the summer of 1990. Mohawk residents of Kanesatake set up blockades to prevent the expansion of a golf course that threatened land the community claimed was sacred and that held a burial ground. Here, an ill-advised raid by Quebec's provincial police, the Sûreté du Québec, led to the death of one of its officers, Corporal Marcel Lemay. The Canadian army was deployed, and massive expenses were incurred, but, in the end, the golf course expansion was halted.

The events at Kanesatake and Kahnawá:ke in the summer of 1990 are important, and there are a number of investigative films and secondary sources that document the blockade and Canada's response. This chapter, though, concerns issues that are perhaps less well known nationally and internationally. The events labelled the "Ipperwash crisis"

---

1 Sam George, Final Submissions of the Dudley George estate and Family Group, before the Honourable Justice Sidney Linden, Commissioner, Ipperwash Public Inquiry, Forest Community Centre, Kimberly Hall, Forest, Ontario, 21 August 2006, p. 18. The quotation appears in document 14.3

took place in 1995 on the shores of Lake Huron in south-western Ontario. The roots of the conflict reach back to at least 1827 when the Huron Tract Treaty resulted in the ceding of over two million acres of land, apparently more land than originally intended and for less compensation than expected. The local Chippewa (Anishinaabe) communities retained four small reserves, including those at Kettle and Stony Point, amounting to less than one per cent of their ancestral territory.

By the early part of the twentieth century, pressure to relinquish even more land was applied to the Kettle and Stony Point First Nation. In 1927, part of the waterfront at Stony Point was surrendered, as was the entire beachfront at Kettle Point in 1928. Canada quickly sold part of the Stony Point land to the Government of Ontario for triple the amount it had paid to the First Nation. This land became Ipperwash Provincial Park. Both the Kettle and Stony Point lands were the subject of land claims in the 1990s, and the former sale was referred to as "tainted" by the Ontario Court of Appeals.

In 1942, the entire reserve at Stony Point was appropriated by the Canadian government under the War Measures Act and used to establish what became Camp Ipperwash, despite community opposition, treaty obligations, and the policy established for the Crown to acquire First Nation lands. Following the war, Canada's Department of National Defence decided not to return the Stony Point land as originally promised. Even early 1970s' appeals for the land to be returned from Minister of Indian Affairs Jean Chrétien were unsuccessful. Finally, more than two decades later, in 1993, members of the Kettle and Stony Point First Nation, frustrated by the endless delays and unsuccessful efforts to have their land returned to them, decided simply to return to that part of their land that had become the army camp. In September of 1995, a few dozen First Nation members, including children, moved their occupation to nearby Ipperwash Provincial Park.

Ontario Premier Mike Harris's provincial government was unwilling to negotiate and was prepared to use extraordinary means to remove the Stony Point community members from the park. On the 6th of September 1995, the Ontario Provincial Police launched a raid in the dark of night during which one of its members, Sergeant Kenneth Deane, shot and killed Dudley George, a young man from the Stony Point community.

Eight years after the death of Dudley George, in 2003, the newly elected provincial government of Dalton McGuinty appointed Justice Sidney Linden to lead an inquiry into the background and events that occurred at Ipperwash in 1995 and to provide recommendations concerning how such tragedies could be avoided in future. For over two years, the Commission of Inquiry into the Circumstances and Events Surrounding the Death of Anthony O'Brien (Dudley) George heard witnesses involved in all aspects of the events, commissioned written research papers from specialists of various sorts, accepted submissions from interested parties, and held a number of public forums and events. In the end, Commissioner Linden made several dozen recommendations intended to improve relations between Canada and Indigenous communities. In 2009, following one of the commissioner's suggestions, a formal process was begun to return the Ipperwash Provincial Park land to the Kettle and Stony Point First Nation.

The documents in this chapter all come from the Ipperwash inquiry. They include testimony from people directly involved in the events of September 1995 and an excerpt from Justice Linden's 2007 report.

1. What are the primary factors that led directly to the death of Dudley George?
2. Was the occupation of Ipperwash Provincial Park a reasonable move in your view? Why or why not?
3. From the testimony of Nicholas Cottrelle and others, were all actions taken by the police appropriate? If not, which actions seem inappropriate?
4. What, in your view, are the main causes of the violence that erupted at Ipperwash Provincial Park? After the occupation began and police response teams were called in, how could violence have been avoided?
5. What did the George family hope to gain from the inquiry? Were they successful?

DOCUMENTS

14.1 *Report of the Ipperwash Inquiry*, 2007

As mentioned in the introduction to this chapter, in 2003 the Ontario Provincial Government appointed Justice Sidney Linden to lead an inquiry into the events that occurred at Ipperwash Provincial Park in September of 1995 and the circumstances that led to these events. The commission held hearings from July 2004 to August 2006. Witnesses included politicians, officials from various government departments, policemen, First Nations people who were present in the park on the night Dudley George was killed, and members of George's family. Many Canadians would find much of the material uncovered by the commission surprising if not shocking. The selections included in document 14.1 come from Commissioner Linden's final report and succinctly illustrate the underlying understandings and attitudes that led to George's death. They also suggest how the occupation and George's death might have been avoided.

Source: Sidney B. Linden, Commissioner, *Investigation and Findings*, vol. 1, *Report of the Ipperwash Inquiry* (Toronto: Queen's Printer for Ontario, 2007), 671–72, 674–77, 681–87, and 689–91.

© Queen's Printer for Ontario, 2013. Reproduced with permission.

The original includes two spellings: Stony and Stoney Point. These have been reproduced as they were.

. . .

1. Why is Ipperwash important?

Over time, questions about the circumstances of Mr. George's death deepened. New information cast doubts on the original explanations of events at Ipperwash when it became clear that many of the initial reports were likely incorrect, particularly the early, unconfirmed reports that the occupiers had guns. Acting Sergeant Kenneth Deane's criminal conviction raised further questions about the propriety of the OPP's actions. Years of media reports and lawsuits intensified the long-standing but unproven allegations of political interference in police decision-making.

Ipperwash raised even more profound questions for Aboriginal peoples. Mr. George was the first Aboriginal person to be killed in a land rights dispute in Canada since the 19th century. To many Aboriginal peoples, the shooting of Dudley George was the inevitable result of centuries of discrimination and dispossession. Many Aboriginal peoples also believed that the explanation for killing an unarmed Aboriginal occupier in a peaceful demonstration was rooted in racism. From this perspective, Ipperwash revealed a deep schism in Canada's relationship with its Aboriginal peoples and was symbolic of a long and sad history of government policy that harmed their long-term interests.

Ipperwash is important because public officials and institutions need to be held accountable for their decisions and actions. Their credibility and legitimacy depend on knowing if, or how, they were involved in the death of an unarmed, peaceful protester.

Ipperwash is also important because it helps us understand the roots and dynamics of an Aboriginal protest. The Aboriginal occupation at Caledonia proves that Ipperwash was not an isolated event. Understanding Ipperwash can help us understand how to prevent Aboriginal occupations and protests in the first place or how to reduce the risk of violence if they occur.

Finally, Ipperwash is important to the future of Aboriginal and non-Aboriginal peoples in this province. There can be no reconciliation without truth. The truth must come out so that Aboriginal and non-Aboriginal Ontarians can move forward together to our collective future.

. . .

3. Was the provincial government prepared for the occupation?

The provincial government's position at both the civil service and political levels in the summer of 1995 was to treat Ipperwash as a "watching brief". This was understandable. A new provincial government had just been elected. Nothing significant had happened to the provincial park. It was summertime and it was easy to blame the federal government for the problem. However, although they were aware that there was the potential for an occupation, provincial government officials did not make sufficient efforts during this period to inform themselves about the Aboriginal peoples' historic grievances or to identify and appoint a mediator who might have headed off the occupation.

Ipperwash might have turned out differently if the provincial government had taken more assertive steps to defuse the growing tension and try to prevent the occupation in the first place. The provincial government could have appointed a mediator or tried to understand the historic grievances of the Stoney Point people, including the claims of an Aboriginal burial site in the park. It could have reached out to Stoney Point people, learned more about the dynamics within the community, or proactively identified potential mediators or facilitators.

We do not know if these actions would have prevented the occupation or Dudley George's death. However, we do know that relationship building and establishing communications *before* an occupation increases the likelihood of peaceful outcomes by helping to build trust and confidence between governments, police and occupiers. These relationships could have proven helpful to defuse tensions when the occupation eventually did take place.

4. Did the provincial government respond appropriately to the occupation?

Premier Harris believed that the occupation was a law enforcement issue, not a First Nation's matter. It was the Premier's position that the park belonged to the province; he therefore concluded that the occupiers were trespassing. As there was no evidence available to him at that time to support the claim of a burial site, he was not prepared to contemplate the occupiers' suggestion that there was one or that the park belonged to them. In light of this, no consideration was given to the possibility of third-party involvement for the purposes of negotiation with the occupiers.

The evidence demonstrated that the Premier and his officials wanted the occupation to end quickly, but there is no evidence to suggest that either the Premier or any official in his government was responsible for Mr. George's death.

The evidence demonstrated that Premier Harris and his officials had a different perspective than the OPP on how the occupation should be handled by the police. The OPP's wish to pursue a go-slow approach contrasted with the government's desire for a quick end to the occupation. Civil service officials agreed in principle with the OPP's approach, but deferred to their political masters on questions of policy.

The provincial government's imperative for a speedy conclusion to the occupation is difficult to justify by events on the ground. The provincial park was closed for the season. There were no campers in the park. Nor was there any proven, substantial risk to public safety that would justify this urgency. In short, there did not appear to be any public safety justification for a "hawkish" response.

The provincial government's priorities reflected its larger concerns about the potential *implications* of Ipperwash. The government was concerned about establishing a precedent for Oka-like occupations in the future. The government also wanted to prove that it was tough on 'lawbreakers' and that Aboriginal peoples would be treated the same as everyone else. The government also did not want a prolonged occupation to deflect it from its larger agenda.

Whether one agrees with these decisions or not, they were within the authority of the provincial government to establish policy, including the policy of how to respond to the occupation at Ipperwash. However, once the Premier and the provincial government established these policies they are accountable for them.

The imperative for speed foreclosed the possibility of initiating a constructive dialogue with the occupiers or others on ways to resolve the occupation peacefully and, as a result, the potential for a peaceful, negotiated resolution became less likely.

5. Was there political interference in police decision-making?

The allegation of political interference in OPP operations and decision-making was one of the most significant concerns about Ipperwash. It was therefore the subject of intense interest at the evidentiary hearings and analyzed in detail in our policy review of police/government relations, found in Volume 2.

The provincial government had the authority to establish policing policy, but not to direct police operations. The Premier and his government did not cross this line. There is no evidence to suggest that either the Premier or his government directed the OPP to march down the road toward Ipperwash Provincial Park, on the evening of September 6.

Incident commander Carson knew of the Premier's desire for a quick resolution to the occupation, as did other members of the OPP directly involved in the policing of the occupation. This was unfortunate and should not have occurred. However, having this information does not constitute political interference nor does it mean that Incident Commander Carson or any other member of the OPP involved in the policing of the occupation were influenced by it, in their operational decision-making. . . .

This is not to say that the interaction between the police and government at Ipperwash was proper or conducive to a peaceful resolution. There was a considerable lack of understanding about the appropriate relationship between police and government. This lack of understanding had significant consequences. An important example is the overlapping and sometimes contradictory reports provided to the provincial government by the OPP and officials from the Ministry of Natural Resources (MNR). MNR officials circulated unverified, inaccurate and extremely provocative reports about automatic gunfire in the park at government meetings. MNR officials did not have the expertise to assess the reliability or accuracy of these reports, nor were they aware of the potential implications of passing this unverified information directly to the Interministerial Committee composed of political staff, civil servants, and seconded OPP officers, one of whom was in contact with the Incident Commander. Lines of communication and chains of command were blurred. There was also a lack of clarity regarding the relationship between political staff and professional civil servants.

Taken together, the interaction between the police and government at Ipperwash created the appearance of inappropriate interference in police operations.

Another fundamental problem in police/government relations at Ipperwash is that key decisions were neither transparent nor accountable. A large part of the Inquiry was devoted to discovering what transpired at several Interministerial Committee meetings and at the "dining room meeting" on September 6, 1995. This is the meeting in which the Premier, several Cabinet ministers and deputy ministers, and other officials discussed the provincial government's response to the occupation at Ipperwash Provincial Park. This is the meeting where [the] former Attorney General testified that he heard Premier Harris say "I want the fucking Indians out of the park". This is the same meeting at which former Deputy Solicitor General Todres testified that she heard former Minister of Natural Resources Hodgson say, "Get the fucking Indians out of my park." Both denied making these comments but the Premier acknowledged at the Inquiry's hearings that the statement attributed to him, would be racist. I have found that the statements were made and that they were racist, whether intended or not.

. . .

7. Why did the OPP march toward Ipperwash Provincial Park on the night of September 6? What went wrong?

. . .

There was a perception by the occupiers of increased police presence on September 6, 1995 in the Ipperwash Provincial Park area. The boat surveillance on Lake Huron, and the low-flying helicopter surveillance caused agitation and anxiety amongst the First Nations people. This caused the occupiers to engage in preparations for what they believed was an aggressive OPP move against them. They collected rocks and sticks, fueled the school bus, and arranged for the women and children to leave the park. On the scanner, they overheard the OPP communicate that they planned to march to the park that evening.

Inspector Carson was a conscientious and competent Incident Commander at Ipperwash during the September 1995 events. He is a man of integrity who clearly wanted the Aboriginal occupation to be resolved peacefully. But on the night of September 6, 1995, I believe it was a mistake to deploy the CMU and TRU down East Parkway Drive toward the sandy parking lot.

CMU officers, dressed in hard Tac equipment with their helmets and shields, marched shoulder-to-shoulder in formation toward the park. There were thirty-two officers, an eight-man arrest team, two canine teams, and two prisoner vans. Several CMU officers were nervous as they marched toward the park in darkness. TRU officers walked ahead of the CMU with assault rifles and semi-automatic pistols, providing cover. The CMU leader yelled commands to his officers as the police marched toward the sandy parking lot. The Aboriginal people were terrified as they saw the officers dressed in "riot gear" marching toward the park. The Aboriginal occupiers were not armed with guns, but some did have baseball bats, stones and sticks.

The OPP's plan to have the occupiers return to the park from the sandy parking lot seemed to work, at least initially. As the CMU advanced to the fence line outside Ipperwash Provincial Park, the occupiers retreated from the sandy parking lot into the park. As the CMU came to a halt, the last few occupiers walked through the turnstiles into Ipperwash Provincial Park. Sergeant Hebblethwaite radioed to the Tactical Operations Centre that "the badgers are in the park." The CMU Incident Commander, Staff Sergeant Lacroix, thought the CMU's mission was complete.

An Aboriginal man, subsequently identified as Cecil Bernard George, whose fear of the police had turned to anger, walked into the sandy parking lot waving a steel pipe that he picked up. He yelled that the park property was Aboriginal land, and that his grandfather was buried on this land. CMU officers had backed up at this time to Army Camp Road. The CMU Incident Commander yelled "punchout". CMU officers ran toward Cecil Bernard George and a confrontation ensued between the OPP and the occupiers. The police fired their guns during the altercation and Dudley George, a thirty-eight year old occupier, was shot and killed by Acting Sergeant Deane.

Deploying the CMU was an offensive not a defensive strategy. It was a show of force. It was designed to clear occupiers or protestors from a particular area. If the strategy does not work, the potential for violence increases. Using the CMU was a calculated risk that was within Inspector Carson's authority to make. The use of any force must be to ensure public safety. Based on the information that he had, Inspector Carson made a decision to use the CMU to clear the sandy parking lot. In his view, public safety required it. But the information upon which Inspector Carson made the decision was incorrect. If Inspector Carson had correct information, I believe that he would not have made a decision to deploy the CMU. If Inspector Carson had waited until the TRU Sierra Teams were in position and reported back to him on what was happening in the sandy parking lot and kiosk, he would have learned that there was not a fire in the sandy parking lot, how many people, if any, were in the sandy parking lot and whether they had guns. . . .

Notwithstanding the many progressive reforms undertaken by the OPP in recent years in relation to policing Aboriginal occupations, the OPP, as an institution needs to be accountable and take some responsibility for the tragedy that occurred on September 6, 1995.

8. Did racism or cultural insensitivity contribute to Dudley George's death?

Cultural insensitivity and racism on the part of some of the OPP officers involved, were evident both before and after Dudley George's death. They created a barrier to understanding and thus made a timely, peaceful resolution of the occupation more difficult. The most obvious instance of racism and cultural insensitivity was a conversation among members of the OPP intelligence team on September 5, 1995, in which an Aboriginal person was referred to as a "big, fat, fuck Indian" and the suggestion was made that they (i.e., the Aboriginal people in the park) could be baited into "a net as a pit" with "five or six cases of Labatt's 50", which "works in the south with watermelons".

These comments were racist against the Aboriginal people who were under surveillance at the time, and they were racist against persons of colour. Not one witness in the hearing tried to defend or rationalize these comments, including the Incident Commander, John Carson, who described the comments as "inappropriate", "unacceptable", and "not to be tolerated".

The racist comments noted above were not an isolated incident; there were a number of other tape-recorded conversations of officers making derogatory remarks about Aboriginal people at the time of the occupation.

The Inquiry also learned of several inappropriate activities after the occupation, including the production and distribution of offensive coffee mugs, and t-shirts containing racist imagery to commemorate the OPP's actions at Ipperwash.

Equally disturbing was the manner in which the OPP dealt with this behaviour. In some instances, they never found out about it. In other cases, senior officials decided that it did not amount to "misconduct." In cases where they did find misconduct, it was determined that the officers should be disciplined under the "informal" procedures set out in the *Police Services Act*.

The OPP's response to these incidents was insufficient. Officers were either subject to internal, informal disciplinary processes or not disciplined at all. Several incidents were not discovered or dealt with until years later when they were "discovered" in the lead up to, or during, this Inquiry. These circumstances call into question the disciplinary regime for this kind of conduct and the internal mechanisms within the OPP for reporting it.

Another example of racism towards Aboriginal people in the period before Dudley George's death was the Ontario Ministry of Natural Resources' race-specific enforcement policy, "Procedures for Dealing with First Nations People". This policy, developed with the assistance of an OPP officer, was issued in August 1995 for the Pinery and Ipperwash Provincial Parks. This policy is an example of inappropriate, racially biased policing and is not acceptable in our society.

Cultural insensitivity and racism did not cause Dudley George's death but it may have contributed to the lack of a timely and peaceful resolution of the occupation. Some members of the OPP held negative stereotypes and thought the worst of the occupiers. While I do not believe this to be true of Inspector Carson, I do believe cultural insensitivity and racism exhibited by some members of the OPP contributed to misunderstandings and misinterpretations of the occupiers' actions and intentions on the crucial days between September 4 and 6, 1995.

Some occupiers also held negative stereotypes and thought the worst of the police. This was also unfortunate but cannot be equated with the stereotypes held by some members of the OPP. Police officers and police services have the authority to enforce the laws and to use force. Accordingly, police officers have a responsibility to treat all persons fairly and to be free of bias and prejudice. Neither cultural insensitivity nor racism has any place in a police force in a civilized society such as Canada.

Cultural insensitivity and racism do not have any place in the highest offices of the province. Both the Premier and the Minister of Natural Resources made racist comments on September 6 that were offensive and inappropriate in any circumstance and particularly when voiced by the leaders of the province. These views also created a barrier to understanding and did not contribute to resolving Ipperwash peacefully.

9. Is the federal government responsible?

The federal government bears the primary responsibility for the occupation of Ipperwash Provincial Park by protesters in September 1995.

The people of the Kettle and Stony Point First Nation, including the occupiers at Stoney Point/Aazhodena have been and continue to be, neglected by the federal government.

Consider this simple chronology:

- Eighty years have passed since the "odour of moral failure" surrounding the 1927 "surrender" of the Kettle Point and Stoney Point lands; the 1928 surrender of the Stoney Point lands had similar characteristics.
- Seventy years have passed since the Kettle and Stony Point Council asked for protection of the burial site in Ipperwash Provincial Park.
- Sixty-five years have passed since the Department of National Defence took over the Stoney Point reserve for military training.
- Sixty-two years have passed since the end of World War Two, at which time the residents of Kettle and Stony Point First Nation expected the land to be returned.
- Twenty-six years have passed since the federal government agreed to return Camp Ipperwash, in whole or in part, when it was no longer needed for military training.
- Thirteen years have passed since the Minister of National Defence announced that the military no longer needed Camp Ipperwash.
- Twelve years have passed since Dudley George died asserting his community's right to the lands reserved by treaty for their exclusive use 180 years ago.

Unfortunately, the issues that were at the heart of the Ipperwash occupation remain unresolved by the federal government, to this day. This inexcusable delay and long neglect, by successive federal governments, are at the heart of the Ipperwash story.

. . .

11. What can be done to prevent violence in the future?

. . .

Aboriginal occupations and protests are not inevitable, nor are they inevitably violent. If I could answer the question above in a single paragraph, it would be this:

The provincial government and other institutions must redouble their efforts to build successful, peaceful relations with Aboriginal peoples in Ontario so that we can all live together peacefully and productively. There have been significant, constructive changes in the law and to key public institutions in the twelve years since Ipperwash. Yet more is needed. We must move beyond conflict resolution by crisis management. And we cannot be passive; inaction will only increase the considerable tensions that already exist between Aboriginal and non-Aboriginal citizens in this province.

Research in the course of the Inquiry showed that the flashpoints for Aboriginal protests and occupations are very likely as intense today as they were during Ipperwash, Oka, Burnt Church, or Gustafsen Lake. No one can predict where protests and occupations will occur, but the fundamental conditions and catalysts sparking such protests continue to exist in Ontario, more than a decade after Ipperwash. Indeed, it appears that the flashpoints for Aboriginal protests and occupations may be intensifying.

Usually, the immediate catalyst for most major occupations and protests is a dispute over a land claim, burial site, resource development, or harvesting, hunting, and fishing rights. The fundamental conflict, however, is about land. Contemporary Aboriginal occupations and protests should therefore be seen as part of the centuries-old tension between Aboriginal peoples and non-Aboriginal peoples over the control, use, and ownership of land. The frequency of occupations and protests in Ontario and Canada is a symptom, if not the result, of our collective and continuing inability to resolve these tensions. Volume 2 of this report, *Policy Analysis*, contains specific recommendations about these matters.

12. What about the land?

. . .

In my view, the most urgent priority is for the federal government to return the former army camp to the Kettle and Stony Point First Nation immediately. This land was appropriated in 1942 for a specific, military purpose and it has been decades since it last served that purpose.

As part of the return, the federal government should undertake and pay for the environmental clean up of the camp that is required. My understanding is that this process has already begun; its completion should not be a reason for delaying the return of the land. In addition, successive federal governments' failure to return the land, for so many years, warrants an apology and appropriate compensation to the Aboriginal people affected. An apology and appropriate compensation will bring a measure of acknowledgement, dignity and justice to the Aboriginal communities affected by the federal government's failure to return the land, in a reasonable period of time, after the war ended.

The solution regarding the future of the park land is more difficult. The one thing I learned during this Inquiry, is that regardless of the solution for the park land, the way forward must be through a process that is fair, inclusive and transparent. This approach would be consistent with the central themes of this Inquiry and report. Furthermore, any process that is designed to resolve the park land issue must promote reconciliation and the long-term interests of all the communities involved. To this end, the communities affected must be actively involved in the process. Therefore, the best I can do is to recommend a process for going forward. Indeed, given the reasons stated above, it would be inappropriate of me to offer a specific solution for the park land.

The park land is adjacent to the former army camp and is not part of the negotiations between the federal government and the First Nation. The park is under provincial jurisdiction as a result of the 1928 surrender and subsequent purchase by the province.

Allowing the status quo to continue, with respect to the park, is not in anyone's interest. The park land is currently not part of the First Nation reserve, nor is it pragmatically subject to provincial management. It is a tribute to the patience and restraint of the occupiers and the local residents that there have been no serious adverse incidents since 1995. But this unresolved status should not continue.

The division that continues to exist between the Kettle and Stony Point First Nation and the residents of Aazhoodena complicates any proposed solution. These communities need to resolve their differences, perhaps with the assistance of the First Nations organizations and, if requested, with the federal and/or provincial government, but these differences should not be used as a reason for not resolving the status of the park.

Unfortunately, there are no perfect solutions and past experience has taught us that solutions that are recommended or imposed by external third parties, are rarely successful. The residents of Aazhoodena must be involved with the First Nation and the non-Aboriginal local community in any discussions regarding the future of the park. I urge all those with an interest in the future of these lands, to put their differences aside and work together to address the common interest of healing and moving forward.

I have already said that I believe the status quo is not an acceptable solution; nor, would it be acceptable in my view, if the park were re-opened unilaterally, by the Government of Ontario, as a provincial park.

One obvious solution is to return the park land, with the army camp, to the Kettle and Stony Point First Nation with the participation of residents of Aazhoodena as I have indicated above. This solution has considerable attraction given the Aboriginal peoples' historical connection to the land, the circumstances of the occupation in 1995, the fact that the occupiers have been cccupying [sic] the land since that time, and the fact that the two parcels of land have effectively merged into one—as they once were—due to twelve years of inaction by successive provincial and federal governments.

The circumstances of the 1927 surrender of West Ipperwash beach remained contentious with the First Nation for decades. The Kettle and Stony Point First Nation challenged the legality of that surrender in the 1990s, and although the courts found the surrender legally valid, the Court stated that the transactions had "the odour of moral failure". The Ontario Court of Appeal subsequently suggested that the federal government's "tainted dealings" might amount to a breach of its fiduciary duty to the First Nation. Although the courts have not considered the 1928 surrender of the Stoney Point beach lands, that included Ipperwash Provincial Park, the evidence before me indicated that the circumstances of that surrender had similar characteristics.

This solution of returning the park land is not as simple as it might seem, as it would require the co-operation of the Aboriginal communities as well as the federal and provincial governments. The provincial government would have to transfer the land to the federal government if it is to be re-constituted as part of the reserve.

In my view, another solution worth considering is a co-management arrangement whereby the Aboriginal communities operate a re-opened park for the benefit of all Ontarians and visitors alike. . . .

This option has some attraction because it would enable the Aboriginal people to be responsible for the stewardship of the park land, including the identification and protection of burial sites. In addition, any proceeds from the operation of the park would flow to the Aboriginal community. This solution provides an opportunity for the provincial government and Aboriginal and non-Aboriginal communities to work together in a joint enterprise, with mutual benefit.

There may be other potential solutions for the park land that could be developed by those most directly affected. However, any solution to the situation at Ipperwash should not be regarded as a precedent for other land disputes; each situation requires its own solution, crafted by the people most directly affected.

Following Dudley George's death, Sam George and his siblings expressed their fundamental wish:

> In the beginning, all we asked them to do was tell us the truth. We just wanted someone to tell us something. I would much rather not have gone down that path myself. I didn't expect to be in litigation for seven years. I didn't think asking for the truth would become such a hard thing to get at.

. . .

14.2 Testimony of Nicholas Cottrelle, 2005

Nicholas Cottrelle was a 16-year-old high-school student in September of 1995 and a member of the Kettle and Stony Point First Nation. He was learning the traditions of his people from family and community elders and was one of those present in the park on the night the police moved in to remove the protestors. These selections from his testimony before the Ipperwash Public Inquiry, include Cottrelle's responses to the questions put to him by Commission Counsel Derry Miller and outline some of what he witnessed immediately before, after, and during the night of September 6th. It should be kept in mind that, like the other witnesses, Cottrelle is asked to remember events that occurred almost a decade earlier.

Source: Testimony of Nicholas Abraham Cottrelle, before the Honourable Justice Sidney Linden, Commissioner, Ipperwash Public Inquiry, Forest Community Centre, Kimberly Hall, Forest, Ontario, 18 January 2005, pp. 7, 17–20, 48–50, 64–65, 69, 77–83, 107–15, 120–21, 133–35, 146–48, 155–59.

© Queen's Printer for Ontario, 2013. Reproduced with permission.

. . .

NICHOLAS ABRAHAM COTTRELLE, Sworn

EXAMINATION-IN-CHIEF BY MR. DERRY MILLAR:

Q: *Morning, Mr. Cottrelle.*

A: Morning.

Q: *I understand you were born on March 8th, 1979?*

A: Yes.

Q: *And so that at the beginning of September 1995 you were sixteen (16) years old?*

A: Yes.

. . .

Q: *And the—during the summer of 1993, were you involved in learning about the traditions of your people from Marcia Simon or others?*

A: Yeah. A lot of people sat around the fire, nighttimes, during the day, and they talked about traditions and the people and stuff about the land.

Q: *And did you become involved in a society, when you moved on to the Army Camp in 1993?*

A: Yes. It was brought to my intention.

Q: *And can you tell us a little bit about that? And could you speak up a bit, Mr. Cottrelle—*

A: Yeah.

Q: *—I think people may be having trouble hearing you. And there's a glass of water there if you need it.*

A: Okay. It was brought to my attention about the Warrior Society.

Q: *Yes.*

A: About their roles in protecting the land as well as the well-being of the people that lived down there.

Q: *And who brought that to your attention?*

A: I believe it was Glenn.

Q: *And can you tell us a little bit more about what you understood the role of the Society was?*

A: It was more or less to protect the ways of our people.

Q: *Yes.*

A: And to protect the land.

Q: *Yes. And by protecting the land, what do you mean by that?*

A: Just against all aggressors.

Q: *And were you to protect the land using weapons or in peaceful ways, or how?*

A: Peaceful ways.

Q: *And—and can you tell us a little bit more about what you learned about that?*

A: Well, with—with the Park it was always everybody's understanding that it was going to be done peacefully, with no weapons. The same with the occupation of the territory as a whole too, was to be done peaceful.

Q: *And did you talk to your grandfather, Abraham George, about the Society?*

A: I can't really remember.

Q: *And the—did part of your duties involve assisting old people, the elderly—*

A: Yes.

Q: *—the Elders?*

A: Wood cutting, running errands for them.

Q: *And that was part of your—your obligation as a member of the Society?*

A: Just common knowledge, just out of respect.

Q: *And you told me before that you would not call—call it a Warrior Society but would give it a different name; can you tell me what that name was?*

A: Myself, I prefer Peacekeepers.

Q: *And why do you prefer Peacekeepers?*

A: Well, that's what we're—that's what we're doing, is trying to keep the peace with the situation in a whole, I guess.

Q: *And the situation in this case, in 1993, it was at the Army Camp?*

A: Yes.

Q: *And along the ranges and then later in a larger part of the area?*

A: Yes.

Q: *And then later at the Park?*

A: Yes.

. . .

Q: *And turning now to the Provincial Park and prior to September 4th, 1995, had you had any discussions with anyone about the Provincial Park and did you learn anything about the Provincial Park, from anyone?*

A: I knew it was a piece of the land, of the territory.

Q: *You knew that it was a piece of land that was part of the Stoney Point land?*

A: Yes.

Q: *And who did you learn that from?*

A: My grandfather.

Q: *And that's Abraham George?*

A: Yes.

Q: *And did your grandfather tell you anything else about the land, the Park?*

A: He had said that there was burial grounds along the maintenance shed road.

. . .

Q: *And so, what did your grandfather tell you about that?*

A: Just said along that ridge there, there was burial sites there. He had talked about them having picnics down there when he was a kid. I guess he used to clean the tables off and stuff for—I forget, I think he said a nickel or something—he would clean up after the picnics they had down there.

Q: *There were picnics down—*

A: When—

Q: *—when it was a provincial park or before it was a provincial park?*

A: Ah, way—no, way before. He was just a kid then.

Q: *Oh, when he was a kid.*

A: Yeah.

Q: *Yes.*

A: And really didn't say too much more that I can remember.

Q: *And they—now, that road, what's happened to that road that ran north from the maintenance area?*

A: We blocked it off.

Q: *And it's—today it's overgrown?*

A: Pretty much, yeah.

Q: *And why did you block—why was it blocked off?*

A: Just, he had asked us to block it off just because of the fact that I believe that the road actually goes over some grave sites; it's pretty—kind of disrespectful.

Q: *And that was your grandfather—*

A: Yes.

Q: *—asked the—the group to do that?*

A: Yes.

. . .

Q: *And on the evening of September 4th, did you observe any firearms in the Park, in the hands of the occupiers?*

A: No.

Q: *And the—so, you stayed in the Park or you—you can't recall if you stayed in the Park the evening of September 4th or went back to the barracks. Can you tell me, did you hear any firearms, gunshots or what sounded like gunshots, during the night of September 4th–September 5th?*

A: No.

. . .

Q: *And on the 5th or on the 6th, do you recall anything else—on the 5th, excuse me, do you recall anything else happening?*

A: I'm not sure—we barricaded all of the entrances, gates and stuff.

Q: *And the—you barricaded the entrances and gates, are you referring to the gate just to the west of the park store?*

A: Yeah, by the Sandy parking lot there.

Q: *Now, it's part of—*

A: Oh, yeah, okay, right here. The main entrance and Matheson Drive.

Q: *So that there was a—and why did you barricade the entrance by the Sandy parking lot, the main entrance and Matheson Drive?*

A: Just to lock everything down, block all entrances.

Q: *And why were you doing that?*

A: Just to keep people out.

. . .

Q: *And so why were you trying to block off the access to the beach?*

A: We, more or less, kind of, I don't know, just, kind of, get, like, a—a little barricade around the fire there—the gate to the Park. We start moving the tables out there and all these OPP cruisers showed up they had, like, the ram bars on front and they start hitting all of—all of the tables.

Q: *So, let's just go step by step. The—you started to move picnic tables out into the eastern part of the Sandy Parking Lot just east of where is says "Sand Covered Parking Lot"—*

A: Yeah.

Q: *—on Exhibit P125? And how many picnic tables were in the Sandy Parking Lot when the police cruisers arrived?*

A: I'd say maybe nine (9).

Q: *And how were they set up? Were they set up blocking the whole parking lot or you said they were around the fire?*

A: No, they were just—they were just, initially, just getting moved. They were just, kind of, scattered.

Q: *Okay. And did you know what the plan was—*

A: No.

Q: *—or was it—you don't know what the plan was to what to do with them after you got them there?*

A: Yeah. We were just kind of moving them.

Q: *So, how many cruisers arrived?*

A: I believe there was four (4) or five (5).

Q: *And what did the cruisers do?*

A: They start ramming the picnic tables.

Q: *And when you say "they started ramming the picnic tables" the—how fast was the cruiser—were the cruisers going?*

A: Well, they had a—they probably had a run at it from the paved road because they kind of lined up here at the paved road. So that's got to be, I don't know, maybe or thirty (30) or forty (40) feet maybe. They had a run at it. I can't say how fast they were going.

Q: *And—*

A: They were busting tables though, and that, they were hitting them.

Q: *And so where were they pushing the tables, the police?*

A: Right against the fence.

Q: *They were pushing them towards the fence?*

A: Yes.

Q: *And where were you when the police cars arrived?*

A: Right next to the turnstile. Myself and Stewart George were moving a table—

Q: *Yes.*

A: —and the cruiser actually hit it when we were still holding it. I believe I jumped out of the way. I almost got run over.

Q: *And the—what happened, the cruisers pushed the—the picnic tables against the fence; what, if anything, did the Occupiers do?*

A: We started throwing rocks at their cars.

Q: *Yes. And how long did this incident take place?*

A: It wasn't too long. Five (5)—five (5) minutes. Maybe a little bit more.

Q: *And after the police officers left were the picnic tables moved back out into the Sandy Parking Lot?*

A: No, we left them there.

Q: *Pardon me?*

A: We left them there backed against the fence there.

Q: *And did you have any other interactions with the Ontario Provincial Police officers on September 5th or September 6th before the incident in the evening of September 5th—September 6th?*

A: It was—can I—kind of mixed up on my days. We were all around the sandy parking lot when, I'd say, approximately eight (8) tactical members walked up to the fence line.

Q: *So were you on the inside or the outside of the Park?*

A: The inside.

Q: *There's a sandy parking lot on the inside of the Park as well; isn't there?*

A: Yeah, we were on—we were on the inside.

Q: *You were on the inside?*

A: Yeah.

Q: *And in the parking area on the west side of the fence line inside the Park?*

A: Yeah, right by the turn—turnstile.

Q: *Yes. And what happened?*

A: They walked up. There was nobody really said anything. And this little short fellow there he come over to the—out from the back of the crowd of the cops and singled—singled Dudley right out. Told him that he was going to be the first one to go.

Q: *And did this just happen out of the blue that this officer—*

A: Yeah. They—

Q: *—came up to the fence—*

A: They came out of—they came out of nowhere. Like,—

Q: *Did they—did they say anything before this police officer arrived? Were you—did you shout at the—your group shout at the police officers?*

A: Not that I can remember, no. 'Cause we were all just standing around and they just come out of—like, they didn't drive up or anything, they walked from somewhere.

Q: *Yes?*

A: And none of the other officers said nothing, but just that one fellow did.

Q: *And did he say anything else? Tell us exactly what he said.*

A: From what I remember it, he had told Dudley to—that he was going to be the first one (1) to go. He was saying stuff like, welcome to Canada, trying to call one (1) of us to the other side of the fence, calling us on, like, for a fight.

Q: *Yes?*

A: And I believe it was Marlin Simon, he picked up a handful of sand and threw it in his face.

Q: *Yes?*

A: And—or as soon as after he done that he grabbed some pepper spray, and he was trying to pepper spray us.

Q: *And what did your group do?*

A: We just backed up and we watched them, and they just took off.

. . .

Q: *And later in the afternoon and the early evening of September 6, were you aware of any change with respect to the police presence?*

A: I had noticed, myself, that there had—there was a lot more police in the tactical gear, the grey suit that you had up on the screen.

. . .

Q: *And where were the Occupiers . . . ? Were they inside the Park or outside the Park?*

A: Inside the Park.

Q: *And where were they?*

A: Lined up along the fence.

. . .

Q: *. . . And can you tell us what you observed?*

A: They were hitting their shields with their batons.

Q: *Yes?*

A: And they were doing a real heavy march.

Q: *What do you—*

A: Like a real stomp.

Q: *But they—when you say, "A real heavy march," can you describe that for us, Mr. Cottrelle?*

A: They were—they were all in sync and—with their march, though, when they would step forward, it was—they were stepping down heavy so we could hear it.

Q: *Yes?*

A: So we kind of heard the march—march of their boots and then, plus, on top of that, you could hear the—them hitting their shields with their batons.

Q: *And how were the—the police officers dressed?*

A: Full riot gear.

Q: *And when you say, "Full riot gear," what do you mean by that?*

A: They had these big gloves, reminded me of hockey gloves, shin pads, full face shields and black helmets on that come down to their shoulders. They also had the shields and telescopic batons.

Q: *And how do you know that they were telescopic batons?*

A: When they got up closer a few of them never had them and when they pulled them out you could—they made a motion down and you could see—you could see the baton coming out.

Q: *It would come out?*

A: Yeah.

Q: *It came out? So, the police officers were at the Point Number 3 on the East Parkway Drive when you arrived. What were the Occupiers doing?*

A: They were standing there at the fence line taking it all in, I guess.

Q: *Were there any lights on? Spotlights?*

A: I can't remember if there was any spotlights or anything.

Q: *And how did—what was the lighting like when you arrived back?*

A: It was fairly dark.

Q: *And how could you see the police officers?*

A: From the—the reflection off the fire from the sandy parking lot.

Q: *The fire that was on the inside of the park side of the turnstile?*

A: Yes.

Q: *I take it that fire was on the inside of the Park?*

A: I believe so, yes.

Q: *And can you recall, was it a full moon, or what was the moon like that night?*

A: I don't even remember. It was—it was dark.

Q: *And so then what happened?*

A: I jumped out of the car there, and had an old baseball bat in the back, I went up to the fence line with everybody else, and the Police, I believe they changed their position a couple of times, kind of like an advance forward, somebody was shouting commands, saying, advance forward, move left, just kind of getting in—getting in line, and stuff.

And I think that's when Bernard went out there.

Q: *And did—did anyone say anything to you when you arrived at the fence line about the Police?*

A: Just—no, I can't remember.

Q: *So, Cecil Bernard George, what did Cecil Bernard George do?*

A: He walked out the—the turnstile and started walking out towards the line of Police, and he was telling them that they had to go, that the Police had to leave, and he was also telling them that they'd never remove the Aboriginal people from the lands, stuff along that lines.

Q: *Well, can you tell us—*

A: That's his—that's all I can remember him saying.

Q: *Okay.*

A: Okay.

Q: *Thanks. And what, if anything, do you recall Cecil Bernard George having in his hand?*

A: His scanner maybe.

Q: *Yes.*

A: Maybe a small stick, club or something, I don't know.

Q: *Well, Cecil Bernard George has testified that he had a steel pipe in his hand, do you recall that?*

A: I—no, I don't.

Q: *Do you recall something in his hand?*

A: I knew—I knew he had something, I don't know if it was a pipe or a stick or something—

Q: *Okay.*

A: —but I know he had something.

Q: *And then what happened? How—why was—Cecil Bernard George went out into the Sandy parking lot from the turnstile, he was saying things to the Police Officers, what happened?*

A: There was an order given, I'm not too sure what—what the Officer had said, but there was a group on the—it would have been the right, the right side of the formation.

Q: *And at this point, where was the formation?*

A: It was right along—just on the inside of the paved road, right in here.

Q: *The—so the officers were lined up across the roadway, just to the—*

A: North side.

Q: *—east—northeast side of where you've got Item number 1?*

A: Yeah.

Q: *And so the Officers were lined up there, and how many Officers were there, do you recall?*

A: Forty (40), maybe thirty (30), forty (40).

Q: *So, what happened?*

A: The right side of that formation of the Police—Police line, they—they came out and they rushed Bernard.

Q: *And when you say the right side of the formation, that would be the—the Officers on the eastern part of the line?*

A: Yes.

Q: *Yes. And they—so they rushed Bernard, Cecil Bernard George—*

A: Yes.

Q: *—then what happened?*

A: They rushed out, hitting him with their shields, knocked him down and they just started beating on him.

Q: *And how many Police Officers were involved?*

A: Eight (8).

Q: *And where were the other occupiers at this point?*

A: We were still on the fence line.

Q: *And what, if anything, did the—you do?*

A: Myself, we were just, kind of, looking around, kind of taking it in for a second. And I believe it was his sister that was beside me and she was screaming around, somebody's got to do something. Somebody's got to get out there.

Q: *And what was—and that was Gina—Gina George or Gina Johnson?*

A: Johnson.

Q: *Yes. And what was happening—what was Cecil Bernard George at this point?*

A: He was probably in—maybe in this area here.

Q: *And was that the area where he was when he was grabbed by the police officers?*

A: Yes. I believe so.

Q: *And could you mark an "X" where you observed Cecil Bernard George being taken by the police officers and put beside it a number 4?*

A: (INDICATING)

Q: *And did you see Cecil Bernard George hit at the police officers?*

A: No, I don't think he had the chance to.

Q: *And so the group of police officers that had Cecil Bernard George at X4 they grabbed him at that, what did they do with him?*

A: They circled around him and they were kicking him and, you know, with their batons.

Q: *Yes. And then what happened with—*

A: They just kept beating on him and couple of guys—well, I don't know how many guys went across, including myself, and I believe we—that's when we had our first fight with the cops.

Q: *And the—where were the other—when you went across the fence line how many of your group went across the fence line with you; do you remember?*

A: I can't remember.

Q: *And do you recall how many people were along the fence line?*

A: Thirteen (13), fourteen (14) maybe.

. . .

Q: *And were the—were the police officers that were around near Cecil Bernard George when he was at item 5, were they—how were they dressed?*

A: They all had the same gear on, the riot—full riot gear.

Q: *And did they have—did they have shields?*

A: Yes.

Q: *So, Cecil Bernard George is at the point where you've marked number 5. Someone said, Get the bus. What did you do?*

A: I ran over to the bus and I had jumped in. It was—it was already running. And I was just getting ready to put it in gear when Leland George came to the door and wanted to go for a ride. I told him just to get in, get in the back.

Q: *And when you—the bus was located where?*

A: I think just north of the gate.

. . .

Q: *And so when you were on the bus when you went out into the Park and when you came back into the Park; did you have a firearm?*

A: No.

Q: *Did you observe whether Leland—did Leland George have a firearm?*

A: There was absolutely no firearms in the Park.

Q: *When you say "there was absolutely no firearms in the Park" on—why do you say that?*

A: Because it was a peaceful occupation.

Q: *And—and so what does that mean, to you?*

A: To me, it means that we knew that we were right what we were doing by reclaiming the Park out by the burial grounds and there was no need for any kind of violence whatsoever.

There was to be no firearms. Nobody was to be drinking, anything like that.

Q: *And the—did you observe any firearms in the hands of the occupiers on September 6th?*

A: No.

Q: *And on the evening of—during the confrontation?*

A: No.

Q: *And after the—after the confrontation you went to the hospital?*

A: Yes.

Q: *And did—but did you observe any before you went to the hospital?*

A: No.

. . .

Q: *Now, you told us that when you got off the bus you looked around for your father, and you could feel the back of your shirt was wet, is that correct?*

A: Yes. Yes.

. . .

Q: *And you got your—you went to the gate and you saw your father, you—you called him back in, I take it he came back in?*

A: Yes, and we walked towards the Park store.

Q: *And then what did you do?*

A: He'd . . . said, I was shot. And we jumped in the car and went through the front gate.

. . .

Q: *. . . Then what happened?*

A: We went out the gate and we pulled up at—at the intersection out there, and—

. . .

A: We stopped and just out of nowhere there's all these cops come flying out the ditch, they had rifles, telling us to put our hands up and kept circling the car and my mother was screaming at them, don't shoot. She was screaming at them about something. And they cleared the car, like, they made sure there was no guns or anything in there, and then they let the ambulance attendants come over.

Q: *So, at the point the Police Officers came out of the ditch, they were pointing rifles at the occupants in the car?*

A: Yes.

. . .

Q: *And where were you taken?*

A: Strathroy Hospital.

. . .

Q: *And when you were in your room what happened?*

. . .

A: They just put me in the room and then they had OPP guards inside and outside the room.

Q: *And how many, when you say OPP guards on the inside of the room, how many police officers were inside the room?*

A: Two (2) on each side of the bed, and there was a couple out in the hallway at all times.

Q: *So there was—you were in a bed against—I take it the head was against the wall?*

A: Yeah.

Q: *And there was one (1) Police Officer on both—on each side of the bed?*

A: Yeah, both corners.

Q: *And then there were—you—could you see the Police Officers outside the room?*

A: Yeah, you could see, there was always one (1) standing by the door and a couple walking by here and there.

Q: *And what if anything did the Police Officers say to you that were in the room?*

A: Nothing, I never talked to them.

Q: *Did they try to talk to you?*

A: Well, they might have, I don't—can't remember.

Q: *Okay. And what happened? This is—*

A: I was—I was trying to stay awake.

Q: *And why were you trying to stay awake?*

A: I was still scared, I didn't trust them. I didn't trust Police.

Q: *Yes.*

A: I didn't know what they were going to try to do to me, while—if I fell asleep or anything, and so I was just trying to stay awake for as long as I could, and eventually I fell asleep, and I woke up and there was cops all around my bed, and the one (1) technical Police Officer, a big guy, he was—my right hand was already wet and he was rubbing this stuff on there with—like a cotton gauze, cotton balls and stuff.

Q: *Yes.*

A: And I kind of come to, and said what are you guys doing? And he just dropped my hand and they went over to the garbage and they got all my clothes and they took off.

Q: *And did they tell you what they were doing?*

A: No.

Q: *And when you woke up, your one (1) hand was wet and the—the other hand was—*

A: Yeah, they were rubbing stuff on it, later I learned it was testing for gunshot residue.

. . .

Q: *. . . So, you were then taken to an interview room?*

A: Yes.

Q: *And then what happened?*

A: Just taken in that room, and all there was a table in there, a couple of chairs. A Detective came in there, Martin, I believe his name is.

Q: *Martin? Yes?*

A: He had sat me down and start talking, asking me what happened, and he had told me that I wasn't allowed to leave or make a phone call until I gave a statement.

Q: *Did you ask him to—*

A: I believe I asked him for to call my mother or my lawyer.

Q: *And—*

A: I'm pretty sure I did that.

Q: *And—*

A: And that's—that was his reply.

Q: *That he said to you that you couldn't do that until you made a statement?*

A: Yes.

Q: *And did—do you know if Constable Martin or the Detective from the Ontario Provincial Police knew how old you were when you were at the Strathroy Detachment?*

A: I'd imagine they would.

Q: *And when you say you imagine they would,—*

A: Because I told the doctor at—at the hospital, how old I was.

Q: *That you were—*

A: They knew—they knew my age and . . .

Q: *Okay. And, so, the officer said that you couldn't call your mother or a lawyer or leave until you made a statement, and did you make a statement at that time?*

A: No, I waited them out for about four and a half (4 ½), five (5) hours.

Q: *And what happened then?*

A: Finally I just told them to come in and I start telling them what was going on and I think we got up to about 9:00 o'clock and then he quit writing. And he was trying to get me to say other stuff.

Q: *When you say, you were telling him what happened on the evening of September 6th,—*

A: Well, I told him everything that happened right up to—right up 'til I went up to the highway,—

Q: *Yes?*

A:—and when I got into the ambulance, but he didn't want to hear from when I showed up to do—at the fence line, before the altercation. From that time to when I got to the highway, he didn't want to listen to it, he already had his own version.

Q: *Well, can you explain that to me, Mr. Cottrelle, how do you know he had his own version? Just tell me exactly what happened, please.*

A: He was—he was trying to say, he goes, oh, well we got a reason to believe there was heavy gunfire coming out of the—coming out of the bus, out of the car, and he was trying to get me to say that, so he can write it in that statement. And it's clear on that statement that I give him, that the time line goes up so far and then he quit writing, and he knew he wasn't going to get anywhere.

Q: *And so you—you disagreed with what he was saying?*

A: Oh yeah. Yes.

Q: *And the conversation came to an end?*

A: Yes, and it was shortly after that I was able to make a phone call.

Q: *Okay. And you called—who did you call?*

A: I believe I phoned Spike.

Q: *And Spike is Ron George?*

A: Yes.

Q: *And Ron George at the time was a lawyer?*

A: Yeah, he was my lawyer at the time.

Q: *And Ron George had been before and subsequently became an OPP Officer?*

A: I think it was before that, when he was a lawyer, and he's an OPP Officer Inspector.

Q: *And so you spoke to Ron George. Did you speak to your mother as well?*

A: I can't remember. I knew, they came—that was who came and picked me up though.

Q: *Was?*

A: Ron and my mother.

. . .

14.3 Presentation of Sam George, 2006

Below is the brief final statement of Maynard Donald "Sam" George before the Ipperwash Public Inquiry. Sam George, Dudley George's older brother, had already been on a journey of more than a decade in length by the time of this statement. The elder George's journey began with a telephone call on the night of September 6, 1995, lasted through Ontario Provincial Police Sergeant Kenneth Deane's criminal trial for the wrongful death of his brother, and finally culminated in the two-year-long Ipperwash Inquiry. Sam George always recognized that Deane was only part of the story at Ipperwash. The more important question was what led to Deane being there in the first place. In this selection, George outlines some of his own experiences and his hopes for the results of the inquiry.

Source: Sam George, Final Submissions of the Dudley George Estate and Family Group, before the Honourable Justice Sidney Linden, Commissioner, Ipperwash Public Inquiry, Forest Community Centre, Kimberly Hall, Forest, Ontario, 21 August 2006, pp. 15–21.

. . .

MR. MURRAY KLIPPENSTEIN: With your permission, Commissioner, the—Mr. Sam George who's been with us for much of the Inquiry would like to make a few comments on behalf of the Estate and Family of Dudley George and then I will complete the submissions if that's all right.

COMMISSIONER SIDNEY LINDEN: Thank you very much. Yes. Welcome. Welcome, Mr. George.

FINAL SUBMISSIONS BY DUDLEY GEORGE ESTATE AND FAMILY GROUP:

MR. SAM GEORGE: Good morning, Mr. Commissioner.

The last eleven (11) years has been a real journey, one I would not like to wish on anyone. The start of it was not very pleasant for—to my family, myself, or to my community.

I have learned a lot over these years and I've also lost a lot. There are things I can never replace or ever re-live. I have seen so much hurt towards other people just because they are upset at something or at someone so they try to make themselves feel better by doing things to—to others.

I know there are people who don't like what I—what I did, but they never saw things through my eyes or felt my heart hurt the way it did and it still hurts when I think about that night.

In the beginning people told me I would never find out the truth—what the truth was, but I had to try. As one (1) of the children of Reg and Jenny George I am a member of a proud family with other siblings; Reg Jr., Cully, Perry, Joan, Pam, Laverne.

We also knew that things were not right about the death of our brother, Dudley. I knew from the time I arrived at the hospital that night, the way everyone was acting, it was like walking into a movie. After hearing what they had to tell me, it was in—it was time to start helping Dudley get ready for that final journey he was now going to make.

We also had to get back home to let the rest of the family know, but before I could do that, I had to find out where my brother and sister were.

The police at the hospital told me they were at the OPP station, so I went over and then asked to see them and after a little time, the police let me in to talk to them.

The first question they asked was, how was Dudley? I had to tell them he had died from the gunshot wound. I had to leave them there in those jail cells.

Once I got close to Forest on my way back I was stopped at—OPP road block and told to get out of my van. I had a gun pointed at me. My wife and son were also in the van with me and it was only a short time ago that I found out that they had guns pointed at them that night.

I was asked by an officer where I was going, so I told them I was going home to tell my family about Dudley and they let us go. But the image stayed in my head for a long time because I've never had a gun pointed at me before and never again since that night.

This was the start of a journey which I had no idea where it was going to take me until today.

On that evening, Dudley did not think he would have been shot at, much less shot dead. I wished it would have never happened. I think it should have never happened.

I'm very proud of Dudley because of the way he stood up for himself and his people. He believed why he was there and it was time to protect our lands where the burial grounds were and which had been promised to us, and for this he gave up his life.

I would like to thank my brother for the time he spent here with me.

(BRIEF PAUSE)

MR. SAM GEORGE: And as my brother—for all the happy times and for all he had taught—taught us and for all he has done for his family and his people.

His work is still being done and that is what we ought—now have to learn to work together and listen to each other in a good way.

But Dudley can now rest because he has given us the work that we need to do.

I would like to thank the Commissioner so much for the way he had listened so carefully to our people. Whatever happens, I will always be grateful.

I would like to thank the present leaders of Ontario, the people of Ontario who have chosen to spend a lot of time and money on this Inquiry, not to fight against us but to listen to us and to try and understand what Dudley and the others were saying about our lands and our burial grounds.

I would like to thank Commission Counsel and Commission staff; they worked so very hard and we are very grateful for what they have done.

I would like to thank the many witnesses who came forward and told the truth. I know it was a difficult thing to go through and I want you to realize that we are very grateful.

I want to thank the other parties and their legal Counsels in the Inquiry who were often so considerate. I would like to thank our legal Team—Counsel on behalf of Dudley and his family.

This is a team that came together to help bring out the truth and also believe in our story. The only bad thing that—was that they had to put up with me all them years.

I also believe that—that when there is work like this it has to be done, the Great Spirit sends us to each other. We would have never got this done without a legal time [sic] like the one we have. We are—we are a very lucky family and we would like to thank them now for all their hard work, sleepless nights working on the files with us. Thank you from the Dudley George family.

There comes a time when one must look back and thank some of the ones who watched me as I went through this. I went through this trying to get where we are today.

My children, who when asked to help, never said no and they were always there to support their uncle Dudley. I would like to thank my sisters and my brothers for trusting me to do the—this work with them. I hope I did a good job. But the one who stood behind me the most was my wife. She watched me I went—as I went through this journey. I thank my wife, Veronica, for being there for me and with me. So to my wife, Veronica, and my children who helped me and to my family, thank you.

Dudley can now rest in peace. And as we come to the end of the Inquiry we can start our healing. We can start to learn how to forgive but we will never forget the night of September 6th, 1995. Thank you.

COMMISSIONER SIDNEY LINDEN: Thank you, Mr. George.

. . .

SUGGESTIONS FOR FURTHER READING

The full text of the *Report of the Ipperwash Inquiry* as well as research and discussion papers prepared for and by the commission and transcripts of evidence presented at the hearings of the commission along with other materials are available on line at http://www.attorneygeneral.jus.gov.on.ca/inquiries/ipperwash/index.html. Of special interest for those seeking more context are the research papers prepared for the commission, some by distinguished Indigenous scholars such as Taiaiake Alfred and John Borrows. These are available by following the links from the "Policy and Research" button at the URL included previously. For an overview and analysis of the events at Ipperwash, including suggestions for resolution of similar grievances in the future, see Edward Hedican, *Ipperwash: The Tragic Failure of Canada's Aboriginal Policy* (Toronto: University of Toronto Press, 2013). For a journalist's rendition of the events at Ipperwash, see Peter Edwards, *One Dead Indian: The Premier, the Police, and the Ipperwash Crisis* (Toronto: Stoddart Publishing, 2001). This book was made into a television movie by CTV: Tim Southam, *One Dead Indian* (Thornhill, ON: Mongrel Media, 2006).

CHAPTER 15

"A UNIQUE TRUST-LIKE RELATIONSHIP"[1]

MODERN TREATY MAKING

As mentioned in Chapter 2, treaty making was a fundamental component of the earliest encounters between Indigenous peoples and the newcomers to their territories in what became Canada. Although the Crown's reasons for entering into treaties changed over time from ensuring peace and friendship to the acquisition of land, the importance of treaty making was always understood and was codified in the Royal Proclamation of 1763. Yet, in the third quarter of the twentieth century, many areas of Canada remained unceded by any Indigenous nation. Since then, beginning with the James Bay and Northern Quebec Agreement in 1975, over a dozen comprehensive claims have been negotiated between Indigenous peoples and the Crown. Even at that, though, there are large tracts of land that still have not been treated for in the second decade of the twenty-first century.

As part of its early 1990s investigation into the relationship between Indigenous peoples and Canadians, the Royal Commission on Aboriginal Peoples (RCAP) engaged in a comprehensive exploration of the historic and modern treaties and the importance of future agreements. The commissioners soon realized that there was a general lack of understanding among non-Indigenous Canadians about the meaning and present-day significance of historic treaties. Further, the commissioners recommended that steps be taken to both recognize the spirit and intent of treaties already made and to create a process whereby future agreements could be made in a way that recognizes the nature of the nation-to-nation relationship between the Crown and individual Indigenous nations. Selections from the RCAP report on modern and future treaties appear below.

---

1 *Restructuring the Relationship*, vol. 2 of *Report of the Royal Commission on Aboriginal Peoples* (Ottawa: Aboriginal Affairs and Northern Development Canada, 1996), 16. This quotation appears in document 15.1.

One of the regions in Canada that remains largely untreated is Canada's most western province. In the nineteenth century, the only treaties signed in what became British Columbia were the 14 "Douglas treaties" (also known as the Fort Victoria or Vancouver Island treaties) covering less than 1,000 square kilometres of Vancouver Island and the BC section of Treaty 8 in the north-east corner of the province. This paucity of treaty making is not for any lack of trying on the part of First Nations. Nisga'a chiefs, for example, travelled to Victoria in 1887 to press their case for a treaty that would recognize their title to ancestral territory in north-western BC. Close to a century later, in 1976, Canada finally agreed to begin negotiations with the Nisga'a. Fourteen years after that, the province of British Columbia joined in. The 12 years of negotiations that followed resulted in an agreement that came into force in April of 2000. Even then, the agreement was challenged by the Opposition, at that time the BC Liberal Party, which unsuccessfully sought to have the agreement declared unconstitutional. Included below is the transcript of a speech made to the Legislative Assembly of British Columbia in December of 1988, a few months after the initialling of the final agreement, by Chief Joseph Gosnell, president of the Nisga'a Tribal Council.

While the tripartite Nisga'a negotiations were underway, representatives of First Nations in British Columbia came to an agreement with the governments of Canada and BC to form the British Columbia Claims Task Force in 1990. The task force, in turn, recommended a six-stage process for negotiating new treaties. The result was the creation of the British Columbia Treaty Commission and the BC treaty process. More than 20 years after the process began, only two treaties have been ratified using it: the Tsawwassen and Maa-nulth treaties.

In 2007, the British Columbia Treaty Commission and the Nisga'a Lisms Government hosted a conference in Vancouver in which the representatives of 69 First Nations and First Nations organizations from across Canada were asked this question: "Are treaties the answer?" Two competing perspectives appear in document 15.3. There are, of course, many other views on treaties and the BC treaty process that are not included here. Some Indigenous leaders, for example, argue that the process, as it stands, is simply a more sophisticated method of promoting assimilation. In the end, each community will decide whether the treaty process, the courts, or some other strategy will provide the best hope for a secure future.

QUESTIONS FOR DISCUSSION

1. Are the historic treaties still relevant and important in twenty-first century Canada? Why or why not?
2. Why do you suppose there is a general lack of understanding regarding the treaty relationship between Indigenous peoples and Canada? How might this problem be resolved?
3. Which of the recommendations of the RCAP report on treaties do you find the most important? Why?
4. Could the Nisga'a have done anything different to expedite the process of securing a treaty?

5. What are Chief Robert Louie's concerns about the BC treaty process?
6. Why might some say that the treaty process, as it stands at present in British Columbia, is nothing more than a contemporary strategy of assimilation?

DOCUMENTS

15.1 Royal Commission on Aboriginal Peoples, "Treaties," 1996

This selection contains further excerpts from the 1996 Report of the Royal Commission on Aboriginal Peoples. In their chapter on treaties, the commissioners presented findings on the nature and modern-day relevance of historic treaties, their conclusions regarding Canadians' general lack of understanding of the treaty relationship, and their recommendations for future treaty making and treaty implementation. Like many of the other problems identified by RCAP, issues related to treaties and the appropriation of the land and resources of Indigenous people remain unresolved even today.

Source: *Restructuring the Relationship*, vol. 2 of *Report of the Royal Commission on Aboriginal Peoples* (Ottawa: Aboriginal Affairs and Northern Development Canada, 1996), 9, 11, 13, 15–18, 60–65, and 68–70.

Reproduced with the permission of the Minister of Public Works and Government Services Canada, 2012.

Footnotes appearing in the original have been removed.

2

TREATIES

When our peoples entered into treaties, there were nations of peoples. And, people always wonder why, what is a nation? Because only nations can enter into treaties. Our peoples, prior to the arrival of the non-indigenous peoples, were under a single political society. They had their own languages. They had their own spiritual beliefs. They had their own political institutions. They had the land base, and they possessed historic continuity on this land base.

Within these structures, they were able to enter into treaties amongst themselves as different tribes, as different nations on this land. In that capacity they entered into treaty with the British people. So, these treaties were entered into on a nation-to-nation basis. That treaty set out for us what our relationship will be with the British Crown and her successive governments.

Regena Crowchild
President, Indian Association of Alberta
Edmonton, Alberta, 11 June 1992

. . .

Treaties were made in the past because the rights of Aboriginal and non-Aboriginal people occupying a common territory could come into conflict unless some means of reconciliation was found. Contemporary Canadian law recognizes Aboriginal rights as being based on practices that are "an integral part of their distinctive culture". The unique nature of Aboriginal rights, as understood in Canadian law, makes it difficult to fit them into the context of rights and obligations our courts are accustomed to addressing. By entering into treaties, the parties can clarify how these rights should interact with one another.

Treaty making can enable the deepest differences to be set aside in favour of a consensual and peaceful relationship. The parties to a treaty need not surrender their fundamental cultural precepts in order to make an agreement to coexist. They need only communicate their joint desire to live together in peace, to embody in their own laws and institutions respect for each other, and to fulfil their mutual promises.

1. A Need For Public Education

We have an agreement as treaty Indians and we believe that these treaties cannot be broken or changed or negotiated because a sacred pipe was used when the treaties were signed and sealed.

Nancy Louis
Samson Cree Nation
Hobbema, Alberta, 10 June 1992

Prejudice has prevented non-Aboriginal society from recognizing the depth, sophistication and beauty of our culture. . . . But this must change, or there will be immense suffering in the future in this beautiful land which the Creator has bestowed upon us.

Chief Eli Mandamin
Kenora, Ontario, 28 October 1992

In Volume 5, Chapter 4 we discuss in detail a program of public education on Aboriginal issues. Here we focus on the state of public knowledge about the treaties, which, unfortunately, are poorly understood by most Canadians.

. . .

The Commission undertook historical and legal research on the treaties on a scale unprecedented in our country's history. We heard at length from First Nations leaders and elders in all parts of the country about the treaties that were made. We heard from Inuit about their land claims agreements, which are modern-day treaties. We heard from the Métis Nation about their hope for a new accord or compact to formalize their relationship with Canada. We heard from leaders and elders of other nations, which were denied the opportunity to make a treaty with the Crown, that they want to do so now, if it can be done upon a proper foundation of mutual respect.

The Canada that takes a proud place among the family of nations was made possible by the treaties. Our defining national characteristics are tolerance, pluralism and democracy. Had it not been for the treaties, these defining myths might well not have taken hold here. Had it not been for the treaties, wars might well have replaced the treaty council. Or the territory might have been absorbed by the union to the south. Canada would have been a very different place if treaty making with the Indian nations had been replaced by the waging of war.

Each of the European nations that came to America to plant a flag and assert imperial pretensions had a particular approach to the people of the continent. The French settled in the St. Lawrence Valley and made such short-term military alliances as were necessary to secure peace and trade. The British brought the common law, reinvented the Indian treaty on the basis of that law, and used it as their primary tool for relating to the Indian nations. This led to what might be termed a friendlier form of expropriation. Certainly the British honed the process of treaty making for purposes of land cession to a fine art.

In the treaties, the British Crown and the Indian nations pledged undying loyalty to one another. The Crown's honour was pledged to fulfilling solemnly made treaty promises. When these promises were dishonoured, the results were shameful. As Alexis de Tocqueville wrote in 1840, "the conduct of the United States Americans towards the natives was inspired by the most chaste affection for legal formalities. . . . It is impossible to destroy men with more respect to the laws of humanity." Substitute 'British' or 'Canadians' for 'United States Americans' and the statement remains as valid and as provocative.

Indian treaties bear the strong imprint of the British legal system. Treaties are of course universal means of arranging alliances, enabling disparate peoples to keep the peace, and establishing mutually beneficial arrangements. What the British did uniquely was to establish unilaterally, in the *Royal Proclamation of 1763*, a set of rules to govern treaty making with the Aboriginal peoples of North America. These rules, as Canadian courts have since declared, gave rise to a unique trust-like relationship, which continues to have legal and political effect today.

The British legal system regarded the creation of these rules as an assertion of British sovereignty and dominion over the land occupied by the Aboriginal nations. Courts in Canada have accepted that it is not their role to question the legality of this assertion of authority. Within the boundaries of our mandate, however, the Commission can and does challenge the legitimacy of certain conclusions based on the Crown's assertions, particularly when they call into question the Crown's declared policies of honourable dealing and its legal duty so to deal (see our recommendations in Volume 1, Chapter 16). It is the Commission's duty to examine the Crown's role in making and fulfilling treaties with First Nations and to make recommendations to the Crown in relation to these historical actions.

The view described earlier—that treaties are no more than outdated scraps of paper—has led many Canadians to consider that the specific obligations described in the treaty documents are trivial and can therefore be easily discharged. In this view, treaties are ancient and anachronistic documents with no relevance today. Like Prime Minister Trudeau in 1969, many Canadians still do not understand how, in a modern democratic society, treaties can continue to exist between different parts of society.

The other view—that treaties were weapons in a war fought not by combat but by deception and the systematic dishonouring of the sovereign's solemn pledges—leaves many Canadians puzzled, even appalled, by the prospect of giving renewed effect to treaties made in the distant (or even the recent) past. They react even more strongly to the prospect of making new treaties. There remains a view among Canadians that old treaty obligations might have to be fulfilled—grudgingly—but that the making of new ones is anathema to a vital and modern nation.

Canadian law and public policy have moved well ahead of these widely shared opinions about treaties. A mere twelve years after his 1969 speech, Prime Minister Trudeau agreed to a constitutional amendment that gave constitutional protection to "existing aboriginal and treaty rights". By that time the courts had given strong indications that these rights had considerable legal significance. A year after the patriation of the constitution, Prime Minister Trudeau endorsed a further constitutional amendment that recognized the contemporary land claims process as the making of new treaties.

Canadians' knowledge and understanding of treaties have not kept pace with these changes. Canadians are not taught that Canada was built on the formal treaty alliances that European explorers, military commanders and later civil authorities were able to forge with the nations they encountered on this continent. Today, with increasing awareness of Aboriginal issues, young Canadians may learn more about the treaties than their parents did, but there is still little in the way of teaching material and curriculum development to dispel this ignorance. It is especially unfortunate that the younger members of the treaty nations may be losing a sense of their own history. If, as Justice Reed said, "every schoolboy knows" that the treaties were a sham used to disguise the expropriation of land, then this is the direct result of schoolboys having been misled or at least deprived of the truth about the treaties and about the peoples that made them.

Our discussion of the historical treaties will of necessity be dominated by a discussion of First Nations. Treaties were not generally made with Métis people or Inuit. As a result, this chapter may appear to focus on only one of the three Aboriginal peoples of Canada. Nevertheless the making of treaties in the future can and should be open to all Aboriginal nations that choose a treaty approach. Many of the future treaties may well be termed accords or compacts or simply land claims agreements. But the Commission believes that treaties, by any name, are a key to Canada's future. We will propose processes to implement and renew the historical treaties, which will involve an examination of the spirit and intent of those treaties. We will also make recommendations to revitalize treaty making for Aboriginal nations that have not yet entered into treaties with the Crown.

We will propose a rethinking of the treaties as a means to secure justice for Aboriginal nations and a reconciliation of their rights with the rights of all Canadians. The result could be a new, satisfying and enduring relationship between the Aboriginal and treaty nations and other Canadians. It is within the treaty processes we propose that our substantive recommendations on matters such as governance, lands and resources, and economic issues will ultimately be addressed.

Treaties need to become a central part of our national identity and mythology. Treaties have the following attributes:

- They were made between the Crown and nations of Aboriginal people, nations that continue to exist and are entitled to respect.
- They were entered into at sacred ceremonies and were intended to be enduring.
- They are fundamental components of the constitution of Canada, analogous to the terms of union under which provinces joined Confederation.

- The fulfilment of the spirit and intent of the treaties is a fundamental test of the honour of the Crown and of Canada.
- Their non-fulfilment casts a shadow over Canada's place of respect in the family of nations.

. . .

5.1 Implementation of Modern Treaties

Our essential conclusions about the historical treaties are equally applicable to treaties that will be made in the future. We regard the treaty-making process as a continuing and vital part of Canadian life. We do not regard modern treaties as any less binding or enduring than earlier ones. We agree that treaties made in the future, like those made in the recent past, will be made largely on the basis of a common language and greater sensitivity on both sides to the matters that can produce difficulties of interpretation. Having said this, modern treaties and future treaties alike will benefit from the perspective that they are, above all, embodiments of a nation-to-nation partnership.

Our assessment of the comprehensive claims policy leads us to conclude that implementation of modern treaties made under that policy should involve two main themes. First, they should be reopened to permit the addition of constitutionally entrenched rights of self-government. The full implications of this conclusion will be fleshed out in the next chapter. Second, where a modern treaty contains a provision for the blanket extinguishment of the Aboriginal party's land rights, that party might elect to have the treaty reopened for renegotiation.

Renegotiation would require *both* parties to begin again at the starting point of those treaties. Logically, this would require the revival of Aboriginal rights to land that were extinguished in blanket fashion. However, it would also require the Aboriginal party to account for all benefits received in exchange for extinguishment. It is quite possible that the federal, provincial or territorial governments involved in the renegotiation would be unwilling to pay as much as was provided in the original agreements, given their view that renegotiation could diminish the degree of certainty and finality involved.

We must also emphasize that renegotiating modern treaties would require untangling the complex arrangements that have grown up around them. Unlike historical treaties, modern treaties call explicitly for frequent renegotiation of particular issues and contain dispute-resolution mechanisms negotiated by the parties and tailor-made for the circumstances of the original agreement. In this sense, they are 'living' agreements to a greater extent than the historical treaties. We would therefore urge the parties to modern treaties to exercise caution in discussing implementation and renewal of these treaties. Nevertheless, to the extent that these treaties do not meet the requirements of a modern relationship as outlined in this chapter, they warrant modification.

It may well be that the treaty principles we have identified can be implemented without wholesale renegotiation. It may also be possible for the negotiations we envisage to take place within the framework of the modern treaties. We encourage the parties to explore all their options and the implications of their treaty partnership before concluding that wholesale renegotiation must occur.

. . .

5.3 Making New Treaties and Equivalent Agreements

The Commission does caution that not all groups of Aboriginal people will be eligible for treaty nation standing. The basic unit of Aboriginal self-determination and self-governance is the nation (see Chapter 3), and in our view only nations can have treaty relations with the Crown. There must be some objective criteria that define a nation, and we discuss what these might be in the next chapter.

First Nations, Inuit and Métis presenters at our hearings pointed out that their peoples are distinct from each other, with different political and cultural traditions, including their traditions of forming relationships with the Crown and with other peoples. Treaty making has been the traditional method whereby First Nations and the Crown have made compacts for coexistence. To avoid misunderstanding, we emphasize that we are not advocating the adoption of First Nations traditions by Inuit and Métis groups.

Our focus is the formalization of new relationships. Internationally, the treaty is used to achieve this between nation-states. In Canada, although treaties have been used to fashion *sui generis* relationships with Aboriginal peoples, the term has been used primarily in connection with First Nations. The agreements made in the future between the Crown and Aboriginal nations might well be called accords, compacts, land claims agreements, settlement agreements or other appropriate terms. They would reflect different world views and priorities. Indeed, if they are true treaties, they would necessarily give expression to the unique rights and cultures of the Aboriginal nations signing them. Our point is that treaty relationships and access to treaty institutions should be extended to all nations of Aboriginal people that want to have them.

We must also caution that we regard treaty making as the exclusive preserve of nations. In the case of the treaty implementation and renewal process described earlier in this chapter, the nation status of the treaty nations was determined by the original act of treaty making. In the case of Aboriginal nations seeking to enter the treaty process today, their status as nations will have to be established.

To open the treaty-making process to Aboriginal groups that do not meet the criteria of a nation would detract from the fundamental nature of treaties and the integrity and status of the nations that make them. This does not preclude a variety of other initiatives to give effect to the rights and aspirations of groups that do not qualify as nations. It simply preserves the essential nation-to-nation nature of the treaties.

Inuit land claims agreements

The Inuit experience with treaties has been restricted to the modern comprehensive land claims process, beginning in 1975 with the James Bay and Northern Quebec Agreement and continuing with the Inuvialuit Final Agreement in 1984 and the signing of the Nunavut Land Claims Agreement on 25 May 1993. These agreements are often termed modern treaties. Negotiations on the Labrador Inuit claims continue. The Inuit leadership, like that of First Nations that have signed comprehensive claims agreements, has questioned the legitimacy of the extinguishment clauses in those agreements.

The Inuit leadership has sought constitutional recognition of Inuit Aboriginal rights, including the right of self-government, and has generally striven for forms of public government. Inuit refer to themselves as a people rather than as a nation or nations. This terminology does not alter the fact that many Inuit groups would likely meet the criteria of nationhood and would be eligible to establish a treaty process if they wanted to do so.

Again, we emphasize that there is no reason why treaties with Inuit have to resemble those with other Aboriginal peoples. As Inuit land claims agreements show, the negotiation of a modern treaty can result in public government and include many other elements tailored to the circumstances of Inuit.

Métis treaties

Some persons regarded as Métis were included as 'Indians' in some of the historical treaties, but Métis people generally have been excluded from treaty making. More recently the Métis Association of the Northwest Territories signed the 1990 final agreement on the Dene/Métis claim in the Northwest Territories. That agreement has not been ratified, however, because of objections to its reference to blanket extinguishment of Aboriginal rights to land. The Sahtu Métis (along with the Sahtu Dene) have since signed a comprehensive claims agreement.

The Commission regards Métis people as eligible to negotiate a treaty relationship with Canada subject to the criteria defining 'nation' or 'people'.

The western Métis Nation has pursued negotiations for a Métis Nation accord, but the latest attempt was thwarted by the failure of the Charlottetown Accord in 1992. In our view, such an accord, being based on nation-to-nation dealings, would be a treaty. The Métis Nation must have full access to all processes and institutions to assist in the negotiation of a satisfactory treaty or accord. The unique situation of Métis people may of course give rise to agreements that have little resemblance to treaties made by First Nations.

RECOMMENDATION

The Commission recommends that

2.2.6

The federal government establish a process for making new treaties to replace the existing comprehensive claims policy, based on the following principles:

Making New Treaties and Agreements

(a) The blanket extinguishment of Aboriginal land rights is not an option.

(b) Recognition of rights of governance is an integral component of new treaty relationships.

(c) The treaty-making process is available to all Aboriginal nations, including Indian, Inuit and Métis nations.

(d) Treaty nations that are parties to peace and friendship treaties that did not purport to address land and resource issues have access to the treaty-making process to complete their treaty relationships with the Crown.

6. Establishment of Treaty Processes

Regarding those parts of Canada which have not yet been covered by land claims settlements, we believe the government should now, belatedly, endorse the principle underlying the *Royal Proclamation of 1763*. Following the consolidation of British North America, this proclamation enunciated the principle of leaving Aboriginal people in possession of all the lands outside the settled colonies of the time and forbidding European settlement of these Aboriginal-held lands until agreements had been reached between the Aboriginal peoples of each region and the Crown. While the terms of the Royal Proclamation were never carried out, this policy still makes admirable sense.

Modern Aboriginal policy, particularly with regard to those groups in the undeveloped or partially developed frontier regions not yet ceded to Canada by Aboriginal people, including much of the interior and some of the coast of Newfoundland and Labrador, needs a 1990s version of the Royal Proclamation, that is, a renewed commitment by Canada to bring about, with utmost urgency, freely-negotiated agreements which will create a new set of partnerships within Confederation with Aboriginal nations and, to a large extent, retroactively legitimate the process of development and non-Aboriginal settlement.

Dr. Adrian Tanner
Native Peoples' Support Group of Newfoundland and Labrador
St. John's, Newfoundland, 22 May 1992

The Commission believes that treaty processes should be established pursuant to a formal declaration of the Crown and have an explicit statutory foundation. We also propose the creation of new institutions to facilitate these processes.

. . .

RECOMMENDATIONS

The Commission recommends that

2.2.7

Royal Proclamation The federal government prepare a royal proclamation for the consideration of Her Majesty the Queen that would

(a) supplement the *Royal Proclamation of 1763*; and
(b) set out, for the consideration of all Aboriginal and treaty nations in Canada, the fundamental principles of

(i) the bilateral nation-to-nation relationship;
(ii) the treaty implementation and renewal processes; and
(iii) the treaty-making processes.

The federal government introduce companion treaty legislation in Parliament that

Federal Companion Legislation

- (a) provides for the implementation of existing treaty rights, including the treaty rights to hunt, fish and trap;
- (b) affirms liberal rules of interpretation for historical treaties, having regard to

  - (i) the context of treaty negotiations;
  - (ii) the spirit and intent of each treaty; and
  - (iii) the special relationship between the treaty parties;

- (c) makes oral and secondary evidence admissible in the courts when they are making determinations with respect to historical treaty rights;
- (d) recognizes and affirms the land rights and jurisdiction of Aboriginal nations as essential components of treaty processes;
- (e) declares the commitment of the Parliament and government of Canada to the implementation and renewal of each treaty in accordance with the spirit and intent of the treaty and the relationship embodied in it;
- (f) commits the government of Canada to treaty processes that clarify, implement and, where the parties agree, amend the terms of treaties to give effect to the spirit and intent of each treaty and the relationship embodied in it;
- (g) commits the government of Canada to a process of treaty making with

  - (i) Aboriginal nations that do not yet have a treaty with the Crown; and
  - (ii) treaty nations whose treaty does not purport to address issues of lands and resources;

- (h) commits the government of Canada to treaty processes based on and guided by the nation-to-nation structure of the new relationship, implying:

  - (i) all parties demonstrating a spirit of openness, a clear political will and a commitment to fair, balanced and equitable negotiations; and
  - (ii) no party controlling the access to, the scope of, or the funding for the negotiating processes; and

(i) authorizes the establishment, in consultation with treaty nations, of the institutions this Commission recommends as necessary to fulfil the treaty processes.

The governments of the provinces and territories introduce legislation, parallel to the federal companion legislation, that

Provincial and Territorial Companion Legislation

- (a) enables them to meet their treaty obligations;
- (b) enables them to participate in treaty implementation and renewal processes and treaty-making processes; and

(c) establishes the institutions required to participate in those treaty processes, to the extent of their jurisdiction.

7. Content of Treaty Processes

We agreed to maintain peace and friendship among ourselves and with the Crown. Peace and friendship can only be nurtured through processes which allow treaty partners to talk and resolve any differences through negotiations and goodwill.

The unique and special relationship which is evidenced by the existence of our treaty places upon both partners a duty to take whatever steps are necessary toward creating mechanisms or processes for resolving difficulties and differences which from time to time will arise in the course of such a relationship. . . .

We seek urgent action aimed at commencing the task of addressing and resolving the many outstanding issues which have arisen in our treaty relationship. We want to make clear our position that treaty framework is a framework we wish to utilize for redressing the many inequities which presently exist. We want the results of that process recognized, affirmed and protected by the Canadian constitution.

Chief Bernie Meneen
High Level Tribal Council
High Level, Alberta, 29 October 1992

Treaty parties will devise the appropriate process for reviewing, implementing and renewing the treaty relationship or for making new treaties. In this section, we provide some guidance on the possible content of treaty processes and the results they may be designed to achieve.

The treaty-making process we envisage represents an evolution from the present comprehensive claims process toward a process that is less exclusionary with respect to the parties and the subject matter of agreements and predicated on the affirmation rather than the extinguishment of Aboriginal title (see Chapter 4).

The Crown saw the historical treaties, as the federal government has seen modern treaties, as one-time final transactions. This perspective must be overcome. The treaties must be acknowledged as living instruments, capable of evolution over time and meaningful and relevant to the continuum of past, present and future. They should not be frozen as of the day they are signed.

15.2 Speech by Chief Joseph Gosnell to the British Columbia Legislative Assembly, 1998

The Nisga'a First Nation, from the north coast of British Columbia, had been trying to negotiate a treaty since 1888 when their representatives travelled to Victoria to demand recognition of title to their lands. Getting little satisfaction, they formed the Nisga'a Land Committee as a vehicle through which to continue to pressure government. For decades, they made presentations, sent petitions, lobbied politicians, and, in 1967, began legal action that ended up with a Supreme Court of Canada decision in 1973. Though the Supreme Court was split on whether the Nisga'a continued to hold title to their territories, six of seven justices agreed that the Nisga'a did so historically. In 1976, soon after this case, which is cited as Calder v. British Columbia, *was decided, Canada began to negotiate with the Nisga'a. Fourteen years after that, British Columbia, too, joined the negotiating table. Finally, in the summer of 1998, a final agreement was completed, and, in May of 2000, after more than a century of effort, the Nisga'a Final Agreement came into effect.*

The document here is the transcript of a speech made by Nisga'a Tribal Council President Chief Joseph Gosnell to the Legislative Assembly of British Columbia only a few months after the final agreement was initialled and approved by the Nisga'a but before it had been ratified by British Columbia or Canada. Chief Gosnell explains the history of the Nisga'a effort to secure a treaty.

Source: Joseph Gosnell in British Columbia, Legislative Assembly, *Debates of the Legislative Assembly* (Hansard), vol. 12, no. 17, 2 December 1998, pp. 10859–61.

Address from the Bar of the House

J. Gosnell: Thank you, Madam Speaker, hon. members, ladies and gentlemen. [Nisga'a spoken.]

Madam Speaker, today, I believe, marks a turning point in the history of British Columbia. Today aboriginal and non-aboriginal people are coming together to decide the future of this province. I am talking about the Nisga'a treaty, a triumph, I believe, for all British Columbians and a beacon of hope for aboriginal people around the world.

It's a triumph, I believe, which proves to the world that reasonable people can sit down and settle historical wrongs. It proves that a modern society can correct the mistakes of the past. As British Columbians, as Canadians, I believe we should all be very proud. It's a triumph because under the treaty, the Nisga'a people will join Canada and British Columbia as free citizens, full and equal participants in the social, economic and political life of this province and, indeed, of this country. It's a triumph because under the treaty, we will no longer be wards of the state, no longer beggars in our own land. It's a triumph because under the treaty, we will collectively own approximately 2,000 square kilometres of land, far exceeding the postage-stamp reserve set aside for us by colonial governments. We will once again govern ourselves by our own institutions but within the context of Canadian law. It is a triumph because under the treaty, we will be allowed to make our own mistakes, to savour our own victories, to stand on our own feet once again. It's a triumph because, clause by clause, the Nisga'a treaty emphasizes self-reliance, personal responsibility and modern education. It also encourages, for the first time, investment in Nisga'a lands and resources and allows us to pursue meaningful employment for our own people from the resources of our own territory.

To investors, it provides economic certainty, and it gives us a fighting chance to establish legitimate economic independence, to prosper in common with our non-aboriginal neighbours in a new and, hopefully, proud Canada. It's a triumph, Madam Speaker and hon. members, because the treaty proves beyond all doubt that negotiations—not lawsuits, not blockades, not violence—are the most effective, honourable way to resolve aboriginal issues in this country. It's a triumph, I believe, that signals the end of the Indian Act, the end of more than a century of humiliation, degradation and despair for the Nisga'a nation.

In 1887 my ancestors made an epic journey from the Nass River to here, Victoria's Inner Harbour. Determined to settle the land question, they were met by a Premier who barred them from this Legislature. He was blunt. Premier Smithe rejected all our aspirations to settle the land question. Then he made this pronouncement: "When the white man first came among you, you were little better than wild beasts of the field." Wild beasts of the field. Little wonder, then, that this brutal racism was soon translated into narrow policies which plunged British Columbia into a century of darkness for the Nisga'a and other aboriginal people.

Like many colonists of the day, Premier Smithe did not know or care to know that the Nisga'a is an old nation—as old as any in Europe. From time immemorial, our oral literature—passed down from generation to generation—records the story of the way the Nisga'a people were placed on earth and trusted with the care and protection of our land. Through the ages, we lived a settled life in villages along the Nass River. We lived in large, cedar-plank houses, fronted with totem poles depicting the great heraldry and the family crests of our nobility. We thrived from the bounty of the sea, the river, the forest and the mountains. We governed ourselves according to ayuuk Nisga'a, the code of our own strict and ancient laws of property ownership, succession and civil order.

Our first encounters with Europeans were friendly. We welcomed these strange visitors—visitors who never left. The Europeans also valued their encounters with us. They thought we were fair and tough entrepreneurs and—no doubt today—negotiators. In 1832 traders from the Hudson's Bay Co. found our people living, in their words, "in two-storey wooden houses the equal of any in Europe." For a time our people prospered, but there were dark days yet to come.

Between the late 1700s and mid-1800s the Nisga'a people, like so many other coastal nations of the time, as well as other tribal groups across this great land, were devastated by European diseases such as smallpox, measles and fevers. Our population, I'm told, was at one time 30,000 strong. We dwindled to about 800 people. Today I am pleased to report that our population is growing. According to our census, we now number approximately 5,500.

We took to heart the promises of King George III, set out in the Royal Proclamation of 1763, that our lands would not be taken away without our permission and that treaty-making was the way the Nisga'a would become part of this new nation. We continued to follow our ayuuk, our code of laws. We vowed to obey the white man's law. And we expected him to obey our laws and also to respect our people.

But unfortunately, the Europeans would not obey their own laws and continued to trespass on our lands. The King's governments continued to take our lands from us, until we were told that all of our land had come to belong to the Crown and that even the tiny bits of land that enclosed our villages were not ours but belonged to the government. Still we kept the faith that the rule of law would prevail one day, that justice would be done, that one day the land question would be settled fairly and honourably.

Madam Speaker, in 1913 the Nisga'a Land Committee drafted the petition to London. The petition contained the declaration of our traditional land ownership and governance, and it contained the critical information that in the new British colony our land ownership would be respected. In part the petition said:

> We are not opposed to the coming of the white people into our territory, provided this be carried out justly and in accordance with the British principles embodied in the Royal Proclamation. If therefore, as we expect, the aboriginal rights which we claim should be established by the decision of His Majesty's Privy Council, we would be prepared to take a moderate and reasonable position. In that event, while claiming the right to decide for ourselves the terms upon which we would deal with our territory, we would be willing that all matters outstanding between the province and ourselves should be finally adjusted by some equitable method to be agreed upon, which should include representation of the Indian tribes upon any commission which might then be appointed.

The above statement was unanimously adopted at a meeting of the Nisga'a nation, or tribe of Indians, held at the village of Kincolith on the 22nd day of January, 1913. Sadly, this was not to be the case.

Also in 1913, Duncan Campbell Scott became deputy superintendent of Indian Affairs. His narrow vision of assimilation dominated federal aboriginal policy for years and years to come and was later codified as the Indian Act. Mr. Scott said: "I want to get rid of the Indian problem. Our objective is to continue until there is not a single Indian in Canada that has not been absorbed into the body politic and there is no Indian question." One of this man's earliest efforts was to undermine the influence of the Nisga'a petition to London and to deflect away from political action. But these men, Smithe and Scott, failed and are now deservedly only dusty footnotes in history.

Still the situation of the Nisga'a worsened. In 1927, Canada passed a law to prevent us from pursuing our land claims, from hiring lawyers to plead our case. At the same time, our central institution of tribal government, our potlatch system we know in Nisga'a as ayuuk, was outlawed by an act of Parliament. It was against the law for us to give presents during our ceremonies, which is central to our tradition; our law instructs us to do that. It was made illegal for us to sing and dance, which again is a requirement of our culture. But still we did not give up, and finally, under the leadership of Dr. Frank Calder, the Nisga'a Land Committee was reborn as the Nisga'a Tribal Council in 1955.

In 1968 we took our land question to the B.C. Supreme Court. We lost but appealed to the Supreme Court of Canada, where in 1973, in what is now known as the Calder case, the justice ruled that aboriginal title existed prior to Confederation. This initiated the modern-day process of land claims negotiations. The government of Canada agreed it was best to negotiate modern-day treaties. Canada agreed it was time to build a new relationship based on trust, respect and the rule of law. In time, as you will know, Madam Speaker, the province of British Columbia came to the negotiating table as well. For the past 25 years, in good faith, the Nisga'a struggled to negotiate this treaty, and finally it was initialled in August in our home community of New Aiyansh.

How the world has changed! Two days ago—and 111 years later, after Smithe's rejection—I walked up to the steps of this Legislature as the sound of Nisga'a drumming and singing filled the rotunda. To the Nisga'a people it was a joyous sound—the sound of freedom. Freedom is described in the dictionary as "the state or condition of being free, the condition of not being under another's control, the power to do, say or think as one pleases." Our people have enjoyed the hospitality and the warmth of this Legislature, this capital city, its sights and its people. In churches, schools and malls, streets and public places our people have been embraced, welcomed and congratulated by the people of British Columbia.

People sometimes wonder why we have struggled so long to sign a treaty. Why, we are asked, did our elders and elected officials dedicate their lives to the resolution of the land question? What is it about a treaty?

To us a treaty is a sacred instrument. It represents an understanding between distinct cultures and shows a respect for each other's way of life. We know we are here for a long time together. A treaty stands as a symbol of high idealism in a divided world. That is why we have fought so long and so hard. I have been asked: "Has this been worth it?" I would have to say, with a resounding yes, it has.

But believe me and my colleagues; it has been a long, hard-fought battle for those that went before us. Some may have heard us say that a generation of Nisga'a men and women have grown old at the negotiating table. Sadly, it is very true. I was a much younger man when I began, became involved in the tribal council; I was 25 years old. Today I'm 63; today my hair is greying. I've gone through six terms of Prime Ministers and their chart. I recall their names—the Rt. Hon. Pierre Trudeau, Joe Clark, John Turner, Brian Mulroney, Kim Campbell and Jean Chrétien—and five British Columbia Premiers—Bill Bennett, William Vander Zalm, Rita Johnston, Mike Harcourt and, yes, Glen Clark. I will spare you the list of deputy ministers, senior bureaucrats and other officials. There are numerous names that we have met across these many years. Their names, I believe, would paper the walls of this chamber at least twice.

We are not naïve. We know that some people do not want this treaty. We know that there are naysayers—some sitting here today. We know that there are those who say Canada and British Columbia are giving us too much, and a few who want to reopen negotiations in order to give us less. Others, still upholding the values of Smithe and Scott, are practising a wilful ignorance. This colonial attitude is fanning the flames of fear and ignorance in this province and reigniting a poisonous attitude that we as aboriginal people are so familiar with.

But these are desperate tactics, doomed to fail. By playing politics with the aspirations of aboriginal peoples, these naysayers are blighting the promise of the Nisga'a treaty not only for us but for non-aboriginal people as well, because this is about people. We're not numbers. The issue that you will deal with over the next weeks. . . . You will deal with the lives of our people, the future of our people. It is about the legitimate aspirations of our people, no longer willing to step aside or be marginalized. We intend to be free and equal citizens. Witness the flags that have been waved in this chamber over the past two days by the Nisga'a people of British Columbia, the Nisga'a people of Canada.

Now, on the eve of the fiftieth anniversary of the Declaration of Human Rights, this Legislature embarks on a great debate about aboriginal rights. The Nisga'a people welcome that debate, one of the most important in the modern history of British Columbia. We have every confidence that elected members of this Legislature will look beyond narrow politics to correct the shameful and historic wrong. I ask each and every one of you, hon. members, to search your hearts deeply and to allow the light of our message to guide your decisions.

We have worked for justice for more than 100 years. Now it is time to ratify the Nisga'a treaty, for aboriginal and non-aboriginal people to come together and write a new chapter in the history of our nation, our province, our country and indeed the world. The world, I believe, is our witness to the endeavours that we have encountered. [Nisga'a spoken.]

Madam Speaker, on behalf of the Nisga'a nation, I greatly appreciate the privilege that has been accorded to me to address this chamber. Thank you. [Applause.]

15.3 Are Treaties the Answer?: Panel Discussion at the *Preparing for the Day After Treaty* Conference, 2007

*This document comes from the transcript of a panel discussion at a Vancouver conference on treaties jointly hosted by the **BC** Treaty Commission and the Nisga'a Lisims Government. Two panel members are represented here, Chief Robert Louie of the Westbank First Nation in the British Columbia interior and Chief Robert Dennis of the Huu-ay-aht, a Nuu-chah-nulth First Nation on Vancouver Island. The Huu-ay-aht is one of the five First Nations signatories to the Maa-nulth final agreement, one of only two treaties negotiated through the BC treaty process. Although Louie and Dennis have different views on the efficacy of the treaty process in British Columbia, there are many other positions on these issues, as mentioned in the introduction to this chapter. The wide range of views on the treaty process within First Nations communities is at least part of the reason that so few agreements have been reached in the more than two decades of the BC Treaty Commission's existence.*

Source: "Panel Discussion: Are Treaties the Answer?" in *Preparing for the Day after Treaty: A Conference for First Nations*, Conference Presentations, November 14–16, 2007, Vancouver, British Columbia.

Reproduced with the permission of the British Columbia Treaty Commission.

Panel Discussion: *Are treaties the answer?*

Perhaps that depends on the question . . . our panel presenters will outline why they believe treaties are the way to a more prosperous future for their First Nation or why they aren't. Identifying what is wrong with the current treaty process and what First Nations need to conclude treaties that work will be up for discussion. Exploration of possible alternatives to the treaty process is encouraged and the audience is invited to be a part of the action! Come prepared with your questions for panel presenters. This debate is meant to stimulate discussion on some of the most pressing issues facing the BC treaty process and First Nations today in a serious but good-natured and inclusive forum.

. . .

Presenter: Chief Robert Louie

Chiefs, elders, commissioners, councillors, negotiators, government officials, distinguished guests, ladies and gentlemen. It does give me great pleasure to be here, to talk to you about the treaty process. The topic we have is "What We Need to Conclude Treaties that Work." What's wrong with the treaty negotiation process? What do we do?

Right now there's over 60 First Nations in this province that are part of the unity protocol and that represents over 35,000 people. It's backed up by the Union of BC Indian Chiefs with approximately 140 First Nations in this province who agree with positions that we're taking.

I'm here to tell you about the treaty process. Don't be fooled that it's working. It's not. And that's a big, big problem.

I'm here to also talk about the future of treaty negotiations. I believe that there is a strong, imminent potential of court action. It is being seriously contemplated against the two governments and it may well proceed in the imminent future unless mandates and things change.

I want to talk to you a bit about the self-governance by First Nations and the fact that some of the First Nations, including my own, are being held hostage by the treaty negotiation process. I'm going to touch upon the problem areas with the treaty process. There are six main mandated areas that are real problems. I'd like to compare the treaty process with other processes—some of which are working—things that are happening in Sechelt, Squamish, McLeod Lake and my own community at Westbank.

I'll talk a bit about the treaty land entitlement in the prairie provinces. Much of that is working and they're not giving up their lands or paying taxes and giving up the jurisdictional basis to do so. And talk briefly about land management and land codes and what's happening there as an alternative.

To say the least, I believe that the vast majority of First Nations in this province are vastly disappointed with the treaty process.

There was so much promise made 17 years ago, a made-in-BC approach. We all expected collectively that we'd be much further ahead today. The fact is: we're not. The future of the treaty process is really dependent on the goodwill and common sense of British Columbia and Canada. The question that has to be asked, therefore: will the honour of the Crown be maintained? Will there be goodwill and common sense?

I recognize that there's been progress made at some of the tables. I see what's happening there and I congratulate Tsawwassen. I congratulate those other communities that have signed, Maa-nulth and some of the other tables that have reached AIPs.

Nothing against those communities, and I applaud those communities for making their decisions.

Sadly, for the vast majority of First Nations in this province it's not working, nor will it ever work under the current mandates. Settlement is a long ways off and, again, court may be the only direction, sadly.

Simply put, Canada and BC are asking First Nations to give up far too much including the successes we have made on our existing reserves and that's ironic, to say the least. At the end of the day, it's the Crown that really needs treaties. It's not the First Nations. Our aboriginal title will not go away with certainty over who really owns BC and what will happen in this province is only going to deepen.

For Westbank, signing a treaty under the current federal and provincial approaches would actually set us back and reverse much of the amazing progress we've made and that would hurt our economy. I came directly from the Westbank lands management seminar, at my community and my gymnasium. We had over 200 people there. First Nations people, lawyers, realtors, people that are looking at business, developers and so forth. We had a gymnasium full of professional people and they're looking at our model of land management, our self-government. We've looked at and have introduced the federal lands registry regulations that came into effect on November 5th [2007]. Our land-use planning laws and plans, development processes that we're doing, there is real economy happening in my community, there's a very thriving real estate and that's not because of treaty, I can assure you. It's because of our location, but more importantly, it's about good governance and what the alternatives are.

We have land management jurisdiction, we have self-government and it's working. Governments have told us at the negotiating table, you're going to be far better off by signing under our mandated positions of treaty. That's baloney. It's not there.

Our proof is in the pudding. We asked our negotiators, come, come to Westbank. Come look and see what's happening. See the amount of development that's happening. It's booming. It is truly booming, over 5,000 residential units right now on the books that are planned. We've got over 9,000 people, most of who are non-natives. We've got 30-storey residential apartment complexes and resort developments that we're contemplating right now. This is real. 29 major projects, $1 billion worth of business. Two years now and we've got over a hundred million dollars of development in permits. That's the type of activity that's happening there. It's not, again, because of treaty.

Does government really think we're going to give that up? I don't think that's going to happen. In treaty negotiations incredibly federal and provincial mandates mean Westbank would have to disrupt our own government. We'd have to re-write most of our laws that we've been working on now for 17 years. And that's after our lawyers have tried to figure out the extent of our jurisdiction and they have complicated restrictions and harmonization rules under the treaties. Because of powers available under the current treaty[,] mandates are not as extensive as ours right now under Westbank self-government. That's a fact. There'd be far more provincial interference with exercise of the limited jurisdiction we would have. Our land status would change, it would disrupt our economy that we've built and worked hard to deliver.

Our primary relationship, believe it or not, is not with Victoria, the provincial government; our primary relationship is with other First Nations and with Canada. This is fundamental and treaty mandates seeks to change this? That's wrong. I assert to you. It's unfair and it would create long term uncertainty for us.

We're not alone in the expressions with regard to self-government. Sechelt, for example, has been successful, they've been [a] self-governing First Nation. They withdrew from the treaty process in part because both governments, Canada and BC, would not recognize their 91.24 self-government model under the treaty. That's a problem for them; it's a problem for us. There's been much progress made outside of this province in other areas, and within this province—Squamish, for example. They're not involved in the treaty process, they're doing very, very well and I commend the people of Squamish for what they've achieved. They've achieved it, not with treaty and the mandated positions, but they've done it because of the position that they're in and the negotiating strength that they have with the province. That's why they're being successful, not to mention the good people that they have there.

Land codes, under the framework agreement, that's an alternative. It's happening across this province. It's major. There are over a hundred First Nations in line waiting to develop their land codes, all with 91.24 jurisdiction; they're not giving up the 91.24 jurisdiction and accepting the 92 model. It's not happening. I assert even, and I apologize if it upsets anyone, but I believe Chief Leah, your community as well, is doing fantastically well and that's a success story and it's outside the treaty process.

McLeod Lake, Treaty 8, the adhesion agreement; they didn't give up their 91.24 lands and they're doing very, very well. The list goes on.

Treaty land entitlements throughout the provinces: there's Alberta, Saskatchewan, Manitoba. They're not being forced to give up their positions so government has done certain things in mandates that they don't do with other communities outside this province. There's something wrong with that picture.

If we, any one of us, goes to Alberta, Saskatchewan, I've been there. Manitoba, I've seen, I've seen Ontario, I've seen the Maritimes. I work in my capacity as chairman of the lands board and I hear the communities. They tell me when I raise the issue about 91.24, what's happening in BC? What are you people doing? Are you giving up all your tax benefits? You're giving up your reserve status? What's wrong with you? That's the actual fact and that's what I hear time and time again across this country.

I think some people seem to have forgotten what we are supposed to be doing in the treaty process. Let's remind ourselves, we are settling the outstanding land question because we, as aboriginal peoples, have an unextinguished aboriginal title to our territories.

You've heard it from Grand Chief Matthew Coon Come and I think that's an actual reality. In treaty we should not attempt to try and settle every issue between us for all time. Treaties should not be used as a back door assimilation of our peoples by making our governments and our peoples and those that do business or live on our lands subservient to provincial standards of law making.

There's a whole bunch of other points. But I'm going to cut to the chase a bit more and just list in summary some of the key problems I see in the mandates of government. Quite frankly, I see at least five.

Firstly, I think self-government is limited by British Columbia through concurrence of law making authority and positions on delegation. That's a problem, the concurrence law model. They want jurisdiction on reserve lands. That's why they're at the table.

Secondly, compensation amounts are limited. They're limited, an aggregate of land and cash not exceeding $70,000 per capita. That's the position that they have, so the compensation amounts are limited.

Thirdly, provincial governments want all settlement lands including reserves to then be 92 lands under the provincial domain. Fee simple, basically, having the title registered in the provincial lands system.

Fourthly, both governments want concurrent taxation jurisdiction and assess the tax revenues of First Nation citizens. We've done our own studies at Westbank, we know the impact that that would be and I'll tell you, we would be dumb and crazy and belligerent to even think that we would sell it to our community. Very clearly, they told us loud and clear, no way. It's not going to happen. I wouldn't expect to be chief much longer if that was the position I took to our people and said here, this is what we're going to do. Not going to happen.

Fifthly, land quantums are not factored in, rather only land value. That's a problem. It's a problem right now in today's market. We have a market right now of lands that are rapidly increasing in property prices, yet land quantums are not factored into this equation, only the land value. That means that our lands are going to be worth less and less in treaty settlement. That is a big, big problem.

So, ladies and gentlemen, I submit that treaty as a mandated position of governments are simply not working.

You know, they're not.

We've got six major areas of contention that I know that unity protocol group supported by the Union of BC Indian Chiefs have agreed and they're problem areas and they've got to be solved, whether we go to a common table, if we can't do a common table approach and settle this, then, again court is the unfortunate answer.

Those key issues include one, certainty. That's the extinguishment policy.

Secondly the constitutional status of treaty lands—do we have to give up our existing reserve lands simply to get a treaty?

Thirdly, governance, do we want the concurrent model of jurisdiction to allow the governments to have a say in our lands.

Fourthly, co-management throughout our traditional territories—that hasn't been offered quite fairly at the tables.

Fifthly, fiscal relations and taxation—are we forced, as aboriginal peoples, to give up our rights that we have lived with all this time? We've given up enough right now, to give up a benefit that exists since the late 1800s. So, it's a problem.

And fisheries; there isn't enough being put on the table. That's loud and clear and we hear that time and time again by the coastal fisheries group.

So, ladies and gentlemen, yes big problems in treaty process. It's not working and don't let anybody be fooled in this room or outside this room to say that, hey, things are rosy and they're working well because they are absolutely not.

We've got a handful of First Nations, maybe that might end up finally settling a treaty under the mandated positions but the vast majority are saying absolutely no way. Governments, wake up, listen. Wei lum lum.

Presenter: Chief Robert Dennis

You probably noticed that I'm the only one here without a pen in my hand and I don't have any papers.

That's for a reason, because I want to talk to you today from my heart, not from my mind because when I let my mind talk it's emotion, it becomes anger, it becomes frustration.

So, from my heart I say, where I come from I firmly, utterly believe the hawiih of the Huu'ay'aht First Nation. That is I firmly believe in the hereditary chiefs of our nation, that is who I recognize first before I do anything on behalf of my nation.

If the hereditary chief says, "I'm willing to accept this," who am I to question the ultimate traditional authority of our nation? And for that matter, who is it for anybody else to question the authority of my head chief. My head chief does not question the authority of any other First Nation. My head chief does not question what other First Nations are doing in their non-treaty environment or their treaty environment. He says I respect whichever path you've chosen.

So today, he has chosen along with the people, the who's of our nation have said we want to be in the treaty process. We want to negotiate a modern day treaty. Kah'li'chen gets his chiefs together and they decide we are going to negotiate a modern day treaty.

Let us gather our people together and see what they want in the treaty. I think that fancy negotiating word is called mandate. I'm not a full fledged negotiator and I'm not a lawyer, I'm just ordinary Robert Dennis. I don't have any education except I went to Grade 12. But what I do know is when your people speak and give you a mandate of what they want to see in the treaty you go out and do it.

In 1994 the Huu'ay'aht community appointed Chief Arthur Peters a permanent member on the Huu'ay'aht treaty committee because he was hereditary chief of the nation. That was the first man they wanted; the hereditary chief had to be on that committee or else it could not exist.

Secondly, we're going to appoint the speaker of that chief to be on that committee and that speaker happened to be myself.

Thirdly, we're going to appoint another chief amongst the Huu'ay'aht and we're going to appoint him to the committee. His name is [Native language] Tom Happynook who is now the president of the NTC. So he was appointed to the committee.

And the people said we want somebody on that team that has a technical and an educational background and can write documents on behalf of the people. And that was Angela Wesley. When we formed that committee, our first responsibility was to visit every one of our people to say: what do you want in the treaty? We spent about three, four months just going around to each of the homes, community meetings, meeting with people. What do you want to see in the treaty?

We didn't ask them what's the mandate you're going to give us. We talked in terms that our people understood. No discredit to the educated people that are sitting up here.

I have a hard time because I'm not as educated as them. In some senses I have an advantage as well. I'm talking to people that are at my educational level, people that can understand what I'm saying.

So we heard what they were saying. The Huu'ay'aht treaty committee, one day we would like to regain that place in the fishing industry that we once had. Our people went from 71 licensed fishermen down to, I believe, we have four or five now. 71 to four or five licensed fishermen. We want to get back up there somehow. So we knew that was a task.

They said we want to see that Sereta River and other rivers in our territory restored. Go out and get some money so that we can restore the resources of the rivers, the salmon, the steelhead and the wildlife, the mink that live in around the rivers, the bears, the eagles. And then they told us when we did a land survey what they would like in the treaty. It wasn't me, Robert Dennis, telling the Huu'ay'aht people what kind of land holdings we should have. We asked the people: what kind of land holdings do you want to see in the treaty? I remember that survey took quite a while.

And some more of the what? I remember this one, 1996, because I work in forestry. We had done a forestry survey and we asked the people: what would you like to see in forestry? Well, I remember the very first thing I almost got knocked out of my chair and one of our members said we want to see 100,000 cubic metres of wood that is allocated to the Huu'ay'aht First Nation. We want to see that in the treaty. I said holy smokes, you know, we only got two guys employed in the forest industry I don't know how we're going to do that. But that became a task. That became a mandate and in that forestry survey they identified cultural and heritage resource in the forest must be preserved, must be protected.

And in that survey they also said sustainable forest management must be one of the guiding principles. So what did we do? We entered into interim negotiations with the province of British Columbia, right up front on that document "Guiding Principles of Sustainability for the Huu'ay'aht First Nation."

We heard what our people wanted to see in the treaty. To me, that's what it's all about so that when you finally do go for ratification, it's not what people outside of your nation say that the treaty is the right answer or not, it's whether you go back and they gave you the mandate. In our case, in the Huu'ay'aht First Nation case, in the case of the Uchucklesaht tribe, in the case of the Ucluelet First Nation, in the case of the Ka:'yu:'k't'h/Che:k:tles7et'h First Nation and in the case of the Tla-o-qui-aht First Nation. Each of our communities overwhelmingly supported that treaty. Why? Because we went out and asked them what they wanted to see in the treaty. We weren't negotiators up here telling them what we're going to put into the treaty and that's probably why we ended up with these incredible results.

I can't tell you the numbers for the other First Nations, but I sure memorized ours: 90 per cent of our people approved the treaty. That's an incredible result and I believe that result came about because we went out and asked the people: what do you want to see in the treaty[?]

So, is the treaty the answer for us? Absolutely. Yes. Because the people have decided it is the right thing for us.

The full text of the "Treaties" section of the Report of the Royal Commission on Aboriginal Peoples, excerpted as document 15.1, is available on line at http://www.collectionscanada.gc.ca/webarchives/20071124125834/http://www.ainc-inac.gc.ca/ch/rcap/sg/shm2_e.html. The full text of treaties completed or in the final stages of ratification through the current British Columbia treaty process, as well as a range of other material, is available on the BC Treaty Commission's website: http://www.bctreaty.net/. For a collection of short essays on treaty making and the BC treaty process, see the BC Treaty Commission and The Law Commission of Canada, *Speaking Truth to Power: A Treaty Forum* (Ottawa: Minster of Public Works and Government Services Canada, 2001), available on line at http://www.bctreaty.net/files/pdf_documents/truth_1_book.pdf. For an analysis that is critical of the BC treaty process, see Taiaiake Alfred, "Deconstructing the British Columbia Treaty Process," *Balayi: Culture, Law and Colonialism* 3 (2001). A version of this article is also available on line from the University of Victoria at http://web.uvic.ca/igov/uploads/pdf/GTA.bctreatyprocess.pdf. See also Andrew Woolford, *Between Justice and Certainty: Treaty Making in British Columbia* (Vancouver: UBC Press, 2005). For information on historic as well as modern treaties from across Canada, including those presently in various stages of development, follow the links from the "Treaty-Making in Canada" section of the Aboriginal Affairs and Northern Development Canada website at http://www.aadnc-aandc.gc.ca/eng/1100100028574/110010000 28578. Of special interest to readers of this chapter is the material accessible from the link to "comprehensive claims" in the main body of the text on the "Treaty-Making in Canada" page. Most First Nations or Indigenous treaty organizations also have their own on line presence that includes information on their treaty or land claims agreement. For an example of the Nunavut Land Claims Agreement, see the Nunavut Tunngavik Incorporated (NTI) website at http://www.tunngavik.com/. For an overview of historic treaties that also includes studies of more modern ones, see J.R. Miller, *Compact, Contract, Covenant: Aboriginal Treaty Making in Canada* (Toronto: University of Toronto Press, 2009), especially Chapters 10 through 12.

Appendix

❋

KEY PEOPLE

There are very many individuals who played important roles in the relations between Indigenous people and settler society in the more than a century covered by this reader. There is a little personal information about some key individuals in the chapter and document introductions, and a few more people have been selected for a slightly fuller biographical treatment here.

Bryce, Peter Henderson, 17 Aug 1853—15 Jan 1932 (See Chapter 6.)
Peter H. Bryce was born in Mount Pleasant, Ontario, the second son of Catherine (Henderson) and George Bryce. He attended the University of Toronto where he focused on the physical sciences with a concentration in geology. He taught at the University of Guelph for a short time before returning to study medicine in Toronto. After earning his MD, he took a position as the first secretary of the Board of Health of Ontario in 1882, a position he held until 1904. The year he left the Board of Health he accepted an appointment as chief medical officer with the Department of the Interior and, in this capacity, split his time between the Department of Immigration and the Department of Indian Affairs. In 1907, Dr. Bryce spent several months travelling through the Prairie West and visiting 35 residential schools established for Indigenous children. His report, which was widely publicized, was a damning indictment of the conditions in the schools. The situation was so bad, according to Bryce, that it threatened the well-being of Indigenous people in Western Canada even outside of the schools. He recommended a large-scale program to improve school buildings and that a more systematized inspection regimen be established to evaluate the health of residential school students. Bryce's recommendations were largely unheeded, though, apparently due to the department's concern for economy. Frustrated by departmental inaction, and after he was forced to retire in 1921, he published *The Story of a National Crime*, segments of which appear in Chapter 6.

Cardinal, Harold, 27 Jan 1945–3 June 2005 (See Chapter 10.)
Harold Cardinal was born into a Cree family on the reserve of the Sucker Creek First Nation in North Central Alberta. In 1968, at age 23, Cardinal was elected president of the Indian Association of Alberta, just in time to respond to the Pierre Trudeau government's "White Paper" discussed in Chapter 10. Cardinal studied the traditional legal structures of his people throughout his life and also earned a law degree and taught at the University of Saskatchewan before moving on to Harvard to earn his masters of law degree. He wrote and published two books—*Unjust Society: The Tragedy of Canada's Indians* and *Rebirth of Canada's Indians*—and co-authored and contributed to several others. Cardinal also served a short, somewhat controversial, term as Canada's regional director for Indian affairs in Alberta. He returned as elected chief of his home community in 1982 and was later awarded an honorary doctorate from the University of Alberta and served as Indigenous Scholar in Residence at the U of A's law school. Just before he died, he was also awarded a doctorate of laws from the University of British Columbia. He continued to maintain that treaties had to function as the primary mechanisms governing relations between First Nations and settler society.

Corbiere-Lavell, Jeannette Vivian, born 21 June 1942 (See Chapter 11.)
Jeanette Corbiere-Lavell is an Anishnaabe woman from the Wikwemikong Unceded Indian Reserve on Manitoulin Island in Ontario. Among other things, she has worked as a teacher, principal, and consultant on issues related to status and justice. She was a founding member of several rights and justice organizations, such as the National Committee on Indian Rights for Indian Women and the Ontario Native Women's Association of Canada. She also served as president of the Native Women's Association of Canada beginning in 2009. In 1970, Jeannette Corbiere married David Lavell, a non-Indigenous journalism student. Almost immediately, she received notification from the Department of Indian Affairs and Northern Development that, due to her marriage, she was no longer an Indian according to the Indian Act. She decided to challenge the discriminatory provisions of the act, and, in 1973, her case was heard before the Supreme Court of Canada along with a similar case initiated by Yvonne Bédard, a Six Nations woman from near Brantford, Ontario. In its decision, the Supreme Court ruled that Canada's 1960 Bill of Rights did not prohibit this sort of discrimination and so did not override the Indian Act. The controversy that surrounded this case and others led eventually to amendments to the Indian Act to bring it in closer alignment with the 1982 Charter of Rights and Freedoms.

Crosby, Thomas, 21 June 1840–13 Jan 1914 (See the introduction to document 4b.2, p. 97.)

Crowfoot (Issapo'mahkikaaw), c. 1830–25 Apr 1890 (See Chapter 2 and 3.)
Issapo'mahkikaaw, or Crowfoot, was born into the Kainai (Blood) First Nation in what is now southern Alberta but spent his formative years among the Siksika (Blackfoot). He developed a reputation for bravery during combat while still a teenager and was awarded his name following a battle with the Apsáalooke (Crow). He soon assumed leadership roles within the Siksika and was one of the signatories to Treaty 7 in 1877. Though Canada's representatives at the treaty negotiations dealt with Crowfoot as if he led the entire

Blackfoot Confederacy, Crowfoot himself, of course, understood the actual political structure of the Blackfoot and was sure to consult other leaders before making any agreements. Although he was an active supporter of the treaty, before long he became critical of the way the Department of Indian Affairs and its agents treated his people. Crowfoot is perhaps best remembered for his efforts to secure friendly relations with non-Indigenous fur traders, missionaries, and mounted policemen and with neighbouring First Nations. Issapo'mahkikaaw was also the adopted father of Pītikwahanapiwīyin (Poundmaker) who became an important Cree leader.

Crozier, Leif Newry Fitzroy (See the introduction to document 3.3, p. 64.)

Davin, Nicholas Flood (See the introduction to document 6.1, p. 153.)

Deskahe (Hi-wyi-iss or Levi General), 1873–27 June 1925 (See the introduction to document 5b.5, p. 143.)

Dewdney, Edgar, 5 Nov 1835–8 Aug 1916 (See Chapter 4.)
Edgar Dewdney was born into a family of privilege in Bideford, England. He trained as a civil engineer before immigrating to British Columbia in 1859. He soon found work with the Royal Engineers, and, in 1865, after a number of gold strikes in the Kootenays, he was appointed to supervise a trail that would connect the interior of the province to the coast. This became known as the Dewdney Trail, parts of which are still in use. In 1869, he was appointed to the colony's legislative council, and, in 1872, following British Columbia's entry into Confederation the previous year, Dewdney was elected as the Conservative member of Parliament for Yale. He was extremely loyal to Prime Minister John A. Macdonald, and, when he was asked, he resigned his seat in 1879 to accept the newly created post of Indian commissioner of the then North-West Territories, a position he held until 1888. For much of this term, from 1881 to 1888, Dewdney also served, as lieutenant governor of the same region. Following his term as lieutenant governor, he was elected again as an MP in 1888 and served in cabinet as minister of the interior and superintendent general of Indian affairs until 1892, when he took up the post of lieutenant governor of British Columbia. He held that position until he retired in 1897.

Dumont, Gabriel, December 1837–19 May 1906 (See Chapter 3.)
Gabriel Dumont was born in 1837 at Red River (present-day Winnipeg), the son of Métis hunter Isidore Dumont (Ekapow) and Louise Laframboise. Dumont grew to be a very able shot both with a bow and with a rifle and, in his twenties, became leader of the sizable annual Métis buffalo hunts. He took no active part in the Red River Resistance of 1869–70 but is remembered primarily for his efforts as a military commander during the North-West Resistance of 1885. Dumont's guerrilla campaign had several successes and won the first battle against the North-West Mounted Police at Duck Lake in March of 1885. As the result of overwhelming odds against them, Dumont and his relatively small Métis force were ultimately defeated at Batoche in May. After Louis Riel surrendered to Canadian authorities, Dumont fled to the United States and eventually used his talent as a marksman when he joined Buffalo Bill's Wild West Show.

Erasmus, Georges, born 8 Aug 1948 (See Chapter 7, Section B and Chapter 9.)

Georges Erasmus was in born Behchokǫ̀, a Dene community in the Northwest Territories before his family moved to Yellowknife when he still an infant. He attended a Catholic high school there before becoming involved with the Company of Young Canadians, a relatively short-lived volunteer organization of the late 1960s established to assist with community development. Erasmus was active in the Indian Brotherhood of the NWT from its inception in 1969 and eventually became president of the organization and its successor, the Dene Nation, founded in 1978. During this time, he fought against the proposed Mackenzie Valley Pipeline. He was elected northern vice-chief of the Assembly of First Nations (AFN) in 1983 and became national chief of the AFN in 1985. After serving two terms leading the AFN, Erasmus was appointed as co-chair of the Royal Commission on Aboriginal Peoples, which is referenced throughout this reader. Erasmus was appointed to the Order of Canada in 1987 and became an officer of that order in 1999. He has also been awarded honorary doctorates from Queen's University, the University of Toronto, the University of Winnipeg, York University, the University of British Columbia, and the University of Western Ontario.

Gosnell, Chief Joseph (Sim'oogit Hleek), born 21 June 1936 (See Chapter 15.)

Chief Gosnell grew up in the Nisga'a village of Gitlaxt'aamiks (formerly New Aiyansh), about 100 km north of Terrace in the north-west corner of British Columbia. He is hereditary chief in the Laxsgiik pdeek (Eagle clan) of the Nisga'a Nation. As a child, he attended St. Michael's Indian Residential School at Alert Bay, near the northern tip of Vancouver Island. He worked most of his life as a commercial fisher and was advisor to Canada during the negotiation of the Pacific Salmon Treaty with the United States. He served many terms as a councillor before being elected chief councillor for the community of Gitlaxt'aamiks. He also spent many years working with the Nisga'a Tribal Council and, in 1990, was elected its president. He was the lead Nisga'a representative during the negotiations for the Nisga'a Treaty, the first modern treaty in British Columbia, which came into effect April 13, 2000. Gosnell was the first elected president of the Nisga'a Lisims Government. Among many other honours, Chief Gosnell received the Order of British Columbia in 1999, and, in 2001, he was named an officer of the Order of Canada. He was elevated to companion of that order in 2006.

Graham, William Morris, 11 Jan 1867–28 Mar 1940 (See Chapter 7.)

W.M. Graham was born in the Ottawa area to Mary Wright Morris and James F. Graham. James Graham was part of the force that travelled in 1870 to suppress the Red River Resistance, and he later became the clerk in the Department of Indian Affairs office in Winnipeg before being appointed Indian superintendent for Manitoba. At 18 years of age, William Morris Graham began his own career in the DIA when he became clerk at the Birtle Agency in Manitoba. He spent 10 years as clerk, first at Birtle, then at Wood Mountain, and finally at the commissioner's office in Regina. In 1896, Graham was promoted to the position of Indian agent for the File Hills Agency in Saskatchewan; in 1904, he became inspector for the South Saskatchewan Inspectorate. By all accounts, Graham was autocratic in his dealings with Indigenous people and self-assured and ambitious in his career. He seems to have been confident that he would become deputy superintendent general of Indian affairs when the position became vacant in 1913, but, when the job went to Duncan Campbell Scott instead, he developed an animosity against the new DSGIA, and bad feelings between the two lasted for the rest of Graham's career. In 1918, Graham was appointed commissioner of greater production for Alberta, Saskatchewan, and Manitoba with the responsibility of increasing agricultural output on reserves. Though this work put him in even greater disfavour with Indigenous reserve residents, Graham was appointed Indian commissioner for the three provinces in 1920 and held the position until he retired in 1932.

Halliday, William May (See the introduction to document 4b.3, p. 101.)

Jenness, Diamond (See the introduction to document 8.1, p. 233.)

Johnson, Pauline, 10 Mar 1861–7 Mar 1913 (See Chapter 3.)
Emily Pauline Johnson (Tekahionwake) was born to a Mohawk father and an English mother on the Six Nations Reserve near Brantford in what became Ontario. Her father served in a number of capacities within the community and became an important liaison in Mohawk-settler relations for most of his adult life. The younger Johnson grew up in a life of relative privilege and was tutored, for the most part, in her family home. When her father died in 1884, she was forced to move to rental accommodations in Brantford. Because of her changed economic status, she turned to writing as a means of earning a living. Though she had some early success in getting her work published, it was several years before she was able to earn an income from writing. Soon Johnson was touring across Canada performing her poetry at dozens of venues. She became one of the few Canadian women ever to make her living writing and performing poetry. In 1906, she travelled to London and was there at the same time as a First Nation delegation, which included Squamish Chief Joe Capilano (Sa7plek), arrived to present grievances against Canada's potlatch ban and overly restrictive hunting and fishing regulations in British Columbia. Johnson became friends with Capilano, which served to increase her already growing attraction to Canada's West Coast. Although the popularity of Johnson's work suffered a decline after her death in Vancouver in 1913, it has enjoyed a resurgence in the last half-century as it came to be re-evaluated by feminist and post-colonial scholars and others.

Laird, David, 12 Mar 1833–12 Jan 1914 (See Chapter 1 and 2.)
David Laird was the son of Janet Orr and Alexander Laird, a well-known farmer and shipbuilder who served on Prince Edward Island's Executive Council. David attended the Presbyterian Theological Seminary in Truro, Nova Scotia, and planned to enter the ministry. Instead, he turned to journalism and founded the *Protestant and Evangelical Witness* in 1859. He began a political career a year later when he was elected to the Charlottetown City Council in 1860. In 1871, Laird became a Liberal member of PEI's House of Assembly, and, in 1873, he was part of a small delegation that travelled to Ottawa to negotiate PEI's entry into Confederation. That same year, he won a seat in the House of Commons and was appointed minister of the interior and superintendent general of Indian affairs. He resigned in 1876 to take up an appointment as lieutenant governor of the North-West Territories. In 1877, along with James Farquharson Macleod of the North-West Mounted Police, Laird negotiated Treaty 7 on behalf of Canada with the Siksika, Kainai, Piikani,

Tsuu T'ina, and Nakoda First Nations. He resigned from the lieutenant governorship in 1881, but, in 1898, he was appointed Indian commissioner for the North-West Territories and Manitoba. Laird transferred back to Ottawa in 1909 and became an advisor to the Department of Indian Affairs.

Loft, Frederick Ogilvie (Onondeyoh), 3 Feb 1861–5 July 1934 (See the introduction to document 5b.1, p. 129.)

Macdonald, John Alexander, 11 Jan 1815–6 June 1891 (See Chapter 1, 3, and 6 especially.)
John A. Macdonald was born in Glasgow, Scotland, and came to Canada with his parents when he was five years old. Macdonald grew up in Kingston, Ontario, and in neighbouring communities. At age 15, he took up an articling position with a well-known Kingston lawyer. The law became a lifelong calling for Macdonald, and he set up practices first in Kingston and later in Toronto. By his late 20s, he began to play an active role in conservative politics and was elected to the Legislative Assembly of Upper Canada in 1844. He took on increasingly important positions within government and opposition ranks, and, between 1857 and 1862, he served, along with Étienne-Paschal Taché and later George-Étienne Cartier, as joint-premier of the Province of Canada. In the mid-1860s, Macdonald joined in a coalition with Cartier and George Brown that, in 1867, brought together Ontario, Quebec, Nova Scotia, and New Brunswick in the Confederation of Canada. Macdonald became the first prime minister of the new nation, and, through this and later terms (1867–73 and 1878–91), he worked to expand Canada's geographic boundaries and to extend Anglo-Canadian control over territories that had been controlled by Indigenous peoples. He led Canada into the Red River and North-West resistances and, as minister of the interior, was at the helm of the Department of Indian Affairs from 1878 to 1887 in addition to fulfilling his responsibilities as prime minister. Though he played a prominent role in the formative days of Canada's Indian policy and its extension to Western Canada, Macdonald made only one trip west, by private rail car in 1886.

Macleod, James Farquharson, 25 Sep 1836–5 Sep 1894 (See Chapter 2.)
James F. Macleod was born in Scotland but moved with his family to a farm his parents purchased in Richmond Hill, just north of Toronto. He attended Upper Canada College and then Queen's College in Kingston and finally pursued legal studies at Osgoode Hall. He was called to the bar in 1860 and, for the next ten years, practiced law in Bowmanville, Ontario. Macleod was also involved in the local militia, and, with his legal training, he rose quickly to the rank of major. As a militia officer, he was with the force that garrisoned Fort Garry following the Red River Resistance of 1869–70. In 1873 Prime Minister Macdonald offered him a position as superintendent and inspector in the newly formed North-West Mounted Police (NWMP). Macleod accepted, returned to Ontario, and, in the fall, was headed back to Fort Garry with a force of 150 mounted policemen. In 1874, Macleod was promoted to assistant commissioner while the force was ordered to the area that became southern Alberta to establish Canadian authority in the north-west. The "march west" was far more difficult than expected. The land was unfamiliar and the force lost its way before turning up in Fort Benton, Montana. Here, Macleod retained

the services of a guide named Jerry Potts who was able to lead Macleod and his force to the area of the whiskey trading post, Fort Whoop-Up, in the heart of Blackfoot territory. By October, Fort Macleod had been built and the following year both Fort Calgary and Fort Walsh had been constructed. Macleod was appointed commissioner of the NWMP in 1876 and was one of Canada's representatives in the negotiations leading to Treaty 7. In 1880, he resigned from the force to become a magistrate in the North-West Territories.

Manuel, Chief George, 17 Feb 1921–15 Nov 1989 (See Chapter 10 and 12.)
George Manuel was born into the Neskonlith community of the Secwepemc (Shuswap) Nation. He attended the Kamloops Indian Residential School until he contracted tuberculosis and was sent to the Coqualeetza Indian Hospital on the Sto:lo reserve near Chilliwack, BC. As a young adult, Chief Manuel served in several Indigenous leadership positions before taking a job with the Department of Indian Affairs in Quw'utsun' (Cowichan) territory on Vancouver Island as a community development officer in 1965. After his three-year tenure with the DIA, Chief Manuel went on to work alongside Harold Cardinal in the Indian Association of Alberta. Then, in 1970, he began a six-year term as president of the National Indian Brotherhood, the precursor to the Assembly of First Nations. From 1975 until 1981, he served as the first president of the World Council of Indigenous Peoples. Near the end of his term as president of the Union of BC Indian Chiefs, he was instrumental in organizing "The Constitutional Express" to ensure that Canada included protection for Aboriginal and treaty rights in its new Constitution. Manuel became an officer of the Order of Canada in 1986 and was nominated several times for a Nobel Peace Prize.

Marshall, Donald Jr., 13 Sep 1953—6 Aug 2009 (See Chapter 13.)
Donald Marshall Jr. was the son of Donald Marshall Sr., a long serving Mi'kmaq grand chief from the Membertou First Nation. In 1971, while he was still a teenager, Marshall Jr. was wrongfully convicted of the murder of another teenager in Sydney, Nova Scotia. After serving over a decade in prion, he was finally exonerated, and, following a royal commission struck to investigate his wrongful conviction, Marshall became a symbol of the racism that remained endemic and systemic in Canada. In 1996, Marshall re-entered the public stage when he was charged with selling eels without a licence. Marshall and his supporters won a somewhat limited victory at the Supreme Court of Canada by demonstrating that he had a treaty right to fish and to sell his catch.

McIvor, Sharon Donna, born 9 Oct 1948 (See Chapter 11.)
Sharon McIvor is a Nlaka'pamux woman from the Lower Nicola First Nation whose traditional territory is in the vicinity of what is now Merritt, British Columbia. She was awarded a law degree in 1986 and went on to earn her masters of law degree and to teach at the Nicola Valley Institute of Technology. For decades, McIvor has been deeply involved in the struggle to advance Indigenous rights and to bring justice to Indigenous women and children especially. She has played important leadership roles in the Native Women's Association of Canada and has worked with the Feminist Alliance for International Action and the British Columbia Committee on the Elimination of Discrimination against Women (CEDAW), a group of non-profit organizations dedicated to

pursuing the interests of women and girls. She has also been heavily involved with efforts to bring the hundreds of cases of missing and murdered Indigenous women and girls to public attention. McIvor is perhaps most widely known for challenging the continuing discrimination of women in the Indian Act. Although it took almost two decades for her case to reach the Supreme Court, McIvor was successful in forcing Canada to amend the act. The changes, though beneficial to many women and their children, did not completely eliminate the discriminatory provisions of the legislation, so McIvor continues her efforts to seek equitable treatment for Indigenous women and their children.

Paull, Andrew, 6 Feb 1892–28 July 1959 (See Chapter 8 for Paull and Chapter 5, Section B for the Allied Tribes).

Andy Paull grew up in the village of Sta'a7mes a Sḵwx̱wú7mesh (Squamish) community near Squamish, British Columbia. When his family moved to the village of Eslha7an (Mission Reserve) in North Vancouver, Paull attended the newly opened St. Paul's Indian Residential School. He attended the residential school for six years but never lost the teachings of his Sḵwx̱wú7mesh elders. In his mid-teens, Paull began work at a Vancouver law firm, and, though he never formally practiced law, the training he received at this firm served him well in his work as an activist. After it was formed in 1916, Paull served on the executive committee of the Allied Tribes of British Columbia, an amalgamation of First Nations groups organized to advance issues related to land and Aboriginal title. He appeared before the special joint committee of the Senate and House of Commons appointed to inquire into their claims, discussed in the introduction to document 5b.6. After the 1927 ban on raising funds to pursue land claims and the collapse of the Allied Tribes, Paull shifted his efforts to promoting Indigenous well-being in more directly localized ways. He went on to lead the North American Indian Brotherhood and to make a presentation on its behalf in 1946 to the Special Joint Committee of the Senate and the House of Commons Appointed to Examine and Consider the Indian Act. For his evidence, see Chapter 8.

Prince, Thomas George (Tommy), 25 Oct 1915–25 Nov 1977 (See Chapter 7.)

Tommy Prince was one of 11 children born to Harry and Elizabeth Prince of the Brokenhead Ojibway Nation. He was a descendant of Chief Peguis, one of the signatories to the Selkirk Treaty of 1817, which was among the first treaties negotiated between Indigenous people and settler representatives in Western Canada. Prince volunteered for the Canadian Army soon after World War II broke out and served first with a company of engineers and then with a parachute battalion. Later, he was selected to be part of a specialized assault team that became known to enemy forces as the "Devil's Brigade." Prince distinguished himself throughout the war by his bravery and initiative, and he became the most decorated Indigenous Canadian soldier in World War II. He was decorated for his valour in both Italy and France and was presented with a Military Medal by King George VI, who also awarded him a Silver Star on behalf of the president of the United States. On his return to Canada, Prince found that he was denied the benefits awarded to non-Indigenous veterans and, facing a life of unemployment, re-enlisted in the army. He served two tours of duty in the Korean War until he was wounded and honourably discharged. Prince continued to find the treatment he faced in civilian life a challenge, and, though he overcame many of his personal demons in time, he spent the last years of his life living in a Salvation Army shelter. Even though it was not particularly evident during his lifetime, Prince played an important role in changing attitudes toward Indigenous people in Canada.

Reed, Hayter, circa 26 May 1849–21 Dec 1936 (See Chapter 3 and 4.)
Hayter Reed was the son of an English father, George Reed, and a Canadian-born mother, Harriet. After attending Upper Canada College and the Model Grammar School for Upper Canada, Reed attended the School of Military Instruction in Kingston. Following his graduation in 1865, he served in the militia and was part of the force that garrisoned Fort Garry following the Red River Resistance of 1869–70. He was called to the bar in Manitoba in 1872, but he seems never to have practiced law. When Reed's Provisional Battalion of Rifles was disbanded in 1878, he went to work in the Department of the Interior. In 1881, he moved to the Department of Indian Affairs as an agent for the Battleford Agency. He subsequently went on to hold a number of positions within the department, including assuming in 1893 its highest civil service position, that of deputy superintendent general. By all accounts, Reed was uncompromising and inflexible in his work with the Indigenous people under his purview. He seemed convinced, for example, in the justness and utility of the never-quite-legal pass system (discussed in Chapter 4). When his Conservative connections became less helpful because of the election of Laurier's Liberals in 1896, Reed was all but forced from his position. He left the employ of the DIA and went on to work for the Canadian Pacific Railway, becoming manager of CP's hotel division in 1905.

Riel, Louis, 22 Oct 1844–16 Nov 1885 (See Chapter 3.)
Louis Riel could easily be in contention for the most controversial figure in Canadian history. He was born in 1844 at Red River (present-day Winnipeg), became bilingual, and studied for both the priesthood and the law. His education put him in an obvious position to emerge as a leader among the Métis. In 1869, he was elected secretary of the Comité National Métis (Métis National Committee) and led the provisional government that eventually negotiated the entry of Manitoba into Confederation with Canada. During the Red River Resistance of 1869–70, the provisional government under Riel's leadership made the decision to execute the radical Protestant Orangeman Thomas Scott, whom it had convicted of treason. This action inflamed anti-Catholic sentiment in primarily English Protestant Ontario and led to Riel's exile. During this period, he spent time in asylums in Quebec and came to believe that he had a religious duty to lead the Métis in Canada's North-West. By 1884, Riel was teaching at a Jesuit mission in Montana when he was visited by a Métis delegation from the South Saskatchewan River area and asked to present their concerns to the Canadian government. When John A. Macdonald's government continued to ignore Métis grievances, they once again declared a provisional government. Thus began the North-West Resistance of 1885, which is discussed in Chapter 3. After the final defeat at Batoche in May, Riel surrendered to Canadian forces, was tried for treason, and was quickly hanged at the North-West Mounted Police barracks in Regina on November 16th.

Scollen, Father Constantine (See the introduction to document 2.5, p. 39.)

Scott, Duncan Campbell, 2 Aug 1862–19 Dec 1947 (See Chapter 5 and 7 especially.) Duncan Campbell Scott was born in Ottawa to a Methodist clergyman, Reverend William Scott, and Janet McCallum. Although the younger Scott had hopes of going to medical school, his family's finances would not allow it. Instead, in 1879, he joined the Department of Indian Affairs as a clerk. In 1913, he became superintendent general and led the department until he retired in 1932. During his tenure, Scott was particularly interested in assimilating Indigenous people into mainstream Anglo-Canadian society while at the same time reducing departmental expenditures. Scott was also a poet of some prominence and published a number of collections of poetry. The policy objectives Scott sought as head of the Department of Indian Affairs were often reflected in his poetry as well.

Steele, Samuel Benfield (See the introduction to document 4a.4, p. 88.)

Trudeau, Joseph Philippe Pierre Yves Elliott (usually known as Pierre Elliott Trudeau), 18 Oct 1919–28 Sep 2000 (See Chapter 10 and 12.) Pierre Trudeau was born into a wealthy Montreal family and was educated at the Jesuit Collège Jean-de-Brébeuf, the Université de Montréal, Harvard University, and the London School of Economics. After a decade of practicing law, Trudeau moved to teaching at the Université de Montréal in 1961 where he became an outspoken critic of Quebec nationalism in favour of a unified federal state. He was elected as a Liberal member of parliament for the first time in 1965 and was appointed minister of justice. Three short years later he was sworn in as Canada's fifteenth prime minister. Within a couple of years of his election, Trudeau had to deal with the 1970 October Crisis and decided to invoke the War Measures Act for only the third time in Canada's history; until this time, the act had never been invoked outside of global conflict. Trudeau spearheaded the patriation of Canada's Constitution in 1982; the constitutional documents included the Charter of Rights and Freedoms. Although many of the reforms that he inspired were progressive, he was never really willing or able to see Indigenous cultures as separate and unique nor Indigenous communities as the holders of special rights or entitlements. As a result of this way of thinking, his government attempted to remove existing Aboriginal and treaty rights with the White Paper of 1969 (see Chapter 10). Later, and only after considerable Indigenous agitation and political pressure, his government made some accommodation for Indigenous concerns in the 1982 Constitution, presented in Chapter 12. Trudeau remains one of Canada's longest-standing prime ministers and is perhaps the country's best-known politician, both at home and abroad.

Wuttunee, William (See the introduction to document 10.3, p. 302.)

Sources

✳

CHAPTER 2

2.1　Area of Treaty 7 and the Traditional Territory of the Blackfoot Confederacy. Reproduced from Treaty 7 Elders and Tribal Council with Walter Hildebrandt, Dorothy First Rider, and Sarah Carter, *The True Spirit and Original Intent of Treaty 7* (Montreal: McGill-Queen's University Press, 1996), xvii, with permission from McGill-Queen's University Press.

2.2　Boundaries of the Numbered Treaties. Reproduced from Treaty 7 Elders and Tribal Council with Walter Hildebrandt, Dorothy First Rider, and Sarah Carter, *The True Spirit and Original Intent of Treaty 7* (Montreal: McGill-Queen's University Press, 1996), xviii, with permission from McGill-Queen's University Press.

2.6　Interview with Cecile Many Guns (Grassy Water), 1973. Interview with Mrs. Cecile Many Guns conducted by Dila Provost and Albert Yellowhorn Sr., n.d. University of Regina, *oURspace*, http://ourspace.uregina.ca/handle/10294/586. Reprinted with permission from the University of Regina.

2.7　Interview with Mrs. Annie Buffalo (Sitting Up High), 1975. Interview with Mrs. Buffalo conducted by Johnny Smith, 12 March 1975, University of Regina, *oURspace*, http://ourspace.uregina.ca/handle/10294/504. Reprinted with permission from the University of Regina.

CHAPTER 3

3.4　The Account of Gabriel Dumont, 1888 (1949). George Stanley, "Gabriel Dumont's Account of the North West Rebellion, 1885," *Canadian Historical Review*, 30, no. 3 (Sept. 1949): 251–56. Reproduced with the permission of the University of Toronto Press.

3.5　The Recommendations of Assistant Indian Commissioner Hayter Reed, 1885. Hayter Reed, "Memorandum for the Honourable the Indian Commissioner relative to the future management of Indians," 20 July 1885, Library and Archives Canada, Department of Indian Affairs, RG 10, vol. 3710, file 19550–3, reel C-10124. © Government of Canada. Reproduced with the permission of the Minister of Public Works and Government Services Canada (2012).

3.6　Address Presented to Chief Crowfoot from the Council of the Corporation of the City of Ottawa, 1886. Address Presented to Chief Crowfoot from the Council of the Corporation of the City of Ottawa, 1886, with W.M. Graham, Indian Commissioner, to Norman H.H. Lett, City Clerk, Ottawa, 14 October 1925, Glenbow Museum and Archives, William Morris Graham Papers, M8097, box 1, file 1. Reproduced with the permission of the Glenbow Museum Archives.

CHAPTER 4

4a.1　Letter from Robert Sinclair to Edgar Dewdney, 1892. R. Sinclair to E. Dewdney, SGIA, 23 June 1892, Library and Archives Canada, Department of Indian Affairs, RG 10, vol. 6817, file 487–1–2 pt. 1, reel C-8539. © Government of Canada.

Reproduced with the permission of the Minister of Public Works and Government Services Canada (2012).

4a.2 Letter From Hayter Reed to Edgar Dewdney, 1885. Hayter Reed to Edgar Dewdney, 16 August 1885, LAC, Edgar Dewdney Fonds, MG 27-IC4. © Government of Canada. Reproduced with the permission of the Minister of Public Works and Government Services Canada (2012).

4a.3 Letter from A.E. Forget to Blackfoot Indian Agent, 1889. A.E. Forget, Assistant Indian Commissioner, to Indian Agent at Blackfoot Crossing, 29 March 1889, Library and Archives Canada, Department of Indian Affairs, RG 10, vol.1137, reel T-1467. © Government of Canada. Reproduced with the permission of the Minister of Public Works and Government Services Canada (2012).

4a.4 Extract from NWMP Superintendent Steele's Monthly Report, June 1890. "Extract from Supt. Steel's monthly report, Fort Macleod, June 1890," Library and Archives Canada, Royal Canadian Mounted Police Fonds, RG 18, series A-1, vol. 45, file 953–90. © Government of Canada. Reproduced with the permission of the Minister of Public Works and Government Services Canada (2012).

4a.5 "The Mounted Police and the Sarcees," *Calgary Herald,* June 8, 1892. "The Mounted Police and the Sarcees," *Calgary Herald*, June 8, 1892. Reproduced with the permission of the *Calgary Herald.*

4a.6 Letter from Fred White to L. Vankoughnet, 1893. Fred White, Comptroller, NWMP to L. Vankoughnet, DSGIA, DIA, 16 June 1893, Library and Archives Canada, Department of Indian Affairs, RG 10, vol. 6817, file 487–1–2, pt. 1. © Government of Canada. Reproduced with the permission of the Minister of Public Works and Government Services Canada (2012).

4a.7 Letter from Hayter Reed to the Deputy Superintendent General of Indian Affairs, 1893. Hayter Reed, Indian Commissioner, to DSGIA, 14 Jun 1893, Library and Archives Canada, Department of Indian Affairs, RG 10, vol. 6817, file 487–1–2, pt. 1, reel C-8539. © Government of Canada. Reproduced with the permission of the Minister of Public Works and Government Services Canada (2012).

4a.8 Chief Dan Kennedy, *Recollections of an Assiniboine Chief*, 1972. Dan Kennedy, *Recollections of an Assiniboine Chief*, ed. James R. Stevens (Toronto: McClelland and Stewart, 1972), 87–88. Reproduced with the permission of Tanya Harnett for the family of Chief Kennedy.

4b.4 "A Plea for Potlatches," 1896. "A Plea for Potlatches," *Victoria Daily Colonist*, February 20, 1896, 5. Reproduced with the permission of the *Victoria Times Colonist.*

4b.5 *Assu of Cape Mudge*, 1989. Harry Assu with Joy Inglis, "Renewal of the Potlatch at Cape Mudge," in *Assu of Cape Mudge: Recollections of a Coastal Indian Chief* (Vancouver: UBC Press, 1989), 103–8. Reprinted with permission of the publisher © University of British Columbia Press 1989. All rights reserved by the publisher.

CHAPTER 5

5a.3 Evidence of D.C. Scott on the Indian Act Amendments of 1920. Evidence of D.C. Scott to the Special Committee of the House of Commons Examining the Indian Act Amendments of 1920, Library and Archives Canada, Department of Indian Affairs, RG 10, vol. 6810, file 470–2–3, pt.7, pp. K-4, L-1 to L-4, M-1 to M-4, N-1 to N-4, reel C-8533. © Government of Canada. Reproduced with the permission of the Minister of Public Works and Government Services Canada (2012).

5b.2 Letter from J.P. Wright to D.C. Scott, 1919. © Government of Canada. Reproduced with the permission of the Minister of Public Works and Government Services Canada (2012).

5b.3 Letter from D.C. Scott to J.P. Wright, 1919. Duncan C. Scott, DSGIA, to J.P. Wright, Indian Agent at Fort Frances,

31 December 1919, Library and Archives Canada, Department of Indian Affairs, RG 10, vol. 3211, file 527,787. © Government of Canada. Reproduced with the permission of the Minister of Public Works and Government Services Canada (2012).

CHAPTER 6

6.4 Mary Carpenter, "No More Denials Please," 1991. Mary Carpenter, "Recollections and Comments: No More Denials Please," *Inuktitut* 74 (1991): 56–61. Reprinted with the permission of *Inuktitut* magazine.

6.5 Isabelle Knockwood, *Out of the Depths*, 2001. Isabelle Knockwood, *Out of the Depths*, 3rd ed. (Lockport, NS: Roseway Publishing, 2001), 32–34, 88–89, 99–100, 124–26, 143, and 157–61. Reprinted with the permission of Fernwood Publishing.

CHAPTER 7

7b.1 Testimony of Gordon Ahenakew, Saskatchewan Indian Veterans Association, 1992. Transcripts of the Hearings of the Royal Commission on Aboriginal Peoples, vol. 50, Saskatoon Indian and Metis Friendship Centre, Saskatoon, Saskatchewan, Tuesday, October 27, 1992, vol. 1, pp. 101–7. Privy Council Office, 1992. Reproduced with the permission of the Minister of Public Works and Government Services Canada, 2013.

7b.2 Testimony of Norman Quinney, Indian Veterans Association, 1992. Transcripts of the Hearings of the Royal Commission on Aboriginal Peoples, vol. 36, Edmonton Inn, Edmonton, Alberta, Thursday, June 11, 1992, vol. 1B, pp. 301–4. Privy Council Office, 1992. Reproduced with the permission of the Minister of Public Works and Government Services Canada, 2013.

7b.3 Testimony of Ray Prince, Northern Region of National Aboriginal Veterans Association, BC Chapter, 1992.

Transcripts of the Hearings of the Royal Commission on Aboriginal Peoples, vol. 141, Prince George, British Columbia, Monday, May 31, 1993, vol. 1, pp. 58–63 and 66–70. Privy Council Office 1993. Reproduced with the permission of the Minister of Public Works and Government Services Canada, 2013.

7b.4 Testimony of Harry Lavallee, National Aboriginal Veterans Association, 1993. Transcripts of the Hearings of the Royal Commission on Aboriginal Peoples, vol. 150, Vancouver, British Columbia, Wednesday, June 2, 1993, vol. 1, pp. 208–12 and 213–16. Privy Council Office 1993. Reproduced with the permission of the Minister of Public Works and Government Services Canada, 2013.

7b.5 *The Aboriginal Soldier after the Wars*, 1995. Canada, Senate, The Standing Senate Committee on Aboriginal Peoples, "Assessment," in *The Aboriginal Soldier after the Wars: Report of the Standing Senate Committee on Aboriginal Peoples* (Ottawa: The Senate of Canada, 1995), 25–34. Reproduced with the permission of the Senate of Canada, 2013.

CHAPTER 9

9.1 The High Arctic Relocation, 1953. Reproduced with the permission of the Minister of Public Works and Government Services Canada, 2013.

9.2 Testimony of Markoosie Patsauq and Samwillie Elijassialuk, 1992. Testimony of Markoosie Patsauq and Samwillie Elijassialuk, Transcripts of the Hearings of the Royal Commission on Aboriginal Peoples, vol. 27, Inukjuak, Quebec, 8 June 1992, vol. 1, pp. 53–63. Reproduced with the permission of the Minister of Public Works and Government Services Canada, 2013.

9.3 Examination of Bent Sivertz, 1993. Examination of Bent Sivertz, Transcripts of the Hearings of the Royal Commission on Aboriginal Peoples, vol. 173, Citadel Inn Ottawa, 29 June 1993, vol. 2, pp. 409–17, 423–29, 438–40, and 457–60. Reproduced with the permission of the Minister of Public Works and Government Services Canada, 2013.

9.5 The Hickling Report, 1990. *Assessment of the Factual Basis of Certain Allegations Made before the Standing Committee on Aboriginal Affairs Concerning the Relocation of Inukjuak Inuit Families in the 1950s: Report*, submitted to the Department of Indian Affairs and Northern Development (Ottawa: Hickling Corporation, 1990), 3–6. Reproduced with the permission of the Minister of Public Works and Government Services Canada, 2013.

9.6 Report of the Royal Commission on Aboriginal Peoples, 1994. Royal Commission on Aboriginal Peoples, *The High Arctic Relocation: A Report on the 1953–55 Relocation* (Ottawa: Supply and Services, 1994), 134–46. Reproduced with the permission of the Minister of Public Works and Government Services Canada, 2013.

CHAPTER 10

10.1 *Statement of the Government of Canada on Indian Policy* (White Paper), 1969. Canada, Government of Canada, *Statement of the Government of Canada on Indian Policy, 1969* (Ottawa: Indian Affairs, 1969), 5–8, 11–15, and 18–22. Reproduced with the permission of the Minister of Public Works and Government Services Canada, 2013.

10.2 Indian Association of Alberta, *Citizens Plus* (Red Paper), 1970. Indian Chiefs of Alberta, *Citizens Plus* (Edmonton: Indian Association of Alberta, 1970), 1–10. Reproduced with the permission of the Indian Association of Alberta.

10.3 William Wuttunee, *Ruffled Feathers*, 1971. William I.C. Wuttunee, *Ruffled Feathers: Indians in Canadian Society* (Calgary: Bell Books, 1971), 10–13, 23–25, 106–09, and 138–41. Reproduced with the permission of William I.C. Wuttunee.

10.4 National Indian Brotherhood, "Statement, on the Proposed New 'Indian Policy,'" 1969. National Indian Brotherhood, "Statement on the Proposed New 'Indian Policy,'" 26 June 1969. Reproduced with the permission of the Assembly of First Nations.

CHAPTER 11

11.3 Cathy Bailey, "Indian Women Struggle for Rights," *Poundmaker*, 1974. Cathy Bailey, "Indian Women Struggle for Rights," *Poundmaker*, 25 February 1974.

11.4 Report of the Royal Commission on Aboriginal Peoples, 1985. Canada, Royal Commission on Aboriginal Peoples, *Report of the Royal Commission on Aboriginal Peoples*, chapter 2, "Women's Perspectives" in vol. 4, *Perspectives and Realities* (Ottawa: Communications Group, 1996), 33–43 and 96. Reproduced with the permission of the Minister of Public Works and Government Services Canada, 2013.

11.6 Letter from Sharon McIvor to Members of Parliament, 2010. Reproduced with the permission of Sharon McIvor.

CHAPTER 12

12.1 Union of BC Indian Chiefs at the Russell Tribunal, 1980. Union of British Columbia Indian Chiefs, Submission to the Russell Tribunal on the Rights of the Indians of the Americas, November 1980, pp. 45–46, 55–57, 59–60, and 66–70. Reproduced with the permission of the Union of the British Columbia Indian Chiefs.

12.2 Petition by the Indian People of Canada to Queen Elizabeth II, 1980. Petition by the Indian People of Canada to Her Majesty Queen Elizabeth II, Ottawa, November 1980. Reproduced with the permission of the Center for World Indigenous Studies.

CHAPTER 14

14.1 *Report of the Ipperwash Inquiry*, 2007. Sidney B. Linden, Commissioner,

Investigation and Findings, vol. 1,
Report of the Ipperwash Inquiry
(Toronto: Queen's Printer for Ontario,
2007), 671–72, 674–77, 681–87,
and 689–91. © Queen's Printer for
Ontario, 2013. Reproduced with
permission.

14.2 Testimony of Nicholas Cottrelle,
2005. Testimony of Nicholas Abraham
Cottrelle, before the Honourable Justice
Sidney Linden, Commissioner, Ipperwash Public Inquiry, Forest Community
Centre, Kimberly Hall, Forest, Ontario,
18 January 2005, pp. 7, 17–20, 48–50,
64–65, 69, 77–83, 107–15, 120–21,
133–35, 146–48, 155–59. © Queen's
Printer for Ontario, 2013. Reproduced
with permission.

14.3 Presentation of Sam George, 2006.
Sam George, Final Submissions of
the Dudley George Estate and Fam-
ily Group, before the Honourable
Justice Sidney Linden, Commissioner,
Ipperwash Public Inquiry, Forest
Community Centre, Kimberly Hall,
Forest, Ontario, 21 August 2006,
pp. 15–21. © Queen's Printer for
Ontario, 2013. Reproduced with
permission.

CHAPTER 15

15.1 Royal Commission on Aboriginal Peoples, "Treaties," 1996. *Restructuring the
Relationship*, vol. 2 of *Report of the Royal
Commission on Aboriginal Peoples* (Ottawa:
Aboriginal Affairs and Northern Development Canada, 1996), 9, 11, 13, 15–18,
60–65, and 68–70. Reproduced with the
permission of the Minister of Public Works
and Government Services Canada, 2012.

15.2 Speech by Chief Joseph Gosnell to the British Columbia Legislative Assembly, 1998.
Joseph Gosnell in British Columbia, Legislative Assembly, *Debates of the Legislative
Assembly* (Hansard), vol. 12, no. 17, 2 December 1998, pp. 10859–61. Reproduced
with the permission of the Speaker of the
Legislative Assembly of British Columbia.

15.3 Are Treaties the Answer?: Panel Dis-
cussion at the *Preparing for the Day
After Treaty* Conference, 2007. "Panel
Discussion: Are Treaties the Answer?"
in *Preparing for the Day after Treaty: A
Conference for First Nations*, Conference
Presentations, November 14–16, 2007,
Vancouver, British Columbia. Repro-
duced with the permission of the British
Columbia Treaty Commission.

Index

Maps and photos indicated in italics

Métis and, 58
organization of, 114
Peter Bryce as Medical Inspector, 167
on potlatch, 102
power over First Nations, 82
on restricting movement, 82
White Paper on, 291
Department of Veterans Affairs, 223, 224.
    See also veterans, Indigenous
deputy superintendent general of Indian affairs
    (DSGIA), 114. *See also* Scott, Duncan
    Campbell
Deschamps, Baptiste, 69
Deskaheh (Cayuga chief)
    The Redman's Appeal for Justice, 128, 143–48
    suggested reading on League of Nations
        appeal, 149
Desterres, Philo, 322, 324–25
Dewdney, Edgar, 74n9, 84n2, 453
DIA, *see* Department of Indian Affairs (DIA)
Dick, Colleen, 110
doctors, medical
    enfranchisement of, 14
Dominion Elections Act (1920), 254
Dominion Land Act (1883), 57
Dorchester, Lord (governor of
    Quebec), 347
double mother rule, 313–14
Douglas treaties, 428
drugs, in Indian Act, 12
DSGIA (deputy superintendent general
    of Indian affairs), 114. *See also* Scott,
    Duncan Campbell
Duck Lake confrontation (1885)
    account in *Daily Mail*, 57
    Crozier report on, 64–68
    DIA annual report on, 60
    Dumont on, 69–73
    See also North-West Resistance (1885)
Dufferin, Earl of (governor general of Canada),
    340, 347
Dumont, Edouard, 69, 70, 71, 72
Dumont, Gabriel, 69, 453
    in *Daily Mail*, 57
    on Duck Lake confrontation, 69–73
    suggested reading on, 80
Dumont, Isidore, 71, 72
dumps, *see* garbage dumps
Dussault, Rene, 212
Dutch, 144, 145

Eagle Head (Piikani [Peigan] chief), 34
Eagle Tail (Piikani [Peigan] chief), 33, 62
earth, as mother, 51
education
    agriculture as part of, 194
    Allied Indian Tribes of BC on, 141
    Diamond Jenness on, 235–36
    higher, 164–66
    League of Indians for, 130
    Mohawk of Kahnawà:ke [Kahnawake,
        Caughnawaga] on, 252
    North American Indian Brotherhood
        on, 239
    Red Paper on, 299
    in return for surrendering land, 157
    Six Nations on, 126
    spirituality and, 160
    See also residential schools
Edwards, Henrietta Muir, 311
Elijassialuk, Samwillie
    testimony on High Arctic relocation,
        259–60
Elizabeth II, Queen
    petition to on constitutional changes,
        345–51
Ellesmere Island, 263, 269–70, 271, 272
enfranchised Indian, defined, 11
enfranchisement
    amendments to Indian Act on, 115, 118–24,
        126–27, 145
    as assimilation, 3, 4, 114, 120
    conference on Bill 79 and, 254
    House of Commons debate on, 3, 4, 6, 7–9
    Indian Act on, 14–16, 118–19
    Mohawk of Kahnawà:ke (Kahnawake,
        Caughnawaga) on, 251
    North American Indian Brotherhood on,
        239
    numbers of Indians enfranchised, 119
    resistance to, 114
    vs. traditional communal land use, 341
    Union of Saskatchewan Indians on,
        246–47
    See also enfranchisement, compulsory;
        self-governance
enfranchisement, compulsory
    Duncan Campbell Scott on, 118–24
    Six Nations on, 125–26, 145
    text of amendment to Indian Act (1920),
        126–27

National Indian Brotherhood on, 308–9
North American Indian Brotherhood on, 239
Red Paper (1970) on, 299
White Paper (1969) on, 294
Huron Tract Treaty (1827), 396
Huu-ay-aht First Nation
  treaty process, 443, 448–49

I Have Lived Here Since the World Began
  (Ray), xxiv
IAA, *see* Indian Association of Alberta
Idaho, Indian titles in, 138
identity, Indian
  White Paper on, 292
  See also Indian status
Immaculate Conception Residential School,
  Aklavik, 175–77
Indian
  character, described by Nicholas Davin,
    155–57
  concept of, and identity, 332
  death rate, 170, 343
  defined in Indian Act, 10–11
  at Duck Lake confrontation, 69, 71
  man power valued, 171
  no longer defined as (enfranchisement), 3,
    16, 114, 123
  non-treaty, defined in Indian Act, 11
  in North-West Resistance, Crozier on, 67
  in North-West Resistance, DIA view of,
    59–60, 61–62, 63
  population decreases, 172–73
  status, determining, 241
  vital statistics lacking, 172
  See also aboriginal; First Nations;
    Indigenous peoples
Indian Act (1876)
  1985 amendment to (Bill C-31), 312,
    315–16
  2011 amendment to on gender equity
    (Bill C-3), 312–13
  Allied Indian Tribes of BC on, 141
  amendment on acquiring off-reserve land,
    224
  amendment on leasing of reserve land, 196
  amendment on seizure of reserve land, 192
  amendment on use of funds, 192, 196
  amendment to prevent legal action, 149

amendments on enfranchisement, 115,
    118–24, 126–27, 145
  amendments on potlatch, 96–97
  amendments on Soldier Settlement Act,
    210–12
  assumptions in on Indigenous cultures, 115
  on councils and chiefs, 13–14
  on enfranchisement, 14–16
  House of Commons debates on, 2–9
  impact of, xxiii
  opposed by Six Nations, 16–17
  overview, 2
  on potlatch, 95, 101–2
  preamble, 10
  purpose of, 3, 9
  on reserve surrender, 12–13, 365–66
  suggested readings on, 17–18
  terms used in, 10–12
  trespass provisions, 81, 82
  Veterans' Land Act and, 226
  White Paper on, 290, 292
  William Wuttunee on, 304–5
  See also Indian Act (1951 amendments)
Indian Act (1951 amendments), 232, 253–55,
    287, 313–15
  suggested readings on, 255
  See also SJC
Indian Association of Alberta (IAA), 305, 429,
    452
  Red Paper (*Citizens Plus*), 295–302
  suggested reading on SJC presentation, 255
Indian Brotherhood of the NWT, 454
Indian identity
  White Paper on, 292
  See also Indian status
Indian land controversy, 128, 133–42, 309
  suggested reading on, 150
Indian lands, defined, 12
Indian organizations, 302–3
Indian Register, 315–16
Indian Rights for Indian Women, 317–19
Indian status
  1951 Indian Act amendment on, 313–15
  Bill C-31 (1985 Indian Act amendment)
    on, 315–16
  children and, 322, 323–24, 325, 326–27
  constitution patriation and, 342
  importance of determining, 320
  importance of for identity, 332

A Cry from an Indian Wife (Johnson),
    78–79
  in DIA annual report, 59–62
  history course example, xv–xix
  pass system and, 83
  recommendations made after by Hayter
    Reed, 74–76
  suggested readings on, 80
  See also Duck Lake confrontation
North-West Territories, and enfranchisement,
    16
Norwest, Lance-Corporal (WWI sniper),
    207–8
Nova Scotia, Mi'kmaq from in WWI, 206–7
numbered treaties, 19, *22. See also specific*
    treaties
Nunavut Land Claims Agreement
    (1993), 434
  suggested reading on, 450
Nungak, Anna, 259, 262
Nuyumbalees Cultural Centre, 107
Nuyumbalees Society, 107, 109
NWMP, *see* North-West Mounted Police
    (NWMP)
NWT Game Ordinance, 274

Oblates of Mary Immaculate, 175–76, 266
occupations, *see* resistance
October Crisis (1970), 460
officious bystander test, 381–82
Oka crisis, 395
Old Bow Fort, residential school near, 159
Old Sun (Siksika [Blackfoot] chief), 33, 34,
    36, 62
Oliver, John, 133
One Arrow's band, 75
Oneida Nation, *see* Haudenosaunee (Iroquois)
    Confederacy; Six Nations
Onondaga Madonna, The (Scott), 116
Onondaga Nation, *see* Haudenosaunee
    (Iroquois) Confederacy; Six Nations
Ontario
  in Ipperwash crisis, 396, 398–99
  relations with Indigenous people, 404
Ontario Native Women's Association of
    Canada, 452
Ontario Provincial Police (OPP), *see* OPP
opium, in Indian Act, 12
OPP (Ontario Provincial Police)

  in Ipperwash Inquiry, 396, 397, 399–400,
    400–403
  Nicholas Cottrelle on, 409–15, 416–18,
    419–22
oral terms, legality of, 366, 378–79
  suggested reading on, 393
organizations, *see* Indian organizations; *specific*
    Indigenous organizations
original documents, *see* primary sources
Oronhyatekha, 165
Ottawa
  address to Crowfoot, 77–78
  tuberculosis in, 175
  Ouellet, Baptiste, 69
Out of the Depths (Knockwood), 177–86
outcast mentality, 234
ownership, property, *see* enfranchisement

Pacific Salmon Treaty, 454
Padloping Island, 271, 272
Pan-Indianism, xxii
paper blood system, 327
Parlby, Irene, 311
pass system
  A.E. Forget letter on parental visitation to
    schools, 87–88
  Cecile Many Guns on, 46
  Dan Kennedy (Assiniboine chief) and, 94
  fear of conflict with Indians over, 85
  Frederick White letter on NWMP and,
    90–92
  Hayter Reed and, 75, 84, 86, 92–93
  illegality of, 82, 85
  overview, 81–82, 82–83
  Robert Sinclair letter on, 84–85
  Sarcee (Tsuu T'ina) in *Calgary Herald*
    article, 90
  suggested readings on, 111
  See also movement, restricting
Paterson, William
  House of Commons debates on Indian Act
    (1876), 4, 5, 7, 9
patriation, *see* Constitution Act (1982)
patrilineal descent, 311–12, 324
Patsauq, Markoosie
  testimony on High Arctic relocation,
    259–62
Paull, Andy, 458
  testimony to SJC, 237–40

R. v. Sparrow (1990), 360, 367–75
    suggested reading on, 393
racism
    in Ipperwash crisis, 398, 402–3
    in justice system, 375
radar stations, 269, 270
railroad, as progress, 77
Railway Act, 240
Rainy Chief (North Blood chief), 34–35
rations, 32, 33, 45, 161
Ray, Arthur
    I Have Lived Here Since the World Began,
        xxiv
RCAP, *see* Royal Commission on Aboriginal
    Peoples
RCMP (Royal Canadian Mounted Police)
    at Cape Herschel, 271
    High Arctic relocation and, 264, 266, 280,
        282
    returning of Inuit by, 275
    sovereignty in Arctic and, 274
    viewed by Inuit, 278
    See also North-West Mounted Police
        (NWMP)
reading against the grain
    DIA annual report (1885), xvi–xix
    technique of, xxi–xxii
Red Crow (Mekasto; South Blood chief),
    35, 62
    suggested reading on, 51
Red Deer River, 29
Red Paper *(Citizens Plus)*, 295–302
Red Pheasant (Battle River Cree chief), 28
Red Power, 302, 303
Red River Resistance (1869-70), 459
Redman's Appeal for Justice, The (Deskaheh),
    128, 143–48
Reed, Hayter, 73–74, 459
    on agents, 86
    on agriculture for Indians, 86
    complaints about NWMP, 87
    letter on NWMP and pass system, 92–93
    Little Poplar (chief) and, 87n3
    on pass system, 84, 86
    recommendations on management of
        Indians, 74–76
regalia, potlatch, 103–4, 107, 108n4,
    108–10
Regina v. Walter Johnston, 300–301
religion, *see* spiritual practices

relocations, 256–57. *See also* High Arctic
    relocation
*Report of the Aboriginal Justice Inquiry of
    Manitoba* (1991), 327
reserves
    Allied Indian Tribes of BC on, 136–37
    in BC, 128
    British North America Act (1867) on, 1
    constitution patriation and, 342
    David Laird on, 33, 35
    defined, 12
    Diamond Jenness on, 233, 235
    House of Commons debates on Indian Act
        (1876), 5–6
    land expropriated for WWI effort, 192
    land possession on, 225
    National Indian Brotherhood on, 308
    Piikani (Peigan), 45–46, 49
    purpose of, 1, 81
    Red Paper (1970) on, 299
    residential schools on, 163
    restored Indian status (Bill C-31) and,
        322–23
    surrender of, in Indian Act, 12–13, 242,
        365–66
    as transitional measure, 341
    in Treaty 7 (1877), 24–25, 37–38
    White Paper (1969) on, 294, 295
    See also Greater Production program;
        Indian land controversy;
        land claims
residential schools
    All Saints Residential School, Aklavik,
        175–77
    apologies for, 151, 176, 186
    Battleford, 63
    generational effect, 152
    Grollier Hall, 175
    health report by Peter Bryce, 166–75
    High River, 63
    House of Commons debate on (1920),
        162–66
    Isabelle Knockwood on, 177–86
    Nicholas Flood report on, 153–61
    "No More Denials Please" (Carpenter),
        175–77
    number of, 164
    overview, 151–53
    passes for parental visits to, 87–88
    Qu'Appelle, 63